LONGMAN
GUIDE TO ENGLISH USAGE

Sidney Greenbaum
Janet Whitcut

Introduction by Randolph Quirk

Longman

Longman Group UK Limited,
Longman House, Burnt Mill, Harlow,
Essex CM20 2JE, England
and Associated Companies throughout the world

First published 1988

Set in Harris Intertype Times

Produced by Longman Group (FE) Ltd.,
Printed in Singapore

ISBN 0-582-55619-8

Publisher

Della Summers

Lexicographers

Brian O'Kill, Susan Engineer

Editor

Stephen Crowdy

INTRODUCTION
by Randolph Quirk

None of us can afford to be complacent about our command of English. For most of the time, of course, there is no problem: we are dealing with family and friends on everyday affairs; and what is more, we are usually talking to them, not writing. It is in ordinary talk to ordinary people on ordinary matters that we are most at home, linguistically and otherwise. And fortunately, this is the situation that accounts for the overwhelming majority of our needs in the use of English.

Problems arise as soon as the context is somewhat out of the ordinary. We suddenly need to address a cousin about the death of her husband; or we are writing to our employer to explain temporary absence; composing the minutes of a particularly delicate committee meeting; even just drafting an announcement to pin on the club noticeboard. This is when we may — or should — pause and wonder about idiom, good usage, the most appropriate way of putting things. There is the risk of sounding too casual, too colloquial, too flippant. There is the converse risk of seeming ponderous, distant, pompous, unnatural; of using an expression which, instead of striking a resonant note, falls flat as a hackneyed cliché.

It is true that pausing so as to express ourselves better has its own dangers. We may break the flow of our thought, lose spontaneity and warmth. Educational fashion of the twentieth century has often seemed to encourage 'free expression' at the expense of correctness or elegance of composition: even to have a somewhat contemptuous disregard for traditional conventions. This has been excused as a healthy reaction from a heavy-handed mode of teaching which is alleged to have insisted on correctness of expression in relative disregard of content. This was the absurd extreme that Francis Bacon ridiculed as 'Pygmalion's frenzy', when people 'hunt more after words than ... weight of matter'. Clearly, matter matters more. Since correctness was sometimes taught rather mechanically as though all that counted was the inflexible application of some crude rules of thumb, a reaction was to be expected and indeed welcomed. It coincided, moreover, with the increasing interest of academic linguists in speech as opposed to writing, in the natural free flow of dialectally various language as opposed to the traditionally recognized standard form of language associated with the official organs of state. In consequence of this interest, it even came to be felt (and sometimes said) that any form of a language was as 'good' or 'correct' as any other form, irrespective of purpose or occasion.

It is widely believed that the reaction against teaching to a strict standard is responsible for a decline in the general quality of writing. Whether in fact there has been such a decline (and what, if so, has caused it) cannot be regarded as other than speculative and controversial. What is certain is that very many people indeed feel uneasy about their own usage and the usage around them. University professors of English receive a steady stream of serious inquiries on these matters from people in all walks of life: accountants, local government officers, teachers, clergymen, bank managers, secretaries, journalists, broadcasters, trade union officials, doctors. A recent selection from my own postbag: What is the difference between *what* and *which* in questions like 'What/which is the best way to cook rice?' Should we compare something *to* or *with* something else? Should one write 'The time is past' or 'The time is passed'? Please tell me if it is all right (?alright) to say 'I didn't know he was that rich', 'Every patient should note the time of their next appointment', 'She hopes to completely finish', 'Aren't I ...?', 'They are deciding who to elect', 'The firm we wrote to', 'I will do my best', 'As regards to your inquiry', 'Thinking over your idea, here is a proposal'. Since we can say 'out of the window', why does my husband object to 'off of the window-ledge'? When I am asked to state my name, should I write 'Mr John Smith' ('Miss Joan Smith') or just 'John Smith' ('Joan Smith')? How is the word *amateur* (or *privacy*) pronounced? Is it 'The garment shrunk' or 'The garment shrank'? 'Half of our customers prefer' or '...prefers'? Should I write 'managing director' (or 'head teacher') with an initial capital?

These are real issues for real people. And rightly so. It is right that we should think before we write — and if possible before we speak too. It is right that we should care about and take pride in the way we express ourselves. This is not to inhibit full and free expression; this is not to lose spontaneity, authenticity, and the important sincerity we communicate simultaneously. Rather, by training ourselves in sensitivity and delicacy of expression, carefully adjusted to subject, occasion, and addressee, we actually enhance our ability to express our thoughts and desires more fully and freely. The feeling of being tongue-tied through self-consciousness is speedily overcome when we realize that being actively conscious of the language we use not merely helps us to adjust what we are saying to the particular addressees we have in mind, but also enables us to release the full range of linguistic expression we might have thought was beyond us. We achieve an added richness and precision of language.

We need constantly to remind ourselves that it is a characteristic of human language to present its users with a wide range of words and of ways in which these words can be combined into sentences. This wealth of choice serves two purposes. It enables us to make new observations and to give any such observation the form that is appropriate to the particular occasion. For the first, we need to go on increasing and adjusting our 'word-power' throughout our lives, becoming more practised in using complicated phrase and sentence structures which will put across our ideas and proposals with precision and clarity. For the second, we must go on increasing our 'repertoire' of alternative formulations so as to be able to fit what we have to communicate to particular situations and addressees.

And in both respects we need to be responsive to the demands and conventions of good usage.

Now, however much we might wish that the rules of good usage were simple, they are not, nor can they ever be. Standards are different in different periods of *time*; in different *places*; and on different *occasions*. Let me illustrate each of these in turn.

First, time. In the nineteenth century it was quite common for educated people to say 'It don't signify' and 'She dresses well, don't she?' Characters in Dickens can use *an't* or *ain't* for 'isn't' without any hint that such forms are other than fully acceptable. By contrast, most people would have found it strange (and many incorrect) to read expressions like 'She prefers her woollen gloves to her fur *ones*', 'They happened to *be having* a meal there', 'He *was sent* a note about it'. Many would still at that time prefer 'Their new house *is building*' to 'Their new house *is being built*', 'Her parties *are* grown tedious' to 'Her parties *have* grown tedious'. Parents were commonly addressed as 'Mama' and 'Papa' (both accented on the second syllable); the verb *oblige* was regarded by many as being correctly pronounced only when it rhymed with *siege*; and *gynaecology* (always then so spelled in Britain) began with the same consonant sound as *join*. And of course some changes take place within a decade or so. It is only since about 1970 that the preference has grown for stressing the second syllable instead of the first in words like *despicable* and *hospitable*; that we have come to expect that *billion* means 'a thousand million'; and that women can be conveniently addressed with the title *Ms*.

Secondly, while the present book is written from a British standpoint, we must never forget that there are different standards in different places. Even with comparable education and social position, a present-day New Yorker and a present-day Londoner can find themselves using forms of English which are equally correct but which are quite distinct: in vocabulary, in grammar, in pronunciation (especially), and (even) in spelling. In other words, there are rules and norms for American English which are independent of the corresponding rules and norms for British English. All of these are stamped on the way our New Yorker would write and speak the sentence, 'They have gotten a new automobile the same color as their last'. A Londoner may, but a New Yorker will not, add the final *done* in 'She asked him to feed the dog and he has done'. In *Foreign Affairs* (1984), by the American professor Alison Lurie, we find a comment on the British Library Reading Room in summer 'when all the tourists ... come out and ... the staff (perhaps understandably) is harassed and grumpy'; perfectly correct for American usage, but in British English *are* would have been preferred. People who are chiefly versed in British English are puzzled if an American airline pilot announces to passengers: 'We shall be in the air momentarily'. In American English the adverb can mean '*in* a moment'; in British English only '*for* a moment'. But each usage, in its place, is perfectly correct. What is correctly *aluminum* in the USA is correctly *aluminium* in the UK.

Thirdly, different standards for different occasions. The same person may apologize for non-participation as follows:

(a) Pressure of other work, ladies and gentlemen, must regrettably preclude my pursuing the subject further on this occasion.

(b) Daddy's just a weeny bit too busy to read any more to his Jennykins tonight, poppet.

It would be as absurd to regard either of these as in itself more 'correct' than the other as it would be to regard both as equally correct for either of these two sharply different occasions. Indeed, both *(a)* and *(b)* readily suggest modified versions that might be more appropriate (and hence more correct). If the child were rather older than the toddler to whom *(b)* is addressed, the language would be appropriately adjusted:

(b') I'm afraid I'm a bit too busy tonight, Jennifer.

Similarly, if the addressees were rather closer associates than those implied by *(a)*, a somewhat less distant and formal apology would naturally suggest itself to the practised speaker who had developed a properly wide repertoire of language appropriate to specific occasions.

In a ceremonious resolution at a board meeting, it might be appropriate to state:

> She will henceforth be styled Deputy Director.

But in a report of the same resolution in the firm's house journal, it might be equally justifiable to write one of the following:

> She will be called Deputy Director in future.

> From now on, her title will be Deputy Director.

It is not merely correct but obligatory in air traffic control by VHF to say 'Speak slower': but one would not approve such an instruction in a speech therapy manual.

A correct form is one that is felt to be acceptable at the relevant period, in the relevant place, and on the relevant occasion. This means that there cannot be a single standard by which an expression must be correct in all places, on all occasions, and at all periods of history. It does not of course mean that 'anything goes'. We are usually faced with a choice between expressions, any of which would be admirable in certain circumstances, but one of which is best for the particular occasion with which we are concerned. And there are some constructions which for practical purposes we can say are admirable in no circumstance at all. If we wish to claim that Mr Smith declined to support us, it would be universally regarded as incorrect grammar to state that 'Mr Smith would not give us no help'. In a long sentence, the best of us can all too easily get lost and fail to make a subject agree with a verb:

> The area in most countries that my friends and I are keen on choosing for our holidays are those that are furthest from big towns.

Or we may slip into other types of mismatch:

> It was their intention to experiment with plants of different species in this heavy clay soil and of ultimately discovering one that flourished.

The two parts of this sentence linked by *and* should be grammatically parallel ('to experiment ... and ultimately discover'), just as they should have been in the following sentence, found in a *Daily Telegraph* news item:

> They were unable to assess whether the world's climate was becoming hotter or cooler, and that it was premature to call a ministerial conference ...

But such errors are not usually resolved satisfactorily by merely correcting the grammar: they betray the need for somewhat more radical revision. Thus it is likely that the writer about clay soil should have been distinguishing between the *intention to* experiment and the *hope of* discovering. Again, correcting the *Daily Telegraph* item to read 'assess whether the world's climate was becoming hotter ... and *whether* it was premature' is only a superficial improvement. The writer probably used the improper *that* because a different verb should have been used for the second clause:

> They were unable to *assess whether* the world's climate was becoming hotter or cooler, and they *considered that* it was premature to call a ministerial conference.

Indeed, it is rare to find errors where single-word emendation is completely satisfying. Take for instance the blatant 'hypercorrection' in the following quotation from the *Radio Times*:

> Those of us who can face the wettest Sunday with equanimity still shower bitter judgment on he who warned us.

Altering *he* to *him* achieves technical correctness, but it is precisely because this 'sounds wrong' that the writer has fallen into error: better not to use a pronoun at all here, and write 'on the person who'.

It is commonplace to notice errors that are equally absolute in the usage of those for whom English is not their native language: indeed, these are especially noticeable since they are often not the kind of errors made by native speakers. In consequence, while we are quick to recognize such errors (and are usually able — just as quickly — to offer the correct alternative) we find it difficult to explain the rule that has been broken. For example 'I am in London since six months' (instead of 'I have been in London for six months' or 'I came to London six months ago'); 'He went out to buy washing powder or so' (instead of '... or something'); 'I am knowing your sister very well' (for 'I know ...').

Sometimes, however, the foreign speaker's error is in a more subtle area of usage such that, if we do not ourselves appreciate the range of usage among native speakers, we may misunderstand the meaning intended. Thus, we are used to *quite* being whole-hearted in 'Her sonata is quite superb' (*ie* if anything *better* than 'superb') but only half-hearted in 'Her sonata is quite good' (*ie* rather *less* than 'good'). However, in 'They were quite satisfied', a difference of context and intonation will allow either interpretation. By contrast, in negative expressions only the 'whole-hearted' sense is possible in correct English, so when we read a foreign critic's comment

> Her sonata was broadcast last week, but she was not quite pleased with the way it was played

we cannot know whether the writer should have used *satisfied* instead of *pleased* (thus giving the 'whole-hearted' meaning: 'She was not entirely satisfied with the playing — though it was very good') or whether the writer was carrying over the 'half-hearted' meaning into a negative clause where it is disallowed (in other words intending to say 'She was rather displeased with the playing'). Now that more than half of the people who use English in the world have not learned it as their first language, it is necessary for us all, if we are to grasp and sympathetically react to communications, to be watchful of the deviations from our own norms that may proceed from native and foreign users of English alike. In an English-language newspaper published in the Orient, there was a report of an interview with 'a few of the do-gooders in public service'. These included nurses and prison officers, and it gradually became apparent that the journalist was using *do-gooders* in a straightforward literal sense, 'those who do good', with none of the pejorative overtones of naivety and ineffectiveness associated with the expression by native-English speakers.

But it would be wrong to think that uncertainty over usage is especially prevalent among non-natives or indeed that particular lexical or grammatical errors point to the linguistic origin of the writer. In a report on an air disaster inquiry, a native English-speaking journalist wrote in the *Daily Mail* that the pilot 'took the brunt of the blame'. This is an idiom where the expectation is raised that whoever bears the brunt of something actually *feels* it, consciously: but in the case of the air disaster in question, the pilot was one of those who had been killed.

Again, it was a native English-speaking writer who formed the following sentence in *The Times*:

> We need, not to return to the last century, but progress to integrating more people into a balanced agrarian life.

So also the journalist who wrote the following in the *Daily Mail*:

> The official skated round the report on the way companies broke sanctions by swopping supplies. Instead, he spoke of the worsening situation ... .

And it was a British judge who was reported in the *Daily Telegraph* as having said that the accused man

> had made the attack 'in the sort of situation that someone else might have simply left the room and slammed the door'.

Nor is it only the cold clarity of print that can reveal our embarrassing slips. When Ms Libby Purves said on BBC radio 'Pauline is nodding her head vociferously', and Ms Angela Rippon said in a television programme 'That's something that makes it not only unique but very special indeed', it was hearers, not readers, who reacted.

In this book, the authors offer expert guidance on points of English where any of us can feel uncertainty, where any of us can go wrong. One general message cannot be overstated: we must think before we write — not just think of how we are to express ourselves, but think first of what exactly it is that we wish to express. Take for example the matter of negotiating to buy a house. If we write to the owner or the agent that we are going to 'take things a stage further', or 'explore the issue a little', or 'continue to investigate the matter', we say very little, and this may well mean that we have not decided what it is we want to say. If we are at the stage of *thinking* in the muffled way these phrases suggest, we are not at the stage of communicating at all; we have not yet expressed to *ourselves* what we mean. This must be the first discipline. Thereafter comes the discipline of selecting the right language: a discipline that must persist beyond first draft to the all-important revisions leading to the final draft.

And the right language will primarily be the clear language and the consistent language. Let me give just one illustration of the latter. English — especially British English — offers us the choice of saying 'The committee is' or 'The committee are'; 'The committee which' or 'The committee who'. In the former we are concerned with the committee as a single institution, in the latter with the committee as a collection of individual people. It often matters a great deal which of these to choose, as we seek to influence our addressee's orientation towards our own. Having chosen, we must then be consistent, since it matters perhaps even more that we should not wrench our addressee from thinking of the body as an impersonal institution at one moment to thinking of a group of individuals at the next:

> The committee, who have been arguing bitterly among themselves, was dissolved at the last meeting of the cabinet.

In a recent article on church affairs in *The Times*, there was just such an unfortunate switch:

> It was the Vatican *who* originally insisted on one uniform English version, and *which* set up an international committee ...

Thinking before we write is not just a matter of clarifying ourselves to ourselves, but of putting ourselves in our addressees' position. How will it sound to *them*? What will *they* understand from what I have written? It is not enough for the author to know what is meant:

The Council ruled that taxis only pick up passengers at the rear of the Town Hall.

It probably did not dawn on the writer of this sentence that — without any wilful intent to misinterpret — a reader could understand it in any of several sharply different ways. But just as destructive as ambiguity is the diversion of an addressee's attention by an unintentional absurdity or double entendre. In a Sussex newspaper it was reported that

A burglar at the Berwick Inn forced a fruit machine to steal £40.

In an American Sunday paper, a thoughtless failure to anticipate a misreading resulted in the following:

Buckingham Palace said that 22-year-old Prince Andrew, son of Queen Elizabeth and a Navy helicopter pilot, would sail with the Invincible.

As we have seen with '(bear) the brunt', clichés and idioms are often used vaguely or improperly, and a writer in *The Times* some years ago made a trap for himself with the phrase *cock a snook*. If we take the phrase 'sign a cheque', this can be made into a noun expression by putting the object in front, 'cheque-signing', and we can do this without hesitation or error as part of our knowledge of the language. But an idiom like *cock a snook* is more opaque than *sign a cheque* and the *Times* writer failed to make the analogous grammatical change in converting to a noun expression, thus achieving a doubly unfortunate effect:

Terrorists have never before carried out such blatant cock-snooking against the security forces.

Let me give one final example to show that writing that is poor in one respect is likely to be poor in another. In an article on Roald Dahl, published in 1985, we find the question:

How does he account for the success of bad children's books, like Enid Blyton?

This is of course grammatically sloppy: Enid Blyton is not a book but an author. But worse if anything than the grammatical sloppinesss is the communicative sloppiness. Just as in the positioning of the word *only* we must train ourselves to hear or read our message as though we were our own addressee, so also we must always be sure our addressee knows the authority for what we are saying. Who is the real speaking 'subject'? We come upon this as a relatively simple grammatical point with the unattached participle:

Returning from church this morning, two horses nearly ran into the car.

Here, improperly, we have not been told that *I* was returning from church. But in a more serious way, communicatively and indeed morally, a 'subject' is lacking in the above sentence about Dahl. There is a covert claim that 'Enid Blyton's books are bad' but no indication as to who is making the claim. And unlike the sentence about the horses, this one does not respond to common sense ('Horses don't go to church, so ...'). The context does not suggest that Roald Dahl himself has said that Blyton books are bad, and in fact the quoted sentence is the first to make reference to her or her work. So the reader is apparently encouraged to think that their badness is well-established as common knowledge. A well thought-out (and fair-minded) version of the question would therefore have been:

How does he account for the success of children's books, such as Enid Blyton's, which *in my opinion* (or *as many people think*) are bad?

Good usage, in short, is a matter of combining the rules of grammar and the acceptable meanings of words with an appreciation of our relationship with the addressee.

PREFACE
by Sidney Greenbaum and Janet Whitcut

We have written this book as a practical guide to contemporary English usage. In it we offer clear recommendations in plain English to those who look for guidance on specific points of pronunciation, spelling, punctuation, vocabulary, grammar, and style. We hope that those who come to consult will stay to browse.

We address ourselves primarily to those wanting advice on standard British English. At the same time, many of our entries draw attention to differences between British English and American English. We believe that our readers will find this information interesting in its own right, but there are also practical reasons for referring to American usages in a guide to British usages. One obvious reason is that British speakers are constantly exposed to American speech and writing through the mass media and need to be warned against possible misunderstandings. Another is that many present American usages may eventually be adopted into British English, and some may be already entering the language of sections of the British population.

Most entries deal with specific words or expressions. We note that *accommodate* is spelled with two *c*'s, two *m*'s, and two *o*'s; that the accent is usually omitted in *régime*; that *indigestible* ends in *-ible* not *-able*; that both *jailer* and *jailor* are current spellings; that both *judgment* and *judgement* are permissible everywhere, but the first is the more usual American choice and the second is often a British preference. Our entries on pronunciation refer not only to individual sounds (*dour* rhymes with *tour*, not with *hour*), but also to the stress patterns of words (the noun *essay* is stressed on the first syllable, but the rare formal verb *essay* is stressed on the second syllable). Punctuation is mainly treated in entries on the individual punctuation marks, such as the comma and the dash, but there is also an entry ('run-on sentence, comma splice') that discusses two common types of punctuation errors as well as a long article on punctuation in general.

Numerous entries are concerned with questions of vocabulary. There are the confusibles: words that resemble each other in sound or spelling but differ in meaning (*homogeneous* and *homogenous*) and words that

xiii

are similar in meaning but are certainly not interchangeable (*artificial* and *synthetic*). Words and expressions are characterized stylistically: some are to be avoided or at least used with restraint because they are fashionable, overused in at least some meanings (*feedback, low profile*); some are clichés (*in this day and age*); some can seem rather pretentious in most contexts (*eventuate*) or are facetious (*nuptials*); others are euphemisms (*underachiever*) or genteelisms (*soiled* in *soiled laundry*); words may be formal (*interment* for *burial*) or informal (the verb *peeve*). Some entries refer to idiomatic combinations: One is *indifferent to* or *as to* (not *for*) something. There are warnings against excessive use of foreign expressions as well as against their incorrect use (*modus operandi, soi-disant*).

Entries on grammar deal with such matters as the forms of verbs (the past of *dive* is *dived*, but there is a common variant *dove* in American English), the plurals of nouns (the plural of *matrix* is *matrices* or *matrixes*), the choice of pronoun forms (when to use *I* and when to use *me*), and the rules for agreement between the subject and its verb. Entries on style draw on both vocabulary and grammar to discuss choices that affect such matters as verbosity and clarity.

Many entries provide generalizations on matters that are raised elsewhere in relation to individual words and expressions. For example, there are general entries on spelling and the plurals of nouns, as well as entries that explain and illustrate terms used in the book (*back-formation, cliché, pretentious, euphemism*). And a number of articles discuss such general topics as grammatical analysis, the parts of speech, dictionaries, the origins of words, change of meaning, and (under the entry 'vocabulary size') the number of words in English.

We are grateful to Brian O'Kill of Longman for his helpful comments on our work. In the course of our writing we have consulted many works of reference, including *A Comprehensive Grammar of the English Language* (Longman) (of which one of us is a co-author). We have drawn on our considerable experience as writers and researchers: one of us is a grammarian and the other is a lexicographer. And we have brought to bear on the writing of this book our long and fruitful association with the Survey of English Usage at University College London.

Aa

a, an

1 Write **a** before words beginning with a consonant sound: *a bicycle*, *a house*, *a one*; and **an** before words beginning with a vowel sound: *an apple*, *an hour*. Words beginning with *eu* have an initial 'yoo' sound, and so do many words beginning with *u*; write *a European, a union*, but *an uncle*. The same rules apply before the names of letters and before groups of initials. Write **a** before B, C, D, G, J, K, P, Q, T, U, V, W, Y, Z: *a PhD, a BBC spokesman*. Write **an** before A, E, F, H, I, L, M, N, O, R, S, X: *an MP, an FBI agent*. Words beginning with *h* and an unstressed syllable formerly took **an,** but most people now prefer **a** here also: *a hotel, a historian*. If you choose **an** before these *h*-words, do not also pronounce the *h*.

2 **A** is often stressed in speech, with the pronunciation as in *ape*. This is particularly common in formal American discourse, but may arise when any speaker pauses to select the following word: *There's been a –slight confusion*. If one genuinely does not know what is coming next, one may then say **a** where **an** is required: *There's been a – embarrassing incident*. The stress should be avoided in the formal reading of prepared material.

3 **A** should be capitalized if it is the first word of a title: *Southey wrote 'A Vision of Judgment'*.

4 **A** is subject to inverted word order in a few constructions, particularly after *too* and *so*, but this tendency to INVERSION should not be allowed to get out of hand. *Too hard a task* is acceptable; *so hard a task* is formal, and may be better changed to *such a hard task*; while *even harder a task* is unnatural, and should certainly be changed to *an even harder task*.

a-, an-

This is a Greek prefix meaning 'not' or 'without', as in *atypical* or *anarchy*. Some scholars have objected to its use with words not of Greek origin; but *amoral* and *asexual* are now well established.

abaft

See ABEAM.

1

abbreviations

See ACRONYMS.

abeam, abaft, astern

Anything exactly on a line at right angles to a ship's keel at its midpoint is **abeam**. Anything behind this line, whether on board the ship or diagonally to left or right, is **abaft**. Anything directly behind the ship is **astern**. The first two words are used only, and the third chiefly, in the technical language of seamanship.

abetter, abettor

Abetter is the common spelling, **abettor** the legal one.

abide

The past tense **abode** is confined to the archaic sense of 'dwell' or 'stay'. Use **abided** for the modern sense of 'obey' or 'accept': *We abided by the rules.*

ability, capacity

The normal constructions are **ability** *to* do something, **capacity** *for* doing something. Some writers distinguish between **ability** as being acquired and **capacity** as being innate: *her ability to solve equations; his capacity for remembering facts.* However, the distinction between what is acquired and what is innate is often unclear.

abjure, adjure

Abjure means 'renounce': *to abjure one's religion.* **Adjure** is a formal word for 'command' or 'entreat': *She adjured them to deny any knowledge of the negotiations.*

able

The use of **able** with a passive infinitive, and particularly with a nonhuman subject (*able to be fried*), sounds awkward; perhaps because **able** suggests a skill or expertness more appropriate to a person who performs an action than to a person or thing that undergoes it. Instead, use *can* or *could* (*It can be fried*), or recast the sentence (*We'll be able to fry it*).

-able, -ible

These endings form adjectives meaning 'liable to, or able to, undergo something': *breakable*; *reliable*; or 'having a particular quality': *fashionable*; *comfortable*. When these adjectives are built up from native English words, the ending is always **-able**: *washable*; *get-at-*

able. The much rarer ending **-ible**, as in *credible*, occurs in certain borrowed words of Latin origin.

This constitutes a spelling problem. Since they form a minority, we append here a list of the **-ible** adjectives, and of those that can end in either **-able** or **-ible**. When there are alternative spellings, we give both; and if one is less frequent, we put it second with *also* before it. Any adjectives not listed here end in **-able**.

accessible
addable, -ible
admissible
apprehensible
ascendable, -ible
audible
coercible
collapsible
collectible, -able
combustible
comestible
compactible
compatible
comprehendible
comprehensible
compressible
concupiscible
condensable,
 also -ible
conductible
connectable,
 also -ible
constructible
contemptible
contractible
controvertible
convertible
corrigible
corrodible
corruptible
credible
deducible
deductible
defeasible
defensible
depressible
descendible
destructible

diffusible
digestible
dirigible
discernible,
 also -able
discerptible
discussable, -ible
dismissible
dispersible
distendible
distractible
divisible
edible
educible
eligible
emulsible
erodible
eruptible
eversible
evincible
exhaustible
expansible
explosible
expressible
extendable, -ible
extensible
extractable, -ible
fallible
feasible
flexible
forcible
frangible
fungible
fusible
gullible, *also* -able
horrible
ignitable, -ible
illegible

immersible
immiscible
impartible
impassible
 (*compare*
 impassable)
imperceptible
impermissible
implausible
impossible
imprescriptible
impressible
inaccessible
inadmissible
inapprehensible
inaudible
includable, -ible
incoercible
incombustible
incompatible
incomprehensible
incompressible
incontrovertible
inconvertible
incorrigible
incorruptible
incredible
indefeasible
indefectible
indefensible
indelible
indestructible
indetectable,
 also -ible
indigestible
indiscernible
indivertible
indivisible

3

inducible
inedible
ineligible
inexhaustible
inexpressible
inexpungible
infallible
infer(r)able, -ible
inflexible
infrangible
infusible
ingestible
insensible
insuppressible
insusceptible
intangible
intelligible
interconvertible
interruptible
invertible
invincible
invisible
irascible
irreducible
irrefrangible
irremissible
irrepressible

irresistible
irresponsible
irreversible
legible
miscible
negligible
nondeductible
omissible
ostensible
partible
passible
  (compare
  passable)
perceptible
perfectible
permissible
persuasible
plausible
possible
preventable,
  also -ible
processible, -able
producible
protrusible
putrescible
reducible

refrangible
remissible
reprehensible
repressible
reproducible
resistible
responsible
reversible
revertible
risible
sensible
submergible
submersible
submissible
suggestible
supersensible
suppressible
susceptible
tangible
terrible
transfusible, -able
transmissible
unintelligible
vendable, -ible
vincible
visible

ablution(s)

Apart from its religious sense of ritual purification, or its use in military contexts for a place where soldiers wash, this can seem a somewhat PRETENTIOUS word, as in *ablution facilities*; or a FACETIOUS one, as in *perform his ablutions under the tap*. It may be better to say *wash*.

abode

This can seem a somewhat PRETENTIOUS or FACETIOUS word when used as a noun: *Welcome to my humble abode*. It may be better to say *home* or *house*. For its use as the past tense of the verb, see ABIDE.

about

1 When I am **about** *to* do something I am on the point of doing it: *I'm about to tell you*. The negative of this, however, *I'm not about to tell you*, usually means that I am certainly not going to tell you. This emphatic way of expressing unwillingness is common in informal American use and is coming into British English.

2 About is unnecessary when the idea of approximation is expressed elsewhere in the sentence: *They're (about) 12 to 15 years old*; *The population is estimated at (about) 30,000*. See AT (1).

3 See AROUND.

above

This can refer to what has been mentioned on a previous page or higher up on the same page: *the remarks quoted above*; *the above remarks*; *the above*. This device has long been established in written English, and is very useful. It is, naturally, inappropriate in writing that is intended to be read aloud. Available alternatives for those few writers who dislike it are *the preceding/earlier remarks*, or *these remarks*. Compare BELOW.

abridg(e)ment

The spelling without *e* in the middle is correct in both British and American English; the spelling with *e* is chiefly British.

abrogate, arrogate

Abrogate means 'annul' or 'repeal': *to abrogate a treaty*. **Arrogate** means 'seize without justification': *to arrogate power to oneself*.

absence

Do not say *in the absence of* when *without* or *not having* will do: *In the absence of further information we cannot proceed*.

Conspicuous by his/her absence, meaning 'noticeably not there', is a CLICHÉ.

absolute

This means 'complete', as in *absolute nonsense* or *absolute proof*. It is also used to express an extreme degree, as in *exposed to absolute danger*, but some writers object to this use.

absolute constructions

The first part of the following sentence is an absolute construction: **Christmas being only one week away,** *we were busy buying presents*. The absolute construction is loosely attached to its sentence: it has its own subject (*Christmas*) and is not joined to the sentence by a linking word (contrast the use of the conjunction *since* in *Since Christmas was only one week away, we were busy buying presents*). Other examples of absolute constructions: **The resolution having been put to the vote,** *the chairman refused to allow any further discussion of the* *matter*; **The inspection now over,** *the soldiers were ordered to return to their barracks.* Apart from a few set expressions (such as *weather permitting* and *present company excepted*), absolute constructions are suitable only for very formal contexts.

An absolute construction is separated from the rest of the sentence by a comma. It is wrong to put an additional comma after the subject of the construction, as in **The resolution, having been put to the vote,** *the chairman refused to allow any further discussion of the matter.*

absorb

See ADSORB.

abstract nouns

If you use too many abstract nouns, you make your writing difficult to understand. You can reduce the number of abstract nouns by changing some of them into verbs or adjectives and providing appropriate subjects where necessary. In these three pairs, the (b) sentence is clearer than the (a) sentence.

1a. There is a *need* for *formulation* of a national policy to encourage the *development* by private enterprise of our national resources in *balance* with the *prevention* of *deterioration* of our environment.

1b. The government should formulate a balanced national policy that will encourage private enterprise to develop our national resources but will at the same time prevent the environment from deteriorating.

2a. The report is an *evaluation* of the *effectiveness* of the Federal regulations in *terms* of the *extent* to which there has been a *reduction* of exposures to carcinogenic substances.

2b. The report evaluates how far the Federal regulations have been effective in reducing exposures to carcinogenic substances.

3a. The British public lacks an *understanding* of the *inevitability* of *exhaustion* of supplies of North Sea oil.

3b. The British public does not understand that supplies of North Sea oil will inevitably run out.

Abstract nouns with a very general meaning are often unnecessary. The style is clearer and more direct when the noun is omitted (other adjustments sometimes being necessary), as in the (b) sentences below:

1a. Almost all the new words and definitions are of a scientific and technological *nature*.

1b. Almost all the new words and definitions are scientific and technological.

2a. The country is falling into a debt *situation*.

2b. The country is falling into debt.

3a. Doctors are particularly susceptible to a stress *factor*.

3b. Doctors are particularly susceptible to stress.

The nouns that tend to be unnecessarily used in this way include ASPECT, BASIS, CASE, CHARACTER, NATURE, PROBLEM, SITUATION.

abstractly, abstractedly

Abstractly means 'in the abstract' or 'by itself': *to discuss the matter abstractly rather than in context*. **Abstractedly** means 'with mind elsewhere': *gazing abstractedly out of the window*.

abut

Other forms are **abutted, abutting**.

abysmal, abyssal

These both mean 'very deep'. **Abysmal** is now used figuratively to mean 'deplorably great' (*abysmal ignorance*), or somewhat informally to mean 'very bad' (*the food was abysmal*). **Abyssal** is the technical term for the ocean depths, especially below 1000 fathoms: *abyssal mud*.

Academe

This is a somewhat OVERUSED literary word for a place of learning or the university environment. It perhaps comes from Milton's reference (*Paradise Regained*, iv. 244) to the garden near Athens where Plato taught as *the olive grove of Academe*.

academic

This word has acquired, besides its earlier associations with learning, a later somewhat derogatory implication of 'useless, having no practical bearing on anything': *a purely academic question*. People who use it in its more literal senses should be aware of this possible implication.

accede, exceed, succeed

To **accede** *to* something is to 'consent' or 'become a party' to it: *accede to their demands*. To **exceed** something is to 'go beyond' it: *exceed my budget*. In the sense 'enter upon an office or position', **succeed** is interchangeable with **accede**: *She succeeded/acceded to the throne*.

accelerator

The word ends in *-or*, not *-er*.

accent

An accent is a type of pronunciation. We can speak of a British accent, an American accent, an Australian accent, and so on. We may also refer to regional accents within a country (Yorkshire, Glasgow, Texan, New York) and to social or ethnic accents (Received Pronunciation, Cockney, Irish American, Black American). There are an indefinite number of English accents, depending on how detailed we wish to be. See PRONUNCIATION; DIALECT.

accent, accentuate

These two verbs overlap in meaning. To **accent** chiefly means to 'pronounce with stress' (*accented the first syllable*), while **accentuate** is commoner in the figurative sense of 'make prominent' (*a trimming that accentuated the waistline*).

accent marks

Although the words are well-established in English, accent marks are still required in words such as *attaché*, *café*, *fiancé*, *pâté* and *protégé*, where the lack of an accent mark might suggest a different pronunciation. The acute accent, as in *café*, is by far the most common of the accent marks, though it is sometimes omitted in American English.

Some words have alternative forms, with or without accents; for example, you may choose whether to retain or drop the accents in *élite*, *entrée*, *première*, *régime*, *rôle*, and *soirée*. You can look for guidance on the use of accent marks under individual entries in this book.

The diaeresis (spelled *dieresis* in American English) in *naïve* is optional, but prefer *naive*.

accept

An organization or college **accepts** a potential member or aspiring student; the member or student is **accepted** *by* the organization or college. The muddled construction **accept** *to* (*I was accepted to the class*) arises out of confusion with *admit* (*I was admitted to/into the class*), which allows *to* as well as *into*.

accept, except

Accept means 'receive willingly', and is slightly formal: *Did you accept the position* (ie take the job)? **Except** as a verb means 'leave out', and is decidedly formal: *You will all be punished – I can except no one*. Do not use **except** when *leave out* will do.

acceptable

This means 'worthy of being accepted', not 'able to accept'. Do not write *They are acceptable to indoctrination,* where *receptive* is intended.

accepter, acceptor

The word is spelled **accepter** in the general sense, **acceptor** as a technical term in law or science.

access, accession

These two apparently similar words have few senses in common. **Access** as a noun means chiefly 'opportunity to reach or have something': *access to classified information*; it has existed as a verb in data processing since the 1960s, meaning 'gain access to': *Accumulator and index registers can be accessed by the programmer.* **Accession** as a noun means chiefly 'entering on a high office': *his accession to the papacy.* Librarians use **accession** as a verb meaning 'to enter (books) in the order in which they are acquired'.

accessary, accessory

In British English **accessary,** noun and adjective, has traditionally meant '(someone) involved in a crime without actually committing it': *Her actions made her (an) accessary to the murder*; while **accessory,** noun and adjective, has meant '(something) inessential to something else but added to it': *car accessories such as wing mirrors.* American English uses **accessory** for both ideas, and the distinction has become blurred in Britain too.

accidentally

The word is not spelled *accidently,* though it has only four syllables in rapid speech. Compare INCIDENTALLY.

acclimatize, acclimate

Acclimatize is the standard British and the chief American English form, with **acclimatization** for its associated noun: *to acclimatize sheep to the hills/academics to jobs in industry.* (See also -IZE). The verb **acclimate** and the noun **acclimation** are secondary alternatives in American English, used particularly with reference to physiological condition rather than in the extended meaning of 'accustom'.

accommodate

The word is spelled with two *c*'s, two *m*'s, two *o*'s.

accommodation(s)

This word, often plural in American English (*overnight accommodations*), may be official jargon for *house* or *lodging*: *to provide alternative accommodation.*

accompanist

This, not *accompanyist*, is now the standard word for an accompanying musician.

accompany

A person is **accompanied** *by* a companion or, if a musician, *by* an accompanist. When one thing has another added to it, it is **accompanied** *with* it: *He accompanied the advice with a warning.*

accomplish

The OED and most American dictionaries give the pronunciation of the second syllable as 'kom', but most British dictionaries still advise the older 'kum', or show it as the first of two alternatives.

accord, account

The idioms associated with these two words are *of one's own accord* (ie voluntarily) and *on one's own account* (ie on one's own behalf, or at one's own risk): *They gave generously of their own accord*; *He did some financial deals on his own account.*

according

1 According *as* means 'depending on whether': *They move into the next class according as they pass or fail the examination.* It is normally followed by two or more choices, here *pass or fail.* But prefer the more usual *depending on whether.* Where only the criterion, rather than the choices, is mentioned, prefer **according** *to*: *They move into the next class (or not) according to their performance in the examination.*

2 According *to* should be used with care when it refers to someone's reported testimony. It may suggest that we are sceptical: *According to George, their housing is adequate.* (Do we believe him?) This implication of scepticism is not present in long-established phrases such as *The Gospel According to St Mark.*

account

On **account** *of* means 'because of', not merely 'because'. It introduces a clause only in very informal (and chiefly American) usage: *On account of I don't want to* should not be used in writing.

accountable

This means 'personally answerable': *The president is accountable to his conscience for his behaviour.* Many writers prefer *responsible* rather than *accountable* when it refers to things: *The bad weather was responsible for our failure.* The word should not be used to mean merely 'explicable', the opposite of *unaccountable*: *This strange custom is scarcely accountable.*

accumulative, cumulative

These two words overlap in meaning. It is probably best to reserve **accumulative** for the person or thing that *accumulates* something (*an accumulative collector of manuscripts*) and to use **cumulative** for what is built up by successive additions (*the cumulative effect of small daily doses*).

accursed

This is often pronounced with three syllables when a stressed syllable follows: *this accursèd devil* (Shakespeare).

accuse

1 The construction is **accuse** *of*, not *with*: *accused of manslaughter.* See also CHARGE.

2 One may refer to someone who has been charged but not convicted as *the accused*, or as *the accused person/man/woman*, or say that he or she is *accused of* a crime. It is tendentious to refer to an *accused thief*, since the question of whether the person is a thief is precisely what is in dispute. It is for the same reason tendentious to call someone an *alleged forger* or a *suspected blackmailer*; but doctors commonly, and harmlessly, speak of *suspected measles*.

accustom

One is **accustomed** *to*, not *with* something: *accustomed to comfort*; *He had to accustom himself to the climate.*

acerbic

See ACID.

ache (*verb*)

Other forms are **ached, aching.**

achieve, achievement

Achieve(ment) implies successful effort in reaching a definite goal. It should not be used of what is undesirable: *employees achieving redundancy*; nor to mean merely 'reach': *She achieved the age of 18*; and is perhaps better not used of things: *The car achieved a speed of 120 mph*. It is somewhat OVERUSED, with no specified goal, in managerial and educational contexts: *the desire to achieve*; *to reward achievement*; *students who are under-achievers*.

acid, acerbic, acrid

These all mean 'sharp and stinging'. **Acid** means 'sharp in taste', like a lemon, or 'caustic and biting': *acid wit*. **Acerbic** is like **acid** but is more often used figuratively: *an acerbic review*. **Acrid** applies particularly to pungent smells, such as that of burning wood, but is also often used figuratively; an **acrid** remark is decidedly more unpleasant than an **acid** one.

acid test

This means a 'crucial trial of value', and is a CLICHÉ.

acknowledg(e)ment

This is spelled either with or without *e*; the latter is more usual, the former is chiefly British.

acoustic

The second syllable is usually pronounced like *coo*, not *cow*.

acquaint

One **acquaints** somebody *with* (rather than *of*) a fact. The phrase can easily seem a PRETENTIOUS substitute for *tell*; and *Are you acquainted with* . . . ? can be rephrased as *Do you know* . . . ?

acquaintanceship

This is a needlessly long variant. Use **acquaintance**: *Their acquaintance was of long standing.*

acquiesce

One **acquiesces** *in*, not *to* or *with*, things: *reluctant to acquiesce in a swindle.*

acquire

This seems a somewhat PRETENTIOUS word for 'get', 'buy', etc, when it is used of physical objects, but less so with abstractions: *She acquired a good command of English.*

acquit

Other forms are **acquitted, acquitting**; the noun is **acquittal**.

acreage

The word is spelled with two *e*'s.

acrid

See ACID.

acronyms

Acronyms are words formed from the initial letters of parts of a word or phrase, commonly the name of an organization. Established acronyms generally do not have full stops between the letters. They are often pronounced as a series of letters: *EEC* (European Economic Community), *ID* (identity or identification card), *UN* (United Nations), *VCR* (videocassette recorder), *FBI* (Federal Bureau of Investigation), *LA* (Los Angeles), *TB* (tuberculosis), *TV* (television), *PAYE* (Pay As You Earn), *GP* (General Practitioner). But often they are pronounced as if they formed a word: *UNESCO* (United Nations Educational, Scientific, and Cultural Organization), *SAM* (surface-to-air-missile), *ASLEF* (Associated Society of Locomotive Engineers and Firemen), *Aids* (acquired immune deficiency syndrome). Some of these pronounceable words are written without capitals and are therefore not recognizable as acronyms: *laser* (light amplification by stimulated emission of radiation), *radar* (radio detection and ranging). Some acronyms are chosen to make suitable words: *WASP* (White Anglo-Saxon Protestant), *BASIC* (Beginners' All-purpose Symbolic Instruction Code), *ASH* (Action on Smoking and Health).

See CLARITY (3).

acrophobia, agoraphobia

Acrophobia is 'fear of heights', **agoraphobia** is 'fear of open spaces'.

across

This should not be spelled or pronounced *acrost*.

act, action

1 Both these nouns refer to doing, and they are partly interchangeable: *do a kind act/action*. **Act** stresses the thing done, and is usually momentary or of short duration, while **action** stresses the process of doing, and may take some time and involve several **acts**. The two words are enshrined in various fixed phrases: *an act of cruelty/folly/ mercy*; *Act of God*; *to take action*; *a civil action*. People speak of the **action**, not the **acts**, of things, meaning the way they work: *the action of a machine/of a medicine*.

2 The modern colloquial uses of **action** in *where the action is*, meaning the place of most exciting activity, and *a piece of the action*, meaning a share in this activity, should be avoided in formal writing.

action (*verb*)

The use of **action** as a verb, meaning 'take action on' (*Please action this report*), is a piece of managerial jargon.

activate, actuate

Activate means 'make (a thing) active or reactive or radioactive': *activated sewage*. **Actuate** means 'motivate (a person) to action': *He was actuated by ambition*.

actual, actually

These words are often OVERUSED as unnecessary emphasizers. *In actual fact* means no more than *in fact*, although *He actually paid* conveys some idea of astonishment. In *She didn't come, actually*, **actually** means *in fact*. In general, the adverb is more often used loosely than the adjective.

actuate

See ACTIVATE.

acuity, acumen

Acuity means 'keenness of perception': *acuity of hearing*. **Acumen** means 'shrewdness of judgment': *her political acumen*.

A.D., AD

This is an abbreviation of *anno Domini*, 'in the year of the Lord'. It

14

comes before the year (*A.D. 30*), but generally is needed only if there are B.C. dates in the context or if there are other reasons to suspect a possible misunderstanding. Orthodox Jews, and perhaps also followers of other non-Christian religions, prefer to use C.E., for *Common Era*. Compare B.C.

ad, advert

These are CLIPPED forms of *advertisement*, used rather informally. **Advert** is British only.

-ada

See -ADE.

adagio

The plural is **adagios**.

adapt, adopt, adept

Adapt means 'make suitable': *to adapt a novel for the stage*. **Adopt** means 'take up': *to adopt new methods*. **Adept** (adjective and noun) means 'skilled' and 'skilled performer': *an adept machinist; an adept at chess*.

adaptation, adaption

The longer form is usually preferred.

adapted

This word cannot replace *suited* or *suitable*, because it implies change. Do not write *He's not adapted to violent exercise*.

adapter, adaptor

A person who adapts something is usually an **adapter** (*the adapter of the play for television*); a device, such as a piece of electrical apparatus, that adapts is an **adaptor**.

add(ed)

Strictly speaking, you can only **add** something when there is already something to be added to. Do not write *an added inducement* unless there is some other inducement. See ADDITIONAL(LY).

addendum

1 The plural is **addenda**, except where the word means part of a tooth of a gear wheel, and then the plural is **addendums**.

2 The plural form is sometimes used as a singular, as in *This addenda contains many new words*; but this should be avoided.

addict

One is **addicted** *to* something, or *to* doing it, but not *to* do it. Do not say *He's addicted to lie*.

additional(ly)

Addition and **additional** lend themselves to VERBOSITY. Replace *in addition (to)* by *besides* or *as well (as)*, and leave out **additional** altogether if you use *add*, as in *add an additional few words at the end*.

address

This can seem PRETENTIOUS if it is used inappropriately for *speech*, *lecture*, or even *talk*. It suggests a very formal prepared speech.

addresses

If you are writing an address as a sequence, separate the units by commas: *76 Rowland Avenue, London NW11 2BL, England; 5130 N. Carpenter Road, Skokie, Illinois 60007, U.S.A.* There is no need to separate the house number from the street name by a comma (*76, Rowland Avenue*).

For letter headings and envelopes, it is old-fashioned to indent each line or to put a comma at the end of each line and a full stop at the end of the address. Prefer the block style without end-punctuation:
76 Rowland Avenue
London NW11 2BL
England

adduce, deduce

Adduce means 'bring forward' as reason or evidence: *He adduced various statistics to prove his point*. **Deduce** means 'draw a conclusion': *I deduce from your silence that you disagree*.

-ade, -ada, -ado, -ato

Words borrowed from foreign languages with these endings have been gradually anglicized in pronunciation from 'ahd, aht' to 'aid, ait': *brocade, tornado, potato*. This has not happened, however, to all such words: in British English the 'ah' pronunciation is used in *avocado*, *tomato*, *armada*, and *promenade*; American English has variant pronunciations with 'ai', or actually prefers 'ai', for all these except *avocado*.

adept

See ADAPT.

adequate

1 This can seem PRETENTIOUS when it is merely an equivalent of *enough*. To have *adequate money* is to have enough money.

2 Since **adequate** by itself implies 'enough for a requirement,' it is TAUTOLOGOUS to say *My income is adequate to/for my needs*.

3 Adequate often implies 'only just good enough' (*Her performance was adequate but hardly exciting*), so you should be careful that this is what you intend to imply.

adherence, adhesion

Both words are related to the verb *adhere*, and have some overlap of meaning; but **adherence** is usually preferred for 'support' or 'loyalty' (*adherence to monetarist economics*), and **adhesion** for the literal senses of 'sticking' or 'gluing'.

ad hominem, ad infinitum, ad interim

Avoid such LATINISMS where possible. They can usually be replaced by 'personal' (*an ad hominem attack*), 'endless(ly)' (*They talked ad infinitum about the budgets*), and 'temporary' or 'for the time being' (*ad interim arrangements*).

adieu

The plural is either **adieus** or **adieux**.

adjacent

This can mean either 'near' or 'adjoining', so that the position of a hotel *adjacent to the shore* is not clear. It can in any case seem somewhat PRETENTIOUS.

adjectivally

The word is not spelled *adjectively*, though it has only four syllables in rapid speech. It is formed from *adjectival*, not from *adjective*.

adjectives and adverbs

Many words are recognizable as adjectives or adverbs by their suffixes. Adjective suffixes include -*able* (*reliable*), -*ive* (*defective*), -*less* (*careless*), -*ful* (*hopeful*), -*al* (*cultural*), -*ic* (*romantic*). The typical suffix for adverbs is -*ly*. However, many common adjectives (*old, wise*) and many common adverbs (*then, here*) do not have suffixes, and some adverbs have the same form as adjectives; for example *early, fast, hard, long, well*.

When the word follows a verb, there is occasionally confusion as to whether to use an adjective or an adverb. Use the adjective if the word refers to the subject, and use the adverb if it refers to the activity. In the following pairs, the (a) sentences correctly have an adjective and the (b) sentences correctly have an adverb.

1a. That pianist is (very) *good*.

1b. That pianist plays *well*.

2a. I subsequently felt (quite) *bad* [also *unhappy, sorry*] about my behaviour.

2b. I slept *badly* last night.

3a. They sounded *cheerful* (enough) when I last saw them.

3b. They spoke *cheerfully* when I talked to them.

The verbs in the (a) sentences are linking verbs, which are typically used to link the subject with an adjective (or a phrase with an adjective as the main word). Further examples of linking verbs and adjectives are *grow nervous, look thin, taste fine, seem foolish, remain firm, become sullen*. Such verbs are not always used as linking verbs. Contrast:

4a. Your cat looked *greedy*. ('appeared to be greedy')

4b. Your cat looked *greedily* at my parrot.

5a. I feel *strong*. ('I feel myself to be strong')

5b. I feel *strongly* about the matter.

Well is an adjective in *I feel well*.

In informal style (especially in American English), adjective forms such as *real* and *sure* are often used as emphasizers with the function of adverbs: *That was real good*; *I sure wouldn't want to be there now*. In formal style use *That was really good*. Rephrase sentences to avoid *sure*: *I certainly would not want to be there now*.

For adjectives and adverbs that are sometimes confused, see also individual entries: BAD, CHEAP, CLEAN, CLEAR, DEAR, DEEP, EASY, FAIR, FALSE, FINE, FIRM, FLAT, FREE, FULL, HARD, HIGH, LARGE, LOUD, QUICK, SHARP, SHORT, SLOW, SOFT, SOUND, STEADY, STRAIGHT, STRONG, SURE, TIGHT, WIDE, WRONG.

See also COMPARISON, GRAMMATICAL.

adjoin, adjourn

Adjoin means 'be next to' (*adjoining rooms*). **Adjourn** means 'postpone' (*to adjourn a meeting*) or, informally, 'move to another place' (*adjourn to the garden after lunch*).

adjudge

See JUDGE.

adjudicator

The word ends in *-or*, not *-er*.

adjure

See ABJURE.

administer, administrate

The shorter first form is better. **Administrate** is a BACK-FORMATION from *administration*.

administrator

The word ends in *-or*, not *-er*.

admissible

The word ends in *-ible*, not *-able*.

admission, admittance

Although both words are related to the verb *admit*, and have some overlap of meaning, **admission** is the only one for 'confession': *his admission of guilt*. While **admittance** is preferred for 'permission to enter a place' (*No Admittance*), **admission** is used for permission to enter in a more abstract sense, perhaps as a member of a society, and also for the cost of being admitted (*Admission £5*).

admit

Other forms are **admitted, admitting**.

-ado

See -ADE.

adopt

See ADAPT.

adoptive

Parents who adopt a child are **adoptive**. The child is **adopted**.

adsorb, absorb

Adsorb is a technical word meaning 'to hold (molecules of gas or liquid) in a layer on the surface', **absorb** means 'to soak up and incorporate': *to absorb the liquid/the atmosphere*.

adult

1 This is usually pronounced with the stress on the first syllable.

2 In the context of films, magazines, and other entertainments, **adult** now implies 'pornographic'.

advance, advanced

Advance as an adjective means 'coming before': *an advance party*; *an advance copy of a book*. **Advanced** means 'far on in development': *advanced studies*; *advanced ideas*.

advance, advancement

Advance means 'progress': *advances in space travel*. **Advancement** means 'promoting or being promoted': *to work towards the advancement* (ie the encouraging) *of our cause*. Do not say *in advance of* when *before* or *in front of* will do.

advantage, vantage

These both mean 'a favourable position', but **advantage** is the better word for figurative use: *Her fluent French gave her an advantage over the other students*; *He watched the riot from the vantage (point) of the roof.*

advantageous

The word is spelled like this, retaining the final *e* of *advantage*.

adverbs, position of

1 within parts of a verb
2 between a verb and an object

1 within parts of a verb

There is no justification for refusing to allow an adverb between the parts of a verb, either between auxiliaries (*should* **probably** *have written*) or between an auxiliary and a main verb (*may* **often** *complain*). These positions are natural for many adverbs. The position after the first auxiliary is in fact obligatory for certain adverbs in particular meanings: *may* **well** *be there*; *can't* **possibly** *go*. And of course *not* comes after the first auxiliary (and perhaps an adverb): *should* **not** *have written*; *may* **also not** *have noticed*. See also SPLIT INFINITIVES.

2 between a verb and an object

Normally, an adverb should not separate the verb from the object. Instead of *The official explained* **convincingly** *her decisions*, put the adverb *convincingly* at the end of the sentence. (The same restriction applies with even greater force to longer insertions than a single adverb; for example, *in her usual forceful manner*.) But there are circumstances that justify the separation. If the object is long, the position at the end of the sentence is clumsy; it is better to put the adverb before the verb or after the verb: *He* **calmly** *repeated/He repeated* **calmly** *the many reasons for his recent actions*. Avoid final position in writing if the object is a clause, since the adverb could be misinterpreted as belonging to the object clause rather than the sentence as a whole. Instead of *He repeated what he had previously said* **calmly**, write *He repeated* **calmly** *what he had previously said* or *He* **calmly** *repeated what he had previously said*.

adversary

This is usually pronounced with the stress on the first syllable.

adverse, averse

Adverse means 'unfavourable': *an adverse decision*. To be **averse** *to* is to 'dislike': *I am averse to violence*.

advert

See AD.

advert, avert

To **advert** *to* is to 'mention': *He adverted to the subject of housing*; but prefer the less formal *refer to*. To **avert** something is to prevent it from happening: *to avert an accident*; or to turn something away: *to avert one's attention from the scene*.

advertise

This is the only correct British English spelling; it is also the predominant one in American English, where the word is sometimes spelled **advertize.**

advice, advise

Advice is a noun; **advise** (not spelled *-ize*) is a verb. The verb is often used in business English for *tell*: *Advise us (of) when the consignment is due.*

adviser, advisor

Both spellings are correct.

-ae, -as

The plural of nouns such as *formula*, with the Latin ending *-a*, may be either **-ae** or **-as**. Consult your dictionary, bearing in mind that since **-s** is the regular English plural ending, a dictionary that shows only irregular plurals may show no plural at all for a noun such as *idea*. In general, the tendency is towards an increasing use of **-as** in general writing (*political formulas*); but the Latin form should be retained in scientific contexts (*mathematical formulae*).

ae-, e-, oe-

Words of Greek and Latin origin may represent the sound 'ee' by the spellings **ae** and **oe**, or, formerly, by the joined letters *æ* and *œ*; or increasingly today, particularly in American English and in scientific and technical contexts, by **e** alone. The following choices are recommended, but usage is changing all the time.

For both British and American English: *aegis* (*egis* is only American), *aesthete/aesthetic* (*esthete/esthetic*, pronounced 'es' not 'ees', is only American): *aeon* or *eon*; *amoeba* (*ameba* is only American); *archaeology* or *archeology*; *encyclopedia* or *encyclopaedia*; *fetid* (pronounced 'fet' not 'feet' in American and increasingly in British English) rather than *foetid* (pronounced 'feet'); *fetal* and *fetus* (*foetal* and *foetus* are only British); *hem-* or *haem-* in compounds (ie blood), as in *h(a)emoglobin*, *h(a)emophilia*, *h(a)emorrhoids* (pronounced 'hem'); *medieval* or *mediaeval*; *paleo-* or *palaeo-* in compounds (ie old), as in *pal(a)eolithic*, *pal(a)eontology*.

for *British English*	*for* *American English*
anaemic, anaemia	anemic, anemia
anaesthetic, anaesthesia	anesthetic, anesthesia

faecal, faeces	fecal, feces
oesophagus	esophagus
oestrogen	estrogen

aegis

See AE-.

aeon, eon

See AE-.

aer-, air-

Words formed from the Latin *aer* = 'air' are pronounced like *air* and are no longer written with a dotted *e* as in *aerated*. American English has replaced *aeroplane* by *airplane*, and **air-** rather than **aer-** has become general in most of the words connected with aviation such as *airborne*, *aircrew*, *airlift*, and *airport*.

aesthete, aesthetic

See AE-.

affect, effect

To **affect** something is to 'influence' it: *The appointment of a new Minister will affect the department's policy*. To **effect** something is to 'bring it about' or 'carry it out': *The new Minister will effect changes in the department's policy*. Confusingly, one meaning of the noun **effect** is close to that of the verb **affect**: to *affect a policy* is to *have an effect on* it. The noun **affect** exists only as a technical term in psychology, meaning the conscious subjective aspect of an emotion, considered apart from any bodily changes it may produce. The noun **effect** in the plural can mean one's property: *my personal effects*.

affection, affectation

In modern use, **affection** is 'tender attachment' and **affectation** is 'insincerity' or a deliberately artificial way of speaking or behaving. There is, however, a second noun **affection**, of different origin, which means 'a disease' (*a pulmonary affection*) or 'an attribute'.

affinity

An **affinity** exists *between* things or people, or *with* another thing or person. The use of *to* or *for* is becoming common in scientific writing (*the affinity of a virus to the nervous system*) but should be avoided outside such technical contexts.

affirmative

The answer was in the affirmative is a PRETENTIOUS way of saying that it was 'yes'.

affluent

This can seem a somewhat PRETENTIOUS word for 'rich'..

affront, effrontery

An **affront** is a show of disrespect, usually deliberate: *His enormous car was an affront to their poverty.* **Effrontery** is barefaced impudence which may cause shocked amusement: *He had the effrontery to ask the Queen to dance.*

à fond

See AU FOND.

aforementioned, aforesaid

See SAID.

Africander, Afrikaner

An **Africander**, or **Afrikander**, is a kind of South African cow or sheep. An **Afrikaner** is a South African of Dutch descent.

after

1 Do not use **after** in formal writing to mean 'afterwards' (*We had dinner and went home after*), except with an accompanying word for a unit of time: *go there the year after*; *in Chaucer's day and for long after* (G. M. Trevelyan).

2 The characteristic Irish use of **after** (*I'm after doing it*) does not mean 'I want to do it' (as *What are you after?* means 'What do you want?') but 'I have just done it', 'I'm in the middle of doing it', or 'I'm in the habit of doing it'.

afterward(s)

Afterwards is the usual form in British English, **afterward** in American English.

age

This is better omitted from phrases such as *at (age) 60*, except in legal and actuarial contexts, as when one is speaking of pension rights or the like.

aged

In such phrases as *aged 21*, and when **aged** is a technical word for 'fully developed', as in *aged wine* or *an aged horse*, this word has one syllable. When it means 'old and infirm', as in *an aged man* or *help for the aged*, it has two.

ag(e)ing

This is usually spelled *ageing* in British English, *aging* in American English.

agenda

Although **agenda** is a Latin plural, it is now always treated as a singular noun: *This agenda is too long*. It has the plural **agendas**: *the agendas for the next two meetings*. It is usual to call any of its parts *an item on the agenda*, or an *agenda item*, rather than to use the rare singular **agendum**.

aggravate, aggravation

In informal speech and writing, *aggravate* ordinarily means 'annoy': *to aggravate her parents* (Samuel Richardson). It has been so used by reputable writers since the early 17th century; but since careful stylists continue to dislike this use, it is best to confine the word in formal contexts to the sense 'make worse': *The problem has been aggravated by neglect*.

aggregate

This is often a PRETENTIOUS word for *total* or *sum*: *the aggregate of our scientific knowledge*. You can sometimes rephrase the sentence and use *all*, though the phrase *in the aggregate* is unobjectionable.

aggressive

This word has acquired a favourable meaning in addition to its earlier one of 'hostile and destructive'. In modern business language, and even elsewhere, it also means 'full of thrusting ambition, energy, and enterprise': *an aggressive salesman*.

aggressor

The word ends in *-or*, not *-er*.

agitator

The word ends in *-or*, not *-er*.

ago

This should not be used in combination with *since*, as in *It is many years ago since World War II ended*. Write either *many years since it ended* or *many years ago that it ended*.

agoraphobia

See ACROPHOBIA.

agree

One **agrees** *with* somebody or something and **agrees** *to* do something. Two or more people **agree** *on* a concerted plan. In addition, **agree** is now correctly used without a preposition, especially in British English and especially in the *-ed* form of the verb, as a verb meaning 'reach agreement about': *to agree a price/a procedure*; *to issue an agreed statement*; *the following articles were agreed* (Winston Churchill).

agreement, grammatical

See NUMBER AGREEMENT; PERSON AGREEMENT.

aid

This word is used, rather than *help*, in the context of providing resources and money for a public cause: *overseas aid*. Where there is no reason to strike this rather impersonal note, the word is journalese. Do not use it when *help* will do.

aid, aide

Both can mean 'a person who helps'. **Aide** is, however, the preferred military spelling, being short for *aide-de-camp*, and is now also used in nursing, welfare work, and diplomacy. In American English it is used even for Administration officials at the level of cabinet ministers.

aim

The older British expression was **aim** *at* doing something. Under American influence, however, **aim** *to* do something has become accepted on both sides of the Atlantic: *She aims to become a doctor*.

ain't

This means 'are not', 'is not', 'am not', 'has not', or 'have not'. Some educated American English speakers use it in informal conversation, particularly in the phrase *Ain't I*; but the expression should be avoided altogether in educated British usage and in all formal writing, except for humorous effect: *Things ain't what they used to be*.

air-

See AER-.

aisle

See ISLE.

akin

Things are **akin** *to*, not **akin** *with*, other things.

à la

Although *la* is feminine in French **à la** is correctly used in English to mean 'in the fashion of' (compare the French *à la mode*), irrespective of the sex of the person whose name it introduces: *unshakable resolution à la Winston Churchill*. The accent is sometimes dropped in American but not in British English.

à la carte

See TABLE D'HÔTE.

albeit

This is often regarded as PRETENTIOUS when used, unless for humorous effect, as an alternative to *(even) though*. It is perhaps justified as a convenient way of linking pairs of adjectives (*a small albeit crucial mistake*), although *but*, *yet*, and *though* will also do in this case.

albino

The plural is **albinos.**

albumen, albumin

Albumen is the white of an egg; **albumin** or **albumen** is a protein that occurs not only in egg white but in blood, milk, muscle, and many plant juices.

alibi

This originally meant a legal plea that someone accused of a crime was elsewhere at the time. Some people strongly object to its newer meaning of simply any excuse or defence (*What's your alibi for being late again?*) and even more to its use as a verb meaning 'to offer an excuse'.

alien

Although earlier writers preferred **alien** *from*, the modern usage is **alien** *to*: *Their ideas are quite alien to ours*.

-(al)ist

See -IST.

all

1 All *of* before a noun (*all of the time; all of these girls*) is commoner in American than in British English, but it is preferable to use *all* alone in formal writing on both sides of the Atlantic. There is no reason to rephrase **all** *of* before a pronoun; *all of us*, *all of whom* are as acceptable as *we all*, *who all*.

2 All *that* with an adjective or adverb (*It's not as cold as all that*; *We don't go there all that often*) is normal in conversation after negatives and in questions, but is inappropriate for formal writing. Rephrase as appropriate: *It's not very cold, not cold enough to freeze the pipes*, etc.

3 See also ALMOST; ALREADY; ALRIGHT; ALTOGETHER; NUMBER AGREEMENT (7).

allege

This means 'assert without proof', and may suggest guilt, for example if we speak of someone's *alleged innocence*. To preserve neutrality, prefer some such word as *declare*, *maintain*, or *affirm*, and rephrase the sentence to make it clear who is responsible: *His colleagues maintain that he is innocent*. See also ACCUSE.

allegro

The plural is **allegros**.

alleluia, hallelujah

The spelling **alleluia** derives from Hebrew through Greek, and appears to be the prevalent form today. **Hallelujah** derives directly from Hebrew, and is the form used by Handel for the Hallelujah Chorus. Other variants are less usual: **alleluiah, alleluja, alleluya, halleluia, halleluiah, halleluja**.

allergic, allergy

In its figurative meaning, this is often a useful word for a strong irrational dislike: *She's allergic to children.* It is, however, somewhat OVERUSED. We may rephrase the sentence and use alternatives such as *repugnance, antipathy, aversion*; but there is no convenient single adjective to replace **allergic** (*averse*, for instance, seems not quite strong enough).

allot

Other forms are **allotted, allotting**; the noun is **allotment**.

allow

This can be used with or without *of* to mean 'admit the possibility of': *His statement allows (of) several possible interpretations.*

all-round, all-around

The first is the only British form, but both are equally acceptable in American English: *an all-(a)round athlete.* See also AROUND.

all told

This is correctly used, not only for counting (*5000 varieties all told*) but in a more general sense of 'taking everything into account': *All told, it was an unsuccessful holiday.*

allude, elude

To **allude** *to* something is to mention it indirectly: *He alluded to 'various technical problems'.* To **elude** someone or something is to escape from them: *He eluded his captors.* See also ALLUSION.

allusion, reference

Strictly speaking, one makes an **allusion** *to*, or **alludes** *to*, an item that is not actually named; one makes a **reference** *to* or **refers** *to* an item when one names it: *a letter alluding to some unspecified problems*; *a speech referring to Mrs Thatcher's monetarist policies.* This distinction is, however, now often ignored. See also DELUSION.

ally

This is usually pronounced with the stress on the first syllable for the noun (*They were allies in wartime*), on the second syllable for the verb (*Its beak allies it to the finches*). But the adjectival form *allied* can be stressed in either way (*families allied by marriage*).

almost

1 Do not confuse **almost** with *all most*: *It's all most* (ie all of it is very) *interesting*; *It's almost* (ie nearly) *interesting*.

2 The word is sometimes used as an adjective before a noun, meaning 'virtual' (*in a state of almost hysteria*), perhaps on the analogy of *near* (*his near defeat*); but it is safer to avoid this practice, particularly in American English.

alone

The position of **alone** in a sentence affects its meaning. Compare *He can lift it alone* (ie unassisted); *He alone can lift it* (ie only he). As the second example shows, **alone** is sometimes used as a more formal and elegant substitute for *only*. This is usually acceptable enough after a noun or pronoun, as with *he* in our example. Elsewhere, it should be changed to *only*, as in the following: *The proof does not rest alone upon the statement.* (Replace by *only*, or put **alone** after *statement*.) Even where **alone** is positioned after a noun or pronoun, there may be ambiguity. *He travels by car alone* can mean either only by car, or without a passenger (*travels alone by car*).

along

In the combination **along** *with* it is usually better to omit **along**: *working along with the other girls*. Where appropriate, you could use *as well as*: *a plane carrying supplies along with passengers*. **Along** *of*, meaning either 'because of' (*went home along of the rain*) or 'with' (*come in along of me*), is to be avoided in standard writing.

alongside

This should not be used with *of*: *Park the car alongside mine* (rather than *alongside of mine*).

already

Do not confuse **already** with *all ready*: *They're all ready here* (ie all of them are ready); *They're already here* (ie even now).

alright

This combination of *all* and *right* is widely considered to be uneducated, and should be avoided in formal writing. Some people, however, would argue that, just as *already* is different from *all ready* and *altogether* from *all together*, the two spellings **alright** and *all right* are needed to distinguish between *The answers are all* (ie all of them are) *right* and *The answers are alright* (ie OK).

also

This is sometimes used instead of *and* in speech, when we
spontaneously introduce an afterthought: *He likes fried potatoes – also
onions*. This trick of speech may be imitated in writing as a deliberate
device of style: *They breed cattle and horses; also children*; but unless,
as here, there is some reason for it, **also** should not normally be used
for *and*, although the combinations *and* **also,** *but* **also** are perfectly
permissible. There is some question as to whether **also** can correctly
begin a sentence. It sometimes does so as the result of INVERSION, in
journalese: *Also present were the Mayor and Mayoress*. The effect of
this device is to give greater, and perhaps not always justified,
importance to the postponed subject. In general prose writing,
however, the information introduced by **also** should be more firmly
integrated with the structure of the sentence.

altar, alter

Altar is a noun referring to a place or structure used in religious
ceremonies. **Alter** is a verb meaning 'make different'.

altercation

This can sometimes be a rather PRETENTIOUS or FACETIOUS word for
'quarrel'.

alternate, alternative

Alternate(ly) means 'every other' (*alternate days* are Monday,
Wednesday, etc), or 'by turns' (*They laughed and cried alternately*).
There is also a verb **alternate**, which means 'do or happen in turns':
Wet and fine days alternated. **Alternative(ly)** means 'as an
alternative': *You can go by sea or alternatively by air*.

alternative

1 There has been a traditional objection, based on etymology, to using
alternative where more than two choices are involved, since the word
is ultimately derived from the Latin *alter* (= 'other', of two).
According to this view, it is correct to say *We have no alternative*, or
What is the alternative?, but not *What are the various alternatives?*
Similarly, it is thought redundant to speak of *the only alternative*.
Good writers have long recognized, however, that there is no other
acceptable way of saying 'What are the other things we can do?', since
choice or *option* does not always cover this idea, and today it seems
mere pedantry to object to this usage.

2 The expressions are **alternative** *to* and *choice between*: *There are* *several alternatives to your plan*; *You have a choice between going by plane and by road.* A sentence such as *There is no alternative between going by plane and by road* could be rephrased as *You must go either by plane or by road.*

3 Since at least the early 1950s, **alternative** has been overused in official jargon as a substitute for *other* or *new*, perhaps by extension from the phrase *alternative accommodation*. For some time people have been making *alternative arrangements*, fixing up an *alternative date* for a cancelled meeting, and offering each other *alternative employment*. Since the late 1960s, however, this meaning of the word has been taken up and extended: first by the hippie youth culture which spoke of itself as the *alternative society*, with different cultural values from those of the surrounding social order, and then by radical leftists in general. These support *alternative newspapers* and *alternative cinema*, independent of established commercial financing; derive *alternative energy* from windmills and the sun rather than from nuclear power or fossil fuels; avail themselves of *alternative medicine*; and advocate *alternative technology*, the use of small cheap tools by people typically working in small self-sufficient groups. It would be churlish to complain about this latest extension of meaning, since here the word can no longer be replaced by *new* or *other*, but has developed a specific social and political colouring in response to what its users want to say.

altho

This informal spelling of *although* does not belong in serious writing.

although

See THOUGH.

alto

The plural is **altos**.

altogether

1 Do not confuse **altogether** with *all together*: *They sang all together* (ie all at the same time); *It's altogether* (ie completely) *different*.

2 *In the* **altogether**, meaning 'nude', is FACETIOUS, not to say old-fashioned.

alumin(i)um

This is spelled with one *i* (**-num**) in American English, two *i*'s (**-nium**) in British English. Pronunciation of the end of the word differs accordingly; in addition, the main stress falls on the second syllable in American English and on the third syllable in British English.

alumnus

A male former student is an **alumnus**, plural **alumni** (not -*nuses*). The rarer word for a female former student is **alumna**, plural **alumnae** (not -*nas*). A mixed group are **alumni**, but a neutral equivalent in British English is *graduates*. In American English, however, the word *graduates* is commonly used as an equivalent of the British English *postgraduates*, for students engaged in studies beyond the first degree.

a.m.

See TIMES OF DAY.

amateur

There are several possible pronunciations: the last syllable may rhyme either with *purr* or with *pure*; the last consonant may be a 't' sound, or like that in *furniture*; or the whole word may rhyme with *parameter*, which is probably the best choice. In British English the stress should probably be on the first syllable, in any case.

amatory, amorous

These words, concerned with sexual love, have some overlap of meaning. **Amatory**, the more literary word, chiefly means 'connected with love': *his amatory affairs*. **Amorous** chiefly means 'moved by love': *amorous women*. Both words can mean 'expressing love': *amatory/amorous glances*.

ambiguity

1 general
2 initial misinterpretation
3 ambiguous position
4 unclear pronoun reference

1 general
An expression is ambiguous if it can have more than one meaning. Ambiguity is prized in certain uses of language (where the two or more meanings are intended to co-exist): poetry, advertising, and humour. In other writing it is a source of confusion for readers.

2 initial misinterpretation
Ambiguous wording may become clear in the wider context, but you should rephrase the wording if it is likely to mislead readers and require

them to reread and puzzle out the meaning. Readers may initially misinterpret *stylistically effective repetition* as one phrase in *The author explains how stylistically effective repetition of formulas is in Old English poetry*. Even merely the insertion of *the* before *repetition* would prevent that misreading. A more radical rephrasing would be clearer: *The author explains the valuable stylistic effects that are achieved through the repetition of formulas in Old English poetry*.

3 ambiguous position

Take care that you do not put an expression in a position that allows the reader to connect it either with what precedes or with what follows. Either move the expression to an unambiguous position or rephrase the sentence. Here are three examples with alternative corrections.

Exercising *often* keeps one healthy and fit.

(*Frequent exercising keeps* . . . or *Exercising will often keep* . . .)

Drinking *normally* did not worry them.

(*Normal drinking did not* . . . or *Normally, drinking did not* . . .)

He promised to exercise more control *at the committee meeting*.

(*At the committee meeting he promised* . . . or *He promised that he would exercise* . . .)

4 unclear pronoun reference

Make sure that it is clear what the pronoun refers to. Avoid ambiguous or vague reference. *Their* is ambiguous in *The teachers made the students put their names on the top of each sheet*; replace by either *their own* or *the teachers'*. What the pronoun refers to must be actually present, not merely implied:

The aircraft made a crash landing. *They* had to leave by the emergency chutes. (*The passengers and crew*)

Experience shows that when abortion laws are liberalized *they* skyrocket. (*abortions*)

In some instances, the vague pronoun is unnecessary: *In the Bible* **it** *says we should love our neighbour* (The Bible says . . .); *In France* **they** *do not have political prisoners* (In France, there are no political prisoners).

ambiguous, ambivalent

Ambiguous means 'having more than one possible meaning', **ambivalent** means 'having simultaneous opposed feelings'. If my attitude towards you is **ambivalent** (ie I don't know whether I like you), you may find my consequent behaviour **ambiguous** (ie you don't know whether I like you).

ameliorate

This can seem a PRETENTIOUS word for 'improve' or 'make better'. Do not use it when *counteract* or *mitigate* is intended; one can *ameliorate conditions* but not *hardships*.

amen

The first syllable can be pronounced either as *ah* or as in *day*.

amend, emend

These words are both concerned with the correction of mistakes: one can **amend** or **emend** a document or a regulation. **Amend** chiefly means 'alter'; it emphasizes the idea of making a change that will improve something, and is the term used of alterations to the US Constitution; but one can also **amend** one's behaviour. **Emend** chiefly means 'correct', and suggests the correction of defective wording: *to emend statistical errors in the annual report*.

amenity

1 The chief American pronunciation of the second syllable, and the older British one, is 'men'. The newer British one is 'mean'.

2 Amenity has become a somewhat OVERUSED word for anything either pleasant or convenient, so that a rubbish dump may be an *amenity site*. It would be clearer if the word could be kept for environmental pleasures of no economic use, such as woodland not harvested for timber and lakes used for boating rather than for civic water supplies.

American

This is so widely used to refer to the USA that it seems too late to do anything about it, and indeed in this book we freely speak of *American English*. There is no other convenient adjective for the USA, corresponding to *Canadian* or *Brazilian*. Canadians are, understandably, offended both at being included (as when Europeans suppose them to be Americans) and at being excluded. In certain contexts, **American** must be taken to cover the whole of North America, or indeed the whole of the western hemisphere, as in *pan-American*. *American Indians* or *Native Americans* are the original peoples of both American continents, and *all-American* may refer to some transaction between Mexico, Venezuela, and Uruguay.

American English

See STANDARD ENGLISH.

Americanism

When we speak of Americanisms in language, we mean words or other language features that are characteristic of the English used in the USA. Many usages that were originally Americanisms (some of them objected to for that reason) have been fully integrated into British English and their origin is no longer recognized: *radio*, *immigrant*, *squatter*, *teenager*, *lengthy*, *to advocate*, *to locate*, *to belittle*, *live wire*, *hot air*, *third degree*, *cold war*, *mass meeting*. Some Americanisms or recent usages that are thought to originate in the United States are resisted by some British writers and speakers: *OK*, *I guess*, *to check up on*, *to win out*, *to lose out*, the sentence adverb *hopefully*. It seems reasonable to evaluate new arrivals from American English as loanwords, which we gratefully accept if we find them useful for British English, but which we may reject if British English already has an exact equivalent. In practice, however, mere fashion dictates what is absorbed into British English.

Many Americanisms never cross the Atlantic: spellings such as *color* and *theater*; forms such as *gotten* (British *got*), *dove* (*dived*), *snuck* (*sneaked*); and grammatical features such as the use of *he* to refer back to *one* (*One must support his team*; British *one's team*) or informal *real* (*That was real good*; British *really good*). Some of them (*real*, for example) may be recognized by British speakers because of their frequency in the mass media. There are numerous words or phrases that are found (at least in the specific meaning) exclusively or almost so in American English: *sidewalk* (pavement), *candies* (sweets), *gas* (petrol), *blank* (form), *faucet* (tap), *comforter* (eiderdown), *first floor* (ground floor, with corresponding changes for other floors), *name for* (name after), *public school* (school maintained by public funds), *pacifier* (baby's dummy), *wash up* (wash face and hands).

amicable

This is usually pronounced with the stress on the first syllable rather than the second. Compare DESPICABLE.

amid(st)

Use either form of this word, which is somewhat literary. See AMONG(ST) (3); -ST.

ammunition, munitions

Ammunition is anything fired from a weapon, such as bullets, shells, and guided missiles. It includes pellets for an airgun, and also bombs, mines, and grenades. The **munitions** made by a munition factory are strictly military, and include not only the larger sorts of **ammunition** but the guns to fire them. **Ammunition**, but not **munitions**, is used figuratively: *The speech provided ammunition for his political enemies.*

am(o)eba

See AE-.

amok, amuck

Both spellings are correct.

among(st)

1 Either form can be used.

2 Where more than two participants are involved, **among** is usually preferred to *between*: *divided it between the two children/among the three children*; but when we speak of exact position, or of precise individual relationships, *between* is the only choice: *a treaty between four European powers; Ecuador lies between Colombia, Peru, and the Pacific Ocean.*

3 There is considerable overlap of meaning between **among** and the somewhat literary *amid(st)*. **Among** is particularly appropriate when followed by a plural (*among themselves*) or by some word indicating a separable group of people or things (*among the congregation*), and is the only choice when we mean 'in or from the number of': *Among so many only a few can survive. Amid(st)* is preferred for the idea of being surrounded by something vague (*amid the confusion*) or for two events accompanying each other in time: *He climbed the rope amid shouts of applause.*

amoral, immoral

Amoral, as well as the rarer **nonmoral** and **unmoral**, means 'outside the sphere of moral judgments': *Babies and animals are amoral.* **Immoral** means positively wrong: *In most societies, incest is considered immoral.*

amorous

See AMATORY.

amount, number

Amount is correctly used of nouns with no plural because they refer either to substances viewed as an undifferentiated mass or to abstractions, but **number** should be used of plurals: *a considerable amount of butter/of influence*; *a certain number of people/of mistakes*.

ampersand

This is the name of the sign &, meaning 'and'. As a space-saver, it is appropriate in formulae and business addresses rather than in ordinary writing. Since it may suggest a closer relationship than *and*, it has the use of indicating that three or more items are to be considered in groups: *Oliver & Boyd and Longman* are two, not three, publishing houses.

ample

This is often no more than a rather PRETENTIOUS word for *enough*. Properly used, it emphasizes plenty rather than mere adequacy, and may seem more appropriate with abstractions (*ample time/opportunity*) than with quantities (*ample coal/sugar*).

amuck

See AMOK.

an

See A.

an-

See A-.

an(a)emic, an(a)emia

These are usually spelled with the *a* in British English, without it in American English. See AE-.

an(a)esthetic, an(a)esthesia, an(a)esthetist

These are usually spelled with the *a* in British English, without it in American English. See AE-.

analogous

Things are **analogous** *in* stated respects *to* or *with* each other. Properly speaking, the word means more than merely *similar* or *like*, suggesting a correspondence in form or function that makes it possible to draw a sustained comparison: *The wings of a bird are analogous to those of an* *aircraft*. The *g* of **analogous** is pronounced as in *get*, rather than as in *gem*.

analogy

There may be an **analogy** *in* stated respects *between* things, or *of* one thing *to* or *with* another.

analyse, analyze

The word is spelled **analyse** in British English, **analyze** in American English.

analysis, synthesis

1 Analysis is the examination of something by separating it into parts, whether the thing separated is a chemical substance or a grammatical sentence. **Synthesis** is the creation of something by combining parts into a whole, whether the thing created is a complex sentence or a chemical dye.

2 *In the ultimate* (or *final* or *last*) *analysis* can seem a rather PRETENTIOUS way of saying 'in the end'.

analyst, annalist

An **analyst** analyses things, or psychoanalyses people; an **annalist** writes annals (historical records).

ancient, antique, antiquated

Ancient refers either to very old things or (facetiously) to very old people: *an ancient book/lady*. It looks back to a more distant past than do the other words, and differs from them also in being applicable to what has long since disappeared; an *ancient civilization* may mean China, which still exists, but it may also mean Babylon. **Antique** refers to a more recent past, and to things rather than people, particularly to things made valuable by age: *an antique clock*. **Antiquated** things are discredited because outmoded: *antiquated machinery/notions*.

and

1 **and** at the beginning
2 **and** joining sentence elements
3 compound subjects with **and**
4 comma after **and**

1 and at the beginning
It is often perfectly legitimate, and very effective, to begin a sentence or even a paragraph with **and**, but the habit should not be allowed to become a mannerism.

2 and joining sentence elements
And joins sentence elements of the same kind and of equal rank: *cats and dogs*; *John and I*; *pink and white*; *They shouted and laughed*; *They were shouting and laughing*; *We boiled the potatoes and fried the eggs*; *John boiled the potatoes and I fried the eggs*. The pitfalls here are of five kinds:

(a) the joining of unlike sentence elements: *To drink heavily and taking too many drugs is bad for you* (either change *to drink* into *drinking*, or change *taking* into *to take*); *They complained about the food and that they were tired* (change to *They complained that the food was bad and . . .*).

(b) the omission of **and** where it is needed in lists, a problem related to the previous one. It is usual to end a list with **and**, either with or without a comma: *cats, dogs, and rabbits*; *red, white and blue*; *They sang, shouted, and drank*. But since **and** must link like to like, a sentence such as *She plays the piano, goes swimming and dancing* needs another **and** before the verb *goes* to link it to the earlier *plays the piano*. (It is quite legitimate to form a list with no **and** in it at all, suggesting that perhaps the list could be continued: *The hedges were full of primroses, daffodils, stitchwort*; but the device should not become a mannerism.)

(c) the insertion of **and** where it is not needed. Again, this is the fault of joining unlike sentence elements. It arises particularly before *who, whom, whose, which*. Nelson wrote of Lady Hamilton: *She is a young woman of amiable manners and who does honour to the station to which he has raised her*. Since like should be linked with like, the clause introduced by *who* should be linked to a preceding clause of the same kind, preferably one that also begins with *who*. Nelson would have done better to write: *She is a young woman who has amiable manners and who . . .* , or simply to omit *and*.

(d) the joining of too many clauses with a string of **and**'s, as children often do, rather than by some more sophisticated system of linkage. The child writes: *I got up and I cleaned my teeth and I had breakfast and I went to school . . .* , but the mature stylist will rephrase into something like *After getting up and cleaning my teeth I breakfasted, went to school, and . . . . .*

(e) ambiguity as to what is being linked. The *New Yorker* quotes: *The play tells of the historical moment when Pocahontas saves the life of Captain John Smith and runs for an hour*; commenting 'That's nothing for a young Indian girl'. The writer meant to link *runs* with *tells*, but inadvertently implied a link with *saves*, so that the subject of *runs* is wrongly *Pocahontas* instead of the intended *The play*.

3 compound subjects with and

Compound subjects joined by **and** are correctly plural: *The Walrus and the Carpenter were walking close at hand* (Lewis Carroll). Some apparent compounds, however, are thought of as single entities and can rightly take a singular verb: *The hammer and sickle* (ie one flag) *was flying from the flagpole*; *The Bat and Ball* (ie one pub) *sells good beer*; *Your whisky and soda is on the table*. Probably Henry Kissinger thought of the compound as one entity when he said *We're at the beginning of a period in which real negotiation and compromise is possible*. (See NUMBER AGREEMENT (3).) A related problem, though not one of verb agreement, is illustrated by the following, heard on the BBC: *the growing link between universities and institutions of higher education and British business*. The link is presumably between the *universities and institutions* on the one hand, and *business* on the other, but there is some ambiguity here; the matter would be clearer if the *link* were described as *between British business on the one hand and universities and institutions on the other*, putting the shorter item first. The ambiguity becomes worse in the letter written by a professor who recommended *the books by Crystal and Crystal and Davy*. How many authors are involved, and in what combination? (See AMPERSAND.)

4 comma after and

Do not use a comma after **and** unless the comma is the first of a pair: *And, as their numbers and morale rise, they may become bolder* (the comma after *and* is correct because it pairs with the comma after *rise*); *The guide book is too bulky for tourists to carry around and, even more unfortunately, the print is too small* (the comma after *and* pairs with the one after *unfortunately*).

and/or

This form is useful in legal and other official contexts; *soldiers and/or sailors* is shorter than *soldiers or sailors or both*. It should be avoided in general writing. It can often be replaced by *or* alone.

anemic

See AN(A)EMIC.

anesthetic

See AN(A)ESTHETIC.

angle

This is legitimately used to mean 'standpoint', but is a somewhat OVERUSED word: *to consider the matter from an administrative angle*. It can sometimes be neatly replaced by an adverb; here, perhaps, by *administratively*. The use of **angle** to mean 'approach or technique for accomplishing something' (*He has a new angle for solving our financial problem*) should be avoided in serious writing.

Anglo-Indian

This formerly meant a British person living mostly in India. Today it means a person of mixed British and Indian descent. The distinction should be remembered when reading older literature.

angry

One is **angry** *at* or *about* things or events, and **angry** *with* people: *She was angry at the delay, and angry with me for causing it*. If one is **angry** *about* people one is displeased, not with them but at what has happened to them: *I was angry about poor George; they've treated him badly*.

annalist

See ANALYST.

annex(e)

The verb is spelled without the final *e*: *to annex new territory*. The noun (*slept in the hotel annex(e)*) usually ends with *e* in British but not American English.

annual, perennial

An **annual** plant completes its life cycle in one growing season; a **perennial** one lives for several years, usually with new growth each year.

annul

Other forms are **annulling, annulled**; the noun is **annulment**.

annunciation, enunciation

Both words can mean an 'announcement'. However, the **Annunciation** now refers specifically to the announcing by the angel to Mary that she was to give birth to Christ; while **enunciation**, besides meaning distinctness in pronouncing (*the enunciation of his consonants*), means the systematic formulation or listing of what is announced: *the enunciation of our political doctrines*.

anodyne

This means 'soothing and comforting': *anodyne medicines*. Its users should be aware that it has also the derogatory sense of 'bland, expurgated, or inducing unconcern': *He wrote a doctored and anodyne account of the riots*.

another

1 Another should be followed by *than*, rather than by *from* or *to*: *another century than ours*.

2 See EACH OTHER.

Antarctic, Antarctica

In careful speech, the first *c* should be pronounced clearly. The second syllable should not sound like 'art'.

ante-, anti-

Ante- means 'earlier than' (*antenatal*) or 'in front of' (*antechamber*). **Anti-**, which is much commoner, has various meanings, including 'against' (*antivivisection*) or 'opposite to' (*anticlockwise*). See also ANTI-.

antenna

Insects and (figuratively) people have **antennae**, television aerials are **antennas**; but see -AE.

anterior

Anterior *to* can seem a PRETENTIOUS way of saying *before*, as in *drama anterior to Shakespeare*.

anti-

1 See ANTE-.

2 Anti- rhymes with *panty* in British English, rather than having the second syllable like *tie*.

3 Anti- in the sense of reversing the usual characteristics has given rise to many compounds. Thus, an **anti-hero** is an ignoble feckless creature, **anti-novels** and **anti-art** flout the traditional values of their kind. The humorist Paul Jennings referred to a particularly rebarbative cat as an **anti-pet**.

anticipate

The very common use of **anticipate** to mean 'expect' has been established in English since the 18th century, and does not appear to cause confusion with the other senses. Some writers prefer, however, to confine **anticipate** to the senses 'use in advance' (*He anticipated his salary*) and 'forestall' (*We anticipated our competitors by publishing first*), and to use *expect* or *foresee* for the other sense; they therefore avoid using **anticipate** *that*, since it must mean 'expect that' (*It is anticipated that the interest rate will rise*). **Anticipate** with an infinitive (*His book is anticipated to be a popular success*), which also means 'expect', is incorrect.

antique, antiquated

See ANCIENT.

antiseptic, aseptic

Both words refer to what prevents infection, but while **antiseptic** applies mostly to the killing of bacteria (*antiseptic ointment*), **aseptic** usually means 'surgically clean' (*an aseptic bandage*).

antisocial, asocial, unsociable, unsocial, nonsocial

As opposites of *social*, these words have some overlap of meaning. **Antisocial** often means 'harmful or hostile to society': *It's antisocial to leave litter about*; and is today a common euphemism for the jocular censure of quite deplorable doings: *It's antisocial to set fire to the college*. The rarer word **asocial** refers mainly to the rejection of society: *the asocial life of a recluse*. **Unsociable** means reserved and perhaps shy: *He's too unsociable even to say good morning*. **Unsocial** may be a synonym for **asocial**, but its chief use in British English today is in the phrase *unsocial hours*, meaning those worked outside the normal working day so that the worker is excluded from social activity. **Nonsocial** is a neutral word, mainly used in technical contexts, meaning 'not socially oriented': *nonsocial bees*.

antithetical

This can often seem a PRETENTIOUS way of saying 'against' or 'opposed': *behaviour quite antithetical to the spirit of the school*. It is, however, a useful word when one needs to highlight the idea of diametrically opposite poles: *a combination of antithetical elements which are at eternal war with one another* (W S Gilbert).

anxious

1 One is **anxious** *about* something; **anxious** *for* something to happen or *that* something should happen; **anxious** *to* do something.

2 Some writers avoid using **anxious** for *eager* (*He's anxious to improve his tennis*) and like to confine the word to contexts of worry or solicitude. There seems no reason for objecting to this extension of the sense.

any

1 Even when **any** is used as an adjective before a singular noun, it is sometimes followed by a plural pronoun: *I'm sorry to see any employee lose their job so suddenly.* This avoids using either *he* for both sexes or the awkward *he or she*, but some writers object to the plural pronoun. See SEXISM.

A similar point applies to the pronouns **anybody**, **anyone**, **everybody**, **everyone**, **nobody**, **someone**, **somebody**. These go with a singular verb, but often take plural pronouns in speech: *Has anybody lost their glasses?*; *Everyone does their best.* This use is not established in formal writing. See NUMBER AGREEMENT (7).

When **any** is a pronoun, it can be plural in a plural context: *Are any of them ready?* But *Is any of them* . . . is equally correct.

2 Many people feel it illogical to use **any** in comparing things of the same class, as in *She's a better dentist than any I know*; *the most beautiful of any English cathedral*, and prefer to replace it by **any** *other* (*a better dentist than any other I know*) or by *all* (*the most beautiful of all English cathedrals*).

3 Any is correctly used as an adverb before an adjective or another adverb: *I can't work any faster.* It is used adverbially, in informal American English, with no following adjective or adverb: *You certainly aren't helping me any*; but the construction may still be felt to be exotic in Britain.

anybody, anyone

See ANY (1); ELSE.

anymore

1 The joining of **any** and **more** into one word is common in American English though not in British English. It occurs only when the combination means 'any longer': *They don't live here anymore.* The words are always spelled as two when they mean 'even the smallest quantity': *I can't eat any more.*

2 The dialectal American use of **anymore** in positive statements, with the meaning 'now, at the present time' (*I really feel sorry for him anymore*), is avoided by careful writers.

anyone

This means 'any person, anybody': *Marry anyone you like*. **Any one** means 'any single' (thing or person): *open any one of the three boxes*; *I don't think any one man could lift it*.

anyplace

This is common in informal American use, meaning 'anywhere': *Put it anyplace you like*. It is, however, avoided by careful writers of serious American prose, who prefer **anywhere**.

anytime

This spelling of **any** and **time** as one adverb is common in informal American English: *We can pick it up anytime*. British English prefers *(at) any time*.

anyway(s)

1 Any and way are combined into one word in both American and British English when the combination means 'in any case': *I don't want to go; anyway, I can't*. But they must be two separate words when they mean '(in) any direction or method': *Any way we go will involve climbing*.

2 The form **anyways** is used in a casual style in American English.

anywhere(s)

Any and **where** are always combined into one word in American and British English, unless for jocular reasons one wants to put an adjective between them: *I don't want to go just any old where*. The form **anywheres** is dialectal.

apart from, aside from

Apart from is both British and American, **aside from** is chiefly American. They both mean 'besides': *Quite apart from the expense, I don't enjoy it*. They also mean 'except': *It was the worst period of my life, apart from the war*. They should thus be avoided where confusion is possible.

aperture

Apart from its meaning in optics and photography, this can often seem merely a PRETENTIOUS way of saying 'opening' or 'hole': *peer through a small aperture in the wall.*

apex

The plural is either **apexes** or **apices**.

apiary, aviary

Bees are kept in an **apiary**, birds in an **aviary**.

apiece

This is spelled as one word when it means 'each, singly': *I gave them £5 apiece.* It is a slightly quaint or dialectal word, which may be better replaced by *each*.

apogee

This is a technical word in astronomy for the farthest point reached by an orbiting satellite from the body that it orbits. Otherwise, **apogee** can seem a somewhat PRETENTIOUS way of saying 'peak': *Her brilliant career reached its apogee in the 1970s.*

apology, apologia, apologetics, apologue

The first three all refer to matter offered in explanation. An **apology**, with its related adjective **apologetic**, is an expression of regret for something admittedly done wrong: *an apology for his rudeness; an apologetic smile*. **Apology** is also an alternative word for **apologia**, which means a formal explanation of why one does or believes something, without necessarily any idea of guilt: *the finest apologia or explanation of what drives a man to devote his life to pure mathematics* (*British Book News*). **Apologetics** is close to this in meaning, but while an apologia commonly refers to a person's actions, **apologetics** is systematic argument in defence of a doctrine, often a theological one, and the word emphasizes the combatting of criticism: *Marxist apologetics*. The rare word **apologue** is nothing to do with any of the above, but means a moral tale, like Aesop's Fables.

a posteriori, a priori

A posteriori argument looks back from observed facts and draws a conclusion as to what must have caused them, as when we argue that it must have been raining because the road is slippery. **A priori** argument looks forward from a cause to what we assume must be the effect, as when we argue that the road will be slippery because it is raining.

apostrophe

1 genitive
2 contractions
3 plurals of letters, digits, cited words

1 genitive

The apostrophe signals that a noun or an indefinite pronoun (such as *someone, anybody, everyone, nobody*) is in the GENITIVE (or possessive) case. See – 's.

The general rules (a)-(c) are straightforward:

(a) If the word is singular, add *'s*.

the *woman's* job (the job held by the *woman*)
Hamlet's indecision (the indecision shown by *Hamlet*)
her *niece's* school (the school attended by her *niece*)
a full *day's* work (the work lasting for a full *day*)
nobody's fault (the fault that can be ascribed to *nobody*)
everyone's need (the need that *everyone* has)
the *boss's* daughter (the daughter of the *boss*)
the young *actress's* success (the success achieved by the young *actress*)
Morris's views (the views held by *Morris*)

(b) If the word is plural but does not end in *s*, add *'s*.

the *women's* objectives (the objectives formulated by the *women*)
the *Irishmen's* reasons (the reasons given by the *Irishmen*)
our *children's* toys (the toys belonging to our *children*)
the *people's* votes (the votes cast by the *people*)
the *police's* actions (the actions by the *police*)
the *clergy's* opinions (the opinions held by the *clergy*)

(c) If the word is plural and ends in *s*, add just an apostrophe.

our *parents'* letters (letters from our *parents*)
the *Kennedys'* supporters (the supporters of the *Kennedys*)

The next sections (d)-(f) state exceptions to rule (a), which requires *'s* for singular names:

(d) Some names ending with an *s* have variant pronunciations in the genitive, either no addition or an added 'iz' sound at the end. They also have variant spellings – apostrophe alone (the more common) or apostrophe *s*.

Burns' poetry	*Jones'* house
Dickens' novels	*Keats'* poetry
Jesus' life	*Moses'* teachings

(e)   Greek names of more than one syllable that end in *-s* take only the apostrophe. There is no added 'iz' sound at the end.

Aristophanes' plays   *Socrates'* life
Euripides' characters   *Xerxes'* defeat

(f)   Words ending in a 's' sound that combine with *sake* may take either the apostrophe alone (*for goodness' sake*) or nothing (*for goodness sake*). Prefer the spelling without the apostrophe: *for goodness (conscience, appearance) sake*. (But the plural form as in *for old times' sake* requires an apostrophe.)

Here are some other special cases:

(g)   The *'s* is added at the end of a compound or noun phrase (where the noun is modified by an *of*-phrase).

my *daughter-in-law's* parents   the *Duke of Edinburgh's* opinion
a *notary public's* signature   The *University of Chicago's* President
a *passer-by's* evidence   the *director of the museum's* secretary
the *court martial's* verdict   the *captain of the team's* bat

In informal style a final *'s* appears after other modifiers (*the boy at the back's grin, the man sitting in the armchair's hat*) and in nouns linked by *and* (*Bill and Mary's house*). On the latter, see LINKED GENITIVES.

An interesting problem is posed in this quotation from *The Times*: *The Prince of Wales's (later Edward VII) passion for the turf began about 1886. . . .* It is odd to add the apostrophe to *The Prince of Wales* and not to the parallel phrase, the appositive *Edward VII*, but to do so would also be odd – *The Prince of Wales's (later Edward VII's) passion* – because it was the Prince of Wales that later became Edward VII, not the Prince of Wales's passion that later became Edward VII's passion. The sentence should have been rephrased to avoid the genitive, eg: *The passion for the turf shown by the Prince of Wales (later Edward VII) . . . .*

(h)   The genitive noun may refer to a place.

We'll see you later at *Mary's*.

I'm going to the *hairdresser's*.

With large businesses, the genitive is sometimes interpreted as a plural. The result is that there may be more than one possible form.

	Woolworths.
We shop at	*Woolworth's.*
	Woolworth.

| | *Macy's.* |
| I'm going to | *Macys'.* |

(i)   The apostrophe is obligatory in singular time expressions such as *in an hour's time* and *a month's postponement*. It is preferable in similar plural expressions: *a five hours' flight*, *three months' notice*. Contrast the hyphenated *a five-hour delay* and *that two-year course*.

(j)   The apostrophe should not be used with the possessive pronouns *hers*, *its*, *ours*, *theirs*, *yours*. The spelling *it's* is a contraction of *it is* or *it has*.

2   contractions

The apostrophe is used to mark the place in a contraction where something is omitted.

can't	she'll	o'clock (of the clock)
don't	it's (it is *or* it has)	the '80s (the 1980s)
isn't	there's (there is *or* there has)	shan't
we're	won't	they've

3   plurals of letters, digits, cited words

The apostrophe *s* is sometimes used to mark the unusual plurals of letters, digits (including year dates), and words that are cited as items of language, but the simple addition of *s* is more frequent. Use *'s* for lower-case letters where the presence of the apostrophe avoids misinterpretation or confusion:

Dot your *i*'s and cross your *t*'s.

Otherwise, prefer *s* alone:

They are now emphasizing the three *R*s once more.

That occurred in the *1960s*.

There are too many *ifs* in that sentence.

Except for the types of instances mentioned earlier in this section, it is incorrect (though not uncommon in shop notices) to use *'s* for plurals that are not genitives (*1lb of tomato's*).

appal(l)

This is spelled with one *l* in British English, usually two *l*'s in American English, but, in either case, other forms are **appalled**, **appalling**.

apparatus

The third syllable is pronounced 'rate' in British English, but 'rate' and 'rat' are equally acceptable in American English.

appear

This can mean 'seem': *The manager appeared anxious*; or 'arrive': *The manager appeared in the office before nine*. When the word is followed by a verb in the infinitive, confusion is possible between the two senses. Does *The manager appeared to explain his views* mean that he seemed to explain them, or that he came in order to explain them?

appellation

This is rather a PRETENTIOUS or FACETIOUS word for 'name' or 'title': *He was unworthy of the appellation of 'critic'*.

appendix

The plural can be either **appendices** or **appendixes**, but **appendices** is probably better for supplements (*useful appendices at the back of the book*) and **appendixes** for internal organs (*They've both had their appendixes out*).

apposition

1 general
2 restrictive and nonrestrictive apposition
3 appositive as pseudo-title
4 pronoun form
5 *and* and *or*

1 general
When two units are equivalent, they are in apposition and generally the second unit is an appositive to the first: *My daughter has received* **the first prize, a dictionary**. (The first prize was a dictionary.) Typically, as in this example, the two units are noun phrases (phrases having a noun as the main word).

2 restrictive and nonrestrictive apposition
Appositives may be restrictive (defining) or nonrestrictive (descriptive) (see RELATIVE CLAUSES). The appositive is restrictive in *The government ignored* **the objection that the antipollution measures would greatly increase the cost of the products**; *the objection* is defined by the following appositive (*that the antipollution measures would . . .*). On the other hand, it is nonrestrictive in *The government ignored* **their main objection, that the antipollution measures would greatly increase the cost of the products**. The first unit – *their main objection* – is sufficiently identified; the nonrestrictive appositive gives explanatory information that could be introduced by *namely* or *that is (to say)*. Restrictive apposition is not punctuated, but it is usual to separate nonrestrictive appositives by commas or occasionally by dashes or brackets, or (at the end of a sentence) by a colon. A nonrestrictive appositive may refer back to the whole of the sentence that precedes it: *The scientists wanted their research to be useful*, **an indication of their desire to work for the benefit of humanity**.

51

When both units are noun phrases, the appositive tends to be nonrestrictive: *I have visited* **their home, a rambling Victorian house**; *The book is about* **Jane Austen, my favourite author**. Compare the nonrestrictive phrase in *Meet Norman,* **my husband** with the restrictive phrase in *Meet* **my husband** *Norman*. Other examples of restrictive apposition are **The physicist** *Albert Einstein*, *John* **the Baptist, the word** *'and'*.

3 appositive as pseudo-title
In journalistic style, appositives are often used as if they were titles: **35-year-old department store heir** *Ann Johnson*; **chairman of the committee for social security** *Mark Smith*; **vice-president for personnel** *Norma Riley*. Prefer the construction with the appositive in second place and introduced with *the* or *a*: *Ann Johnson,* **the 35-year-old department store heir**. See FALSE TITLES.

4 pronoun form
The choice of pronoun form for an appositive (*I* or *me*, *we* or *us*, etc) depends on whether it is part of the subject or object, etc: **Both of us, Alice and I,** *were nominated to the committee* (*Both of us, Alice and I* is subject); *The police interviewed* **both of us, Alice and me** (*both of us, Alice and me* is direct object). The objective form is correct after *let us*: **Let us, you and me,** *attend to the business* (*us* is objective, and so should be the appositional *you and me*); *Please* **let us, Mary and me,** *join your group*. But see LET.

5 *and* and *or*
The conjunctions *and* and *or* sometimes introduce an appositive: *I turned for advice to my sister* **and my closest friend**; *They preferred the weather in the British Isles,* **or the United Kingdom and Eire**. Take care in using these appositions, since they can cause misunderstandings. For example, if *my sister and my closest friend* are in apposition, then 'my sister' is the same person as 'my closest friend'. But unless the readers are aware of this, they are more likely to think that *and* here indicates two different people.

appraise, apprise

To **appraise** something is to assess its value: *to appraise the cost of a project*. The word is often wrongly used instead of **apprise**, which means 'inform, notify': *They apprised him of the facts*. **Apprise**, not **appraise**, would have been the right word in a British legal document which declared that the purchaser *has been appraised of details of the accommodation and premises*.

appreciate

1 The third syllable is usually pronounced 'she'. An alternative pronunciation 'see' exists, but may sound rather too genteel to ears that are not used to it. Compare NEGOTIATE.

2 One central sense of **appreciate** is 'esteem at full value', or 'recognize with gratitude': *I appreciate all you have done for us*. This sense has been extended in business English to express polite requests: *We should appreciate an early answer; It would be appreciated if you would return the documents*. By a further extension, **appreciate** can now mean 'realize' or 'understand': *I appreciate that things have been difficult*. In both these senses, **appreciate** is now an OVERUSED word. To prune its exuberance, replace it in the first sense by *We should be glad/ grateful/obliged*; in the second by *admit, realize, recognize, understand*; and avoid following it with a clause beginning with *that*. When the word is followed by a noun (*I appreciate your difficulties*), the sense is closer to the earlier meaning of 'esteem'.

apprehend, comprehend

There is considerable overlap of meaning between these two words; both mean 'understand'. **Apprehend** chiefly means 'discern, become aware of', or 'recognize the existence of' something, as in *apprehend eternal truths*. **Comprehend** means 'grasp mentally, get to the bottom of' something, and emphasizes the thought-processes involved: *He may not comprehend that type of argumentation*.

apprise

See APPRAISE.

appropriate (*adjective*)

This somewhat OVERUSED word has its uses, but can often be replaced by *right, suitable, proper*, or *fitting*. Bureaucrats use it in their jargon to hide behind. There, *in appropriate cases* may mean 'whenever I feel like doing it'.

a priori

See A POSTERIORI.

apropos

1 This is one word, with no accent, in modern English; *à propos* is French.

2 As a preposition, the word means 'with reference to', and is properly used either with no following preposition or with *of*: *apropos (of) the recent dispute*. **Apropos** should not be followed by *to*.

apt, liable, likely

Apt and **liable**, before an infinitive verb, mean 'having a general timeless tendency': *It's apt/liable to rain in Scotland*. They are both coming to mean that something will probably happen in the future: *It's apt/liable to rain this afternoon*. Some writers still prefer **likely** in this sense, and confine **liable** to undesirable things: *liable to get dirty* rather than *liable to stay clean*.

aqueduct

This word has only one *a*, in contrast with such words as **aqualung** and **aquamarine**.

Arab, Arabian, Arabic

Arab means 'of the Arab people': *an Arab sheikh*. **Arabian** today refers to Arabia, the peninsula between the Red Sea and the Persian Gulf: *Arabian fauna*; it is also an older word for **Arab**: *an Arabian horse*. **Arabic** refers to the language, literature, or script of the Arabs: *Arabic numerals*.

arbiter, arbitrator

In British English, an **arbiter** has a decisive influence (*an arbiter of fashion*) whereas an **arbitrator** is called in to decide a dispute between parties, but is not necessarily obeyed. The distinction is less absolute in American English.

arc

Despite their spelling, the verb forms **arced, arcing** are pronounced to rhyme with *parked, parking*. They are sometimes spelled **arcked, arcking**.

arch-, archi-

When this prefix means 'chief', **arch-** is pronounced 'artch' except in *archangel*. In its form **archi-**, the pronunciation is always 'arki': *architect, archidiaconal*.

arch(a)eology

See AE-.

archaism

An archaism is a word or expression formerly in general use but now rarely used except in restricted contexts. Examples: *anon, howbeit, perchance, quoth*. Archaic words and expressions occur in some religious language (for example, *thou, thee, thy*, and the corresponding verb forms such as *doth* and *saith*) and in some legal language. Skilled writers may occasionally make good use of archaisms in poetry or in humorous writing, but they are inappropriate in normal prose.

archetype

1 This is pronounced 'arki-'.

2 It can mean the original pattern from which other things are copied: *the House of Commons, the archetype of all the representative assemblies which now meet* (T B Macaulay). In Jungian psychology, an **archetype** is an inherited idea derived from the experience of the whole human race. Today this rather OVERUSED word often means a perfectly typical example of something: *the archetype of the golden-hearted strumpet*.

Arctic

In careful speech, the first *c* should be pronounced clearly. The first syllable should not sound like 'art'.

ardo(u)r

This is spelled **ardour** in British English, **ardor** in American English.

aren't I

This is the commonest British contraction of the formal *am I not*; but although perfectly acceptable in Britain, it is felt to be somewhat affected in American English. See AIN'T.

Argentina

This, rather than *the* **Argentine**, is the recommended name for the South American republic. The people are **Argentinians**, rather than **Argentines**, and the related adjective is also **Argentinian.**

arguably

This can mean 'as may be shown by argument': *She is arguably the best cellist in Europe*. See SENTENCE ADVERBS.

arise, rise

Arise is chiefly abstract: *if the occasion arises; A problem has arisen*. **Rise** is literal: *The water is rising*; *The sun has risen*. Both words are excessively literary for the meaning 'get out of bed'. Compare AROUSE.

aristocrat

The recommended, conservative British pronunciation is with the stress on the first syllable. The largely American pronunciation, with the stress on the second syllable, is also heard in Britain.

arithmetical, geometrical progression

An **arithmetical progression** is a sequence such as 3, 5, 7, 9 in which each number differs from the one in front of it by the same amount; a **geometrical progression** is a sequence such as 3, 6, 12, 24 in which each number differs from the one in front of it in the same ratio. Both expressions are loosely used to suggest a fast rate of increase: *The number of families holidaying abroad grew in geometrical progression*. In fact, both sorts of progression may be very slow if they grow by a small enough increment: 1000, 1000½, 1001 is an **arithmetical progression**, too. Mathematicians more often use the expressions *arithmetic sequence* and *geometric sequence*.

armada

The second syllable is now usually pronounced 'ahd', rather than 'aid'.

armamentarium

This word has extended its range from its original sphere of medicine (*an armamentarium of new antibiotics*) to mean any array of abstract tools or weapons: *equip them with a formidable armamentarium of skills*. In this sense, it occurs in managerial and business school jargon.

armed with

This is often a journalistic way of saying 'carrying; equipped with': *He arrived armed with a box of chocolates*. It should be avoided unless an actual weapon is involved.

armo(u)r

This is spelled **armour** in British English, **armor** in American English.

around, round, about

In American English, **around** is a preferable substitute for nearly all senses of the other two words. In British English, the situation is more complicated. Here, the use of **around** for **about** to mean 'approximately', as in *around 60%* or *around three o'clock*, is becoming more common, although some people still feel it to be an Americanism. British speakers may prefer to use **round** for the idea of 'revolving' (*The wheels go round*; *They danced round the tree*) and also for the idea of 'circuitousness', or the other side of something (*the shop round the corner*), but they are willing to use **around** as the Americans do for the idea of 'surrounding' (*seated around the fire*) and for 'here and there' (*travelling around*). American and British speakers alike use **about,** not **around** or **round,** informally where *almost* would be better in formal writing (*I'm about ready*); for 'concerning' (*a book about rabbits*); for 'on one's person' (*I've no money about me*; most people prefer *on me* here); and for 'out of bed' (*he's already up and about*).

arouse, rouse

These can both mean 'awaken'. On the whole, **arouse** is more often abstract, meaning 'excite': *arouse curiosity/suspicion; sexually aroused.* **Rouse** is more usual for the literal sense: *rouse the sleeping children.* Compare ARISE.

arpeggio

The plural is **arpeggios.**

arrant, errant

Arrant means 'deplorably great': *arrant nonsense.* **Errant** means 'straying': *errant sheep*; or 'misbehaving': *an errant husband.*

arrogate

See ABROGATE.

art(s)

When it is used as an adjective, **art** refers to aesthetic creation: *art pottery*; *an art theatre*; *an art school.* **Arts** as an adjective means those fields of study normally distinguished from the physical and social sciences: *History is an arts subject.* Such subjects are also called the *humanities.* In American education, the *liberal* **arts** include the natural and social sciences, though not the applied ones such as medicine and engineering.

artefact, artifact

1 In Britain, **artefact** is probably the commoner spelling; in the USA, **artifact** is usual.

2 From its earlier sense, of an object produced by human workmanship, this word is now loosely extended to mean a typical and usually bad consequence or effect: *Drug abuse has been regarded as* *an artefact of mass unemployment.* This tendency should be resisted by careful writers.

articulate

The verb is OVERUSED. As a variation, one can often replace it by *express* (*to articulate one's grievances*). The adjective is coming into use as a general term of critical praise, where nothing verbal is involved. A painter's design or a violinist's performance can now be **articulate**, meaning 'coherent' or 'well-arranged'.

artificial, synthetic

Both words refer to what is produced by human agency rather than found in nature; but **artificial** tends to be used of things that are not really what they imitate (*artificial flowers* are not really flowers), while **synthetic** things, though highly processed, usually are what their names indicate (*synthetic dyes* and *fibres* really are dyes and fibres).

artiste, artist

An **artiste** (rhyming with *beast*) is a male or female professional performer, especially a singer or dancer: *circus artistes.* An **artist** is particularly a painter or sculptor, but **artist** is also used in admiration of anyone, such as a gifted cook or hairdresser, who makes an art of an occupation. The modern tendency is for **artist** to supersede **artiste** in all contexts.

as

1 **as** *me* or **as** *I*	10	**as** *is*, **as** *was*
2 **as** or **so** in comparisons	11	**as** *from*, **as** *of*
3 omitted **as**	12	**as** *to*, **as** *for*
4 unnecessary **as**	13	**as** *if*, **as** *though*
5 **as** *such*	14	**as** *far* **as**; see FAR
6 **as** = 'in the capacity of'	15	**as** *follows*; see FOLLOW
7 **as** = 'while' or 'because'	16	**as** *long* **as**; see LONG
8 **as** (*how*) for **that**	17	**as** *well* **as**; see WELL
9 **as** or **like**		

1 **as** *me* or **as** *I*

In formal writing, *She is as tall* **as** *I/he/she/they* is preferable to *She is as tall* **as** *me/him/her/them*. (See CASE, GRAMMATICAL.) The point at issue is whether **as** in this context is a preposition, like *on* or *after* (nobody would write *on he* or *after we*); or whether it is a conjunction, with a following verb that has been omitted: *as he is, as we are.* It is often better to include the verb, since *as fat as I* may sound too formal, and *as fat as me* be frowned on, but nobody can object to *as fat as I am*. It is actually safer to include the verb where the comparison might otherwise be ambiguous. *He sees me as often as Mary* may mean either . . . *as he sees Mary* or . . . *as Mary does*.

2 as or so in comparisons

There is no foundation for the old-fashioned doctrine that **so** is better than **as** in negative sentences: *It's not as cold as yesterday* is just as correct as *It's not so cold as yesterday*. We must, of course, use **as**, not **so**, in a positive sentence: *It's as cold as yesterday*. In the sentence *Ask for a hundred pounds a week, if you can find anyone who thinks you worth as much*, *as much* suggests that the sum is paltry, while *so much* would mean it was considerable. For **as/so long as,** see LONG.

3 omitted as

Do not leave out the second **as** in sentences such as *She can play as well as or better than you can*. (See ELLIPSIS.) If the sentence sounds clumsy with the repeated **as**, rephrase it as *She can play as well as you, or better*. Rephrase it in any case if correct English would require two **as**'s in a row. *He regarded it not so much as an insult as as a waste of time* sounds better as *He regarded it more as a waste of time than as an insult*. It is, however, respectable informal English to leave out the first **as** in *(as) dry as a bone, (as) old as the hills*.

4 unnecessary as

As can be omitted from expressions like these: *They appointed him (as) caretaker*. It is better omitted here: *as and when the Bill becomes an Act* (leave out *as and* or *and when*, according to the sense). But omission is not the solution in the following, from the *Daily Telegraph*: [The Archbishop] *said that part of the meaning of yesterday's service was as a re-assertion of public faith*. The neatest improvement might be *yesterday's service was partly meant as* (or *intended as*, or *meant to be*) *a re-assertion of public faith*.

5 as *such*

As *such* often means 'in itself, intrinsically considered': *Money, as such, cannot buy happiness*. It needs to be used with caution. In the sentence *There is no difficulty in the allocation of overheads as such*, the expression **as** *such* might mean overheads as overheads, or the allocation as an allocation, or the difficulty as a difficulty. The idea would be more clearly expressed as *There is no difficulty in principle*, if that is what is intended.

6 as = 'in the capacity of'

This sense is closely related to **as** *such*: *I give you this warning as a director of the firm*. This sort of phrase introduced by **as** is apt to become displaced in the sentence, with nonsensical results rather like those of the DANGLING PARTICIPLE. *As a director of the firm, you should* *accept my warning* should be used only if 'you' are the director, not 'me'.

7 as = 'while' or 'because'

As can mean 'while': *As she picked the gooseberries, she sang*; or 'because': *As I can't speak Greek, her charm was lost on me*. Both of these are perfectly good English; but **as** should be replaced by *while*, *because*, etc according to the intended meaning where there is any possibility of confusion: *As we were walking, he showed us the map*; *As we have yielded to their demands, the pressures have become greater*.

8 as (*how*) for that

Avoid the use of **as**, or **as how**, for **that**, except when deliberately representing regional speech: *not as* (replace by *that*) *I know of*; *He says as how* (replace by *that*) *he's thirsty*.

9 as or like

Use **like**, not **as**, before a noun, to mean 'similarly to, in the same way as', where no verb follows: *to sing like a bird*. When a verb does follow, **as** is to be preferred today for formal writing, although the construction with **like** as conjunction has long been current in English: *We are overrun by them, like the Australians were by rabbits* (Winston Churchill). Use **as,** not **like,** before adverbs: *occasions when, as now* (not *like now*), *we have no option*; and before prepositions, or where there should be prepositions: *a book in which, as in his last* (not *like his last*), *he discusses the implications of modern genetics*. There is a difference between *Let me speak to you like a father* (ie in the way your own father might) and *Let me speak to you as a father* (ie in my capacity as your father). Some people insist on **such as**, not **like,** in formal writing to introduce examples: *a subject such as physics*. Do not use **like** for **as if**: *lying on the floor* **like** (use **as if**) *he was dead*. (But see section 13 below.) In an overzealous effort to avoid the excessive use of **like**, some people err in the opposite direction and use **as** in the wrong places: *He trembled as* (use *like*) *a leaf*; *As* (use *Like*) *his father before him, he preferred brandy*. See HYPERCORRECTION.

10 as *is*, as *was*

The idioms **as** *is* (*bought the clock at an auction as is*) and **as** *was* (*This is a picture of my boss as was*) belong to informal rather than to formal English.

11 as *from*, as *of*

The somewhat bureaucratic expressions **as** *from* and **as** *of* are useful for saying that something is to take effect retrospectively, from some named earlier date: *This charge is payable as from the 1st January last*. There seems no point in them when we speak of the present or future: *This charge is payable as of today* (use *from*); *This charge will be* *payable/will cease to be payable as from the 1st January next* (use *payable from, cease to be payable on*).

12 as *to*, as *for*

When it is used of doubts, arguments, and questions, **as** *to* is often better replaced by *about*, *on*, or *of*: *I have no information as to* (use *about*) *his plans.* When possible, it is better omitted altogether, particularly before *whether: There is some doubt/some question (as to) whether they will be available*; *Have you the least notion (as to) what it means?*; *Nobody could decide (as to) what to do.* But both **as to** and **as for** are a useful way of bringing something important to the front of a sentence. They refer to an earlier topic, and mean 'when we come to the matter of': *You can have a bed, but as for/as to the children, they'll have to sleep on the floor.*

13 as *if*, as *though*

As *if* and as *though* are normally followed by the subjunctive *were* rather than *was* in formal writing: *He spoke as if I were deaf*; *She behaves as though she were a millionaire.* But the ordinary present tense is required where the emphasis is on truth rather than falsity: *It's not as if he's dishonest* (ie he's honest); *It looks as though we're landing* (ie fasten your seatbelts). See SUBJUNCTIVE.

-as

See -AE.

ascend

This is a very formal way to say 'go up': *He ascended into heaven.* Outside appropriate contexts it can seem rather PRETENTIOUS.

ascendancy, ascendant

These two nouns can also be spelled **-ency, -ent**. The expressions *have an ascendancy over*, *be in the ascendant*, *the ascendancy of* are borrowed from astrology, and all imply dominance and controlling influence, not the tendency to rise. Thus, *political ideas now in the ascendancy* are those that are dominant now, not the ones that are on the increase. The adjective **ascendant**, as distinct from the noun, can mean 'rising': *ascendant stems of a plant.*

ascent, assent

Ascent is 'going up': *the ascent of the Matterhorn.* **Assent** is 'agreement': *He gave his assent to the plan.*

ascertain

This is a formal way of saying 'find out', and may sound PRETENTIOUS: *ascertain what time the train arrives*. Since it suggests 'find out definitely', it also sounds odd to combine it with an expression of uncertainty, as in *ascertain the approximate height of the wall*.

aseptic

See ANTISEPTIC.

Asian, Asiatic

Asian is the preferred word for the peoples and cultures of Asia. **Asiatic** may be considered offensive.

aside from

See APART FROM.

asked

Some people prefer to pronounce the *k* in careful speech; others find this pronunciation unnatural and fussy.

asocial

See ANTISOCIAL.

aspect

This is sometimes superfluous. Instead of *She was not a success from a social aspect*, prefer the neater and more economical *She was not a social success* or *She was not a success socially*.

assay, essay (*verb*)

In modern use, to **assay** is to 'evaluate' or 'test' (something, originally a metal): *to assay their ability*; to **essay** is to 'attempt': *to essay a task*. Both verbs are somewhat archaic and very formal.

assemblage (or assembly), nouns of

See NAMES FOR GROUPS.

assent

See ASCENT.

assertive

In business-school jargon, this means 'forceful' and 'striking' in approving contrast to 'dim and retiring'. Firms will advertise for *an assertive and highly-motivated salesman*, and there are educational courses devoted to *assertiveness training*.

assignment, assignation

An **assignment** is a 'job' or 'task': *The reporter's assignment was to interview the dancer*. An **assignation** is an 'agreement to meet', particularly to meet a lover secretly.

assist, assistance

This is a rather formal way of saying 'help' and may sound PRETENTIOUS. It usually suggests less physical involvement; you might *help* someone who is washing a car, but **assist** someone who is looking for a flat. The construction is **assist** (someone) *in* doing something, rather than **assist** (someone) *to* do it. The use of **assist** *at* to mean 'be present at', whereby one can **assist** *at a banquet* without actually passing round the gravy, is borrowed from the French and is somewhat affected in modern English.

association

The expression *in* **association** *with* (*working in association with an oil company*) is often VERBOSE. It can be shortened to *with* alone, unless it is important to suggest a looser connection. To work *with* an oil company might mean to be employed by it.

assume

See PRESUME.

assuming

Modern convention permits the use of **assuming** for 'it can be assumed that': *Assuming he agrees, the work will start on Monday*. See DANGLING PARTICIPLE.

assurance, insurance

In British English **assurance** is the technical word for **insurance** in respect of certainties such as death, rather than possibilities such as theft or fire. Thus, a British **insurance** company will offer you *life* **assurance**, although ordinary people call it *life* **insurance**. In American English **insurance** is used for both.

assure, ensure, insure

1 All these words can mean 'make safe or certain', but they are used in different phrases and contexts: *to ensure accuracy* (in American English also *to insure accuracy*); *an assured position*; *you may rest assured that* . . . (ie you may be certain). To protect something against financial loss is to **insure** it.

2 You **assure** someone *of* a fact, or **assure** someone *that* something is true.

asterisk (*)

This sign draws attention, usually to a footnote; it is placed at the end of what is being noted, and again before the note at the bottom of the page. In modern linguistic writing it introduces a piece of 'wrong' language: **three boy*. Older authors used it where today we would use spaced full stops, to show omitted words or letters.

astern

See ABEAM.

asthma, asthmatic

This is pronounced 'assma' in British English, 'azma' in American English. To pronounce the medial *th* would sound rather unnatural.

astronaut, cosmonaut

Astronaut is the general term for a spaceman; **cosmonaut** is used only for Soviet spacemen.

astronomical

The word is used of enormous numbers and distances, but not in formal writing: *an astronomical sum of money*. It becomes an OVERUSED word when applied to less measurable matters: *an astronomical improvement in housing conditions*.

at

1 **at** *about*
2 **at** *all*
3 **at** or **in**
4 *we* **at**, *here* **at**

1 at *about*
Some people object to this combination, arguing that one must arrive

either *at seven o' clock* (ie exactly) or *about seven o' clock* (ie approximately). The objection seems odd, since **at** can be followed by other similar adverbs (*at exactly/approximately/almost seven o' clock*); and indeed must be, if that is what you want to say, since *He arrived almost seven o' clock* is not English.

2 at all

This means 'ever' (*seldom if at all*) or 'to the least extent' (*not at all far*). It sounds odd when applied to things that are all-or-nothing, as in *not at all married*, or as one secretary asked when filling in a hospital admittance form, *Have you a religion at all?*

3 at or in

(a) **At** suggests a point, **in** suggests an area: we say **at** *the North Pole* but **in** *France*. But the distinction is delicate. A large city is considered to be an area (*He works in London*) but even it, or its airport, may be regarded as a point on the map if global distances are in mind: *We refuelled at London on our way from New York to Moscow*. A small town or village is more likely to be thought of as a point (*He lives at Puddleby-on-the-Marsh*), except by those intimate enough with it to see it as an area: *Everyone in Puddleby is furious with him.*

(b) The British tend to say **at** *school*, **at** *college*, where the Americans would prefer **in** *school*, **in** *college*.

4 we at, here at

With company names, where **in** would be traditional, the use of **at** is modern public-relations jargon: *We at Toadflax Ltd believe* . . . ; *Here at Toadflax we try* . . . .

-ato

See -ADE.

ate

The standard British pronunciation rhymes with *bet*; to rhyme the word with *bait* is either a regionalism or an Americanism. For American English, this position is reversed: the rhyme with *bait* is standard, while the rhyme with *bet* is either a Briticism or substandard.

-ation

Do not write *an enumeration of the flirtations within the organization*; a string of words all ending in **-ation** sounds dreadful. See REPETITION OF SOUNDS AND WORDS.

attempt

The verb **attempt** is more formal than the verb *try*, and may sound

PRETENTIOUS: *to attempt/try to open it.* The noun **attempt,** however, replaces the noun *try* except in rather informal contexts: *to make another attempt/have another try.*

attend

To **attend** *to* a person is to 'look after' or 'pay attention to' him or her: *The hairdresser will attend to you next. To* **attend** an event is to be present at it: *to attend the meeting.*

attire(d)

These formal words are FACETIOUS when used for 'clothes' and 'dressed': *her best Sunday attire.*

attorney general

The plurals **attorney generals** and **attorneys general** are both correct.

attractive

This is an all-purpose word, particularly in journalese, for *beautiful, pretty,* etc, and seems to be applied automatically to young women.

au courant

See AU FAIT.

audible

The word ends in *-ible,* not *-able.*

audit *(verb)*

Besides its technical sense of checking financial accounts *(audit the books),* the word has a chiefly American educational sense, of attending a course without expecting formal credit for it.

auditor

The word ends in *-or,* not *-er.*

au fait, au courant

These both mean 'fully informed and competent': *She's perfectly au fait with financial matters.* **Au courant** emphasizes awareness of the latest developments: to *keep au courant with* the newest publications is to *keep up with* them. **Au fait** sometimes means 'socially correct': *The decorations were perfectly au fait*; but this extension of meaning has not become established. Avoid using such FOREIGN PHRASES.

au fond, à fond

Au fond means 'at bottom' or 'fundamentally': *He's perfectly reliable au fond.* **À fond** means 'to the bottom': *She knows her subject à fond.* Both expressions are somewhat PRETENTIOUS. Avoid such FOREIGN PHRASES.

auger, augur

An **auger** is a tool for boring holes; an **augur** is a person, particularly an ancient Roman, who predicts events. The verb **augur** chiefly means 'give promise of': *Higher pay augurs a better future.*

aught

This means 'all' or 'anything': *for aught I care*; *hard to believe that the outcome can be aught but disastrous.* It belongs to old-fashioned poetic language (see POESY), not to modern writing.

augment

This means 'add more of the same thing': you *augment your staff* by taking on more people. Avoid **augment** where *increase* or *add to* will do; it may seem rather PRETENTIOUS.

au naturel

This means either 'cooked plainly' or 'naked'. It should not be spelled *natural*. Avoid such FOREIGN PHRASES.

aura, aurora

An **aura** is an atmosphere that emanates from someone or something: *The prospectus exudes an aura of respectability.* **Aurora** once meant the dawn, but now chiefly refers to the *Aurora Borealis* – the northern lights – or to the corresponding *Aurora Australis* in the southern hemisphere.

aural, oral

Aural refers to the ears (*a bat's aural apparatus*) and to hearing. **Oral** refers to the mouth (*oral hygiene*) and to speaking in contrast to writing (see VERBAL). The two words are usually pronounced the same, and in certain contexts may overlap in meaning: *aural* and *oral instruction* come to much the same thing.

auspice, augury

These can both mean 'a prophetic sign': *Under these unpromising*

auspices the parting took place (Jane Austen). An **auspice** is
particularly a favourable sign, probably by association with *auspicious*,
which means 'promising future success'. To avoid ambiguity, it is
clearer to retain the neutral **augury** for this sense (*an exciting augury of
the future*), reserving **auspices** (plural) for the chief modern sense of
'kindly support': *a concert arranged under the auspices of the local
Council*. (Since this is a cliché, some writers would prefer to describe
such a concert as *sponsored by* or *supported by* the Council.)

autarchy, autarky

Autarchy means 'absolute sovereignty', or 'autocratic rule'; **autarky**
means 'self-sufficiency', particularly that of a national economy not
dependent on imports. The two words are pronounced the same, but
they come from different Greek words.

authentic, genuine

These both mean that something is exactly what is claimed. So far as
they are distinguishable, **authentic** suggests fidelity to the truth (*an
authentic account*; *a novel's authentic historical background*); **genuine**
means that a thing is not a forgery or substitute (*a genuine Rembrandt*;
genuine maple syrup).

author

1 When a writer refers to himself or herself as *the* **author,** it is a rather
pompous self-important way of saying *I*: *The author* (ie I) *was
hospitably entertained by the villagers to a meal of shellfish.*

2 The verb **author** should usually be avoided where *write* will serve. It
may be defensible where there is some uncertainty as to who actually
sat down at the typewriter, as with reports **authored** (or, better, **co-
authored**) *by* a group, or large undertakings **authored** *by* a
distinguished impresario who delegates the work to a team.

authoress

Most women writers would rather be called *authors*. See FEMININE FORMS

authoritarian, authoritative

Authoritarian means 'favouring or demanding subjection to
authority', rather than allowing freedom, and is chiefly disapproving:
an authoritarian headmaster/system of government. **Authoritative**
means 'possessing acknowledged authority', and is mainly
appreciative: *an authoritative statement/interpretation*. People who are
authoritarian think of themselves as **authoritative**.

authority

Authority *over* an area or domain is the official power to command. One has, in this sense, **authority** *to do* something or *for doing* something: *What authority have you to enter this house?* **Authority** *with* a person or group is the unofficial power to influence: *He has some authority with the students.* A person who knows a lot about something is an **authority** *on* that specific subject or *in* that general field.

autocracy, autonomy

Autocracy is government by one person with unlimited power, an *autocrat.* **Autonomy** is self-government by a country or community: *The member countries of the British Commonwealth have complete autonomy.*

automation

See MECHANIZATION.

automaton

The plural can be either **automatons** or **automata**, but **automata** is the more learned form.

autumn

The word is not usually capitalized.

avail

Normally one **avails** *oneself of* something: *You should avail yourself of the opportunity to learn French.* (This may seem a somewhat PRETENTIOUS substitute for *take* or *seize the opportunity*.) The construction should not be used in the passive as *be* **availed** *of*, so *This chance should be availed of* needs to be rephrased as *This chance should be taken*, or *made use of*.

avenge, revenge, vengeance

These all refer to punishing someone who has wronged either oneself or a person one loves. The less common word **avenge** suggests the vindication of an abstract justice: *Avenge, O Lord, thy slaughtered saints* (John Milton). It is a more highminded word than **revenge**, which just means 'getting even' and may suggest spite and malice. The noun **vengeance** means both **avenging** and **revenging**.

aver

This very formal word means 'declare forcefully'. It should not be used as a mere variation on *say*.

average, median, mean

An **average** is the sum of the quantities in a group divided by their number; the **average** of 3, 8, 10 is 7. Confusingly, mathematicians call this the *arithmetic mean*. The **median** is the quantity above and below which there are an equal number of other quantities; the **median** of 3, 8, 10 is 8. The **mean** is the quantity halfway between the largest and the smallest; the **mean** of 3, 8, 10 is 6½. Of the three, **average** is the only word used outside its statistical sense, to mean 'ordinary', or sometimes 'mediocre': *not a brilliant performance, only average.*

averse

1 See ADVERSE.

2 Although some older writers on usage recommend the constructions **averse** *from*, an **aversion** *from*, because the Latin preposition *a* means 'away', **averse** *to* and **aversion** *to* are now the accepted forms.

avert

See ADVERT; AVOID.

aviary

See APIARY.

avid

This suggests an insatiable desire to have or get something: *avid for praise*; *avid readers*. It cannot legitimately include the desire to make or do something, as in the recent broadcast which referred to *building societies avidly producing housing price figures*.

avocation, vocation

An **avocation** is a hobby that is practised in addition to someone's regular job or **vocation**. It may also mean 'job', though **vocation** is by far the commoner word. If the sense of **avocation** is not clear from the context, it is better to substitute an unambiguous synonym.

avoid, prevent, avert

To **avoid** something dangerous is to keep away from it; to **prevent** it is to stop it from happening; to **avert** it is to ward it off, or deflect it.

Thus, a careful writer distinguishes *avoid the splinters of glass* from *prevent the splinters from hitting us*, and does not write *avoid the splinters hitting us*, though *avoid being hit by the splinters* is legitimate. Similarly, one might *avert a flood* by building a wall, but *avoid a flood* by driving round instead of through it.

avuncular

This means 'of or suitable to an uncle', and is generally used figuratively: *avuncular advice*. There is no corresponding word for aunts.

await

See WAIT.

aware

People used only to be **aware** *of* something, or **aware** *that* something was happening: *I am aware of the difficulty*. The word has since become a blanket term of approval. It can stand on its own (*an aware person*) to mean that one understands oneself and one's surroundings; or it can indicate which area of the surroundings one understands, by combinations such as *politically aware*. In these new uses, **aware** has become an OVERUSED word.

away, way

Away has traditionally been used in both British and American English to intensify expressions of distance and time: *They live away out in the country*; *It happened away back in 1910*. The shortened form **way** is common in informal American English, and is making some headway in Britain in such combinations as *way back*, *way above*, *way up*, *way ahead*.

awful, awfully

Awful (*adjective*) now means 'very bad' (*awful weather*) or 'extreme' (*an awful lot of difference*). **Awfully** means 'very' (*awfully difficult*), as does the nonstandard adverb **awful** (*awful tired*). The word has virtually lost its original association with the idea of *awe*. In 1862 Nathaniel Hawthorne could still write *however awfully holy the subject*; but it is safer today to avoid **awful** and **awfully** altogether in serious writing.

awhile, a while

Awhile is an adverb: *to rest awhile* (ie briefly). **While** is a noun: *to rest* *for a while* (ie for a period of time, like *for a week*). Spell it **a while** when it means a period of time: *for a while*; *in a (little) while*; *It took a while to arrive*.

ax(e)

This is spelled **axe** in British English, **ax** or **axe** in American English.

axis

The plural is **axes**.

aye, ay

In both spellings, this means 'yes' (pronounced like *eye*), and is also a poetic word for 'always' (*for aye*, pronounced to rhyme with *day*).

azure

The older pronunciation was like *pleasure* but with the first vowel as in *bad*. This seems to be giving way, in British perhaps more than in American English, to various newer ones with a second syllable like *pure*; indeed the whole word may now rhyme with *lays your*.

Bb

-b-, -bb-

See DOUBLING.

bacillus

The plural is **bacilli**.

back of

Back of, **in back of**, and **in back** are rather informal American English for *at the back (of)*, and are the logical opposite of *in front (of)*: *a yard (in) back of the house*; *a dress that buttons in back*. These expressions are usually replaced by *at the back (of)* or *behind* in formal writing.

back-formation

One major way of creating new words is to add a suffix or a prefix to an existing word; for example, *driver* is derived from *drive*. In back-formation, the new word is created by removing what was (wrongly) felt to be a suffix. Some examples: *burgle* (*burglar*), *sculpt* (*sculptor*), *negate* (*negation*), *reminisce* (*reminiscence*), *baby-sit* (*baby-sitter*), *chain-smoke* (*chain-smoker*), *televise* (*television*). These are now established words in the language. New or recent back-formations are often felt to be mistakes, though they may later become generally accepted. Some examples that should still be avoided in formal writing: *enthuse* (*enthusiasm*), *self-destruct* (*self-destruction*), *couth* (*uncouth*).

background

This has become an OVERUSED word. While it is reasonable to write *The election took place against a background of widespread unemployment*, or to refer to *applicants with widely different backgrounds* (ie origins, qualifications, experience, interests), there are many cases where a more precise expression would be preferable: *The successful applicant will have had a good background of sales experience* (ie will have had ample sales experience); *The weak state of the pound provides the background of the trouble* (ie causes, or explains, the trouble).

backpack

See RUCKSACK.

backward(s)

Before a noun, use **backward**: *a backward child*. After a verb, use the form with an *s* in British English (*to walk backwards*) and the one without an *s* in American English.

bad, badly

The adjective **bad** is correctly used after 'linking' verbs, ie those which can be rephrased with the verb *be*: *It sounds/looks/seems/remains/feels/ becomes bad*; though *feel badly* is common in speech. The adverb **badly**, not **bad**, is appropriate with other verbs (*He dances badly*) and where it means 'severely' or 'desperately': *It ached badly*; *I want it badly*.

bagman

See SALES REPRESENTATIVE.

bail, bale

In both British and American English, you **bail** *out* a prisoner, who is then *on* **bail**; and you **bale** hay, which then becomes a **bale** or 'bundle'. In American English you also **bail** *out* water from a boat, and **bail** *out* of an aircraft with your parachute, but British English prefers **bale** for both these.

bait, bate

To **bait** is to 'tease' someone (rather old-fashioned); you **bait** a hook, with **bait** such as a worm; and rat poison is **bait** too. A person anxiously awaiting something does so *with* **bated** *breath*.

balance

The **balance** can mean 'what is left over', but some careful writers use it only where there is a clear comparison between two numerical amounts, especially of money: *I bought some shoes and spent the balance of what you gave me on beer*. It is better not to use it to mean simply 'the rest', as in *She will read the balance of the chapter tomorrow*.

balding

This is a rather journalistic adjective, said to have been coined by *Time* magazine: *the balding 50-year-old chairman*. It seems, nevertheless, a useful way to say that someone is getting bald.

baleful, baneful

Baleful means 'gloomy and malignant': *baleful glances*. **Baneful** means 'destructive and ruinous': *baneful habits/effects*.

ballgame

This is an OVERUSED word of American origin, meaning 'situation' or 'set of circumstances': *Now we've computerized we're in a completely new ballgame*. In the USA, though of course not in Britain, a **ballgame** is principally baseball.

balmy, barmy

Balmy means 'soft and soothing': *balmy breezes*. **Barmy** means 'frothy and yeasty'. In addition, they are both used as an informal word meaning 'crazy', for which **balmy** is the preferred American spelling and **barmy** the British one: *I must have been barmy to buy an old car like this*. The two words are more likely to be pronounced exactly the same in British than in American English.

baluster, banister

They both mean a pillar supporting a railing. **Baluster** is the more technical word, and is more likely to be used of stone ones out of doors. **Banisters** (or **bannisters**) are typically wooden, and run alongside an indoor staircase. They may be taken to include the supported handrail, as when one *slides down the banisters*.

bandit

Bandits is the modern plural; **banditti** is old-fashioned, and in any case could probably be used only for the historical sense of **bandit**, 'a member of an organized gang of robbers in Mediterranean countries', not for the modern sense 'terrorist'.

bandwagon

Originally a vehicle for circus musicians, a **bandwagon** can now mean a faction or cause whose fashionable momentum attracts people to *jump*, *hop*, or *climb* onto it. One would not use the expression about oneself, since it implies a stampede to get onto the winning side.

baneful

See BALEFUL.

banister

See BALUSTER.

banjo

The plural is **banjos** or, less usually, **banjoes**.

bank (of river)

The *left* and *right* **banks** depend on the direction of movement of the river. Thus, the Seine flows from east to west, so its *left* **bank** is to the south.

bar

Bar is the neutral word in both American and British English for a counter or room for public drinking. A whole establishment for drinking is more likely to be called a **bar** in American than in British English, because the main British words for this are **pub**, **public house** (formal), **boozer** (slang), or *the* **local** for one's neighbourhood pub. (A British **pub** is often divided into a **public bar** and a more comfortable and expensive **saloon bar** or **lounge bar**.) **Saloon** is the pre-

Prohibition American word for either the room or the establishment. It became a rather disreputable word, though it is now self-consciously revived by places that hope to suggest a flavour of the Old West. A **cocktail lounge** is usually a rather elegant room inside a hotel or club, frequented often by women. **Inn** and **tavern** are older words for a drinking establishment, perhaps offering also food and lodging, and these words survive in the names of particular enterprises, often of a smart sort. A **roadhouse** is an inn on a main road in the country, and has connotations of being large and showy.

barbarian, barbaric, barbarous, barbarity, barbarism

The first three words all mean 'uncivilized' or 'savage'. **Barbarian** is the most neutral adjective: *barbarian tribes*. **Barbaric** may be either condemnatory (*barbaric cruelty*) or admiring (*barbaric splendour*). **Barbarous** is strongly derogatory: *barbarous treatment/ignorance*. Of the related nouns, **barbarity** is savage cruelty (*They treated their prisoners with barbarity*); **barbarism** is fairly neutral; **barbarousness** can usually replace either **barbarism** or **barbarity**.

Barbarous and **barbarism** are both used of the uncultivated use of language: *a barbarous word/writer*; *the barbarism of his style*.

barbecue

The word is normally spelled like this; not **barbeque**. Spellings like *bar-b-q* and *bar-be-q*, which are sometimes used in advertisements, are not suitable for formal use.

barely

See HARDLY.

barmy

See BALMY.

barrage

The original military sense of **barrage** is of a protective curtain of gunfire, later extended to a system of anti-aircraft protection: *barrage balloons*. A misunderstanding of this protective function has led to the modern metaphorical use of the word in an attacking sense: *to face a barrage of questions/criticism*. Those who are worried by this, but would like to preserve the military flavour, may prefer to say *volley* or *fusillade* or *bombardment*.

barring

Modern convention permits the use of **barring** for 'except for':
Barring accidents, the work will start on Monday. See DANGLING
PARTICIPLE.

bar sinister

The correct heraldic term for the symbol of bastardy is **bend sinister** or
baton sinister, but **bar sinister** is so well established that it would be
pedantic to use the other expressions outside technical contexts.

basal, basic

Both adjectives are related to the noun **base**, but while **basal** is chiefly
confined to technical contexts (*basal metabolism; basal ganglion*),
basic is widely used to mean 'fundamental' (*his basic honesty*). In this
sense, **basic** and **basically** are somewhat OVERUSED: *It's a basic fact
that children need exercise*; *Basically, we'll have to wait and see.*

base

See BASS.

based on, upon

This is now sometimes used like a preposition, though not by careful
writers: *Based on present values, we must expect a sharp increase
during the coming winter.* See DANGLING PARTICIPLE.

bases

This can be the plural of *base*, when it ends with the sound 'iz', or of
basis, when it ends with the sound 'eez'.

BASIC, Basic

BASIC is a computer language. **Basic**, with only the *B* capitalized,
may mean the same thing, or it may be short for **Basic** *English*, a
simplified form of English designed by C K Ogden in the 1920s for
international use.

basis

1 The plural is **bases**.

2 This word often gives rise to VERBOSITY. It is shorter, and may be
neater, to replace a phrase involving **basis** with an adverb: *on a
provisional basis* becomes *provisionally*, and *on a temporary basis*

becomes *temporarily*. *On the basis of economy* could become *for economy*.

bass, base

They are pronounced the same, and can both mean 'low'; but **bass** applies to low musical pitch (*bass voice*; *bass clef*; *bass clarinet*), while **base** means 'low' in the sense of inferior (*base metal*) or ignoble (*base betrayal*).

bastion

From meaning a projecting part of a fortification, **bastion** has come to be used figuratively for a 'stronghold' or 'bulwark': *a bastion of freedom*. There seems no reason for objecting to this extension.

bate

See BAIT.

bathos, pathos

Bathos is 'anticlimax', a ludicrous descent from the grand to the trivial; **pathos** is the quality that evokes pity. **Bathos** can also mean false pathos, or maudlin sentimentality. The two words easily become confused, perhaps because what one person finds genuinely moving (**pathos**) another will see as trite and hackneyed (**bathos**).

B.C., BC

This is an abbreviation of 'before Christ'. It should come after the year: *55 B.C.* Orthodox Jews, and perhaps also followers of other non-Christian religions, prefer to use B.C.E., for *Before the Common Era*. Compare A.D.

be

1 The combinations **being** *as*, **being** *as how*, and **being** *that* (*Being as how it's Sunday, he's still in bed*) are nonstandard, and should be replaced in standard English by *because* or *as*.

2 The form **be** *he/you/they etc* for *whether he/you/they etc is/are* is very formal, to be used only with restraint and for particular effect: *Anyone who comes to the door, be it the milkman or a harmless neighbour....* A somewhat less restricted alternative is *whether it be the milkman ...* , and the fixed expression *be that as it may* is still current. See SUBJUNCTIVE.

3 In modern English, we no longer use **be** like the character in Jane

Austen who exclaimed *My father is come!* When **be** is used like this with the *-ed* form of a verb, it means that the participle has either become an adjective, as in *They were interested*, or forms a passive, as in *The job is finished* (ie we've finished it). People who say *The clock is stopped* are using *stopped* as a quasi-adjective, and may go on to say *. . . and it has been for days*.

There may be some ambiguity as to whether a passive or an adjective is intended. Does *People should be enlightened* mean that we ought to enlighten them, or just that they ought to be modern? Where neither of these interpretations is possible, the safer auxiliary verb is not **be** but **have**: *I've finished*, not *I'm finished*.

4 See also AIN'T; CASE, GRAMMATICAL (2) (for *it's me*).

bear (*verb*)

The verb **bear** has many meanings: *bear witness*; *bear fruit*; *I can't bear it*. But where you can replace it by *carry*, as in Shakespeare's *Let four captains bear Hamlet . . . to the stage*, it may sound less PRETENTIOUS to do so in modern English. See also BORN.

bear, bull, stag

These are three kinds of speculator on the Stock Exchange. The **bear** sells shares, assuming that the market will go on falling and that his own selling will contribute to the decline; he plans then to buy back at a lower price. The **bull** buys shares, assuming that the market will go on rising and that his own buying will contribute to the rise; he plans to sell them later at a profit. Thus, a *bull market* is rising, while a *bear market* is falling. **Stag** is a British English word for someone who buys newly issued shares, hoping for a quick profitable resale.

bearskin

See BUSBY.

beat, beaten

Both are participles of the verb **beat**. The shorter form is now used only adjectivally, informally in the sense of 'exhausted' (*I'm dead beat*) or in reference to the *beatniks* of the 1950s and 1960s (*the beat generation*; *beat poets*). Otherwise the form is **beaten**: *She's beaten the record*; *They were beaten on the last lap*.

beau

The plural is either **beaux** or **beaus**, both pronounced 'boze'.

beauteous

In modern writing, the use of **beauteous** for 'beautiful' is either archaic or jocular (see POESY).

beauty

This is now commonly used not only of a beautiful person or thing (*She's a great beauty*; *the beauties of our fair city*) but in the sense of a very attractive feature: *The beauty of it is that everyone can play*. There seems no reason to object to this extension of meaning.

because

1 Careful writers avoid the use of **because** in contexts such as *Because he's old (it) doesn't mean he's stupid*, or *The importance of this rule is because it prevents cheating*, and prefer *The fact that he's old . . .* and *The importance of this rule is that . . . .* The idea of 'explanation' should not be expressed twice in the same sentence (see TAUTOLOGY). For *the reason is because*, see REASON.

2 Negative sentences with **because** may be ambiguous. *He didn't marry her because he was poor* should be rephrased as either *Because he was poor he didn't marry her* or *It was not because of his poverty that he married her*, according to the intended meaning.

3 Where **because** introduces the premise for a conclusion, rather than the cause of an effect, as in *They must be in, because the light is on*, it may be better to rephrase the sentence in formal writing: *Since the light is on, they must be in*, or *They must be in, for the light is on*.

4 See also 'COS; DUE TO; FOR.

become

1 Become goes with adjectives (*He became famous*) or with nouns (*She became a vet*). It is not correctly used, like *come*, with the infinitives of other verbs: *He came* (not *became*) *to be recognized*. (In a different sense it can, of course, be an ordinary verb with an object, as in *This behaviour does not become you*.)

2 Some writers overuse **become** in place of *get*, a verb which they may feel to be unsuitable for serious writing; but it is better, because more natural, to write *get lost*, *get used to it*, rather than using **become** here.

beg

This is legitimately used in such polite phrases as *I beg your pardon* and *I beg to differ*; but it is overused in old-fashioned business English.

Expressions such as *beg to acknowledge* or *beg to remain* should be replaced by something more natural and friendly.

beg the question

This means to base a logical conclusion on something that should not itself be taken for granted, as when one says 'He can't be a policeman, because policemen always wear uniform'. To **beg a question** does not mean, as is sometimes supposed, to avoid giving a straight answer to it.

behalf

In modern English, **behalf** is used with *on*; in American English, with either *in* or *on*. It is possible in American English, and was formerly possible in British English, to distinguish *in your behalf* (ie in your interest) from *on your behalf* (ie as your representative). In any case, *on behalf of* should not be confused with *on the part of*. An *effort on behalf of the members* is made for their sake, one *on the part of the members* is made by the members themselves.

behavio(u)r

The word is spelled **behaviour** in British English, **behavior** in American English.

beholden

Beholden *to* is a rather archaic way of saying 'indebted to': *I'd rather pay for myself and not be beholden to anyone.* The form *beholding to* is obsolete.

behove, behoove

1 Behove is the British English form, **behoove** is American.

2 Behoove rhymes with *move*; so did **behove** at one time, but it now rhymes with *wove*.

3 This very formal word is properly used only in the construction *it* **behoves** (someone to do something): *It behoved us to fight.* It cannot have any subject but *it*, so that *The weather behoved us to close the shutters* is incorrect.

beige

The word is spelled *-ei-*, not *-ie-*.

being as (how), being that

See BE (1).

belabo(u)r, labo(u)r

1 These are spelled **belabour, labour** in British English; **belabor, labor** in American English.

2 Both words can mean 'treat in laborious detail': *to belabour/labour the obvious*; but it is probably best to confine **belabour** to its more usual sense of 'thrash'.

bells

Time on board ship is indicated by strokes of a bell dividing four-hour watches into half-hour intervals. Thus, starting at eight o'clock, *four* **bells** is ten o'clock, not four o'clock as many readers of sea stories might suppose.

belly

The traditional word **belly** has the advantage that it describes both the cavity containing stomach, liver, intestines, and (for females) womb and also the front surface of the body between chest and crotch: *the child in her belly*; *initials tattooed on his belly*. People who find the word too coarse for modern use have the choice between **abdomen**, which means much the same thing but is technical or formal; **stomach**, which is misleading in that its primary meaning is of one of the organs within the cavity; and **tummy**, which is babytalk though now often used by adults, including doctors and nurses when talking to patients. In the modern climate of plain speaking, **gut(s)** is making somewhat of a comeback, though this word is as inaccurate as **stomach**, referring as it does to organs within the cavity, and cannot be used of the external surface.

beloved

1 This is pronounced with only two syllables (*She was greatly beloved*) except when it is used as an adjective before a noun or alone: *my beloved one*.

2 The form **beloved** *of* is more formal than **beloved** *by*, but both are correct.

below

This can refer as an adverb to what is to be mentioned on a later page or lower down on the same page: *the information below*. This device has long been established in written English, and is very useful. It is, naturally, inappropriate in writing that is intended to be read aloud. Available alternatives for those few writers who dislike it are *the following information*, or *the information that follows*. Compare ABOVE.

benefit of

The phrase *without* **benefit of** means 'without the help or advantage of': *a primitive cottage without benefit of electricity*. It may be derived from *without benefit of clergy*, which originally meant 'without the clerical privilege of being tried in a special court'. But there are various legal expressions such as *benefit of discussion* and *benefit of inventory* where **benefit** similarly means an advantage, and the new phrase *without* **benefit of** would be a legitimate extension from any of these.

benzene, benzine

Both are colourless inflammable liquids that can be used as fuels and solvents. **Benzene** is C_6H_6 and comes chiefly from coal, while **benzine** is a mixture obtained from petroleum. **Benzine**, not **benzene**, is another word in American English for *petrol* or *gasoline*.

bereaved, bereft

Bereaved is preferred to **bereft** in the emotional context of being deprived by death: *a bereaved mother*. **Bereft** means more generally deprived, so it is usually necessary to specify what one is **bereft** *of*: *He was bereft of his senses*; *a man bereft of all hope*. This means in practice that **bereft** cannot precede the noun it describes. Only **bereaved** is used like a noun: *The bereaved gathered round the grave*.

Berkeley

The first syllable rhymes with *dark* in British English, as in London's *Berkeley Square*. It rhymes with *lurk* in American English, as in the name of the Californian university campus.

berserk

Nobody seems quite sure how to pronounce this word, or even whether the stress should fall on the first or second syllable. The *s* can be pronounced 's' or 'z', and the first syllable can either rhyme with *fur* or resemble the beginning of *banana*.

beseech

The established form for the past tense and participle is **besought**: *They* *(have) besought admittance.* **Beseeched** also exists: *She (had) beseeched him to be careful.*

besides, beside

In modern English, **besides** is used rather than **beside** to mean 'in addition to': *Besides being old, she is losing her sight.* A possible source of confusion is that some people use it to mean 'other than' or 'except': *Besides John, nobody was there.* If your intended meaning may be misinterpreted in the context, it is safer to use one of the appropriate synonyms. **Besides**, but not **beside**, is used today as an adverb: *Besides, I'm too tired.* As a preposition, meaning 'by the side of', the only form is **beside** (*sit beside me*), which is also used in various idiomatic phrases: *beside oneself; beside the point.*

best

The two/three/hundred best books is probably better than *the best two/three/hundred books*, since the superlative forms of other adjectives are used like that. We say *the three fattest men* or *the five most ridiculous answers*, not *the fattest three men* or *the most ridiculous five answers.*

bet *(verb)*

The usual past tense **bet** is used for definite transactions: *She bet me £5 I couldn't do it.* The rarer past tense **betted** is used in a more general sense, particularly where no object follows: *They betted heavily in the eighteenth century.*

bête noire

This means a 'bugbear', or object of extreme aversion. It is spelled with a final 'e', even when the bugbear in question is male, and both words have a (silent) added 's' in the plural: *Advertising men were his bêtes noires.* Do not use too many of these foreign expressions.

better

1 Informally, *you had better*, expressing a recommendation, is shortened to *you'd better* and now commonly in informal speech to *you better*; but the last is not appropriate for serious writing. Do not write *you would better.*

2 Better can replace *more*, but only where the reference is to choice: *I'd like nothing better (than to go home).* It should not be so used in comparisons of measurement: *It's more than* (not *better than*) *nine miles to the shops.*

3 Some people are irritated by the trick, common with advertisers, of using **better** where there is no true comparison: *the better class of customer*. Better than whom?

between

1 **between** *you and me*
2 **between** *each/every*
3 **between** + *and*
4 repeated **between**
5 **between** or **among**; see AMONG(ST) (2)

1 between *you and me*
In careful English, pronouns after **between** should correctly be in the objective case, since *between* is a preposition: *the difference between us and them* (not *we and they*). See CASE, GRAMMATICAL (3).

2 between *each/every*
Between should be followed either by a plural noun or pronoun or by two or more nouns or pronouns joined by *and*: *the distance between the houses/between my house and hers*; *the time between meals/between tea and supper*. There are therefore objections to the use of a singular noun after **between** *each* or **between** *every*: *three inches between each buttonhole* (prefer *between the buttonholes* or *between each buttonhole and the next*); *He sipped his wine between every sentence* (prefer *after every sentence*). Some critics carry their objection to **between** *each* so far as to ban *between each pair* (since *pair* is singular in form though plural in meaning), and would change *the difference between each pair of words* to *the difference between the words in each pair*. This seems to be going too far, since *the difference between this pair of words* or *the difference between the pair of words* would be unexceptionable. A slight awkwardness arises where one of the two items linked by **between** is omitted by ELLIPSIS, as in *the contrast between working for the Government and for private industry*. It would be more formally correct here to write *working for the Government and working for private industry*. See also CORRELATIVE.

3 between + *and*
Items after **between** should be linked by *and*, not by any other word. Examples of what not to do are *the distinction between centralization as opposed to giving more autonomy to the districts* (use *and giving*); *the conflict between the right of free speech as against the demands of national security* (use *and the demands*); *the period between 1960–1970* (use *and*, or *from . . . to*). Commonest, however, is the error of replacing *and* by *or*: *to choose between going on holiday or buying new clothes*. This probably arises when we first think *We can either go on holiday or buy clothes*, and then attempt to recast the sentence.

4 repeated between

Longer sentences sometimes become so complicated that it is hard to
see which items are linked by **between**: *We have to choose between
arriving early and perhaps having to wait and arriving late and
perhaps missing the beginning*; *There is a considerable climatic
difference between January and February and March and April.* In the
first sentence, the choice is clearly *between* the two times of arriving:
in the second, it is presumably *between* the weather of the first two
months *and* that of the second two, but some clarification is needed.
One mistaken way of attempting this is to introduce a second **between**:
. . . between January and February and between March and April;
this would be reasonable if any other preposition were involved, such
as *in* (*in January and February and in March and April*), but will not
do with **between.** The best way out is to recast the sentence
completely, or perhaps to use *on the one hand*: *. . . between on the
one hand arriving early . . . and on the other hand arriving late.*

bevel (*verb*)

Other forms are **bevelled, bevelling** in British English, but the second *l*
is usually omitted in American English.

bi-

When **bi-** is used in measurements of time (*biweekly, bimonthly*), there
is often doubt as to whether it means 'every two' or 'twice in one'. It is
often safer to avoid such combinations, and say *every two months, half-
yearly*, etc. However, *bicentenary* and *bicentennial* are unambiguously
a two-hundredth anniversary.

biannual, biennial

Biannual properly means 'twice a year', **biennial** means 'every two
years'; but as many people do not recognize this distinction, it may
sometimes be safer to avoid these expressions. See BI-.

bias

Other forms are either **biased, biasing** or **biassed, biassing**.

Bible, biblical

Bible is usually capitalized when it means the Scriptures, but not when
it means a standard reference work: *This book should be the
fisherman's bible.* The adjective *biblical*, with no capital, nevertheless
refers to the Scriptures.

bid (*noun*)

In journalese, this means an 'attempt' or 'aspiration': *swimmer's bid for world record*. In consequence, there can be confusion with the word's other meaning of an 'offer', as made at an auction. A *bid for a supermarket chain* is probably an offer to buy it.

bid (*verb*)

1 In the sense of making an offer to buy, as at an auction or in cards, the verb **bid** has other forms **bid, bid**: *She bid £10*; *£10 was bid*. As a somewhat archaic word for 'command' or 'invite', the forms are **bade** or **bad**, **bidden** or **bid**: *She bade them go*; *We were bidden to the wedding*. Note also *We bade them adieu*; *It bade fair to become a best-seller*.

2 Bade rhymes with either *had* or, increasingly, with *fade*.

biennial

See BIANNUAL.

billion

In older British use, a **billion** is a million million, 10^{12}. The British are now using **billion** increasingly to mean a thousand million, 10^9, which is what the word means in American and in international scientific English. One must be careful to avoid ambiguity between these two possible senses. **Milliard**, which also means a thousand million, is not used technically in modern English. Compare TRILLION.

bimonthly, semimonthly

Correctly, **bimonthly** means 'every two months' and **semimonthly** means 'twice a month'; but as many people do not recognize this distinction, it may be safer to use *every two months* or *twice a month*. See BI-.

birthday

Your **birthday** is normally an anniversary of your birth, not the day you are actually born. On a baby's *first* **birthday**, he or she is one year old. However, if an American printed form asks you to state your **birthday**, it clearly means your date of birth.

bisect

It means 'divide in two', so *to bisect something in two* is a TAUTOLOGY. Compare DISSECT.

bit

1 This word for 'a small amount' is always informal. Some people feel that **bit** in this sense should be used only for solids (*a bit of cake*) and not for liquids (*a bit of rain*), but nobody seems to mind the use, in speech, of **bit** for abstractions (*a bit of trouble*).

2 The informal use of **bit** in the vague sense of 'sphere of activity' or 'piece of behaviour' (*She rejected the whole love and marriage bit*) comes originally from theatrical slang, where **bit** means a 'small role' or **bit** *part*.

bite

In modern English, the past tense is **bit** (*It bit me*) and the participle usually **bitten** (*It's bitten me*; *I've been bitten*). The archaic participle **bit** (*I've been bit*) survives as an alternative, though not a recommended one, in American English.

bivouac (*verb*)

Other forms are **bivouacked, bivouacking**.

biweekly, semiweekly

Correctly, **biweekly** means 'every two weeks' (in British English, *fortnightly*) and **semiweekly** means 'twice a week'; but as many people do not recognize this distinction, it may be safer to use *every two weeks* or *once a fortnight* for one, and *twice a week* for the other. See BI-.

black, blacken

Black as a verb is on the whole more literal than **blacken.** One **blacks** shoes, and may **black** someone's eye. **Blacken** is wider in its application, and can mean 'make dark or dirty': *buildings blackened by smoke*. Only **blacken**, not **black**, can be used intransitively (*the sky blackened*); or figuratively (*blacken her character*), with the curious exception of the trade-union sense: one **blacks** an industry when one imposes a boycott on it.

black, coloured, Negro, nigger

Black is now the term preferred by black people themselves, reflecting the pride in their African origins expressed by the concept of negritude. **Coloured,** except in South Africa where it has the technical meaning 'of mixed race', is sometimes used to cover all nonwhite people, both of African and of Asian descent, but it is disliked by both black and brown people, and should never be used in this sense as a noun. It is better to use the neutral term **nonwhite. Negro**, and particularly

Negress, are now considered insulting by many black Americans because of their historical associations, though they mean merely 'black'. If used at all, they should be capitalized: *two Negroes*; *a Negro girl*. On the other hand **black** and **white** should not be written with capitals: *a black lawyer*; *young blacks*; *white minorities*. The term **nigger** is considered breatnen even more offensive, though black Americans sometimes apply the term without offence to other blacks. It is best avoided even in such combinations as *nigger brown* for a dark chocolate colour and *nigger in the woodpile* for an unforeseen snag.

blame

Some critics have objected to the construction **blame** something *on* someone, as in Kipling's *when all about you are . . . blaming it on you*, on the grounds that the verb *blame* requires as its object a person not a thing. Available unchallenged alternatives are *blame you for it* or *place/lay the blame for it on you*.

blanch, blench

Both **blanch** and **blench** mean 'turn white', the former more literally: *blanched almonds*; *He blenched with fear*. There is also, however, a different verb **blench**, meaning 'flinch' or 'recoil', with some implication of cowardice: *They never blenched in the face of danger*.

blatant, flagrant

From meaning 'vulgarly noisy', **blatant** has now come to mean 'glaring and shameless': *blatant disregard of the facts*. It has thus become almost a synonym of **flagrant**, which means 'conspicuously scandalous': *flagrant neglect of duty*. On the whole, **flagrant** emphasizes the gravity of the offence, and **blatant** the brazenness of its perpetrator, but both should involve some sort of guilt. Careful writers will avoid using either to mean merely 'shocking', as in *blatant poverty*.

blaze, blazon

Both verbs can mean 'proclaim publicly': *blaze the news abroad; blazon the tidings forth*. **Blaze** in this sense comes from older words for *blow* or *blast*, **blazon** from the display of a heraldic emblem.

blends

Blends are words that are produced by combining parts of other words. Some of these are firmly established in the language and can be used in formal writing: *breathalyser* (breath analyser), *brunch* (breakfast, lunch), *cheeseburger* (cheese, hamburger), *motel* (motor hotel), *paratroops* (parachute troops), *smog* (smoke, fog), *workaholic* (work, alcoholic). Others are NEOLOGISMS, eg *fantabulous* (fantastic, fabulous) and *ginormous* (gigantic, enormous), to be avoided in formal writing. On other ways of shortening, see ACRONYMS; CLIPPED WORDS; CONTRACTIONS.

blessed

This is pronounced with two syllables as an adjective before a noun (*every blessèd time*) or alone (*among the blessèd*). It is pronounced with one syllable as the past tense or participle of the verb **bless** (*He has) blessed them*; *blessed with good health* and in the expression *Blessed if I know*. The spelling *blest* belongs only to poetry.

blind, blinded

The participle **blinded** is used when some clear agency or specific time is involved: *blinded by smoke*; *blinded in the war*. Otherwise, the adjective **blind** is the usual word: *He became blind*; *a blind horse*.

blink, wink at

To 'ignore' something deliberately is to **blink** *at* it or, as some people think more correct, to **blink** it: *blink (at) the unpleasant facts*. To 'condone' something, perhaps as a sympathetic accomplice, is to **wink** *at* it: *wink at his small failings*.

bloc, block

A **bloc** is a political grouping of people, parties, or countries: *the Eastern bloc*. **Bloc** occurs also in the expression *en bloc* (ie as a whole). **Block**, which means a great many other things, should not be used in either of these senses.

blond(e)

The French word takes an *-e* as the feminine ending. In English, a fair-haired woman is a **blonde.** The adjective is often spelled **blonde** when applied to women (*a blonde actress*), but is otherwise **blond**: *a blond youth*; *a table of blond walnut*. But the connotation of the noun is mainly female, and as the two forms sound identical in spoken English, it is safer to use only the adjective with reference to men. If one says *There's a blond(e) waiting to see you,* the person will almost certainly be taken to be female. Compare BRUNET(TE).

bloody

Because of the highly emotive (chiefly British) slang sense, as in *not bloody likely*, we can now scarcely use this word to mean 'bloodstained', as when Shakespeare wrote *What bloody man is that?*; though of course in the context of *a bloody battle*, the meaning is clear.

blooming

Because of the British slang sense, as in *blooming fool*, we can now scarcely use this word to mean 'in bloom' outside a clear horticultural context.

bluebell

In England, this is the wild hyacinth, a blue bell-shaped flower of the lily family. In Scotland, it is what the English call the harebell: another blue bell-shaped flower, but of the harebell family and with a slenderer stalk and fewer and larger flowers. In the northern USA the word is used of various more or less blue and bell-shaped flowers, particularly one of the borage family whose blue flowers first appear as pink buds.

blue book

See WHITE PAPER.

blueprint

In a technical drawing office a **blueprint** is a final detailed design in the form of a photographic print. By an extension of meaning, the word can now refer to a detailed programme for future action: *a blueprint for victory*. It has become a somewhat OVERUSED word for any scheme, plan, or prototype, whether detailed or not: *The new method served as a blueprint for future work*.

blush, flush

Both words refer to people turning red with emotion. One **blushes** from shame or shyness; one usually **flushes** from some stronger emotion, such as great pride or anger. **Blush**, but not **flush**, is used when one merely feels embarrassment without showing it: *I blush to remember what I said*; *Spare my blushes*.

boast

Although this word can correctly mean 'possess as a source of pride' (*The village boasts three shops*), when the subject is a person it may suggest discreditable self-praise (*a family who boast three cars*).

boat, ship

Outside nautical circles it is perfectly standard to use **boat** in referring to transport by a passenger vessel, however large: *cross the Channel by boat*. Otherwise, **boats** are small. Naval surface vessels above a certain not clearly defined size are **ships**, but submarines are **boats**.

boatswain

This is pronounced as in the variant spelling **bosun**, with either an *s* or a *z* sound.

bobby

See COP.

bobby pin

See HAIRPIN.

bogey, bogy, bogie

All three spellings can have the same three meanings; but **bogey** is best for the golf score (one above *par*), **bogy** for the goblin, and **bogie** for the item of rolling-stock.

Bohemian, bohemian

This is spelled with a capital *B* for an inhabitant or the language of Bohemia (now in Czechoslovakia), but with a small *b* for a person of unconventional lifestyle.

bona fide(s)

The noun **bona fides** means 'good standing, genuineness'. Though it ends with an *s*, it is not a plural, and should correctly take a singular verb: *His bona fides was questioned*. **Bona fide**, which looks like the singular, is not a noun but an adjective meaning 'genuine': *bona fide antiques*. Do not use too many of these LATINISMS.

born, borne

Borne is the participle of **bear** in all its many senses except those connected with birth: *burdens too heavy to be borne*; *I've borne it as long as I could*. In the 'birth' sense, **borne** is used when the female who gives birth is the subject (*She has borne three sons*) and in the passive with *by* (*children borne by her*), but **born** in the passive without *by*: *Her sons were born in Greece*; *children born to her*.

borrow

One **borrows** things *from* people. To **borrow** something *of* someone is

now old-fashioned, and to **borrow** it *off* him or *off of* her is
nonstandard.

bosom

See BREAST.

boss

This is rather informal, whether it means one's employer or line
manager or an organizer of an American political party.

botanic(al)

The modern form is **botanical,** though **botanic** may be preferred in the
special context of **botanic(al)** *garden*.

both

1 **both** with more than two	5 **both** and **each**
2 unnecessary **both**	6 *the* **both**
3 **both** . . . *and*	7 *we* **both**
4 **both** *their faults*	

1 both with more than two
Both refers to, and emphasizes, 'two-ness': *Both John and Sarah play
tennis*; *It's both useful and interesting.* It should be avoided where
more than two items are involved, as in *both useful, interesting, and
inexpensive*, and is particularly unacceptable with three or more nouns:
The library contains both books and newspapers and records; *Both
Anne and Mary and Sarah are coming tonight.*

2 unnecessary both
It sounds TAUTOLOGOUS to use **both** in addition to *same, equal, equally,
alike, at once,* or *together*, which themselves convey the idea of 'two-
ness': *(both) in France and in England alike*; *They're (both) exactly the
same*; *We're (both) equally hungry.*

3 both . . . and
Both goes with *and* as a pair, not with any other word or words:
interesting both to a lay audience as well as to (write *and to*)
professionals. **Both** and *and* should link parallel constructions.
Compare *both in France and in England* (joining two phrases); *in both
France and England* (joining two nouns); but not *both in France and
England*, which incorrectly joins a phrase to a noun. See CORRELATIVE
(2).
　　With plural nouns, do not use **both** unless it is clear what it refers to.
Both the women and their husbands should be changed to *The two*

women and their husbands, or to *The husbands as well as the women,* according to the intended meaning.

4 both *their faults*

In possessive constructions, it is more formally correct and usually clearer to choose the form *the fault of both* rather than *both their faults.* The latter pattern is ambiguous in *both their houses*; do they share two houses between them, or have one each? It becomes impossible where a single possession or relationship is shared. One must write *She's the mother of both of them,* not *She's both their mother.*

5 both and each

The use of **both** (meaning two things together) for **each** (meaning two or more things separately) can lead to ambiguity. *Both houses cost £50,000* may mean that they cost £50,000 each or £50,000 together. Rephrase as *They each cost . . . ,* or perhaps *Together, they cost . . .* according to the intended meaning. It can also lead to such absurdities as *There's a policeman on both sides of the road,* which somehow implies, as **each** (*There's a policeman on each side of the road*) would not, a single straddling colossus rather than two men, one per side.

6 *the* both

Both should not be preceded by *the.* Expressions such as *the both of us* should be avoided in serious writing.

7 *we* both

The patterns *Both of us wear socks* and *We both wear socks* are equally correct. So are *both of the children* and *both the children,* but the second is shorter and may seem neater.

bottleneck

This word appears never to have been used in connection with actual bottles. It is useful as meaning a 'point of constriction', such as a narrow stretch of road holding up traffic. Our sense of its literal meaning, though, makes it odd to speak of *curing* or *solving* a **bottleneck,** or of a *big* **bottleneck** as an especially serious one. Such absurdities have fallen into deserved disrepute.

bottom line

This is managerial jargon for anything from 'net cost' to 'final result', and is a decidedly overworked expression.

bound, bounden

The idioms are *in duty* **bound** but *one's* **bounden** *duty.* **Bounden** has no other use in modern English.

bourgeois

This used to mean 'not aristocratic enough', as in Molière's *Le Bourgeois Gentilhomme*, but now usually means 'not proletarian enough'. Either way it suggests narrow-minded materialism and boring respectability.

boy

Unlike *girl*, **boy** is rarely used of adults, except in the plural to describe a man's circle of friends: *He's out with the boys*. It was formerly used to address black males of any age, and is very offensive in this sense.

boyfriend

A woman's **boyfriend** is today more likely to be a sexual partner than a mere male companion. A man's **boyfriend** is unequivocally his homosexual partner. Compare GIRLFRIEND, and see LOVER.

boyish, girlish

Boyish tends to be more flattering than **girlish** when the words are used of adults and adult behaviour: *his boyish charm*; *her girlish giggle*.

bracket

This is a statistician's jargon word for 'group' or 'level': *the lower income brackets*; *children in the thirteen to sixteen bracket*; *jobs within the £10,000 p.a. bracket*. It is inappropriate in general writing.

brackets

This is the term for ( ), also called *parentheses* in American English. Use brackets to enclose explanations and digressions:

Supersonic aircraft cause sonic booms *(shock waves of sound)* that resemble the bow waves *(shock waves of water)* caused by a ship.

The vulnerability of ICBMs *(intercontinental ballistic missiles)* is worrying the army.

He spent his last trip in England with a friend and a dog *(a well-meaning creature that got them thrown out of a nonconformist baptism for trying to rescue a lady from total immersion)*.

Many motorists refuse to obey speed limits and warning indicators *(when these are in operation)*.

Unemployment is the lowest in the region *(about five per cent last year)*.

The ministers have vacillated over the English New Towns' debts on government loans *(the Scottish New Towns have been paid for by direct grant)*.

In the last example, the sentence in brackets could have been punctuated as a separate sentence, in which case a full stop would mark the end of the preceding sentence:

The ministers have vacillated over the English New Towns' debts on government loans. *(The Scottish New Towns have been paid for by direct grant.)*

If the part in brackets is not a separate sentence, punctuation marks should always follow the final bracket:

New Hampshire collects taxes on its lottery *(first in the nation this year)*, on horse and dog racing, and on the sale of cigarettes and liquor.

Brackets are commonly used for page numbers, dates, and other note-like references:

His remote, radio-controlled cameras recorded simultaneous images of the event *(page 92)*.

This paper deals with Einstein's works on Special Relativity *(1905)* and General Relativity *(1915)*.

On one side stand three Egyptian gods *(above, left)*.

They are also sometimes used to enclose digits or letters that mark listed items or sections.

Brahman, Brahmin

Brahman is the correct word for a high-caste Hindu, or for a breed of Indian cattle. **Brahmin** is used widely and respectably, both for the Hindu and for an aloof and intellectually cultivated person: *Boston Brahmins*.

bravado, bravery, bravura

Bravado is a swaggering pretence of bravery. **Bravery** is the real thing. **Bravura** is a show of daring or brilliance, or particularly a musical passage requiring florid agility.

breach, breech

A **breach** is a violation *(breach of the law)*, a gap *(breach in the wall)*, or a rift *(breach between friends)*; a **breech** is the buttocks, now chiefly in *breech birth,* or part of a firearm. **Breach**, but not **breech**, is current as a verb: *breach the wall/the agreement.*

breakdown, break down

A **breakdown** can mean a statistical analysis into categories, and to **break** something **down** can mean to classify it. One should avoid the use of these expressions where there is any risk of confusion with the more literal senses: *They demanded a complete breakdown of our exports*; *statistics of the adult population broken down by sex.*

breast, chest, bust, bosom, etc

The difficulty here is to find a neutral term in relation to women. Both men and women have **chests**, from the anatomical and medical point of view: *a chest X-ray*. In addition, men's clothes come in **chest** sizes, while women's are measured round the **bust**, an otherwise rather old-fashioned word suggestive of Edwardian corsetry. **Breast** is used for the front of the chest, for the seat of emotion (*Their breasts swelled with pride*), and in a sartorial sense (*breast pocket*). It is also a frank and serious word for each of the milk-producing organs; the coarser equivalents of **breasts** in this sense include **boobs**, **tits**, **bristols** (British English), and **knockers**. Some people are driven to the GENTEELISM of saying **bosoms**, instead of confining **bosom** to the singular: *the bosom of her dress*; *She held it to her bosom.*

breech

See BREACH.

brethren

This old plural of *brother* is now confined to ecclesiastical contexts (*dearly beloved brethren*) or to sects (*Plymouth Brethren*). It includes women. Members of male religious orders are **brothers**, and so are trade union members.

briar, brier

Briar is the usual spelling for the tobacco pipe or the root used for making it, and **brier** for the prickly plant.

brickbat

In the technical language of bricklaying, a **brickbat** is half a brick, which may also make a convenient missile. People who use this word for an uncomplimentary remark (*dodged verbal brickbats*) may have lost all awareness of the literal meaning.

bring, take

1 Bring implies motion towards the speaker, **take** implies motion either away from or accompanying the speaker: *Take away these dirty plates and bring me some coffee*; *If you're going out, will you take me with you?* Either verb can be used where the point of view is irrelevant: *The obelisk was brought/taken from Egypt to London.*

2 Avoid pronouncing the final *g* in **bring** separately, as in *finger*.

3 The form *brung* is nonstandard.

Britain, British Isles

See GREAT BRITAIN.

British, English, Briton, Britisher, Brit

The people of the United Kingdom are all **British**. They do not like to be called **English** unless they actually are so, though those who are **English** may find the word more emotionally appealing than **British**; the others should be referred to as **Irish**, **Scottish**, or **Welsh**, unless they are immigrants who have become UK citizens, for whom **British** is the only choice. Nobody likes to be called a **Briton**, though it saves space in headlines (*12 Britons die in air crash*), and is the correct way of referring to the *Ancient* **Britons**. **Britisher** is an American English expression. **Brit** is becoming increasingly popular on both sides of the Atlantic, but is informal and may be found rather offensive.

British English

See STANDARD ENGLISH.

broach, brooch

One **broaches** a topic or a container, but wears a **brooch**.

broad, wide

Broad suggests general spaciousness or amplitude: *broad shoulders*; *broad acres*. **Wide** is used for openings (*a wide doorway*) and hence for the idea of practicable passage (*a wide road*) or distance between limits (*widely separated*).

broadcast

The preferred past tense and participle are **broadcast** rather than **broadcasted**, though both forms exist: *He broadcast yesterday*; *The speech was broadcast.*

broke, broken

Today, **broke** is an informal adjective meaning 'penniless': *We're broke*. The adjective from the verb *break* is **broken**: *a broken arm*; *a broken treaty*.

brother

See BRETHREN.

brunet(te)

The French word takes an *-e* as the feminine ending. In British English, a dark-haired (white) woman is a **brunette**, and the adjective is also spelled **brunette** (*brunette hair*). The French masculine **brunet** is a chiefly American word, and is there applied to women as well as men. But the connotation of the noun is mainly female, and as the two forms sound identical in spoken English, it is safer to use only the adjective with reference to men. If one says *There's a brunet(te) waiting to see you*, the person will almost certainly be taken to be female. Compare BLOND(E).

buffet

When it means a sideboard, or a meal where you help yourself, **buffet** is now usually pronounced 'boofay'. The noun and verb meaning 'strike' (*waves buffet the shore*) are pronounced 'buffit'.

bug

As noun or verb, this refers to an electronic listening device: *to bug a phone*. In their informal uses, the noun means 'an unexpected defect' (*iron out the bugs*) and the verb means 'bother' (*stop bugging me*).

bugger

Both noun and verb seem to be more freely used in informal British English than in American English, with no sexual connotation: *cheeky little bugger*; *engine's a bugger to start*; *I felt absolutely buggered after the meeting*. British speakers should be aware that such expressions, which would be avoided in polite British usage, may cause consternation in the USA.

bulk

1 As a noun, *the bulk of* properly means 'the greater part of', not 'the greater number of'. Avoid writing *the bulk of the inhabitants/the crowd*.

2 As a verb, **bulk** forms the idiom **bulk** *large*, not *largely*.

bull

See BEAR.

bumblebee, humble-bee

Bumblebee is the main form. **Humble-bee** is chiefly British.

bureau

The plural is either **bureaux** or **bureaus**, both pronounced 'bew-rose'.

bureaucrat(ic), bureaucracy

These are derogatory words for any large organization and the officials who serve it. The implication is of a complex hierarchy which is inflexible and perhaps also inefficient.

burgeon

Originally meaning 'sprout' or 'blossom', this is now a popular synonym for *flourish* or *expand*: *burgeoning cities*; *his burgeoning talent*. There seems no reason for objecting to this figurative extension, but it is in danger of being OVERUSED.

-burg(h)

When it is spelled *-burg*, as in *Hamburg* or *Pittsburg*, this placename ending is pronounced 'berg'. When it is spelled *-burgh*, as in *Edinburgh* or *Jedburgh*, it is pronounced 'burra' or 'brer', not 'berg'.

burglarize, burgle

The former is chiefly American English, but both verbs are convenient for referring to the act of burglary. Since this specifically involves breaking into and entering a building, the vaguer verb *rob* would not be an adequate synonym. For **burglarize**, see -IZE.

burned, burnt

Burned is the commoner past tense and participle of *burn*, in both British and American English, where the verb has no object: *The fire burned brightly*. **Burnt** is commoner in British English, but **burned** in American English, where the verb has an object: *She burnt/burned her boats*. Both British and American English use **burnt** as an adjective: *burnt toast*.

bus

The plural is either **buses** or **busses**. As a verb, meaning 'transport by bus', it has other forms **bused**, **busing** or **bussed**, **bussing**.

busby, bearskin

The tall black fur hats worn by the five British Guards regiments are officially **bearskins**, though most people call them **busbies**. A **busby** is correctly the shorter fur hat worn by the hussars.

business, busyness

The second form means 'the state of being busy', and is pronounced with three syllables, as distinct from **business** which has two.

businessman

This is now coming to be pronounced with the *-man* as in *postman* or *milkman*, but the older pronunciation with *man* sounding like a separate word is equally correct.

bust *(verb)*

This is an informal variant of **burst**: *laughed fit to bust*. In addition, it has many senses where **burst** could not replace it. It means 'break' (*bust my watch*; *bust up the meeting*; *blockbuster*; *trustbusting*) or '(make) bankrupt' (*go bust*), or 'arrest' (*busted for drug smuggling*), or 'raid' (*police busted the flat*), or a 'flop', or a 'spree' (*go on a bust*). In American English it also means 'tame' (*bronco-busting*) or 'demote' (*busted him to private*).

bust *(noun)*

See BREAST.

but

1 **but** at the beginning	4 **but** *that*, **but** *what*
2 **but** *however*	5 illogical contrasts
3 **but** *him*/*he*	6 *disastrous,* **but** *disastrous!*

1 It is often perfectly legitimate, and very effective, to begin a sentence or even a paragraph with **but**, but the habit should not be allowed to become a mannerism. Where **but** begins a sentence, it should not be separated by a comma from what follows, unless the comma is the first of a pair: *But that's ridiculous*; *But, as you admitted, it's very expensive.*

2 It is neater and shorter not to combine **but** with *however*, *yet*, *still*, or *nevertheless*, which themselves express the idea of contrast, unless you want to emphasize the contrast: *The sky grew darker; (but) nevertheless they struggled on.* See TAUTOLOGY.

3 As a preposition meaning 'except', **but** is used with *him*, *me*, etc rather than *he*, *I* (see CASE, GRAMMATICAL (5)): *nobody but him; all of us but her.* Some writers prefer, however, to use *he* and *I* when a verb follows if the pronoun may be felt to be the subject: *Nobody but I can tell the difference.*

4 There seems no objection in principle to the combination **but** *that*: *I don't doubt but that he's guilty; Who knows but that they might succeed?* The danger here is that an extra negative often creeps in, making nonsense of the sentence: *Who knows but that they might not succeed?* This probably happens by confusion between the two constructions **but** *that* and *that* . . . *not*, because *Who knows that they might not succeed?* would express the intended meaning. The combination **but** *what*, as in *He never goes there but what he gets drunk*, is nonstandard and should be avoided in serious writing. Rephrase, perhaps as *He never goes there without getting drunk.*

5 But should connect two sentence parts of the same kind that are in contrast with each other: *not fierce, but gentle; quickly but accurately; not a cat but a dog; I wear it at home, but not at the office.* With the foregoing short instances there is no problem: *fierce* and *gentle* are opposed. But where longer stretches of language are involved, it is important to ensure that there is a real contrast. Sometimes the relationship between the parts would be more correctly expressed by *and*: *He is shrewd enough to know where his own interests lie, but* (replace by *and*) *perfectly capable of distinguishing between the alternatives we offer him.*

6 But can be used informally to emphasize an utterance by repetition (*lost everything, but everything*), but not in serious writing.

buttocks

It is difficult to find a neutral word for the part of the body that one sits on. **Buttocks** is plain enough but disconcertingly plural, drawing attention to the cleft between the two parts. **Backside** can also be plural in American English. **Bottom** and **behind** are informal and inoffensive; **rump** suggests quadrupeds or meat rather than humans, and **seat** is an extension from a part of the chair or trousers to the part that comes in contact with them. Coarser words are **bum** (chiefly British, since in American English the word also means 'tramp'); **arse**, chiefly British and including the anus; **ass**, American and including both the anus and sexual intercourse; and **fanny**, which in American English means the buttocks but in British English the female genitals.

buy

1 The past tense and participle are **bought**. The form *boughten* survives only as a dialectal word meaning 'bought from a shop; not homemade'.

2 The use of the verb to mean 'accept' (*I'll buy that*) and even of the noun to mean 'something bought' (*a good buy*) is informal and should be avoided in serious writing.

by

Since **by** has so many meanings, one must avoid ambiguity in its use. The writer who reported that *a dead elm tree . . . is to be replaced by Canadian airmen* meant to say that the airmen will plant another tree; but since one normally *replaces* one thing *by* another it sounds, absurdly, as if the airmen were going to be planted instead. If the tree were going to be *removed* by the airmen there would be no problem, but as it is the sentence needs to be entirely recast. A different ambiguity occurs in *An empty aspirin bottle was found by the deceased*, which sounds as though the dead person found the bottle rather than, as was presumably meant, that the bottle was found *beside* him. Where *with* or *at* can reasonably be used instead of **by**, they should be: *pleased with his progress*; *startled at the news*.

by, bye

The word is spelled **by** in *by and by*; either way in *by the by(e)*; **bye** in the sporting senses (a score in cricket, or a free passage to the next round of a tournament) or when it means *goodbye*.

by(e)-

This prefix meaning 'incidental, secondary' is usually spelled **by-**, and is joined to the following word with or without a hyphen: *by(-)product*. *Bylaw* and *by-election* can also be spelled *byelaw*, *bye-election*.

Byzantine, byzantine

This takes a capital *B* when it refers to ancient Byzantium, the modern Istanbul, but not always in its relatively modern sense of 'tortuous and devious': *the byzantine complexity of their politics*.

Cc

-c-, -ck-

Words ending with -c add -k- before adding any of the endings -ed, -er, -ing, -y: *bivouac(ked)*, *mimic(ked)*, *panic(ky)*, *picnic(ker)*, *traffic(king)*. An exception is *arc, arcing* (also *arcking*). Before -ian, -ism, -ist, -ity, -ize there is no -k-: *critic(ize)*, *music(ian)*, *electric(ity)*.

cacao, cocoa, coca, coco

Cacao is the tree whose seeds are roasted and crushed to make **cocoa**, which is drunk or eaten as chocolate. **Coca** is the shrub from which the drug **cocaine** is derived. The **coco** is the coconut palm or its fruit, more familiarly called a coconut.

cachou, cashew

A **cachou** is a lozenge for sweetening the breath. A **cashew** is a tropical tree grown for its nuts or the nut itself.

cactus

The plural is either **cacti** or **cactuses**.

caddy, caddie

Tea is kept in a **caddy**. A person who carries golf clubs is usually a **caddie**, but **caddy** is an acceptable alternative spelling.

cadre

This is pronounced 'kahder', or sometimes 'kadry' in military circles. It means either a nucleus of trained personnel or a member of such a nucleus.

c(a)esarean, c(a)esarian

The name of the surgical operation is usually spelled **caesarean** in

British English, **cesarean** in American English. Less common alternatives are **caesarian** (British), **cesarian** (American).

café

1 The accent is sometimes dropped in American English.

2 The pronunciation 'kaff' is non-standard or jocular.

calculate

It is an American English regionalism to use **calculate** for 'suppose' or 'assume', as in *He'll be here soon, I calculate*. Avoid this use in serious writing.

calculus

In the medical sense, the plural is usually **calculi**: *calculi in his gall bladder*. In the mathematical sense, use **calculuses**: *the integral and differential calculuses*.

calendar, calender, colander

A **calendar** is a list of dates. A **calender** is a machine that presses cloth, rubber, or paper between rollers. A **colander** (or *cullender*) is a perforated utensil for washing food.

Calgary

See CALVARY.

caliber, calibre

The word is spelled **caliber** or **calibre** in American English, **calibre** in British English. It is usually pronounced with the stress on the first syllable.

caliph

The first vowel is probably best pronounced as in *cat*, but the pronunciation as in *cake* is a respectable alternative.

callous, callus

Callous means 'hardened', whereas a **callus** is a hard place on skin or bark. It is thus correct to call hardened skin *calloused* (ie made hard) or *callused* (ie having calluses): *his calloused/callused palms*. Behaviour can be only **callous**, meaning insensitive: *her callous disregard for their suffering*.

Calvary, cavalry, Calgary

Calvary was the hill where Jesus was crucified; **cavalry** are mounted troops; **Calgary** is a city in Canada.

came the ...

This expression, as in *came the dawn*, should be avoided as a journalistic CLICHÉ.

camp (*adjective*)

This is a difficult word to use. It means either 'homosexual' (rather derogatory) or 'amusingly affected and in bad taste': *camp send-ups of old music-hall songs.*

campus

In American English, this means the grounds and buildings of a university, or a division of a university (*The University of California has several campuses*), and is often used of a high school. The word is a relatively recent introduction into British English, and is still used rather more commonly of the grounds and buildings of a geographically self-contained university in a rural setting, and thus chiefly of the new universities.

can, may

The chief modern sense of **can** is to express ability, 'know how to' (*I can swim*), and that of **may** is to express possibility (*It may rain*). In addition, both verbs express the idea of giving permission, 'be allowed to', but **can** is now commoner than **may** in this sense: *You can go now*; *You can't smoke here.* There is usually no real chance of misunderstanding: a little boy who asks *Can I go now?* is obviously not asking whether he knows how to. Where misunderstanding is genuinely possible, **may** is preferred, as in the following from the files of the Survey of English Usage: *What right have we to tell someone in Germany what he may or may not do?* **May** is still preferred for the 'permission' sense in very formal writing: *If the Minister is satisfied that it is reasonable to do so, he may* (ie the regulation permits him to) *award a higher pension.* It is curious that those who claim to find the 'permissive' **can** confusing never say that the use of **may** for permission leads to confusion with the idea of possibility. The above example could theoretically mean that the Minister will *perhaps* award the pension.

can, tin

The familiar often cylindrical food container is usually called a **can** in American English and a **tin** in British English: *a can/tin of tomatoes*. But **can** in this sense is coming rapidly into British English, particularly with reference to a container for drink: *a can of beer*. Both words are also used as verbs: *a canning factory; tinned beans*.

candelabra, chandelier

1 The older word for a branched candlestick is *candelabrum*, plural *candelabra*. The more modern word, in use since the early 19th century, is **candelabra**: *a beautiful candelabra*. It has the regular English plural **candelabras**.

2 A **candelabra** stands on a surface, a **chandelier** hangs from the ceiling.

cannon, canon, cañon, canyon

A **cannon** is a large gun, part of a horse's leg, or a shot in billiards; a **canon** is a law, a kind of clergyman, a kind of musical composition, or the total authentic works of a writer; a **cañon**, now usually anglicized to **canyon** and always pronounced like that, is a deep narrow steep-sided valley.

cannot

1 Cannot and **can't** are correctly used before *but* (*He could not but smile*) and before *help* (*He couldn't help smiling*). There is a long-standing traditional objection to **cannot** *help but* (*He could not help but smile*), which is believed to form a DOUBLE NEGATIVE, but the combination has been widely used by reputable writers for most of this century, and perhaps by now its detractors are outnumbered by its users. However, the use of **cannot** and **can't** with other negatives (*I can't hardly remember*) is still nonstandard.

2 There is some risk of ambiguity in such statements as *I cannot speak too highly of his contribution* and *His contribution cannot be overestimated*. Was his contribution great, or only mediocre?

3 Cannot *seem to* should be rephrased as *seem unable to* in formal writing.

4 Cannot is written as one word, unlike the other such negative combinations, which are either *must not* or *mustn't*, *should not* or *shouldn't*.

canvas, canvass

Canvas (or occasionally **canvass** in British English) is a kind of cloth, and to cover something with **canvas** is to **canvas** it. To solicit votes is to **canvass**, and the solicitation of votes is a **canvass**. **Canvass** forms the inflections **canvassing, canvasses, canvassed**, while **canvas** forms either the same set of inflections or, more usually, a set with a single *s*: *two large canvas(s)es by Picasso*.

canyon

See CANNON.

capacity

1 In the meaning of 'function' or 'role', this word is best confined to such expressions as *in his capacity as judge*; *He served the government in various capacities*. It may seem PRETENTIOUS to ask *What is his capacity?* when enquiring what job someone does, though reasonable to admire *his capacity for hard work*, meaning his ability to do it.

2 See ABILITY.

capital, capitol

A **capital** is a city serving as the seat of government, a **capitol** is the building in which a US legislative body meets.

capital, corporal

Capital *punishment* is the death penalty; **corporal** *punishment* is the infliction of physical pain.

capitalist, capitalism

These are usually pronounced with the stress on *cap*. There is an alternative British English pronunciation with the stress on *pit*, but it is not universally acceptable.

capitals

1	general	**5**	family titles
2	sentence capitals	**6**	verse
3	names	**7**	acronyms
4	titles of works	**8**	God

1 general
It is easy to state the general conventions for capitals, but on many

details there is no established convention. Whatever our choice in such instances, we should (as always) strive for consistency.

2 sentence capitals

Sentences start with a capital, and so do sentences that are quoted:

> She turned to me and said, 'We are looking for someone to type our correspondence.'

> The manager replied curtly: 'There must be no smoking in this room.'

> 'After that episode,' she said, 'relations between us began to disintegrate.'

But if merely part of a sentence is quoted, the quotation is not capitalized:

> The advertisements described the product as 'made with dairy cream'.

When more than one sentence is in brackets or follows a colon, there is no doubt that each sentence should be capitalized. Similarly, a sentence in brackets that is not part of another sentence is capitalized:

> Increasing numbers of people enjoy skiing down mountains in midwinter. (Skiing became popular in the 1920s.) One result is a growing improvement in the design and quality of ski clothes.

But when the sentence in brackets is within another sentence, a small letter is normal:

> He said that the next world war would come in the year 1980 (some newspapers thought so too), then changed the date to 2000.

When a sentence follows a dash, it always starts with a small letter:

> We do not believe that there is a serious problem – the work will certainly be completed on time.

When it follows a colon (apart from a quotation) practice varies, but a small letter is preferable:

> He abandoned his studies: he lacked perseverance.

3 names

All proper names take capitals. They include names of specific people (*Helen Keller*), groups of people (*Norwegians, Roman Catholics*), languages and groups of languages (*Arabic, Indo-European*), places (*New York*), days (*Monday*), months (*January*), holidays (*Good Friday, Independence Day*), and institutions (*the Waldorf Astoria, the Metropolitan Museum, the Bank of England*). But the seasons (*spring* etc) generally do not begin with a capital.

Some words that were originally names are now used in a general sense and are no longer in capitals: *a valentine, scotch (whisky)*. Contrast *Bohemian* (someone from Bohemia) and *bohemian* (someone living an unconventional life); *Bible* (the sacred scriptures) and *the lawyer's bible* (an authoritative work).

When a name consists of more than one word, generally all the words are in capitals apart from the article, the conjunction *and*, and prepositions such as *of*: *the Department of Education and Science, the Library of Congress*. Exceptions are *The Hague* (in contrast to *the Netherlands*) and newspapers that have *the* as part of the title: *The New York Times*. In the latter case, the article is dropped before the genitive: *in today's New York Times*.

Often a multiple-word name is referred to after the first mention by a part of the name that has a general sense. In such cases, it is normal to use small letters, though some people prefer capitals: *Oxford University – the university*; *Senator Hallway – the senator*; *Mexico City – the city*; *the National Union of Mineworkers – the union*; *the American Civil War – the war*.

When the words are used in a general sense, they are always in small letters: *the universities*; *government departments*; *a senator*; *a professor*; *a president*.

On the other hand, to avoid misunderstanding it is normal to use capitals when a partial name is used in a specialized sense: *Scotland Yard – the Yard*; *the United States –the States*; *The Daily Telegraph – the Telegraph*; *the House of Commons – the House* or *the Commons*; *the Canary Islands – the Canaries*; *Petticoat Lane – the Lane*.

Certain high titles as partial names are often, though not invariably, capitalized. If in doubt, prefer capitals: *the Queen*; *the Duke*; *the President*; *the Princess*.

High titles of respect are capitalized. They precede a name or are used alone, often as terms of address: *Her Majesty the Queen*; *His Excellency the Ambassador from Peru*; *Her Royal Highness*; *Your Honour*; *His Holiness*.

4 titles of works

It is normal to capitalize the first and last words of titles of works (including subtitles) and all other words except for the articles (*a, an, the*), prepositions of no more than four letters (such as *to, for*, and *with*), and the conjunctions *and, or*, and *but*: *For Whom the Bell Tolls*; *What's On*; *Iran Under the Ayatollahs*; *The Music Makers: The English Musical Renaissance from Elgar to Britten*; *Lord of the Flies*.

These rules apply to the titles of newspapers, magazines, journals, books, plays, films, television series and programmes, paintings, musical compositions, short stories, poems, songs, chapters in books, and articles in newspapers, magazines, and journals. See also ITALICS; QUOTATION MARKS.

5 family titles
When used alone or before a name, they are usually capitalized:
Mother; *Dad*; *Aunt Helen*; *Uncle Tom*.

6 verse
Traditionally, each line in verse starts with a capital, but some modern poets have abandoned this convention.

7 acronyms
Acronyms (words formed of the initials of words or parts of words) are generally all in capitals, except for plural endings (eg *GPs*): *UNESCO*; *CBS*; *USSR*; *MPS*; *BBC*; *GHQ*. But some acronyms, such as *radar* and *laser*, are not felt to be acronyms and are written with small letters. See ACRONYMS.

8 God
When used to refer to the monotheistic deity, *God* and similar words (*the Lord*, *the Almighty*) are capitalized. Pronouns referring to the deity were once always capitalized (*Thou*, *He*), but most writers no longer follow this convention.

caption

This usually means the words either above or below and accompanying a picture, or a film subtitle. The belief that this word should mean only a heading is based on the mistaken impression that **caption** derives from the Latin *caput*, a head, whereas it seems to have meant a 'seizing' of the point (Latin *capere* to capture).

carat, karat, caret

A unit of purity for gold is a **carat**, or in American English a **karat**, a unit of weight for precious stones is a **carat**, a mark (∧) indicating an insertion in a piece of writing is a **caret**.

carbon monoxide, carbon dioxide

These are both gases. **Carbon monoxide** is a poisonous gas, CO, formed when carbon burns incompletely (as in car exhaust fumes). **Carbon dioxide** is CO_2, formed when we breathe out, absorbed by plants, and used in making fizzy drinks.

carburet(t)or

This is spelled with two *t*'s in British English, one *t* in American English.

111

careen, career

To **careen** a boat is to make it lean over to one side for cleaning or repairing. In American English, **careen** can now legitimately mean 'lurch rapidly along': *The car careened down the bumpy slope*. The word cannot be replaced in this sense by **career**, which means 'move rapidly and out of control' but does not by itself suggest this erratic swaying motion, a combination of speed and heeling over.

careless, carefree

These can both mean simply 'free from care': *careless grace; carefree holidays*. Both can also mean 'not taking enough care', but **careless** then implies a more censorious attitude on the part of the speaker: *carefree with his money; careless slovenly work*.

carillon

This is now usually pronounced to rhyme with *million*, though some people still put the stress on the first syllable: *carol* followed by *on*.

caring

This is OVERUSED in the sense of 'compassionate' or 'affectionate' (*She is a very caring mother*), and in a vaguer sense referring to social welfare (*Medicine is one of the caring professions*; *Our party offers caring policies*).

carnivorous

See CONIFEROUS.

carousal, car(r)ousel

Carousal is drunken revelry. The stress is on the second syllable, pronounced 'ow'. A **carousel** is a rotating device, such as that for delivering baggage at an airport; in American English (where it is more usually spelled **carrousel**) it is also the word for a merry-go-round. The stress is on the last syllable, and the *ou* is pronounced 'oo'.

case

1 This OVERUSED word is often a mark of careless, pretentious writing. Careful writers may prefer to replace *In the case of cigars sold singly, they were made smaller* by *Cigars sold singly were made smaller*; and *In many cases the churches have become derelict* by *Many of the churches have become derelict*; and *Is it the case that pigs have wings?* by *Do pigs have wings?*

2 *In* **case** can mean 'if' in American English. Compare: (American and British) *We'd better insure the house in case it burns down*; (American) *We'll get the insurance money in case it burns down*.

case, grammatical

1 general	**4** after *as* and *than*
2 after the verb *be*	**5** after *but*
3 *and* or *or*	**6** *who* and *whom*

1 general

He and *him* differ in their grammatical case, and so do *I* and *me*, *she* and *her*, *they* and *them*, *we* and *us*. We use *he* and *I* when they are subject, and *him* and *me* when they are object: **I** *know* **him**; **He** *knows* **me**. Old English (like many other languages) had several cases for nouns, pronouns, and adjectives. We lost most of those case distinctions a long time ago, a loss that few regret. However, the loss has reduced our sense of a role for the remaining case distinctions.

Only nouns and pronouns display distinctions in case. Nouns and most pronouns have only two cases, the **common case** and the **genitive** (or 'possessive') **case**: *Susan, Susan's*; *somebody, somebody's* (see GENITIVE). In the written language, we can distinguish the case forms for singular and plural nouns: singular *student, student's*, plural *students, students'* . In the spoken language, however, there is no difference for most plural nouns, since the regular plural (*students*) and the genitive plural (*students'*) are pronounced identically, and indeed share the same pronunciation with the genitive singular (*student's*). Only nouns with irregular plurals, such as *child*, have four distinct pronunciations as well as four written forms: *child, child's, children, children's*. Because we do not have a full set of distinctions for regular nouns in speech, some people make mistakes in the use of the apostrophe in writing (see APOSTROPHE).

A few pronouns have three cases: the **subjective** (or 'nominative') case and the **objective** (or 'accusative') case as well as the **genitive**:

subjective	*I*	*we*	*he*	*she*	*they*	*who*	*whoever*
objective	*me*	*us*	*him*	*her*	*them*	*whom*	*whomever*
genitive	*my*	*our*	*his*	*her*	*their*	*whose*	

The general rules are straightforward. These pronouns are in the subjective case when they are the subject of a finite verb: I *think that* **they** *live in Dartmouth*. They are in the objective case when they are (1) the object (direct or indirect) of a verb: *He can't see* **them**; *She's given* **me** *the money*; or (2) the complement of a preposition: *for* **us**; *I was with* **her**. In effect this means that subjective pronouns come

113

before the verb and objective pronouns come after the verb. This generalization underlies some of the uncertainties and disputed usages.

2 after the verb *be*

The verb *be* is a linking verb, and the pronoun following it is not an object but a complement that refers back to the subject. Consequently, some people think that the pronoun should always be in the subjective case; they object to *It's me* and *This is him*, and require instead *It is I* and *This is he*. On the other hand, these pronouns follow a verb and in that position they are usually in the objective case (see **1** above). Such sentences with *me* and other objective pronouns chiefly occur in speech or in written dialogue, and they are legitimate in those contexts; but in formal writing use *It is* **I** and *This is* **he**.

3 *and* or *or*

People often make mistakes when the pronoun does not immediately follow the verb or preposition: *I hope that you will visit my wife* **and I** *in the near future; These sandwiches are intended for Sheila, you,* **and** **I**; *Let Robert* **and I** *show you the way*. The correct form is **and me** in these three sentences, as is obvious if we replace the phrases by the pronoun alone: *I hope that you will visit* **me** *in the near future; These sandwiches are intended for* **me**; *Let* **me** *show you the way*. (See LET (1).) The common misuse of *I* in such instances – particularly common in the expression *between you and I* in the sense 'confidentially' – is due to a feeling that *you and me* is as wrong here as in *You and* **me** *should be friends*. (See HYPERCORRECTION.) The evasive substitution of **myself**, as in *I hope that you will visit my wife* **and myself** *in the near future*, is inelegant (see REFLEXIVE). The misuse of the objective pronoun for the subject phrase is nonstandard: *My wife and* **me** *will be there*; and it is worse when the polite order is reversed (**Me** *and my wife will be there*).

4 after *as* and *than*

As and *than* are undoubtedly conjunctions, linking equal units. But the question is whether they can also be prepositions when they are followed by just a pronoun. If so, the pronoun should be objective: *as fat as* **him,** *older than* **her**. For formal writing you may treat *as* and *than* as conjunctions, and decide which case to use according to whether the pronoun would be subjective or objective in the equivalent clauses: *She is as fat as* **he** (*is*); *They paid Joan more than (they paid)* **me**; *They treat their children more casually than* **we** (*do*). But since the subjective pronoun in these instances sounds pedantic to many, it is better to use the clause instead: *They treat their children more casually than* **we do**. If the objective pronoun is ambiguous, as in *She doesn't see the children more than* **me**, use the clause: *She doesn't see the children more than* **I do**; *She doesn't see the children more than* **she sees me**. However, *than whom* is always correct, even when *whom* is subject: *We unanimously appointed to the position of managing director the deputy managing director,* **than whom** *none had served our company more effectively.* (Contrast: *None had served . . .* **than she** *had.*)

5 after *but*

The subjective pronoun sounds a HYPERCORRECTION, although some writers use the subjective when the pronoun is in the subject position (*Nobody* **but I** *can tell the difference*) and others use it also when it is related to the subject even though it is at the end (*Nobody can tell the difference* **but I**). However, we cannot expand *but I* to make a sensible clause even when it appears at the end of the sentence (*Nobody can tell the difference but I can*) and therefore *but* cannot be a conjunction. It is more logical to treat *but* in this sense as a preposition and therefore to select the objective case in all instances: *Nobody* **but me** *can tell the difference*; *Everybody can tell the difference* **but me**; *I know everybody here* **but her**.

6 *who* and *whom*

The distinction between subjective *who* and objective *whom* has virtually been lost in most present-day usage. It is perfectly natural to say **Who** *do you want?* or **Who** *should I give it to?* The distinction, however, should be preserved in formal usage: **Who** *selected them?*, but **Whom** *did you select?* or *On* **whom** *do you rely?* The same distinction applies to *whoever* and *whomever*, but *whomever* is restricted to very formal writing: **Whoever** *wants to see me must make an appointment with my secretary*, but **Whomever** *you select will be admitted* or *To* **whomever** *it may concern.* (See also WHOSE.) In relative clauses, you may prefer to replace *whom* by *that* or to omit the pronoun altogether, particularly when the clause is brief. Hence, instead of *the woman whom I met* you may use *the woman that I met* or *the woman I met*.

The correct case in formal usage depends on the function of the pronoun in its clause. Problems may arise when a relative clause is interrupted by a parenthetic expression. If in the middle of *the man who was responsible for the decision* we insert some such expression as *they thought* or *I know*, we may wrongly feel that the pronoun is the object of the parenthetic verb and therefore produce incorrectly *the man* **whom** *they thought was responsible for the decision.* We can avoid this error by reconstructing the relative clause as a separate sentence; we would then see that the personal pronoun must be subjective: *They thought (that)* **he** *was responsible for the decision.* Contrast the correct choice of objective *whom* in *the man* **whom** *they thought to be responsible for the decision*; the corresponding sentence requires objective *him*: *They thought* **him** *to be responsible for the decision.*

Similar problems may arise when the relative clause follows a preposition. The choice of pronoun may be wrongly influenced by the preposition, although the preposition governs the clause rather than the pronoun. Hence, *whoever* is correct in *I explained my predicament to* **whoever** *was there* (*whoever* is subject; compare **She** *was there*), and *whomever* is correct (though very formal) in *I explained my predicament to* **whomever** *I saw* (*whomever* is object; compare *I saw* **her**). So also *You can tell it to* **whom(ever)** *you wish*, since *whom(ever)* is object; compare *You wish to tell it to* **her**.

cashew

See CACHOU.

casket

In American English, this word is chiefly used as a EUPHEMISM for 'coffin', implying a fancy coffin that is rectangular rather than coffin-shaped. In British English, it means a small chest or box, such as one for keeping jewels in.

cast (*verb*)

Avoid using the somewhat PRETENTIOUS word **cast** where *throw* will do: *throw* (rather than *cast*) *one's socks into the laundry basket*. But in a wide range of senses and expressions, **cast** is the better word, for example *cast a gloom; cast a net*.

caste, cast (*noun*)

A **caste** is a hereditary social group in Hinduism, or by extension any system of rigid social stratification. Otherwise the word is **cast**. The actors in a play are the **cast**.

caster, castor

Sugar containers and small wheels on furniture are either **casters** or **castors**; finely ground white sugar is either **caster** *sugar* or **castor** *sugar*; but it is **castor** *oil*.

casual, causal

1 Casual means 'happening by chance', or 'offhand': *casual remarks*. **Causal** refers to cause: *the causal agent of the disease*.

2 Casual has acquired an appreciative implication. Besides the earlier meanings, it now often means 'nonchalantly informal': *casual elegance*.

casualty

It is now perfectly legitimate for **casualty** to mean not only a serious or fatal accident, or a person killed, but any kind of victim: *Small firms will be the first casualties of this policy.*

catacomb, catafalque, cenotaph, hecatomb

These are all connected with death. A **catacomb** is a subterranean cemetery. A **catafalque** is an ornamental platform for a dead body. A **cenotaph** is a monument, particularly a war memorial, to people buried elsewhere. A **hecatomb**, originally an ancient Greek or Roman sacrifice of animals, is a killing of many victims.

catalyst

In the chemical sense, this means a substance that encourages chemical change in other substances without itself being affected. The meaning has been extended to cover anything that by limited action inspires a wider-ranging series of events (*Her question was the catalyst for an interesting class discussion*), but the word is OVERUSED in this wider sense and should not be used as a mere synonym for *cause* (as in *The crash was the catalyst of a multiple pile-up*).

catastrophe, cataclysm

These are both momentous destructive events. **Catastrophe** emphasizes disaster: *the catastrophe of the plane crash*. **Cataclysm** suggests an upheaval that shatters an established order: *refugees from the cataclysm of the revolution*.

categorical(ly)

This is somewhat of a CLICHÉ when it means 'without qualification': *categorical statements*; *He categorically denied it.*

Catholic

Except in specialized theological contexts, **Catholic** can be used everywhere today for *Roman Catholic*: *Catholic schools*. With a small *c*, **catholic** means 'broad in sympathies or tastes': *a catholic taste in music*.

catsup, catchup

See KETCHUP.

Caucasian

It is better to use this word only of the people, languages, etc of the Caucasus. It is used as a technical, and in some places legal, term for the white races, but it is better replaced in general writing by *white* (not *White*). It may even be misunderstood: *'I presume the Loved One was Caucasian?' 'No, why did you think that? He was purely English.' 'English are purely Caucasian, Mr Barlow'* (Evelyn Waugh).

ca(u)ldron

Caldron is the preferred spelling in American English, **cauldron** in British English.

ca(u)lk

Calk is the preferred American spelling for 'stop up the seams of a boat', **caulk** the British spelling.

causal

See CASUAL.

cause

Things and events **cause**, or are the **cause** *of*, other things and events. Since the word **cause** itself covers the idea of the explanation of an effect, it should not be combined with *due to* or *as a result*. Do not write *The cause of the accident was due to icy roads*, or *The delay was caused as a result of fog*, but rather *The cause of the accident was icy roads* or *The delay was caused by fog*.

cavalcade

Originally this meant a procession on horseback or in carriages, but today the word is very generally used of motorized vehicles: *a cavalcade of motorbikes*. It seems unreasonable to object to this extended use, since a **procession** somehow sounds pedestrian, and a **pageant** is not necessarily mobile. Not everyone likes the word **motorcade**, which has been available since 1913, for a procession of motor vehicles.

cavalry

See CALVARY.

-ce

See -E-.

-ce, -cy

Many words ending in -**ant** or -**ent** have a related word ending in -**ce** (*magnificence*), or in -**cy** (*buoyancy*), or in either (*persistence, persistency; competence, competency*). If in doubt which form to use, consult a dictionary. If no dictionary is available, it is worth noting that words of more than three syllables favour -**ce** (*intelligence*, but *frequency*); and that nouns with no plural favour -**ce**, while nouns that can have both singular and plural often prefer -**cy**, -**cies**. Indeed, a noun such as **emergence** 'the act of emerging' may coexist with a related countable noun, such as **emergency** 'an unforeseen crisis'.

cease

Except in certain specialized combinations such as *cease-fire*, this is now a rather formal word for 'stop'.

-cede, -ceed, -sede

Most words ending with this sound spell it -**cede**: *accede, precede, recede*. Exceptions are *exceed, proceed, succeed*, and *supersede* (the only one with -**sede**).

ceiling

This is a convenient, though perhaps OVERUSED, word in the metaphorical sense of an 'upper limit'. Our sense of its literal meaning, however, makes it better not to speak of *increasing*, *extending*, or *waiving* a **ceiling**, or to say that a ceiling is beginning to *bite*.

celebrant, celebrator

Originally a **celebrant** was someone such as a priest at mass, who *celebrates* a public ritual. In modern American English the word is also used of anyone who *celebrates* anything: *the celebrants at his birthday party*.

cello

The plural is **cellos**.

Celsius, Centigrade

These both mean the temperature scale by which water boils at $100°$ and freezes at $0°$. **Centigrade** comes from the French, **Celsius** from the name of the 18th-century Swedish astronomer who invented the scale. **Celsius** is the approved word in technical circles, and has become general in weather forecasts. Fortunately *C* is the abbreviation for both.

Celt, Celtic

These are usually pronounced 'kelt(ic)', not 'selt(ic)', except in the case of the Scottish football team **Celtic**. But a prehistoric axe head is sometimes called a **celt**, pronounced 'selt'.

cement, concrete, mortar

Strictly speaking, **cement** is a powder made by burning clay and limestone. It is mixed with sand, stone, and water to make **concrete** (and without the stone to make **mortar** for plastering or for sticking bricks together). The words **cement**, **concrete**, and **mortar** are often used interchangeably, however, by people other than builders and architects.

cenotaph

See CATACOMB.

censer, censor, censure

A **censer** is a burner for incense. A **censor** is the person who **censors** books, plays, and films. **Censure** is severe criticism, and to **censure** is to blame. **Censorial** refers to **censors** (*his censorial duties*), and **censorious** to **censure** (*censorious comments*).

census

See CONSENSUS.

centenary, centennial

These both mean a 100th anniversary. **Centenary** is the preferred British form for the noun, though some British writers use **centennial** for the adjective. **Centennial** is the American preference for both adjective and noun. The same considerations apply to **bicentennial** (as celebrated by the USA in 1976) versus **bicentenary**, and **tercentennial** versus **tercentenary**. **Quatercentenary** and **quincentenary** are, however, the usual words for 400th and 500th anniversaries.

Centigrade

See CELSIUS.

centre, center

The word is spelled **centre** in British English, **center** in American English. Things **centre** (**center**) *on*, *upon*, or *in* other things: *her hopes centred on her son*. An institution can be **centred** *at* a place: *a*

nationwide organization centred at Tewkesbury. The use of **centre**
with *about*, *round*, or *around* (*Many legends centre around him*) is
now so common as to be virtually established idiom, but still avoided
by some careful writers. Those who dislike the combination **centre**
(a)round, but wish to preserve the idea suggested by *(a)round*, may
prefer to write *revolve around*.

centrifugal

The main stress is usually on the third syllable rather than the second.

centripetal

The main stress may be on either the second or the third syllable.

century

1 The 1900s are the 20th **century** AD, of which the last year will be the
year 2000. Similarly, the period 1801–1900 inclusive was the 19th
century, 1301–1400 was the 14th **century**, and so on. Centuries BC
are counted in the same way but in reverse: Julius Caesar's raid on
Britain in 55 BC was in the first century BC, and 600–501 BC was the
sixth century BC.

2 Expressions such as *during this century* mean 'since 1900', not
'during the past hundred years'.

cereal, serial

A **cereal** is a food grain or a breakfast food; a **serial** is a radio or
television production or a written publication appearing in instalments.

ceremonial, ceremonious

Both adjectives are related to *ceremony*. **Ceremonial** refers to actual
ritual: *a ceremonial occasion*; *ceremonial robes*. The chief meaning of
ceremonious today is 'punctilious, observing the conventions':
ceremonious politeness; *a ceremonious old gentleman*. People can be
ceremonious but not **ceremonial**.

certain

A **certain** implies that the speaker is unable to be more specific, and
may suggest a degree of irony, as in *The house has a certain charm*, or
a certain Mrs Jones. The expression should be avoided if there is
danger of confusion with the other meaning of **certain**, as in *There is a
certain remedy for this ailment*. If we mean *a sure remedy* we should
say so.

121

cervical

There are two pronunciations: one with the stress on the first syllable, like *serve*, the other with the stress on the second syllable, rhyming with *like*. Both are correct, though the second is more technical.

cessation, cession, session

Cessation is a stopping: *the cessation of the noise*. **Cession** is a yielding of rights or territory: *the cession of Alsace-Lorraine to Germany in 1871*. A **session** is a period of meeting: *The Court is in session*; *a recording session*.

ceteris paribus

The first syllables of both words are stressed, and pronounced like the beginnings of *kettle* and *parrot*. This expression means 'all other things being equal'. Do not use too many of these LATINISMS.

chafe, chaff

To **chafe** is to rub, usually painfully: *The shoe chafed his heel*; or to feel iritated: *He chafed at his boring job*. To **chaff** is to tease: *They chaffed him about his silly mistake*.

chain reaction

Strictly, this implies that A causes B which causes C, and so on. The expression is now loosely used for any flood of uncontrollable consequences of A, whether or not they cause each other: *This concession may trigger off a chain reaction of wage demands*. There seems to be no objection to this usage, provided it is understood.

chairperson

Although a **chairwoman** must be female, a **chairman** may be either a man or a woman, so that *Madam Chairman* is not absurd or even unusual. Those who regard **chairman** as having an undesirably strong male implication have the option of using **chairperson**, which is particularly appropriate when the sex happens to be unknown (as when the post has not yet been filled): *A chairperson will be appointed*. A woman is more likely than a man to call herself the **chairperson**. Those who dislike **chairperson** may avoid the problem by saying **chair**: *Who is the chair?*; *Address your remarks to the chair*.

chaise longue

This is a kind of sofa with a head and one armrest. The plural is either **chaise longues** or **chaises longues,** pronounced the same as the singular or with an added 'z' sound at the end of the second word. The form **chaise lounge** is nonstandard.

chamois

This is pronounced 'sham-wah' when it means a small European antelope. When it means a kind of soft leather it is pronounced 'shammy' and often spelled *shammy* or *chammy*.

chancel, choir, chantry

These are all parts of a church. The area in front of the nave (where the congregation sit) is the **chancel**, containing the altar and seats for clergy and singers. These singers are the **choir**, and **choir** also means the part of the **chancel** where they sit, west of the altar rails. A **chantry** is an endowment to sing masses for someone's soul, or a side chapel or altar where such masses are sung.

chancery, chancellery

Chancery is a court of equity in both the British and the US judicial systems. **Chancery** and **chancellery** (or **chancellory**) can both mean the office of an embassy. They can also both mean the department of a *chancellor*, a title which has various meanings in government, in the Church, and in higher education.

chandelier

See CANDELABRA.

change of meaning

All languages are subject to constant change. We notice this even within our own life span, when the young use words and expressions that puzzle their grandparents, and the grandparents perhaps say things that the young find quaintly outmoded. We all need some vocabulary notes to read Shakespeare and a good deal more than that for Chaucer, while we have to learn Anglo-Saxon as a foreign language.

A great deal of this change arises because we have occasion to say something new. We may coin a new word for the new idea, or we may (as is very common in English) borrow a word from another language, but what we often do is simply to give an existing word a new meaning. When it originated in the 18th century, *broadcast* referred to the scattering of seed in all directions, but it is now commonly used to mean 'transmit by radio or television'. *Dilapidated* comes from the Latin *lapis*, 'stone', but we not only use the word of a ruined stone building but speak of a *dilapidated* car or a *dilapidated* old raincoat. *Holiday* comes from 'holy day', but it is used of any day of freedom

from work, not only of religious occasions such as Christmas and
Easter.

Dilapidated and *holiday* are examples of words that have widened in
meaning. Words may also become narrower in meaning, more specific.
Deer used to mean any animal, particularly a small mammal, as it did
when Shakespeare wrote of *rats and mice and such small deer*, but the
word now applies only to antlered ruminants of the family *Cervidae*.

Words can come up or go down in the world. In the 14th century
villain meant a village peasant, but now it can mean only a scoundrel.
Sometimes the word still refers to much the same thing, but social
attitudes have changed towards the thing it stands for. In this sense,
two words that have come down in the world are *imperialism* and
academic. People no longer admire as they once did the policy of
extending national power by territorial acquisition, so that *imperialism*
is now a derogatory term. The traditions of formal learning are less
respected than they once were, so that although *academic* still has a
respectable sense (*academic freedom*) people are now likely to speak of
matters without practical significance as *purely academic*. The opposite
process has happened to *casual* and *aggressive*, for instance, which
have come up in the world. People have come to admire what is natural
and informal rather than what is highly contrived, and to express this
feeling by speaking appreciatively of *casual* clothes or a *casual* life-
style. Modern business methods need the qualities of energy and
enterprise, so that *aggressive*, which used to apply only to hostile
destructive behaviour, is now used in praise of a successful salesperson
or marketing strategy.

People are often conservative about language change. Many entries
in this book advise you to avoid, at least for the purpose of formal
writing, new senses that are not yet well established or that have met
with particular hostility.

chant(e)y, shant(e)y

A **shanty** is a crude hut. The similar word for a sailor's work song is
usually spelled **shanty** or **shantey** in British English, but **chantey** or
chanty in American English.

chaperon(e)

Both spellings are acceptable, but the first predominates, even though
the one ending with -*e* seems more feminine and the word is used of a
role typically fulfilled by a woman.

character, nature

These words are sometimes used in a rather VERBOSE way like *kind* or
sort. It is shorter and often neater to rephrase *advertising of a*

misleading character or *acts of a ceremonial nature* as *misleading advertising* or *ceremonial acts.*

charge (*noun*)

The expression *in* **charge** *of* can mean either 'in control of' or 'under the control of'. The first meaning is certainly more common in British English, where the second is usually expressed by *in the* **charge** *of*: *The general manager is in charge of all transactions*; *All transactions are in the charge of the general manager.* Sentences such as *He is in charge of the doctor* are more likely to occur in American English, and could be seriously ambiguous.

charge (*verb*), accuse

A person is **charged** *with* a crime, but **accused** *of* it.

chart, charter

To **chart** is to plot something on a map or in tabular form. To **charter** is to rent (a means of transport) temporarily (*charter a plane*) or to certify (a person) formally (*a chartered surveyor*). Thus, an unknown island may be *uncharted* but you would not call it *unchartered.*

chastise

The word is spelled like this in both British and American English; not -*ize.*

château

The accent is sometimes omitted in American English. In accordance with the same process of anglicization, the plural is sometimes not **châteaux** but **châteaus.**

cheap, cheaply

Cheap as an adverb is used mainly in contexts of buying and selling: *I can get it for you cheap*. It cannot otherwise replace **cheaply**, the usual adverb: *The room was cheaply furnished.*

check (*verb*)

When this means 'verify' or 'investigate', one can *check (up) on the facts* or, in American English, *check into the facts*; but it is more elegant, particularly in British English, to write **check** alone: *check the facts*. This style should be avoided, however, where **check** alone might be taken to mean 'restrain', as in *The police checked her.* In American English, but not usually in British English, **check** can mean 'deposit in a cloakroom'. An instruction by an American speaker to *check your bag* may be understood in Britain to mean 'inspect' it.

check, checker

These are American spellings for the British **cheque** (ie bank order), **chequer**: *a chequered career*. **Checkers** is the American word for the game called *draughts* in Britain.

cheerful, cheery

Cheerful can mean merely 'contented' or 'ungrudging': *cheerful obedience*. **Cheery** suggests more positive high spirits, as evinced by someone's voice and manner: *a cheery greeting*. One can behave in a **cheery** way without really feeling **cheerful**.

cheers

In both British and American English, **cheers** is the practically universal toast before drinking. For many British speakers it is an all-purpose word used as a form of thanks, as a farewell, and even as an apology.

cheque, chequer

See CHECK, CHECKER.

cherub

When it means an angel in the Bible, the plural is **cherubim**; when it is a beautiful chubby child, the plural is **cherubs**.

chest

See BREAST.

chesterfield

See SOFA.

chicano

This means an American of Mexican origin, and is not a disparaging term. Mexican Americans use it about themselves. It is sometimes, but not always, capitalized.

chick(en)

Chicken is the domestic fowl, or its flesh (*chicken sandwiches*), or its young (*a hen with her chickens*). Informally it can also mean 'young person': *She's no spring chicken*; or 'coward, cowardly': *to play chicken*. **Chick** is either a baby chicken or a dated slang word for 'woman'.

childish, childlike

When these words are used of adults or adult behaviour, **childish** refers to what one ought to have outgrown, such as fretful impatience or immature behaviour (*showed a childish determination to excel*), while **childlike** refers to what one still happily preserves, such as innocent simplicity (*played with childlike enthusiasm*). An actual child can be only **childish**, not **childlike**: *the little boy's round childish face*.

chilli, chili, chile

Chilli is the preferred British English spelling, **chili** the preferred American one. The variant **chile** is American English only.

chimera

The word is usually spelled like this, not **chimaera**.

Chinese

This is the word, both as adjective and noun, for the people of China: *Chinese students*; *We've invited a Chinese/two Chinese*. **Chinaman** is old-fashioned and now regarded as somewhat offensive.

choir

See CHANCEL.

chop, cutlet

Chop is used particularly of lamb and pork. A **chop** usually includes part of a rib. A **cutlet** is a small boneless slice of meat. One also speaks of *cutlets of cod* or *nut cutlets*, where **chop** could not be used.

chord, cord

A **chord** is a combination of musical notes, and also a straight line across part of a curve. A **cord** is any kind of string, including stringlike anatomical parts: *umbilical cord*; *spinal cord*; *vocal cords*.

Christian name

In contrast to *surname* or *family name*, **Christian name** is properly applied only to names given at Christian baptism. A useful and religiously neutral alternative is **first name**, with **middle name** for any second or subsequent one. Other alternatives are **forename** (British English), or **given name** (American English).

chronic

When applied to a disease or longstanding evil, this means 'lingering' or 'continuous' (as opposed to *acute*): *chronic bronchitis*; *chronic unemployment*. The word should not be used, in serious writing, to mean 'bad, terrible', as in *The food was chronic*.

chute

See SHOOT.

-ciate, -tiate

In verbs with the ending **-ciate**, and their related nouns in **-ation**, the *ci* is generally pronounced as 's': *pronunciation, emaciation*. In verbs with the ending **-tiate**, and their related nouns, the *ti* is generally pronounced as 'sh': *propitiation*. But, perhaps because two occurrences of 'sh' sound ugly, some people prefer to pronounce the first *ti* in such nouns as 's': *negotiation*. Such speakers may use 's' in *association* but 'sh' in *associate*. There is also a tendency, disliked by many, to use 's' in *negotiate*.

cinema

The British go to the **cinema** or the **pictures** to see a **picture** or **film**. The Americans go to the **movies** or to a **theater** to see a **movie**, though the associated industry is more formally called the **motion picture industry**. Devotees of the art form call it **cinema** or, in a newer usage, **film**: *a student of film*.

Cingalese

See SINHALESE.

Cinzano

This is pronounced 'chin-zah-noh'. It is the trademark of an Italian vermouth.

cipher, cypher

The usual spelling is **cipher**. **Cypher** is a rarer alternative in British English.

circumcise

This is the only correct spelling, in both British and American English; not *-ize*.

circumlocution

A circumlocution (also called a periphrasis) is a roundabout way of saying something. The shorter expression is generally preferable, but in some contexts you might wish to use a circumlocution out of politeness; for example, *I wonder whether you would mind passing me the salad* instead of the peremptory *Pass me the salad*.

Here are some common circumlocutions and possible replacements:

an X of this description – this kind of X
apart from the fact that – except, but
as a consequence of – because of
at this point in time – today, now
a yard in length – a yard long
because of the fact that – because
be in accordance with – agree to
be of the opinion that – think, believe
by means of – by
by virtue of the fact that – because
due to the fact that – because
during such times as – while
during the course of – during
except for the fact that – except, but
few in number – few
for the reason that – because
in accordance with – under
in addition to – besides
in a few cases/instances – occasionally
in a majority of cases/instances – usually
inasmuch as – since
in close proximity – near
in connection with – about
in isolation – alone
in less than no time – quickly
in many cases/instances – often

in most cases/instances – usually
in relation to – about, for, on
in respect of – about, for, on
in some cases/instances – sometimes
in spite of the fact that – although
in the absence of – without
in the event that – if
in the light of the fact that – because
in the near future – soon
in the neighbourhood of – near, about
in the vicinity of – near, about
in view of the fact that – because
irrespective of the fact that – although
large in size – large
notwithstanding the fact that – even if
of a delicate/menacing etc character – delicate, menacing, etc
on account of the fact that – because
on a temporary basis – temporarily
on the grounds that – because
owing to the fact that – because
pink in colour – pink
prior to – before
regardless of the fact that – although
subsequent to – after
to the extent that – if
until such times as – until
with reference to – about, for, on
with regard to – about, for, on
with respect to – about, for, on
with the exception of – except

Circumlocution is a common fault in official, commercial, and scholarly writing.

See also TAUTOLOGY; VERBOSITY.

circumstances

Some writers insist on using *in*, rather than *under*, the **circumstances,**

because **circumstance** is derived from the Latin *circum* ('around'), and
one is *in* whatever surrounds one; but the phrase *under the*
circumstances has been established in English since the 17th century
and is perfectly legitimate. It means 'because of the situation'. But
when **circumstances** means 'material welfare', as when someone is
said to be *in easy circumstances*, only *in* may be used.

citations

See REFERENCES.

cite

To **cite** is to 'refer to, or adduce, by way of authority': *He cited a*
biblical passage/a previous case. Only facts are cited. You do not **cite**
a person's criminal record unless the person has been proved to possess
one. See also SIGHT.

citizen, subject, inhabitant, resident, denizen

A **citizen,** among other meanings of the word, is a native or naturalized
person who owes allegiance to a particular state, and is entitled to
assistance from it: *a US citizen*. In the case of Britain, a monarchy, its
citizens are also **subjects**: *a British subject*. People who simply live in
a place are **inhabitants** or **residents**, but they may be permanent
residents without the status of **citizens**. **Denizen** is a rather flowery
word for **inhabitant**, but was also applied in the past to naturalized
citizens, and is still used of naturalized plants and animals.

city

Technically, a **city** is more than merely a fair-sized town. It is a legal
corporation, and in Britain the title is conferred by royal charter, or
means that the town has a cathedral, or both; in the USA a **city** has a
charter granted by the state. **Cities** need not in fact be very large: the
City of London occupies only about one square mile, and there are
quite small ones in the American West.

civilian

In modern use, this means a person who is not only not in the armed
forces, but also not in any other uniformed public body, such as the
police or the fire brigade. But a uniformed person out of uniform is
wearing **civilian** dress.

clad

When it means 'clothed' or 'covered', people or things should be **clad** *in* something: *ivy-clad walls*; *clad in armour*. The word should not be used to mean simply 'not naked'.

claim

This primarily means 'demand as a right': *They claimed Supplementary Benefit*; *He went to claim his luggage at the station.* This sense is legitimately extended to mean 'assert in the face of possible contradiction', where the claimant is concerned with obtaining due credit: *He claims to be the Queen's cousin.* The word is now widely used, and perhaps sometimes OVERUSED, as a mere synonym for *assert* or *declare*: *She claims that she was attacked by masked gunmen.*

clarify

This means either 'clear' or 'make comprehensible', but not 'answer'. Thus, to **clarify** *a question* or a *problem* is not to answer it but to state it more clearly.

clari(o)net

This is now spelled without the *o*, and pronounced 'kla-ri-NET'.

clarity

1	general	8	subordinate clauses
2	jargon	9	missing links
3	acronyms	10	postponed verbs
4	misplaced expressions	11	passives
5	abstract nouns	12	superfluous words
6	strings of nouns	13	less familiar words
7	strings of prepositional phrases	14	writing about writing
		15	negatives

1 general
There may be occasions when writers actually want to be vague or obscure: to impress readers with their superior knowledge of the topic or of the English language; to pretend that they understand more about their topic than they really do; to avoid committing themselves or their superiors without saying so explicitly; to conceal unethical actions or attitudes; to avoid open acknowledgment of mistakes. Readers should rightly object to such deceitful manipulations. They are abuses of the language. See DOUBLESPEAK.

Writers may be unclear, however, without intending to be, perhaps because they have not thought clearly enough about their topic. But the reason may be that their vocabulary or grammar is unclear.

2 jargon

It is a basic principle of good writing to adapt one's language to one's readers. Technical terms are justified when an expert addresses others who are similarly expert in the same field: the terms are precisely defined within the expert field. The problem arises when technical terms are used in writing that is intended for non-experts. Specialized vocabulary that is incomprehensible to the general public is known as **jargon** when it is addressed to the general public. Technical terms sometimes enter the common vocabulary. Depending on their level of education and experience, many general readers can understand them sufficiently to make sense of the passage in which they occur; eg *leukaemia* (medicine), *Oedipus complex* (psychology), *habeas corpus* (law), *software* (computers). If you need to use a technical term and you are not sure whether your readers will understand it, define the term or explain it with a paraphrase when you first mention it. Even so, restrict the number of technical terms you introduce into any one piece of writing so as not to make excessive demands on the patience of your readers, since explanations and paraphrases slow down reading.

3 acronyms

Another possible source of obscurity is the **acronym,** a word formed from the initial letters of a word or phrase. Some acronyms are familiar generally (*UN*, *TV*, *PhD*, *GP*, *PR*), but most are not. Again, if you are not sure whether your readers will understand it, give in brackets the complete form from which the acronym derives: *NEB* (New English Bible), *OED* (Oxford English Dictionary), *SAM* (surface-to-air-missile). Sometimes you will need to give an explanation in addition to or in place of the complete form, since that may not give sufficient clues to the meaning: *CAT scanner* (machine which produces three-dimensional X-ray pictures), *SWAPO* (black independence movement in Namibia), *DMT* (dimethytryptamine, hallucinogenic drug).

4 misplaced expressions

If an expression is wrongly placed in the sentence, it may lead to an unintended interpretation, at least initially: *We took somebody to the funeral* **that did not have a car** (We took to the funeral somebody that did not have a car); *I hope that my conscience will prevent me from fighting an unjust war* **if necessary** (I hope that if necessary my conscience will prevent me from fighting an unjust war). In any case, misplaced expressions reduce the clarity of the sentence. See AMBIGUITY; ORDER OF WORDS.

5 abstract nouns

If you use too many **abstract nouns,** you make your writing more difficult to understand: *The entertainment* **aspect** *of reading is a* **factor** *to be emphasized in addition to the informative* **experience** *of reading*

(We should emphasize that reading can entertain as well as inform).
See ABSTRACT NOUNS.

6 strings of nouns
The relationship may be unclear between nouns that are strung
together, one dependent on the other: *government property tax reform
proposals*. You can use prepositions or verbs to clarify relationships:
government proposals for property tax reforms or *property tax reforms
proposed by the government*. It is best to avoid a string of three or more
nouns unless the previous context shows which words go together or
unless one or more pairs of words habitually co-occur (for example,
property tax in *property tax reforms*). Occasionally a shorter string is
potentially ambiguous and you may need to rephrase: *British history
teachers* (*teachers of British history* or *British teachers of history*).

7 strings of prepositional phrases
It may also be difficult to understand a long string of prepositional
phrases, one dependent on the other: *The ambassador took the
opportunity* **for** *a lecture* **on** *the necessity* **for** *improvement* **of** *relations*
between *the Soviet Union and the United States*. Better (also avoiding
too many abstract nouns): *The ambassador took the opportunity to
lecture on why it was necessary to improve relations between the Soviet
Union and the United States*. As a rough guide, keep to a maximum of
four such phrases. But even four is too many if the prepositions are
identical, for example *of* in *I have read* **of** *the achievements* **of** *the Irish*
of *the southern regions* **of** *New England*. It is easy to change some of
the prepositions: *I have read* **about** *the achievements* **of** *the Irish* **in** *the
southern regions* **of** *New England*.

8 subordinate clauses
Sentences can become overcomplex when they have too many
subordinate clauses, particularly when the clauses are the same type.
Sentence 1a. has a clause of reason at the beginning (*Since* . . .) and at
the end (*because* . . .):

> 1a. Since many minor revisions were still required, the second draft
> of the document had to be approved by the committee, contact with
> the individual members of which was made by phone or letter,
> because the committee had by then been dissolved as a standing
> committee by the Board.

You can easily make this sentence simpler by splitting it into two
sentences as well as by eliminating unnecessary passives:

> 1b. Since the second draft of the document required many minor
> revisions, it had to be approved by the committee. Individual
> members were contacted by phone or letter, because the Board had
> by then dissolved the committee as a standing committee.

Similarly, sentence 2a. piles up relative clauses, beginning with *who* or *which*. Version 2b. is an improvement.

2a. If universities must admit all students who apply for admission, they will admit many students who are not capable of pursuing studies at university level, which will force them to withdraw when they find that they cannot cope with the work, which will be a waste of government money.

2b. If universities must admit all students who apply for admission, they will admit many students who are not capable of pursuing studies at university level. These students will have to withdraw when they find that they cannot cope with the work, and the result will be a waste of government money.

9 missing links

Writing may be unclear because logical links are missing and readers cannot easily supply them: *Although single parents cannot fill the roles of both mother and father, they can encourage the relationships of their children with other adults* (. . . the relationships of their children with adults who can fill the missing role); *They want to restore the voting age to 21 because of immaturity* (. . . because people below the age of 21 are immature).

10 postponed verbs

The verb is the pivot of the sentence. It should come relatively early. Make the part before the verb shorter than the part after it. The first sentence in each pair is unbalanced and more difficult to understand than the second:

1a. A more cautious and limited programme of genetic improvement, using wind-pollinated seed from selected trees growing in the wild, is advocated by some plant geneticists.

1b. Some plant geneticists advocate a more cautious and limited programme of genetic improvement, using wind-pollinated seed from selected trees growing in the wild.

2a. The difficulty of devising strategies for imparting computer information about the structure of the language, the situational context, and knowledge of the world poses a major problem for speech recognition by computers.

2b. A major problem for speech recognition by computers is posed by the difficulty of devising strategies for imparting to computers information about the structure of the language, the situational context, and knowledge of the world.

3a. Pressure to prevent the erection of new nuclear power stations and even to demolish existing power stations is increasing.

135

3b. Pressure is increasing to prevent the erection of new nuclear power stations and even to demolish existing power stations.

11 passives

Active sentences (*You* **will hear** *the dialling tone through the loudspeaker*) are easier to understand than passive sentences (*The dialling tone* **will be heard** *through the loudspeaker*). Unless there are good reasons for using the passive, prefer the active. See PASSIVE.

12 superfluous words

Make your sentences shorter and clearer by using fewer words:

(a) Do not use unnecessary repetitions of the same idea: **new** *innovation*, **alternative** *choices*, *loud* **in volume**, *return* **back**. The one word (*innovation*, *choices*, *loud*, *return*) is sufficient. See TAUTOLOGY.

(b) Do not use a longer expression when a shorter one will do:

Birds, dogs, and fish are *the major animal species from which pets are usually selected* (. . . are the most common pets).

British companies *have the inability to produce* that type of computer (. . . cannot produce).

If you still have *a time allocation left*, look for a job (. . . still have time).

See CIRCUMLOCUTION; VERBOSITY.

13 less familiar words

It may sound PRETENTIOUS to use less familiar words when there are equivalent familiar words. Instead of *dwell*, *endeavour*, *initiate*, *terminate*, use *live*, *try*, *start*, *end*.

14 writing about writing

There is no need to describe what you are doing or to evaluate your own writing. Omit signposting such as *I will begin by discussing*, *I should like to add a further point*, *I will now conclude by saying*. Do not unnecessarily use hedging expressions such as *I think*, *rather*, *perhaps*, or *may*; they make you sound timid and unwilling to commit yourself. Do not unnecessarily use emphatic expressions such as *certainly*, *obviously*, *very*, *crucial*, *as everyone would agree*; they make you sound arrogant or dogmatic. Similarly, do not write *It is important to note that*, *It is worth adding that*, *It is interesting to point out*; leave such evaluations to your readers.

15 negatives

Positive sentences are easier to understand than negative sentences. Unless you are denying something, prefer the positive. Sentences become particularly difficult when negative words like *not* and *no* occur with words that imply a negative, like *deny*, *unless*, or *without*:

Unless you *fail* to apply within three months of the accident, compensation will *not* be *denied* to you.

Here is a clearer positive version:

If you apply within three months of the accident, you will receive compensation.

classic, classical

The two forms are only partly interchangeable in meaning. **Classic** means 'of recognized and enduring excellence' (*a classic race*; *the classic work on the subject*), or 'archetypal' (*a classic case of nepotism*), or 'quietly conservative' (*a classic suit*). **Classical** is the preferred form for the arts and literature of ancient Greece and Rome (*classical scholars*; *a classical statue*), and *classical music* is opposed either to light, popular music or to romantic music. Shakespeare's *Julius Caesar* is **classic** as to its literary status and **classical** as to its subject matter.

clean, cleanly (*adverb*)

Both can mean 'in a clean manner': *fight clean/cleanly*. **Clean** also means 'completely' (*got clean away*), and occurs in the proverb *a new broom sweeps clean*.

clean, cleanse, cleanly (*adjective*)

Cleanse is pronounced 'klenz', and is used in a more figurative sense than **clean**: *clean the floor*; *cleanse us of our sins*. Thus, when a scouring powder or skin cream is called a **cleanser** rather than a **cleaner** (*lavatory cleanser*), it suggests 'purity' as well as mere cleanness. A person or thing that has been **cleaned** or **cleansed** is not necessarily **cleanly**, pronounced 'klenli' or 'kleenli', because the rather old-fashioned words **cleanliness** and **cleanly** imply habitual fastidious cleanness.

cleaner

A person who is employed to clean an office or private house is now usually called a **cleaner**, though women in this role are sometimes still referred to in British English as a **charwoman** or **char**, or with the genteelism **charlady**; in American English a woman who cleans in a home is a **maid**.

clear, clearly

Both can mean 'in a clear manner'; **clear** is so used in the phrase (*He spoke*) *loud and clear*. **Clear** also means 'out of the way' (*stand clear*) or 'completely' (*got clear away*), while **clearly** also means 'unambiguously': *He's clearly wrong*. In *Clearly, it's time for us to go*, **clearly** is a SENTENCE ADVERB meaning 'It is clear that'.

cleave

There are two somewhat archaic verbs **cleave**, with almost contrary meanings. One means 'adhere firmly', and forms **cleaved**, **clove**, or sometimes **clave**: *The wet shirt cleaved/clove to his body*. The other means 'divide, separate', and forms **cleaved**, **cleft**, or **clove** in the past tense and **cleaved**, **cleft**, or **cloven** in the participle. It is the participles of this second verb that occur, arbitrarily, in the fixed phrases *cloven hoof, cloven tongue*; *cleft stick, cleft palate*.

clerk

The word is pronounced 'klahk' in British English, 'kluhrk' in American English. A **clerk** in the British sense does paper work of some sort, but American English uses the word of someone employed at a sales or service counter.

clever

This is not always an entirely complimentary adjective. It emphasizes quick, sharp facility and resourcefulness in small matters (*a clever manoeuvre*), perhaps at the expense of profundity and sound reasoning: *a clever but facile remark*. It may be used of physical dexterity: *clever with her hands*. One can be **clever** without knowing very much or having studious tastes.

clew

See CLUE.

cliché

A cliché is an expression that has lost its force and freshness because it is overused. Clichés are substitutes for independent thinking and writing, and they may therefore make the writing seem stale and insincere.

Some expressions are always clichés: *in this day and age, each and every, for love or money, the calm before the storm, none the worse for wear, leave no stone unturned, explore every avenue, food for thought*. On the other hand, a stereotyped expression may be justified as appropriate to the context. There is no need to avoid such expressions if they express precisely what is required: *last but not least, add insult to injury, at a loss for words*. You should use your judgment, and not choose a cliché simply because it is the first thing that comes into your head.

Many clichés are roundabout ways of saying something that could be better said more economically: *in this day and age* (nowadays), *at that point of time* (then), *in the vicinity of* (near), *is of the opinion that* (thinks), *on account of the fact that* (because). See CIRCUMLOCUTION.

client

Lawyers, and people in professions such as accountancy, have **clients**; except for doctors, who have *patients*. **Client** is now widely used as a more prestigious word than *customer* in ordinary business relationships: *the clients of a dress shop*. (An alternative here would be *patron*, which may be avoided because of the association with *patronizing*.) Social workers now also speak of their **clients**, which is more polite than *cases* for the people they deal with. A body of **clients** are a **clientele**, a perhaps rather PRETENTIOUS word.

climactic, climatic, climacteric

Climactic is the adjective from *climax*; **climatic** is from *climate*; **climacteric**, noun and adjective, is a critical stage in life, such as the menopause.

climate

From being confined to weather, **climate** has come to mean 'trend', or 'prevailing mood', particularly in *climate of opinion*. There seems no reason for objecting to this useful extension.

climax

1 Climax comes from the Greek word for *ladder*, and its technical meaning in rhetoric is 'ascending gradation': including, so to speak, all the rungs of the ladder, and not only the top one. In general use it means 'culmination': the top rung only, so that the **climax** of someone's career is its highest point.

2 The use of **climax** as a verb, meaning 'come or bring to a climax' is felt in Britain to be somewhat of an Americanism.

climb

By itself, **climb** means 'go up': *to climb the hill*; *The aircraft climbed slowly*. It is unnecessary to say *climb up the hill/the ladder*, but *up* is needed when one means 'go up an unspecified steep surface, using the hands': *You'll have to climb up and get it*. If one is to **climb** in any direction except *up*, one must say so: *climb down the ladder*; *climb into* *his spacesuit*. The combination **climb** *down* is perfectly standard, both in the literal sense and when it means 'back down, retract'.

clipped words

Clipped words are words that have been shortened from other words. Most are rather informal and are therefore out of place in formal writing: *ad*(vertisement), *bike* (bicycle), *demo*(nstration), *exam*(ination), (in)*flu*(enza), *fridge* (refrigerator), *lab*(oratory), *math*(ematics) in American English and *maths* in British English, *mike* (microphone), *photo*(graph), *pro*(fessional), *prof*(essor), *women's lib*(eration movement).

Certain clipped words have become so firmly established that they are no longer felt to be informal: (violon)*cello*, *movie* (moving picture), (aero, air)*plane*, *soccer* (association football), *zoo*(logical gardens). In some instances the longer form is not used and is generally not known: (omni)*bus*, *cab*(riolet), *mob*(ile vulgus), *taxi*(meter cab).

On other ways of shortening, see ACRONYMS; BLENDS; CONTRACTIONS.

clique

This is usually pronounced to rhyme with *week*, not *chick*.

close (*verb*)

Close is sometimes a more formal alternative to *shut*: *to close (shut) the door/one's eyes*; *The shops close (shut) at six o'clock*. But **close** has many senses for which *shut* is no substitute: *to close a deal/a bank account*; *The museum is closed to the public*; *We closed with their offer*; *The stock market closed steady*. Even in its most literal sense, to *close a door* may be felt to imply, perhaps because of the association with *enclosure*, a shutting *in* (*conversation behind closed doors*); while to *shut a door* suggests a shutting *out*. However, **shut** and not **close** goes with the word **in**, so that we must say *The cat got shut* (not *closed*) *in the cupboard*. **Close** is always more formal than *end* or *finish*: *Let me close by saying* . . . .

close, closed

The phrases are *close company*, and *close shave*; *closed circuit*, and *closed shop*; *close* or *closed corporation*; *closed* or *close scholarship*; *close season* (British English) but *closed season* (American). (In these phrases *close* is, of course, the adjective **close**, pronounced 'klohs', not the verb, pronounced 'klohz'.)

close proximity

(In) close proximity (to) is a rather stilted way of saying 'near'.

clothes

The older pronunciation rhymes with *rose*, as in Ophelia's *Then up he rose, and donned his clothes*; but the pronunciation that includes the *th* is now at least as common.

cloture, closure

In American but not British English, **cloture** is used for **closure** in the sense of the limitation of debate in a legislative body, which conveniently distinguishes it from the other senses of **closure**: *pockets with zip closure*.

cloven

See CLEAVE.

clue, clew

Something that guides one to a solution is a **clue**, sometimes spelled **clew** in American English. In both British and American English, **clew** (so spelled) is an archaic word for a ball of thread, as used for finding one's way out of a labyrinth, and it also means one of the corners of a sail, or a metal loop attached to this.

CO, c/o, co., Co

CO stands for commanding officer, conscientious objector, cash order, Commonwealth Office, or Colorado; **c/o** stands for care of (in envelope addresses); **co.** stands for company (*Jones & Co.*, with a capital *C*) or county; **Co** is the symbol for the chemical element cobalt.

co-

Words beginning with the prefix **co-** (ie 'together, associate') are usually spelled as one word, with no hyphen: *coincide*; *cohabit*. Exceptions are (a) when the combination is felt to be relatively new: *co-worker*; *co-starring*, (b) when it might lead to a wrong pronunciation, or wrong division of syllables. Here British English is more reluctant than is American English to dispense with the hyphen: *co(-)pilot*; *co(-)belligerent*. This problem is particularly acute where **co-** is followed by *o*, and even American English spelling prefers a hyphen in *co-op*, *co-opt*, although *cooperate* is spelled as one word in American English and commonly in British English. The alternative of distinguishing the two vowels by dots on the second *o* (*coöperate*) has fallen into disuse.

coca

See CACAO.

coccyx

This is pronounced 'koksiks' and means the base of the spine. The plural is either **coccyges** or **coccyxes**.

cockscomb, coxcomb

Cockscomb is a garden flower. A **coxcomb** is a conceited fop. The old word for a jester's cap can have either spelling.

coco, cocoa

See CACAO.

coed

In American English, this means a female student in a coeducational college or coeducational high school. In British English, it means a coeducational school: *Bedales, the Hampshire coed* (*Private Eye*).

cohort

Besides being a division of an ancient Roman legion, **cohort** has modern technical meanings in biology, where it is a taxonomic group, and in sociology, where it is a group of people sharing some statistical factor. In modern American English, however, it can mean not a group but a single person who is one's companion, accomplice, or henchman. This usage, perhaps based on the mistaken impression that the word is formed with *co-* like *copilot*, is avoided by careful writers of both American and British English.

colander, cullender

1 This kitchen sieve is usually spelled **colander,** but both spellings exist. **Colander** can be pronounced either 'kol-' or 'kul-', but **cullender** can be only 'kul-'.

2 See CALENDAR.

coliseum, colosseum

They both mean a large stadium or theatre. The ancient Roman amphitheatre should be spelled **Colosseum** with a capital *C*, but **coliseum** is the usual form for a modern public building. It is often capitalized as the name of a cinema or dance hall.

collaborate

See COOPERATE.

collation

Strictly speaking, this means a light informal meal, particularly one served at an unusual time. It is sometimes used as a rather quaint word for *meal*: *a magnificent cold collation after the wedding*.

collectives

A collective noun refers to a group of individuals. Examples: *army, audience, committee, class, company, council, crew, crowd, enemy, family, firm, flock, government, group, herd, jury, majority, minority, nation, public, team*. Collective nouns also include proper names, such as the name of a country denoting a national team (*France*) or the name of a business company (*ICI*). In American English, a singular collective noun normally takes a singular verb. In British English, however, a singular collective may be treated as either singular or plural, depending on the point of view of the writer: when the group is considered as a whole, the singular is preferred; when it is viewed as consisting of individuals, the plural is preferred. Consequently, in British English both these alternatives are correct: *The jury **has** not yet reached a verdict*; *The jury **have** not yet reached a verdict*. (Of course, a plural collective always takes a plural verb: *The committees have just been appointed*.)

Pronouns should be consistent in number with the collective: *The committee **is** discussing whether **it** should open **its** sessions to the public*; *The committee **are** discussing whether **they** should open **their** sessions to the public*. *It* suggests that the committee is being regarded as an impersonal unit, while *they* suggests that the emphasis is on the members of the committee as individuals. The choice between singular and plural verb is also associated with the choice between personal *who* and impersonal *which*: *a family **who** are*; *a family **which** is*. See WHO (2).

college

See SCHOOL.

collide, collision

Some people feel that these words should be used only when one moving object hits another, and not when one of the objects is stationary. Most people, however, find it quite acceptable to write *The car collided with a lamp post*, although they might hesitate to write *The car and the lamp post collided* or *There was a collision between the car and the lamp post.*

collude, collusion

Collude means more than merely 'act together, collaborate'. It implies a secret understanding for a bad purpose: *fined . . . for colluding to raise beer prices* (*Financial Times*). The more common noun, **collusion,** similarly means 'conspiracy' rather than merely 'cooperation'.

colon

1 explanation, example, or list	**4** biblical reference
2 quotation	**5** time of day
3 subtitle	**6** greeting in letter

1 explanation, example, or list

The main use of the colon is to point forward to an explanation, an example, or a list. This book, indeed this entry, is full of examples and lists introduced by colons. The colon is frequently equivalent to expressions such as *namely, as follows, for example, such as.* Such expressions are often unnecessary if you insert a colon:

> Buying the fish was easy: there were plenty of good fish shops in the city, supplied direct from Grimsby.

> At the core of the problem is a political question: how to make choices within an imperfect society.

If you use an introductory expression, insert a semicolon instead of a colon:

> The play has too many scenes; for example, in the second act there are ten scenes and in the third act as many as twelve.

The colon is particularly appropriate to introduce a list of items:

> Many other kinds of conservation activity were planned: buying a pond or field; finding new uses for old buildings; persuading a local school to care for an ancient monument; turning a section of a local park into a nature reserve.

> She enjoyed numerous leisure activities: fishing, tennis, rowing, painting, to name but a few.

But use a semicolon with an introductory expression:

> She enjoyed numerous leisure activities; for instance fishing, tennis, rowing, painting.

Her father was usually away from home in the evening; for example, he was an active member of the city council, he sang in the church choir, he taught pottery in the youth club.

In a formal list, the items are set out on separate lines, each introduced by a number or letter:

You may select one of the following materials:
1. polished aluminium
2. chrome painted copper
3. polished stainless steel
4. satin stainless steel

In such formal lists, prefer small letters for initial words and no end-punctuation, though some writers use capitals and semicolons. Use capitals and full stops if each item consists of one or more sentences.

Do not insert a colon that interrupts the flow of the sentence. No colon is required in these sentences:

Breakfast consisted of: a boiled egg, dry toast, fruit juice, and coffee.

The typical owner of this car is: a businessman or professional who likes to look after himself.

Some writers use a colon in such cases when the items are set out as a formal list, but it is also correct to omit the colon:

We will pay up to the sum insured for loss or damage to the contents in your home caused by
a) fire, explosion, lightning, earthquake
b) storm or flood
c) malicious act
d) theft or attempted theft
e) subsidence or ground heave of the site on which your home stands

2 quotation

You may use a colon to introduce quoted material, particularly if the quotation covers more than one sentence:

I wrote about this sculpture in 1982: 'The head is powerfully conceived . . . '

The colon is similarly used to introduce speech in a dialogue, particularly in plays:

Timothy pressed home his advantage spitefully: 'We must ask poor old Bobby. I've been meaning to do so for a long time.'

SALLY: Who are you?

NORMAN: A friend of your brother's.

145

3 subtitle

Use a colon to separate a subtitle from the main part of the title:

Literary Style: A symposium

4 biblical reference

Use a colon to separate the verse from the chapter in biblical citations:

Genesis 2:1–8   Job 5:17–25

5 time of day

In American English, a colon is used between hours and minutes:

3:25   6:45

In British English, use a full stop:

3.25   6.45

6 greeting in letter

In formal American English, the greeting at the beginning of letters ends with a colon:

Dear Dr. Williamson:
Thank you for . . .

In British English and in less formal American English, use a comma.

Colonial

In American English, this refers to the period before 1776, when the USA became independent. **Colonial** architecture and furniture are thus the equivalent of the British Queen Anne or early Georgian, whether genuine or faked. A British house agent would use the word only in the hope of attracting a prospective American purchaser. To the British, the word has overtones of the days of the British Empire.

colossal

It chiefly means 'awesomely large', and applies particularly to manmade constructions: *a colossal skyscraper*. The word has been somewhat OVERUSED to mean merely 'very great': *colossal speed*; *a colossal blunder*; *colossal heat*; *a colossal joke*.

colosseum

See COLISEUM.

colo(u)r

It is spelled **colour** in British English, **color** in American English. This applies also to the word in most of its various combinations: *colo(u)rful*, *colo(u)ring*, *colo(u)r-blind*. Exceptions include *coloration*, which is not only the sole American spelling but the preferred British one; and the musical term *coloratura*, from the Italian, which has only one spelling.

coloured

See BLACK.

coma, comma

A **coma** is a state of unconsciousness, or (a different word) the head of a comet; a **comma** is the punctuation mark (,). They rhyme with *foam a* and *bomb a* respectively.

combat (*verb*)

Other forms are **combatted**, **combatting** in British English, but the second *t* is often omitted in American English.

combatant

This is usually pronounced with the stress on *com*, not on *bat*.

combine (*noun*)

This means an industrial group: *L'Oréal, France's largest perfume and cosmetics combine* (*The Observer*). There is nothing derogatory about the word in this sense, but when it is used more widely with reference to any association to promote shared interest it may, in American English, have connotations of shadiness and doubtful legality.

combine (*verb*)

It is a TAUTOLOGY to write **combine** *together*.

come

The use of **come** before an expression of future time (*a year ago come March*) should be avoided in serious writing.

come of age

This is the idiom for the reaching of legal majority; not *become of age*.

Comecon

See COMINTERN.

comestibles

This is a largely FACETIOUS word for 'food'.

comforter

See QUILT.

comic(al)

Things that are intentionally funny are **comic**: *a comic opera*; *comic songs*. Unintentionally funny things are **comical**: *comical earnestness*; *the problem has its comical side*.

Comintern, Cominform, Comecon

Comintern (*Com*munist *Intern*ational) was an organization, founded in 1919 and dissolved in 1943, to unite those working for Communism and promote revolutionary measures. **Cominform** (*Com*munist *Inform*ation Bureau) was an organization which operated from 1949 to 1956 to coordinate the activities of the Communist parties of nine countries, not all in the Eastern bloc. **Comecon** (*Co*uncil for *M*utual *Econo*mic Assistance) is an economic federation of Communist countries, founded in 1949 and corresponding roughly to the EEC.

comity

This means 'friendly harmony'. The *comity of nations* is not some kind of 'league' or 'federation', but the code of civilized courtesy between nations, expressed by recognition of each other's laws and customs.

comma

1 general	**4** listing comma
2 joining comma	**5** clarifying comma
3 isolating comma	**6** see COMA

1 general
Of all the punctuation marks, the comma is the most flexible, allowing scope for personal taste and sensitivity. For that reason and also because of the variety of its uses, it is the hardest mark to categorize. We do not attempt to discuss all the complexities of its uses. Instead, we deal briefly with common errors.

2 joining comma
The comma often joins the parts of a compound sentence: *The risks of staging a musical are considerable, and the backers have been known to suffer huge losses.* Here the two parts are joined by *and*; if appropriate, they may be joined by certain other linking words: *or, but, nor, neither, so, yet.* A frequent error is the comma splice: the joining of two or more sentences with a comma alone – without a linking word – when a weightier stop is required: *The hospital is small, it has only*

150 beds (replace the comma with a semicolon). The error is particularly likely to occur when another type of linking word, such as *nevertheless* or *therefore*, is used at the beginning of a sentence: *The power plant has had no accidents, nevertheless, accidents are always possible* (correct to: no accidents; nevertheless, accidents . . .). Experienced writers sometimes use commas alone for literary effect in linking a series of (often three) parallel sentences; a well-known example is *I came, I saw, I conquered.* See also RUN-ON SENTENCE; SEMICOLON; AND.

3 isolating comma

Here the comma isolates a part of the sentence, such as words addressing people directly: *That statement, ladies and gentlemen, has been endorsed by all the members of the committee.* Other examples: *The company gave its employees a Christmas bonus, money and a food hamper*; *On further consideration, I have decided to accept your recommendation*; *When in doubt, you should call a doctor*; *The airport, however, is unpleasantly overcrowded*; *Having found the letter, she immediately dictated a reply.* The point to remember about this use of the comma is that the part must be properly isolated, so that if it comes in the middle of the sentence, there must be two commas, one on either side. It is wrong to omit one of the pair. Nobody would make this mistake with brackets, which also have this isolating use, but it is easy to forget to insert the second comma, as in *The policy has, in this respect been conciliatory* (correct to: . . . has, in this respect, been . . .).

An important use of isolating commas is to mark a **relative clause** as **nonrestrictive**, ie giving non-identifying information. Contrast the nonrestrictive *which*-clause in *My salary, which is paid monthly, is augmented by various fringe benefits* (the *which*-clause merely adds supplementary information about the salary; it does not specify which salary, since that is already specified by *my*) and the restrictive *which*-clause in *Salaries which are paid monthly are augmented by various fringe benefits* (the *which*-clause specifies which salaries – only those paid monthly; *which* can here be replaced by *that*). If we intend to say that all salaries are augmented, then the relative clause requires a pair of commas: *Salaries, which are paid monthly, are augmented by various fringe benefits.* For the distinction between restrictive and nonrestrictive, see APPOSITION; RELATIVE CLAUSES.

Apart from such parenthetic uses, a comma should not come between the subject of a sentence and its verb, or between a verb and its object. Nobody would write *They, pay the highest taxes*, but there is a temptation to make the same mistake with long subjects, since a pause in that position is likely in speech: *The people that are making the most money, pay the highest taxes.* A sensitive writer, however, will flout the no-comma rule to prevent momentary confusion, for example when the same word occurs twice in succession: *Whatever he says or does, does not interest me.* (But it is often possible to avoid such repetition by rephrasing the sentence, and it is preferable to do so; for example, in this instance: *Whatever he says or does is of no interest to me.*)

4 listing comma

These separate a list of words or phrases that have the same grammatical use: *She slowly, carefully, and deliberately placed each book on the desk*; *He eats, drinks, and talks too much*; *The government is supported by moderate opposition leaders, army officers and religious leaders*; *The suits were always grey, pin-striped and immaculate.* As these examples show, you can choose whether to put a comma before *and* in such lists. The final comma may be needed to preserve a useful distinction: *You can buy these products in John Lewis, Selfridges, and Marks and Spencer.* The comma after *Selfridges* helps to show that *Marks and Spencer* is a separate company.

There are exceptions to the rule of listing commas when a string of adjectives and other words or phrases comes before a noun: *the famous iron-and-glass plant houses*; *traditional solid oak panelling.* In these instances we cannot put *and* between the parts: the first are plant houses made of iron and glass that are famous, and the second is traditional panelling made of solid oak. If we can put *and* between the parts, we may (but need not) insert listing commas: *large, flat, square objects* (objects that are large, flat, and square). Commas are necessary if the parts refer to different things: *yellow, blue, and pink flowers* (yellow flowers, blue flowers, and pink flowers).

5 clarifying comma

A comma (otherwise optional) is sometimes necessary to prevent a misunderstanding, if only momentary: *As the police car pulled up, the crowd surged forward* (without the comma, we might read the sentence at first to mean that the car pulled up the crowd): *After a period of calm, college students have begun to demonstrate again* (not: calm college students).

comma splice

See RUN-ON SENTENCE.

commander, commandant, commando

These are personnel in the armed forces. A **commander** is one rank below a captain in both the British and US navies. **Commander** is also used for the commanding officer of a particular unit or installation, who is also called its **commandant**. A **commando** is either a unit trained for surprise raids into enemy territory, or a member of such a unit.

commence

Outside very formal contexts, prefer *begin* or *start* to **commence**. It is bureaucratic jargon.

commentate

This verb is a BACK-FORMATION from *commentator*, and applies particularly to the giving of broadcast commentaries. It should not be used as a grander synonym for *comment*.

commercial traveller

See SALES REPRESENTATIVE.

commissioner, commissionaire, commissar, commissary

A **commissioner** is a member or head of a *commission*, a group of people assigned to a particular duty or entrusted with particular powers: *a Charity Commissioner*; *a Commissioner of Police*. A **commissionaire** is a uniformed attendant at a theatre, cinema, hotel, or office. A **commissar** is a Communist party official; the word was used until 1946 for the heads of government departments in the USSR: *a People's Commissar*. A **commissary** (besides being a café or canteen in American English) is an officer in charge of a military *commissariat*, the department of an army that organizes food supplies.

commit

Other forms are **committed, committing.**

committed, commitment, committal

People are **committed** if they have pledged themselves to a particular system of belief or course of action: *a committed Christian; We are committed to a policy of expansion*. If one is **committed** one has made a **commitment**: *his commitment to radical causes*; *make a firm commitment to fetch your children from school*. The related noun **committal** is usually applied to the act of delivering or transferring someone to an institution: *his committal to a mental hospital*.

common

See MUTUAL.

common sense

The compound noun is written as two words: *full of common sense*; but the adjective as one word: *a commonsense decision*.

communicate, communication

Apart from their other senses, as in *communicate a disease*, **communicate** is often a PRETENTIOUS word for *tell* or *write*, and **communication** for *letter*. As an academic study, however, **communications** (in the plural) includes all the verbal and visual techniques for transmitting ideas, and in this sense it cannot be replaced by another word.

Communist, communism

Use a capital *C* for a party member, or for the official ideology of the USSR, or (usually) for a left-wing revolutionary; a small *c* for the general theory or system of holding goods in common: *the communism of the early Christian church*.

compact

This is generally an appreciative synonym for *small*, useful when one wishes to suggest a convenient smallness made possible by the efficient use of space: *a compact camera/kitchen*. The **compact** American car is in fact medium-sized by European standards.

comparable

This is usually pronounced with the stress on the first syllable, not like the verb *compare*.

comparative(ly), relative(ly)

1 Some writers prefer to avoid the use of these words to mean merely 'fairly' or 'rather' (*a comparatively warm day*) where no true comparison is involved. They are appropriate, however, where we are concerned with proportion: *Of the total number of houses, relatively few have bathrooms*.

2 Do not write *a comparatively/relatively few*. Omit *a*.

comparatives

See COMPARISON, GRAMMATICAL.

compare

One can equally correctly **compare** something *to* or *with* something else, but careful writers recognize a difference of meaning. To state a similarity, use *to*: *Shall I compare thee to a summer's day?* (Shakespeare); *She compared the noise to* (ie said it was like) *that of a road drill*. To make a detailed analysis of resemblances and differences, use *with*, *and*, or a plural: *a report comparing the passenger facilities at Heathrow with/and those at Orly*; *a report comparing the facilities at the two airports*. **Compared** *to* and **compared** *with* are indistinguishable in meaning: *Paris is small compared to/with London*, but *Paris is smaller than London* is better here. When **compare** is used without an object, *with* is the only choice: *Our garden can't compare with theirs*.

comparison

The idiom is *in/by* **comparison** *with*, not *of* or *to*: *Our garden is small in/by comparison with theirs*, but prefer here *Our garden is smaller than theirs*.

comparison, grammatical

1 degrees of comparison
2 absolutes
3 absolute comparatives
4 absolute superlatives
5 case after *as* and *than*; see CASE, GRAMMATICAL (4); see also ELLIPSIS.

1 degrees of comparison

Most adjectives and adverbs have two higher degrees of comparison: comparative and superlative. The comparative is for two items: *the* **better** *of the (two) proposals*. One or both of the two items may in fact be a set of items: *My proposal was far* **better** *(than the others)*; *The girls are* **easier** *to teach (than the boys)*. The superlative is required for more than two items or sets of items: *the* **best** *of the (three) proposals*; *The nine-year-olds were the* **easiest** *to teach (of the various age groups)*.

We make comparatives and superlatives either by changing the form of the word or by adding *more* and *most*. The change in form generally requires the addition of the endings *-(e)r* and *-(e)st*, and perhaps the change of a final *-y* to *i* before the ending.

absolute	comparative	superlative
tall	taller	tallest
brave	braver	bravest
happy	happier	happiest
complex	more complex	most complex
valuable	more valuable	most valuable

Most adjectives of one syllable and some of two syllables normally take the endings, but only a few adverbs (most of them having the same form as adjectives) do so. However, they may sometimes take *more* instead of the normal endings when there is a contrast:

> The children were *not very thin,* but they were *more thin* than I had been led to suppose.

> She is *less happy* in her new job, although I had expected her to be *more happy.*

Do not combine *more* or *most* with the *-(e)r* and *-(e)st* forms: *more taller* and *most tallest* are wrong.

Some irregular comparatives and superlatives may cause difficulties.

absolute	comparative	superlative
good ⎫ well ⎭	better	best
bad ⎫ badly ⎭	worse	worst

The comparison forms for the adjectives (*good*, *well* 'in good health'; *bad*) are identical with those for the corresponding adverbs (*well*; *badly*). *Worser* and *worsest* are uneducated forms.

2 absolutes

Some adjectives and adverbs do not have comparatives or superlatives; they occur only as absolutes. For example, we cannot say *more atomic* or *most medical*. Usage varies for the set of adjectives that seem to express the top end of a scale. We cannot, for instance, say *more entire* or *most entire*; on the other hand, we can use *more full* or *most thorough*. There is some doubt on whether to use comparatives or superlatives with other adjectives in the set: *absolute, complete, equal, excellent, extreme, ideal, perfect, total, unique, utter*. On the whole, it is advisable to avoid the comparison of these and the corresponding adverbs in formal writing. Comparison is perfectly acceptable when the words are used in a different meaning: *more absolute* ('positive') *proof*; *the most extreme* ('radical') *opinions*. See GRADABILITY.

3 absolute comparatives

Advertisers are fond of using absolute comparatives, perhaps to forestall lawsuits. A comparative is absolute when the basis of comparison is not given and is not conveyed elsewhere in the context. Detergents are said to wash *whiter* (whiter than what?), cigarettes to smoke *cooler*, and airline seats to be *more comfortable*. Careful writers will make sure that the basis of comparison is clear to their readers. See also BETTER.

4 absolute superlatives

There is a somewhat informal use of the superlative to express merely a high degree: *You are most kind* ('extremely kind'); *He was most peculiar*. Generally, *most* conveys this meaning, but sometimes the inflected superlative is used in the same way when it modifies a noun: *She is wearing the oddest hat*. In very formal writing, the absolute superlative should be replaced by a degree word, if indeed one is felt to be necessary (*very peculiar, an extremely odd hat*). See also MOST (3).

compass(es)

The instrument that indicates direction is a **compass**. The instrument for drawing circles is either a **compass** or a pair of **compasses**.

compel, impel

1 Other forms of **compel** are **compelled, compelling**.

2 To **compel** is to force irresistibly to do something: *The rain compelled us to stay indoors*. It is stronger than **impel**, which is more often used of feelings and of one's own motivation: *He felt impelled to speak his mind*.

competence, competency

Both forms share the possible meanings. On the whole, **competence** is preferred for 'ability'.

compile

See COMPOSE.

complacency, complacence

They mean the same thing, but **complacency** is now much commoner.

complaisant, compliant, complacent

The rather formal **complaisant** means 'courteously assenting', and may suggest a weak lack of resistance: *She listened with a complaisant smile to their outrageous suggestion*. It is close in meaning to **compliant**, which means 'yielding submissively to others', willingly or otherwise: *We disliked his hectoring tone but were obliged to be compliant*. Neither word should be confused with **complacent**, which means 'self-satisfied and unworried', and suggests gloating superiority: *The team have won so many matches that they have become complacent*.

complete (*adjective*)

1 When **complete** means 'total, whole', as in *two complete revolutions round the sun*, it should not be used with *more* or *most*, *rather* or *very*, *less* or *least*. Do not write *a more complete silence*. This objection does not hold, however, when **complete** means 'thorough'. It is reasonable to refer to *a more complete study* of a subject.

2 See REPLETE.

complete (*verb*)

This means 'make complete or perfect': *to complete my study of Browning*; *The church completes the charm of the village*; or 'fulfil': *to complete a contract*. It may seem rather PRETENTIOUS to use it for 'finish, reach the end of', as in *complete a college course*.

complex

This technical term from psychiatry is often used to mean simply an 'exaggerated reaction' or 'bee in one's bonnet': *He has a complex about flying*. (An informal equivalent would be to say *he has a thing about it*.) The reaction may take the form of either an excessive attraction or a mild phobia. *Inferiority complex* is used loosely for a feeling of being inadequate.

compliant

See COMPLAISANT.

compliment, complement, supplement

A **compliment** is a flattering expression of admiration: *pay him compliments on his work*. A **complement** completes a full quantity: *to have the usual complement of arms and legs*. A **supplement** is added as an extra to what might otherwise be thought complete: *eat fresh fruit as a supplement to their diet*. All three can be used as verbs:

compliment him on his work; *The jacket complements the trousers*; *supplement their diet.*

compose, compile

To **compose** a written work is simply to write it; writers **compose** a sonnet or a symphony. To **compile** a work is to put it together out of materials from elsewhere; one **compiles** a dictionary or an anthology. See also COMPRISE.

compound

To **compound** a crime is to agree for a consideration to condone it, and not to prosecute: *compound a felony*. It does not mean 'aggravate, make worse', although the word is sometimes used like that (*compound an error*), perhaps because people think of *compound fracture* and *compound interest*.

comprehend

See APPREHEND.

comprehensible, comprehensive

Comprehensible means 'understandable, intelligible': *ideas scarcely comprehensible to the average mind.* **Comprehensive** means 'of large scope, inclusive': *a comprehensive insurance policy*; *comprehensive schools.*

comprise, consist, compose, constitute, include

1 There are three possible errors associated with this group of verbs.

When a whole is completely made up of several items, it **comprises**, **consists** *of*, or is **composed** *of* them: *A chess set comprises/consists of/is composed of 32 chessmen.* First error: do not use **comprise** in the same way as **compose**, by writing *A chess set is comprised of 32 chessmen.*

When several items add up to a whole, they **compose** or **constitute** it: *32 chessmen compose/constitute a chess set.* Second error: the subject of **comprise** should be the whole (here, the chess set) but not the items (here, the chessmen). The following is an example of this second error: *More than a million butterflies and insects, comprising the tiny National Butterfly Museum at St Mary's, Bramber, West Sussex, were sold for a total of £130,132 yesterday by Sotheby's* (*Daily Telegraph*). Here, the museum collection **comprises** all those butterflies, but the butterflies **constitute** the museum collection.

When a whole is only partially made up of one or more items, it **includes** it or them: *A chess set includes four bishops.* Third error: do

157

not use **include** for the whole list, by writing *A chess set includes 32 chessmen.* That is the proper place to use **comprise.** See also CONSIST.

2 **Comprise** is spelled *-ise*, not *-ize*, in both British and American English.

compromise

The word is spelled *-ise*, not *-ize*, in both British and American English.

compulsive, compulsory

Compulsive behaviour is caused by a strong impulse or inner compulsion: *a compulsive gambler.* **Compulsory** behaviour is enforced by someone else: *compulsory wearing of seatbelts.*

concave, convex

Concave objects are hollowed inwards, like a cave. **Convex** objects bulge outwards, like an eyeball.

conceal

Where possible, prefer the simpler word *hide.* **Conceal** is appropriate where something abstract is hidden: *to conceal his connection with the case.*

conceit, conceive

Both words are spelled *-ei-*, not *-ie-*.

[concensus]

This is an incorrect spelling of **consensus.**

concept

From its earlier philosophical sense, an 'abstract notion generalized from particular instances' (*He had only seen donkeys, so had no concept of 'horse'*), **concept** has become an OVERUSED word for 'idea', 'programme', 'plan', 'design', etc: *a new concept in beauty care.*

concerned

1 **Concerned** *at, for,* or *about* something, or **concerned** *that* something should or should not happen, means 'anxious' or 'solicitous': *concerned for his safety/at the bad news; concerned that they might get lost.* **Concerned** *with* means 'having to do with': *a letter chiefly concerned with domestic details.*

2 *So/as far as X is* **concerned** is often VERBOSE, and can be replaced by

a single prepositional phrase: *The regulation has had no effect so far as the shopkeepers are concerned* (write *no effect on the shopkeepers*); *He is unknown as far as the wider musical public is concerned* (write *unknown to the wider musical public*). *So far as I am concerned* might be replaced by *To me, For me*, or *For my part*.

concert, recital

A classical **concert** is given by a group of musicians, although in popular music a **concert** may be a solo performance. A **recital** is given by a soloist or small group, not an orchestra, but an amateur performance by music pupils may be called a **recital**.

concerto

The plural is **concertos** or, less usually, **concerti**.

conciseness, concision

Both are correct for the quality of being *concise*. **Conciseness** is more usual; **concision** has also an archaic meaning 'cutting off'.

conclude

This can mean 'decide', but only in the sense of determining something on the basis of evidence: *The judge concluded that they were guilty*. It is possible to say *He concluded that he would wait a little longer*, with the implication that he reached the decision by considering the facts; but **conclude** should not be followed by an infinitive, as in *He concluded to go to bed*.

concrete

See CEMENT.

concur

Other forms are **concurred, concurring**.

condemn

See CONTEMN.

condition

From the meaning 'state of health or fitness' (*The car is in good condition; His heart is in poor condition*), **condition** has come to mean 'defective state of health': *suffering from a heart condition*. Some people find **condition** in this sense an unnecessary EUPHEMISM for 'complaint'.

conditional clauses

See SUBJUNCTIVE.

conducive

Things are **conducive** *to*, not *of*, results: *Exercise is conducive to health.*

conduit

The older British pronunciation rhymes with *fund it*. Most British speakers today, however, rhyme the word with *bond it*, *bond wit*, or *bond you it*, as do American speakers.

confer

Other forms are **conferred, conferring**.

confidant(e), confident

A **confidant(e)** is someone to whom secrets are entrusted. Use **confidant** for either sex, but **confidante** for a woman only. (They have the same pronunciation and are stressed on the last syllable.) **Confident** is an adjective meaning 'bold, assured'.

conform

Traditionally one **conforms** *to* laws and requirements, but **conform** *with* is now common and almost equally acceptable.

confrontation

This word is OVERUSED in the sense of a direct clash between opposing political forces. It may cover anything from acts of unprovoked violence, seen as heroic by the confronters, to mere resistance to someone's demands: *These islands cannot survive on a doctrine of confrontation* (Len Murray). **Confrontationism** is practised by **confrontationists**, who seek to provoke violence by the other side so that they can retaliate.

congenial, genial

Congenial means 'agreeably suited to one's nature; sympathetic', so a group of people whom one likes and gets on with are *congenial company*. **Genial** means 'cheerful and good-tempered', so friendly jolly people are *genial company*. **Genial** can be used in isolation (*our genial host*), but **congenial** involves another person to whom one is 'suited'.

congenital

See GENETIC.

congratulate, congratulations

The second syllable is correctly pronounced 'grat' or 'gratch' in British English, not 'grad'.

Congress

In modern use, the US legislative body is called simply **Congress**, although the Constitution prefers *the* **Congress**. Some recent presidents have attempted to revive the older style.

congressman, congresswoman

A US **congressman** or **congresswoman** is usually in practice a member of the House of Representatives (the lower house of Congress), although technically the word could apply to members of the Senate (the upper house). Compare M.P.

coniferous, carnivorous

Coniferous applies to pines, firs, and similar trees; **carnivorous** means 'meat-eating'. The estate agent who offered a garden with *flower borders and carnivorous trees* had got it wrong.

conjugal, connubial

Both words refer to the married state, but **conjugal** emphasizes the relations between husband and wife in such phrases as *conjugal rights, conjugal friction*, while the rather formal **connubial** suggests the unity of matrimony: *connubial bliss*. **Conjugal** is usually pronounced with the stress on the first syllable rather than the second.

connection, connexion

1 Both spellings are permissible in British English; but **connection** is commoner, and is the only American form.

2 *In* **connection** *with* is often better replaced by *at, concerning, about*, etc: *He expressed his pleasure in connection with* (write *pleasure at*) *this successful outcome*. The phrase is legitimately used, however,

161

when it means 'associated with': *held a whist drive in connection with the dance*.

connive

To **connive** *at* something wrong is to shut one's eyes indulgently: *The policeman connived at the robbery*. **Connive** also means 'conspire': *The criminals and the police connived to rob the bank*; *The police connived with the criminals*.

connote, denote

These both mean 'mean', but in different ways. A word **denotes** its explicit primary meaning: *The word 'father' denotes a male parent*. A word **connotes** its associated secondary meaning: *For Jane, the word 'father' connoted only violence and fear*.

conscientious, conscious

Conscientious means 'scrupulous, careful': *a conscientious researcher*. **Conscious** means 'aware' or 'awake'.

consensus, census

Consensus is not spelled *concensus*, and has nothing to do with a **census**, which is a counting of the population.

A **consensus** is a judgment arrived at by general agreement. Since it is itself an opinion, it is a TAUTOLOGY to say *consensus of opinion*.

consequence

1 *As a* **consequence** *of* and *in* **consequence** *of* are VERBOSE substitutes for *because of*.

2 *As a* **consequence** and *in* **consequence** can often be neatly replaced by *so* and *therefore*.

consequent, consequential

See SUBSEQUENT.

conservative

Use a capital *C* for a member or supporter of the British political party, a small *c* for the other meanings, such as 'moderate' (*a conservative estimate*) or 'traditional in style' (*conservative tailoring*).

consider

When **consider** means 'regard as being', do not use it with *as*: *They* *considered him a bad influence* (not *as a bad influence*); *I consider it essential* (not *as essential*). To **consider** something *as* something means 'think of it in the role of': *We should consider the project both as a training exercise and as a source of profit.*

considerable

This adjective is correctly applied to abstractions: *considerable numbers; to a considerable extent; took considerable trouble*. It is less appropriate with material things. A *considerable garage* would sound better as a *large garage*, and *considerable sugar* as *a good deal of* or *a considerable amount of sugar*.

considering

Modern convention permits the use of **considering** for 'in view of the fact that': *Considering he was new at the job, he did quite well.* See DANGLING PARTICIPLE.

consist

A thing **consists** *of* the material parts that make it up: *Breakfast consisted of cereal, milk, and fruit*. To **consist** *in* something is to 'reside in' or 'lie in' it, and the phrase is used only in defining abstractions: *Liberty consists in the absence of obstructions* (A E Housman); *The game consisted in* (or *of*) *trying to throw a ring over a pole*. See also COMPRISE.

consistency, consistence

Both forms share all the meanings, but **consistency** is much the commoner, both for 'the virtue of not being inconsistent' (*follow his advice with consistency*) and for 'degree of viscosity' (*the gooey consistency of the mud*).

consistently, persistently

Both these adverbs are used of something done repeatedly.
Consistently suggests that the action is performed uniformly, without discrepancy: *a consistently ironic tone throughout the book*.
Persistently implies calculated and perhaps infuriating perseverance: *You have persistently ignored my letters*. Inanimate things can function **consistently** but not **persistently**: *The temperature remained consistently below zero*.

conspicuous

Conspicuous by its/his/her absence (meaning 'noticeably not there') is a CLICHÉ.

constable

The first syllable is pronounced either 'kun' or 'kon'. The former is older.

constitute

See COMPRISE.

constrain, restrain

These can both mean 'hold back; inhibit'. To be **constrained** is abstract, and usually unpleasant: *feel constrained by the narrow routine*. **Restrain** suggests action for the good of the one restrained, and with subduing effect: *restrain one's anger*; *restrain the boy from jumping*. **Constrain**, but not **restrain**, can also mean 'force; compel': *Necessity constrains me to admit it*.

consult

Some British people dislike the combination **consult** *with*, meaning 'ask the advice of', as an Americanism. They prefer to say *consult a doctor* rather than *consult with a doctor*. There is no objection to **consult** *with* in the sense 'confer with': *I intend to consult with (or consult) my colleagues*.

consummate

To **consummate** a marriage is not to perform the wedding ceremony, but to make the marriage effective by sexual intercourse.

consummation

Consummation devoutly to be wished (usually meaning a very desirable goal) is a CLICHÉ.

contact

The use of **contact** as a verb meaning 'get in communication with' (*contact your local agent*) was once disliked, but is now established and very common except in the most formal contexts. It combines concisely the ideas of 'write to', 'telephone', 'visit', and 'send a message to'. The related noun sense, 'person one is in communication with' (*has some useful contacts in Berlin*), is another useful modern addition to the language.

contagious, infectious

Strictly speaking, **contagious** diseases are transmitted by direct bodily contact with a diseased person or something the person has touched. **Infectious** diseases are spread by micro-organisms through the air or water. Both words are used figuratively: *contagious enthusiasm*; *infectious laughter*. See also CONTIGUOUS.

contemn, condemn

Contemn is a rare formal verb meaning 'treat with contempt, scorn' and related to the commoner words *contempt* and *contemptible*. It is not a grander synonym for **condemn**, which means 'declare to be evil' or 'doom': *his own early drawings of moss roses and picturesque castles – things that he now mercilessly condemned* (Arnold Bennett).

contemporary, contemporaneous

Both words mean 'happening or existing at the same time', **contemporaneous** being the more formal: *Akbar was contemporary/ contemporaneous with Elizabeth I*. The chief modern sense of **contemporary**, however, is 'contemporary with ourselves'. One should be careful to avoid ambiguity here. A production of *Hamlet* in *contemporary dress* may be in the costume of either the 16th century or the late 20th century.

contemptible, contemptuous

Contemptible things or people deserve contempt: *contemptible meanness*. **Contemptuous** people or behaviour express contempt: *a contemptuous sneer*.

contend

This can mean 'maintain, assert', but it implies that there is opposition: *He contended that he was right*. Do not use it as a mere synonym for 'say' or 'explain', where no opposition is involved: *He contends that water boils at 100 °C*.

content (*verb*)

One **contents** oneself *with*, not *by*, something, in the sense of 'limit one's desires or actions'. This seems obvious enough in the case of nouns: *He contented himself with two helpings*; but the rule must also be borne in mind with the *-ing* form of verbs: *He contented himself with* (not *by*) *shaking hands.*

contiguous, contagious

Contiguous refers to what touches something else: *France and Belgium are contiguous.* **Contagious** is used of diseases, and means 'transmitted by bodily contact'. See also CONTAGIOUS.

continental

In many contexts this refers to the Continent of Europe as distinct from Britain. **Continental** food purports to be French, whether it is served in Birmingham, New York, or Bombay, and a **continental** breakfast is the kind that the French are believed to eat, without bacon or any other hot dish. In older British literature, expressions such as *the continental Sunday* imply either yearning or disapproval, according to how people felt about the supposed greater freedom and gaiety of France.

continental quilt

See QUILT.

continual, continuous

Strictly speaking, **continual** applies to something that keeps recurring at frequent intervals, and is often used with annoyance: *these continual interruptions.* **Continuous** applies to something in an unbroken line or sequence: *three days' continuous flight*; *rivers connected to form one continuous waterway.* But since the two words are scarcely distinguishable in many contexts (*continual/continuous fear*), writers who wish to convey the one idea and exclude the other may prefer to use *recurrent* or *intermittent* for **continual**, and *unbroken* or *uninterrupted* for **continuous**.

continuance, continuation, continuity

All these words are related to *continue.* **Continuance** is particularly used of the period for which something lasts: *the continuance of the fine weather.* **Continuation** suggests the active prolonging of something: *their continuation of the arms trade.* **Continuity** is the quality of being *continuous* or unbroken. In film production, it means 'consistency' between individual shots that are divided by breaks in the filming.

continue

1 Continue *on* and **continue** *to remain* are TAUTOLOGOUS. They can be replaced by **continue** (or *carry on*) and *remain*.

2 To **continue** *to do* something is to go on doing it, without stopping: *Despite interruptions, he continued to read us the poem.* To **continue** *by doing* something is to add something new: *He talked about Keats' 'Ode to Autumn', and continued by reading us the poem* (ie that was what he did next).

contractions

Contractions such as *I'm, they're, can't, isn't* are fully acceptable in most writing, but are not appropriate to very formal style. Do not use them in official documents or in letters that are headed with a formal greeting such as *Dear Sir or Madam*.

contralto

The plural is **contraltos**.

contrary

1 Both the adjective and noun are pronounced with the stress on the first syllable, except when the adjective means 'obstinately self-willed': in *Mary, Mary, quite contrary* it rhymes with *Mary*.

2 *On the* **contrary** is used for denying a statement: *This problem is not trivial; on the contrary, it is extremely serious.* This expression should not be confused with *on the other hand*, used for adding new and contrasting information: *This problem is not trivial; on the other hand, we have plenty of time to remedy it*.

contrast

One **contrasts** something *with* something else: *He contrasted the microscope with the telescope.* One may also **contrast** a pair of things, either linked by *and* or as a plural: *to contrast the British and French legal systems*; *to contrast the two systems.* One thing **contrast**s *with* another: *His reaction contrasted favourably with theirs* (not *the two reactions contrasted favourably*). When **contrast** is a noun, one may use *with* or *to* (*in contrast with/to what I said earlier*) or, where appropriate, *between* (*the contrast between brother and sister*).

contribute

This is usually pronounced with the stress on the second syllable rather than the first.

controversial

From its original sense 'open to discussion, debatable' (*a controversial issue*), this word has come often to mean 'likely to be disapproved of' or even 'disreputable', as opposed to 'safe and colourless': *a controversial appointment*; *his controversial opinions*. A **controversial** *person* may mean an 'argumentative' one, but this is a rarer meaning.

controversy

This word is now very often pronounced in Britain with the stress on the second syllable, but this pronunciation attracts criticism from some people. The traditional British pronunciation with the stress on the first syllable is normal in American English.

contumely

This is usually pronounced 'KON-tyoom-li', rather than with stress on the second syllable. It is a formal word for 'rude, haughty words or treatment'.

convenience

At your earliest **convenience** is a very formal way of saying 'as soon as you can', and may sound PRETENTIOUS.

converse

See REVERSE.

conversion

Words that originate in one part of speech are frequently 'converted' to another part of speech: *The* **pay** *was good*; *They are* **cornering** *the market in silver*; *Don't* **elbow** *me*. Conversion is a well-established process in the language, but some conversions are informal and should not be used in formal writing: *That book is a* **must** *for jazz fans*; *He* **upped** *and left*; *He's a* **has-been**; *a* **fun** *party*. Avoid introducing conversions of your own, especially when there are recognized alternatives: *Customs agents have been unable to stop the* **ship** *of illegal drugs into this country* (replace by *shipping* or *transport*).

convex

See CONCAVE.

conveyance

This has other legitimate meanings, but it may sound rather PRETENTIOUS as a word for a 'vehicle'.

convince

This means 'persuade to believe'. One can **convince** someone *of* a fact, or **convince** someone *that* something is true or something ought to happen: *He convinced me that I was wrong.* Careful writers avoid the use of **convince** with an infinitive verb to mean 'persuade into a course of action', as in *He convinced them to leave the country.*

cool

The informal uses of **cool** are, as an adjective, to emphasize large sums of money (*They made a cool million on the deal*) or as a general term of approval (*That's a really cool jacket*); as a noun, to mean 'calm detachment': *I managed to keep my cool, however, and told him I wouldn't sign an exclusive contract with anyone* (*The Times*). These do not belong in serious writing, except (as above) for particular effects of style.

cooperate, collaborate

1 Cooperate is now spelled like this in American English, and commonly in British English. A British alternative is **co-operate**. See CO-.

2 Cooperate and **collaborate** can often be used interchangeably. **Cooperate** emphasizes willingness to be helpful: *I can't lift you if you don't cooperate.* **Collaborate** applies particularly to intellectual endeavours (*They collaborated on a film script*) and has the possible sinister sense of assisting an enemy who has occupied one's country.

coordinate

The word is now usually spelled like this. An alternative is **co-ordinate**. See CO-.

cop, copper, bobby

Of the many informal words for 'policeman', **cop** seems to be the most neutral, and is reported to be preferred by the police themselves. **Copper** is perhaps less sympathetic. **Bobby** is British, affectionate and old-fashioned. Slang alternatives include **pig** (very offensive), **flatfoot**, and **fuzz**; the British **rozzer** and **(Old) Bill**; and the American **bull**, **heat**, and *the* **man**.

cope

The use of **cope** by itself, as in *I can't cope*, without stating what it is I cannot **cope** *with*, is now commonplace in all except formal writing.

copy

If you ask for three **copies** of something such as a typescript, make it clear whether or not one of them is to be the original. Otherwise you may, at least in British use, receive either three or four versions altogether.

cord

See CHORD.

core, corps, corpse, corpus

A **core** is the central part of something: *apple core*; *He was honest to the core*. A **corps** is an organized group of people (*the press corps*), and its plural is the same as its singular. Both **core** and **corps** are pronounced 'kore'. A **corpse**, pronounced 'korps', is a dead body. A **corpus** (plural **corpora** or **corpuses**) is a collection of language or writings, particularly the complete works of an author.

co-respondent, correspondent

1 Co-respondent is the usual British spelling for the first of these words, **corespondent** the usual American one. See CO-.

2 A **co-respondent** is the person accused of adultery with the husband or wife in a divorce suit. A **correspondent** writes letters, or contributes to a newspaper or broadcast: *our correspondent in Lagos.*

corn

In British English this means wheat, oats, or barley. In American English it means maize, also known as Indian corn. The latter is what *cornflakes* are made from.

coronary

This is pronounced with the stress on the first syllable.

corporal, capital

See CAPITAL.

corporal, corporeal

These both mean 'of the body'. In modern use, however, **corporal** applies chiefly to what affects the body unpleasantly: *corporal discomforts*; *corporal punishment*. **Corporeal** emphasizes the fact of having a body at all, and may contrast with 'spiritual' or with 'immaterial': *We saw . . . the woman, with a corporeal body as real*

at that moment as our own, pass in through the interstice (Bram
Stoker, *Dracula*).

corps, corpse, corpus

See CORE.

corpus delicti

This means the 'body' of facts showing that a crime has taken place.
The existence of an actual 'body' of a murder victim is, therefore, only
one such possible fact. Outside legal contexts, use these LATINISMS
sparingly.

correctitude

This formal word is a combination of *correct* and *rectitude*, and means
'propriety of conduct'.

correlative

1 general	**3** mistaken correlation
2 misplaced correlatives	**4** more than two

1 general
Correlatives are paired words that occur separately in the sentence.
Here are some common pairs of correlatives: *both* . . . *and*; *either*
. . . *or*; *neither* . . . *nor*; *not only* . . . *but*; *between* . . . *and*;
whether . . . *or*.

2 misplaced correlatives
Correlatives emphasize relationships such as similarity and contrast
between two grammatically similar units. They are misplaced if they
are not positioned immediately in front of the parallel units. For
example, *by the growing crime rate* **and** *by the recurring epidemics* are
parallel phrases and so are *the growing crime rate* **and** *the recurring
epidemics*. The correlatives are therefore wrongly placed in *The tourist
industry was affected* **both** *by the growing crime rate* **and** *the recurring
epidemics*; correct to **both** *by the growing crime rate* **and** *by the
recurring epidemics* or to *by* **both** *the growing crime rate* **and** *the
recurring epidemics*. Other examples of misplaced correlatives: *They*
either *found errors* **or** *misrepresentations in the report* (correct to
found **either** *errors* **or** *misrepresentations*); *He* **neither** *would support*
nor *oppose reforms of the voting procedures* (correct to *would* **neither**
support **nor** *oppose*); **Not only** *would we take part in the project* **but**
could also persuade our neighbours to join us (correct to **Not only**
would we . . . , **but** *we could* . . .).

171

3 mistaken correlation

Some correlations are considered mistakes in formal written English: *The committee* **neither** *supported* **or** *opposed the proposal* (correct to *neither . . . nor*); *The appointment was fixed* **between** *four* **or** *five on the following day* (*between . . . and*); *The motion was* **no sooner** *passed* **when** *the treasurer resigned* (*no sooner . . . than*); **Hardly** *had the meeting started* **than** *demonstrators burst into the room* (*hardly . . . when*; similarly *barely . . . when, scarcely . . . when*); **Why** *I did not reply earlier is* **because** *I have been abroad the last two months* (*The reason . . . that*); *She was* **that** *tired* **that** *she nearly collapsed* (*so . . . that*); *It was* **not so much** *frightening* **but** *embarrassing* (*not so much . . . as*). In negative comparisons both *not so . . . as* and *not as . . . as* are correct: *The guest bedroom was* **not as** (or **so**) *large* **as** *the main bedroom.*

4 more than two

Correlatives generally come in pairs. It is therefore not correct to write *The site is* **between** *a river* **and** *a highway* **and** *a hill* (*The site is bordered by . . .*) or *I have understood* **both** *the contract* **and** *letter* **and** *your explanation* (omit **both**). *Either* and *neither* are exceptional in that clarity may sometimes demand that they be used with more than one conjunction: *On the enclosed form you must complete* **either** *Section A* **or** *Section B* **or** *both.*

correspond

When it means 'be in agreement; be equivalent', things **correspond** *to* or *with* other things: *These goods do not correspond to/with what I ordered.* When it means 'exchange letters', one person **corresponds** *with* the other.

correspondent

See CO-RESPONDENT.

corrode

See ERODE.

'cos

This pronunciation of *because* should be avoided in careful speech.

cosmonaut

See ASTRONAUT.

cost (*verb*)

Besides meaning 'require as a price' (*It cost £5*), **cost** can mean 'estimate the cost of'. Builders and decorators, for example, will **costed** a prospective job. In American English, particularly among economists in government circles, a modern variation is **cost** *out*: *to cost out the new program*.

cost, price

As nouns meaning what one pays, **cost** and **price** are more or less synonymous, but one speaks of the **price** of a cabbage and the **cost** of feeding a family. **Cost** rather than **price** is used of services and immaterial things: *printing costs*; *the cost of having the house painted*; and, of course, *the cost of living*.

cost-effective

This means 'economically worthwhile, profitable': *take cost-effective measures to combat a slump in sales*. It is a fashionable expression in business English.

costume

See SUIT.

cosy, cozy

This is spelled with an *s* in British English, with a *z* in American English.

couch (*noun*)

See SOFA.

couch (*verb*)

This can mean 'express, say': *couched in warlike terms*; but the use may seem PRETENTIOUS in most contexts.

could, might

Both **could** and **might** can be used in estimating probabilities: *Don't try to lift it – you might/could hurt yourself*; *If I hadn't caught him, he might/could have been killed*. Rephrase where there is any danger of ambiguity. *The road might/could be blocked* can mean either that it is perhaps blocked or that blocking it is possible, so write *perhaps it is blocked* or *we could block it*.

couldn't care less

As an expression of lack of concern this is now a CLICHÉ. A later development has been to drop the negative: *I know nothing about it and could care less.* If one is going to use the phrase at all, its traditional form makes more sense, but neither of the two is appropriate in serious writing.

council(lor), counsel(lor)

A **council** is an assembly, organization, or executive body: *the local town council*; *the National Council for Civil Liberties*. A **councillor** or **councilor** (a variant spelling in American English) is a member of a **council**. **Counsel** is a lawyer or group of lawyers, in Britain barristers, who advise and represent a client. It is also 'advice': *gave them wise counsel*. A **counsellor** or **counselor** (a variant spelling in American English) is someone who gives professional advice (*marriage guidance counsellor*); or a senior diplomat; or a supervisor at an American children's summer camp; or an American lawyer who is the equivalent of a barrister.

couple

1 When it means 'two people', **couple** takes a plural verb: *Any young couple want* (not *wants*) *a home of their own.*

2 The vague use of *a* **couple** *of* to mean 'a few' is informal; even more so is **couple** in this sense without *of*, as in *a couple minutes*.

course

1 *In/during the course of* is VERBOSE. *During* is quite enough.

2 *Of* **course** should be used thoughtfully and sparingly. It can be employed with disdainful effect, to suggest that a piece of out-of-the-way knowledge is commonplace: *His last win, of course, was in 1977.* (This device is acceptable, though, when what it introduces is commonly but not universally known, so that a few readers need to be informed without insulting the majority.) *Of* **course** is also used dishonestly, to escape having to defend an unwarranted assumption: *The committee are, of course, totally corrupt.* There can be no justification for that.

courtesy, curts(e)y

Courtesy is politeness. A **curtsy** or **curtsey** is a woman's obeisance of respect.

court-martial

Courts-martial is the traditional plural, but **court-martials** is a common alternative.

coxcomb

See COCKSCOMB.

cozy

See COSY.

cracker

This has several meanings, but the word is a source of international misunderstanding. In British English, it chiefly means the paper tube that one pulls with a bang at Christmas parties; in American English, it chiefly means a crispy bread product, but this meaning also appears in the British English *cream cracker*.

craft (*verb*)

This synonym for *make* or *produce* is often used rather dishonestly in advertisers' English to suggest the loving and leisurely care of the old-fashioned craftsman: *carefully crafted shoes*.

crape, crepe

Crape is the usual spelling for the black mourning material, **crepe** or **crêpe** for the light crinkled fabric and for the pancake.

crash

This is a fashionable and perhaps OVERUSED word for things intended to achieve quick results: *a crash diet*; *a crash course*; *a crash programme to deal with illiteracy*. Beware of possible misunderstanding, as in *a crash course in driving*.

crayfish, crawfish

Crayfish is the British spelling, **crawfish** the American spelling, for any of various edible freshwater crustaceans, and also for the *spiny lobster*, which figures on French menus as *langouste*.

credence, credibility

1 Credence is mental acceptance of what is offered as true. **Credibility** is the quality of being convincing. Thus, to *give credence to* a story is to believe it, to *give credibility to* it is to enable others to believe it.

2 Credibility has become a jargon word in the sense of 'power to impress people'. It is so used, both in such sinister contexts as the **credibility** of the nuclear deterrent, and in advertisements requiring the candidate for a post to have **credibility** as an engineer or accountant.

credible, credulous, creditable

Credible means 'believable': *a credible story*. **Credulous** means 'too ready to believe': *Foreigners were ready to be credulous about America*. The negatives are **incredible, incredulous,** and the associated nouns are **credibility** and **credulity** (or **credulousness**). **Creditable** means 'deserving esteem': *a creditable effort*. The negative is **discreditable.**

crepe

See CRAPE.

crescendo

1 The plural is either **crescendos** or **crescendoes**.

2 This means a gradual increase, particularly in musical volume. A **crescendo** rises to a climax but is not itself that climax. Do not write *reach a crescendo* or *rise to a crescendo*.

crevasse, crevice

These both mean 'crack' or 'fissure', but a **crevasse** is much the larger. A climber may poke a toe into a rock **crevice**, but fall into a **crevasse** in a glacier. American English also uses **crevasse** for a breach in a river embankment.

criterion

Criteria, not **criterions**, is the correct plural. The plural **criteria** is sometimes used as a singular (*this criteria*), but it should not be; write *these criteria*.

criticism, criticize

Although these words have a neutral sense of 'judging and evaluating', as in *literary criticism*, in day-to-day use they imply disfavour. We do not say *His action exposed him to criticism*, or *She was criticized for this decision*, if we mean that they were praised.

critique

This is now quite a popular synonym for *review* or *notice*, both as a noun and (particularly in American English) as a verb: *to critique the play*. It seems no more pretentious than any of the other words for the activity.

crochet (*verb*)

Other forms are **crocheted, crocheting**.

cross

In British English, though not in American, it is old-fashioned to pronounce this as 'kraws'.

crow (*verb*)

The past tense is usually **crowed**. The alternative past tense **crew** is British English only, and applies only to the noise a cock makes, not to a baby's cheerful sound and not to the sense 'exult, gloat': *He crowed over his rivals*.

crummy

This, rather than **crumby**, is the usual spelling of the slang word meaning 'miserable, worthless'.

crumple, crumble

Cloth **crumples**: *a crumpled shirt*. Bread or stone **crumbles**. In the abstract both words mean 'disintegrate' or 'collapse': *His resistance crumbled/crumpled*.

crunch

When it comes to the crunch is a CLICHÉ.

cubic(al)

Use **cubical** for the shape, **cubic** for the more abstract uses: *a cubical box/room*; *cubic equations*; *cubic measure*; *cubic metre*.

cui bono

This is the Latin for 'To whose advantage?'. As a maxim in law, it expresses the principle that the likeliest person to have done an action must be the one who stands to gain from it. The phrase is wrongly used by people who think it means 'What is the use?'. Do not use too many of these LATINISMS.

cullender

See COLANDER.

cultivated, cultured

These both can mean 'refined and educated': *cultivated people*; *cultured tastes*. In addition, **cultivated** distinguishes garden varieties of plants from wild ones (*cultivated blackberries*), while **cultured** is used of other things grown under artificial conditions (*cultured pearls*; *cultured viruses*). It is often safer to use **cultivated** than **cultured** with reference to people's breadth of reading and appreciation of the arts. **Cultured** may carry some trace of snobbery (*cultured accent*).

cum

This preposition means 'combined with', as in *lounge-cum-dining room*. It may be more puzzling to Americans than to the British, who are accustomed to its occurrence in placenames such as *Chorlton-cum-Hardy*.

cumulative

See ACCUMULATIVE.

cupful

The usual plural is **cupfuls**, not **cupsful**.

curate's egg

This means 'something with both good and bad parts', and is a CLICHÉ.

curb, kerb

The **kerb** (British English) or **curb** (American English) is the border of a pavement. Use **curb** for the other senses of the noun, and for the verb. A chain for controlling a horse, or an enclosing fender or frame, is a **curb**. To **curb** anything is to control or restrain it.

currant, current

A **currant** is a fruit: *currants in a cake*. A **current** flows: *current of air*. The adjective meaning 'at the present time, now' is **current**: *during the current week*.

curriculum

The plural is either **curricula** or **curriculums**.

curts(e)y

See COURTESY.

custom

Used as an adjective, chiefly in American English, but increasingly in British English too, this means 'made to personal order': *custom clothes*; *a custom-built car*. The word is now used somewhat indiscriminately of mass-produced goods that make some claim to quality.

customs

See TAX.

cutlet

See CHOP.

-cy

See -CE.

cymbal, symbol

A **cymbal** is a percussion instrument, played by a **cymbalist**. A **symbol** is a sign standing for something else, and a user of symbols is a **symbolist**.

cynosure

See SINECURE.

cypher

See CIPHER.

cypress, Cyprus

A **cypress** is an evergreen tree. **Cyprus** is a Mediterranean island.

Dd

-d-, -dd-

See DOUBLING.

d', de, du, van, von

Except for *du*, these particles meaning 'of' usually begin with a small letter in foreign names, but with a capital when the name has become 'naturalized' as that of an English-speaking family. Compare: *Charles de Gaulle, Thomas De Quincey*; *Vincent van Gogh, Laurens Van der Post*; but the rule is not invariable. The opposite applies to *du*: Louis XV's mistress spelled her name *Du Barry*, whereas the English literary and dramatic family of the *du Mauriers* have preferred a small *d*.

daemon, demon

A **daemon** is an attendant spirit, or a supernatural being in Greek mythology. The spelling **demon** is preferred for the modern sense of 'devil'.

Dáil

The name of the Irish parliament is pronounced to rhyme with either *oil* or *mile*.

dairy, diary

A **dairy** is where milk is produced; a **diary** is a journal. Confusion of the two is a common spelling and printing error.

Dame

See SIR.

damn, dam

Damn, damned, damnedest, and **damning** are pronounced with the *n* silent. This word of all-purpose profanity is spelled **dam** only in the informal combinations *dammit* (for *damn it*) and *damfool* (for *damned fool*). In **damnable** and **damnation** the *n* is pronounced.

dance

Besides meaning a party with dancing (*go to a dance*), or a way of dancing (*The conga is a Cuban dance*), **dance** is now used without *a* to mean 'the art of dancing', with reference to intellectual or exotic kinds of dancing as an art form: *African dance*; *the problems of modern dance*. The alternative word *dancing* would sound less serious here.

danegeld

This annual tax is believed to have been imposed in the 9th century to buy off Danish invaders in England. The word is now used, figuratively, of any shameful payment made to save the trouble of proper resistance: *Nigel Lawson wants electricity prices raised . . . because he needs to milk the profits of this nationalised industry to balance the Treasury books. The Electricity Council says it can pay the danegeld to naughty Nigel without putting up its prices* (*Daily Mail*).

dangling participle

The parts of a verb that end in *-ing* and (for regular verbs) in *-ed* are participles. They can be used to modify a noun, as in *a* **crying** *baby* or *the* **defeated** *army*. They can also be used as the verb in a phrase attached to the subject of the sentence: *A baby,* **crying** *loudly and incessantly on the floor above, woke us all up* (the baby was crying); **Defeated** *in battle, the army surrendered unconditionally* (the army was defeated). A similar attached phrase can be formed with an *-ing* participle and a preceding preposition or conjunction: *After* **working** *for the firm for 20 years, she decided to leave* (she was working; if it is used with a preposition the *-ing* participle is traditionally called a GERUND); *When last* **seen,** *he was in Leeds* (he was last seen).

A dangling participle (also known as an unattached or unrelated participle) occurs when the *-ing* or *-ed* phrase is placed next to the subject but is not related to it. It may in fact be related to another noun in the sentence: **Being** *in charge, the accusation was particularly annoying to me* (the accusation was not in charge; I was in charge); *If* **paid** *generously, we can expect good work from them* (if they are paid, not if we are paid). Possible corrections of these two sentences are *Being in charge, I was particularly annoyed by the accusation*; *If they are paid generously, we can expect good work from them*. The error requires more radical correction if the participle phrase is not related to any noun in the sentence: *By* **applying** *the techniques of these massage therapies, the body will be restored to its natural balance* (presumably the masseur or masseuse applies the technique). Here is a longer example of a dangling participle: **Having** *just hurtled through Noël Coward's Diaries, superficial and unwitty but a unique canter through life at the top of show business, Michael Redgrave's autobiography comes as sober, slow-paced but much more satisfying* (*Daily Telegraph*). It is of course not Michael Redgrave's autobiography but the author who has just hurtled through the diaries, although the author is not referred to in the sentence. Generally, sentences with dangling participles can be easily understood. Nevertheless, they are considered to be incorrect and should be rephrased to avoid criticism.

There are also dangling phrases without participles: **A weak student,** *his teachers gave him extra homework and discussed it with him privately* (he is a weak student, not his teachers); *When* **out of work,** *the state pays unemployment benefit* (the state is not out of work); **Heavy with blossoms,** *I saw the tree swaying in the wind* (the tree is heavy with blossoms). Rephrase such sentences to avoid the error.

Certain *-ing* and *-ed* phrases are allowed to dangle. In the first place, there are several *-ing* and *-ed* words that are no longer participles but have become prepositions: *according (to), barring, concerning, considering, failing, following, including, owing (to), pending, regarding.* Others have become conjunctions: *assuming, granted, provided, providing, seeing, supposing.* Nobody would object to **Barring** *unforeseen circumstances, the meeting will take place next Monday* or to **Provided** *that they pay the full amount, they can join the outing.* Secondly, there are phrases in which the understood subject refers to the writer and the whole phrase involves the writer's comment. Again, no one would object to **Seriously speaking,** *their methods of production are antiquated* or to **To be frank,** *the economic situation is deteriorating* (I, the writer, am being frank in telling you this) or to **Putting it another way,** *they were simply negligent.* Finally, the understood subject of an acceptable dangling phrase may be an understood *it* or *which* that refers to the content of the rest of the sentence: *A mediator will be brought in* **when necessary** (when it is necessary); *The rattling has stopped,* **suggesting** *that the machine is now functioning properly* (which suggests that).

In addition, some dangling participles are conventionally used in particular varieties of the language. In commercial or bureaucratic language, for example, it is conventional to introduce a topic by *arising out of* or *referring to.* In scientific language, a dangling participle is often used when the understood subject is the writer or writers; *using* is particularly common: **Using** *familiar techniques, the cell walls of certain bacteria were examined in detail* (the writer used familiar techniques). With regard to these phrases, it is safest in formal writing to confine yourself to the established forms. When in doubt over a sentence such as **Remembering** *your interest in impressionist* *painting, it seems to me likely that you will want to see the current exhibition at the Tate Gallery*, use instead the full form: *Since I remember your interest in impressionist painting, it seems to me likely that you will want to see the current exhibition at the Tate Gallery.* Or rephrase to introduce the appropriate subject: **Remembering** . . . I *think it likely that* . . . .

dare

Dare can be used in three ways.

As an auxiliary verb like *can* or *must*, followed by another verb without *to*, it is used in questions (*Dare I open it?*), or in negatives (*He daren't answer*), or in subordinate clauses (*I wonder whether they dare go*), or as part of the expression *I daresay*. This is perhaps the preferred construction in British English.

Dare is also used as an ordinary verb, rather like *want*, followed by another verb with *to*: *He didn't dare to disobey.*

The two constructions are blended in a third construction: *He didn't dare disobey*, where *didn't* appears without *to*. This seems to be favoured in American English.

dash

Dashes indicate sharp pauses. Since they are versatile, there is a danger of overusing them. They are especially common in journalistic writing and in personal correspondence. In formal writing they have two main uses, one resembling the colon and the other resembling the isolating commas. In the first use, the dash introduces an explanation or elaboration of what comes before it: *For many years I have been interested in Nigeria – its people, history, art, and music*; *The researchers found that the children had a surprising attachment to their grandparents – an unexpected phenomenon in a society that has no respect for the elderly.* The dash makes a sharper break than the colon, and unlike the colon sometimes introduces merely an emphatic continuation: *The stories create suspense and keep promising full comprehension – later*; *Foreign exchange traders must have all the resources of modern information technology – or go bankrupt.* The second major use of dashes is to mark off a parenthetic part of the sentence. As with isolating commas, parenthetic dashes come in pairs in the middle of the sentence: *The Japanese negotiators were more sensitive – and more courteous – than the American negotiators*; *This description deals with Great Britain – England, Scotland, and Wales – where there is general agreement on the basic shape of the machinery of government.* In the first of these two sentences, the parenthetic dashes make a more emphatic separation than would isolating commas.

In the second, the dashes are needed to make a clearer separation in the presence of other commas with different functions.

dastardly

This rather archaic word means 'cowardly'. It seems inappropriate to refer to personally dangerous crimes or their perpetrators as **dastardly**, however weak or innocent the victim.

data

Although **data** is strictly a plural (from the rarely used singular *datum*), it is now coming to be used as an aggregate singular noun: *All this data is new*. This usage is avoided by careful writers of British English, but is better established in American English and everywhere in the field of data processing. It is still safer to treat the word as a plural, at least in formal writing: *All the essential data . . . are here* (*Times Literary Supplement*). In any case, nobody speaks of *a data*.

dates

The standard British order for dates, increasingly used in the USA, is day, month, and year, without punctuation between the units: *15 July 1964*; *27 December 1985*. The alternative American order puts the month before the day and encloses the year in commas: *July 15, 1964, . . .*; *December 27, 1985, . . .* A more conservative British style indicates that the figure for the day represents an ordinal numeral (first, second, etc) by adding an abbreviation: *1st*; *2nd*; *3rd*; *4th*; *5th*. (An even more conservative style uses full stops after *1st.*, etc.) The ordinal numeral is an unnecessary addition.

In lists and in informal style, the names for the months may be abbreviated, though generally only the longer names (those with more than five letters): *Jan.*; *Feb.*; *Aug.*; *Sept.*; *Oct.*; *Nov.*; *Dec.* In such contexts it is also possible to represent the whole date by figures: *5/3/86*; *5–3–86*; *5.3.86*. But because of the different conventions for the order of the units, 5/3/86 means 5 March 1986 in British usage and 3 May 1986 in American usage. This difference can therefore cause misunderstandings in transatlantic communication. A frequent practice in continental Europe, also found in Britain, is to use small roman numbers for the months, a usage that prevents misinterpretation: *5.iii.86* or *3.v.86*. The year alone may be abbreviated in informal style, and an apostrophe is then used to indicate the abbreviation: *in '45*, *after '84*. For the decades use *s* without an apostrophe: *in the late 1960s and early 1970s*; but informally: *in the late '60s and early '70s*.

Use a dash to represent periods: *In March–August 1985*; *during 18–28 December*; *during 6 April 1985–5 April 1986*; *in the period 1939–1946*. If the years are within the same century, you need not repeat the first two figures and may instead indicate the abbreviation by a dash or slash: *during 1930–46*; *the tax year 1983/84*. Use the full forms with the prepositions *from* and *between*: *from 1985 to 1988* (not *from 1985– 1988*); *between 1939 and 1946* (not *between 1939–46*).

If you use *B.C.*, put it after the year: *55 B.C.* You will only need to add *A.D.* (*anno domini*, Latin for 'in the year of the Lord') if there are *B.C.* dates in the context or if there are other reasons to suspect a possible misunderstanding. The abbreviation *A.D.* comes before the year: *A.D. 70*.

davenport

See SOFA.

day

In this day and age, meaning 'nowadays', is a verbose CLICHÉ.

de

See D'.

de-, dis-

These prefixes can both be used before verbs and nouns to mean 'reverse the action', 'get rid of', 'deprive of': *delouse*; *disinfect*; *decontamination*; *disincentive*. Where possible, good writers try to avoid creating new words on this pattern, preferring perhaps *legalize* to *decriminalize*. Often, however, such a strategy is not possible, because what is needed is a precise term. *Derestrict* does not only mean 'remove restrictions from', but has the special sense of 'remove the speed limit from (a road)'. It could not be replaced by any word such as *relax* or *liberate*.

deadly, deathly

Deadly is the usual word for things that actually cause death: *deadly poison*; *a deadly disease*. **Deathly** is usually figurative, and means 'suggestive of death': *deathly silence*; *a deathly pallor*. **Deadly**, not **deathly**, can mean 'very dull': *a deadly bore*; *spent a deadly afternoon*.

dead reckoning

Dead here does not mean 'unerring' or 'exact', as in *dead shot* or *dead centre*. **Dead reckoning** is the calculation of the position of a ship or aircraft by mathematics alone, without the help of external observation.

deaf, deafened

The participle **deafened** is used when some clear agency is involved: *deafened by the noise*. Otherwise, **deaf** is the usual word: *He became deaf*; *a deaf child*.

Dear

In the phrase of greeting at the start of a letter, **Dear** is an impersonal formality, and does not imply affection. Use **Dear** *Sir*, **Dear** *Madam* in formal letters to complete strangers, **Dear** *Mr Jones* to strike a friendlier note. *My* **Dear** *Mr Jones* is considered more formal than **Dear** alone in American letter-writing, while in British use it may sound a little patronizing. See also LETTER ENDINGS.

dear, dearly

When it means 'expensively', the adverb form is **dear**: *buy/sell dear*; *pay dear for it*; *It cost them dear*. **Dearly** means 'very much': *I love her dearly*; *I would dearly like to go*.

dearth

This means 'scarcity'. *A dearth of good novels* is a slightly PRETENTIOUS way of saying *not many good novels*.

deathly

See DEADLY.

debacle, debut

1 A **debacle** is a complete fiasco, rout, or collapse: *the Wall Street debacle of 1929*. A **debut** is someone's first appearance in public or in society: *She had a daughter making her debut*; *He scored two goals on his debut for the team*.

2 Both words are now usually written without accents, rather than as **débâcle** and **début**.

debar, disbar

1 Other forms are **debarred, disbarred**; **debarring, disbarring**.

2 One **debars** a person from doing something: *His professional status debars him from taking part in amateur events*. To **disbar** a lawyer is to deprive him or her of the right to practise.

debatable

The word is spelled without the final *e* of *debate*.

debate

1 One **debates** a question, or **debates** what to do, whether to do it, or where to go. One does not, correctly, **debate** *on* or *about* something.

2 Debate can mean 'turn over in one's mind', an activity that can be engaged in alone. The word does not necessarily imply joint discussion.

debouch

This is pronounced to rhyme with *pouch*. It means 'emerge' (*a stream debouching into a lake*), and is not to be confused with *debauch*, 'lead into vice'.

debrief

This does not mean 'take away someone's brief', but 'interrogate on return from a mission'. Pilots and diplomats, not lawyers, are **debriefed**, to see what they have found out.

debris

This is now usually spelled without an accent; not **débris**. In British English, the first syllable is stressed and pronounced either 'deb' or 'dayb'. In American English, either syllable is stressed and the word is pronounced either 'd'BREE' or 'DAYbree'.

debut

1 See DEBACLE.

2 Avoid the use of **debut** as a verb: *She debuts next week*; *to debut a new car model*.

deca-, deci-

Deca- means 'ten times': a *decahedron* is a geometric figure with ten faces. **Deci-** means 'one tenth': a *decilitre* is a tenth of a litre.

decade

1 This is usually pronounced with the stress on the first syllable.

2 The names of decades are better written without an apostrophe: *the 1920s*, rather than *the 1920's*. Informally, the first two figures can sometimes be omitted, and are then replaced by an apostrophe: *the '80s*.

decease, deceased

Outside legal contexts, these can seem PRETENTIOUS words for *die*, *death*, *dead*.

deceitful, deceptive

Deceitful people deceive intentionally. **Deceptive** means merely 'misleading'.

decent

See DECOROUS.

decided, decisive

Decided means 'unquestionable': *a decided advantage*. **Decisive** means 'bringing to an issue; conclusive': *a decisive goal*. **Decided** and **decisive** can both mean 'free from hesitation; resolute': *his decisive/ decided manner*. The same differences and overlap exist between the related adverbs: *It is decidedly* (ie unquestionably) *too cold to go swimming*; *Napoleon was decisively* (ie conclusively) *defeated at Waterloo*; *He spoke decidedly/decisively* (ie resolutely) *of his intention to continue the strike*.

decimate

Although **decimate** originally meant 'kill one in ten of' (eg of mutinous soldiers), it now also means 'kill a large proportion of', and this use is accepted as standard: *Typhus fever decimated the school* (Charlotte Brontë). **Decimate** does not, however, mean 'kill nine out of ten', or 'exterminate completely', though its users should be aware that it may be so understood. Do not use this word where any proportion or degree is specified (*seriously decimated*; *decimated by 60 per cent*), and do not use it in relation to a single creature; one cannot say that David **decimated** Goliath.

decision

The *c* is pronounced like 's', not like 'z'.

declare

Apart from its specialized senses (*declare war*; *declare a bottle of vodka at the customs*), **declare** means 'state emphatically': *declare her* *innocence.* Do not overuse it as a mere variant of *say*, as in *She declared that it was late.*

déclassé

The word is spelled with the accents. It means 'fallen from a higher social position'.

decline

This means 'refuse courteously'. You can either **decline** something offered to you (*decline an invitation*) or **decline** *to do* something (*declined to give his name*). You cannot, correctly, **decline** something that you are asked for (*declined the use of his name*).

décolletage, décolleté

Both words are spelled with the accents. The first means a low-cut neckline, and the second means having or wearing such a neckline.

décor, decor

Both spellings are correct.

decorous, decent

These both mean 'conforming to propriety'. **Decorous** applies particularly to appearance and behaviour: *a decorous ankle-length skirt*; *walk decorously to church.* **Decent** is much wider in its application, embracing also the idea of 'suitable, adequate' (*decent housing*) and 'not obscene' (*a decent family film*).

decorous, indecorous

The usual pronunciation is with the stress on *dec*, but there is an American variant pronunciation that stresses *or*.

decoy

The verb is pronounced with the stress on the second syllable; the noun can be either 'DEEcoy' or 'deCOY'.

decry, descry

To **decry** something is to express disapproval of it. To **descry** something is to see it, especially at a distance: *We could descry the Eiffel Tower on a clear day.* **Descry** is a decidedly formal word.

dedicated, dedication

These words are often rather insincerely used to suggest devotion to a noble calling. While it is not unreasonable to speak of a **dedicated** *scholar* or *craftsman*, or the **dedication** of a musician, advertisers seem to be going too far when they refer to the **dedicated** *service* of hotel staff, or demand **dedication** as a prerequisite for a job in insurance.

deduce

See ADDUCE.

deduce, deduct

To **deduce** is to establish (a conclusion) by reasoning: *I deduced from the noise that the dogs had woken up.* To **deduct** is to subtract. The two verbs share the noun **deduction.**

deductive, inductive

These apply to two forms of logical reasoning. The **deductive** process derives a particular conclusion from general known principles, as when one says, 'Cats eat fish, so fish must be the right food for this cat'. **Inductive** reasoning derives a general principle from particular known instances, as when one says, 'The cats I know eat fish, so fish must be what cats eat'.

deem

This very formal word has a necessary meaning in the legal sense of assuming something to be a fact, as when people who make no overt objection to a measure are **deemed** to have consented to it. **Deem** is otherwise a facetious or PRETENTIOUS word for *think*.

deep, deeply

Deep as an adverb means 'far' or 'well within': *a house deep in the woods*; *This superstition had its roots deep in the Dark Ages.* **Deeply,** but not **deep,** can mean 'profoundly': *deeply distressed*.

defective, deficient

Defective means 'faulty in quality'; **deficient** means 'insufficient in quantity'. While there is a clear contrast between a **defective** water supply (ie bad water) and a **deficient** one (ie not enough water), there are many contexts where either word is suitable, as when one speaks of a **defective** or **deficient** memory.

defence, defense

The word is spelled with a *c* in British English, with an *s* in American English.

defensible, defensive

1 Defensible ends in *-ible*, not *-able*.

2 Defensible means 'able to be defended': a **defensible** point of view is a 'justifiable' one. **Defensive** means 'serving to defend': **defensive** play in cricket is concerned with protecting the wicket rather than scoring runs.

defer

Other forms are **deferred, deferring**. The related nouns are *deferral* or *deferment*, meaning 'delay'; and *deference*, meaning 'respect', which is associated with **defer** in the sense of *I defer to your opinion*.

deficit

This is usually pronounced with the stress on the first syllable.

definite, definitive

Things that are explicitly set forth are **definite** or **definitive**, but the two words have otherwise little overlap of meaning. **Definite** things are precise, not vague: *Give me a definite answer, yes or no*. **Definitive** things are final and unalterable, not provisional. A **definitive** biography, or other literary work, is one that will probably not be superseded for a long time. **Definitive** can also mean 'defining precisely': *a report which is definitive of* (ie defines) *our future intentions*. The word should not be used as merely a grander synonym for **definite**: *His answer was a definitive* (use *definite*) *no*.

    Definite and **definitely** are sometimes used for almost meaningless emphasis: *a definite advantage*; *definitely dangerous*. This usage should be avoided in formal writing.

deflection, deflexion

Both spellings are permissible in British English; but **deflection** is commoner, and is the only American form.

defuse, diffuse

To **defuse** something is to remove its fuse (*defuse a bomb*) or, figuratively, to make it less tense (*defuse a crisis*). **Diffuse** as an adjective means 'not concentrated or concise' (*a diffuse literary style*), and is pronounced with a final 's' sound. As a verb, **diffuse** means 'spread or scatter' (*diffused light*), and is pronounced with a final 'z' sound.

dégagé

This is spelled with the accents. It means 'free from constraint' or 'politically uncommitted'.

degree

1 This word often gives rise to VERBOSITY. For example, where possible, replace *to a serious* **degree** by *seriously*.

2 The phrase *to a* **degree,** meaning 'to a remarkable extent', is well established in the language: *The film was boring to a degree.* It can also, however, mean 'in a small way' (*experimented to a degree with new techniques*), so one must make it clear which meaning is intended.

deity

The *e* is pronounced either as in *see* or as in *say*; but some people dislike the *say* pronunciation.

déjà vu

This is spelled with the accents. It means 'the illusion of remembering something which is in fact experienced for the first time'. Do not use it with reference simply to something which has happened before. Avoid such FOREIGN PHRASES where possible.

delectable

This is a rather literary synonym for *delightful* or *delicious*: *delectable coffee/jokes*.

deleterious

This is a formal and somewhat PRETENTIOUS word for 'harmful'.

deliberate, deliberative

Deliberate means either 'intentional' (*deliberate malice*) or 'slow and steady' (*walking with deliberate steps*). **Deliberative** means 'engaged in discussion': *a deliberative assembly*.

delimit

See LIMIT.

192

deliver

Informally, this can now mean 'produce the desired or promised result': *Just because they can't deliver on tax cuts and spending cuts,. Whitehall's mandarins mustn't presume that all other organisations are equally ineffectual* (*Daily Mail*). But this usage should be avoided in serious writing.

deliverance, delivery

Both words are derived from *deliver*. **Deliverance** is chiefly associated with *deliver* in its sense of 'liberate; rescue' (*the deliverance of the prisoners*), although it has the legal sense of 'the publicly communicated verdict of the jury'. **Delivery** is associated with all the other meanings of *deliver*: *milk deliveries*; *a delivery boy*; *the delivery of a speech/of a ball*.

delusion, illusion

These both mean 'something false that seems to be true'. An **illusion** is an impression of the senses, either known nevertheless to be false or awaiting confirmation: *the illusions of childhood*. A **delusion** is a fixed false opinion, such as that held by a mad person, which cannot be removed by any appeal to reason: *his delusion that he is Napoleon*. The idea that the sun moves round the earth was once a **delusion** but is now an **illusion**. In certain circumstances, either word is equally appropriate: *She's under the delusion/illusion that I'm brilliant*. Neither word should be confused with **allusion**, the act of mentioning something indirectly. See ALLUSION.

de luxe, deluxe

This is spelled as two words in British English, as one word in American English. It means 'luxurious and elegant'.

demagog(ue)

The spelling **demagogue** is correct everywhere. **Demagog** is an alternative in American English only.

demand

One **demands** something *of* or *from* someone: *He demanded the time of/from a passerby*. One makes a **demand** *for* something *on* someone: *constant demands on me for advice*.

193

demanding

This is often a EUPHEMISM for *exhausting*, as when employers advertise *demanding work*; or for *selfish*, as in *a demanding invalid*.

demean

This is two verbs. One means 'behave (oneself)', and is associated with *demeanour*: *He must demean himself appropriately in public*. The other means 'debase; degrade': *Don't demean yourself by answering*. Both verbs are long-established, but the first is now becoming obsolete.

demeano(u)r

The word is spelled **demeanour** in British English, **demeanor** in American English.

demesne

The second syllable is pronounced like either *main* or *mean*. Apart from its technical senses to do with land ownership, the word is sometimes used for 'sphere, territory' as a variant of *domain*.

demi-

See SEMI-.

demise

Outside legal contexts, this is a PRETENTIOUS word for *death*.

demo

The plural is **demos**.

democrat, democratic

Use a capital *D* for the US political party or its members, a small *d* for the principles of democracy or its adherents: *It's more democratic to eat in the canteen*.

demon

See DAEMON.

demur

Other forms are **demurred, demurring**. This verb meaning 'raise objections' is not related to **demure**, meaning 'modest'.

denizen

See CITIZEN.

Denmark

Something is rotten in the state of Denmark is a CLICHÉ.

denominator

See NUMERATOR.

denote

See CONNOTE.

dénouement

This is spelled either with or without the accent. It means the resolution of the plot of a literary work, or the outcome of a complex sequence of events.

dent, dint

These can both mean 'hollow made by a blow' (*a dent/dint in the wing of my car*) or 'adverse effect' (*a dint/dent in his reputation*). Only **dint** is used in the phrase *by* **dint** *of*, meaning 'by means of': *She passed the exam by dint of hard work.*

dentures

This is an unnecessary GENTEELISM for *false teeth*.

depend

In speech, **depend** is often used alone: *'What do they eat?' 'It depends!'* Or it can be immediately followed by an indirect question: *It depends what you mean*; *It all depends where they live*. In formal writing, however, **depend** should be followed by *on* or *upon*: *It depends on what you mean*; *It depends upon where they live*.

dependence, dependency

Dependence is the state of being dependent: *dependence on drugs*. A **dependency** is something that is dependent, particularly a territorial unit under the jurisdiction of another nation.

dependent, dependant

In British English, the noun is **dependant** and the adjective is

195

dependent: *He has several dependants/people dependent on him.* In American English the noun may be spelled either way (*He has several dependants/dependents*), but the adjective is **dependent**.

depositary, depository, repository

These three words have some overlap of meaning. A **depositary** is a person to whom something is entrusted. **Depository** and **repository** can also mean this; but in addition they both mean a place where something is stored. A **repository** may be a smaller place, where the things are not stored so much as dumped: *The cupboard was a repository of old jam jars.*

depot

The word is spelled without an accent.

deprecate, depreciate

These two verbs have different origins: **deprecate** comes from the Latin *de-* + 'pray', and **depreciate** from the Latin *de-* + 'price'. **Deprecate** means 'express disapproval of, deplore': *He deprecated the plan to build a new motorway.* **Depreciate** means 'fall in value' or 'lower the price' (*The currency has depreciated*), but it also means 'belittle, disparage': *Don't depreciate their considerable intelligence.* It is this last sense of **depreciate** that comes so close to **deprecate** as to be almost indistinguishable, since what one 'deplores' one often also 'disparages'; a person may have a shy, *self-***deprecating** or *self-***depreciating** manner, meaning much the same thing. The two meanings should, however, be kept apart as far as possible.

derby, Derby

The first vowel is pronounced like the vowel in *garb* in British English, but like the vowel in *herb* in American English.

derisive, derisory

Both these words can mean 'expressing derision, mocking': *derisive/derisory laughter.* In addition, **derisory** but not **derisive** means 'worthy of derision', and particularly 'absurdly small': *a derisory pay offer.*

derrière

This is usually spelled with the accent. The word is a facetious EUPHEMISM for the buttocks.

descendant, descendent

In British English, the noun is spelled **descendant** and the adjective **descendent**. In American English, each word can be spelled in either way.

description

1 When one **describes** something, one gives a **description** *of*, not *about*, it.

2 Description is VERBOSELY used in such expressions as *a car of this description*, where *this kind of car* would be shorter and neater.

descry

See DECRY.

desert, dessert

A **desert**, with the stress on the first syllable, is an arid region. **Dessert**, with the stress on the second syllable, is the sweet course at the end of a meal. **Desert** meaning 'what one deserves' (*He got his just deserts*) and **desert** meaning 'abandon' (*He deserted his post*) have the stress on the second syllable, like **dessert**.

deshabille, dishabille

Deshabille is usually spelled like this, rather than **déshabillé**. The anglicized version **dishabille** is a popular alternative. Both forms mean 'the state of being only partly dressed'.

desiderate

This is not merely a very formal synonym for *desire*. It combines the meanings of *want* and *miss*.

desideratum

The plural is **desiderata.** The fourth syllable is pronounced like *art* or *eight*. The word means 'something desired'.

designed, destined

Designed means 'intended, planned': *a book designed for primary schools*; *a programme designed to appeal to housebound people*. **Destined** means 'set apart for a special purpose' (*freight destined for English ports*), and is somewhat OVERUSED in narrative to express the author's hindsight: *the boy who was destined to write these great symphonies*.

desirable, desirous

Desirable means 'worthy to be desired': *a desirable residence*.
Desirous means 'impelled by desire': *desirous of fame*.

desire

This verb is more dignified than *wish for* or *want*. It is appropriately
used in such ceremonial contexts as *desire the pleasure of your
company*, but seems a little PRETENTIOUS when used of material things,
as in *I desire a clean napkin*.

desist

This is a formal and rather PRETENTIOUS word for *stop*: *desist from
interfering*.

desk

From the desk of is a piece of business jargon. It implies that the great
executive did not write the letter personally.

despatch

See DISPATCH.

desperado

The plural is either **desperados** or **desperadoes**. The third syllable is
pronounced 'ahd', not 'aid'.

despicable

This is now usually pronounced with the stress on *spic*, although the
pronunciation with the stress on *des* is the more traditionally accepted.

despise

This is the only correct spelling, in both British and American English;
it ends in *-ise*, not *-ize*.

despite

As a preposition, this means 'in spite of': *He ran despite his injury*. Do
not say **despite** *of*. **Despite** *the fact that* is a VERBOSE way of saying
although.
    Despite is also used, very formally, as a noun meaning
'disadvantage': *I know of no government which stands to its
obligations, even in its own despite, more solidly* (Winston Churchill).

despoil

This means 'rob, pillage': *They despoiled a monastery of its revenues.* Although *spoil* had this same meaning in biblical English, as when the Children of Israel *spoiled* the Egyptians, the two words are no longer synonyms in modern English.

dessert

See DESERT.

destined

See DESIGNED.

destiny, destination

Destiny is the predetermined course of events. A **destination** is the place to which something is sent or to which someone is going.

destruct

This word is used as a verb and noun in US military and rocketry contexts, with reference to the deliberate destruction of a rocket or military device. It has extended its meaning with *self*-**destruct**: *The junta of Greek colonels self-destructed in 1974* (*Time*). In general, however, **destruct** should not be allowed to replace the verb *destroy* and the noun *destruction*.

destructible

The word ends in *-ible*, not *-able*.

destructive

Things are **destructive** *to* or *of* other things: *destructive to/of antique furniture*.

detail

In modern British English, the stress is on the first syllable for both the noun (*go into details*) and the verb (*He detailed his grievances*). In American English, it is usually on the second syllable.

détente

This can be spelled with or without the accent. It means 'a relaxation of hostile relations'.

deter

Other forms are **deterred, deterring**.

deteriorate

This word should not be pronounced as if it were spelled 'deteriate'. It is not a synonym for *worsen*, since it can be used, as *worsen* cannot, about what is admirable: *allow a tradition of academic excellence to deteriorate*.

determinately, determinedly

Determinately is rare, and means 'conclusively, finally': *The matter is determinately settled*. **Determinedly** means 'resolutely': *I am determinedly opposed to the project*.

determine

This legitimately means 'resolve' (*He determined to marry at all costs*), or 'establish, limit' (*The hedge determines the boundary*; *Demand determines the price*), or, in law, 'set an end to' (*determine an estate*). It can seem a rather PRETENTIOUS alternative to *fix*, *settle*, *decide*, etc, as in *determine where to go before we start*.

detour

This is spelled without an accent, and the first syllable is pronounced 'dee'. It means 'deviation from a direct course'.

detract, distract

Detract means 'take away something desirable': *Nothing can detract from their achievement*. **Distract** means 'draw away the attention of': *He distracted me from my work*.

detrimental

This can sound a formal and somewhat PRETENTIOUS word for 'harmful'.

develop

Among its many other senses, **develop** is legitimately used when people contract diseases (*He developed measles*), or, rather formally, in the sense 'become apparent' (*It developed that they had nowhere to sleep*). Since it carries some sense of gradual evolving, **develop** should not be used as a mere synonym for *occur* or *arise*, as in *A crisis has suddenly developed*.

develc pment

The word is spelled without an *e* after the *p*.

device, devise

1 Device is a noun, meaning 'stratagem', 'convention', or 'piece of equipment': *a clever device*. **Devise** is a verb, meaning 'formulate, invent': *devise a scheme*. It is spelled like this, not *-ize*, in both British and American English. There is also a noun **devise**, used in law in connection with the disposal of property by will.

2 *Leave someone to his/her own devices* is a CLICHÉ.

devil's advocate

Originally, this means the Roman Catholic official who presents all the possible objections to recognizing someone as a saint; by extension, it has come to mean anyone who for the sake of argument champions the less approved course. The expression does not mean either a 'tempter', or someone who whitewashes a bad case. On the contrary, such a person deliberately blackens a good case, but merely to explore the argument.

devise

See DEVICE.

deviser, devisor

A person who *devises* anything in the sense of 'formulating' or 'contriving' it is a **deviser**. A person who leaves property in a will is a **devisor**.

devoid

Devoid *of* (*a book devoid of any literary merit*) can often be neatly replaced by *without*.

dexterous, dextrous

Both spellings are correct. The first is somewhat commoner, particularly in American use.

diabolic(al)

Diabolic is the preferred form in actual reference to the devil: *diabolic laughter*. **Diabolical** usually means 'dreadful': *diabolical cruelty*; *The food was diabolical*.

di(a)eresis

The word is spelled **diaeresis** in British English, **dieresis** in American English. It means the mark of two dots over a vowel to show that it is pronounced as a separate syllable, as in *naïve* or *Brontë*. This typographical device, however, is becoming less common in English; people no longer write *aërate* or *coöperate*.

diagnose

One **diagnoses** a disease, not a person. Do not write *He was diagnosed as having shingles*.

diagnosis

The plural is **diagnoses**, with the last syllable pronounced 'seez'.

diagram (*verb*)

Other forms are **diagrammed, diagramming** in British English, but the second *m* is usually omitted in American English. For both British and American English write **diagrammable, diagrammatic**.

dial (*verb*)

Other forms are **dialled, dialling** in British English, but the second *l* is usually omitted in American English.

dialect

A dialect is a variety of the language with distinctive features of vocabulary and grammar. It should be distinguished from an accent (type of pronunciation), though there may be an association between the two. Dialects may be delimited by region or by social or ethnic group. One major distinction is between the standard (educated) dialects and nonstandard dialects. Standard dialects, which differ little from each other, vary largely by the country as a whole (American, British, Australian). Nonstandard dialects are regionally located, but are also associated with a social class or ethnic group (Cockney, Cornwall, Pennsylvania, Black English). There are an indefinite number of English dialects, since the number depends on how detailed we wish to be. See STANDARD ENGLISH; ACCENT; VARIETIES OF ENGLISH.

dialectal, dialectic, dialectical

Dialectal refers to *dialect*: *dialectal words*. **Dialectic** is, roughly, the testing of a theory by logical processes, but the word has technical meanings in philosophy. It is a noun, and its associated adjective is either **dialectical** or, less usually, **dialectic.**

dialogue

There is no reason for the belief that **dialogue** should apply only to a conversation between two people. As it happens, the Greek words from which it comes are *dia* (= through, across, apart) and *legein* (= to speak). If you want a special word for a dialogue between two people, use *duologue*. In any case, **dialogue** has become somewhat OVERUSED to mean a discussion or negotiation between two parties, as in *East-West dialogue on arms control*.

diarrh(o)ea

This is spelled **diarrhoea** in British English, **diarrhea** in American English.

diary

See DAIRY.

dice, die

The cube used in games of chance was formerly called a **die**, with **dice** as its plural. Today, **dice** is commonly used in the singular (*That dice has rolled under the chair*), though still with **dice** as its plural: *a set of poker dice*. This sense of **die** survives only in the expression *The die is cast*, meaning that an irrevocable step has been taken.

dichotomy

Strictly speaking, **dichotomy** is the division of a whole into two parts, as for binary classification. The word is legitimately used of differentiation into two mutually exclusive groups: *the dichotomy between theory and practice*. **Dichotomy** should not be used, though it often is, to mean no more than 'difference' or 'conflict': *widen the dichotomy between the two political parties*.

dictate

The verb is pronounced with the stress on the second syllable (*dictate a letter*), the noun with the stress on the first syllable (*the dictates of fashion*).

dictionaries

Dictionaries provide information on the vocabulary of a language. In addition to general dictionaries in one language, there are bilingual dictionaries, which give equivalent words in another language. There are also specialized dictionaries, for example those devoted to words used in the fields of medicine, law, or computers, and dictionaries of slang and dialects. Dictionaries vary in size. The largest is the *Oxford English Dictionary* in twelve volumes (also available in a two-volume small-print edition) with a supplement in four volumes; it is a historical dictionary and contains many obsolete words. The largest contemporary dictionary is *Webster's Third New International Dictionary*, 2662 pages long, which has one supplementary volume. All general dictionaries are to some extent 'abridged'; they do not contain all the specialized words in the language. (See VOCABULARY SIZE.) All are fallible in that they miss recent words or meanings. A word or meaning may be in respectable use even if it is not in your dictionary.

Compilers of dictionaries obtain their information partly from consulting existing dictionaries and partly from collecting citations of words in their context. The citations provide the evidence for the word's existence and for its use. Dictionaries are primarily descriptive: they describe the spelling, pronunciation, meaning, etc of a word. They may also add comments on how one should use the word, either by expressions such as *formal*, *slang*, and *nonstandard*, or by usage notes.

It is well worth devoting some time to reading the introductory guide to the dictionary that you consult habitually. The guide explains the range of information that the dictionary provides and the meanings of the terms and abbreviations it uses. It also explains the significance that the dictionary ascribes to its ordering of definitions or variants in spelling and pronunciation. The general dictionary in one language usually supplies the following information:

(1) Spelling, including any variants, eg *judgment, judgement*. The divisions between syllables are sometimes indicated by raised dots. The dictionary tells you whether the word begins with a capital and whether a compound may or should have a hyphen.

(2) Pronunciation, with patterns of stresses for words of more than one syllable, including any variants. The introductory guide contains a pronunciation key, which is sometimes repeated throughout the dictionary.

(3) Parts of speech, such as noun or verb. Often the same word is used for more than one part of speech.

(4) Inflections, such as the plural *-s* of nouns or the past *-ed* of verbs (and possible variants) when these are not added according to the general rules, as in plural *heroes* or past *preferred*. Completely irregular forms are of course also given: plural *children* and past *took*.

(5) Definitions. There are frequently several senses to be defined. Sometimes, as well as a definition, the dictionary explains how the word is used.

(6) Usage. The dictionary may indicate some restriction on a word, its spelling, its pronunciation, or one of its definitions. The restriction may apply to place (*American*), time (*archaic*), language variety (*legal*), or style (*informal*). Or perhaps the entry word is used only with certain other words (*listen* goes with *to*). Some dictionaries provide brief usage notes that give advice on problems of usage, such as whether to use *none* with the singular or plural. It is particularly important to consult the introductory guide for the meaning of some of these usage labels.

(7) Etymology, or history of words. The words are traced back to earlier periods of English and to languages from which they were borrowed.

Dictionaries also list expressions consisting of more than one word (*flog a dead horse*; *vested interest*) as separate entries or under major entries. Again, the introductory guide will give advice on where to find such expressions.

Some dictionaries (particularly American dictionaries) include names as well as words, for example *Kipling* and *Detroit*. Some have separate lists of abbreviations and names and provide lists of abbreviations and symbols and other types of information, such as on weights and measures.

dictum

The plural is **dicta** or, less usually, **dictums**.

didn't I?

It sounds insistent to attach **didn't I?** to the end of one's statements, as in *Well, I got my foot stuck, didn't I?*, if you have no need to invite agreement.

die (*noun*)

See DICE.

die (*verb*)

Other forms are **died, dying**. It is equally correct to speak of **dying** *of*, or *from*, causes: *to die of/from thirst*.

diesel

The word is spelled *-ie-*, not *-ei-*.

dietitian, dietician

Both spellings are correct.

differ

Things or people that are unlike each other **differ** *from* each other.
People who disagree **differ** *with* or *from* each other.

different

1 different *to/than/from*. The use of **different** with either *to* or *than* has
been long established in English: *It's quite a different thing within to
what it is without* (Henry Fielding); *The consuls . . . had been elected
for very different merits than those of skill in war* (Oliver Goldsmith).
Today, however, **different** *from* is the safest choice for serious writing.
Different *to* is a British alternative, censured by grammarians since the
18th century, but defensible in casual speech and writing. It is rare in
American English. **Different** *than*, a mainly American combination,
has the advantage that it can introduce a clause: *He wears different
clothes on Sunday than he does on weekdays.* To avoid disapproval,
however, it would be safer to rephrase this as *different clothes from
those he wears on weekdays.*

2 Different can be used with a singular noun to make a comparison
with something that may or may not be mentioned: *You look different*
(ie from before) *with your hair short*; *They each wanted to see a
different film* (ie from each other). This device is sometimes
dishonestly used in advertising, as in *the soap that's different* (from
what? in what way?).

3 Avoid using **different** with a plural noun to mean 'various, separate':
I visited them on three separate (not *different*) *occasions*; *Various* (not
different) *people have commented on it.*

differentiate, distinguish

Both these words can mean 'tell the difference': *unable to distinguish/
differentiate between red and green.* In addition, they can mean 'point
out the difference', or 'be the difference': *the qualities that distinguish/
differentiate butterflies from moths.*

diffuse

See DEFUSE.

diffusible

The word ends in *-ible*, not *-able*.

digest

The verb is pronounced with the stress on the second syllable, the noun with the stress on the first. The noun means a collection of writings in condensed form.

digestible

The word ends in *-ible*, not *-able*.

digraph

See DIPHTHONG.

dike

See DYKE.

dilapidated

This word derives ultimately from the Latin *lapis*, 'stone', and was originally applied, more literally than the equivalent Latin word, to decaying stone structures. It is now quite legitimately used of anything that is falling to pieces: a *dilapidated car/raincoat*.

dilemma

1 Some people prefer to pronounce the first syllable like *dill*, not *die*.

2 This word is derived from the Greek *di-*, 'two'. A **dilemma** is, strictly speaking, a choice between two unsatisfactory alternatives: *the dilemma whether to lower prices or lose sales*. This idea is, perhaps, legitimately extended to include more than two of such alternatives, provided there is a definite number of them and they remain unattractive; but the word should not be used of a predicament or problem involving an open choice, as in *the dilemma where to go for our holidays*.

dimension

Besides its senses in measurement and mathematics, **dimension** is now somewhat OVERUSED to mean no more than 'aspect; factor': *Car ownership will add a new dimension to their lives*.

diminuendo

The plural is **diminuendos**.

diner-out

The plural is **diners-out**.

dinghy, dingy

A **dinghy** is a small boat. **Dingy** means 'discoloured and shabby'.

dint

See DENT.

diphtheria, diphthong

For both words, it is traditionally recommended to pronounce the first syllable 'diff' rather than 'dip', with the *ph* as in *physics* or *photo*, though the pronunciation 'dip' is also correct. Note the spelling *-phth-*.

diphthong, digraph, ligature

A **diphthong** is a gliding vowel sound of two elements within one syllable, such as the 'oy' of *boy*. The word **diphthong** is sometimes used of what is more correctly called a **digraph**, which is a single sound represented by two letters, such as the *ea* of *bread*. Both **diphthong** and **digraph** are also incorrectly applied to the **ligature**, which means a pair of letters such as œ that are printed as a single character. Ligatures are now rarely used in English.

diplomat(ist)

A person in the profession of diplomacy was called a **diplomatist** in older British English, but **diplomat** is now standard everywhere.

direct, directly

1 Both these adverbs can mean 'in a straight line' (*The road runs direct(ly) to London*) or 'without intervention' (*sell oil direct(ly) to the Government*). Only **directly**, not **direct**, can come immediately before an adjective (*directly relevant*), and only **directly** can mean 'in a straight line of descent' (*directly descended from Queen Victoria*) or 'as a close logical cause' (*not directly affected by the changes*) or 'immediately' (*left directly after lunch*). Be careful to avoid ambiguity in the use of **directly**. *I shall communicate with him directly* might mean either that I shall do it at once or that I shall do it without going through his secretary.

2 The use of **directly** to mean 'as soon as' before a clause (*Directly I received the letter I rang him up*) is common in informal British use, but to be avoided in serious writing.

dirigible

The word ends in *-ible*, not *-able*.

dis-

See DE-.

disability

See INABILITY.

disappoint

The word is spelled with one *s* and two *p*'s.

disapprove

One can, correctly, not only **disapprove** *of* something but **disapprove** it. However, *They disapproved his proposal* usually means that they expressed their disapproval by an act of condemnation or rejection, rather than merely feeling it.

disassemble, dissemble

To **disassemble** something is to take it apart: *disassemble a watch*. To **dissemble** something is to conceal it: *dissemble his boredom*.

disassociate

See DISSOCIATE.

disastrous

This should be pronounced with three syllables, not four; it is not spelled *disasterous*.

disbar

See DEBAR.

disburse, disperse

Disburse means 'pay out': *trustees disbursing funds*. **Disperse** means 'scatter': *The crowd dispersed*; *The sun dispersed the mist*.

disc, disk

In most senses, the word is usually spelled **disc** in British English and **disk** in American English. However, British English prefers **disk** in connection with computers (*floppy disk*; *disk pack*), while American

English prefers **disc** for a gramophone record, for a circular steel tool on a plough, and for a technical sense in botany.

discernible, discernable

The more usual spelling is **discernible**, but **discernable** is also correct.

disciplinary

This is usually pronounced with the stress on the third syllable, whose vowel sound is that of *tin*, not of *mine*.

disclose

This means 'make known what is hidden': *demands that politicians disclose the sources of their income.* **Disclose** often suggests that some fact has been hidden for good reason, being perhaps even discreditable, and definitely implies that the fact is true. It is foolish to use the word where no secrecy is involved, and dishonest to use it when making an unproved accusation: *They announced* (not *disclosed*) *that the baby would be christened on Sunday*; *It has been alleged* (not *disclosed*) *that he accepted a bribe.*

discomfit, discomfort

Discomfit means 'frustrate, thwart'. It is a stronger word than the more common word **discomfort**, which means merely 'make uneasy'; but the two words are both often used in the weaker sense.

discontinue

This word is conventionally used to mean 'cease production': *The line has been discontinued.* Elsewhere, it may seem merely a PRETENTIOUS synonym for *stop*.

discotheque

This spelling, rather than **discothèque**, is becoming common, but both are correct.

discover

See INVENT.

discreet, discrete

Discreet means 'prudently silent'; a **discreet** secretary does not reveal the employer's secrets. The related nouns are **discretion** and **discreetness**. **Discrete** means 'individually distinct': *a picture* *consisting of discrete spots of colour.* It is used wrongly here: *During the 1¼ hour service Special Branch officers moved discretely* (it should be *discreetly*) *along the side aisles watching the congregation* (*Daily Telegraph*). The related noun is **discreteness.**

discrepancy, disparity

These both mean 'difference'. A **discrepancy** arises when the difference ought not to exist at all: *a small discrepancy between two sets of figures.* **Disparity** suggests wide inequality: *the great disparity between their ages.*

discriminate

To make a distinction is to **discriminate** *among* or *between* alternatives, or to **discriminate** one thing from another: *The elephant can discriminate between food and money/can discriminate food from money.* To treat one set of people better or worse than another is to **discriminate** *in favour of* or *against* them: *to discriminate in favour of one's friends/against women employees.*

discus

The plural is now usually **discuses** rather than **disci.**

discuss

Discuss needs an object; you **discuss** a topic, not *about* a topic. There is no reason for resisting such constructions as *as was discussed last night*, where *as* functions like an object.

discussable, discussible

Both spellings are correct.

disembowel

Other forms are **disembowelled, disembowelling** in British English, but the second *l* is omitted in American English.

disfavo(u)r

The word is spelled **disfavour** in British English, **disfavor** in American English.

disfranchise, disenfranchise

1 The first form is more usual.

2 Both words are spelled like this in both British and American English; not -*ize*.

disguise

It is spelled like this in both British and American English; not -*ize*. See also GUISE.

disgusted

One is **disgusted** *at* or *with* a person, **disgusted** *at* or *by* an action, quality, or event: *disgusted at* (or *by*) *what happened*.

dishabille

See DESHABILLE.

dishevel

Other forms are **dishevelled, dishevelling** in British English, but the second *l* is usually omitted in American English.

dishono(u)r, dishono(u)rable

These are spelled with the *u* in British English, without it in American English.

disinterested

The first meaning of **disinterested** was 'lacking interest; apathetic', first recorded in the 17th century. Now, after a long period of meaning only 'impartial', the quality one expects of a judge or umpire, **disinterested** is reverting to its earlier meaning. Since this trend arouses the strong disapproval of many people, it is wiser to use **disinterested** only in the sense of 'impartial' or, indeed, where there may be danger of ambiguity, to replace it by *uninterested* or *impartial* according to the sense.

disk

See DISC.

dislike

Although one may *like to do* things, one can only **dislike** things or **dislike** *doing* things: *I dislike listening* (not *to listen*) *to pop music*. When **dislike** is used as a noun, one feels a **dislike** *of* or *for* things, not *to* them.

dismissible

The word ends in *-ible*, not *-able*.

disorganized

This can mean either 'unorganized; not yet organized', or 'having been thrown into disorder' from the verb *disorganize*.

disorient(ate)

Both **disorient** and **disorientate** are correct. The shorter form is chiefly American, the longer is chiefly British.

disparity

See DISCREPANCY.

dispassionate, impassive, impassioned, impassionate

Dispassionate means 'without passion; calm': *a dispassionate decision*. **Impassive** particularly means 'showing no passion': *her impassive countenance*. Both **dispassionate** and **impassive** involve lack of passion, and are sharply in contrast with **impassioned**, which means 'ardent; full of passion': *His wife, an impassioned grower of green vegetables, continued her work in the rear garden* (John le Carré). The rare word **impassionate** is a synonym both of **dispassionate** and of **impassioned**.

dispatch, despatch

The commoner spelling is **dispatch**.

dispel

1 Other forms are **dispelled, dispelling**.

2 Dispel means 'scatter': *dispel the fog*. By extension, the word is often used of abstractions (*dispel a rumour*), but it sounds odd when applied to one indivisible item, as in *dispel an insinuation*. *Parry* or *rebut* might be better there.

dispense with

See DISPOSE OF.

dispersal, dispersion

These both mean the process of dispersing or the condition of being dispersed, but there is some difference of emphasis. In general use,

213

dispersal is chiefly the process: *the dispersal of the mob by the police.*
Dispersion is chiefly the resultant situation: *the widespread dispersion of the family all over the world.* **Dispersion**, but not **dispersal**, has also many technical senses in statistics, chemistry, and optics, where it can mean either process or result.

disperse

See DISBURSE.

displace, replace

These both mean 'take the place of', but **displace** has more emotional colouring: *I don't want to be displaced by that young fool.*

disposable

The word is spelled without the final *e* of *dispose.*

disposal, disposition

Both nouns are related to *dispose.* **Disposal** emphasizes the idea of getting rid of something (*waste disposal*) and corresponds to *dispose of.* **Disposition**, among its other meanings, is the way something is arranged: *the orderly disposition of the books on the shelves.*

dispose of, dispense with

To **dispense with** something is to do without it. To **dispose of** something is to get rid of it. The two come close in meaning, since one tends to discard what is unnecessary. But while **disposing of** something suggests putting it somewhere, **dispensing with** it may mean causing it not to exist: *dispose of old clothes to a jumble sale*; *try to dispense with the need for a damp course.* To **dispose of** a meal is to eat it, to **dispense with** a meal is to eat nothing.

disputable

This is usually pronounced with the stress on the second syllable rather than on the first.

dispute

The verb is always pronounced with the stress on the second syllable, and the noun is usually pronounced in the same way. The pronunciation of the noun with the stress on the first syllable is disliked by some people.

disqualified

See UNQUALIFIED.

disremember

This synonym for *forget* is a regionalism, chiefly in American English.

disrobe

Outside those circles where people wear actual 'robes', this can seem a PRETENTIOUS or FACETIOUS word for *undress*.

dissatisfied, unsatisfied

Both imply a lack of some kind; but **dissatisfied** means 'discontented'. **Unsatisfied** has a wider range of meaning, as when we speak of an *unsatisfied demand* for something. An **unsatisfied** person has not got enough of something, but may not feel actively **dissatisfied** about it.

dissect

The word is spelled with two *s*'s, and means 'separate into pieces', not 'cut in two'.

dissemble

See DISASSEMBLE; DISSIMULATE.

dissension

The word is usually spelled like this, rather than *dissention*.

dissertation, thesis

In most British universities, a **dissertation** is submitted as part of the requirements for a first or master's degree, while a **thesis** is a longer and more elaborate piece of work, such as that required for a doctorate. In American universities, one submits a **thesis** for the master's degree and a **dissertation** for a doctorate.

dissimulate, dissemble, simulate

One **dissimulates** or **dissembles** something that one has or is: *to dissimulate/dissemble his boredom*. One **simulates** something that one has not or is not: *to simulate interest*.

dissociate, disassociate

The first form is more usual, but both are correct.

distaff

This is the staff that holds the thread in hand spinning. It is symbolic of the female, and is reasonably so used in genealogy: *descended from several eminent statesmen on the distaff* (ie the mother's) *side*; but it can become tiresomely FACETIOUS. Do not refer to cooking, sewing, and the like as **distaff** occupations.

distensible

The word ends in *-ible*, not *-able*. It means 'able to be distended'.

distil(l)

This is spelled **distil** in British English, **distill** in American English. In both cases, other forms are **distilled, distilling**.

distinct, distinctive, distinguished

A thing whose mere existence is clearly noticeable is **distinct**: *There's a distinct smell of beer in the room.* Anything whose characteristics set it apart from others of its class is either **distinct** *from* them, or **distinctive**: *Beer has a very distinctive smell, quite distinct from the smell of wine.* Neither word should be confused with **distinguished**, which means 'eminent, outstanding'.

distinguish

See DIFFERENTIATE.

distract

See DETRACT.

distractible

The word ends in *-ible*, not *-able*.

distribute

The usual pronunciation is with the stress on the second syllable rather than on the first.

distributive number

It is normal to use the plural for items or persons that are matched individually with a plural set; for example, *passes* in *All employees must carry their passes with them at all times* (Every employee has one pass), or *The dentist prefers children under ten to be accompanied by their mothers.* But the singular is sometimes necessary to avoid ambiguity: *The form asked them to name their previous employer* (only one employer); *The children should be accompanied by a parent* (Only one parent is required). Idiomatic expressions may require the singular: *I asked them to keep an open mind on the issue*; *We could not put a finger on what went wrong.*

distributor

The word ends in -*or*, not -*er*, whether it means a person or part of an engine.

ditto (*verb*)

Other forms are **dittos, dittoing, dittoed**.

dive, dived, dove

The past tense of **dive** is **dived** in British English. The alternative past tense **dove** (rhyming with *rove*) is becoming commoner in American English, particularly in speech, and cannot be considered nonstandard, but it is still avoided in careful American writing.

divergent

This means more than 'different'. It suggests that a difference between two things is widening, and there is no possibility of bringing them together: *the divergent aims of workers and management*. Educationists and psychologists use **divergent**, appreciatively, of far-ranging imaginative thought processes as distinct from close logical reasoning; but it is unwise to speak of *divergent thinking* in this technical sense to people who think the word means 'uncooperative' or 'eccentric'.

diverse, divers

Diverse means 'of different kinds, unlike': *hold diverse opinions on the matter*. The rather archaic or FACETIOUS word **divers** means 'sundry, several': *We visited divers bars*.

divisible

The word ends in -*ible*, not -*able*.

divorcee, divorcé(e)

A **divorcee** is a divorced person of either sex. If the word is spelled with an accent in the French manner, it is consistent also to preserve the French distinction between **divorcé**, for a man, and **divorcée**, for a woman.

217

divulge

This means 'make known what is hidden', and should not be used as a mere synonym for *say* or *announce*. Compare DISCLOSE.

djin, djinn

See JINN.

do

In British English **do, doing**, and **done** are often used to avoid the repetition of a verb in a complex verb phrase. In formal writing, they should be omitted here: *We never go there now, but we used to (do)*; *I don't know whether I'll come, but I might (do)*; *John joined the union, and Ann may have (done), too*; *'Are you working?' 'I was (doing), but I'll stop now'*. For *do so*, see SO (4).

dock

In British English a **dock** is an enclosed area of water in a port; in American English **dock** is a synonym of *wharf* or *pier*. It is curious that though in American use you might jump *off* a **dock**, in British use you jump *into* one.

doctor

1 The word ends in *-or*, not *-er*.

2 In Britain, licensed physicians are called **doctor** whether or not they hold a doctorate in medicine, but qualified surgeons usually call themselves *Mr* or a female equivalent. In the USA, dentists and vets are called **doctor** as well as physicians and surgeons. The habitual use of the title **doctor** by the holder of a PhD, though technically justified, may be thought ostentatious outside academic circles, and sometimes leads to confusion with medical **doctors**.

doctrinal

In British English, this is pronounced with the stress on the second syllable, which sounds like *try*. In American English, it is pronounced with the stress on the first syllable, like *doctrine*.

dodo

The plural is either **dodos** or **dodoes**.

doff, don

These are used for ceremonial occasions: *They doffed their mortarboards when the Chancellor entered*. But otherwise they can sound rather PRETENTIOUS or FACETIOUS words for 'take off', 'put on'.

dogged

This is pronounced with two syllables as an adjective meaning 'determined': *work with dogged tenacity*. It is pronounced with one syllable as the past tense or participle of the verb *dog*: *He dogged their footsteps*.

dolce far niente, dolce vita

These Italian phrases mean, respectively, 'pleasant carefree idleness' and 'lazy life of self-indulgence'. They are both CLICHÉS.

doll's house, dollhouse

The first is British English, the second American, for a child's toy house.

dolo(u)r, dolorous

The noun is spelled **dolour** in British English, **dolor** in American English; but the related adjective is always **dolorous**.

Domesday, doomsday

Both are pronounced 'dooms'. The first occurs in the title of William I's *Domesday Book*, the second means 'judgment day'.

domicile

The last syllable is pronounced 'sile' in British English, 'sile' or 's'l' in American English.

dominate, domineer

They both mean 'exercise control'; but **dominate** is a neutral word for 'rule, command', while **domineer** is always derogatory, meaning 'tyrannize'.

domino

The plural is either **dominoes** or **dominos**.

don

See DOFF.

donate

This usually means 'give for a public cause' (*donate a site for a car park*), and is a perfectly good word in such contexts. Otherwise, prefer *give*.

Don Juan, Don Quixote

It is fashionable to attempt the Spanish pronunciation of such names as these. **Juan** becomes not 'JEW-en' but 'hoo-AHN', **Quixote** not 'QUIX-oat' but 'ki-HOTE-y'. The same trend may be noticed in the pronunciation of FOREIGN PLACENAMES.

donor

The word ends in *-or*, not *-er*, in both British and American English.

don't

The use of **don't** for *does not* was very common in educated informal English until well into the 20th century: *I only hope that this letter will reach you, though your loss will not be very great if it don't* (Aldous Huxley). It is now regarded as nonstandard in British English, though it still has some currency in educated American speech, particularly that of the Midland and South Atlantic seaboard areas. It should always be avoided in serious writing.

doomsday

See DOMESDAY.

dope

This is standard English for antiknock, for a cellulose varnish, or for a drug illegally administered to racehorses and greyhounds. It is somewhat informal for narcotic or illegal drugs, and perhaps more so for the senses 'fool' (*Open it, you dope!*) and 'information' (*all the dope about how to operate it*).

double

This is used in British but not in American English for saying letters and telephone numbers. The British version of 9044 is *nine-oh-double four*, the American is *nine-zero-four-four*.

double-barrel(l)ed

This is spelled with two *l*'s in British English, one in American English.

double entendre

This has been accepted since the 17th century as the English form of the phrase. In modern French the expression is in fact *double entente*, but there seems no reason to change back. It means a word or phrase with two meanings, one of them usually rather indecent. See FOREIGN PHRASES.

double negative

In some languages two or more negatives may be used in the same construction to emphasize the negation. This usage was once permissible in English, and is still common in uneducated speech, where *I didn't say nothing* is unambiguously identical with the educated *I didn't say anything* or *I said nothing*. The double or multiple negative is incorrect in educated English when it is used for emphasis. A somewhat less conspicuous error occurs after introductory negative expressions such as *It wouldn't surprise me if* or *I shouldn't wonder if*. The double negative in the sentence *I shouldn't be surprised if he didn't accept the offer* is wrong if the intended meaning is 'I shouldn't be surprised if he accepted the offer' rather than 'I shouldn't be surprised if he refused the offer'. Other examples of the double negative occur in *I hardly said nothing*, where *hardly* is a negative adverb, and in *Under no circumstances will I not permit smoking in private offices*, where *under no circumstances* contains a negative. Correct to *I hardly said anything* and *Under no circumstances will I permit* . . . The writer of the following sentence conveyed precisely the opposite of the obviously intended meaning through using the negative noun *denials* in association with *not*: *Although a majority of MPs and Ministers were ready to accept official denials that the Queen was not personally involved in any attempt to discredit the Prime Minister, they demanded a high-level inquiry to identify the culprit* (*Daily Telegraph*). Clearly, the spokesman denied that the Queen was personally involved, rather than that she was not personally involved.

The double negative is criticized on the grounds that logically two negatives make a positive. It is still criticized when there are three negatives, which according to the logical argument should make it negative again: *I didn't never say nothing* (correct to *I didn't ever say anything* or *I never said anything*). Where two negatives do combine to express a positive, the double negation is legitimate in educated English: *a not unhappy choice* (a quite happy choice); *not infrequently* (quite frequently); *You can't not admire her pluck* (You have to admire her pluck); *None of us have no friends* (All of us have some friends). In the first two examples, a negative word is negated by *not*; the effect of *not* is to reduce the force of the negative and produce a weak positive. The last two examples convey a strong positive. See also NEGATION.

doublespeak

Doublespeak is the dishonest use of public language, particularly by politicians or bureaucrats. It is a misuse of language that distorts words from their accepted meanings to persuade people to acquiesce in policies that they might otherwise reject. It is public language intended to conceal or mislead. It works by indirection and understatement. Expressions like *peace-loving*, *free* (in *the free world*, *free trade unions*), *progress*, *democratic* often lose specific meanings; they become merely generalized favourable terms. The contrary has happened to expressions like *imperialist*, *racist*, and *totalitarian*. As a result, one needs to define such expressions with precision before using them. Public institutions mitigate the harshness of *dismissal* by substituting the *imposition of compulsory early retirement*. It is less abhorrent to drop a *nuclear device* than a *nuclear bomb*; *the inner city* can wait longer for clearance than *slums*; *group self-determination* seems praiseworthy, though it has been a substitute for *apartheid*. See also EUPHEMISM.

doubling

1 Words of one syllable that end in one consonant preceded by only one vowel, double the consonant when adding an ending that begins with a vowel. Thus, *run, runner*; *rob, robbing*; *drop, dropped*; but *want, wanted* (two consonants); *like, liked* (ends with a vowel); *wait, waited* (two vowels); *ship, shipment* (the ending does not begin with a vowel). Note that *y* does not count as a consonant for this purpose: *stay, staying*. *Wool* makes *woollen, woolly* in British English but can also make *woolen, wooly* in American English.

2 Words of more than one syllable behave in the same way if the word is accented on the last syllable. Thus, *begin, beginner*; *refer, referring*; *commit, committed*; *permit, permitting*; *annul, annulled*; but *evict, evicted* (two consonants); *rebuke, rebuked* (ends with a vowel); *remain, remained* (two vowels); *regret, regretful* (the ending does not begin with a vowel); *limit, limited* (accent not on the last syllable). Note that *leapfrog* makes *leapfrogged* in both British and American English, while *worship* makes *worshipped* and *kidnap* makes *kidnapped* in British English but they can also make *worshiped* and *kidnaped* in American English. Words ending in -*c* may take -*ck*: *picnic(ker)*, *panic(ked)*.

3 In American English, words of more than one syllable that end in -*l* are usually treated as in (2) above. In British English, such words always double the -*l* even if the accent does not fall on the last syllable. Thus:

	British English (always)	**American English** (chiefly)
cancel	cancelled	canceled
cruel	crueller	crueler
duel	duelling	dueling
jewel	jeweller	jeweler
label	labelled	labeled
marvel	marvellous	marvelous
quarrel	quarrelled	quarreled
travel	travelling	traveling

But note that *instal(l)* (British and American English) makes *instalment* (British), but *installment* (American); *appalling* is formed from *appal* (British) and *appall* (American); and it is *fulfil, fulfilling, fulfilment* in British English but chiefly *fulfill, fulfilling, fulfillment* in American English. See also DISTIL(L); INSTIL(L).

doubt, doubtful

In positive sentences **doubt** (both verb and noun) and **doubtful** are correctly followed by *whether* or, less formally, by *if*. Such sentences assert that there is some uncertainty: *I doubt whether he'll come*; *There's some doubt/It's doubtful whether he'll come*. In negative sentences, which deny that there is any uncertainty, **doubt** is followed by *that* or *but that*: *I don't doubt (but) that he'll come*; *There's no doubt (but) that he'll come*. In American use, and increasingly in British, **doubt** *that* is also used in positive sentences, meaning 'think it unlikely'. *I doubt that he'll come* means 'I think he will not come'. In questions, **doubt** *that* and **doubt** *whether* are both available, according to the degree of likelihood. *Do you doubt that he's honest?* suggests greater confidence in his honesty, on the part of the speaker, than *Do you doubt whether he's honest?*

doubtless

This is an adverb, not an adjective: *Doubtless she forgot*. Do not say **doubtlessly**.

dour

This Scottish word usually rhymes with *tour*, not with *hour*. It means 'sullen'.

douse, dowse

Douse means 'drench' or 'extinguish': *douse the candle*. To **dowse** is

223

to search for water or minerals with a divining rod, but **dowse** is sometimes used as a spelling of **douse.** See DOWSE.

dove (*verb*)

See DIVE.

dove (*noun*)

See PIGEON.

dowel (*verb*)

Other forms are **dowelled, dowelling** in British English, but the second *l* can be omitted in American English.

dower, dowry

In older legal use, a **dower** was a widow's life interest in her deceased husband's property. A **dowry** is property brought by a woman to her husband in marriage.

downplay

This is journalese for 'de-emphasize': *The strike was downplayed in the national press.* Prefer *play down*.

down to

See UP (2).

downward(s)

Before a noun, use **downward**: *a downward glance.* After a verb, use the form with *s* in British English (*to look downwards*) and the one without an *s* in American English.

dowse, divine

One **dowses** *for* (ie searches for) hidden water or minerals with a divining rod. To **dowse** them or **divine** them is actually to find them by this means. See also DOUSE.

drachma, drachm, dram

The **drachma** is the Greek monetary unit. A **drachm** and a **dram** are small units of weight (there is also a *fluid* **drachm**), but **dram** is now chiefly used for a tot of spirits.

draft, draught

In British English, a preliminary version of anything is a **draft**, and someone **drafts** it: *a draft treaty*. If it is a legal document, the person who drafts it is a **draftsman**, but a preliminary sketch for a machine or structure is drawn by a **draughtsman.** A money order is a **draft**. One drinks a **draught** of **draught** beer, and drives **draught** horses. A current of air is a **draught**. The game is called **draughts**.

In American English, all these words are spelled **draft**, but the game is called *checkers*.

dragoman, dragoon

1 The correct plural of **dragoman** is **dragomans**, but **dragomen** is common.

2 A **dragoman** is an interpreter in the Near East. A **dragoon** is a member of a military unit formerly composed of mounted infantrymen with carbines.

dram

See DRACHMA.

drawer

When it means 'person who draws something', this is pronounced with two syllables. When it is part of a chest of drawers, or when **drawers** means 'pants', it is pronounced like *draw(s)*.

drawing

Some speakers dislike the pronunciation 'draw-ring'.

drawing room

See SITTING ROOM.

dream

Dreamed and **dreamt** are equally common in British English for the past tense and participle, but **dreamed** is the usual American form.

drier, dryer

Prefer **drier** for 'more dry', **dryer** for a drying device: *a hair dryer*. But both spellings are available for both.

drily, dryly

Both spellings are available. **Dryly** is strongly favoured in American English.

drink (*verb*)

The past tense is **drank**: *He drank* (not *drunk*) *it*. The participle is **drunk**: *She has drunk* (not *drank*) *it*. See also DRUNK(EN).

drivel (*verb*)

Other forms are **drivelled, drivelling** in British English, but the second *l* is usually omitted in American English.

drought, drouth

Drought is the main international form of this word for dry weather. The form **drouth** survives in Scottish, Irish, and American English, but is otherwise archaic and is less suitable in formal writing.

drown

1 The past tense and participle are **drowned**. **Drownded** is nonstandard.

2 An accident by drowning may be described as either *He drowned* or *He was drowned*. The latter, however, does not exclude the possibility that someone drowned him. Beware of misunderstanding here.

drunk(en)

Drunk is used chiefly after a verb: *She got drunk*. **Drunken** is used chiefly before a noun and can apply both to animate beings and to actions: *the drunken sailor*; *drunken merriment*. Since **drunken**, not **drunk**, is the word for habitual intoxication, **drunken** is sometimes used after a verb to make that distinction: *The sailors were both drunken and lecherous*. There is no equivalent reason for putting **drunk** before a noun, but people sometimes do: *a pub full of drunk/ drunken football fans*.

dryer

See DRIER.

dryly

See DRILY.

du

See D'.

dual, duel

Dual means double: *dual carriageway*; *dual citizenship*. A **duel** is a fight between two people to settle a quarrel.

dub

Other forms are **dubbed, dubbing**. It can mean 'confer a title on', or 'provide a film with a soundtrack'.

duel

1 See DUAL.

2 Other forms of the verb **duel** are **duelled, duelling** in British English, but the second *l* is usually omitted in American English.

due to

Due is an adjective: *He got his due reward*. In consequence, when it is followed by *to* it should, strictly speaking, be attached to a noun; something is **due** *to* something else. The phrase is now commonly used like *because of* or *owing to*, either at the beginning of a sentence or after an ordinary verb: *Due to the extreme cold, we were unable to plant the trees*; *We were delayed due to the fog*. This usage now seems thoroughly established, and is adopted by many educated speakers and writers: *Due to inability to market their grain, prairie farmers have been faced for some time with a serious shortage* (Queen Elizabeth II, Speech from the Throne). It still, however, arouses strong disapproval, and should be avoided by careful writers. Confine your use of **due to** to a position after linking verbs such as *be* or *seem*, or directly after a noun: *The delay was due to the fog*; *Rheumatism due to bad housing was very common*. If in doubt about the legitimacy of **due to**, use *because of* or *owing to*, which are always safe.

due to the fact that

This is a VERBOSE way of saying 'because'.

dul(l)ness

Both spellings exist, but **dullness** with two *l*'s follows the analogy of **smallness**, **illness**, and should be preferred.

duly, dully

Duly means 'in a due way; properly'. **Dully** means 'in a dull way'.

dumb

Since **dumb** can mean 'stupid', it is more polite to refer to people who cannot speak as *mute*.

dumbfound, dumfound

Both spellings are correct, but the first is rather more usual.

duodecimo

The plural is **duodecimos**. It is a size of book.

duplication, duplicity

Duplication is the act of copying or repeating something. **Duplicity** is malicious deception.

duplicator

The word ends in -*or*, not -*er*.

durance, duress

Durance is 'confinement', as in the CLICHÉ *in durance vile*. **Duress** is chiefly 'illegal coercion': *acted under duress*.

Durex (*trademark*)

In Australia this is the trademark of a sticky tape, in Britain of a contraceptive. Both parties should be aware of the misunderstandings that may arise.

during

During the course of is VERBOSE, and can be replaced by **during** alone. The same is true of *during such time as* and *during the time that*, which can be replaced by *while* or *so long as*.

duty

See TAX.

duvet

See QUILT.

dwarf

Prefer **dwarfs** to **dwarves** for the plural; or at any rate confine **dwarves** to the sense of small legendary men, as in *Snow White and the Seven Dwarves*.

dwell

This is rather PRETENTIOUS in the sense 'live as a resident', but normal in the sense 'keep one's attention on': *dwell on her grievances*.

dyeing, dying

Dyeing comes from the verb **dye**, 'give colour to'; **dying** comes from **die**, 'stop living'.

dyke, dike

Both spellings are correct for both noun and verb. **Dyke** may be preferred as a derogatory word for 'lesbian'.

dynamo

The plural is **dynamos**.

dynasty

The first syllable is usually pronounced like *din* in British English, but like *die* in American English.

dyslexic

This, not **dyslectic**, is the adjective from the noun **dyslexia**, 'impaired reading ability'.

Ee

There is often some uncertainty over the spelling of words formed from other words ending with a silent *e*; does *sale* make *salable* or *saleable*?

The best answer in this case is 'Either', and the best general advice one can give, to which there are unfortunately many exceptions, is as follows:

Words that end with a silent *e* drop the *e* when adding an ending that begins with a vowel: *debate, debatable*; *write, writing*; *white, whitish*; *continue, continuous*. The chief exception to this rule is that words ending in *ce, ge* often retain their *e* so as not to affect the sound of the *c* or *g*: *enforce, enforceable* (but *forcing* and *forcible*); *advantage, advantageous*; *age, ageing* or *aging* (but *raging, charging*). *Singeing, swingeing*, and *tingeing* (also *tinging*) retain the *e* which is dropped from other verbs ending in *nge* (*hinging, sponging, lunging*). Some other exceptions are *acreage, mileage, hieing, gluey*.

Words that end with a silent *e* usually retain the *e* when adding an ending that begins with a consonant: *use, useful*; *home, homeless*; *safe, safely*; *move, movement*. Some exceptions here are *truly, duly, wholly, argument, ninth*. A further group of words ending with *dge* can either drop or retain their *e*: *abridg(e)ment*; *acknowledg(e)ment*; *judg(e)ment*. There is a general tendency, in such debatable cases, to retain in British English some *e*'s that are usually dropped in American English.

e-

See AE-

each

1 When **each** is the subject of a sentence it should correctly, in formal writing, be followed by a singular verb and pronoun: *Each has done his best*. Plural pronouns (and, more controversially, plural verbs) are often used, however, in educated speech, in cases where **each** is followed by *of* and a plural noun, and particularly where one wishes to avoid the awkward *he or she*: *Each of the members must clean their own equipment*. When **each** follows a plural subject, the following verb and pronoun are correctly plural: *They each clean their own equipment*. See NUMBER AGREEMENT (4; 7).

2 *Each and every*, as in *each and every time they enter*, is VERBOSE. Use either **each** or *every*.

each other

1 When **each** and **other** form an undivided sequence, the genitive is **each other's**: *They borrow each other's shirts*.

2 Do not use **each other** as the subject of a verb: *They each know what the other is thinking*, not *They know what each other is thinking*.

3 There is no basis for the superstition that **each other** should refer to two people or things, and **one another** to more than two.

early on

This expression, originally a Briticism, is now established in American as well as British English: *earlier on in the experiment*. There can be no objection to it except in the most formal writing, where it is better to omit *on*.

earth, Earth

When **earth** means, not soil but the planet we live on, it is often though not always capitalized. It is normal to treat **Earth**, with or without *the*, as the name of one planet among others, on the analogy of *Mars*, *Venus*, and so on.

earthly, earthy, earthen

Earthly means 'of the world' (*earthly paradise*) as opposed to 'heavenly'. **Earthy** means either 'like earth' (*an earthy taste*) or 'crude, coarse' (*earthy jokes*). **Earthen** means 'made of earth' (*earthen floor*) or 'made of baked clay' (*earthen pots*).

east, eastern

See NORTH.

eastward

Before a noun, use **eastward**: *an eastward flight*. After a verb, use the form with an *s* in British English (*driving eastwards*) and the one without an *s* in American English.

easy, easily

Easy as an adverb is used only in certain fixed phrases: *Easy does it*; *Easy come, easy go*; *Take it easy*; *Go easy with the sugar*; *Easier said than done*. It cannot replace **easily**, the usual adverb: *The door opens easily*.

eat

See ATE.

eatable, edible

Eatable means 'reasonably pleasant to eat; not spoiled': *The stew was* *so salty it was scarcely eatable.* **Edible** can mean this too, but it also means 'capable of being treated as food; not poisonous': *edible fungi.*

echelon

This originally meant a steplike arrangement of ships, troops, etc: *planes flying in echelon.* The word is now freely used to mean 'level, grade': *the highest echelons of the Civil Service.* There seems no reason to object to this extension of meaning.

echo

The plural is **echoes.**

éclair, éclat, élan

These are all spelled with the accent. An **éclair** is a little cake: *chocolate éclairs.* **Éclat** is ostentatious brilliance: *pass the test with éclat.* **Élan** is zest and vigour: *dance with élan.*

eclectic

This means 'choosing or chosen from various sources'; it does not mean 'fastidious'. A person with an **eclectic** taste in music enjoys many, often unusual, sorts of music but not necessarily the best music.

ecology

This properly means 'the balanced relationship between living organisms and their environment'. With the increase of concern about pollution and the protection of our surroundings, **ecology** has come to be used loosely as a synonym for *environment.* You can *damage the environment*, but *upset the ecology* (ie disturb the balance).

economic(al)

1 The first syllable is pronounced either 'e' or 'ee'.

2 Economic is related to **economics**, the science of the production, distribution, and consumption of goods and services: *an economic crisis.* It can also mean 'reasonably profitable': *economic deposits of coal.* **Economical** means 'thrifty': *an economical housekeeper/meal.*

ecstasy

The word is spelled like this, not *extasy* or *ecstacy.*

-ection

Some words that end in **-ection**, such as *connection, deflection,* *inflection*, *reflection*, have the alternative British spellings *connexion*, *deflexion*, etc; but the **-ection** endings are commoner, and are the only American form.

ecumenical

This is the usual spelling in both British and American English, rather than **oecumenical.**

-èd

One of the uses of the ending **-ed** is to form adjectives such as *walled* or *polo-necked*. This ending does not normally constitute a syllable on its own, except after the sounds 't' and 'd' (*pointed*; *simple-minded*) and in a few other cases such as *wretched* and *ragged*.

Some such words, however, can have an extra syllable in certain circumstances. *Aged* has one syllable when it means 'fully developed' (*aged wine*) and two when it means 'old and infirm' (*aged man*); *beloved* has two syllables in such situations as *He was greatly beloved*, but three when it stands before a noun or alone (*my beloved (one)*); *learned* has one syllable when it means 'acquired by learning' (*learned behaviour*) and two when it means 'erudite' (*learned man*); and any **-ed** ending can be pronounced as an extra syllable in poetry if the metre makes it necessary. Poets sometimes write **-èd** with the accent to show what is intended, but the device is not common elsewhere; one must simply check the pronunciation in a dictionary.

edema

See OEDEMA.

edible

See EATABLE.

edifice

The chief use of this word for 'structure' is now abstract: *the keystone which holds together the social edifice* (R H Tawney). In literal use, **edifice** may sound a rather PRETENTIOUS or FACETIOUS word for *building*.

editress

Call her an *editor*. See FEMININE FORMS.

-ee

In its basic use, **-ee** is attached to a verb to mean someone who undergoes the action of that verb: *trainee*; *addressee*; *examinee*. There has been some criticism of new words such as *amputee* formed on this pattern, and still more of **-ee** words that mean someone who behaves in a particular way. Although *refugee* and *absentee* are well enough established, you may perhaps dislike *retiree* for a person who retires, and feel that an *escapee* or *attendee* would be better called an *escaper* or *attender*. Use such words with caution.

e'er, ere

These two words occur in old-fashioned poetic language and may be confused. Both are pronounced like *air*. **E'er** means 'ever' and **ere** means 'before'.

effect

See AFFECT.

effective, effectual, efficient, efficacious

These all apply to what has an effect. **Effective** emphasizes the high degree of the effect: *take effective measures*; *an effective speech/speaker*. **Effectual** applies only to the action, not to the doer, and suggests that it was completely successful: *His remark put an effectual end to the conversation.* (A person, however, can be *ineffectual*.) **Efficient** describes people or measures that achieve results with the least fuss and the best use of resources: *an efficient manager/machine*. **Efficacious** applies only to things and usually to medicines, and stresses the power to achieve a result: *an efficacious remedy against spots*.

effete

Originally this meant 'worn out, exhausted', but in modern use it means 'decadent, effeminate': *effete civilizations/young men*. It is not usually used of women.

effluvium

The plural of this word meaning 'offensive smell' is either **effluvia** or **effluviums. Effluvia** is often treated as singular (*a noxious effluvia*), but not by good writers.

effrontery

See AFFRONT.

e.g., i.e.

They are not synonyms: **e.g** stands for the Latin *exempli gratia* and means 'for example'; **i.e.** stands for the Latin *id est*, 'that is'. Compare: *a portrait, e.g. the Mona Lisa*; *a portrait, i.e. a representation of a person*. In print, the full stops are sometimes omitted, as in this book.

egis

See AE-.

ego

The plural is **egos.**

egoist, egotist

There is considerable blurring of sense between these two words. On the whole, a boastful self-important person is an **egotist**, while the **egoist** is someone who believes that self-interest is the best goal of all action.

egress

This has a technical meaning in astronomy. It is otherwise a very formal and rather PRETENTIOUS word for 'going out' or 'exit'.

eiderdown

The word is spelled *ei-*, not *ie-*. See also QUILT.

either, neither

1 As a subject, **either** and **neither** are correctly followed by a singular verb and pronoun: *Here are two books*; *either is perfectly suitable*. Plural verbs and pronouns are often used with *neither* in educated speech though not in formal writing, in cases where a plural noun follows: *Neither of the books are really suitable*. The plurals are used even in educated writing when **either** . . . *or* or **neither** . . . *nor* is followed by a plural noun next to the verb: *Either my father or my brothers are coming*. The same principle holds when there is a change of grammatical 'person' between the two items; we say *Neither you nor he has answered* but *Neither he nor you have answered*. Plural verbs and pronouns are also used informally when one wishes to avoid the awkward *he or she*: *If either David or Janet come, they will want a drink*. See NUMBER AGREEMENT (7), PERSON AGREEMENT.

2 Either and **neither** should stand next to the part of the sentence they concern. Compare: *Either you must improve your work or you will be dismissed* (ie two clauses); *You must improve either your work or your appearance* (ie two nouns).

3 There is nothing wrong with using **either** and **neither** as adjectives for more than two: *Come on either Friday, Saturday, or Sunday.* When they are used as pronouns, they are replaced by *any* and *none* for more than two: *either/neither of the twins*; *any/none of the triplets.*

4 Either may correctly be used for *each*: *On either side the river lie Long fields of barley and of rye* (Tennyson); but this use should be avoided where there is danger of confusion with the other sense of **either**. A vein that runs *on either side of the heart* might be taken to run sometimes on one side and sometimes on the other, so use *each* here.

ejector

The word ends in *-or*, not *-er*.

eke out

To **eke out** a supply of something is to make it go further by supplementing it: *He eked out his income by getting a second job.* The expression also means 'get (a living) with difficulty': *He eked out a precarious existence by selling garden produce.* This second sense is now well established.

élan

See ÉCLAIR.

elder, older

Elder and **eldest** are used chiefly of people, and then almost exclusively of family relationships (apart from the special phrase *elder statesman*, meaning an eminent retired one). It is more formally correct to speak of *my elder brother, his eldest sister* than to use **older** and **oldest** there. Where a close group rather than a family is involved, **older** and **oldest** are common alternatives: *the eldest/oldest partner.* **Elder** and **eldest** are used of things only in the rather rare sense of 'former': *He writes in an elder tradition.* **Older** and **oldest** are used of things as well as of people, and **older**, but not **elder**, can be used with *than*: *She's older* (not *elder*) *than I am.*

elector

The word ends in *-or*, not *-er*.

electric(al), electronic

Systems that use electricity as a direct source of power are **electric**: *an electric plug/clock.* **Electrical** expresses a rather less direct and more general connection with electricity: *electrical appliances*; *an electrical engineer*; *electrical fault in the system*. **Electronic** refers to systems whereby one electric current controls another by means of an intervening device such as a transistor or thermionic valve: *electronic music*. It may mean 'computerized': *an electronic office*.

elegant variation

Elegant variation is an overingenious variation of expressions to avoid repetition of the same words. It may mislead readers into thinking that the expressions refer to different things, and it can sound pompous or facetious: *The debate intensified when a draft of the **treaty** was produced, but the few issues blocking the **pact** were soon resolved* (*treaty* and *pact* refer to the same document; repeat *treaty* to avoid any misunderstanding); *The man who had attempted to assassinate **the pope** was forgiven by **the pontiff** during a visit to the prison by **the Holy Father*** (replace *the pontiff* by *him* and *a visit* by *his visit* and omit *by the Holy Father*; better still, reword in the active: *During his visit to the prison, the pope met the man who had attempted to assassinate him, and forgave him*). Unnecessary repetition is a stylistic fault; good writers use pronouns and other means of substitution instead. See REPETITION OF SOUNDS AND WORDS.

elegy, eulogy

An **elegy** is a poem lamenting someone's death. A **eulogy** is a formal speech in praise of someone.

elemental, elementary

Both these words can mean 'being an element' (*elemental/elementary sulphur*) and both, in consequence, convey a general sense of primary simplicity; but **elemental** refers chiefly to the simplicity of the great forces of physical nature, and **elementary** to the simplicity of first principles: *the elemental rage of a stormy sea*; *elementary arithmetic*.

elevator

The word ends in *-or*, not *-er*.

elicit, illicit

These two words have the same pronunciation, but no connection in meaning. To **elicit** something is to evoke or bring it out: *to elicit the facts from the children*. **Illicit** means 'unsanctioned, illegal': *illicit love*; *an illicit still*.

eligible, illegible

Eligible means 'qualified, worthy': *eligible for promotion.* **Illegible** means 'undecipherable': *illegible handwriting.*

eliminate

One can **eliminate** only what is there already; the word is not a synonym for *prevent.* Compare: *eliminate terrorism*; *prevent future acts of terrorism.* **Eliminate** is a rather formal and sometimes PRETENTIOUS way of saying 'get rid of' or 'do away with', or sometimes a EUPHEMISM for *kill.*

élite

This can be spelled with or without the accent; the accented form is more favoured in British than in American English. It means a small powerful superior group of people.

ellipsis

Ellipsis is the omission of words that we can readily supply to complete the meaning of the sentence. Some kinds of ellipsis are likely to be found only in casual speech or its representation in writing: (I) *Told you we'd be late*; (Do you) *Know anybody here?*; (It's a) *Pity you didn't see her.* Other kinds are typical of certain restricted uses of writing, for example notices or headlines: *Children* (are) *not admitted*; (The) *STRIKE ENDS.* Many kinds of ellipsis, however, are common in both speech and writing: *I cannot explain the discrepancy, but I am sure that my accountant will be able to* (explain the discrepancy).

Ellipsis is useful in reducing repetition. It can also contribute to a pleasing rhythm in parallel constructions, and can sharpen contrast: *I am responsible for efficient production and you* (are responsible) *for increased sales*; *Norma is flying to Rome this week and* (she is flying) *to Lisbon next week.*

Mistakes, however, can arise in the handling of ellipsis. Some elliptical sentences can simultaneously be interpreted in more than one way. If there is a doubt about the interpretation, it is better to give the full form: *She agreed to return the documents that she had deposited in a bank, but she would not say* **which** (documents *or* bank). Or a sentence can be interpreted as either elliptical or not: *We sell electronic clocks and* (? electronic) *typewriters.* If there is a possibility of misinterpretation, rewrite to obtain the intended interpretation; for example: *We sell electronic clocks and electronic typewriters* or *We sell typewriters and electronic clocks.*

Ellipsis in the verb can cause problems. It is often possible to omit the last part of the verb phrase and perhaps other words as well: *The letters could have been* **forged** *but they weren't* (weren't forged); *My daughter* **drives** *a car, but I can't* (can't drive one); *The other candidates are* **questioning** *the impartiality of the tellers but I don't intend to* (I don't intend to question it). One problem occurs when the understood verb has a form different from that of the verb that is present later in the sentence. It is perfectly correct to write: *The restaurant can* (can improve) *and must* **improve** *the quality of its food*, where the forms are identical. It is also correct to write: *The Chinese restaurant is* **improving** *the quality of its food, but the French restaurant can't* (can't improve the quality of its food), where the understood verb and direct object come later. But is is wrong to write: *The French restaurant won't* (correct to *won't improve*) *and the Chinese restaurant is* **improving** *the quality of its food*; *All future editions will or have* **been amended** (correct to *will be amended or have been amended*) *by deleting the objectionable reference.*

The passive is more restricted than the active. You may omit an understood passive as long as the other verb is also passive: *The change in his manner was* **noticed** *by most of his friends, but may not have been by his family* (may not have been noticed). But even if the forms of the two verbs are identical, they must be repeated in full if the understood verb alone is passive: *Most of his friends* **noticed** *the change in his manner, but it may not have been by his family* (correct to the passive *may not have been noticed* because the previous *noticed* is active).

Comparisons may become faulty because an essential part of the comparison is omitted: *In the first six months after bereavement the death rate of widowers is higher than other men* (higher than the death rate of other men, higher than that of other men) *of the same age and social class*; *I prefer watching television to the cinema* (prefer watching television to going to the cinema, or prefer television to the cinema); *Unlike Greece, British summers* (Unlike Greek summers, British summers) *are sometimes wet and chilly*; *The novels of Mark Twain are as good or better than* (as good as or better than) *those of Charles Dickens.*

If you omit a preposition, it must be identical with one that is present: *My clients are aware and unhappy* **with** (aware **of** and unhappy **with**) *the public statements that your clients have issued*; *You can hardly hope, let alone insist* **on** (hope **for**, let alone insist **on**), *a detailed account.*

In a series of three or more linked units, if you omit something in the second unit you must also omit it in all the subsequent units: *The office is open* **on** *Monday, Wednesday, and* **on** *Friday* (on Monday, Wednesday, and Friday, or on Monday, on Wednesday, and on Friday); *I can produce* **my** *passport,* **my** *birth certificate, and driver's* *licence* (my passport, my birth certificate, and my driver's licence, or my passport, birth certificate, and driver's licence).

See also CASE, GRAMMATICAL (4); NEGATION (3).

else

1 The usual possessive forms of *anybody* **else**, *someone* **else**, etc are *anybody* **else's**, *someone* **else's**, not *anybody's*/*someone's* **else**: *Nobody else's house is big enough*. In the case of *who* **else**, the usual form is *who* **else's**, which is preferable to *whose* **else**.

2 Else is correctly followed by *than* or *but* or *except*: *Where else than/but/except in France could this happen?*

elude

See ALLUDE.

elusive, illusive, illusory

Elusive means 'hard to catch, grasp, or identify': *an elusive hare/concept/aroma*. **Illusive**, or more usually **illusory**, means 'deceptive, unreal' and applies particularly to what turns out to be unsatisfactory when attained: *illusory hopes/success*.

embargo

The plural is **embargoes**.

embarrass

The word is spelled with two *r*'s and two *s*'s.

embed

Other forms are **embedded, embedding**.

embryo

The plural is **embryos**.

emend

See AMEND.

emergence, emergency

Emergence is the act of emerging: *the emergence of Venus from the waves*. An **emergency** is an unforeseen crisis.

emigrant, immigrant, migrant

An **emigrant** *emigrates* from his or her country, and the practice is *emigration*: *a ship full of emigrants leaving Liverpool.* An **immigrant,** who may be the same person at a later stage of the journey, *immigrates* into another country, and the practice is *immigration*: *Immigration Control at the airport.* **Migrants** are people (or creatures) that *migrate* between countries, and the practice is *migration*: *migrant workers*; *the spring migration of the wild ducks.* An **immigrant** into Australia may be called a **migrant** in Australian English.

émigré

The first accent is occasionally omitted, but not the second. It means a political refugee.

eminent, imminent, immanent

These three words sound somewhat alike, but have no connection in meaning. **Eminent** means 'outstanding, prominent': *an eminent lawyer.* **Imminent** means 'threatening, about to happen': *The collapse of the building seemed imminent.* The rarer word **immanent** means 'existing within, inherent'. Theologians use **immanent** with reference to God, meaning that he is present everywhere in the universe.

emotional, emotive

These can both mean 'of the emotions': *an emotional/emotive disorder*; or 'arousing emotion': *Capital punishment is an emotive/emotional issue.* Only **emotional** can mean 'showing emotion' (*an emotional person*), and **emotive** particularly means 'expressing emotion' (*the emotive use of language*).

empanel, impanel

This is usually spelled **empanel** in British English, **impanel** in American English. Other forms are **-elled, -elling** in British English, but the second *l* is usually omitted in American English. The word means 'enrol on a panel': *empanel a jury.*

empathy, sympathy

These both mean 'sharing in another's feelings'; but while **sympathy** often emphasizes the idea of pity for distress, **empathy** involves imaginative identification with the other person.

emperor

The word ends in *-or*, not *-er*.

employ

One **employs** workers: *employ a secretary*. As a synonym for *use*, as in *employ a sharp pencil*, this can seem a rather PRETENTIOUS word.

employee, employé

Employee, the last syllable rhyming with *tea*, is the better choice here; but **employé**, often spelled without the accent in American English, also exists. In either case the stress is normally on the second rather than the third syllable.

emporium

The plural is either **emporiums** or **emporia**. This word means a large shop: *a product seldom found in West End emporia*. In British English it is a FACETIOUS or old-fashioned word.

enable

Correctly, **enable** means 'make able': *enable them to evade taxation*. It is better not to use the word in the sense 'make possible' (*enable tax evasion*), although there are respectable precedents for the practice.

enamel (*verb*)

Other forms are **enamelled, enamelling** in British English, but the second *l* is usually omitted in American English.

enamo(u)red

This is spelled **enamoured** in British English, **enamored** in American English. The word is usually jocular, and is better followed by *of* than by *with*: *I am not enamoured of the way you stub your cigarettes out in your saucer*.

encomium

The plural is either **encomiums** or **encomia**. It means an expression of praise.

encyclop(a)edia

See AE-.

end

At the end of the day is a CLICHÉ. It means 'at the time of final reckoning'.

endeavo(u)r

1 The word is spelled **endeavour** in British English, **endeavor** in American English.

2 The verb **endeavour** is more formal than the verb *try*, and may sound PRETENTIOUS: *to endeavour/try to climb in*. The noun **endeavour**, like the noun *attempt*, replaces *try* except in rather informal contexts: *to make an endeavour/an attempt*; *to have a try*.

endemic, epidemic, pandemic

These words are used of diseases. An **endemic** disease is habitually common in a particular area. **Epidemic** and the rarer **pandemic** refer to outbreaks of disease, an **epidemic** affecting many individuals in a community at the same time, a **pandemic** extending over a larger area and affecting a higher proportion of the population. All these can refer to diseases of animals as well as of people.

ending, ended

Use **ending**, not **ended**, with reference to future time: *figures for the year ending next December*. Use either **ending** or *that* **ended** for past time: *figures for the year ending/that ended last December*.

ending with a preposition

See PREPOSITION (4).

endorse, indorse

Endorse, not **indorse**, is the main form in both British and American English. An established sense of the word is now 'express approval of': *9 out of 10 dentists endorse our product*. The related sense 'express public support for a political candidate' is, however, confined to American English.

enema

The usual plural is **enemas**; the alternative plural **enemata** is very technical and pedantic.

energize, enervate

To **energize** is to make energetic: *Oats are an energizing food for horses*. To **enervate** is to weaken, physically or mentally: *Heat enervates people*.

enforce

You can **enforce** a regulation; or you can **enforce** behaviour *on* a person: *enforce obedience on the children*. You cannot properly **enforce** a person *to do* something or *into doing* something. Use *force*, *compel*, *coerce*, etc for this second construction: *force* (not *enforce*) *them to obey*; *coerce* (not *enforce*) *them into obeying*.

enforceable

The word is spelled like this, retaining the final *e* of *enforce*.

enfranchise

The word is spelled with *-ise*, not *-ize*, in both British and American English.

English, England

1 See BRITISH.

2 Sports commentators often speak of the **England** rather than the **English** *team*, perhaps because **English** would suggest 'English people' rather than 'representing England'.

enhance

Things and qualities may be **enhanced**, but not people: *a hillside location enhanced by a broad vista*; *The election enhanced his political prestige*; not *He was enhanced in prestige by the election*.

enjoin

It is confusing that the rather formal **enjoin** can mean either 'command' or 'forbid': *She enjoined obedience on the children* (ie commanded it); *Conscience enjoined him from telling a lie* (ie forbade him). Instead of writing something like *His religion enjoins fasting*, which might have either meaning, make matters clear by using the verb in some other construction; either *His religion enjoins him to fast* (ie commands him) or *His religion enjoins him from fasting* (ie forbids him).

enormity, enormousness

Enormity means 'great wickedness', or 'a very evil act': *the enormity of his crime*; *to commit enormities*. Do not use it to mean 'great size', as in *amazed at the enormity of the compliment*. If **enormousness** seems a clumsy word, use *immensity* or *vast extent*.

enough, sufficient

1 Enough and the more formal **sufficient** are used in different constructions. Compare: *enough people/money*; *people/money enough*; *I was fool enough to believe him*; *sufficient people/money*; *a sufficient number*; *long enough*; *sufficiently long*. Where there is a real choice, as with *enough/sufficient money*, it can seem PRETENTIOUS to use **sufficient** for **enough. Enough**, but not **sufficient**, can properly be used as a noun: *Have you had enough* (not *sufficient*) *to eat?*. One may prefer, however, to use **sufficient** for kind or quality, **enough** for quantity. *Sufficient reason* is a 'good enough' reason rather than a 'large enough' one.

2 The construction **enough** *that*, as in *He's old enough that he can go to the theatre*, is now common, but careful writers still prefer *He's old enough to go to the theatre*.

enquire, inquire

Some British writers use the spelling **enquire, enquiry** for the 'asking' sense (*enquire after his health*) and **inquire, inquiry** for the 'investigation' sense (*hold a formal inquiry*). The two are not distinguished in American English, which prefers **inquire, inquiry** for both.

enrol(l)

It is spelled **enrol** in British English, **enroll** or **enrol** in American English. In either case, other forms are **enrolled, enrolling.**

ensure

See ASSURE. **Ensure** and **insure** usually have the same pronunciation.

enterprise

The word is spelled with *-ise*, not *-ize*, in both British and American English.

enthral(l)

Enthral is the chief British spelling, **enthrall** the chief American one. In either case, other forms are **enthralled, enthralling.**

enthuse

This informal verb is a BACK-FORMATION from *enthusiasm*. It means 'make enthusiastic' or 'show enthusiasm', but should be avoided in serious writing. There are plenty of alternatives, such as *thrill, inspire, be enthusiastic*.

entitled

This means either 'named, called' (*a book entitled 'Emma'*) or 'having a just claim to something good' (*entitled to a prize*; *entitled to enter the hall*). In this second sense, the word cannot properly be used of payments or penalties. Do not write *He is entitled to suffer for his mistake*.

entomology, etymology

Entomology is the study of insects; **etymology** is the study of the origins of words.

entrée

The spelling with the accent is preferred for British English, but **entree** is legitimate. When meals had more courses, it meant a dish served between the fish and the meat, but it is now usually the main course.

entrust, intrust

Entrust is the commoner spelling. One can **entrust** something *to* someone, or **entrust** someone *with* something: *He entrusted his savings to the bank*; *He entrusted the bank with his savings*. Do not use **entrust** like *trust*; one cannot simply **entrust** someone, nor **entrust** someone *to do* something.

enunciation

See ANNUNCIATION.

envelop, envelope

Envelop, with the stress on *vel*, is the verb: *envelop herself in a cloak*. **Envelope** is the noun: *a stamped addressed envelope*. Of the two ways of pronouncing the noun, the anglicized 'EN-ve-lope' is rather better than 'ON-ve-lope'.

envious, enviable

Envious means 'feeling or showing envy': *envious glances*. **Enviable** means 'worthy of envy': *an enviable position*.

envisage, envision

These can both mean 'conceive of as a future possibility': *The committee envisages an entirely new system of education.* **Envision** is an American rather than a British English word, and is preferred by American writers where *that* follows: *I envision that we shall extend our markets*; but it is also used as a somewhat PRETENTIOUS synonym for *imagine*: *One cannot envision a world without the internal-combustion engine.*

envoy, envoi

A diplomatic agent is an **envoy**. The postscript of a poem is an **envoi** or **envoy**.

eon

This is an alternative spelling of **aeon** in both British and American English.

epaulet(te)

The word is usually spelled **epaulette** in British English, **epaulet** in American English.

épée

This is spelled with both accents. It is a kind of fencing sword.

epic

The original sense of **epic** is of a long classical narrative poem of heroic deeds, such as Homer's *Odyssey* or Milton's *Paradise Lost*. The word is now applied, perhaps too freely, to a novel, play, film, or series of events of unusual size or scope or of heroic content: *the epic defence of Stalingrad*; *that great environmental epic, the wreck of the Torrey Canyon* (*The Guardian*).

epidemic

See ENDEMIC.

epigram, epigraph, epitaph, epilogue, epithet

An **epigram** is a short witty statement; an **epigraph** is an engraved inscription, or a motto at the beginning of a book; an **epitaph** is an inscription or statement commemorating a dead person; an **epilogue** is a concluding part of a book or play; an **epithet** is a descriptive term, or term of abuse.

episcopal, Episcopalian

Episcopal refers to bishops: *his episcopal authority*. Broadly, an **episcopal** church is any church governed by bishops; but, more specifically, the **Episcopal Church** is an Anglican church in Scotland and the USA whose members are **Episcopalians**.

epistle

This can mean one of the letters in the New Testament, or a verse composition in letter form. The word is FACETIOUS when used merely as a synonym for *letter*.

epithet

This originally meant a 'characterizing word or phrase attached to a name', as with *the Conqueror* in *William the Conqueror*. It now usually means 'term of abuse': *hurling epithets at the other driver*; but strictly speaking one should say *abusive epithets* here. See also EPIGRAM.

epitome

This means a 'typical example', or 'embodiment', of something whether good or bad: *The monarchy is the epitome of tradition*; *He was the epitome of laziness*. **Epitome** does not mean 'climax' or 'culmination', as in *reach the epitome of his political career*.

epoch, epoch-making

An **epoch** is a momentous event, a turning-point: *Her first sight of the sea was an epoch in her life*. One can thus say that the steam engine was an **epoch-making** invention; but **epoch-making** is somewhat OVERUSED with reference to things that are not particularly significant or memorable.

equable, equitable

Equable means 'pleasantly free from variations, not extreme': *an equable climate*; *her equable temperament*. **Equitable** means 'fair and just, reasonable': *an equitable distribution of wealth*.

equal (*adjective*)

1 One is **equal** *to* (ie capable of) a task, or **equal** *to doing* it, but not **equal** *to do* it. Do not write *He's quite equal to find his own way home*.

2 Since there can be no degrees in equality, things can be *almost* **equal** or *exactly* **equal** but not *more* **equal** or *very* **equal**. Do not write *a more* *equal distribution of income*, but prefer *equitable*. George Orwell infringed this rule with devastating ironic effect when he wrote *Some animals are more equal than others*. See GRADABILITY.

equal (*verb*)

Other forms are **equalled, equalling** in British English, but the second *l* is usually omitted in American English.

equally

1 Do not write **equally** *as*, as in *Exercise is equally as important as food*. Prefer *Exercise is (just) as important as food*, or *Exercise and food are equally important*.

2 Two or more items after **equally** should be joined by *and*, not by any other word: *She paid attention equally to the flowers and* (not *as*) *to the vegetables*.

equate

One **equates** one thing *and* or *with* another: *to equate dissension and/ with disloyalty*.

equator

The word ends in *-or*, not *-er*.

equerry

Put the stress on either the first or second syllable. In court circles the latter is apparently favoured.

equilibrium

The plural is either **equilibriums** or **equilibria**.

equip

Other forms are **equipped, equipping**.

equitable

See EQUABLE.

equivalent

One can say *This pill is the equivalent* (noun) *of ten oranges*, or *This pill is equivalent* (adjective) *to ten oranges*. Do not say *the equivalent to*.

-er, -est

See COMPARISON, GRAMMATICAL (1).

-er, -or

The ending **-er** is attached to a verb to form a noun meaning 'person or thing that does something': a *worker* is a person who *works*, a *silencer* is a device that *silences*. It appears also in compounds such as *taxpayer*, *lawnmower*, and *language teacher*. It can, if necessary, be attached to any verb in the language.

In certain borrowed and neo-classical words, however, the ending is spelled **-or**: *elector*; *generator*. Such words are not always related to any English verb: *author*; *doctor*. Some words can end with either **-er** or **-or**: *adviser/-or*; *impostor/-er*. In certain cases, such as *adapter/ adaptor*, there may be a difference of meaning.

-er, -re

Some words that end with **-re** in British English have the ending **-er** in American English: *calibre, caliber*; *centre, center*; *fibre, fiber*; *theatre, theater*. There is some inconsistency here: American spelling retains *acre, lucre, massacre, ogre*, where the change to **-er** would make the preceding *c* or *g* change its sound; British spelling has adopted *meter* for the measuring instrument, retaining *metre* for the unit of length and for the verse rhythm.

ere

See E'ER.

ergo

This is a FACETIOUS way of saying 'therefore', often used of other people's illogical inferences: *He thinks that because they can't talk, ergo they must be stupid.*

erode, corrode

These both mean 'eat away'; wind and water **erode** rock, acid **corrodes** metal. In figurative use, **corrode** is the more damaging: *Hot weather erodes the willpower*; *Envy corrodes the judgment.*

erotic, exotic, esoteric

Erotic means 'feeling or arousing sexual desire': *erotic poems*. **Exotic** means 'foreign' or 'excitingly unusual': *an exotic dish*. **Esoteric** means 'restricted to a small initiated group': *esoteric school slang*.

errant

See ARRANT.

errata

Strictly, this is the plural of **erratum**, meaning 'error'. It is often used to mean 'list of printing errors', but even in this sense it should not be treated grammatically as a singular noun (*The errata are* (not *is*) *on page 2*) and should not be given a plural *erratas*. If you need to refer to the lists of printing errors in two books, you could say *errata lists*.

erstwhile

In general, this can seem a rather PRETENTIOUS word for *former* or *formerly*, and is to be avoided.

erupt, irrupt

To **erupt** is to 'break out', like a volcano or a skin rash. To **irrupt** is to 'break in', like an angry crowd rushing onto a football field. In figurative use the two words have become interchangeable: *Violence erupted/irrupted in the ghetto*.

escalate

This is a BACK-FORMATION from *escalator*. It means 'increase step by step', and is well established in modern English, applying particularly to military strategy in which each side counters the action of the other by a more drastic move. **Escalate** has been OVERUSED as a vague synonym for *rise* (*escalating prices*) or *expand* (*escalate the company's interests overseas*).

escalator

The word ends in *-or*, not *-er*.

escape

To **escape** a danger is to 'avoid' it, with or without conscious action: *escape the family tendency to grey hair*. One **escapes** *from* actual confinement or danger: *escape from* (not just *escape*) *the burning building*.

escapee

See -EE.

Eskimo

The plural is **Eskimos**.

esophagus

See OESOPHAGUS.

esoteric

See EROTIC.

especial(ly)

See SPECIAL(LY).

espresso

The plural is **espressos**. Pronounce this word as it is spelled, not 'ex-press-o'.

Esq.

This abbreviation of **esquire** is more commonly used for addresses in Britain, where it may be applied to anyone who would otherwise be called *Mr*, than in the USA, where it is now rare except for writing to lawyers. Even in Britain *W. Jones Esq.* is less frequent than *Mr W. Jones* or just *W. Jones*.

-ess

For **waitress, authoress**, etc see FEMININE FORMS.

essay

Pronounce it, as a noun, with the stress on the first syllable: *write an essay*. Pronounce it, as a rare formal verb meaning 'try', with the stress on the second syllable: *He essayed to speak*. See also ASSAY.

Establishment

'*The* **Establishment**' is a term popularized in the 1950s for the people and institutions in power, regarded as arrogant and fusty and as having a vested interest in supporting the existing order. It applies particularly to government, the armed forces, and (in Britain) the Church of England, but more widely to any controlling group; their critics speak of *the literary* **Establishment** or *the theatrical* **Establishment**. The word has been OVERUSED as an expression of the dislike felt for those in authority.

esthete, esthetic

These are alternative spellings of **aesthete, aesthetic** in American
English only.

estimate, estimation

An **estimate** is a calculation or opinion: *Give me a rough estimate of
the cost*. **Estimation** is the process of arriving at such a calculation or
opinion. Nevertheless, *in my estimation* is an established way of saying
'in my opinion'.

estrogen

See OESTROGEN.

et cetera, et al.

1 Do not pronounce *et* as 'ek'.

2 Et cetera (nearly always abbreviated to **etc.**, **&c.**, which are
sometimes printed without a full stop) means 'and other things' and
belongs in footnotes and works of reference only. In formal continuous
prose, lists of items can instead be preceded by *such as* or *for example*,
or followed by *and so on* or *and so forth* (for things) or *and others* (for
people). **Et cetera** should be confined to things, and not used of
events, as in *The ball bounced up and down, up and down, etc.* It is
somewhat offensive when used of people. In legal documents, and in
the condensed style of footnotes and bibliographies, people are referred
to as **et al.**, an abbreviation of the Latin *et alii* (= and others).

3 Do not write *and etc.*, since *etc.* includes the meaning 'and'. Do not
use *etc.* at the end of a list beginning with expressions such as *include*,
including, *such as*, or *for example*. Put a comma before **etc.** unless
only one item has been mentioned: *cats, dogs, etc.*; *cats etc.* See LISTS.

ethic(al)

Ethical, not **ethic**, is the established form of this adjective, both for the
sense 'morally correct' and for the technical sense used of a drug
'available on prescription only'.

ethnic

Ethnic used to be the adjective associated with *ethnology*, the study of
the physical characteristics and cultural behaviour of the various human
races. **Ethnic** *minorities* were thus people within a community who
were a minority from the ethnological standpoint; in the New World,
people who had preserved the national traditions and language they

253

brought with them as immigrants. **Ethnic** then car ᵋ to be applied to
those national traditions themselves, as a synonym for *exotic* or
foreign, particularly suggesting a traditional peasant culture; **ethnic**
dresses are likely to be made of handwoven Indian cotton. In the USA,
more than in Britain, **ethnic** is also used as a noun meaning 'member
of an ethnic minority'. American **ethnics** tend, in practice, to be people
of Central European origin.

étude

This is usually, though not always, spelled with the accent. It is a piece
of music written chiefly for the practice of technique.

etymology

See ENTOMOLOGY.

eugenics, genetics

Eugenics deals with the improvement of the human race by selective
breeding; **genetics** with the mechanisms and structures involved in
heredity.

eulogy

See ELEGY.

euphemism

A euphemism is the substitution of an inoffensive expression, or one
with favourable associations, for an expression that may offend
because of its disagreeable associations. *Pass away* is a euphemism for
die, *put* (animals) *to sleep* for *kill*, *perspire* for *sweat*, *nurse* for *suckle*,
agent for *spy*, *dentures* for *false teeth*. Euphemisms are particularly
common for the processes of reproduction and excretion and for
activities, people, and bodily parts involved in those processes. People
vary in what they consider to be offensive, and toleration for blunt
language also varies from period to period. A euphemism may
eventually acquire unpleasant associations and give way to later
euphemisms: *toilet* and *lavatory*, themselves euphemisms, are
frequently replaced by other euphemisms, such as *cloakroom*.
Euphemisms can be used legitimately for politeness and tact, but they
are dishonest when they are used to avoid facing unpleasant activities
or to conceal and deceive. Dishonest uses are frequent in political and
military language: Hitler's plan for the extermination of the Jews was
called *the final solution*, *protective custody* has been used for
imprisonment, *industrial action* for *strikes*, *police action* for *war*, and
armed reconnaissance for *bombing*.

euphuism, euphemism

Euphuism was an artificial style of English fashionable in the late 16th and early 17th centuries. Compare EUPHEMISM.

evacuate

One can either **evacuate** (ie empty) a place, or **evacuate** (ie remove) the people from it. Both senses are perfectly standard. The people who are evacuated are *evacuees*.

evaluate

This means 'estimate the value of'. It cannot replace *value* to mean 'rate highly'. If you intend the second meaning, do not write *His contribution has never been sufficiently evaluated*.

even

In formal writing, **even** should go next to the word it concerns: *Even John* (ie so certainly everyone else) *works on Sundays*; *John works even on Sundays* (ie so certainly on weekdays). The natural place for **even**, however, is often next to the verb (*John even works on Sundays*), and such an arrangement is usually clear enough in speech, where the stress of the sentence helps to convey the meaning.

event

The chiefly British English idiom with *of* (*in the event of my death*) corresponds to the chiefly American idiom with *that* (*in the event that I die*). Both are a formal and rather VERBOSE way of saying *if I die*.

eventuate, eventuality

These can seem rather PRETENTIOUS words. Prefer *happen* or *result* for **eventuate**, and perhaps *development* or *possible outcome* for **eventuality**.

ever

1 Ever is used, rather informally, to give force to various expressions: *my first ever road accident*. In this sense it can be combined with *how*, *where*, *what*, etc, but the combination should not be written as one word: *How ever* (not *however*) *did you manage it?*; *Who ever* (not *whoever*) *can it be?* **Ever** *so* and **ever** *such* (*thanks ever so*; *ever such a nice girl*) do not belong in serious writing.

2 The informal *ever so often* means 'very often'; *every so often* means 'now and then'.

every

1 Every is used with a singular noun and, correctly, with a singular verb: *Every employee was a union member*. The verb should remain singular even after a plural noun: *Every one of the employees was a union member* (not *were union members*). In speech, **every** is sometimes permissibly followed by plural pronouns to avoid using *he* for both sexes: *see every student before they go away*. See NUMBER AGREEMENT (4); SEXISM.

2 Prefer *There's a dishwasher in every kitchen*, rather than *There are dishwashers in every kitchen*, unless the kitchens have more than one dishwasher each.

everybody, everyone

See ANY (1).

every day, everyday

Every day means 'each day': *go there every day*. **Everyday** means 'ordinary': *everyday life*; *my everyday clothes*.

everyone

This means 'every person, everybody': *invite everyone to the party*. **Every one** means 'every single thing or person': *He ate every one of the biscuits*.

everyplace

This is rather informal American English for 'everywhere': *I looked for it everyplace*.

evidentially, evidently

Evidentially refers to *evidence*: *evidentially proved*. The much commoner word **evidently** means 'as seems evident': *Evidently he was born in Leeds*.

evilly

There are two *l*'s.

evince, evoke

The formal word **evince** means 'reveal (a state of mind)': *The chairman evinced a desire* (ie 'showed that he wanted') *to obtain higher profit margins*. **Evoke** means 'produce a state of mind': *This place evokes memories of happier years*.

ewe, yew

A **ewe** is a mature female sheep; the identically pronounced word **yew** is a kind of evergreen tree.

ex-, late

Ex- means 'former': *the ex-president*; *his ex-wife*. **Late**, in one sense, means 'recently dead': *the late James Dawson*; *his late wife*. One's **ex** is one's divorced spouse.

exalt, exult

To **exalt** is to 'raise high, elevate': *personages of exalted rank*. To **exult** is to 'rejoice, glory': *exulting in their victory*.

exceed

See ACCEDE.

exceedingly

See EXCESSIVELY.

excel

Other forms are **excelled, excelling**.

excellence, excellency

The two words are partly interchangeable; but **excellence** is the more usual for the quality of being excellent, and **excellency** for the title of certain dignitaries such as ambassadors.

excellent

There can be, or should be, no degrees in excellence. Things can be *quite* **excellent** but not *more* **excellent** or *very* **excellent**. *Most* **excellent**, as in *the Queen's most excellent Majesty*, is permissible; since here *most* is an absolute superlative, expressing merely a high degree (see COMPARISON, GRAMMATICAL (4)).

except, excepting

The ordinary word is **except**: *nobody except me*; *can do everything except cook*. **Excepting** is used only after *always* and *not*. Compare: *They were all saved except the captain*; *They were all saved, not excepting the captain*. Alternatives are *except for* and *with the exception of*.

See also *accept*.

exception

1 *With the exception of* is usually no more than a VERBOSE way of saying *except*.

2 *The exception proves the rule* has been variously interpreted. As a formula in law, it means that the stating of an exception leads one to infer the existence of an unstated rule. What most people mean by the expression is either (a) that the existence of an exception heightens by contrast our sense of whatever it is an exception to, or (b) that exceptions can always be discounted if they seem to upset the pattern of regularity. One of these two meanings underlies dialogues such as the following: 'All the Greens are pretty stupid'. 'Oh, I don't know. Ann Green's quite bright'. 'She's the exception that proves the rule'.

excess

In excess of is VERBOSE. Use *more than* or *over*.

excessively, exceedingly

Excessively means 'too much' and **exceedingly** means 'very much': *I am exceedingly* (not *excessively*) *grateful*.

exchangeable

The word is spelled like this, retaining the final *e* of *exchange*.

excise

The word is spelled with *-ise*, not *-ize*, in both British and American English. See also TAX.

excitable

The word is spelled like this, dropping the final *e* of *excite*.

excitement, excitation

Both words are formed from *excite*, but **excitation** is preferred in scientific contexts: *the excitation of atoms by electron impact*; *They opened their Christmas presents with shrieks of excitement*.

exclamation mark

The exclamation mark indicates a forceful utterance. It conveys great emotion, surprise, or excitement. Use it for:

(1) sentences introduced by exclamatory *how* or *what*: *How well you look! What a marvellous performance that was! What an excellent idea!*

(2) exclamatory questions: *Isn't she tall! Wasn't that a wonderful meal!*

(3) expressions of surprise introduced by *to think that* or (more formally) merely *that*: *To think that you might have been killed too! That I should live to hear such words from my son!*

(4) negative expressions of surprise introduced by *well, if* or *why, if*: *Well, if it isn't the devil himself! Why, if it isn't my old friend Caroline!*

(5) wishes introduced by *if*: *If only you had told me! If I could just explain!*

(6) wishes or curses introduced by *may*: *May the sun always shine on you!*

(7) other conventional wishes or curses: *Long live the Queen! God forbid! Heaven help us! Bless you! Damn!*

(8) urgent warnings or alarm calls: *Be careful! Look out! Help!*

(9) peremptory commands, often without a verb: *Fire! Hands up! Attention! Not a sound!*

(10) certain interjections when used emphatically: *Oh! Hey!*

Otherwise, use the exclamation mark sparingly. Never use repeated exclamation marks or combinations of exclamation and question marks in serious writing.

excludable, excludible

Both forms are correct.

excreta

It is spelled like this, not *excretia*; it rhymes with *heater*, not with *Esher*; and it is a plural noun, not a singular.

excusable

The word is spelled like this, without the final *e* of *excuse*.

executor, executioner

An **executor** carries out the provisions of a will. An **executioner** inflicts capital punishment.

executrix

This is the formal legal word for a woman *executor*. See FEMININE FORMS.

exercise

1 The word is spelled with *-ise*, not *-ize*, in both British and American English.

259

2 *The object of the exercise* is a CLICHÉ.

exhaustible

The word ends in *-ible*, not *-able*.

exhausting, exhaustive

Exhausting means 'very tiring'. **Exhaustive** means 'covering all possibilities, comprehensive': *an exhaustive investigation*.

exhibit, exhibition

An **exhibit** is an item or set of items forming part of an **exhibition**: *our firm's exhibit at the Ideal Homes Exhibition*.

exhibitor, exhibitionist, exhibitioner

1 Exhibitor ends in *-or*, not *-er*.

2 An **exhibitor** displays something in a public exhibition: *the exhibitor of the winning roses at the flower show*. An **exhibitionist** behaves so as to attract attention, in some cases by indecent exposure. An **exhibitioner** is a student holding a scholarship at certain British schools and universities.

exorcise

The word is usually spelled with *-ise* in both British and American English; but *-ize* is a possible alternative. It means 'drive out evil spirits'.

exotic

See EROTIC.

expansible

The word ends in *-ible*, not *-able*.

expatriate

The word is spelled like this, not *expatriot* or *ex-patriate* or any other form. It means a person who lives abroad, and is not formed from *patriot*.

expect

In very formal writing, **expect** should be limited to the senses 'anticipate' (*expect a telephone call*; *expect to be forgiven*) and 'take for granted as reasonable' (*He expects us to work on Saturdays*). In speech and ordinary writing, **expect** is quite correctly used of present or past events, meaning 'suppose, think': *I expect he was tired.*

expectorate

This is an unnecessary GENTEELISM for *spit*.

expedient, expeditious

Expedient as an adjective means 'appropriate' or 'advantageous'; **expeditious** means 'prompt, speedy'.

expediter, expeditor

Both spellings are correct.

expel

Other forms are **expelled, expelling**.

expensive

Do not use **expensive** about prices. Goods may be **expensive**, but prices can be only *high*.

experiential

This means 'derived from or based on experience'. It gives rise to a good deal of jargon, such as *experiential deprivation* (ie cutting creatures off from natural experiences) and *experiential referent* (ie something one has experience of). Use it with restraint.

expertise (*noun*), expertize

Spell the noun with *-ise* in both British and American English. It means 'expert opinion or skill'. There is also a verb **expertize** or **expertise**, which means 'give an expert opinion'.

explain

If you report that someone **explained** something, as in *He explained that the economy was rapidly reviving*, you imply that what was said was true, or at any rate that you agree. If you disagree with the reported assertion, introduce it by some other verb such as *maintained* or *asserted*.

explicate

Explicate and **explication** are properly used of a detailed and learned analysis. Elsewhere, they sound PRETENTIOUS as alternatives to *explain* and *explanation*.

explicit, express, implicit

Explicit and **express** can both mean 'clearly stated and specific': *He disobeyed my explicit/express orders*. **Express** is preferred to **explicit** where a particular intention is involved: *She came for that express purpose*. **Explicit**, rather than **express**, is the opposite of **implicit**, meaning 'implied but not directly expressed': *an implicit assumption*.

explore

Explore every avenue is a CLICHÉ. There is nothing wrong, though, with this use of **explore** to mean 'investigate', as in *explore the possibilities*.

exposé, exposition

Exposé (spelled with the accent) chiefly means 'disclosure of something discreditable': *a newspaper exposé of organized crime*. **Exposition** means 'detailed explanation of something difficult': *a brilliant exposition of structuralism*.

exposed

One normally thinks of people who are **exposed** *to* something as being laid open to what they would rather be shielded from: *exposed to ridicule/to enemy gunfire*. The word is increasingly and rather oddly used of useful experiences: *students who have been exposed to two years of oral French*. This is jargon.

express (*adjective*)

See EXPLICIT.

express (*verb*)

Express *oneself* can mean 'say that one is': *He expressed himself as happy*. The construction *He expressed himself happy* is also common.

expressible

The word ends in *-ible*, not *-able*.

exquisite

This is pronounced with the stress on either the first or the second syllable; the former is the more traditional, but may sound old-fashioned.

extant, extinct, extent

Extant means 'still existing; not yet destroyed': *extant manuscripts.*
Extinct means 'no longer existing or active': *extinct animals/
volcanoes.* **Extent** means 'range; limit': *the extent of the forest/of our
patience.*

extempore, impromptu

These both apply to something done without much preparation. Strictly
speaking, an **extempore** speech may have been premeditated to some
extent, but it is not memorized or read and is made without notes,
whereas an **impromptu** one is absolutely spontaneous; but the two
words are often used interchangeably. **Impromptu** is the preferred
word for spontaneous action as distinct from public speaking: *an
impromptu change of plan.*

extemporize, temporize

Extemporize means 'improvise': *extemporize a lecture.* **Temporize**
means 'speak or act vaguely so as to gain time'.

extend

This verb is properly used in all its meanings connected with stretching
and making longer: *extend one's arms*; *extend our visit till Tuesday.* It
can sound PRETENTIOUS when used merely as a synonym for 'give':
extend credit to customers; *extend our thanks.*

extension

The word ends in *-sion*, not *-tion.*

extensive, extended

Extensive means 'long' or 'widespread'; **extended** means
'lengthened'. An *extensive tour* is a long or thorough one, an *extended
tour* is longer than was originally planned.

extent

See EXTANT.

extenuate

To **extenuate** a crime is to lessen its seriousness; *extenuating
circumstances* are facts that to some extent excuse the crime and should
be taken into account. One does not **extenuate** a person who
misbehaves, but the misbehaviour itself.

exterior, external, extraneous, extrinsic

These all mean 'outside'. **Exterior** and **external** are used of things that have a corresponding 'inside': *an exterior/external door* (ie leading out of a building). A football, being hollow, has an **exterior** surface, but one would not so readily use the word of an apple. **External** is used particularly of outer surfaces: *medicine for external use* (ie on the skin); or of surfaces as seen by an outsider: *the external appearance of the house*. Something **extraneous** has come in from outside: *extraneous light*; *an extraneous body in my eye*. **Extrinsic** applies particularly to qualities that do not form part of the thing itself. One can contrast the **extrinsic** value of a £5 note, as money, with its *intrinsic* value as a mere piece of paper.

extinct

See EXTANT.

extol(l)

Extol is the only British spelling and the chief American one, with **extoll** as a lesser American variant. In either case, other forms are **extolled, extolling**.

extract, extricate

Extract means 'draw forth against resistance': *extract a tooth/a confession*. **Extricate** means 'set free from entanglement': *extricate oneself from brambles/from debt*.

extraordinary

This is usually pronounced with the second syllable like *straw*. There is no need to pronounce it like *extra* plus *ordinary*.

exult

See EXALT.

-ey

See -Y.

eye dialect

Eye dialect is misspelling intended to represent mispronunciation: *ennything, fer, goin', iz, licker, wimmin, wot, woz*. It is used in literary dialogue that purports to render uneducated dialect, and is a common device for the same purpose in comic strips. In fact, the misspelling is usually a fair representation of educated pronunciation.

Ff

-f, -fe

There is no rule about whether a word ending with *f* or *fe* will form its plural *-f(e)s* or *-ves*. We say *loaves* but *oafs*, *thieves* but *chiefs*. Here is a list of words ending in *f* or *fe* that form their plurals in *-ves*:

calf - calves
elf - elves
half - halves
knife - knives
leaf - leaves
life - lives
loaf - loaves

self - selves
sheaf - sheaves
shelf - shelves
thief - thieves
wife - wives
wolf - wolves

The reflexive pronouns *ourselves*, *themselves*, and *yourselves* also form their plural in *-ves*.
Both forms are found with:

dwarf - dwarfs, dwarves
hoof - hoofs, hooves
scarf - scarfs, scarves
wharf - wharfs, wharves

The phrase *still life*, used to refer to paintings, has the regular plural *still lifes*.

fabricator

The word ends in *-or*, not *-er*.

fabulous

This is OVERUSED as an informal term of approval: *a fabulous hairdo/bathroom*.

façade

This can be spelled with or without the mark (called a cedilla) under the *c*.

facetiousness

Expressions that are intended to be funny but annoy the audience whom they are trying to amuse are facetious. It must always be a matter of personal judgment whether one's reader will be too sophisticated to laugh at a particular joke, but one should be cautious about it.

One of the commonest ways of being facetious is to use a pretentious or archaic word out of context, such as *ablutions* for *washing*, *disrobe* for *undress*, *impecunious* for *poor*, or *imbibe* for *drink*. Another is the use of jocular made-up words, such as *galumph* or *splendiferous*.

Facetiousness becomes bad taste when it treats a sad event frivolously. One would not announce the death of someone's near relative by saying that poor old George *kicked the bucket*.

face up to

Some critics advise that **face up to** should be dropped, in favour of using the verb **face** alone; but there is a shade of difference in meaning here. **Face** may mean simply 'confront' (*face a drop in profits*), while **face up to** decidedly means 'confront without flinching' (*We must face up to the situation*). It is probably better, in view of the criticism, to use **face** alone if it will cover what you want to say.

facilitate

Correctly, one **facilitates** (ie makes easier) something that is done: *This new software facilitates our stock control*. One does not **facilitate** (ie help) the people doing it. Do not say *We are facilitated in our stock control by this new software*.

facility, faculty

Facility can mean 'ability to do something easily': *She has considerable facility as a pianist*. It should be distinguished from the related sense of **faculty**, 'ability to do something at all': *He has a faculty for saying the right thing*. **Facility** is also a blanket term for anything that makes it possible to do something: *books and other facilities for study*. It may mean 'premises, establishment'; if so it is better, because more precise, to say *laboratory*, *factory*, *airport*, *theatre*, or whatever one has in mind, rather than referrring to them all as **facilities**.

facing

The word is spelled without an *e* in the middle.

fact

1 *True* **facts** or *real* **facts** is a TAUTOLOGY.

2 *The fact that* is often VERBOSE. *He admitted the fact that* . . . can be reduced to *He admitted that* . . . . Where the matter cannot be dealt with so simply, it may be well to recast the sentence: *Despite the fact that he was ill* can be changed to *Although he was ill* or *Despite his illness. Owing to the fact that* . . . means no more than *Because* . . . .

factious, fractious

Factious means 'tending to break up into groups; divisive': *the factious parties of the Left*. **Fractious** means 'unruly' or 'quarrelsome'.

factitious, fictitious

Factitious means 'produced artificially, engineered'. One may create a **factitious** demand for a product by spreading rumours of possible shortage, in which case the demand will then exist. A **fictitious** demand would not exist at all, because **fictitious** means 'not real': *fictitious characters in a novel; a fictitious name*.

factor

A **factor** is, properly, something contributing to a result: *the factors determining the rate of unemployment*. The word is OVERUSED as a blanket term when more precise alternatives such as *component, element, occurrence, feature*, or *consideration* are available, as in *There are four main factors in this problem*.

factotum

The plural is **factotums**.

faculty

See FACILITY.

faecal, faeces

The words are usually spelled like this in British English, but **fecal, feces** in American English. See AE-.

faerie

See FAIRY.

fag, faggot

In British English a **fag** is a cigarette, a tiresome task, or a junior schoolboy who does menial jobs for a senior; a **fag** is also a male homosexual, chiefly in American English (see HOMOSEXUAL). In British English, a **faggot** is a bundle of sticks or a meatball. In American English a **faggot** is a homosexual, and the bundle of sticks is usually distinguished by being spelled **fagot**.

fail

It can be misleading to use **fail** *to* when you mean merely *do not/did not*, since **fail** carries the implication of neglect or particularly of unsuccessful attempt. The same is true of **failure** *to*. Do not write *He failed to arrive* when you mean merely that he never arrived, or *the failure of the water to go through the pipe* when you mean that it did not go through.

failing

Modern convention allows the use of **failing** as a preposition meaning 'in the absence of': *Failing specific instructions, use your own judgment*. (This means 'if there are no instructions', so **failing** could not be replaced by *without*.) See DANGLING PARTICIPLE.

fair, fairly

These both mean 'in a fair way'. **Fair** as an adverb is used in certain fixed phrases: *fight fair*; *play fair*. In some uses, it can replace **fairly** to mean 'utterly': *It fair/fairly makes you sick*. **Fairly**, not **fair**, can mean 'moderately': *a fairly easy job*.

fair, fare

Fair means 'fine', 'just', 'blonde', and so on. **Fare** is either the price of transport, or food: *Christmas fare*. A fête is a **fair**. The verb is **fare**, as in *How are you faring?*

fairy, faerie, faery, fay

These all mean a small creature with magic powers, in fairy stories. In addition, a **fairy** is a male homosexual, but the context must usually make it quite clear which one is talking about (see HOMOSEXUAL). **Faerie**, **faery**, and **fay** are alternatives to be used only in certain poetic

contexts, as in the title of Edmund Spenser's *The Faerie Queene*.
Faerie and **faery** can also mean 'fairyland'.

fait accompli

The plural is **faits accomplis**. It means 'something already
accomplished and irreversible'. Use these FOREIGN PHRASES with
restraint.

faithfully, truly

Yours **faithfully**, or more rarely *Yours* **truly**, ends a formal letter in
British English to a stranger that begins *Dear Sir*, *Dear Madam*, *Dear
Sirs*, etc. See LETTER ENDINGS.

faker, fakir

A **faker** is an impostor, a swindler. A **fakir** is a wandering Muslim or
Hindu holy man.

fallible, fallacious

Fallible ends in *-ible*, not *-able*. It means 'capable of error': *Generals
are never more fallible than when they are winning.* **Fallacious** means
'deceptive, delusive' or 'illogical': *fallacious evidence*; *fallacious
arguments*.

false, falsely

They both mean 'in a false way'. **False** as an adverb is used only in the
expressions *play someone false*, *ring false*, and cannot replace **falsely**,
as in *falsely accused*.

falsehood, falseness, falsity

These all mean 'lack of truth, inaccuracy'. A **falsehood** is usually a lie:
to tell falsehoods. **Falseness** and **falsity** usually mean 'lack of truth'
without the imputation of deliberate lying: *the falseness/falsity of this
belief.* **Falseness**, in addition, can mean 'treacherousness': *the
falseness that lay behind his plausible manners.*

false illusion

This is a TAUTOLOGY. All illusions are false.

false titles

The 'false title' device was popularized by the magazine *Time* and is
now a commonplace of journalese. It consists of writing *footballer*

Matthew Green or *famous British footballer Matthew Green* rather than *Matthew Green, the/a footballer*. Its two advantages are that it saves some space, and that it exempts its users from making the delicate distinction between *the* footballer (for famous ones) and *a* footballer (for obscure ones).

The false title is useful to journalists, but does not belong in ordinary writing. Where it is used, it should not be too long; it should not be capitalized (*Footballer Matthew Green*) as if it were a real title; and it should not be separated by a comma (*famous footballer, Matthew Green*) from the name it precedes. See APPOSITION (4).

falsetto

The plural is **falsettos**.

famed

The use of **famed** for the longer word *famous*, as in *famed cricketer*, is journalese. Do not use it in general writing.

familiar

Things are **familiar** *to* people: *That idea was familiar to them*. People are **familiar** *with* things: *They were familiar with that idea*. Things cannot be **familiar** *to* other things, as in *methods familiar to our educational system*. Use **familiar** *in* the system, or *typical of* it.

fanatic, fanatical

Fanatic is the noun (*a football fanatic*) and **fanatical** the usual form of the adjective (*fanatical enthusiasm*).

fandango

The plural is **fandangos**. It is a Spanish dance.

fantastic

This is OVERUSED as an informal term of approval: *He looked fantastic in his velvet jacket*.

fantasy, phantasy

This is spelled with an *f* when it means 'imaginative fiction' (*fantasy and science fiction*) or a 'daydream' (*sexual fantasies*). The literary and archaic spelling **phantasy**, if used at all, is confined to the sense 'image-making power': *the schizophrenic's phantasy-life*.

far

1 *As far as* and *so far as* should not be used to replace *as for* or *as far as X is concerned*. Do not write *As far as clothes, they are well provided*, but *As for clothes* or *As far as clothes go*.

2 *Far be it from me* is a CLICHÉ, and is disliked by some people for its combination of pomposity with ostensible self-deprecation.

faraway, far away

This is written as two words, except when it is used as an adjective before a noun: *The house isn't far away*; *faraway villages*; *a faraway look in her eyes*.

fare

See FAIR.

farouche, louche

Farouche means 'sullen and shy': *country boys with farouche manners*. **Louche** means 'shifty and disreputable': *louche waterfront bars*.

farrago

The plural is **farragoes**. It is a rather literary word for 'hotchpotch': *a farrago of lies*.

farther, farthest

See FURTHER.

fascinate, fascination

One is **fascinated** *by* other people, or **fascinated** *with* or *by* things; those people or things then have a **fascination** *for* one. Do not write *people who have a fascination for power politics*, which suggests that the people fascinate the politics rather than being fascinated by them.

fatal, fateful

These can both mean 'involving dreadful consequences': *a fatal/fateful decision*. **Fatal**, not **fateful**, means 'causing death': *a fatal accident*. **Fateful** means 'decisive for the future', and can refer to cheerful events: *the fateful night when we first met*.

father

This is spelled with a capital *F* when it means God, or something personified as an old man (*Father Thames*), or when it is used as a title for a priest (*Father Brown*).

fault

The verb **fault**, meaning 'find a fault in', is both well established and useful, particularly in negative contexts: *We can't fault his logic.* It should be avoided, however, where *blame* or *censure* would do instead: *One can scarcely blame* (not *fault*) *her for publicizing the incident.*

faun, fawn

A **faun** is a Roman god with the horns and legs of a goat; a **fawn** is a young deer.

fauna

The plural is either **faunas** or **faunae**, but is rarely needed. **Fauna** means all the animals of a particular region or period: *desert fauna.*

faux pas

The plural is also **faux pas**. It means 'a social blunder'. Do not use too many of these FOREIGN PHRASES.

favo(u)r

The word is spelled **favour** in British English, **favor** in American English. It is archaic business English to call a business letter a **favour**.

fawn

See FAUN.

fay, fey

Fay is a poetic word for 'fairy'; see FAIRY. **Fey** means 'in an elated otherworldly state', as was formerly said of people doomed to early death.

fayre

This is a would-be quaint spelling either for *fair* in the sense of 'fête' (*a charity fayre*) or for *fare* in the sense of 'food' (*dine on Elizabethan fayre*).

faze, phase

Faze is informal American English. It means 'daunt, disconcert', and is usually used negatively: *Nothing seems to faze her*. It should not be spelled **phase**. **Phase** is a noun meaning 'stage, episode' (*going through an unpleasant phase*) or a verb meaning 'schedule in stages': *phase a development programme*.

-fe

See -F.

fearful, fearsome

These can both mean 'frightening', or 'extremely bad': *fearful/ fearsome weather*. **Fearful** is the more usual word in the sense of 'frightened', and is the only choice where the cause of the fear is mentioned: *fearful of reprisals*.

feasible

1 The word ends in *-ible*, not *-able*.

2 Feasible means 'able to be done', and should not be used to mean 'probable' or 'credible'. A protest march or a surgical operation may be **feasible**, but a snowstorm or an epidemic is not.

feature

Feature as a verb properly means 'play a part, figure': *other lesser known figures who feature in the book* (*Times Literary Supplement*); or 'give special prominence to', as in cinema advertisements: *featuring* (or *starring*) *Robert Redford*. Do not use **featuring** when you mean simply 'with', as in *Venice, featuring its celebrated canals*.

February

Some speakers dislike the pronunciation 'feb-you-ri'; the word has two *r*'s in it.

fecal, feces

See FAECAL.

feckless, reckless

Feckless means 'incompetent and irresponsible': *a feckless wastrel*. **Reckless** means 'boldly incautious': *reckless driving*.

fecund

The first syllable can rhyme with either *deck* or *beak*.

feedback

In its strict scientific sense, **feedback** is the return to an input of part of the output of a machine, producing changes (as in an automatic control device) that provide self-correcting action. The word has been OVERUSED for any kind of response to a process that is passed back to the originator: *They got a lot of feedback from their advertising campaign.*

feel

1 Feel is widely and correctly used as a synonym for *think* or *believe*: *I feel that your behaviour was unwise.* This generally suggests a discreet diffidence, where *I think* would be more baldly outspoken.

2 Feel followed by an adjective means 'be conscious of a sensation': *feel cold; feel sure I posted it.* An adverb used after **feel** describes the way of feeling rather than what is felt: *feel very differently about it; feel strongly that we should object.* In talking about one's health, one can *feel bad* or *ill, well* or *good.* In talking about one's state of mind, it is common in speech to say *feel badly,* as in *I feel very badly about how we treated him;* but in formal writing, *badly* should be replaced here by an adjective, such as *guilty* or *sorry.*

felicitate, felicity

These are formal and sometimes PRETENTIOUS words for 'congratulate' and for 'happiness'. **Felicity** is appropriately used to mean 'aptness': *a style, which adapts itself with singular felicity to every class of subjects* (J H Newman).

fellow

When **fellow** means 'associate', there is a problem of whether to spell the resultant compounds as one word, or two, or with a hyphen. *Fellowship* is one word in both British and American English. American English, avoiding the hyphen, spells *fellowman* as one word and *fellow creature, fellow feeling, fellow passenger, fellow sufferer, fellow traveller, fellow worker* as two. British English uses more hyphens, and tends to favour *fellow-citizen, fellow-feeling, fellow-countryman, fellow-man, fellow-traveller.*

feminine forms

Feminine endings such as *-ess* should be used with caution. It is

perfectly correct to use *-ess* of animals (*lioness*) and in female titles
(*baroness*; *countess*); a woman who waits in a restaurant is a *waitress*
(the new non-sexist word *waitron* is not established), and the superior
of a convent of nuns is an *abbess*; and probably no one cares whether a
murderess is offended or not. But a serious woman writer does not like
to be called an *authoress* or *poetess*, female business executives regard
themselves as *managers* (*manageress* might mean a woman who runs a
launderette or small shop), and *instructresses* and even *actresses* may
prefer to think of themselves as *instructors* and *actors*. *Shepherdess*
belongs rather to pastoral poetry than to modern sheepfarming. *Jewess*
and *Negress* are decidedly impolite, and should be avoided.

Some *-ess* words, such as *seamstress*, have no precise masculine
equivalent. A *governess* is not a female *governor*, so that if she dislikes
the term she must call herself a *teacher* or *tutor*. *Hostess* is a harmless
word, but she is likely to be a woman steward on a ship or plane rather
than merely a female *host*. An *adventuress* is an unscrupulous seeker
after wealth rather than a gallant woman explorer. Women *mayors* and
ambassadors are not *mayoresses* or *ambassadresses*, because those
titles are reserved for the wives of their male counterparts or perhaps
for their own female escorts. A *paintress* decorates ware in a
commercial pottery rather than being a woman artist. A *conductress*
conducts a bus, not an orchestra. A *priestess* operates in a non-
Christian religion and is not simply a woman *priest*.

The same is true of the smaller group of *-ette* words. An *usherette*
shows people to their seats in a cinema rather than being, for instance,
the kind of *usher* who is a doorkeeper in a lawcourt. A *drum majorette*
twirls her baton in front of an American marching band, rather than
being a woman *drum major*, the non-commissioned officer in charge of
a military drum corps. (Women army officers use the masculine titles.)

The general tendency, however, is increasingly to allow masculine
words, especially those ending with *-er* and *-or*, to do duty for both
sexes. *Executrix* and *testatrix* may still have some currency in legal
contexts, but they are often replaced by *executor* and *testator*. Words
ending in *-man* and *-master* can refer to women; a woman may be a
craftsman or *postmaster*, and a woman hospital doctor a *houseman*.
Alternatively they may be replaced by *-person* words (*chairperson*;
salesperson), or the official policy both in Britain and the USA of
devising asexual job descriptions may have abolished them, as British
Rail has replaced *stationmaster* by *station manager*. One British
teachers' union is called the *Association of Schoolmasters and Women
Teachers*. The *-woman* and *-mistress* forms still survive, however,
though less so in official use: *horsewoman*.

An alternative to using a feminine ending is to prefix the word with
woman, *lady*, or *girl*: *woman doctor*; *lady barrister*; *girl student*. Many

modern women dislike this practice, however, unless there is definite need to specify the sex.

The only 'feminine forms' that are almost inescapable are the possession of a female first name, and the use of *Mrs/Miss/Ms* rather than *Mr*. Women who wish to avoid sexual classification, and who are not fortunate enough to be called something like Leslie or some foreign name unrecognizable as feminine, can use initials alone. Women doctors and professors can announce themselves on paper without revealing their sex. It is not fair, however, to do this on a letter and then be offended if the answer to the letter begins *Dear Sir*.

See also SEXISM.

femur

The plural is either **femurs** or **femora**.

ferment, foment

Literally, to **ferment** is to produce a chemical reaction releasing bubbles of gas; to **foment** is to apply hot wet poultices to the body. In their figurative use, both words mean 'incite to disorder'; one can **foment** or **ferment** rebellion.

ferrule, ferule

A **ferrule** is a protective metal ring or cap on something such as a shaft or umbrella; a **ferule** is a ruler used for punishing children.

fervent, fervid

Fervent describes deep, sincere emotion: *a fervent believer in free speech*. **Fervid** usually describes outward behaviour that is too fervent: *His fervid manner of lovemaking offended her* (Arnold Bennett).

festive, festal

These both mean 'of or suitable for a feast': *festive/festal garlands*. **Festive** also means 'joyous': *a festive party of students*.

fetal, fetus

This is the usual spelling in American English, and increasingly in British English too. The British English alternatives **foetal, foetus** are becoming less common.

fête

This is usually spelled with the accent in British English, but either **fete** or **fête** in American English.

fetid

The word is usually spelled like this, and pronounced with 'fet', rather than being spelled **foetid** and pronounced with 'feet'.

fever

See TEMPERATURE.

few

1 The adjectives **few, fewer** do not correctly accompany either 'numbers' that give the size of a quantity or the word *number*. Write *less* (not *fewer*) *than six weeks* (ie a length of time); *less* (not *fewer*) *than £50* (ie a sum of money); *The number of people was less* (not *fewer*) *than usual*; *They arrived in smaller* (not *fewer*) *numbers than we expected*; but *fewer than 50 people*. See LESS.

2 The phrase *few in number* is VERBOSE, just like *large in size* or *pink in colour*. Use **few** alone.

fey

See FAY.

fez

The plural is **fezzes** or, less usually, **fezes**.

fiancé(e)

These words are spelled with the accent. A **fiancé** is a man, a **fiancée** is a woman.

fiasco

The plural is **fiascoes** or, less usually, **fiascos**.

fibre, fiber

The word is spelled **fibre** in British English, **fiber** in American English.

fictitious, fictional

Both words mean 'invented'; one can speak of **fictitious** or **fictional** characters in a novel. But **fictional** chiefly applies to imaginative literature (*fictional writing*), and **fictitious** chiefly means 'false' (*gave a fictitious address*). See also FACTITIOUS.

fiddle

Musicians familiarly describe as a **fiddle** what other people nowadays call a *violin*; but classical musicians do not call themselves *fiddlers* or call what they do *fiddling*. To most of us, **fiddle** and its associated verb means 'swindle': *He fiddled his expenses.*

fidget

Other forms are **fidgeted, fidgeting**.

field, province, sphere, realm

A **field** is often a limited area of knowledge: *the field of cartography.* By contrast, **province** suggests someone's special responsibility: *behaviour which is the province of the psychiatrist rather than of the lawyer.* A **sphere** is an area of activity or interest: *the political/the domestic sphere.* The more literary word **realm** applies particularly to levels of reality: *the realms of the imagination; within the realms of possibility.*

fiend, fierce, fiery

All three are spelled *-ie-*, not *-ei-*.

fifth

In careful speech, the second *f* should be pronounced.

fight

Britain fought with the USA or *John and Bill fought* may mean 'fought against each other' or 'fought side by side in the war'. Unless the context makes it clear, write *X fought against Y*, or *X fought Y*, or *X and Y fought each other*, or *X fought together with Y*, according to the sense.

figure

1 In British English, **figure** rhymes with *bigger*, but in American English it often sounds like 'fig-yer'.

2 The use of **figure** to mean 'conclude' (*They figured it was no use trying*) or 'consider' (*I figure him for a crook*) or 'plan' (*I figure on going into town*) is American English and also rather informal. Its use to mean 'solve' or 'fathom' (*I just can't figure him out*) or 'seem reasonable' (*That figures*) is informal, but not confined to American English.

film

See CINEMA.

final

Final culmination, *final upshot*, *final outcome*, and *final end* are
TAUTOLOGOUS.

finalize

Many people who have no objection to other verbs, such as *modernize*,
that are formed by adding *-ize* to an adjective, strongly dislike **finalize**.
It is a genuinely useful word in bureaucratic contexts, where it means
'put into conclusive unalterable form' and could not be replaced by
complete or *finish*. It should probably be confined to abstract contexts
(*finalize the new guidelines*) and not extended to concrete objects, as in
finalize the new science wing.

financial

In informal Australian English, this can mean 'having money, well
off': *Motherhood is a blessing, whether you're financial or not*
(*Australasian Post*).

fine, finely

Fine as an adverb means either 'by an irreducible margin' (*You're
running it very fine if you want to catch the 8.40*) or, informally, 'very
well' (*We're doing fine*). It cannot replace **finely** in any of the many
other meanings.

finicky, finicking, finical

These all mean 'too meticulous, fussy'. **Finicky** is the usual word,
finical is rather literary.

fiord, fjord

Both spellings are correct. **Fiord** seems to be slightly commoner in
British English, **fjord** in American English.

firm, firmly

Firm as an adverb is used only in certain fixed phrases: *stand firm;
hold firm*. It cannot replace **firmly**, the usual adverb: *spoke firmly to
her*.

first

1 In giving lists of items, **first** *two*, *next three*, and *last four* should be preferred to the more old-fashioned *two* **first**, *three next*, and *four last*, though either style is permissible. In any case, a large number must come at the end: *the first seventeen chapters*.

2 *First and foremost* is VERBOSE. Use **first** alone.

3 *First come first served*, not *first serve*, is the proper form of that idiom.

firstly

Some people object to **firstly** as a redundant variant of *first* (which is an adverb as well as an adjective), and therefore use *first* in lists of items even when the others in the series end in *-ly*: *first, secondly, lastly*. Others hold that in any case such lists should be formed with the adverbs *first, second, last*, rather than with **first(ly)**, *secondly, lastly*, but there seems to be no basis for this prejudice. Perhaps *first, second, last* should be preferred where the words can be interpreted as adjectives: *There are three important reasons for my decision: first. . . .* . Most writers feel free to choose either *first, secondly* or *first, second* or **firstly**, *secondly*; but it is better to avoid the inconsistent form **firstly**, *second*.

first name

See CHRISTIAN NAME.

fish

Fish, regarded as a food, is a noun with no plural: *a wine that goes well with fish*. Otherwise, there are two plurals, **fish** and **fishes**. The plural **fish** is much commoner: *We caught several fish*. **Fishes** is now used chiefly for different species: *valuable food fishes such as the haddock and turbot*.

fit (*verb*)

In British English, the past tense and participle are **fitted**. American English has the alternative **fit**, used particularly for the sense 'be of right size', as in *My suit fit beautifully*, or figuratively 'be suitable', as in *The name fit him*. There is disagreement among American writers as to whether **fit** or **fitted** is the better form here, but they prefer **fitted** elsewhere, as in *a fitted raincoat* or *We fitted new locks on the door*.

fix

The verb **fix** is used much more widely in American than in British English to mean 'prepare, get ready', as in *fix a drink* or *I must fix my face*, but the British use it as much as the Americans to mean 'repair', as in *get the radio fixed*. As a noun meaning 'predicament', **fix** is somewhat informal: *We're in a real fix*. It is decidedly slang when it means 'a shot of a narcotic', but that sense is now so widely known that it can be used figuratively: a *Daily Mail* journalist writes of the Chancellor of the Exchequer's *addiction to ever-increasing fixes of energy tax revenue*.

flaccid

This is usually pronounced 'flak-sid', but 'flas-sid' is also acceptable.

flack, flak

Flack is an informal American word for 'press agent'. It is also a less usual spelling of **flak**, meaning originally 'antiaircraft gunfire', but now usually (and informally) 'heavy criticism': *His proposals ran into a lot of flak*.

flagrant

See BLATANT.

flair, flare

Flair is natural aptitude, particularly where this involves intuitive discernment: *a flair for playing the stock market*. It does not mean 'liking', so do not write *a flair for flimsy dresses*. A **flare** is a blaze of light (*The aircraft dropped flares to illuminate the target*) or a spreading outwards (*jeans with wide flares*).

flambé(e)

The adjective is usually spelled **flambé**, but **flambée** is also acceptable. It means 'served in burning spirit': *pineapple flambé*. Other forms of the verb are **flambéed, flambéing:** *pineapple flambéed with kirsch*.

flambeau

The plural is either **flambeaux** or **flambeaus**. It means a flaming torch.

flamenco

The plural is **flamencos**. It is a Spanish gipsy dance.

flamingo

The plural is either **flamingos** or **flamingoes**.

flammable

See INFLAMMABLE.

flan

See TART.

flannel

Other forms of the verb are **flannelled, flannelling** in British English, but the second *l* is usually omitted in American English. **Flannelette** has one *l* in the middle.

flare

See FLAIR.

flat, flatly

These can both mean 'completely' or 'positively', but are each used in certain fixed phrases. One can *flatly refuse*, *deny*, or *oppose* something, *turn* a person or suggestion *down flat*, *go flat* against something, or be *flat broke*.

flaunt, flout

To **flaunt** something is to parade it ostentatiously: *flaunting her expensive clothes in front of her poor relatives*. To **flout** a rule or law is to disregard it contemptuously: *They openly flouted the regulations*. They have in common a certain quality of barefaced impudence, which may be why many people use **flaunt** incorrectly for **flout**, as in *He has flaunted my authority*. Nobody seems to use **flout** for **flaunt**.

flautist, flutist

A fluteplayer is a **flautist** in British English, a **flutist** in American English. **Flutist** is in fact the older word.

flavo(u)r

The word is spelled **flavour** in British English, **flavor** in American English.

fledg(e)ling

The spelling **fledgling** is correct everywhere, but **fledgeling** is a possible British alternative.

flee

See FLY.

fleshy, fleshly

Fleshy means 'consisting of flesh, plump' (*his thick, fleshy neck*) or 'succulent, pulpy' (*the fleshy texture of a ripe melon*). **Fleshly** means 'carnal', referring to the sensual aspect of human nature as opposed to the spiritual: *fleshly lusts*.

fleur-de-lis

This is the heraldic lily of France. The plural is either **fleurs-de-lis** or **fleur-de-lis.** The ending is usually spelled **lis** but sometimes **lys**, and is pronounced 'lee' in the singular, but often 'leez' in the plural.

flexible

The word ends in *-ible*, not *-able*.

flier, flyer

Both spellings are available for all senses. British writers tend to prefer **flyer** and Americans to prefer **flier,** except for the American English sense of 'an advertising circular'.

floor

In American English, the ground level of a building is the *first* **floor,** and those above it the *second*, *third*, etc. In British English the ground level is traditionally the *ground* **floor,** with the *first*, *second*, etc above it, but some high buildings in Britain are beginning to adopt the American system of numbering. Where it exists, the **mezzanine** is an intermediate floor like a balcony between the ground and first floors (British) or the first and second floors (American).

flora

The plural is either **floras** or **florae**, but is rarely needed. Flora means all the plants of a particular region or period: *alpine flora*.

flotsam and jetsam

Literally, **flotsam** is the wreckage or cargo that remains floating after a ship has sunk; **jetsam** is whatever is thrown overboard or washed ashore. Both words also mean miscellaneous discarded odds and ends, or sometimes vagrants, tramps: *drifting human flotsam*.

flounder, founder

Literally, to **flounder** is to struggle clumsily about (*floundering in the mud*); to **founder** is to go lame (of a horse) or sink (of a ship). Since both are ways of coming to grief, they are sometimes confused in the figurative sense. **Founder** implies utter failure: *the point on which the whole conference foundered* (ie broke down); while someone who **flounders** is still functioning, however ineptly: *floundered through his speech*.

flout

See FLAUNT.

flu

This is not spelled '*flu*, although it is a CLIPPED form of *influenza*. It is slightly informal, but is now much commoner than *influenza* in all but the most formal contexts.

fluid

Technically, anything that will flow to conform to the shape of its container is a **fluid**, so that gases are fluid as well as liquids. In daily life, **fluid** is a synonym for *liquid*, as when a doctor tells someone to drink lots of fluids.

flush

See BLUSH.

flushed, flush

Flushed means 'red in the face' (*flushed with running*) or 'excited' (*flushed with victory*). **Flush** means 'not indented or projecting' (*flush panelling*) or, informally, 'having plenty of money'.

flutist

See FLAUTIST.

fly, flee

The past tense and participle of **fly** are **flew, flown**; those of the rather literary **flee** are both **fled**. Both words can mean 'hurry away', or 'run away from', but **fly** is not used in that sense in the past tense. One can say *We must fly/flee the country*, but *We fled* (not *flew*) *the country*. In consequence, **fled** is more commonly used than the other forms of the verb *flee*.

flyer

See FLIER.

fob

See FOIST.

fo'c'sle

See FORECASTLE.

focus

The plural of the noun is either **focuses** or **foci**. Other forms of the verb are **focused, focusing** or, less usually, **focussed, focussing**.

foetal, foetus

See FETAL, FETUS.

foetid

See FETID.

foist, fob

You can **foist** something unwanted *on* or *upon* a person: *foist these dirty jobs on me*. You can **fob** a person *off with* something spurious or inferior: *I won't be fobbed off with that excuse*. You can also **fob** something *off on* a person: *fobbing off inferior goods on his customers*; but you cannot properly **foist** a person *off with* something.

folio

The plural is **folios**.

folk, folks

The use of **folk** or **folks** for 'people' adds a somewhat archaic and sentimental colouring, at least to a British ear. (The word is more widely used in American English.) A group of **folk** waiting in the rain for a bus sounds unpretentious, and therefore more pitiable. **Folks** in the plural often means a particular group of people: *the old folks*; *my folks* (ie my family); *Do you folks want some tea?* In all these contexts, *people* should be preferred in formal writing, and **folk** reserved for such combinations as *folk song* or *folk traditions*.

follow

Even when *as* **follows** has a plural subject, and introduces a list of several items, it should not be pluralized to *as follow*: *The afternoon's events were as follows . . . .*

following

1 Following is correctly used as an adjective: *Trains will leave at the following times*; and as a noun: *He attracted a numerous following*. Its use as a preposition has attracted a good deal of adverse criticism, but may be found more acceptable when it means 'after and because of' than when it means 'after' alone. Compare: *Following a multiple pileup on the northbound carriageway, the M1 was closed for three hours*; *After* (rather than *following*) *the lecture, tea will be served*. See DANGLING PARTICIPLE.

2 When it means 'the one or ones to be mentioned next', British usage requires *the following*, but in American English it is correct to write *Following were present*.

foment

See FERMENT.

foot

When **foot** means the unit of length, use **-foot** in hyphenated combinations (*a 10-foot drop*), but elsewhere, both *foot* and *feet* are possible: *He's six foot tall*; *He's six feet tall*. In combinations with inches, *foot* is preferable: *He's six foot two.*

footnotes

Footnotes are usual in technical and scholarly articles, papers, or books, but in other types of writing you should avoid them. They document the sources that the writer has used: quotations and also the source of facts, argumentation, and results if these are not common knowledge. They also add points that would disturb the flow of the writing if they were included in the main text; but one should avoid such digressions as far as possible, since they distract readers. In some styles of documentation, the sources are briefly referred to in the text and a list of detailed references appears at the end, thereby dispensing with the need for reference footnotes. If you need to refer to sources in ordinary writing it is best to do so by citing in the text merely the author and perhaps the title of the work, eg: *Walter Nash, The Language of Humour, pages 38–53.* In the natural and social sciences the normal method is to give the last name of the author and the year of publication, eg: *Nash 1985, 38–53.* (See REFERENCES.)

Number the footnotes consecutively by a raised number in the text. Then put the same numbers with a full stop after them at the beginning of the footnotes. There are two possible positions for footnotes: at the end of the complete text or at the foot of the page. When footnotes are at the end of the text, start with a new page if the work is to be printed. When they appear at the foot of the page, separate them from the text by a line. For the forms of references in the text, see REFERENCES.

for

1 For as a preposition must be followed by *me, us, him, her, them*, not by *I, we, he, she, they*. Write *for us* (not *we*) *farmers*; *for John and me* (not *I*). See HYPERCORRECTION.

2 Do not write *I want for her to answer*, or *She said for me to open it*, or *I'll tell you for why*; rephrase as *I want her to answer*, and *She said I was to open it* or *She told me to open it*, and *I'll tell you why*.

3 The conjunction **for** can mean 'and the reason is that': *The old lady never goes out in the snow, for she is afraid of slipping*; or 'and the proof is that': *They must be in, for the light is on.* In both these examples, where **for** links two statements of equal importance, it is better than *because* for formal writing. In the first example it is actually clearer in meaning, as *because* after a negative is ambiguous; with *because* the sentence could (absurdly) mean 'It isn't because she's afraid of slipping that she goes out'. **For** as a conjunction must be preceded by a comma or semi-colon, and can even begin a new sentence after a full stop.

4 For **for** or **in**, see IN (3).

forbid

1 The past tense is either **forbade** or **forbad,** and the participle **forbidden**: *The law forebad(e) sedition; You are forbidden to go.* **Forbade** rhymes with either *mad* or *made*, **forbad** rhymes with *mad*.

2 Do not write *Circumstances forbid me from revealing the truth*; but rephrase it as *Circumstances forbid my revealing the truth* or *Circumstances forbid me to reveal it.*

forceps

The plural is **forceps**.

forcible, forceful

1 Forcible ends in *-ible*, not *-able*.

2 Both **forcible** and **forceful** can mean 'possessing force, powerful': *a forcible/forceful argument*. **Forcible**, but not **forceful**, means 'done by force': *forcible entry/expulsion*. **Forceful**, but not **forcible**, can be used of people: *a forceful speaker/personality*.

for(e)bear

The verb meaning 'refrain from' is **forbear**, with the stress on *bear*: *He forbore to answer*. The noun meaning 'ancestor' is either **forebear** or **forbear**, with the stress on *for(e)*.

forecast

The preferred past tense and participle is **forecast** rather than **forecasted**, though both forms exist: *He forecast(ed) a wet summer*; *A wet summer has been forecast(ed)*.

forecastle, fo'c's'le

Whichever way one spells this word for part of a ship, it is pronounced 'FOKE-sl'.

forego, forgo

A verb **forego**, meaning 'precede', survives chiefly in the form **foregoing**: *The foregoing statement is open to challenge*. Another verb, usually spelled **forgo** but sometimes **forego**, means 'renounce': *to forgo a privilege*.

forehead

This is traditionally pronounced to rhyme with *horrid*, but a newer alternative pronunciation rhymes with *warhead*. See SPELLING PRONUNCIATION.

foreign phrases

English has constantly borrowed words and phrases from other languages, and most have become fully naturalized. Some familiar words retain one or more indications of their foreign origin: their plural is un-English (*bacterium–bacteria*) or they have an alternative un-English plural (*antenna–antennas, antennae*); they retain their original accents (*protégé*); or they have spellings that diverge from the usual spelling-pronunciation correspondences (*concerto, debris*).

Foreign words or phrases that are not in general use are often italicized in printed material and underlined elsewhere: *ad hoc*, *ad infinitum*, *a priori*, *bête noire*, *laissez-faire*, *vis-à-vis*. When foreign expressions are in the process of becoming naturalized, practice is likely to be varied, but in formal writing you should use italics or the equivalent underlining if you are in doubt.

The safest rule over foreign words and phrases in English is to avoid them where you can, since they are liable to be misused and misunderstood. It is, for example, easy to confuse *à fond* (ie 'thoroughly') with *au fond* (ie 'fundamentally'), or to misinterpret *in petto* as 'in miniature' rather than 'in secret'.

This can be a matter of tact, and of judgment as to your intended audience. One has no hesitation over such well-naturalized words as *café* or *concerto*, but one will usually be careful over *tête-à-tête* or *hoi polloi*. (It is, of course, another matter if unethically one actually wants to make someone feel inferior.)

There are situations, however, where a borrowed term has no reasonable English equivalent. The French words *blasé*, *manqué*, and *détente*, the Italian *imbroglio*, and the German *schadenfreude* express ideas that could otherwise be conveyed only by unwieldy circumlocution. These are justifiably used in suitable contexts.

See ACCENT MARKS; FOREIGN PHRASES; LATINISMS; ORIGINS OF WORDS.

foreign placenames

The names of countries, and of the world's most important cities and natural features, have always been translated into various languages. Just as the French language calls *London Londres* and the *United States* the *États-Unis*, so English uses *Italy* for the country which its inhabitants call *Italia*, and both English and French call its capital *Rome* rather than *Roma*.

Even if we do not change the spelling of foreign placenames, we often modify their pronunciation for our own comfort, pronouncing *Paris*, for instance, to rhyme with the English surname *Harris*.

But all of this seems to be changing. The English language anglicizes the pronunciation of placenames less than it did even a generation ago. Whether because of increased foreign travel or from a becoming increase in national modesty, we now try to pronounce *Marseilles* and *Rheims* more or less as their citizens do, whereas our forebears made them rhyme with *Wales* and *dreams*. We also have to learn the names of many towns in their own languages, if only to catch the right plane to *Geneva* or *Florence* when the airport departure board announces flights to *Genf* or *Firenze*.

Here are a few foreign placenames and their English versions:

own language	*English*
Bruxelles	Brussels
Firenze	Florence
Gdansk	Danzig
Genève, Genf, Ginevra	Geneva
Livorno	Leghorn
München	Munich
Reims	Rheims

For Chinese names, see PINYIN.

foreign plurals

1	general	4	French plurals
2	Latin plurals	5	Italian plurals
3	Greek plurals	6	Hebrew plurals

1 general

Most foreign words that have been borrowed into English take the regular English -*s* plural, eg *kindergartens*. Some have both a foreign plural, generally for technical usage, and an -*s* plural, for everyday usage; eg *formulae* in mathematics and science, and *formulas* otherwise. Others have only the foreign plural.

The lists of foreign words below indicate which you should use only with the foreign plural and which you may use with either plural, the choice generally depending on the type of context. The headings refer to the language of origin for most of the words in each list.

2 Latin plurals

(a) singular -*us*

Latin plural in -*i*: *alumnus, alumni*; *bacillus, bacilli*; *locus, loci*; *stimulus, stimuli*. Both plurals: *cactus* (*cactuses* or *cacti*); *focus*; *fungus*; *nucleus*; *radius*; *syllabus*; *terminus*. Latin plural in -*a*: *genus, genera*. Both plurals: *corpus* (*corpuses* or *corpora*).

(b) singular -*a*

Latin plural in -*ae*: *alga, algae*; *alumna, alumnae*; *larva, larvae*. Both plurals: *antenna* (*antennas* or *antennae*); *formula*; *nebula*; *vertebra*.

(c) singular -*um*

Latin plural in -*a*: *addendum, addenda*; *bacterium, bacteria*; *corrigendum, corrigenda*; *desideratum*; *erratum*; *ovum*. Both plurals: *aquarium* (*aquariums* or *aquaria*); *candelabrum*; *curriculum*; *maximum*; *medium*; *memorandum*; *millennium*; *minimum*; *moratorium*; *podium*; *referendum*; *spectrum*; *stratum*; *symposium*; *ultimatum*. Do not use *media* in the sense of news media as a singular. In American

English, *data* (from the rarely used singular *datum*) is often treated as singular (*this data*; *The data was* . . .), but in British English it should be treated as plural, except when it is a technical term in data processing.

(d) singular *-ex* or *-ix*
Latin plural in *-ices*: *codex, codices*. Both plurals: *apex* (*apexes* or *apices*); *appendix*; *index*; *matrix*; *vortex*.

3 Greek plurals

(a) singular in *-is*
Greek plural in *-es*: *analysis, analyses*; *axis, axes*; *basis, bases*; *crisis*; *diagnosis*; *ellipsis*; *hypothesis*; *oasis*; *paralysis*; *parenthesis*; *synopsis*; *synthesis*; *thesis*.

(b) singular in *-on*
Greek plural in *-a*: *criterion, criteria*; *phenomenon, phenomena*. Both plurals: *automaton* (*automatons* or *automata*); *ganglion*. Do not use *criteria* or *phenomena* as singular or make plural forms from them (*criterias, phenomenas*).

4 French plurals

(a) singular in *-eau* or *-eu*
Both the French plural in *-x* and the regular plural in *-s*: *adieu* (*adieus* or *adieux*); *bureau*; *chateau*; *flambeau*; *milieu*; *plateau*; *tableau*. The plural of *nouveau riche* (a person who has recently become rich) *is nouveaux riches*.

(b) singular in *-s* or *-x*
The French plural is the same as the singular: *chamois*; *chassis*; *corps*; *patois*; *rendezvous*. The plural is, however, pronounced differently. The final *-s* of the singular is not pronounced at all, but in the plural it has a 'z' sound.

5 Italian plurals
The singular in *-o* has a plural in *-i*. Both plurals: *libretto* (*librettos* or *libretti*); *tempo*; *virtuoso*. *Graffiti* is plural, but the singular *graffito* is not often used. The plural *banditti* is occasionally found instead of the regular *bandits*.

6 Hebrew plurals
Hebrew plural in *-im*: *kibbutz, kibbutzim*. Both plurals: *cherub* (*cherubs* or *cherubim*); *seraph*. *Matzo* (unleavened bread) has the Hebrew plurals *matzoth* and *matzot* as well as the regular *matzos* (which also represents one pronunciation of the Hebrew plural).

forename

See CHRISTIAN NAME.

forever

In American English, **for** and **ever** are regularly combined into one word. British writers often prefer to keep them apart when the phrase means 'for all future time' (*to live for ever*; *diamonds are for ever*) but to combine them to mean 'persistently' (*He's forever complaining*) or 'a very long time' (*It took me forever to find the house*).

foreword, forward

A **foreword** is a preface to a book, especially one not written by the author. **Forward** means 'to the front'.

forgivable

The word is spelled without the final *e* of *forgive*.

former, latter

1 Former refers to the first of two things, **latter** to the second of two. Where more than two items are involved, use *first* or *first-named*, *last* or *last-named*, or simply repeat the words involved: *John, Bill, and Sarah met at John's* (not *at the former's*) *house*; *Of silver, gold, and platinum, the last* (not *the latter*) *is the most valuable*.

It is usually better, however, to recast one's sentence so as to avoid using **former** or **latter**. People sometimes use them unnecessarily, as a sort of ELEGANT VARIATION, where repetition would be clearer; they oblige the reader to look back through the sentence and see what they refer to, whereas the eye and attention should be encouraged to travel uninterruptedly forward.

Boswell reports that Dr Johnson always 'contrived to construct his sentences so as to have no occasion for them'. Instead of writing something like *Of puppies and kittens, the former are harder to train*, one can often rephrase the sentence simply as *Puppies are harder to train than kittens*. There is more excuse for using **former** and **latter** in some longer sentences where a simple pronoun would be confusing, as it would be here: *When news of the disaster came, Cornwallis sought to retrieve it by cutting off Morgan, but the latter had dropped back with such celerity that the force sent out was too late*. If *the latter* were replaced by *he,* we should be in doubt as to which general was in question. It would be best, though, to say *Morgan*.

2 A **former** bank clerk (or criminal, or Conservative) remains a former bank clerk for the rest of his or her life. It is illogical to say that any living person *was a former* anything. Do not write *Our new Chairman was the former company secretary*. You can say either that he *is the former secretary* or that he *was formerly the secretary*.

formerly, formally

Formerly means 'previously'. **Formally** means 'in a formal way'.

formidable

Some speakers dislike the pronunciation with the stress on the second syllable, rather than the first.

formula

The tendency is to prefer the Latin plural **formulae** in scientific contexts (*mathematical formulae*), and **formulas** elsewhere (*political formulas*).

formulate, formulation

Formulate means 'express in a systematic form' (*formulate an opinion*) or 'develop' (*formulate a policy*). The related noun is **formulation**: *his concise formulation of the problem*. **Formulation** is now somewhat OVERUSED to mean 'theory' (*the formulation that parents should be more closely involved in the learning process*) or 'formula' (*a new varnish formulation*).

forte

When it means a person's 'strong point', it is pronounced 'for-tay' or 'fort'. In the musical sense, it is 'for-ti' or 'for-tay'.

forth, fourth

Forth means 'onwards'. **Fourth** is 4th.

fortissimo

The plural is either **fortissimi** or **fortissimos**.

fortuitous

Fortuitous properly means 'happening by chance': *the fortuitous rencounters, the strange accidents of fortune* (Henry Miller). It is often misused to mean 'fortunate', as in the headline: *Fortuitous try helps All Blacks to survive their uncertainty* (*The Times*). The article goes on to describe how the scrum half scored 'a try which Wilson, his captain, described as lucky'. The use of **fortuitous** in this sense is open to objection, since strictly a **fortuitous** event may be an 'unfortunate' one.

forty

The word is spelled without a *u*.

forum

The usual plural is **forums**; but in reference to an ancient Roman marketplace it is **fora**.

forward(s)

1 See FOREWORD.

2 Before a noun, use **forward**: *forward planning*; *forward players*. After a verb use **forward** in American English. In British English, use **forwards** only when it means 'moving straight ahead': *run backwards and forwards*; *This wheel rotates only forwards*. Otherwise, prefer **forward**: *bring the date of the meeting forward*; *I look forward to seeing you*.

forward (*verb*)

Use **forward** for 'send on' (*forward the letters to your new address*); but it is unnecessary to use it merely for 'send', as in *forward the goods on receipt of your cheque*.

foul, fowl

Foul means 'dirty' or 'treacherous'. A **fowl** is a bird.

founder

See FLOUNDER.

fourth

See FORTH.

fowl

1 See FOUL.

2 The plural is usually **fowls** (*feed the fowls*) except in such compounds as *wildfowl*, *guinea fowl*.

fraction

Fraction often means 'a tiny bit': *come just a fraction closer*. Yet, correctly, a **fraction** is any proportion of a whole number. This ambiguity is played upon dishonestly by advertisers who tell us that something can be got at *a fraction of the cost* of something else. It could in theory mean $^{49}/_{50}$ of the cost, but it sounds much less.

fractious

See FACTIOUS.

framework

Within the framework is a CLICHÉ. It is better to write *problems within* (not *within the framework of*) *the organization*, and *deal with the matter in conformity with* (not *within the framework of*) *EEC regulations*.

Frankenstein

In the original novel of that title by Mary Shelley, **Frankenstein** was the name of the monster's creator, not of his monster, but the term is now commonly used of any creation that destroys its maker.

frantic(al)ly

The longer form **frantically** is now more usual.

frappé

The accent is sometimes omitted in American English. It is used of a drink to mean 'chilled'.

fraught

The rather literary **fraught** *with* means 'charged with': *a situation fraught with peril*. In informal British English **fraught** can mean 'tense and anxious' (*fraught and complex relationships*), but the word should not be used like that in formal writing.

free, freely

1 These adverbs both mean 'in a free manner'. **Free,** meaning 'without restriction', is used in certain phrases (*let the rope run free*) but cannot replace **freely,** the usual adverb, elsewhere: *She freely admitted her mistake.* Only **free** means 'without payment'. Children educated **free** do not pay fees, children educated **freely** are allowed a lot of liberty.

2 *For* **free** means 'without payment', but the phrase does not belong in formal writing.

free rein

This means 'unrestricted scope': *give free rein to one's feelings*. As the phrase is associated with horses and not kings, the word is **rein**, not *reign*.

freeze, frieze

Freeze means 'turn to ice'; a **frieze** is a decorative band on a wall.

French pronunciation

It is very difficult to pronounce a French word correctly in the middle of an English sentence. (When a French person does so, it is often at the cost of pronouncing the rest of the sentence as if it were French.) Even if one does succeed in saying the French perfectly, the result may sound ostentatious and affected.

The conventional compromise is to make some approximation to the French sound, without going beyond the repertoire of the English pronunciation system. We do this when we rhyme *machine* with *green*, rather than with *line* as the spelling would suggest, or when we pronounce *café* with two syllables rather than rhyming it with *safe*.

fresco

The plural is either **frescos** or **frescoes**.

fresh

Fresh often replaces *new* when a writer wants to emphasize the attractive qualities of vigour and originality: *a fresh approach to the question*; *some fresh evidence*; *to gain a fresh skill*. In this sense, **fresh** is a somewhat OVERUSED word.

freshman, fresher

They both mean a first-year student, of either sex. **Fresher** is a British English alternative, and may be preferred because it lacks the *-man* ending. The word *freshwoman* barely exists. See FEMININE FORMS.

friable

This means 'crumbly', not 'able to be fried': *friable soil*.

friend

1 The word is spelled *-ie-*, not *-ei-*.

2 It is perfectly correct to say *I am friends with him* or *I made friends with him*.

friendly, friendlily

Although it ends with -ly like *quickly* and *easily*, **friendly** is not an adverb but an adjective: *a friendly smile*. The related adverb **friendlily** (*He smiled friendlily*) looks and sounds so odd that some writers have experimented with using **friendly** as an adverb; but *He smiled friendly* is not yet acceptable, and it is better to write *in a friendly way*, or to rephrase the sentence as *He gave me a friendly smile*.

frieze

See FREEZE.

frock

This is a somewhat old-fashioned word for a girl's or woman's dress, and tends to sound quaint or facetious.

frolic

Other forms are **frolicked, frolicking**.

from

1 Do not write *from hence*, *from thence*, *from whence*. These rather archaic words mean 'from here', 'from there', 'from where', and can stand alone. Write *the village whence* (not *from whence*) *he came*, or (better) *the village he came from* and (more formally) *the village from which he came*. *From here*, *from there*, and *from where* (*We walked from where you left us*) are perfectly correct and are preferable.

2 When numbers indicate a range, **from** is often unnecessary after another preposition such as *of* or *with* (*at a cost of (from) £5 to £10*; *men with (from) three to six years' experience*), or after certain verbs (*It cost (from) £5 to £10*; *He spent (from) three to six years on the project*).

frontier

Countries have **frontiers** *with* other countries: *France's frontier with* (not *to*) *Belgium*.

front-runner

This originally meant a contestant who does best when racing in front position. It has since been so much used to mean 'leader of the field, pacemaker' that the original sense is likely to be misunderstood.

froward

This is an archaic word for 'perverse' or 'unfavourable'. It does not mean 'forward'.

fruition

This means 'realization, fulfilment'. Surprisingly, the word is not connected with the literal sense of *fruit*; but *come to fruition* and *bear fruit* both mean 'reach a satisfactory result'.

fuchsia

It is spelled like this, not *fuschia*, and pronounced 'FEW-sha'. It is called after a German botanist named Fuchs.

fuel (*verb*)

Other forms are **fuelled, fuelling** in British English, but the second *l* is usually omitted in American English.

-ful

This forms the ending of words such as *roomful* or *handful*. The usual plurals of such words are *roomfuls*, *handfuls*, and so on, although plurals such as *cupsful* and *teaspoonsful* are sometimes used for the words common in measuring. The following is odd, but not wrong: *long, overcrowded, earnest television debates in which studiosful of people competed in failing to get across their point of view* (*Daily Telegraph*).

fulfil(l)

The word is spelled **fulfil** in British English, **fulfill** in American English. In both cases, other forms are **fulfilled, fulfilling**. The related noun is **fulfilment** in British English, **fulfillment** in American English.

full, fully

In older English and poetry, **full** as an adverb means 'very' (*was full glad*) or 'entirely': *Full fathom five thy father lies* (Shakespeare). In modern English, **full** means 'exactly' or 'squarely' (*hit him full in the face*) while **fully** means 'at least' (*fully half of us*).

full stops

Use a full stop (also called **period**, especially in American English) to mark the end of a sentence or a sentence fragment (eg the response *Much better, thank you.*) that is not a question or an exclamation. You may also use a full stop instead of a question mark if the question has the force of a request: *Would you please send me the forms as soon as possible.* See also REPORTED SPEECH.

Use full stops to mark abbreviated words, including initials of names: *Prof.*, *Rev.*, *Nov.*, *Inc.*, *B.C.*, *U.K.*, *a.m.* There is, however, an increasing tendency in British English to omit the full stop when the first and last letters of an abbreviation are present: *Mr, Mrs, Ms, Dr*, and so on. The same tendency is found in other instances (*MA, PhD, pm*), but it is safer to insert the full stops if you are in doubt. In both British and American English it is usual not to punctuate ACRONYMS: *NATO*, *CBS*, *BBC*. If an abbreviation full stop comes at the end of a sentence, it serves also as the full stop of the sentence.

Use ellipsis dots (or ellipsis periods) to mark the omission of part of a quotation:

> The writer asserted: The City of London, Britain's financial centre, has always been a place apart from the rest of the country . . .
> Today the City is more different and separate than ever.

If the omission comes at the end of a sentence (as in this example), a fourth dot is added in American English and sometimes in British English, especially in scholarly writing.

Use full stops before decimals (*65.5 per cent*), between units of money (*£10.50; $15.75*), and in British English between hours and minutes (*5.30 p.m.*; in American English *5:30 p.m.*).

fulsome

The oldest sense of the word is 'abundant, copious': *described it in fulsome detail*. In modern English, however, the word chiefly means 'too effusive' or 'overdone': *fulsome praise*; *the fulsome chromium glitter of the escalators* (Lewis Mumford). **Fulsome** will certainly be understood in a derogatory sense, whether or not this is intended.

fun

Fun is now used informally in both British and American English as an adjective before nouns: *fun people*; *a fun party*. This is a pleasant and lively device, but it does not belong in serious writing.

funds

This is a proper word for an available supply of money (*funds allocated to research*), but it can seem PRETENTIOUS or FACETIOUS when it means small sums of cash.

fungus

The usual plural is **fungi**; but **funguses** is sometimes used.

funnel (*verb*)

Other forms are **funnelled, funnelling** in British English, but the second *l* is usually omitted in American English.

funny

This can mean 'amusing', or more informally 'peculiar', 'dishonest' (*funny business*), or 'slightly unwell' (*feel funny*). Only the 'amusing' sense is appropriate to formal writing, and one must be careful that the word is not understood in one of the other senses.

furnish

This is the right word for 'equip with furniture', but it may seem rather PRETENTIOUS as a substitute for *provide* or *give*. To *furnish particulars* means no more than 'tell'.

furor(e)

In British English, this word is usually spelled **furore**, rhyming with *Tory*. In American English, it is usually spelled **furor**, rhyming with *more*. It chiefly means 'uproar, commotion'; an older sense 'craze, fad' has fallen into disuse.

further, furthest, farther, farthest

All these words can be used for literal distance: *farther/further down the corridor*; *Who can jump the farthest/furthest?* Only **further**, not **farther**, can be used in the abstract sense: *closed until further notice; was further annoyed by a second intrusion*; and only **further** can be used as a verb: *to further your chances*. **Farthest** and **furthest** are synonyms: *the subject farthest/furthest removed from my comprehension*. Many careful writers choose **farther** and **farthest** for the literal sense, but it is not wrong to use **further** and **furthest** throughout.

fuse, fuze

The electrical safety device is a **fuse** in both British and American English. In American military use, a detonator for setting off an explosive charge is a **fuze**, and this distinction has been adopted by NATO.

fused participle

The *-ing* participle is traditionally called a GERUND when it is the verb in a phrase that is a noun equivalent: *She likes* **playing golf** (compare *She likes that*). The traditional rule is that the noun or pronoun before the gerund must be in the genitive case:

> They were afraid of *the workers' demonstrating* against the new rules.

(Compare: They were afraid of *the workers' demonstration* against the new rule.)

> I cannot remember *his borrowing* the file.

The alternative construction is the fused participle, where the noun or pronoun is not genitive:

> I cannot remember *him borrowing* the file.

> They were afraid of *the workers demonstrating.*

Some writers object to the fused participle because it is initially misleading: the above sentences do not mean 'I cannot remember him' or 'They were afraid of the workers'. On the other hand, English has a parallel construction with the infinitive that escapes criticism. The following sentences are identical except that the first has the participle and the second has the infinitive:

> I do not want *them making* a noise during the service.

> I do not want *them to make* a noise during the service.

To avoid objections, prefer the genitive in formal writing for pronouns and names. In many other instances the genitive is clumsy or impossible, so that the fused participle is either preferable or the only alternative:

> We are interested in *the building being* sold before the end of the year.

> I am not sure of *the information being* correct.

> They remember *a car with a broken rear window passing* through a red light.

> The council was afraid of *the teachers and parents protesting* against the cuts.

> I did not see *him signing* the letter.

It is usually possible to rephrase the sentence to avoid using the *-ing* form; for example:

I am not sure whether the information is correct.

The council was afraid that the teachers and parents would protest against the cuts.

Both the gerund and the fused participle are to be distinguished from the modifying participle that follows a noun. Contrast:

1. I cannot risk *Norman's talking* to her. (gerund)

2. I cannot risk *Norman talking* to her. (fused participle)

3. I do not know *the boy talking* to her. (modifying participle)

There can be ambiguity between types 2 and 3:

I do not like the boy talking to her. ('I do not like it that he talks to her' (2) or 'I do not like the boy who is talking to her' (3))

Since *-ing* words can be nouns, there can also be ambiguity between the gerund and a noun: *I did not like his writing* (gerund: the fact that he wrote; noun: his handwriting or what he wrote). If your intention is not clear in the context, rephrase the sentence.

future

In the near future is a VERBOSE way of saying 'soon', and so is *in the not too distant future* for 'eventually'. *Future plans* is often TAUTOLOGOUS; see PLAN (2).

-g-, -gg-

Words ending in *-g* double the *-g* even where a word of more than one syllable is not accented on the last syllable: *humbug(ged)*, *leapfrog(ged)*, *sandbag(ged)*, *zigzag(ged)*. Such words therefore disobey rule (2) given under DOUBLING.

gabardine, gaberdine

The modern fabric is usually spelled **gabardine**, but the medieval garment **gaberdine**.

Gaelic, Gallic

Gaelic refers to the Celts or to their Celtic languages; **Gallic** to Gaul, or France, meaning 'typically French'.

gage, gauge

A token of defiance or pledge of performance is a **gage**. A measurement (*narrow gauge railway*) or instrument for measuring, or the verb meaning 'measure; estimate' (*hard to gauge his moods*), is **gauge** in British English but often **gage** in American English. In both spellings, the word rhymes with *cage*.

gainfully employed

This is official jargon. In ordinary contexts, *working* is preferable.

gainsay

This is a rather literary synonym for *deny* or *dispute*, and almost always used in the negative: *There was no gainsaying the statistics.*

gal

This spelling of *girl* is used to represent a pronunciation that is either Cockney, American, or old-fashioned British upper class.

gala

The chief modern pronunciation in British English is 'gah-la' rather than 'gay-la', but the latter is standard in American English.

gallant

When it means 'courteous to ladies', **gallant** is sometimes pronounced with the stress on the second syllable rather than on the first; the pronunciation, like the concept, is old-fashioned.

Gallic

See GAELIC.

gallon

There are 8 pints, or 4 quarts, in a **gallon**. But the British and Canadian *imperial* **gallon** is about 4.546 litres and the US **gallon** about 3.785 litres. The *wine* **gallon** is the same as the US one.

gallop (*verb*)

Other forms are **galloped, galloping**.

gallows

This is a singular noun: *a gallows*. The plural is **gallows** or, less usually, **gallowses.** Either a singular or a plural verb can be used with reference to a single gallows in its literal sense (*The gallows was/were erected on a hill*), but only the singular when it means the punishment of hanging (*The gallows has been abolished*).

galore

This is a rather informal word for 'abundant': *bargains galore*.

galumph

This informal and FACETIOUS word means 'move heavily and joyfully'. It was coined by Lewis Carroll, the author of *Alice in Wonderland*, as a BLEND of *gallop* and *triumphant*.

gambit

In a game of chess, a **gambit** is a deliberate sacrifice made to gain an advantage. By extension, the word often means 'stratagem' or merely 'opening topic': *a useful conversational gambit*. The idea of sacrifice is lost, but that of a calculated move should be preserved.

gamble, gambol

To **gamble** is to play games of chance for money; to **gambol** is to skip about. Other forms of **gambol** are **gambolled, gambolling** in British English, but the second *l* is usually omitted in American English.

gam(e)y

The word is spelled either with or without the *e*. It means 'smelling slightly decomposed' or 'scandalously spicy': *all the gamy details*.

ganglion

The plural is **ganglia** or, less usually, **ganglions**.

gantlet

See GA(U)NTLET.

gaol, gaoler

These spellings of *jail, jailer* are going out in Britain, and are obsolete in American English.

garage

The pronunciation 'GA-rahzh' is the one that many British speakers prefer. There seems no real reason to object to the anglicized alternative 'GA-ridge', on the analogy of similar words such as *courage* which are borrowed from the French. The chief American form is 'ga-RAHZH', which is rather disliked in Britain.

garb

This is a rather FACETIOUS noun meaning 'clothes' (*His garb was bizarre*) or verb meaning 'dress' (*garbed in black*).

gargantuan, gigantic

These both mean 'huge', but **gargantuan** applies almost solely to food and appetite (*a gargantuan meal*) while **gigantic** refers to either literal or figurative size: *a man of gigantic stature*; *a gigantic bill for repairs*.

garments

As a plural, this can seem a rather PRETENTIOUS word for 'clothes'. **Garment** in the singular is a useful alternative to 'item of clothing'.

gar(r)ot(t)e

The British tend to spell it **garrotte** or **garotte**, the Americans to prefer **garrote**. It means 'strangle'.

gas

Other forms are **gases** or **gasses, gassing, gassed**. In American English the noun means 'gasoline, petrol', and one must thus be careful to avoid confusion with cooking gas, also often sold in liquid form at filling stations.

gaseous, gassy

Gaseous begins with the sound 'gas' or 'gash' in American English, but sometimes also with 'gay' in British English. **Gaseous** is more formal and scientific than **gassy**, which chiefly means 'fizzy': *gassy beer*.

gasoline, gasolene

Gasoline is the commoner spelling, but both are correct.

gaucho

The plural is **gauchos**. It means either a South American cowboy or, in the plural, short wide trousers.

gauge

See GAGE.

ga(u)ntlet

Gauntlet is the British spelling, both for the protective glove and for the ordeal by beating. **Gantlet** is an American alternative, but more for the ordeal than for the glove.

gay

As both adjective and noun, this is the preferred word used by homosexuals of themselves. 'Homosexual' has become such an important sense of **gay** that one may be misunderstood if one uses it simply to mean 'cheerful' or 'brightly coloured'. See HOMOSEXUAL.

gazebo

The plural is **gazebos.** It means a roofed but usually wall-less structure built to command a view.

-ge

See -E-.

geezer

See GEYSER.

gelatin(e)

The form without the second *e* is preferred in American English, and in scientific use everywhere; **gelatine** is chiefly British. The American pronunciation ends with 'tin' or 't'n', the British usually like 'teen'.

gender

This is a word for grammatical classification: *nouns of the masculine gender*. It is sometimes used to mean 'quality of being male or female' (*prejudices based on the gender of candidates*) where the more usual word *sex* might suggest 'sexual behaviour' in a physical sense. It should not be used FACETIOUSLY, as in *persons of the feminine gender*.

gender, grammatical

Gender is a grammatical classification of words that corresponds largely with distinctions of meaning, particularly differences of sex. In English, unlike many other languages, nouns and other parts of speech do not have inflectional endings that indicate their gender. A few sets of pronouns, however, express natural distinctions. Masculine pronouns (eg *he*, *him*, *his*, *himself*) refer to males, and feminine pronouns (*she*, *her*, *hers*, *herself*) refer to females. The neuter pronouns *it*, *its*, *itself* are used to indicate something other than a person; for example, an inanimate thing (*some beef*), an abstraction (*truth*), an event (*the riot*), a collection of people (*the government*), and most animals (*a snake*). If we think of an animal (for example a pet) as a person or if we need to distinguish its sex, we may use *she* or *he* instead of *it*. And if we think of an inanimate thing in personal terms (for example, a car, a ship, or a country) we generally use *she* instead of *it*, though people sometimes refer to a computer as *he* and some women use *he* for their car. On the other hand, we can use *it* for a baby, though it is more polite in the presence of the parents to refer to the baby as *he* or *she*.

The pronouns *who*, *whom*, *whoever*, *whomever* always indicate people. They contrast with the nonpersonal *which* and *whichever*: *Margaret*, **who** *knows me well*; *your parents' house*, **which** *I have often visited*.

There are a few pairs of nouns where one has a feminine ending (eg *hostess*, *heroine*, *usherette*) or a masculine ending (*bridegroom*, *widower*). There are of course other nouns that refer to males or females but they have no distinctive forms for that purpose: *wife/husband*; *mother/father*; *sister/brother*.

Most of the pronouns can refer directly to something in the situation: *Look at* **her**, but they commonly refer to something that appears in the same sentence or in a previous sentence: **Joan** *is the eldest daughter and I like* **her** *best*. All nouns belong to gender classes indirectly because of the choice of pronouns that go with them. For example, we use *he* for *uncle* and *man*, but *she* for *aunt* and *woman*. Depending on the sex of the person, we refer back to the words *doctor* and *student* by *she* or *he*.

See also SEXISM; WHOSE.

general

When **general** forms the second part of a military title, the plural is regular; *lieutenant generals* and *major generals* are particular kinds of

general. When **general** is an adjective at the end of a nonmilitary title, the traditional plural is as in *attorneys general*, *secretaries-general*, *postmasters general*, but such combinations are tending to fall in line with the military practice, so that *attorney generals* is also acceptable.

generalissimo

The plural is **generalissimos**.

generally

This can mean 'usually' (*He generally drinks tea*) or 'as a whole' (*of interest to the public generally*). One must be careful not to write things like *They are generally hungry*, which probably means 'all of them most of the time', if it might be taken to mean 'most of them always'.

generator

The word ends in *-or*, not *-er*.

genesis

The plural is **geneses**. It means 'origin'.

genetic, congenital

Inherited conditions are **genetic**; **congenital** ones date from one's birth (*congenital brain damage*).

genetics

See EUGENICS.

genial

See CONGENIAL.

genitive

The genitive or possessive is a grammatical case in English that indicates a relationship between two nouns or between a pronoun and a noun. In *the* **child's** *father*, *the* **workers'** *complaints*; **her** *father*, **their** *complaints*, the words *child's*, *workers'*, *her*, and *their* are in the genitive case. In writing (though not always in speech) the genitive has a distinct form. The genitive noun is marked by an apostrophe, with or without an additional *s*. *The child has a father – the child's father*; *The workers have complaints – the workers' complaints*. The genitive pronoun also has a distinctive form: *She has a father –* **her** *father*;

They have complaints – **their** *complaints*. The apostrophe is sometimes attached to the last word of a phrase rather than to the main noun: *the chairman of the company's speech.*

Instead of a genitive noun, we can often put an *of*-phrase after the other noun: eg instead of *the* **child's** *father* we can have *the father* **of the child**. The genitive is more usual if the noun refers to living things, particularly human beings. It may also be used if the noun refers to certain things closely associated with human beings, eg **London's** *water supply*, *the* **school's** *board of governors*, *the* **book's** *first sentence*, *the football* **season's** *first matches*. Otherwise, it is normal to use the *of*-phrase (*the end* **of the garden**) or to use the noun as a modifier without the genitive (*the* **door** *handle*).

See APOSTROPHE; CASE, GRAMMATICAL; LINKED GENITIVES; OF; -'S.

genius

When it means 'very great intelligence', or a person possessing this, the plural is usually **geniuses**. When it means 'attendant spirit', the plural is **genii**. See also JINN.

gent

This is FACETIOUS as a short form of *gentleman*.

genteelism

This is a kind of EUPHEMISM, which means the substitution of a mild or indirect expression for one that might be offensive. Many euphemisms are entirely justified. We use them not only for decency, with reference to bodily parts and functions, but out of generous feeling towards people whom we should otherwise have to call *poor*, *fat*, *old*, *crippled*, or *stupid*. But the kind of euphemism here called genteelism is favoured by people who think the frank and obvious word is vulgar. Since the most effective users of the language are seldom afraid of being frank (or even abrupt when the occasion warrants it), it is a mistake to try to sound genteel.

Some expressions that used to be genteel, such as (in Britain) *toilet* for *lavatory*, have passed into such general use as no longer to deserve censure. The following list contrasts a few genteelisms, still identifiable as such, with their more direct equivalents.

genteel	plain
bosom	breast, chest
dentures	false teeth
expectorate	spit
odour	smell
perspire	sweat

| retire | go to bed |
| soiled | dirty |

gentle art

This is a CLICHÉ, as used in *the gentle art of procrastination*.

gentleman

There is a slightly archaic ring to this word. Men do not use it of other men with whom they are at all intimate, and it sounds somewhat coy on the lips of a woman (*her gentleman friend*). Its chief uses are half-humorously to emphasize courtesy and chivalrousness (*He's a perfect gentleman*); or as a polite form used in someone's presence (*Bring the gentleman a clean glass*); or in the plural in public address (*ladies and gentlemen*) where *Men* would savour of the army or the football field; or perhaps with *old*, because *old gentleman* sounds more respectful than *old man*. Compare LADY.

genuine

In British English the final *-ine* is pronounced as in *tin*; in American English it is also pronounced as in *mine*. See AUTHENTIC.

genus

Genera is the correct plural of this technical word, but some biologists use **genuses.**

geographic(al)

Geographical is the main form.

geometric(al)

Mathematicians prefer the form **geometric**: *geometric progression*; *geometric mean*; *geometric series*. **Geometrical** usually refers to the simple abstract shapes of geometry: *a skirt with a geometrical pattern of squares*.

geometrical progression

See ARITHMETICAL, GEOMETRICAL PROGRESSION.

geriatric

This is the adjective associated with *geriatrics*, the branch of medicine concerned with the health of old people. The fact that **geriatric** can now be used jocularly for 'decrepit' (*my geriatric car*) reminds us unpleasantly of our society's often insensitive attitude to old age.

German sounds

People often have to make some attempt to pronounce in the German way certain German words and names that have passed into English (compare FRENCH PRONUNCIATION). Without going beyond the equivalent customary English sounds, it is reasonable to deal with the matter as follows. Pronounce:

ie as in 'field':	*diesel.*
ei, ai as in 'height':	*Heine, Mainz.*
äu and *eu* as 'oy':	*Fräulein, Freud.*
ee as in 'day':	*Beethoven.*
au as 'ow':	*Frau.*
ch as in the Scots 'loch':	*Bach.*
ö, oe as in 'bird':	*Röntgen.*
sch as 'sh':	*Schiller.*
j as 'y':	*Jaeger.*
w as 'v':	*Wagner.*
z as 'ts':	*Mozart.*

gerund

The gerund is a word ending in *-ing* that behaves in some ways like a noun and in some ways like a verb: *I have not yet received an explanation for their* **postponing** *the meeting*. *Postponing* is here a gerund: it resembles a noun in that it is introduced by the genitive *their* (compare *their postponement of the meeting*), but it is also followed by the object *their meeting* (compare *They postponed the meeting*). Other examples of gerunds: *Norman was not aware of your* **applying** *for the position*; *Ruth likes* **using** *a computer*; *You can save electricity by* **switching** *off lights whenever you leave the room*; *We have no intention of* **restricting** *your right to join any trade union*. See FUSED PARTICIPLES.

In a similar construction, the gerund is linked to the following noun by *of*. Prefer the simpler structure without *of*: *I have not yet received an explanation for their* **postponing of** *the meeting* (omit *of*); *You can save electricity by* **the switching** *off of lights whenever you leave the room* (omit *the* and *of*).

Some verbs allow a gerund but not an infinitive to follow (eg *They*

regretted asking *me*; *He* **resented waiting** *for them*); others allow an infinitive but not a gerund (eg *I* **hope to see** *you soon*; *She* **asked to meet** *us*); others allow both a gerund and an infinitive (*They* **like going/ to go** *to the supermarket*; *I* **remembered writing/to write** *to my sister*). In general, the gerund expresses that the situation has occurred at the time indicated by the main verb of the sentence, and the infinitive that it has not occurred. Contrast:

Did you remember *writing* to your sister? (that you had written)

Did you remember *to write* to your sister? (that you should write)

The entries for individual verbs in this book and in a good dictionary will often tell you whether you should use a gerund or an infinitive and whether you may use either.

gesticulate, gesture

In the literal sense, to **gesticulate** usually involves waving one's arms excitedly. It is more theatrical than to **gesture** or make **gestures**. The noun **gesture**, but not *gesticulation*, is used of anything done for its effect on others: *send them flowers as a friendly gesture*.

get

1 In really formal writing it is better not to use **get** very much. It can usually be replaced by *become*, *receive*, *buy*, *obtain*, according to the sense. In certain contexts, though, **get** is almost unavoidable. *They got married last week* means that they underwent the ceremony then, whereas *They were married last week* may only mean that they were husband and wife at the time. (One could, of course, say *They married last week*.)

2 Gotten, rather than **got**, is an alternative past participle in American English. It is used for the sense 'obtain' (*He's just gotten a new passport*), not for the sense 'possess' (*He has* (not *he's gotten*) *big ears*). British English allows *He's got big ears*, but not in formal writing.

geyser, geezer

A **geyser** is a hot spring, or (in British English) a bathroom gas boiler; **geezer** is an informal word for a peculiar fellow. The British usually pronounce them in the same way, with the first syllable rhyming with *breeze*, but in American English the first syllable of the 'hot spring' sense usually rhymes with *size*.

ghetto

The plural is **ghettos** or, less usually, **ghettoes**.

ghoul

It rhymes with *fool*, not *owl*.

gibe, gybe, jibe

These three words are all pronounced alike. **Gibe** (sometimes spelled **jibe**) means 'to tease', or 'a taunt'. **Gybe** (British English) or **jibe** (American) is a nautical word, used of a sail that swings suddenly across the vessel. A third verb **jibe** means 'be in accord; agree' in American English: *His account of the accident jibes pretty well with theirs.*

gift

Do not use **gift** as a verb as in *They gifted him with a book*, since we can convey the same sense with *They gave him a book*. **Gifted** meaning 'highly intelligent' (*gifted children*) is perfectly acceptable.

gigantic

See GARGANTUAN.

gigolo

The plural is **gigolos**.

gild, guild

1 Gild means 'to cover with gold'; **guild** (less usually spelled **gild**) means 'an association of merchants or craftsmen'.

2 Other forms of **gild** are **gilded** or **gilt**, but in the figurative sense 'make deceptively attractive' it has to be **gilded**: *gilded corruption*.

gill

When the word means a fish's breathing apparatus or a mountain ravine, the *g* is pronounced as in *giggle*. When it is a unit of liquid capacity, it is pronounced like *Jill*.

gilt, guilt

Gilt means 'covered with gold', from the verb *gild*; **guilt** means 'blame'.

gimmick

This is a useful word for a novel device, scheme, or attention-getting angle: *a new gimmick for our political campaign*. One can scarcely advise anyone not to use it in serious writing, because judicious writers plainly do use it.

gipsy, gypsy

Gipsy is the chief British spelling, **gypsy** the American one. It is often spelled with a capital *G* for the people or their language.

girdle

See GRIDDLE.

girlfriend

A man's **girlfriend** is today more likely to be a sexual partner than a mere female companion. A woman's **girlfriend** may be a female companion (*She's out shopping with a girlfriend*) or her homosexual partner. Compare BOYFRIEND, and see LOVER.

girlish

See BOYISH.

given name

See CHRISTIAN NAME.

glacé

The word is spelled with the accent.

gladiator

The word ends in *-or*, not *-er*.

glamo(u)r

It is spelled **glamour** in British English; this is also the preferred spelling in American English, although **glamor** is an acceptable alternative there. Related words are **glamorize** and **glamorous** or, less usually, **glamourize** and **glamourous**.

glance, glimpse

A **glance** is a quick look at something; a **glimpse** is a quick sight of something.

glycerin(e)

The form without the *e* is preferred in American English and in scientific use. **Glycerin** ends with the sound 'in', **glycerine** with 'in' or 'een'.

gneiss

The word is spelled *-ei-*, not *-ie-*. It is a kind of rock.

go

1 Go has always been used with adjectives (*go blind*; *go grey*); and the same construction is used in many combinations (*go public*; *go comprehensive*; *go metric*) which are perfectly appropriate to serious writing. By contrast, **go** with a noun, meaning 'change to' (*go wheels*), **go** *and* expressing surprise (*She went and won first prize*), and **going** *for* meaning 'favourable to' (*He hasn't much going for him*) are somewhat informal.

2 Some people find **going** *to go* (*He's going to go to Paris*) rather clumsy, because it uses **go** twice, and prefer to express the idea in some other way, such as *He's about to go* or *He'll soon be going*.

gobbledygook

See VARIETIES OF ENGLISH.

god

God, the supreme being, is spelled with a capital *G*, but a small *g* is usual for those worshipped in polytheistic systems: *Hindu gods*.

gold, golden

Things actually made of gold are **gold** rather than **golden**: *a gold watch*; *golden curls*.

golf course, links

Originally, a **golf links** was a **golf course** at the seaside, but now the two expressions are often used interchangeably.

good, well

1 Use **well**, not **good**, as an adverb: *He sings well* (not *good*). Both **well** and **good** can be used as adjectives after verbs such as *be*, *seem*, *look*, and *feel*; but there can be a difference between *I feel good* (ie cheerful) and *I feel well* (ie healthy).

2 Good *and* meaning 'completely' (*I'll come when I'm good and ready*) is informal.

goodbye, good-by

1 The spelling without *e*, and with the hyphen, is American rather than British.

2 Although **goodbye** comes from 'God be with you', there is nothing wrong with saying *Goodbye to you*. The internal construction of the word has been obliterated by time.

goodwill, good will

In both British and American English, **goodwill** is spelled as one word when it means the favour and prestige attached to a business, and also when it is used before a noun: *a goodwill gesture*. Many British writers prefer the form **good will** for the general sense: *a gesture of good will*.

gorilla, guer(r)illa

A **gorilla** is a large African ape; a **guer(r)illa** (with either one or two *r*'s) wages irregular warfare. The pronunciation of the two words is usually identical, but some people try to distinguish them by pronouncing the first vowel sound of **guerrilla** like that of *get*.

gossip (*verb*)

Other forms are **gossiped, gossiping.**

got, gotten

See GET.

gourmet, gourmand

A **gourmet** is a connoisseur of fine food and drink, a **gourmand** is simply greedy; the one is a polite term and the other rather rude. A hotel will advertise a complicated expensive meal as a **gourmet** dinner, not a **gourmand** one.

government

In careful speech, the first *n* should not be left out.

governor

The word ends in *-or*, not *-er*.

graceful, gracious

They are both associated with 'grace'. **Graceful** applies chiefly to physical movement: *a graceful dance*; but one may also speak of *a graceful* (ie handsome) *apology*, since **gracious** here would suggest that the person was being condescending. **Gracious** implies kindly courtesy, particularly from a superior: *by the gracious permission of Her Majesty*. In brochures and advertisements, it suggests the dignified elegance available to the rich in the past: *gracious living*; *gracious entertaining*.

gradability

Words are gradable when it is possible to view them as on a scale of more or less. Gradable words may be nouns (*a big* **fool**, *a bigger* **fool**, *the biggest* **fool**), verbs (**admire** *her a little*, **admire** *her greatly*), adjectives (*somewhat* **careless**, *extremely* **careless**), and adverbs (*very* **painfully**, *much more* **painfully**).

Most adjectives and adverbs are gradable, allowing comparison (*less wise*, *as wise*, *wiser*, *most wise*) and modification by degree words. The degree words show how far along the scale they are: *slightly uneasy*; *rather quickly*; *so neatly*; *very happy*; *thoroughly disgusted*. Some adjectives and adverbs are not gradable; we cannot, for example, say *very atomic* or *more previously*. Writers are divided on the gradability of certain adjectives and adverbs, either because the words are thought to express the highest degree (*excellent*; *perfectly*) or because they are thought not to be measurable on a scale (*equal*; *uniquely*). If you are in doubt, it is safer to avoid treating as gradable these adjectives and the corresponding *-ly* adverbs: *absolute, complete, equal, excellent, extreme, ideal, perfect, total, unique, utter*. See COMPARISON.

graduate

In both British and American English, a student is said to **graduate**: *She graduated in 1983*. The older usage by which a university was said to **graduate** a student (*He was graduated from Harvard*) is now less current. The American English *He graduated Harvard* should be replaced by the more correct *He graduated from Harvard*. Americans also use **graduate** for the completion of primary and high school studies.

graffiti

This word for writings on walls is really the plural of the much rarer singular **graffito.** It is now often, though still incorrectly, used with a singular verb (*This graffiti has been painted over*) but should properly be treated as a plural (*These graffiti have been painted over*).

grammar

The word **grammar** is used in various ways, one of which is as a name for the study and description of human languages. One common use takes in *syntax* (the ways in which words combine into phrases and sentences) and *inflections* (changes of form that words undergo to make distinctions such as number and tense). The usual modern name for the scientific study of language is *linguistics*, which includes the study of *grammar* (syntax and inflections), *morphology* (the ways in which words are formed), *phonetics* (speech sounds), *phonology* (the sound system), *semantics* (meaning), and *pragmatics* (language in actual use). *Philology* is an older word for linguistics, used particularly for historical and comparative language study and also for the study of the language of earlier literature.

grammatical analysis

1 general	**7** complement
2 parts of speech	**8** adverbial
3 phrases	**9** sentence types
4 sentence components	**10** clauses
5 subject and verb	**11** nonfinite subordination
6 object	

1 general
This book is a guide to grammatical as well as vocabulary usage, and it makes use of a limited number of grammatical terms. Readers may find it convenient to have the main terms brought together here in one place as a very brief outline of what English grammatical analysis is about.

2 parts of speech
In talking about the ways in which words combine, we need to refer to classes of words. Word classes are usually called **parts of speech.** If we take an example sentence *The chief accountant in the company has explained the new procedures*, a traditional analysis assigns each word to a part of speech:

The	article
chief	adjective
accountant	noun
in	preposition
the	article

company	noun
has	verb
explained	verb
the	article
new	adjective
procedures	noun

Grammarians usually make further distinctions. For example, *has* is said to be an **auxiliary** ('helping' verb), and *explained* a **full** verb. (See also PARTS OF SPEECH.) Many words belong to more than one part of speech. We can only know what they are from their use in a particular sentence. So, *light* is a noun in *The light hurts my eyes*, an adjective in *I prefer light colours*, and a verb in *I cannot light my pipe*.

3 phrases

A sentence consists of words, but the words cluster into **phrases**, groups of words that belong together. Our example sentence consists of three phrases:

The chief accountant in the company

has explained

the new procedures.

The first of these contains another phrase:

in the company.

And that also divides into two parts: *in* and *the company*.

Phrases are called after the main word in the phrase. If we reduced each of the three main phrases in our sentence to one word, the most important word, we would arrive at the sort of sentence that might appear in a newspaper headline: *Accountant explained procedures*. These three words give their names to their phrases:

The chief *accountant* in the company –	noun phrase
has *explained* –	verb phrase
the new *procedures* –	noun phrase

There are five types of phrases, which are named after parts of speech: noun, verb, adjective, adverb, and preposition phrase. *In the company* is a prepositional phrase, named after the introductory preposition (here *in*) that characterizes this type of phrase:

in the company –	prepositional phrase

Notice that the preposition is followed by a noun phrase:

the *company* –   noun phrase

Two types of phrases are not illustrated in our sentence:

very *new* –   adjective phrase

quite *recently* –   adverb phrase

4   sentence components

Our sentence has three noun phrases:

The chief accountant in the company

the company

the new procedures

They have different uses in the sentence. We distinguish between the type of phrase and its function as a **component** of a sentence or a phrase. *The company*, as we have shown, is a component of a prepositional phrase; the other two noun phrases are components of the sentence. In our sentence, *the chief accountant in the company* is the **subject** of the sentence. One traditional division of the sentence is in two parts: the subject and the predicate:

The chief accountant in the company –   subject

has explained the new procedures –   predicate

The predicate can be further analysed into its components; in our sentence they are:

has explained –   verb

the new procedures –   direct object

The verb and the direct object may also be viewed as components of the sentence.

There are seven possible components of the sentence:

subject
verb
direct object
indirect object
subject complement
object complement
adverbial

5 subject and verb

The essential components of typical sentences are the **subject** and the **verb**, and in statements they appear in that order:

subject	*verb*
Alice	skis.
Robert	was reading.
Most of the work	is finished.
Your bicycle	has been stolen.

When we make the sentence into a question that can be answered by *yes* or *no*, the verb comes before the subject. (Usually there is more than one word in the verb phrase, in which case it is the first that precedes the subject.)

Does *she* ski?

Was *he* reading?

Is *most of the work* finished?

Has *your bicycle* been stolen?

The subject is usually what is talked about in the sentence. We can therefore put *who* or *what* before the verb and ask a question about the subject:

Who skis?	Alice.
Who was reading?	Robert.
What is finished?	Most of the work.
What has been stolen?	Your bicycle.

(The question is meaningless, however, when *it* is the subject in sentences like *It is raining*.)

The subject is normally left out in directives (see section 9 below): *Leave at once!*; *Don't argue*. There are also certain minor types of sentences where the verb is left out, eg: *The more, the merrier*; *Hands up!*; *Cigarette?*. And the verb is often left out in response sentences like those in the previous paragraph.

6 object

Many verbs can be followed by a **direct object**:

subject	verb	direct object
Robert	was reading	the newspaper.
Janet	has written	another letter.
The man with the beard	knows	you.
Nobody	can find	my glasses.

We can ask a question with *who* or *what* about the direct object. (We use the subject and verb in our question.)

What was Robert reading?	The newspaper.
What has Janet written?	Another letter.
Who does the man with the beard know?	You.
What can nobody find?	Your glasses.

Some verbs can also take an **indirect object**, which comes before the direct object:

Janet has written *me* another letter.

I have sent *them* the documents.

That has saved *us* some money.

Another way of expressing the same thing is to use a prepositional phrase: *Janet has written another letter* **to me**; *That has saved some money* **for us**.

7 complement

The **subject complement** follows **linking verbs** such as *be*, *become*, and *seem*. It identifies or characterizes the subject:

subject	verb	subject complement
The next station	is	Piccadilly Circus.
My work	has become	more interesting.
This question	seems	far easier.
The chair	looks	comfortable.

Similarly, the **object complement** identifies or characterizes the direct object: *They made her* **their representative**; *I find my work* **more interesting.**

8 adverbial

The **adverbial** refers to such circumstances of the situation as place, time, manner of action, reason, purpose, condition:

We can meet *at my office*.

The last report was published *fifteen years ago*.

The gas mains were cut *accidentally*.

Some adverbials comment on the sentence as a whole or show logical connections between sentences or parts of the sentence:

Unfortunately, no further rises are possible.

One of the directors, *however*, has issued a public statement of protest.

A sentence can have more than one adverbial:

Surprisingly, snowstorms were *still* occurring *in late May*.

9 sentence types

There are four major sentence types: statement, question, directive, and exclamation. Most sentences are statements, such as this: *We provide suitable schooling for the average child, not just the academically gifted one.* There are three types of question: *yes–no* questions expect the answer *yes* or *no* (*Does this make sense to you?*); *wh-* questions, so called because most are introduced by a word beginning with *wh-*, ask for information (*What was their response?*); alternative questions ask for a choice between alternatives (*Is the letter on my desk or in the file?*). Directives express commands, requests, invitations, and the like: *Send the next person in*; *Take another piece*; *Be careful.* Exclamations express the strong feeling of the speaker: *How simple the answer is! What a good time we had!*

It is possible to use one sentence type to convey the meaning of another. The question *Would you please send the next person in?* is a request and the directive *Tell me your name* asks for information.

10 clauses

Sentences within sentences are **clauses**. A sentence that consists of two or more clauses joined together by the conjunctions *and*, *or*, or *but* is a **compound sentence**:

We have not received any reply to our last letter *and* we are therefore referring the matter to our solicitors.

Will you come straight to my house *or* will you go home first?

The climate is excellent, *but* the economy is in bad shape.

These three conjunctions balance the two parts of the sentence; they are **coordinators** and the clauses are **coordinate clauses**.

A sentence containing one or more clauses that are subordinate to it is a **complex sentence** and the clauses are **subordinate clauses**:

> *When you next write a report*, please make sure *that your secretary sends me a copy.*

> *If you have not made an appointment*, you cannot see the dentist.

Subordinate clauses are usually introduced by **subordinators**, such as *if*, *when*, *although*, *that*.

11 nonfinite subordination

Instead of the subordinate clauses illustrated at 10 above, it is possible to use subordination with nonfinite verbs. The three types of nonfinite verbs are: the **infinitive** (usually with *to*), the **present participle** (ending in *-ing*), and the **past participle** (usually ending in *-ed*).

> Please ask your secretary *to* send *me a copy.*

> *When next* writing *a report*, check your spelling.

> Asked *about the allegation*, he would not reply.

Sometimes there is no verb at all:

> *When in doubt*, check your spelling.

gramophone, record player, phonograph, music centre

Gramophone is now old-fashioned, having been superseded by **record player**, the usual term for the modern electronic device. **Phonograph** is still current in American English. **Music centre** is the chiefly British term for a unit combining record player, radio, and cassette tape recorder.

gratis

It is often better replaced by *free*, and the combination *free (and) gratis* is a TAUTOLOGY.

gratuitous

This can mean 'costing nothing', but the usual sense is 'uncalled-for': *gratuitous insolence*. It has nothing to do with 'gratitude'.

gratuity

In British English, this is the proper word for a lump sum given to a soldier on discharge. It may sound PRETENTIOUS or FACETIOUS to use it simply for a 'tip'.

gray

See GREY.

Great Britain, United Kingdom, British Isles

Great Britain, or **Britain**, is the land mass of England, Scotland, and Wales. The **United Kingdom**, or **UK**, adds Northern Ireland to these, its full title being the *United Kingdom of Great Britain and Northern Ireland*. The **British Isles** includes also the Republic of Ireland, and is a geographical term only.

Grecian, Greek

In modern use, **Grecian** applies only to the art of classical Greece and to human features that remind one of this art: *Grecian columns*; *Grecian nose*. It cannot elsewhere replace **Greek**, the usual adjective.

green paper

See WHITE PAPER.

grey, gray

Grey is the usual British spelling, **gray** the American.

griddle, girdle, gridiron, grill

A flat cooking surface is a **griddle** or **girdle**. A metal frame for cooking over a fire is a **gridiron** or **grill**, but **grill** today chiefly means the gas or electric device that throws heat downwards.

grief, grievous

Both words are spelled *-ie-*, not *-ei-*. **Grievous** is neither pronounced nor spelled 'grievious'.

griffon, griffin, gryphon

A **griffon** is a kind of dog. A **griffin**, also spelled **griffon** or **gryphon**, is a mythical animal combining the eagle and the lion.

grill, grille

A **grill** is a piece of cooking equipment (see GRIDDLE); or a restaurant; or a grating, such as that between a bank clerk and a customer or in front of a car radiator. A **grille** can be only a grating.

grind

Grind to a halt is a CLICHÉ.

grisly, grizzly, gristly

Grisly means 'gruesome': *a grisly account of the murder*. **Grizzly** means 'grey', or else a large American bear. **Gristly** refers to the tough *gristle* in meat.

groin, groyne

A **groin** is the join between thigh and abdomen or the line along which two intersecting vaults meet. The wall built from the shore to control erosion is usually spelled **groyne** in British English and **groin** in American English.

grotto

The plural is **grottoes** or, less usually, **grottos.**

ground(s)

Either **ground** or **grounds** can mean 'basis; reason': *ground(s) for complaint. On the grounds that* is a rather VERBOSE way of saying 'because'.

grovel

Other forms are **grovelled, grovelling** in British English, but the second *l* is usually omitted in American English.

gruel(l)ing

Gruelling is the usual spelling in British English, **grueling** in American English.

Gruyère

The word is spelled with a capital *G* and an accent.

gryphon

See GRIFFON.

guarantee, guaranty

Guarantee is both verb and noun, while **guaranty** is only a noun. It is never wrong to use **guarantee** in all the noun senses. Its synonym

guaranty is used only in legal and commercial contexts: *to enter into a guaranty*.

guarantor

The word ends in *-or*, not *-er*. It means 'person or bank that guarantees something'.

guer(r)illa

See GORILLA.

guest

One thinks of a **guest** as being hospitably entertained and paid for by someone else. The use of the same word for people paying to stay at a hotel, and for the immigrant **guest** *workers* in EEC countries, doubtless springs from an attempt to convey this same friendly feeling. It is a fiction, but it would be hard to know what else to call them.

guild

See GILD.

guilt

See GILT.

guilt, guilty

Guilty means 'responsible for an offence', and **guilt** is 'responsibility for an offence'. People who feel **guilty** are often said to be suffering from **guilt** feelings, perhaps because **guilty** *feelings* would suggest that the feelings themselves were blameworthy; but no such problem arises over **guilty** *conscience*.

guise, disguise

These both can mean 'external appearance': *under the guise of friendship*; *blessings in disguise*. **Disguise**, however, is necessarily a false appearance, while **guise** is neutral: *old ideas in a new guise*.

gullible, gullable

The first spelling is usual; the second is rare.

gunwale, gunnel

Whichever way it is spelled, this word for the upper edge of a boat's side rhymes with *tunnel*.

guts

This is informal in the sense of 'courage; determination'. Used in serious contexts, it creates an atmosphere of coarse vigour: *was a tower of strength, holding everything together by sheer unrelenting guts* (Nicholas Monsarrat). See also BELLY.

gybe

See GIBE.

gymnasium

The plural is either **gymnasiums** or **gymnasia**. When it means a German secondary school, not a hall for gymnastics, it is usually pronounced 'gim-NAHZ-ium', with the *g* as in *gift*.

gyn(a)eco-

This means 'of women', and forms words such as *gyn(a)ecology*. The *a* is normally included in British spelling and omitted in American spelling.

gypsy

See GIPSY.

Hh

habiliments

Apart from its figurative use to mean 'fittings' (*the habiliments of civilization*), this is a FACETIOUS word for 'clothes'.

habitable, inhabitable

They both mean 'livable-in'; but **habitable** is usually used of buildings (*make the flat habitable*) and **inhabitable** of larger areas (*The tundra was barely inhabitable*).

habitual

This is usually preceded by *a* rather than by *an*: *a habitual joker*.

habitué

This is spelled with the accent. It means 'a person who regularly visits a place'.

had

See BETTER (1); HAVE.

h(a)emophilia, h(a)emorrhage, etc

See AE-.

hail, hale

Hail means 'summon' or 'acclaim': *hail a taxi*; *His invention was hailed as a major advance*. To **hale** is to compel forcibly: *hale a vagrant into court*. To **hail** *from* a place is to be a native of it; and **hail-fellow-well-met** is used as an adjective meaning 'hearty and genial'. This last is sometimes confused with **hale** *and hearty*, where **hale** means 'healthy'.

hairdo

The plural is **hairdos**.

hairpin, hairgrip, kirby-grip, bobby pin

A **hairpin** is U-shaped, like a **hairpin** *bend* in a road, and is used for holding a mass of long hair in place. A **hairgrip** or **kirby-grip** (both British English) or **bobby pin** (American) is a flat hairpin whose prongs spring together to hold a small quantity of hair.

half

1 Half, as a noun or adjective, is followed by a singular verb after a singular noun or pronoun, and by a plural verb after a plural: *Half (of) the lake was frozen*; *Half (of) the children are absent*. See NUMBER AGREEMENT (7).

2 The traditionally recommended form is as in *a half dozen*, *a year and a half*, *a million and a half*; but **half** *a*, as in *half a dozen*, or the form *one and a half years*, *one and a half million* is probably now more usual. Do not, in any case, write *a half a*.

3 In British English, **half** can mean **half-past**; *half nine* is 9.30. This sometimes confuses learners of German, who find that *halb neun* is 8.30.

4 One *cuts* (or *slices*, or *breaks*) things *in half*, not *in halves*. See also HALVE.

half-

See -IN-LAW.

half-past

In careful British speech, the *half* is pronounced as 'hahf', not 'hah'.

hallelujah

See ALLELUIA.

hallo

See HELLO.

Hallowe'en

Halloween is the preferred American spelling, **Hallowe'en** the British one; but both are acceptable everywhere.

halo

The plural is either **halos** or **haloes**.

halve

This means 'divide into two equal parts' or 'reduce by half' (*The cost has been halved*). If something now costs 30% or 40% of its former price you can say it costs *less than half*, but do not say that the cost has been *more than halved*.

hamstring

The past tense and participle are **hamstrung**: *teachers hamstrung by an obsolete syllabus*. An alternative form **hamstringed** is now rare.

hand

To **hand** means 'available' or 'within reach': *Use whatever comes to hand*. The phrase is used to say that a letter has been received, but only in very old-fashioned business English. There is a shade of difference between *to* **hand**, *at* **hand**, which means 'near in time or place' (*The* *great day is at hand*), and *on* **hand,** which means 'ready for use' (*He kept his rifle constantly on hand*). For *on the other hand*, see CONTRARY.

handful

The plural is **handfuls** or, less usually, **handsful**. See -FUL.

handicap (*verb*)

Other forms are **handicapped, handicapping**.

handiwork, handwork

These both mean work done manually and not by machine, **handiwork** perhaps suggesting crafts such as embroidery and **handwork** referring to manual industrial processes. **Handiwork,** not **handwork,** is the result of someone's personal efforts: *This must be the handiwork of an experienced burglar.*

handkerchief

The plural is **handkerchiefs** or, less usually, **handkerchieves**.

handsome, hansom

Handsome means 'good-looking'. A **hansom** is a two-wheeled carriage.

hang

The past tense and participle are **hung** (*hung the picture*), except in the sense 'suspended by the neck until dead'. Here, they are correctly **hanged** (*They hanged him for murder*), although **hung** is often used informally in this sense also: *Wasn't D'Alton's father hung?* (Hilaire Belloc).

hangar, hanger

A **hangar** is a shed for housing aircraft. A **hanger** is anything that hangs, or that has things hung from it.

hanger-on

The plural is **hangers-on**.

hapless, haply

Hapless means 'unfortunate', **haply** means 'by chance'. Both words are somewhat literary; **haply** belongs to old-fashioned poetic language (see POESY).

happy

See SATISFIED.

hara-kiri

This is the usual way to spell this Japanese ritual suicide, rather than **hari-kari**.

harass, harassment

The traditional pronunciation of both these words is with the stress on *har*. A new pronunciation with the stress on *ass* is gaining ground, but not yet to be recommended for British English. The words are spelled with only one *r*.

harbinger

The *g* is pronounced as in *messenger*. It means 'something that foreshadows the future'; the cuckoo is traditionally known as the **harbinger** of spring.

harbo(u)r

The word is spelled **harbour** in British English, **harbor** in American English.

hard, hardly

1 These can both mean 'badly': *Things went very hard/hardly with us*. It is safer, however, to confine the use of **hardly** to the commoner meaning 'scarcely', and not to use it at all where there may be ambiguity. In *We were hardly hit by the recession*, replace **hardly** by *hard* or *scarcely* according to the intended meaning.

2 Hard *put* and **hard** *put to it* both mean 'barely able', and are both correct: *We were hard put (to it) to find an explanation*.

hardly, barely, scarcely

1 These should be used with *when* or *before*, not with *than* or *till*: *We had hardly arrived when* (not *than*) *she started scolding us*; *Scarcely was I in bed before* (not *till*) *the telephone rang*. See CORRELATIVE (3).

2 Since they mean 'almost not', none of these words should be used with another negative: *I can* (not *I can't*) *hardly tell*; *Hardly anyone* (not *no one hardly*) *goes there any more*. See DOUBLE NEGATIVE.

harmony, melody

Harmony is the combination of simultaneous musical notes into a chord. **Melody** is the combination of successive musical notes into a tune.

have

1	**have** *got*	**4**	*would* **have**
2	**have** *got to*	**5**	**have** *my watch stolen*
3	*If I* **had**		

1 The use of **have** *got* is commoner in British than in American English. Some British speakers use **have** *got* to express the idea of momentary possession (*'Have you got a cold?' 'Yes, I have.' 'No, I haven't.'*), as opposed to habitual possession (*Do you have many colds?*), but the distinction is disappearing under American influence: *'Do you have a cold?' 'Yes, I do.' 'No, I don't.'*

2 Have *got to* means 'must'. Again, American usage prefers **have** *to* and does not, as the British do, distinguish habitual necessity (*I have to wear special shoes*) from momentary necessity (*I've got to go now*). The usual American question form here is *Do you have to?* and the British is *Have you got to?* The following is a somewhat regional alternative: *pupil looked at his teacher and asked: 'Have we to swank a bit, Miss?'* (*The Times*).

3 Be careful not to introduce an extra **have** before a participle in an *if*-clause by analogy with the main verb phrase: *If I'd* (not *If I'd have*) *known, I'd have told you*.

4 *Would*, *could*, and *might* can all be followed by **have**, but not by *of*, which sounds much the same in speech: *I might have* (not *of*) *known*.

5 To **have** something *done* means either to cause it to be done (*had my hair cut*) or to undergo it (*had my watch stolen*). Both are legitimate, but one should avoid the construction if it leaves any doubt as to whether the person instigated the action.

haversack

See RUCKSACK.

havoc

Play havoc and *wreak havoc* are CLICHÉS.

he, him, his, himself

These pronouns have traditionally been used to refer to either sex, since there is no English singular pronoun of common gender; but the use of **he** to mean 'he or she' is often absurd, and today may be found offensive. The following should have been rephrased: *Everyone will be able to decide for himself whether or not to have an abortion* (Albert Bleumenthal, New York State Assembly). There are several possible ways of making this sentence acceptable. See SEXISM.

headquarters

The singular takes either a singular or plural verb, and the plural has the same form as the singular. You can say *Our firm's headquarters is* (or *are*) *in Sheffield*, or *Their respective headquarters are too far apart. Headquartered* now often appears as a participle (*a company headquartered in Paris*), but many people regard this usage as jargon.

head up

Careful writers prefer to use *direct*, or *lead*, or *head* alone, rather than **head up**, to mean 'be chief of': *a new manager to head (up) the sales department.*

healthy, healthful

These can both mean 'conducive to health': *healthy/healthful exercise*; or 'enjoying good health', though here **healthful** is used chiefly in a figurative sense: *healthy children; Dickens' relatively healthful exuberance.* **Healthy** is the commoner word, and the only one for the sense 'showing health': *a healthy appetite.*

heaps

When it means 'a lot', **heaps** is singular unless a plural noun follows: *There is heaps of time; There are heaps more reasons.* The use is informal.

heart, rote

Something that one has learned *by* **heart** or *by* **rote** can be recited from memory, but *by* **rote** emphasizes the idea of mechanical memorizing without understanding.

heave

The past tense and participle are either **heaved** or **hove**. **Heaved** is the usual choice (*His chest heaved with sobs*) except in **hove** *into sight* and **hove** *to.*

heavenward(s)

Before a noun use **heavenward**: *a heavenward glance*. After a verb, use the form with an *s* in British English (*gazed heavenwards*) and the one without an *s* in American English.

Hebrew

See JEW.

hecatomb

See CATACOMB.

hectare

The second syllable can be pronounced to rhyme with either *care* or *car*. But an **are,** which is one hundredth of a **hectare**, can only rhyme with *car*.

hegemony

This is usually pronounced with the stress on the second syllable, rather than the first, and the *g* as in *get* rather than *gem*. It means 'dominating authority': *aiming at world hegemony*.

hegira, hejira

The spelling with *g* is commoner. It is pronounced with the stress on the first syllable, which sounds like *hedge*. It means 'exodus, emigration', and with a capital *H* refers to the flight of Muhammad from Mecca in A.D. 622.

heifer

The word is spelled *-ei-*, not *-ie-*.

height, heighten

Both words are spelled *-ei-*, not *-ie-*. **Height** rhymes with *night*, and does not end with a 'th' sound.

heinous

The word is spelled *-ei-*, not *-ie-*. The first syllable is usually pronounced 'hay' rather than 'hee'.

heir

The word is spelled *-ei-*, not *-ie-*. An **heir** *apparent* cannot be displaced

by any possible birth; an **heir** *presumptive* can be displaced by the birth
of a child with a superior claim. **Heir** *apparent* is often used loosely of
someone whose succession appears certain: *heir apparent to the
presidency*.

heist

The word is spelled *-ei-*, not *-ie-*. It is slang, chiefly in American
English, for 'armed robbery'.

helicopter

The first two syllables rhyme with *jelly*.

helix

The plural is **helices** or, less usually, **helixes**. It means something
spiral in shape.

hello, hallo, hullo

Hallo and **hullo** are chiefly British alternative spellings of **hello**. All
have the plural **-os**.

help

1 When **help** means 'assist', it is correctly used either with or without
to, but the construction with *to* is more formal: *Help me (to) clean the
windows*.

2 It is perfectly correct to use **help** in the sense 'refrain from, avoid':
He couldn't help smiling. For *can't* **help** *but*, see CANNOT.

helpmate, helpmeet

They both mean 'wife or husband'. **Helpmeet** is archaic, and comes
from Genesis 2:18, where Eve is referred to as a *help meet* (ie
'suitable') *for him*. **Helpmate** is the present form, a mistaken
reinterpretation ('folk etymology') of **helpmeet**.

hemophilia, hemorrhage, etc

See AE-.

hemi-

See SEMI-.

hence

For *from* **hence**, see FROM.

henna (*verb*)

Other forms are **hennas, hennaed, hennaing**.

her

See SHE; HERS. For *as she*, *than her*, etc see CASE, GRAMMATICAL (4).

herculean

It is usually pronounced with the stress on *le*, but sometimes on *cu*. It means 'of extraordinary size, strength, or difficulty': *a herculean task*.

here

1 Before a plural it should correctly be **here** *are*, though **here** *is* is more common in spoken English: *Here's some more blackberries*.

2 *This* **here** and *these* **here** (*this here book*) are always wrong; but there is nothing wrong with *this book here* and *these children here*.

hereby, herein, hereof, hereon, herewith

Hereby is a formal word, appropriate in such contexts as *I hereby declare him elected*. The others are both formal and archaic, at one time normal in legal contexts. They sound PRETENTIOUS if they are used where *in this*, *with this*, etc would do.

hereditary

This is usually preceded by *a* rather than by *an*: *a hereditary peer*.

heritage, inheritance

These both mean something acquired from a predecessor. A **heritage** may be a privilege to which one is entitled by birth: *a rich heritage of folklore*. **Inheritance** is the usual word for property passed on to an heir, and also for transmitted genetic qualities.

hero

The plural is **heroes** rather than **heros**, except when, in American English, it means a large sandwich made from a long split roll.

heroic

This is usually preceded by *a* rather than by *an*: *a heroic gesture*.

heroin, heroine

Heroin is a narcotic drug; a **heroine** is a female hero.

hers

This means 'the one belonging to her': *the house became hers* (not *her's*).

herself

See REFLEXIVE.

hesitancy, hesitance, hesitation

Hesitancy (or, rarer, **hesitance**) is the tendency to indecision: *the timid hesitancy of his character.* **Hesitation** is the act or fact of hesitating: *He agreed without hesitation.*

hew, hue

To **hew** is to chop with heavy blows; a **hue** is a shade of colour.

hiccup, hiccough

Other forms of **hiccup** are either **hiccuped, hiccuping** or **hiccupped, hiccupping**. The variant spelling **hiccough** is less frequent and is pronounced like **hiccup**.

hide

The participle is usually **hidden**, but **hid** also exists: *Where has he hidden* (or *hid*) *the key?*

hie

This belongs to old-fashioned poetry, or else is FACETIOUS. It means 'hurry': *Thither we advise you to hie* (*New Yorker*).

high (*noun*)

Some people dislike the use of **high** to mean 'a highest point', as in *Sales have reached a new high.*

high, highly

High as an adverb means 'at or to a high place': *climb high*; *to aim high*; *The company is flying high.* Both **high** and **highly** can mean 'to a high degree' (*pay high/highly*), but only **highly** can be used before

adjectives and participles (*highly intelligent*; *highly paid*) and only
highly can mean 'with approval' (*She speaks highly of you*).

hijack, hijacker

These are the usual spellings, though *high-jack* also exists. These
words for seizing control of a vehicle must surely be regarded as
standard, rather than informal, in modern use. There is no other way of
expressing the idea.

him, his

See HE. For *as he, than him*, etc see CASE, GRAMMATICAL (4).

Himalaya(s)

The traditional pronunciation rhymes **Himalayas** approximately with
dimmer players. There is a newer tendency to pronounce the word with
the stress on the second syllable, which sounds like 'mahl', and also to
refer to this mountain range in the singular as *the* **Himalaya**. See
FOREIGN PLACENAMES.

himself

See HE; REFLEXIVE.

Hindi, Hindustani, Urdu, Hindu

Hindi is an official language of India. **Hindustani** is an older word for
Hindi, **Urdu**, or any mixture of the two languages before they were
distinguished. **Urdu** is an official language of Pakistan, and is used
also by Muslims in India. A **Hindu** is an adherent of Hinduism, and is
in most cases a person of Indian nationality or descent.

hippo

The plural is **hippos**. This is an informal word.

hippopotamus

The plural is **hippopotamuses** or, less usually, **hippopotami**.

[hisself]

The correct word is *himself*.

historic, historical

1 Historic means 'memorable; likely to be famous in history': *a
historic occasion*. **Historical** means either 'having really existed' (*Was*

339

King Arthur a historical character?) or 'because of past events' (*For historical reasons the boundary runs down the middle of the stream*) or 'belonging merely to the past': *'Yes, sir, "an extinct case of purely historic concern", sir'. Strickland went on into the telephone . . . 'Historical', Lacon corrected him irritably. 'Not historic concern. That's the last thing we want! Historical'* (John le Carré). In accounting, however, **historic cost** is established as a variant of **historical cost**, meaning the original cost of an asset as opposed to the current cost of replacing it.

2 Historic, historical, historian, and **history** are usually preceded by *a* rather than by *an*: *a history of France*.

histrionics, hysterics

Histrionics are a deliberate exhibition of temperament, for emotional effect. **Hysterics** is (or are) involuntary, an uncontrollable fit of laughter or weeping.

hither, thither

These somewhat archaic words can sometimes, but not always, be replaced by *here* and *there* respectively. They mean 'to this place' and 'to that place', and are still needed where it is important to emphasize direction rather than position: *goods in transit thither*. For the same reason, the still current phrase *hither and thither* cannot be replaced by *here and there*, which means 'scattered around'.

hoard, horde

A **hoard** is a supply stored for future use; a **horde** is a tribe or crowd.

hobnob

Other forms are **hobnobbed, hobnobbing**.

hobo

The plural is **hoboes** or, less usually, **hobos**. It means a vagrant, in American English.

hocus

Other forms are **hocussed, hocussing** in British English, but the second *s* is usually omitted in American English. It means 'hoax' or 'befuddle'.

hodgepodge

See HOTCHPOTCH.

hoe (*verb*)

Other forms are **hoed, hoeing**.

hog (*verb*)

Other forms are **hogged, hogging**.

hoi polloi

This is a derogatory term for 'the common people, the masses'. Although **hoi polloi** means 'the many' in Greek, it is correct idiomatic English to speak of *the hoi polloi*. But use these FOREIGN PHRASES with restraint.

holey, holy, wholly

Holey means 'having holes'; **holy** means 'sacred'; **wholly** means 'entirely'.

home

1 It is correct in American English to use **home** where British usage would prefer *house*: *new homes for sale*; *She has a beautiful home*. Estate agents in Britain use **home** enthusiastically in this sense, to the annoyance of some people.

2 Home is used as an adverb, without **to,** when one speaks of or implies movement towards one's home: *We went home*. This is true even with the verb *be*: *We're nearly home*. Where no movement is involved, prefer *at* **home,** rather than **home** alone, in formal British writing: *to stay at home*; *Is Henry at home?*

3 For **home** as a verb, see HONE.

Homeric

Besides referring to the poet Homer, this means 'of epic proportions': *a Homeric feat of endurance*. **Homeric** *laughter* is inextinguishable and perhaps cruel mirth, often shared by a group, at the sight of something ludicrous, as when all the gods laughed at the limping Hephaestus.

hom(e)y, homely

Homy, usually spelled **homey** in American English, means 'homelike': *a hom(e)y atmosphere*. **Homely** means 'commonplace and

341

unpretentious': *a homely meal of bacon and eggs*. In American use, **homely** also means 'not good-looking': *a homely face*.

homo-

This Greek prefix means 'same' or 'similar'. It should not be confused with the Latin *homo* (= man). Thus, *homosexuality* is preference for sexual activity with people of one's own sex, not necessarily with men.

homogeneity

The second *e* is better pronounced as in *see*, not as in *say*. It means 'sameness of composition'.

homogeneous, homogenous

Homogeneous chiefly means 'same in composition': *a culturally homogeneous neighbourhood*. The first syllable rhymes with *Tom*, and the main stress is on *gen*, pronounced as in *genius*. The somewhat technical word **homogenous** means 'corresponding in parts or organs, owing to descent from the same ancestral type or to similar evolutionary adaptation'. The main stress is on *mog*, rhyming with *dodge*.

homograph, homonym, homophone, synonym

Homographs are words, such as the noun *conduct* and the verb *conduct*, that are spelled alike but are different in meaning and possibly in pronunciation. **Homonyms** are words, such as the noun *quail* and the verb *quail*, spelled and pronounced alike but different in meaning. **Homophones** are words such as *two* and *too*, pronounced alike but different in meaning or spelling. **Synonyms** are words, such as *full stop* and *period*, that are the same in meaning.

homosexual

1 In British English, the first syllable is usually pronounced to rhyme with *Tom*: but Americans and some older British speakers prefer the pronunciation *home*. See HOMO-.

2 Both male and female **homosexuals** prefer to be called **gay**, though some aging males use **queen** of themselves. **Lesbian** refers to women only. **Invert** and even more **pervert** are derogatory. **Queer, pansy, poof, poofter, nancy, fairy,** and the chiefly American **fag** or **faggot** are offensive informal terms for homosexual males.

hone, home

Hone means 'sharpen, make more acute': *finely honed sarcasm*. **Home**

as a verb is used of missiles **homing** *in on* a target. The author of the following should have used **home**: *as your interest hones in on a particular facet of landscape* . . . .

honorarium

The plural is either **honorariums** or **honoraria**. The *h* is silent. The word means 'fee paid for a nominally free professional service'.

hono(u)r

The word is spelled **honour** in British English, **honor** in American English except on formal invitations.

hono(u)rable, honorary, hon.

1 Hono(u)rable is spelled with the *u* in British English, without it in American English.

2 Honourable is used as a title for the children of British viscounts and barons and for the younger sons of earls, and for various holders of high office in both Britain and the USA. See TITLES OF PEOPLE. MPs refer to each other as *the* **honourable** *member* inside the House of Commons. The title should be used with an initial or first name, or with *Mr, Mrs*, etc, not with the surname alone: *(The) Honourable J Smith*; *(The) Honourable John Smith*; *(The) Honourable Mrs Smith.* **Honorary** means 'conferred or elected without the usual obligations' (*honorary degree*; *honorary member*), but its chief meaning is 'unpaid': *the honorary secretary*. Confusingly, the abbreviation **Hon.** stands for either *the* **Honourable** or *the* **Honorary,** according to the context: *the Hon. Secretary*; *(The) Hon. John Smith.*

hoof

Hooves is the commoner plural, but **hoofs** is also correct.

hopefully

Besides meaning 'in a hopeful way' (*They waited hopefully for the results*), this now very commonly means 'it is hoped': *Hopefully they will arrive in time*. There is a strong prejudice both in Britain and in the USA against this usage, and the British believe it to be an Americanism. Its users may justify their decision by analogy with adverbs such as *naturally*, which can mean either 'in a natural way' (*His hair curls naturally*) or 'it is natural' (*Naturally I'm coming*). The device with **hopefully** is often useful, since one is not obliged to state who is doing the 'hoping'. If you use it, be careful to leave no room for ambiguity between the two possible meanings. *They will leave* *hopefully in the morning* might mean either that they will leave with optimism, or that I hope they will succeed in leaving. See SENTENCE ADVERBS.

hoping, hopping

Hoping comes from *hope*, **hopping** from *hop*.

horde

See HOARD.

horrid, horrible, horrifying, horrendous, horrific

In order of emphasis, **horrid** is the weakest of these words, meaning often no more than 'nasty': *horrid little boy*. **Horrible** (which ends in *-ible,* not *-able*) is stronger: *horrible accident*. **Horrifying** suggests the really shocking or gruesome: *horrifying stories of bloodshed*. **Horrendous** and **horrific** have become debased, to mean something like 'perfectly horrid': *horrendous taxes*.

hors d'oeuvre

The usual plural is **hors d'oeuvres** (rhyming with *serves*), but **hors d'oeuvre** is also acceptable.

hose

This word is used in shops as a noun meaning socks, stockings, and tights collectively, but *hosiery* is commoner. The verb meaning 'wash with a hose' is usually used with *down* or sometimes *out*: *hose down the car*; *hose out the pigsty*.

hospitable

The stress can fall on either *hos* or *pit*, but the first is the recommended British pronunciation.

hospitalize

This verb meaning 'put in hospital' is official jargon, though quite a useful word. See -IZE.

host

This is now commonly used as a verb (*hosted a TV series*), but careful writers avoid it. You can say *act as host*.

hotchpotch, hodgepodge

Hotchpotch is an obsolescent word for a thick soup or stew. A jumbled mixture of things is a **hotchpotch** to the British, but usually a **hodgepodge** to the Americans.

hotel

This is usually preceded by *a* rather than by *an*, and the *h* is pronounced and not silent as in *hour*: *a hotel bedroom*.

housewife

When it means a woman who runs a house, **housewife** is pronounced as spelled, but when it means a small sewing kit it is pronounced 'HUZ-if'. The masculine equivalent *househusband* is not, or not yet, in serious use. In American English *homemaker* is used as a neutral equivalent for both men and women.

hovercraft

See HYDROFOIL.

how

1 This can mean 'the way in which': *I know how it works*; or 'the fact that': *told them how he had a situation* (Charles Dickens). It is nearly always safer, however, to replace **how** by *that* in this second sense, since a sentence such as *I remember how they fought* may mean that I remember their way of fighting or the fact of their fighting.

2 Do not use *as* **how** for *that*: *He says that* (not *as how*) *he'll be late*.

3 How *come?* meaning 'why is it?' (*How come we never meet?*) is too informal for serious writing.

howbeit

This is often regarded as PRETENTIOUS. Like *albeit*, it should usually be avoided, except for humorous effect, when *though* will do, but it is sometimes useful as a way of linking contrasted adjectives: *The room is comfortable, howbeit small*.

however

1 It is better not to use **however** and *but* together: *We were afraid we should be late; but when we arrived* (or *however, when we arrived* or *when we arrived, however,*) *the doors were still closed*.

2 However should be separated from the rest of the sentence by a comma or pair of commas when it means 'nevertheless', as in the above example, but not when it means 'no matter how', as in *however fast I eat*.

3 For **however** misused for 'how ever', see EVER.

hue

See HEW.

hullo

See HELLO.

human, humane

1 As both noun and adjective, **human** means not only 'not an animal' but also 'not a supernatural being'. Expressions such as *human being, human race* are becoming increasingly useful owing to the feminist dislike of *man, mankind* in this general sense, but it is also possible to say *person, people*.

2 Human can refer to the bad as well as to the good qualities of our species: *human error*. When used appreciatively, it often means 'warm and friendly': *He's really very human when you get to know him*. **Humane** means 'merciful, compassionate': *humane killing of animals*.

humanity, humanism, humanitarian

Humanity is either the quality of being *humane* or the quality of being *human*, and *the* **humanities** are the cultural branches of learning. **Humanism** in the modern sense is a philosophy asserting the intrinsic worth of *humans* and rejecting religious belief, and **humanists** are its adherents. **Humanism** and **humanist** also refer to the asserting of literary cultural values. Neither kind of **humanist** should be called a **humanitarian**. **Humanitarians** are philanthropists, people who promote human welfare. **Humanitarianism** is thus close to *humaneness* and to one sense of **humanity**, but is specifically concerned with people.

humankind

See MANKIND.

humble

This is usually preceded by *a* rather than by *an*: *a humble apology*. The phrase *in my humble opinion* is unnecessary; one can say *I think*, or nothing at all.

humble-bee

See BUMBLEBEE.

humbug (*verb*)

Other forms are **humbugged, humbugging**.

humility, humiliation

Humility is meekness, the virtue of being humble. **Humiliation** is mortification, the misfortune of being humbled. One radio announcer was heard to say *He has got to recover from the humility* (it ought to be *humiliation*) *of his recent defeat.*

hummus, humus

Hummus (also spelled **houmous** and **houmus**) is a paste of chick-peas and sesame seeds, served as an appetizer. **Humus** is rotted organic material in the soil.

humo(u)r, humorist

Humour is the spelling in British English, **humor** in American English. **Humorous** and **humorist** are spelled in the same way everywhere.

hunting

In Britain, **hunting** is pursuing a fox, deer, or hare with a pack of hounds and usually on horseback, whereas pursuing birds or animals with a gun is called *shooting*. In the USA, **hunting** is the word for both activities.

hurdle, hurtle

To **hurdle** is to jump over hurdles. To **hurtle** is to move very fast: *police cars hurtling along the road.*

hurt

This can correctly mean 'be painful': *My foot hurts*; *It hurts to move my foot*; *The tax increases really hurt.* It is somewhat informal to use **hurt** to mean 'suffer', as when one says *I hurt*, or that an educational programme is *hurting from financial cuts.*

hy(a)ena

Hyena is the usual spelling, in British as well as in American English.

347

hydrofoil, hovercraft

A **hydrofoil** travels over water, and its hull rises out of the water only when it is going fast. A **hovercraft** is supported on a cushion of air, and can travel over both land and water.

hydrometer, hygrometer

A **hydrometer** measures the density of liquids. A **hygrometer** measures the humidity of the atmosphere.

hyper-, hypo-

Hyper- means 'beyond' or 'excessive': *hypersensitive*. The opposite is **hypo-**, meaning 'below' or 'deficient'. A very high body temperature is *hyperthermia*, a very low one is *hypothermia*.

hyperbola, hyperbole

A **hyperbola** is a geometric figure, a kind of curve. **Hyperbole** is extravagant exaggeration, as in *mile-high icecream cones*. Both words have the related adjective **hyperbolic** or, less usually, **hyperbolical.**

hypercorrection

A hypercorrection is a grammatical mistake caused by a false analogy. For example, people who have been taught to avoid *me* in certain contexts (*It is me; You and me should get together*) may extend the rule to instances where *me* is correct, thereby producing the hypercorrection *between you and* **I** instead of the grammatically correct *between you and me*. Other examples are the incorrect *whom* in *You may remember the young girl* **whom** *it now seems gave us the right directions* (*who* is correct); and the incorrect *as* in *They are singing* **as** *nightingales* (*like* is correct).

hypercritical, hypocritical

Hypercritical means 'too critical, fault-finding'. **Hypocritical** comes from *hypocrisy*, the pretence of possessing virtues or beliefs that one lacks.

hypermarket

See SUPERMARKET.

hyphen

1 for joining parts of a word **2** for word division between lines

1 for joining parts of a word

The main purpose of the hyphen is to indicate that two or more parts belong to the same word. Dictionaries and writers often differ on whether particular combinations should be written as separate words, as a hyphenated word, or as a solid word. American English tends to use fewer hyphens than British English, preferring words to be either separate or solid rather than hyphenated. The advice that follows gives general guidance on the use of the hyphen. For guidance on particular words, consult a dictionary.

(a) compound modifiers

When two modifiers come before a noun, they may separately modify the noun (*a small pleasant court*; the court is small and pleasant), or the second may combine as a compound with the noun (*a small tennis court*; the tennis court is small), or the first may combine with the second to form a compound modifier of the noun (*a small-claims court*; the court is for small claims). Compound modifiers sometimes need a hyphen to prevent misunderstanding: *a light-green dress*; *free-world trade*; *long-dead animals*; *a first-class discussion*. Since the hyphen is always correct for compound modifiers, use it whenever there is any chance of misunderstanding. In long noun phrases it may be difficult to decide where to put hyphens if the compound modifier itself contains compounds: *the New York San Francisco flight*; *the air pollution lung cancer correlation*. It is clearer to rephrase with prepositions: *the flight from New York to San Francisco*; *the correlation between air pollution and lung cancer*. See CLARITY (6).

If the first word of a compound modifier ends in *-ly* (*a happily married couple*) there is no need for a hyphen, since the suffix shows that the first word modifies the second and that therefore the two words form a compound modifier. Contrast *a slowly moving train* with *a slow-moving train*, and *a badly conducted meeting* with *a well-conducted meeting*.

Some combinations, such as *habit-forming* (see (b) below), always take a hyphen. Others do so only when they are compound modifiers. If they do not come before a noun, they are not hyphenated: *a well-conducted meeting*, but *The meeting was well conducted*; *her much-talked-about visit*, but *Her visit was much talked about*; *an on-the-spot investigation*, but *The investigation was conducted on the spot*.

(b) adjective compounds in *-ing* and *-ed*

Adjective compounds whose second word ends in the suffixes *-ing* or *-ed* often take a hyphen even when they come after a noun:

Her secretary was *hard-working*.

They were on a *fact-finding* mission.

The couple were *middle-aged*.

These are *hand-baked* rolls.

Irregular passive participles that do not end in *-ed* follow the same rule: *weather-beaten*, *poverty-stricken*, *hand-sewn*.
The compounds are also written solid (*hardworking, handbaked*), especially in American English, except where the result would juxtapose vowels, as in *middle-aged*.

(c) noun compounds ending in an adverb
In many noun compounds, the first word is derived from a verb and the second is an adverb. If the first word ends in *-er* or *-ing*, use a hyphen: *passer-by*, *runner-up*, *summing-up*, *dressing-down*. If it has no ending, a hyphen may be used: *break-in*, *follow-up*; but many such compounds are normally solid: *handout*, *breakdown*. These combinations are always separate words when the first word is a verb: *They intend to* **follow up** *my inquiry*; *The car may* **break down** *at any time*.

(d) coordination compounds
Use a hyphen when the relationship between the two words expresses an addition: *bitter-sweet chocolate* (chocolate that is bitter and sweet); *secretary-treasurer* (person who is both secretary and treasurer); *Chinese-British talks* (talks between the Chinese and the British).

(e) number compounds
Use a hyphen for number compounds: *twenty-one*; *thirty-fifth*. Put a hyphen between the numerator and denominator of fractions, unless one or both are compounds and already have a hyphen: *one-sixth*; *twenty-one fiftieths*. Note also the hyphens in compound modifiers such as *a ten-year-old boy*; *a 50-mile-an-hour speed limit*; *twenty-odd students*. *Twenty odd students* (twenty peculiar students) is of course very different from *twenty-odd students* (about twenty students).

(f) compounds with a single capital
Always put a hyphen after an initial single capital: *T-shirt*; *U-turn*; *X-ray* (also *x-ray*).

(g) family compounds with *great-* and *-in-law*
They require hyphens: *parents-in-law*; *great-aunt*.

(h) prefixes
Most prefixes do not require a hyphen, but there are some exceptions. A hyphen is usual after *ex-* (former), *half-* (except *halfway*), *quasi-*, and *self-* (except *selfsame*): *ex-wife*; *half-asleep*; *quasi-mystical*; *self-assurance*. It is also usual if the prefix comes before a capital or a figure: *un-American, pre-1914*. A hyphen may be required to distinguish different words: *re-form* (form again), *reform* (improve); *co-op* (cooperative), *coop* (enclosure). It may also be required to avoid doubling a vowel: *semi-illiterate*. British English often uses a hyphen after a prefix to prevent mispronunciation: *non-equivalence*; but there is

a growing tendency to write the words solid, as would be normal in American English.

(i) coordination with hyphens
Two or more hyphenated items may be joined: *pre- and post-war Britain*; *gas- or oil-heated furnaces*. This first hyphen (sometimes called a suspension hyphen) is used even when the words are normally written solid, but the second word is then solid: *hetero- and homosexual partners*. Because the absence of the hyphen in this last instance means that the two items are treated differently, it is better to write out the two words in full.

2 for word division between lines
Since dividing a word makes the word somewhat more difficult to read, it is better to start a word on a new line than to divide it. There can be no justification in having just one or two letters of a word on a line. Traditional British practice is to make the break at a point that represents a division in the structure of the word, and American practice is to follow the pronunciation by dividing between syllables. American writers can therefore legitimately divide the word *meteorology* as *mete-orology* as well as the possible British division *meteor-ology*. For most words the result is the same, and in any case British practice is increasingly based on pronunciation.

Here are some general principles to consider:
(a) Divide a compound (whether otherwise hyphenated or solid) only between the parts of the compound: *self-justification* (not *self-justifi-cation*); *camera-ready*; *basket-ball*.
(b) Divide a prefix from the rest of the word: *hyper-active*; *over-simplification*.
(c) Make the break before *-ing*: *consider-ing*; *overwhelm-ing*; *discuss-ing*. If the final consonant is doubled when *-ing* is added, divide the word between the consonants: *commit-ting*; *occur-ring*.

hypocritical

See HYPERCRITICAL.

hypothesis

The plural is **hypotheses**. It means 'a proposed possible explanation; a theory'.

hysterical

This is usually preceded by *a* rather than by *an*: *a hysterical outburst*. The use of **hysterical** to mean 'extremely funny' is informal.

hysterics

See HISTRIONICS.

Ii

I

1 *And* **I** is often, but incorrectly, used instead of *and me* as the second of the two objects after a verb or preposition. See CASE, GRAMMATICAL (3); HYPERCORRECTION.

2 There is no reason whatever against using **I** at the beginning of a letter, or wherever else it is appropriate. It is pleasanter and more direct than referring to yourself as *the undersigned* or *the author*. (See WE.) **I** is often omitted in the informal style of diaries (*Went shopping with Susan*), and the same device is appropriate enough in the kind of light journalism that imitates the diary form.

3 **I** *am* and **I** *remain* are old-fashioned as ways of ending a letter.

i before e

Many people have trouble over whether to write *ie* or *ei* when those vowels appear in combination. The regular rule, applying where the combination sounds like 'ee', is:
    i before *e*
    except after *c*,
    or when sounded like 'ay'
    as in 'neighbour' or 'weigh'.
Some words that exemplify this rule are: *believe*; *fiend*; *hygiene*; *niece*; *relieve*; *shield*; *siege*; (after *c*) *ceiling*; *conceit*; *deceive*; *receipt*; (sounded like 'ay') *beige*; *freight*; *heinous*; *inveigle*; *sleigh*; *veil*. Exceptions are: *seize*; *caffeine*; *codeine*; *protein*.

The rule operates, however, in respect only of the sounds 'ee' and 'ay'. There is also some regularity in words with a long 'i' sound, which usually have *ei*: *eiderdown*; *either*; *height*; *neither*; *heist*; *gneiss*; *sleight*; *kaleidoscope*. Thereafter all rules break down. The following words, grouped by their sounds, must simply be memorized: *friend, heifer, leisure*; *fierce, pier, weird*; *fiery*; *forfeit*; *heir*; *view*. And there is no rule about the pronunciation and spelling of proper names, such as *Leigh* and *Reith*.

ibidem

Ib., **ibid.**, and **ibidem** mean 'in the same book, chapter, etc as was mentioned before'. They always refer to what immediately precedes: *Edmund Spenser, The Faerie Queene, bk I, c.IV.v . . . Ib.c.V.i* (ie in the same book but the next canto) *. . . Ib.xviii* (ie later on in the same canto). In modern scholarly use, **ib.** and **ibid.** are often replaced by the author's name and a date and page number: *Austin 1982, (p.)82.* Such references are then spelled out in full in a list at the end of the book or chapter. Compare OP. CIT.

-ible

See -ABLE.

-ic, -ical

Two adjectives formed from the same noun with **-ic** and with **-ical** may have different meanings, as with *economic* and *economical*, both from *economy*, or *historic* and *historical*, both from *history*. Or there may be no (or little) difference of meaning, as with *heroic, heroical* or *botanic, botanical*; in which case one usually tends to supersede the other with the passage of time, though there is no rule as to which of the two will prevail. Where the **-ic** form can also serve as a noun, as with *fanatic* or *cynic*, it seems sensible to use **-ical** for the adjective, but unfortunately language does not always develop on such rational lines.

-ics

For the choice between *politics is* and *politics are*, see NUMBER AGREEMENT (14).

idea

One has an **idea** *of* or *on* or *about* or *for* something or doing something, or an **idea** *that* something happens or happened, but one cannot have an **idea** *to do* something. Write *He had the sudden idea of opening* (not *to open*) *a bookshop*.

ideal

Since there can be no degrees in the **ideal**, some people object to expressions such as *one of the most ideal spots for a holiday*. Avoid such combinations in careful writing.

ideally

This can mean either 'perfectly' (*ideally suited to each other*) or 'for best results' (*Ideally, we should allot twice as much time to the project*). Be careful to make it clear which meaning is intended. A sentence such as *They are(,) ideally(,) planted on a sunny slope* may mean, with commas before and after **ideally**, that that is where you ought to plant them or, without the commas, that they are already planted in the best possible place.

identical

It is always correct to say that one thing is **identical** *with* another. The combination **identical** *to* is also now common in educated usage, and there seems to be no reason against it: *a house identical with/to mine*.

identify with

This combination is somewhat OVERUSED in such contexts as *groups that are identified with conservation*. Here it could be replaced by *associated with*, or *closely linked with*. **Identify with** is normally used to mean 'feel psychological kinship with' (*identify with the hero of the novel*), but sounds odd when it is used for 'share the aims of', as in *to identify with the Company's marketing policy*.

ideology

This word originally meant 'visionary theorizing', but it is valuable in our century in its newer sense of 'social and political programme': *Marxist ideology*. The modern world needs a word without religious associations to embrace the secular doctrines that move it. **Ideology** should probably not be used of trivial or individual beliefs; one person can scarcely have a private **ideology.**

idiom

This may sometimes seem a rather PRETENTIOUS word for 'style' or 'manner': *the modern jazz idiom*.

idiosyncrasy

The word is spelled -*crasy*, not -*cracy*. It means 'a characteristic peculiarity of behaviour'. The adjective is *idiosyncratic*.

idle, idol, idyll

1 Idle means 'not working'. An **idol** (same pronunciation) is an object of worship. An **idyll** (rhyming with *fiddle* or *bid ill*) is a literary or musical work reflecting a simple, happy rustic scene.

2 Idle need not mean 'lazy'; machines can *stand* **idle**. It implies a cause for inactivity, such as unemployment or leisure, and that cause may be laziness.

i.e.

See VIZ.; E.G.

if

1 **if** and **whether**   4 **if** . . . *then*
2 **if** meaning 'though'   5 **if** . . . *was/were*; see WERE
3 **if** *and when*

1 Where there is a choice between **if** and **whether**, prefer **whether** in formal writing: *I wonder whether* (rather than *if*) *he heard*. **Whether** is often clearer than **if**, since *Let me know if you intend to come* might mean that you need not mention the matter unless you are coming. **If** should not introduce a set of alternatives: *They swim whether* (not *if*) *it's dark or light*.

2 There is no objection in principle to the use of **if** to mean 'even if, though' (*an interesting if untenable argument*), but here again, some ambiguity is possible. *They are intelligent, if untrained* may mean either that only the untrained ones are intelligent or that they are intelligent despite their lack of training.

3 It is usually unnecessary to use **if** and *when* together: *I'll pay if* (or *when*, not *if and when*) *I see you*.

4 It is usually unnecessary to introduce with *then* the conclusion of a condition that starts with **if**: *If it rains, (then) we'll get wet. Then* here merely adds unnecessary emphasis. It is justifiable, however, in the following long sentence, since without it a hasty reader might conclude that the writer admits to being 'an imperialist racialist': *If* [the fact] *that I am not ashamed of the achievements of men and women from this country both here and overseas in the past makes me an 'imperialist racialist' – then I am one* (Lord Clifford, in *The Times*). It was important here to show that *I am one* is merely the conclusion that would follow on a rejected premise.

ignoramus

The plural is **ignoramuses**. **Ignoramus** means 'we do not know' in Latin, and since it is not a Latin noun, it does not form a Latin plural.

-ile

Most words ending with **-ile,** such as *fertile* and *docile*, are pronounced in modern British English so that the last syllable rhymes with *mile*. In American English the last syllable is usually so reduced that, for instance, *fertile* rhymes with *turtle* and *missile* rhymes with *thistle*. But in British English some technical terms of statistics, such as *decile*, are pronounced with the last syllable like *ill*; and in both British and American English, words of recent French origin such as *automobile* end with the sound of *wheel*.

ilex

The plural is **ilexes**. The tree is either the holly or the evergreen oak.

ilk

In its original Scots sense, this means 'same', and relates the names of Scottish landed families to their property. *Balwhidder of that ilk* means 'Balwhidder of Balwhidder'. **Ilk** has now been extended, often humorously or disparagingly, to mean 'sort, kind': *Virginia Woolf and her ilk*; *politicians and others of that ilk*. People who know what the word originally meant may be offended at its use in this well-established broader sense, at least in serious writing.

ill, sick

They both mean 'in bad health'; but since in British English the primary sense of *be* **sick** is to vomit (*The dog was sick on the rug*) and of *feel* **sick** to feel like vomiting, the British prefer to talk of general bad health by saying *I was ill last week*.

   Ill cannot usually precede a noun in British English, however, so that it is normal to speak of *a sick child*, and of *sick leave* and *sick pay*. People who are **ill** are *the* **sick**. It is common in British journalism to use **ill** to describe the state of people who have been injured. A person may be reported as being *seriously* **ill** as a result of gunshot wounds.

   In American English, **ill** and **sick** are interchangeable, **ill** being somewhat more formal and used of more serious complaints, and one can speak of *an ill child*. The 'vomiting' sense is distinguished in American use by the phrase *sick to one's stomach*; but see NAUSEATED.

illegal, illegitimate, illicit

See LAWFUL.

illegible

See ELIGIBLE.

illegible, unreadable

1 These words are spelled with *-ible* and *-able* respectively.

2 A piece of writing is **illegible** if it cannot be deciphered (*illegible handwriting*), **unreadable** if it is too boring, too technical, or too incompetently written. Avoid using **unreadable** for **illegible.**

illicit

See ELICIT.

illiterate, innumerate

Illiterate in the strictest sense means 'unable to read or write'. Since it can also mean 'badly educated' (*too illiterate to have heard of Milton*), educationists have evolved the term *functional* **illiterate** for the person who has actual difficulty in extracting information from the printed page. The British English words **innumerate, innumeracy** refer to ignorance of mathematics and of the scientific approach, implying that numbers as well as words are part of education. However, **illiterate** and **illiteracy** are the usual words for ignorance of a particular field of knowledge, so that one may speak of *computer* **illiteracy** and of someone being *scientifically* **illiterate.**

illusion

See DELUSION.

illusive, illusory

See ELUSIVE.

illustrative

The main stress is usually on *ill* in British English, on *lust* in American English.

illustrator

The word ends in *-or*, not *-er*.

image

This can mean 'a conception of a person, institution, etc, created in the public mind by manipulation'. It is what public relations experts are concerned with. The word is OVERUSED in this sense, though a word for it is needed in our times: *his public image*; *brand image*; *image-building*; *to project a corporate image of warmth and humanity.*

imaginable

The word is spelled without the final *e* of *imagine*.

imaginary, imaginative

Imaginary means 'imagined, not real': *to fear imaginary dangers.*
Imaginative means 'able to imagine, inventive' (*an imaginative child*)
or 'produced by the imagination'. Both words can apply to something
invented, but an **imaginative** *biography* uses the imagination to
supplement known sources, while an **imaginary** *biography* either does
not exist at all or recounts the life of someone who never existed.

imbibe

This is a FACETIOUS word for 'drink', though unexceptionable in its
figurative sense, as in *imbibe knowledge.*

imbroglio

The plural is **imbroglios.** It means 'a tangled situation'.

imbue

One can **imbue** a person *with* a quality: *imbue them with a sense of
duty.* One cannot properly **imbue** a quality *into* a person. Use *instil* or
infuse for this second construction: *instil* (not *imbue*) *a sense of duty
into them.*

imitator

The word ends in -*or*, not -*er*.

Immaculate Conception

In Catholic dogma, this means the conceiving of the Virgin Mary, not
the conceiving of Jesus.

immature, premature

Immature means 'not yet mature; not fully developed': *immature
fruit; emotionally immature adults.* **Premature** means 'happening or
arriving too soon': *premature babies; premature reports.*

immediately

The chiefly British use of **immediately** for 'as soon as' has been
established in English since early in the 19th century: *I came
immediately I'd eaten*; but it is perhaps better avoided in formal
writing.

immigrant, immigration

See EMIGRANT.

imminent, immanent

See EMINENT.

immoral

See AMORAL.

immovable, irremovable

1 Both words are spelled without the final *e* of *move*.

2 Immovable means 'impossible to move', **irremovable** means 'impossible to remove'. People who cannot be dismissed from an official position are **irremovable.**

immune

One is **immune** (ie 'exempt') *from* taxation or punishment, but **immune** (ie 'resistant') *to* disease or persuasion.

immunity, impunity

Immunity is either 'exemption' (*immunity from arrest*) or 'lack of susceptibility to disease'. **Impunity** is 'freedom from bad consequences': *trespassing with impunity.*

impact

This is rather OVERUSED in the sense of 'effect' or 'influence', or of 'ability to impress': *the impact of computerization on society*; *a production with great dramatic impact.*

impair

This suggests deterioration rather than total loss: *The continual noise impaired his hearing for a time*; *The strike seriously impaired community services.* It can seem somewhat PRETENTIOUS when used merely for *hurt* or *damage.*

impanel

See EMPANEL.

impassable, impassible

These are different words, not variant spellings. **Impassable** means 'impossible to traverse or surmount': *an impassable obstacle*; *Snow made the road impassable*. The rarer word **impassible** means 'unable to feel, impassive'. They sound the same in American English; but those British speakers who pronounce *pass* with a long 'a' use that sound in **impassable,** while rhyming the *pass* of **impassible** with *ass*.

impasse

The first syllable of this word for 'deadlock' is usually pronounced 'am' in British English but 'im' in American English. Since the word is borrowed from the French, one is confronted by the choice of how far to anglicize it.

impassionate, impassioned, impassive

See DISPASSIONATE.

impeach

This means 'bring a charge against', not 'dismiss from office'. The word is used of offences against the state, and in the USA of misconduct by public officials.

impecunious

This can seem a rather PRETENTIOUS or FACETIOUS word for *poor*.

impedance, impediment

These are both formed from *impede*. **Impedance** is used in physics and electronics, while **impediment**, the more general word, is also the physiological and legal one: *a speech impediment*; *an impediment to a marriage*.

impel

Other forms are **impelled, impelling** in both British and American English. See also COMPEL.

imperative, imperious, imperial

In the grammatical sense, **imperative** applies to commands; *Stop!* and *Go home!* are **imperative** forms. Otherwise, it means that a duty is urgent: *It was imperative to finish the job by Friday.* **Imperious** means 'arrogant, overbearing': *an imperious voice.* **Imperial** means 'of an empire' (*imperial crown*), or else it refers to the British nonmetric system of weights and measures (*imperial gallon*).

imperceptible

The word ends in *-ible*, not *-able*.

imperialism, imperialist

Imperialism is the policy of extending the rule of a nation outside its established boundaries, or broadly any extension of power and authority: *cultural imperialism*. People who advocate such a policy are **imperialists.** These words have declined from appreciative to derogatory use as people have ceased to admire what they represent. In 1899 Lord Rosebery could speak of *the greater pride in Empire which is called Imperialism*; whereas in the late 20th century **imperialist** is the blanket adjective of Communist condemnation for the foreign policies of any non-Communist country.

imperil

Other forms are **imperilled, imperilling** in British English, but the second *l* is usually omitted in American English.

impersonate, personate, personify

To **impersonate** is to pretend to be someone else, either in a theatrical performance or for fraudulent purposes: *The dancers impersonated animals*; *He was caught impersonating an officer*. To **personify** something is to embody or typify it in human form: *He is kindness personified*. The rarer word **personate** can replace either of the others.

impetus

The plural is **impetuses**.

impinge, infringe, impugn

Both **impinge** and **infringe** can mean 'encroach': *to impinge/infringe on my rights*. **Infringe**, but not **impinge**, can mean 'encroach on': *infringe a patent*. Neither word should be confused with **impugn,** which means 'question the integrity of': *to impugn his rival's motives*.

implausible

The word ends in *-ible*, not *-able*.

implement

As a verb meaning 'fulfil, execute, accomplish', this is somewhat OVERUSED, particularly in official writing: *plans not yet implemented owing to lack of funds*.

implicit

See EXPLICIT.

imply

See INFER.

import (*noun*)

This may sound a rather PRETENTIOUS word in the sense that can be replaced by *meaning* or *importance*: *It was hard to determine the import of this decision.* Its use is better confined to the sense of goods *imported* into a place.

importantly

Besides meaning 'in an important way' (*He cleared his throat importantly*), this now often means 'as is important; it is significant that . . .': *He's experienced with poultry, and more importantly he's a good worker*. This usage is disliked by some people in both Britain and the USA, and in Britain may be felt to be an Americanism. Its users may justify themselves by the analogy with other adverbs such as *naturally*, which can mean either 'in a natural way' (*His hair curls naturally*) or 'as is natural' (*Naturally I'm coming*). If you wish to avoid it you can usually neatly replace it by *more important* or *most important*: *He's experienced with poultry and, (what is) more important, he's a good worker.*

impossible

1 The word ends in *-ible*, not *-able*.

2 Since things either are or are not **impossible**, some people object to expressions such as *even more impossible*. Such combinations should be avoided in careful writing.

impostor, imposter

The usual spelling is **impostor,** but **imposter** is a permitted variant.

impotent, impudent

Impotent means 'powerless' (*impotent fury*) or, when used of a man, 'unable to copulate'. **Impudent** means 'shameless, insolent'.

impractical, impracticable

Impractical means 'not sensible or prudent': *an impractical dreamer.* **Impracticable** chiefly means 'impossible to carry out'. A plan, method, or suggestion that cannot be carried out is both **impractical** and **impracticable**, so that the two words are often interchangeable, but a shade of difference may remain: *It was impracticable to open the window, because it was locked*; *It was impractical to open the window, because of the rain.* If it is important to make a clear distinction, **impractical** may be better replaced by *useless, imprudent, not sensible,* etc.

impregnable

It is disconcerting that this can mean both 'unconquerable, unassailable' (*impregnable fortress*; *impregnable social position*) and also (though rarely) 'able to be impregnated'.

impresario

The plural is **impresarios.** It means 'the sponsor or manager of a public entertainment'.

impromptu

The plural of the noun is **impromptus.** See also EXTEMPORE.

improvable

The word is spelled without the final *e* of *improve*.

improvement

When something has improved, there is an **improvement** *in* it; or one can *make improvements to* it. When two things are compared, one can be an **improvement** *on* the other: *Today's weather is an improvement on yesterday's.*

improvise

The word is spelled like this in both British and American English; not *-ize*.

impudent

See IMPOTENT.

impugn, impute

To **impugn** is to 'question the integrity of': *to impugn his rival's motives.* To **impute** is to 'attribute', often unjustly: *imputing to him a guilt of which he was innocent* (Edith Sitwell). See also IMPINGE.

impunity

See IMMUNITY.

in

1 in, into	4 in, on
2 in, within	5 verbose phrases with in
3 in, for	6 in, at; see AT (3)

1 in, into

The central meaning of **in** is to convey the idea of position (*in a box*) or state (*in public*). It is very often, and quite correctly, used also to convey the idea of motion, but may be less vivid than **into**: *jump in/ into the lake*. See INTO.

2 in, within

When **in** means 'not beyond' it may be clearer to replace it by *within* or *inside*. *It'll arrive in a week* may mean either that it will arrive before the end of the week or that it will arrive on the seventh day.

3 in, for

The British say *the coldest spring for years*. The Americans say *in years*, and the American idiom has passed into British use alongside the older form.

4 in, on

In American English one gets **on, onto,** or **off** a train, bus, or boat; in British English it is also possible to get **in, into,** or **out of** them. Americans live **on** a street, the British live **in** one: *a house in Baker Street*; *a hotel on Broadway*.

5 verbose phrases with in

Expressions such as **in** *length*, **in** *number*, **in** *shape*, **in** *size* are VERBOSE. Instead of *few in number* say *few*, instead of *five feet in length* say *five feet long*, and for **in** *excess of* prefer *over* or *more than*.

in-, un-

These both mean 'the opposite of': *incoherent*; *unfair*. **In-** is generally preferred in learned words of Latin or French origin, but its use has declined. Before words beginning with *l* it becomes **il-** (*illogical*), before *b*, *m*, or *p* it becomes **im-** (*improper*), and before *r* it becomes **ir-** (*irrelevant*). With very few exceptions **un-**, not **in-**, forms the negative of *-ed* and *-ing* words: *unexpected*, *unassuming*. See also NON-.

inability, disability

Inability is lack of the capacity to do something: *his inability to pay*

the bill. A **disability** is a physical or mental handicap, which of course may also prevent one from doing things. It can mean 'legal disqualification': *disability of infancy*.

inaccessible, inadmissible

Both words end in *-ible*, not *-able*.

inapt, inept, unapt

These all mean 'not apt'. In careful modern use, **inapt** chiefly means 'not appropriate' (*an inapt quotation*), **inept** means 'foolish' or 'clumsy' (*inept interference*), and the rarer **unapt** means 'unlikely' (*unapt to argue*).

inasmuch as, insofar as, insomuch as

Each of these formal phrases is now conventionally spelled as two words, not four, although **insofar as** still often appears as *in so far as* in British use. **Inasmuch as** chiefly means 'since, because': *The drug should be used sparingly, inasmuch as it has unpleasant side effects.* **Insofar as** means 'to the extent that': *I'll help you insofar as I can.* **Insomuch as** can mean either of these, and **inasmuch as** occasionally also means 'to the extent that', so that *I'll help you inasmuch as/ insomuch as I can* may mean either 'because I can' or 'as much as I can'. It is less ambiguous to use *since* or *because* rather than **inasmuch as, insomuch as** for the one meaning, and less old-fashioned to use *so far as* rather than **inasmuch as, insofar as** for the other.

inaudible

The word ends in *-ible*, not *-able*.

inaugurate

This is a formal word, appropriate to formal and ceremonious occasions: *The President was inaugurated on 20 January*. It can seem PRETENTIOUS to use it merely for 'start' or 'begin', as in *The new dealing system on the Stock Exchange was inaugurated in 1986*.

incarnate

This word of theological origin means 'made flesh; embodied in human form', but its chief modern meaning is 'in an extreme form; utter': *a fiend incarnate*; *The scene was confusion incarnate*.

inception

This means 'starting-point, beginning of a process': *At its inception, the movement consisted of only five members*. It can seem PRETENTIOUS to use it merely as a substitute for *start* or *beginning*.

inchoate, incoherent

These both mean 'imperfectly organized'. **Inchoate** (pronounced 'in-KOH-ayt') means particularly 'not yet in full operation; still unformed': *inchoate longings*. Its superficial similarity to the word *chaos* has probably led some of its users to emphasize the idea of 'muddle'. **Incoherent** usually refers to disconnected or inarticulate words: *an incoherent story*; *a voice incoherent with rage*.

incident

From meaning 'a subordinate or trivial event', **incident** has come often to mean 'a violent disturbance': *a serious border incident*. The use seems to have arisen in Britain during World War II, as a euphemism for 'bomb explosion'.

incidentally

1 This is not spelled *incidently*, though the word has only four syllables in rapid speech. Compare ACCIDENTALLY.

2 Incidentally is often used, meaning 'by the way', to introduce a digression: *Incidentally, I never thanked you for the marmalade*. Consider carefully whether you need to use it at all in a piece of formal writing. It sounds like an apology for saying something irrelevant, even though it may be intended as a quick way of changing the subject.

incise

The word is spelled like this in both British and American English; not *-ize*.

incisor

The word ends in *-or*, not *-er*.

inclined

I am inclined to think is a diffident way of saying 'I think'. Since it suggests that I have a 'disposition' or 'impulse' to think, the expression **inclined** *to* may sound odd when used about things, as in *The clutch is inclined to slip*. Prefer *tends to* or *is liable to* here for serious writing.

include

See COMPRISE.

incognito

The plural is **incognitos**, but is rarely needed: *We dropped our incognito*. In modern English use a woman is **incognito**, not *incognita* as in Latin.

incoherent

See INCHOATE.

incommunicado

The fifth syllable is pronounced 'ahd' rather than 'aid'. The word is used of prisoners, and means 'deprived of communication'.

incompatible, incomprehensible

Both words end in *-ible*, not *-able*.

inconsequential, inconsequent

They are almost indistinguishable. **Inconsequential** chiefly means 'unimportant', but so does **inconsequent**. **Inconsequent** chiefly means 'illogical; irrelevant', but so does **inconsequential**.

inconsolable, incontrovertible, incorrigible, incorruptible

The first ends in *-able*, the other three in *-ible*.

incredible, incredulous

Incredible means 'unbelievable, impossible to believe' (*an incredible story*) or, loosely, 'wonderful, amazing' (*an incredible view*). **Incredulous** means 'disbelieving, unable to believe' (*an incredulous stare*).

incubator

The word ends in *-or*, not *-er*.

incubus

The plural is either **incubuses** or **incubi**. An **incubus** was a male demon who was believed to have sexual intercourse with sleeping women, but it can now mean something that weighs oppressively on one: *free from the incubus of our mortgage*.

inculcate

One can **inculcate** ideas or information *in* or *into* a person: *She inculcated a sense of social responsibility in her children*. Some careful writers dislike the construction **inculcate** a person *with* an idea, and prefer to use *imbue*: *students imbued* (not *inculcated*) *with the desire for knowledge*.

incumbent

1 The **incumbent** is the present holder of an office or post, so it is TAUTOLOGOUS to speak of *the present incumbent*, though *the previous incumbent* would be reasonable.

2 Incumbent can mean 'imposed as a duty'. *It is incumbent on us to* . . . is official jargon for 'we must'.

incur

Other forms are **incurred, incurring.**

indecorous

See DECOROUS.

indefensible, indelible

Both words end in *-ible*, not *-able*.

independent

Both the noun and the adjective are spelled like this in both British and American English. Compare DEPENDENT.

in-depth

This OVERUSED word means 'detailed; comprehensive': *an in-depth study*; *in-depth discussions*. It is also oddly used to mean 'profound': *in-depth determination*.

indestructible

The word ends in *-ible*, not *-able*.

index

The plural is usually **indices** in the mathematical sense, but **indexes** elsewhere.

Indian

It is still possible to confuse the two meanings of **Indian**, particularly when Americans are reading British English or vice versa. In the USA, **Indian** is more likely than in Britain to mean 'member of one of the indigenous peoples of the Americas', while in a British context it usually means 'person from India'. It is safer to specify *American Indian* or (chiefly American use) *Native American* for the first meaning, unless the context is perfectly clear. *Red Indian* and the facetious *Injun* should be avoided. Pakistanis and Bangladeshis are not **Indians**, though they are often the proprietors of **Indian** restaurants.

indicate

1 The medical use of **indicated**, as in *Radical surgery was indicated*, is not appropriate to nonmedical writing. Use *necessary*, *advisable*, *appropriate*, etc: *Prompt action is advisable*; or rephrase as *We should act promptly*.

2 Indicate can usefully combine the functions of *say*, *show*, *hint*, etc, as in *He indicated his desire to cooperate*, if one does not wish to state whether he actually spoke. Otherwise, use one of the alternatives.

indicator

The word ends in *-or*, not *-er*.

indict, indite

They are both pronounced 'in-dite'. To **indict** is to charge with a crime. **Indite** is a quaintly FACETIOUS word for 'write': *indite a poem*.

indifferent

One is **indifferent** *to* or *as to* (not *for*) something, or **indifferent** *whether* something happens.

indigestible

The word ends in *-ible*, not *-able*.

indiscriminating, indiscriminate

See UNDISCRIMINATING.

indispensable

The word ends in *-able*, not *-ible*.

indisputable

The main stress is usually on *put*, but an alternative pronunciation with the stress on *dis* is also correct.

individual

This word should properly be used to distinguish one person from the rest of the group: *to safeguard the rights of the individual in society*. It should not be used, in serious writing, as a jocular or disparaging synonym for *person*, as in *He's a cantankerous individual*.

indivisible

The word ends in *-ible*, not *-able*.

indoor, indoors

The adjective is **indoor**: *indoor games*. The adverb is **indoors**: *to go indoors*.

indorse

See ENDORSE.

inductive

See DEDUCTIVE.

indulge

One **indulges** either a person (*He indulged himself by opening another bottle*) or a taste or emotion (*indulge my curiosity*); or one **indulges** in something enjoyable. By a reasonable extension, **indulge** in now often means 'engage in, undertake', with some implication that the occupation is a trivial one: *indulging in the curious hobby of raising tropical fish* (*Times Literary Supplement*).

industrial, industrious

Industrial means 'relating to manufacturing industry': *an industrial nation*; *industrial diamonds*. **Industrious** means 'hardworking'.

industry

This is usually pronounced with the stress on *in*, not on *dust*.

inebriated

This is a FACETIOUS word; it is better to say *drunk*.

inedible

See EATABLE.

inept

See INAPT.

inequity, inequality, iniquity

Inequity is unfairness: *to correct inequities in the wage rates.*
Inequality is lack of equality. *Inequalities in the wage rates* may of
course also be 'unfair', but they need not be. **Iniquity** is wickedness or
a sin.

inevitable

This means 'bound to happen', and in daily life applies chiefly to
things that we would rather avoid: *the inevitable results of overeating.*
In the specialized language of criticism, however, it has the
appreciative sense of 'dramatically convincing; true to nature'. A critic
who calls a phrase **inevitable** is not expressing censure.

infallible

The word ends in *-ible*, not *-able*.

infamous, notorious

These both mean 'having a bad reputation; deserving hatred'; but
despite its apparent similarity to *famous*, **infamous** does not
necessarily imply, as **notorious** does, that the person or thing in
question is known widely as well as unfavourably: *infamous treatment
of prisoners*; *a notorious drunkard.*

infant

In law, an **infant** is a person below the age of majority. In British
education, it is a child between five and eight. Otherwise, it is a *baby*,
and it may seem less PRETENTIOUS to say so.

infectious

See CONTAGIOUS.

infer, imply

1 Other forms of **infer** are **inferred, inferring.**

2 Correctly, the writer, speaker, or performer **implies** (ie 'expresses indirectly'): *His silence implied consent*; the reader, listener, or observer **infers** (ie 'guesses by reasoning'): *I infer from your letter that all is well*. The two are often confused, usually by using **infer** for **imply** rather than **imply** for **infer**, but careful writers avoid both misuses. In case of ambiguity, it is often safer to provide either word with an adequate context: *I infer from their silence that they disagree*.

inferior

Things are **inferior** *to*, not *than*, other things: *a man of inferior abilities to mine*.

inferno

The plural is **infernos**.

infinite, infinitesimal

An immeasurably small thing is better described as **infinitesimal** than as **infinitely** *small*; but there is nothing wrong with using **infinite(ly)** in respect of abstractions that cannot be quantified: *infinitely more/less attractive*.

inflammable, flammable, inflammatory

Despite appearances, **inflammable** and **flammable** are not opposites, but synonyms. Since **inflammable** looks as though it might mean 'not flammable', on the analogy of *independent* or *insensitive*, those concerned with the risk of fire prefer to use **flammable** in technical contexts. (Things that will not burn are *nonflammable* or *noninflammable*.) Only **inflammable** can be used in the figurative sense of 'easily excited': *an inflammable temper*. **Inflammatory** means 'tending to cause inflammation' or 'tending to agitate people': *inflammatory propaganda*.

inflatable

The word ends in *-able*, not *-ible*.

inflection, inflexion

Both spellings are permissible in British English; but **inflection** is commoner, and is the only American form.

inflexible

The word ends in *-ible*, not *-able*.

inflict

One can **inflict** damage or trouble *on* or *upon* a person: *inflict punishments on the children*. One cannot properly **inflict** a person *with* something. *Afflict* should be used for this second construction: *afflict* (not *inflict*) *them with punishments*.

inform

This is a formal word, appropriate in certain contexts: *inform a prisoner of his rights*. It can seem PRETENTIOUS to use *inform* where *tell* will do, and it is incorrect to use it for *tell* or *ask* someone *to do* something: *Please ask* (not *inform*) *the customer to wait*.

informant, informer

An **informant** is anyone who tells anyone anything, particularly one who supplies an investigator with data. An **informer** informs against others to the police.

information

It is reasonable, and indeed soothing, to say *for your information* if you mean to reassure your audience that no action is necessary: *For your information, we have already notified the department concerned*. It can add nothing to an instruction to act (*For your information, the witnesses should sign their names on page 4*), and is therefore better omitted.

infringe

See IMPINGE.

infuse

One can **infuse** a quality into a person: *infuse confidence into the team*. One cannot properly **infuse** a person *with* a quality. *Imbue* should be used for this second construction: *imbue* (not *infuse*) *them with confidence*.

infusible

The word ends in *-ible*, not *-able*. It means 'impossible to fuse', not 'possible to infuse'.

-ing

The pronunciation of the **-ing** ending known as 'dropping the *g*', by which *hunting* sounds like 'huntin', has now virtually passed out of educated use in both Britain and the USA, though it is still recorded in novels as a feature of old-fashioned upper-class speech.

ingenious, ingenuous

Ingenious means 'clever, inventive' (*an ingenious little gadget*), and the associated noun is *ingenuity*. **Ingenuous** means 'innocently candid, artless' (*his ingenuous enthusiasm*), and the noun is *ingenuousness*.

ingénue

The accent may be omitted, but is usually retained in British English. It means 'an artless young woman', particularly as a stage role.

ingest

This rather PRETENTIOUS word means 'eat; drink; swallow; take in', and is useful when one does not wish to specify which is meant. It is often used figuratively: *ingest information*. *Eat*, *swallow*, etc should be preferred in normal contexts.

ingratiate

One **ingratiates** *oneself*, not anyone else. It means 'gain favour for', not 'please': *He tried to ingratiate himself with his colleagues* (not *to ingratiate his colleagues*) *by relaxing the rules*.

ingress

This has a technical meaning in astronomy, but is otherwise a very formal and PRETENTIOUS word for 'entering' or 'entrance'.

inhabit

This means 'live in', not 'house' or 'contain': *an area inhabited by* (not *inhabiting*) *various flora and fauna*.

inhabitable

See HABITABLE.

inhabitant

See CITIZEN.

inherent

The common British pronunciation of the second syllable is like *here*, but a variant as in *herring* is also legitimate.

inheritance

See HERITAGE.

inheritor

The word ends in -or, not -er.

inhibit, prohibit

1 They both mean 'prevent'. **Inhibit** chiefly means 'discourage by moral or social pressure': *The presence of their father inhibited them from speaking freely.* To **prohibit** is to forbid by outside authority: *They were prohibited from striking.*

2 One can **inhibit** or **prohibit** an action or **inhibit/prohibit** someone *from doing* it, but not someone *to do* it. Write *He inhibited/prohibited us from leaving* (not *to leave*).

initial

As an adjective, **initial** is a formal and sometimes PRETENTIOUS word for *first*. Other forms of the verb are **initialled, initialling** in British English, but the second *l* is usually omitted in American English.

initiate

One can **initiate** a person *into* something: *initiate students into the mysteries of algebra.* One cannot properly **initiate** something *into* a person. Use *instil* or *infuse* for this second construction: *instil* (not *initiate*) *mathematics into them.*

-in-law, step-, half-

1 The plurals of *mother-in-law*, *sister-in-law*, etc are *mothers-in-law*, *sisters-in-law*.

2 One's relations **in-law** are the husbands or wives of one's blood relations; or else one's husband's or wife's blood relations. In older use, the same expression was also used for the relationship we now call **step-**, relations by remarriage. A *brother-in-law* is one's husband's brother, or sister's husband; a *stepbrother* is the son by a former marriage of one's father's or mother's new spouse. Neither of these are blood relations, but a *half-brother* is related through one parent, as when a child is born of the new marriage.

inning(s)

In cricket, it is one **innings**, two **innings**, and this is also the figurative use: *He lived to 94, so he had a good innings*. In baseball, it is one **inning**.

innocent

1 In law, one does not plead **innocent**, but *not guilty*.

2 It is no longer very funny, but rather FACETIOUS, to use **innocent** *of* for *without* or *lacking*: *a face innocent of make-up*. Use it only when you particularly want to suggest 'lacking something bad': *innocent of any evil intent*.

innovation

New **innovation** is a TAUTOLOGY. All innovations are new.

innovative

This is an appreciative jargon word for 'full of new ideas; creative': *an innovative role in the expansion of overseas sales*.

innuendo

The plural is either **innuendos** or **innuendoes**. It means a hint, particularly a veiled slight on someone.

innumerate

See ILLITERATE.

inoculate

See VACCINATE.

in order that, in order to

See ORDER.

in petto

Besides its original meaning 'in secret', used technically in the Vatican, this has come to be used incorrectly for 'in miniature', probably because it sounds like *petty*: *School is the world in petto*. Do not use many of these FOREIGN PHRASES.

input

From its use in electronics and computer technology, this has become an OVERUSED word for anything coming into a system, from purchases to teaching: *He has contributed a valuable input to our project*. As a verb used in data processing, its other forms are **inputted, inputting**.

inquire

See ENQUIRE.

inquisitor

The word ends in *-or*, not *-er*.

insanitary

See UNSANITARY.

insensible

The word ends in *-ible*, not *-able*. It is not the opposite of *sensible* in the sense 'reasonable, judicious', but means 'without feeling, unconscious'.

inside of

Informally, this means 'in less time than': *We should be there inside of an hour*. It is better to say *within an hour* in formal writing, and to use **inside** alone with reference to position: *inside my mouth*.

insignia

This word for 'badges of honour' is correctly used as a plural in British English, though its singular form **insigne** is rare. In American English it is permissible to speak of *an* **insignia**, with the plural **insignias.**

insinuate

This is used either in the sense 'worm one's way into' (*He insinuated himself into their favour*) or in the sense 'hint something discreditable' (*He insinuated that the witness had been bribed*). It cannot be used for 'enter artfully', without an object (*He insinuated into our organization*).

insofar as

See INASMUCH AS.

insouciance

This borrowed French word is now usually pronounced as the English spelling would suggest, with the first syllable like *in* and the last like that in *influence*. It means 'unconcern, nonchalance'.

inspector

The word ends in *-or*, not *-er*.

inspire

You can **inspire** a person *with* a quality: *The sight inspired him with nostalgia*. You can also **inspire** a quality *in* a person: *It inspired nostalgia in the tourists*. Both constructions are correct.

inst.

This is old-fashioned business English for 'this month'. It is better to write the name of the month.

instal(l)

This is usually spelled with two *l*'s, but **instal** is also correct. In any case, other forms are **installed, installing**, and the noun is **installation**; but **instal(l)ment** has one *l* in British English and two in American.

instance

This word gives rise to many VERBOSE phrases. *In this* **instance** can often be replaced by *here*; *in most/some/a few* **instances** by *usually/sometimes/occasionally*; and *in the first* **instance** by *first*. Careful writers may prefer to rephrase such a sentence as *They live at home in the majority of instances* as *Most of them live at home*. See CASE (1).

instigate

One may **instigate** a person to disobey orders, **instigate** legal proceedings, or **instigate** a plot to overthrow the government. The word means 'provoke action', often discreditable action: *instigate a race riot*. It should not be used merely for 'set up', as in *instigate a new accountancy system*.

instil(l)

1 The word is spelled **instil** in British English, but usually **instill** in American English. Other forms are **instilled, instilling.**

2 One can **instil** a quality *in* or *into* a person: *instil a love of learning into the children*. One cannot properly **instil** a person *with* a quality. Use *imbue* for this second construction: *imbue* (not *instil*) *them with a love of learning*.

institute, institution

Certain organizations, and the buildings that house them, which have been set up (*instituted*) for some purpose are called **institutes**, others are called **institutions**. **Institute** is more likely to be used as part of a title: *the British Film Institute*. It is also used of a short intensive study course in US education: *an urban studies institute*. **Institution** has also the wider sense of 'an established practice within a culture': *the institution of marriage*.

instructional, instructive

The material and processes of *instruction* are **instructional**: *an instructional course*. Anything that succeeds in imparting *instruction* is **instructive,** which means 'enlightening': *a very instructive experience*.

insufficient

This can sound PRETENTIOUS, and should be avoided where *not enough* will do.

insurance

See ASSURANCE.

insure

See ASSURE. **Insure** and **ensure** have the same pronunciation.

intaglio

The plural is **intaglios**. An **intaglio** is carved with a sunken design, as opposed to a *cameo*, which projects in relief. The *g* is silent.

intangible

The word ends in *-ible*, not *-able*.

integral

The usual pronunciation is with the stress on *in*, rather than on *teg*.

integrate

This has proper technical senses in mathematics, in psychiatry (*integrated personality*), and in connection with racial desegregation (*to integrate school districts*). It is loosely used, and perhaps OVERUSED, in the sense 'blend, combine, incorporate': *to integrate the economies of two countries*; *integrate the West German divisions into the Atlantic defence system* (*New Statesman*). But one should not be censorious where no obvious alternative presents itself, as in *integrate criminals into society*.

intellectual, intelligent

The adjective **intellectual** can mean either 'of the intellect' (*an intellectual difficulty*) or 'guided by intellect rather than by feeling or experience; interested in the things of the mind; highly educated' (*an intellectual family*). The noun means a person who is **intellectual** in this second sense, and it is often used with some distrust and even scorn for the deficiencies it implies. Bertrand Russell wrote: *I have never called myself an intellectual, and nobody has ever dared to call me one in my presence. I think an intellectual may be defined as a person who pretends to have more intellect than he has, and I hope this definition does not fit me.*

Intellectual people must of necessity be **intelligent,** but an **intelligent** person need not be **intellectual.** To be **intelligent** is to have a quick understanding, but one can be **intelligent** without having any interest in scholarly matters and without knowing very much; indeed, the word is often used of small children and of animals.

intelligible

The word ends in *-ible*, not *-able*.

intend

One **intends** something to happen, or **intends** *that* something should happen, but one cannot correctly **intend** *for* something to happen. Write *I didn't intend her* (not *for her*) *to hear.*

intense, intensive

Intense chiefly means 'extreme': *intense heat/pleasure.* **Intensive** means 'highly concentrated' (*intensive effort*), and has a number of specialized meanings in grammar, in medicine (*intensive care*), and in industry (*intensive farming*).

intent

1 One is **intent** *on* something or *on doing* something. Write *He was intent on marrying* (not *to marry*) *her.*

2 *To all intents and purposes* is a VERBOSE way of saying 'in effect, virtually'.

intention

One speaks both of **intention** *to do* something and **intention** *of doing* it. There is some degree of leeway here, but the normal idiom after *the, no, any, some, every,* is **intention** *of*: *He has no intention of going; He spoke with the intention of annoying me; I have every intention of* *coming back.* After *it is*, *it was*, use **intention** *to*: *It wasn't my intention to hurt her.* Elsewhere, use **intention** *to*: *He spoke with intention to annoy.*

inter

Other forms of this formal word for 'bury' are **interred, interring.**

inter-, intra-

Inter- means 'between': *international*; *intercity*; *intermarry*. **Intra-** means 'within': *intrauterine*; *intrastate commerce.*

inter alia

This means 'among other things'. If you mean 'among other people', write *among others*, rather than the correct but pedantic Latin *inter alios*. In general, avoid these LATINISMS.

interceptor, intercepter

Both spellings are correct.

interchangeable

The word is spelled like this, retaining the final *e* of *interchange.*

interesting

1 The word is usually pronounced with the stress on *in*, not on *est*.

2 To say that something is **interesting** may mean just that one does not want to commit oneself to an opinion. When possible, use some more specific adjective such as *puzzling*, or *important*, or no adjective at all.

interface

This means 'surface forming the common boundary between two spaces or bodies': *an oil-water interface*. It is OVERUSED in the figurative sense of 'common frontier, meeting point': *the interface between literary studies and social history*; or 'liaison, connection': *a strong interface with the Ministry*. It is also OVERUSED figuratively as a verb: *to interface* (ie combine, cooperate) *with the design department.*

interior, internal

See EXTERIOR, EXTERNAL, of which these are opposites.

interlocutor

The word ends in -*or*, not -*er*. It is a formal word for 'person with whom someone is talking'.

interment, internment

Interment is a formal word for burial. **Internment** is imprisonment during a war: *the internment of enemy aliens.*

intermezzo

The plural is either **intermezzi** or **intermezzos.**

in terms of

See TERMS.

internecine

1 This is pronounced 'in-ter-NEE-sign' in British English, but the endings 'NESS-in' and 'NESS-een' are also acceptable as American pronunciations.

2 Although **internecine** formerly meant 'mutually destructive', it now usually means, and will be taken to mean, 'involving conflict within a group': *an internecine union dispute.* Such conflict need not even be particularly 'destructive'.

interpersonal

This is a jargon word for 'face to face': *learning in an interpersonal situation* (ie with a teacher); *interpersonal skills* (ie the ability to get on with people).

interpret(at)ive

Both **interpretative** and **interpretive** are acceptable, and mean the same thing.

interregnum

The plural is either **interregnums** or **interregna**.

interval

This means 'a distance between two points' (*lamp posts placed at regular intervals*) or 'a period between two events', such as the **interval** (in American English, the *intermission*) between two parts of an entertainment. **Interval** does not mean 'length of time', so do not write *an interval of two years* unless the two years in question obviously separate one event from another.

intervene, intervention

These can mean 'interfere, interference', but usually in an appreciative sense: *The Bank of England intervened to stabilize the pound.* Welfare bodies speak of *social work intervention*, which means doing something rather than nothing about a bad state of affairs.

intestinal

The pronunciation with the stress on the *test* is acceptable everywhere; that with the stress on *tin* (which is then pronounced 'tine') is a British variant.

intimate (*adjective*)

Besides its usual meanings, **intimate** can mean 'small', with the appreciative implication of 'cosy' rather than 'poky': *an intimate cocktail lounge.* Or it can be a EUPHEMISM for 'involved in sexual intercourse': *In six months they were intimate six times in the car and twice on a mountainside* (*News of the World*).

intimidate

One can **intimidate** someone *into doing* something, but not *from doing* something: *They intimidated him into leaving* (not *from staying*).

into, in to

1 Do not confuse **into,** meaning 'so as to be inside' (*They came into the house*) with **in to**: *They came in to see me*; *We went in to breakfast.*

2 The use of **into** for 'involved with, keen on' (*into 'hard drugs*; *Are you into yoga?*) is too informal for serious writing.

intolerable, intolerant

Intolerable means 'too bad to be tolerated, unbearable': *intolerable pain*. **Intolerant** means 'unable to tolerate', and often 'narrow-minded': *intolerant of new ideas*.

intoxicated

This is a rather formal word. It is often better to use *drunk*.

intra-

See INTER-.

intricacy, intricate

These are usually pronounced with the stress on *in*, not on *tric*.

intrigue

In French, *intriguer* means 'tangle, perplex'. Nevertheless, the English verb is properly used in the sense 'fascinate': *I was intrigued to learn* . . . It conveys better than any other word available a notion of amused and slightly ironical curiosity.

intrinsic

This is the opposite of **extrinsic**. See EXTERIOR.

intrude, obtrude, protrude

To **intrude** is to thrust in without good reason: *He intruded a trite moral into his play*. To **obtrude** is to thrust forward without good reason: *not a man to obtrude his beliefs casually*. Thus, **intrusive** means 'entering unwanted' and **obtrusive** means 'too noticeable'. To **protrude** is, literally, to 'jut out': *protruding teeth*.

intrust

See ENTRUST.

intuit

This is a well-established BACK-FORMATION, meaning 'know by intuition': *She was able to intuit what they were thinking*.

inured

One is **inured** (ie 'hardened') *to* something disagreeable: *inured to a life of drudgery*. In relation to pleasant or neutral things, use *accustomed to* or *used to*.

invalid

The adjective meaning 'not valid' is pronounced with the stress on *val*. The noun meaning 'sick person' is pronounced with the stress on *in*; the pronunciation of its last syllable like 'lid' is acceptable everywhere, while 'leed' is a British variant.

invaluable

This means 'more valuable than can be estimated; priceless'. It is thus the opposite of *valueless* or *worthless*, not the opposite of **valuable.**

inveigh, inveigle

Both words are spelled -*ei*-, not -*ie*-, but while the second syllable of **inveigh** always has the vowel sound of *day*, that of **inveigle** can also have the vowel sound of *we*. To **inveigh** *against* something is to protest against it forcefully; to **inveigle** is to cajole.

invent, discover

One **invents** something new, such as a machine. One **discovers** something already in existence, such as an island or a scientific law.

inventor

The word ends in -*or*, not -*er*.

inventory

The stress is on *in*, not on *vent*.

inverse

See REVERSE.

inversion

Inversion is a change in order of elements within a sentence that results in the main verb appearing before the subject (*Here comes the coffee*) or the auxiliary appearing before the subject (*Can you see them?*). The circumstances in which inversion is normal include:

(1) questions: *Have you put your signature at the end of the form?* (The exception is when the question begins with an interrogative word that functions as the subject: *Who has told you?*; contrast the inversion in *What have you heard about them?*, where *what* is the object.)

(2) after an introductory negative element: *Under no circumstances should you apologize*; *She would not speak to them, nor would she write to them*.

(3) after *so* (as well as negative *nor* and *neither*) in an elliptical clause: *I recalled the incident, and so did my parents*; *The hotel room was excellent, and so was the food*; *I did not understand the letter, and neither did the others*.

(4) in conditional clauses without a conjunction: *Had I been there, it would not have happened* (contrast *If I had been there, . . .*); *Should you want some help, please let us know*. The inverted forms are more formal.

Inversion is possible in some other circumstances, but requires discretion:

(1) reporting clauses in direct speech: *'The writer', said one critic,*

385

'has no sense of style.' This type of inversion can become irritating if overused. In any case, do not use it if the subject is a pronoun (*said he*).

(2) to prevent a long subject from overbalancing the sentence: *Surrounding the market stalls were two hotels, several public houses, an expensive restaurant, and several coffee shops; At the entrance stood a statue of a blind goddess holding a bow and arrows.* This type is sometimes clumsily used in journalistic writing without the justification of a long subject: *Opening the new building will be the mayor.*

(3) to place emphasis on the subject: *From the car sprang a fierce tiger; Here comes the manager.*

(4) to bring to the front an element that links with something preceding; it also places emphasis on the last element: *The principal was not to blame; equally blameless were the teachers; He was angry, and even angrier was his wife.*

inverted commas

See QUOTATION MARKS.

investigation

Make an investigation into something is a VERBOSE way of saying *investigate* it.

investigator, investor

Both words end in *-or*, not *-er*.

invincible, invisible

Both words end in *-ible*, not *-able*.

invite (*noun*)

Do not use this word for 'an invitation', except perhaps humorously.

involve, involvement

Involve is lazily OVERUSED in place of many other words such as *include, require, mean, affect, encroach on,* and *lead to*. It is perhaps best reserved for situations of 'complication' or 'entanglement', as when one speaks of an **involved** argument: *We hope not to involve them in our difficulties.* In the following, **involve** would be better either replaced or omitted: *The cost involved* (omit *involved*) *would be excessive; There was a collision involving* (use *between*) *a bus and a private car; The disease threatened to involve* (use *affect*) *his kidneys;*

Your decision will involve (use *mean*) *addressing all the letters by hand.*

Involve is also used in the appreciative sense of 'occupy oneself absorbingly; commit oneself'. A firm may invite job applicants to become **involved** *with* the company, suggesting a more profound commitment than that of merely working for it. From this sense of the word has developed a corresponding jargon sense of the noun **involvement**: *total career involvement.*

invulnerable

Since one either is or is not **invulnerable,** it seems better to avoid such expressions as *make us fairly invulnerable.*

inward(s)

Before a noun, use **inward**: *to achieve inward peace.* After a verb, use the form with an *s* in British English (*The door opens inwards*) and the one without an *s* in American English.

ion, iron

Ion is a technical term in atomic physics. The word is not a printer's error for **iron,** the metal. The adjective formed from **ion** is *ionic*; but, confusingly, *Ionic* with a capital *I* refers to the region of ancient Greece called *Ionia*, and to a style of architecture associated with it. *Ironic* is related not to **iron** but to *irony*.

-ion

See -NESS.

irascible

The word ends in *-ible*, not *-able*.

Irish

See BRITISH.

ironic(al), ironically

The adjective now often means 'paradoxical' (*It was ironical that he should be taxed at the top rate on his unemployment benefit*), or simply 'odd' or 'unexpected': *It's ironic that we should both have been ill at the same time.* Likewise, the adverb, besides meaning 'in an ironical way' (*He smiled ironically*), means 'strangely enough': *Ironically, the cupboard was empty.* There is considerable prejudice in Britain against these usages.

iron out

This useful expression means 'settle by discussion and compromise; solve': *iron out our differences*. It need no longer be regarded as particularly informal.

irony

This is the use of words to express a meaning other than, and often opposite to, what is directly said, as when a large man is known as *Tiny*. Dramatic **irony** is the effect produced when the characters in a play speak or act in ignorance of something known to the audience. What these senses have in common is the listener's pleasure in recognizing something that has not been explicitly stated, and thus being admitted to an inner circle. The word **irony** is often and perhaps excessively used of an incongruity between what actually happens and what one thinks ought to happen: *The irony of it was that meat prices dropped the year I went over to raising beef cattle.* The expression *irony of fate* means this last kind of irony, and is a CLICHÉ.

irreducible

The word ends in *-ible*, not *-able*.

irrefutable

This is pronounced with the stress either on *ref* or on *fut*; both are correct.

irregardless

This means the same as *regardless*, which is itself negative; probably the added negative prefix was mistakenly introduced by analogy with *irrespective*. It should not be used.

irrelevant

This should not be pronounced or spelled *irrevelant*. Properly, things are **irrelevant** *to* (ie have nothing to do with) other things: *That statement is irrelevant to your argument.* The word has been somewhat OVERUSED, particularly by students about proposed subjects of study, to mean 'nothing to do with our needs; not applicable to modern life'.

irreligious, nonreligious, unreligious

Irreligious means 'against religion, ungodly'. **Nonreligious** means 'not religious, secular'. **Unreligious** may mean either.

irremovable

See IMMOVABLE.

irreparable, unrepairable

Harm and damage are **irreparable,** pronounced with the stress on *rep*: *an irreparable loss*. Material objects that cannot be mended are **unrepairable.**

irreplaceable

The word is spelled like this, retaining the final *e* of *place*.

irrepressible, irresistible, irresponsible

All three words end in *-ible*, not *-able*.

irrespective of

This means 'without reference to; regardless of': *a college open to all irrespective of race, colour, or creed*. Do not use *irrespectively* here.

irreversible

The word ends in *-ible*, not *-able*.

irrevocable

This is usually pronounced with the stress on *rev*; except when the word is used with reference to letters of credit, in which case *voc* is the stressed syllable.

irrupt

See ERUPT.

isle, aisle

An **isle** is an island. Apart from its use in placenames (*the Isle of Wight*), the word belongs to old-fashioned poetry. An **aisle** (same pronunciation) is a gangway, or a side passage in a church.

-ism

From being used in the names of doctrines and theories (*socialism, Buddhism*), **-ism** has developed a modern sense of 'discrimination on the grounds of something'. Besides *racism*, there are *sexism, classism, ageism* (which usually means discrimination in favour of the young), *heterosexism* (prejudice in favour of heterosexuals), *disablism* or *handicappism* (discrimination against the disabled), *smokeism* (against smokers), and several others. If this usage stems from a real desire to be fairer to people, it should probably be welcomed.

isolation

It is rather VERBOSE to use *in isolation* when *alone* will do.

Israelite, Israeli

See JEW.

issue

1 As a noun, **issue** is somewhat OVERUSED for *subject* or *topic*: *a controversial issue.* Careful writers try to confine this use to such topics as are matters for dispute: *discussing the issue of who is to govern*; *I don't want to make an issue of it.*

2 In both British and American English one can **issue** (ie provide officially) something *to* someone: *The school issued uniforms to the players.* In British English, one can also **issue** someone *with* something: *Why are we being issued with Privy Council stationery?* (*Punch*).

-ist, -alist

When a word can be formed with either **-ist** or **-alist,** as with *agricultur(al)ist* or *education(al)ist*, it is reasonable to prefer the shorter version; but sometimes, as with *conversationalist*, one form rather than the other has established itself.

it

1 See ITS.

2 Avoid using **it** if the meaning is not clear in the context. *I didn't drink coffee because it was too hot* may mean that the coffee was too hot, or that the weather was.

3 For *it's me*, see CASE, GRAMMATICAL (2).

Italian sounds

Some Italian words and names have passed into English, particularly in the field of music, and one should make some attempt to pronounce them in the Italian way. (Compare FRENCH PRONUNCIATION.) Without going beyond the equivalent customary English sounds, it is reasonable to adopt the following system.

Pronounce:

c or *cc* before *e* or *i* as in *church*: *Cinzano*.

c or *cc* before *a*, *o*, or *u* as *k*: *concerto*.

ch as *k*: *Chianti*.

g or *gg* before *e* or *i* as *j*: *Genoa*.

g or *gg* before *a*, *o*, or *u* as in *get*: *Garibaldi*.

gh as in *get*: *ghetto*.

The *g* of *gli* is silent: *intaglio*.

gn as *ny*: *gnocchi*.

z or *zz* as *ts* or *dz*: *scherzo*; *intermezzo*.

italics

Italics in print are the equivalent of underlining in manuscript. There are several uses of italics or the equivalent underlining:

(1) For titles of books, newspapers, magazines, journals, plays, operas, long musical compositions, ballets, films, long poems that are often published separately, paintings and other works of art. See TITLES OF BOOKS AND NEWSPAPERS.

(2) For referring to phrases, words, or parts of words:

Spell *limited* with one *t*.

I never use *in view of the fact that*.

The past of *take* is *took*.

(3) For emphasis, corresponding to a heavy stress in speech, to make sure that the reader understands the main point:

There is no doubt that children grow more when asleep, but the growth may not depend on *length* of sleep.

Use italics sparingly for this purpose.

(4) For foreign words or phrases that have not become naturalized in English:

The evidence is *prima facie* sufficient to justify prosecution.

item

This useful word can mean any thing, abstract or concrete (though not any person): *an item of sportswear*; *the next item on the agenda*; *grammatical items such as a noun*. It is correctly used where only an uncountable noun is available; we can speak of *several items of furniture* but not of *several furnitures*. It is sometimes lazy, however, to use **item** where a more precise word exists. *Items of clothing* are *clothes*, and one of them is a *garment*.

its, it's

Its means 'the one belonging to it': *its climate*; *its kennel*. **It's** means
'it is', or 'it has': *It's ready*; *It's arrived*. **It's** is often, but quite
wrongly, used for **its**: *It's roadholding puts Viceroy in the forefront of
cars* (*The Times*). Let us hope this example is a misprint.

ivory tower

This CLICHÉ means 'a retreat to which one can escape from practical
concerns'. It is derogatory, suggesting the selfishness of the highbrow
who is unwilling to become involved in real life: *viewing college as an
ivory tower*.

-ize, -ise

1 Verbs like *liquidize* and *sympathize* and nouns like *crystallization* can
be spelled with either *z* or *s*. The spelling with *z* is the only American
form, and is also a common British one, endorsed by the 'house style'
of several British publishing houses and newspapers. The following,
however, must be spelled with **-ise** in both British and American
English: *advertise, advise, apprise, chastise, circumcise, comprise,
demise, despise, devise, disenfranchise, disfranchise, disguise,
enfranchise, enterprise, excise, exercise, improvise, incise, premise,
revise, supervise, surmise, surprise, televise*. Sooner than learn the
foregoing list, some British writers find it safer to use **-ise** all the time.
Whichever way you decide, try to be consistent. The spelling of verbs
ending in **-yse**, such as *analyse*, with a *z* is purely American.

2 New verbs are constantly being formed with **-ize**: *burglarize*;
comprehensivize; *containerize*; *decimalize*; *personalize*; *privatize*;
prioritize. This is a useful resource of the language, but it should not be
allowed to get out of hand. Where there is a simpler way of expressing
the same idea, avoid the **-ize** alternative, as by replacing the verb
martyrize by the verb to *martyr*.

Jj

Jacobean, Jacobin, Jacobite

They all come from *Jacobus*, the Latin for 'James'. **Jacobean** refers to James I of England (reigned 1603–1625): *Jacobean furniture*. A **Jacobin** was a member of an extremist radical group during the French Revolution, who met in a convent near the church of St Jacques (St James) in Paris. A **Jacobite** was a supporter of James II and of the later Stuarts after the revolution of 1688.

jailer, jailor

Both spellings are correct. See also GAOL.

jamb

This is an upright piece forming the side of a door or window; it is not spelled *jam*.

janitor

The word ends in *-or*, not *-er*.

Jap

The term is considered offensive by those to whom it is applied. Use *Japanese* for the adjective and for the singular or plural noun.

jar (*verb*)

Other forms are **jarred, jarring**.

jargon

See VARIETIES OF ENGLISH.

jetsam

See FLOTSAM AND JETSAM.

393

Jew, Israelite, Israeli, Hebrew, Yiddish

Believers in Judaism are **Jews**, and the word is also used of those who identify themselves with, or are identified by others with, the Jewish people. The **Israelites** were the descendants of Jacob (also called Israel) in the Bible, who inhabited the ancient land of Israel. The citizens of modern Israel are **Israelis**, many of whom are not Jewish. The ancient language is **Hebrew**, chiefly a written language for some 2000 years, and revived for all purposes in modern Israel. There is no language called **Jewish**, though there are a number of Jewish languages. The best known is **Yiddish**, spoken by some Jews of Eastern European origin. It is a Germanic language with Hebrew and Slavonic elements that is usually written in Hebrew characters. In contemporary use, **Hebrew** refers to the language, not to the people, although an older use survives in some titles such as the *Young Men's* and *Young Women's Hebrew Associations.*

The proper adjective is **Jewish**: *my Jewish* (not *my Jew) friend.* A **Jewess** may prefer to be called a *Jewish woman* or *Jewish girl*; see FEMININE FORMS.

jewel(l)ed, jewel(l)er

These are spelled with two *l*'s in British English, but the second *l* is usually omitted in American English.

jewel(le)ry

Jewellery is the usual British spelling, **jewelry** the American one.

jibe

See GIBE.

jinn, djin, djinn

The Arabic word for this class of supernatural spirits in Muslim folklore is also rendered in English as *jinni, djinni, djini,* and *genie.* This last has the plurals *genies* and (less usually) *genii,* the second being easily confused with one of the plurals of *genius* (*geniuses* or *genii*) in the sense 'guiding or guardian spirit', but *genius* and *jinn* are of quite different origins.

job, position

Job is a homelier word than the formal **position,** but does not necessarily suggest less prestige. Though **job** may be used of the most exalted sorts of work, perhaps in the effort to avoid pomposity (*the exhausting job of Prime Minister*), **position** is less likely to be used of dishwashing. **Job** is used in all such combinations as *job description*, *job evaluation*, and *job satisfaction*, popular in management jargon.

join together

This very common combination is TAUTOLOGOUS. **Join** implies 'togetherness'.

jolly, jollily

As an adverb, **jolly** is an informal word for 'very': *It was a jolly good thing I was there*. For 'in a jolly way' one must either use **jollily,** awkward though it sounds (*He laughed jollily*), or say *in a jolly way*.

journalese

See VARIETIES OF ENGLISH.

judge, adjudge

These two words overlap in usage. In the legal senses, one **judges** or **adjudges** a case, **judges** or **adjudges** a prisoner guilty; one **judges** an accused person and **adjudges** (ie 'awards') legal costs. In the more general senses, one **judges** or **adjudges** something to be true (*Everyone adjudged the play a success*), one **judges** a flower show or beauty competition, **judges** (ie 'estimates') time or distance or temperature, and **judges** between rival choices.

judg(e)ment

Both spellings are permissible everywhere; but **judgment** is the more usual American choice, and **judgement** often a British preference.

judging by

This expression is often used for 'if we are to judge by': *Judging by the noise, the race must have started*. It is almost, but perhaps not quite, within the class of *-ing* and *-ed* forms such as *talking of* (*Talking of music, what's the programme for Thursday?*) which are conventionally permitted to be used in this way; see DANGLING PARTICIPLE. A safe alternative would be *If we may judge by the noise . . .*

judicial, judicious

Judicial is the word for courts of law and legal administration: *the judicial branch of government*; *judicial proceedings*. **Judicious** means 'sound in judgment, discreet': *a very judicious decision*. The two words are sometimes confused when *judicial* is used of the sort of behaviour that one expects from a judge. A *judicial* (ie thoughtful and critical) comment or statement may also be a *judicious* (ie discerning) one.

junction, juncture

A **junction** is a place where things join: *a railway junction; an electrical junction box.* A **juncture** is chiefly a critical moment in time. The expression *at this juncture*, if used at all, should be reserved for occasions of impending crisis and should not mean merely 'now'.

juror, jurist

The word **juror** ends in *-or*, not *-er*; it means a member of a jury. A **jurist** is a person versed in the law, particularly one who writes on legal subjects. The term is used more widely in American than in British English of any lawyer.

just

1 One meaning of **just** is 'exactly': *It's just five o'clock.* It is therefore TAUTOLOGOUS to say *just exactly five o'clock*; use **just** or *exactly* alone.

2 The use of **just** to mean 'very, completely' (*just wonderful; just perfect*) is not appropriate to serious writing.

3 When **just** means 'only a moment ago' it is traditionally used in British English with the perfect tense (ie with *had, have*, etc): *He's just arrived; The bell has just rung.* Increasingly, however, British English under American influence has come to use **just** in this sense with the simple past tense: *He just arrived; The bell just rang.*

4 It is important to distinguish **just** *not* from *not* **just. Just** followed by a negative means either 'by a small margin not' or 'simply not'; a person who is *just not old enough* is 'almost old enough' or 'simply too young', and *I just couldn't reach it* covers the same two possible meanings. When the negative comes before **just,** the combination means 'not only'. *He's not just old enough* means that he is old enough, and has also other attributes. We expect it to go on . . . *he's also tall enough.*

Justice

This is the title of various judges, such as a British High Court judge (*Mr Justice Smith*) or a Justice of the US Supreme Court.

juvenile, puerile

Juvenile may mean simply 'young' (*his juvenile appearance*) or 'for young people' (*juvenile literature*); but it can mean, as **puerile** must mean, 'silly and childish': *puerile/juvenile humour*.

Kk

kaleidoscope

The word is spelled *-ei-*, not *-ie-*.

kangaroo

The plural is **kangaroos**.

karat

See CARAT.

kerb

See CURB.

kerosene, paraffin

Kerosene (or **kerosine**) is the American, Australian, and New Zealand English word for one sense of **paraffin**, the British word for the familiar fuel oil produced by distilling petroleum. **Kerosene** does not replace **paraffin** in the technical senses of the word.

ketchup, catsup, catchup

All forms are acceptably used. **Ketchup** is probably the commonest British form, but **catsup** may be favoured in American English. The word has, of course, nothing to do with cats.

key, quay

A **key** fits a lock, provides a solution, or is to be pressed on a piano or typewriter. Another kind of **key** is a low island, such as one of those off the coast of Florida. A **quay** is a wharf.

kibbutz

The plural is **kibbutzim.** It means 'a collective settlement in Israel'.

kidnap

Other forms are **kidnapped, kidnapping** in British English, but the second *p* is often omitted in American English.

kids

This is widely though informally used for 'children', even in educational journals by teachers who wish to sound friendly and human, but that usage irritates many people in Britain. The word is conveniently vague, since it can also apply to teenagers and young adults: *college kids.* It is more informal in British than in American use.

kilo-, milli-

In the metric system, **kilo-** means 'thousand' and **milli-**'thousandth': *kilometre; millimetre.*

kilometre

The traditional, and recommended, British pronunciation is that with the stress on *kil.* This is consistent with the pronunciation of such related words as *kilolitre* and *centimetre*; but many British speakers now pronounce the word with the stress on *om*, either under American influence (since this is the chief American pronunciation) or by association with such words as *speedometer* and *gasometer.*

kind, sort

1 In formal writing, one should write *this* **kind**, *that* **sort** (*That kind of book is dull*) and not *these* **kind**, *those* **sort**, although the incongruous combination of plural *these* and singular **sort** (*Those kind of books are dull*) is common in speech. The plural is perhaps more acceptable in questions after *what* or *which*: *What sort of things are they?* The idea of plurality can be expressed correctly by rephrasing: *Those kinds of books/Those kinds of book/Books of that kind are dull.*

2 Some critics object to **kind** *of a*, **sort** *of a* (*a kind of a wheelbarrow*), and advise that *a* should be omitted here. The construction is certainly informal, but there may be a delicate distinction in speech between *What kind of job is that?* (ie what does the work entail?) and *What kind of a job is that?* (ie you should be ashamed of it!).

3 Kind *of* and **sort** *of* are often used in informal speech to mean either 'rather' (*We felt kind of hungry*) or 'in a manner of speaking' (*You sort of wiggle your toes*), but these phrases have no place in serious writing.

4 Where **kind** *of* and **sort** *of* are correctly used, they should not be pronounced *kinda*, *sorta* in formal speech.

kindly

1 Though **kindly** ends with **-ly** like *quickly* and *easily*, it can be not only an adverb (*She smiled kindly*) but an adjective (*her kindly smile*).

2 Kindly is often used for *please*, in business English and elsewhere: *Kindly fill in the attached questionnaire.* Since, however, it can also mean 'in a kind way' (*They greeted her kindly*), some people take exception to the phrase *kindly requested* (*You are kindly requested not to smoke*) because they think that it sounds as if the person who is making the request is being kind about it. This objection seems unreasonable.

kimono

The plural is **kimonos.**

kirby-grip

See HAIRPIN.

kith and kin

This rather archaic expression is still sometimes used with FACETIOUS effect. Originally, **kith** meant 'friends' as distinct from **kin,** 'relations'.

knapsack

See RUCKSACK.

knee-jerk

This is OVERUSED in the sense of 'involuntary automatic response': *knee-jerk radicalism.*

kneel

The past tense and participle are **knelt** or **kneeled. Knelt** is on the whole the preferred British form, but American English uses both.

knickers

See PANTS.

knife

Knives is the plural of the noun, but is not part of the verb: *He knifes him.*

knight-errant

The plural is **knights-errant.**

knit

The past tense and participle are either **knit** or **knitted**. **Knit** is commoner in the general sense of 'united' (*a closely knit group*), and **knitted** in the sense of making things from wool (*a knitted jacket*).

knock up

In British English this chiefly means 'awaken by knocking', and in American English it chiefly means 'make pregnant', a state of affairs which gives rise to amusing misunderstandings.

knot

Technically, this means the speed of one nautical mile per hour. Since it is not a distance, one should not properly speak of *knots per hour*, although this loose usage is common.

know

1 It is the sign of an inept speaker to have to keep appealing to the knowledge shared with the listener by repeatedly saying *you know*.

2 In negatives particularly, **know** is often followed by *that*, *if*, or *whether*, but it should not be followed by *as*: *I don't know that* (not *as* or *as how*) *he can.*

know-how

This is a useful though somewhat OVERUSED word for 'knowledge of how to do something; expertise', particularly with reference to the faculty of overcoming technical problems. Since it applies chiefly to the practical and commercial, one would not speak of the *know-how* of a musician or mathematician.

knowledgeable

The word is spelled like this, retaining the final *e* of *knowledge.*

krona, krone

The **krona** is an Icelandic or Swedish unit of currency, plural **kronur** (Icelandic) and **kronor** (Swedish). The **krone** is a Danish or Norwegian unit of currency, plural **kroner**, and was an Austrian unit from 1892 to 1925, plural **kronen**.

kudos

This means 'fame, prestige'. It is not a plural, any more than *pathos*, and one cannot speak of one *kudo*.

Ll

_____

-l-, -ll-

See DOUBLING.

lab

This CLIPPED form of *laboratory* is only slightly informal.

label (*verb*)

Other forms are **labelled, labelling** in British English, but the second *l* is usually omitted in American English.

laboratory

This is usually pronounced with the stress on the second syllable in British English, on the first syllable in American English.

labo(u)r

It is spelled **labour** in British English, **labor** in American English. The related adjective is always spelled **laborious**. See also BELABOUR.

lacerations

This can seem a rather PRETENTIOUS word where *cuts* will do, as in *multiple lacerations on the legs*.

lachrymose

This can seem either PRETENTIOUS or FACETIOUS. Prefer *tearful*.

lack

Careful writers avoid **lack** *for*, and write *He will not lack* (not *lack for*) *advisers*.

lacuna

The plural is either **lacunae** or **lacunas**. It is a rather formal word for some senses of *gap*.

lad

This means any male person, who need not even be young. A jolly word, expressing male togetherness (*having a few jars with the lads*) particularly in sport, it may irritate those who feel less jolly. Note that in its special sense of 'groom in a racing stable', a **lad** may well be a woman.

lady

It is a GENTEELISM to refer to oneself as a lady, except humorously. Modern women at the upper end of the social scale tend to avoid the word, at least when speaking of their social equals, and to say *a woman doctor* or *the woman next door*. There is, however, some evidence that the word is coming back among feminists, as in *She's a very able lady*. Most people prefer to use **lady** rather than *woman* when they speak of a woman in her presence (*Bring this lady another sherry*); or with *old*, because *old* **lady** sounds more respectful than *old woman*. The plural is used in public address (*ladies and gentlemen*). For **lady** as a title, see TITLES OF PEOPLE.

lady-in-waiting

The plural is **ladies-in-waiting**.

lama, llama

A **lama** is a Buddhist monk of Tibet or Mongolia. A **llama** (same pronunciation) is a South American ruminant mammal.

lamentable

In British English, this is usually pronounced with the stress on *lam*, but the pronunciation stressing *ment* is equally current in American English.

landward(s)

Before a noun, use **landward**: *the landward side*. After a verb, use the form with an *s* in British English (*sailing landwards*) and the one without an *s* in American English.

languor

The word is spelled like this in both British and American English; not *-or* or *-our*. It rhymes with *anger*.

large

1 *A large number/portion/proportion of* is a VERBOSE way of saying 'many/much of'.

2 Things *bulk* **large**, *loom* **large**, or are *writ* **large**; not *largely*. *Largely* means 'to a large extent', not 'in a large way': *Success was largely due to his efforts*.

large-scale, large-sized

Large-scale is correctly applied to maps. When used of other things than maps, it implies 'wide-ranging' or 'extensive': *a large-scale statistical survey*. It is VERBOSE to use it, or **large-sized**, merely for 'big'.

largess(e)

This is spelled with or without the final *e*. The commoner pronunciation is that with the stress on *gess*, but many people stress *lar*.

largo, lento

The plurals are **largos** and **lentos**. They are musical instructions; **largo** means 'slow and dignified', while **lento** means merely 'slow'.

larva

The plural is **larvae** or, less usually, **larvas**.

larynx, pharynx

The plurals are either **-rynges** or **-rynxes**. The **larynx** is the upper part of the windpipe, containing the vocal cords, and is where one suffers from *laryngitis*. The **pharynx** connects the mouth to the gullet, and so lies above the **larynx**.

lasso, lariat

1 The plural of **lasso** is either **lassos** or **lassoes**. It is pronounced either 'LASS-oh' or 'lass-OO'.

2 Lasso and **lariat** are both of Spanish origin, and both mean the same running noose for catching livestock; but **lariat** is chiefly an American word, and is also used of a rope for tethering grazing animals.

last, latest

1 Last can mean 'final': *famous last words*; or 'next before the present': *I saw her last week*; *This is better than his last film*. These two senses can sometimes cause misunderstanding, since *his last film* might be taken to mean his final one; in this case a clearer word would be **previous**. It can also mean 'most recent', but for that sense it is clearer to use **latest**: *her latest, but not we hope her last, book*.

2 It is better to write *the last chapter but one* than *the last but one chapter*.

3 For *last four* or *four last*, see FIRST.

lastly

See FIRSTLY.

late

See EX-.

lateral thinking

This means the sort of creative thinking that attacks a problem or topic from unorthodox angles instead of proceeding on rigidly logical lines. The expression is OVERUSED, perhaps because some people wish to indicate that there is a type of thinking that human beings can do that machines cannot do.

lath, lathe, lathi

A **lath** is a thin strip of wood. A **lathe** is a machine on which work is rotated and shaped. A **lathi** is a heavy stick used as a weapon in India.

lather

This can rhyme with either *gather* or *father*. On the whole the *gather* pronunciation is preferred in the USA and the *father* one in Britain.

Latinisms

Everything that has been said about FOREIGN PHRASES applies even more strongly to the use of Latin words and phrases in general English. The trouble is that very few people today know Latin, and mistakes are made not only by misunderstanding the meaning but by using the wrong grammar. The noun *bona fides*, for instance, is singular: *His bona fides was questioned*. It is not the plural of *bona fide*, which is an adjective: *a bona fide offer*.

If one has occasion actually to say a Latin word or phrase as part of an English sentence, the safest course is to pronounce it more or less in the English manner, rather than attempting the system believed to have been employed by the ancient Romans: pronounce *Cicero* as 'sis-e-roh' not 'kik-e-roh'. Latin technical terms in law and medicine, and the Latin of the Roman Catholic Church, have their own established pronunciations.

latish

The word is spelled without the final *e* of *late*.

latter

See FORMER.

laudable, laudatory

Laudable means 'worthy of praise, admirable': *He controlled himself with laudable restraint*. **Laudatory** means 'expressing praise': *She spoke in laudatory terms of their work*.

launch

1 This is sometimes pronounced to rhyme with *branch*, but the pronunciation rhyming with *paunch* is now preferred for British English.

2 Launch is rather OVERUSED in the sense of 'start, initiate': *launch a programme/a subscription campaign*.

lavatory

See TOILET.

law

Some speakers dislike the pronunciation of a nonexistent *r* ('intrusive *r*') sound between **law** and a following word that begins with a vowel, as in *law (r) and order*. See R.

lawd

This spelling of *lord* is often used to suggest an uneducated pronunciation, but the pronunciation it implies is in fact exactly that of standard British English. See EYE DIALECT.

lawful, legal, legitimate, licit

These all mean 'permitted by law'. **Lawful** can imply conformity with divine law or natural justice, and thus may mean 'rightful': *the lawful heir*; *your lawful Queen*. **Legal** means 'recognized by the law of the land', so that a **lawful** marriage is one to which there is no **legal** impediment. (**Legal** also means, as the other words do not, 'connected with the law', as in *legal formalities* and *the legal profession*.) **Legitimate** applies particularly to a status accorded by legal authority (*his legitimate ruler*) and most usually to the status of being born in wedlock (*his legitimate children*). The rarer formal word **licit** means 'not forbidden by law; permissible': *The licit use of property does not include creating a nuisance*. The meanings of *unlawful, illegal, illegitimate*, and *illicit* may be more or less deduced from the above; but **illicit** is a good deal commoner than its opposite, and applies to secret activities carried on regularly, particularly to those which the law might allow if certain conditions were satisfied: *illicit amours*; *an illicit whisky still*.

lawman

This American English word means a sheriff or police officer. It should not be used of a lawyer.

lawyer

This is the general word for anyone who makes a profession of the law. In the USA, such a person may call himself or herself an **attorney**, particularly if he or she appears for clients in court. In Britain, **attorney** is an old word for **solicitor**, surviving today only in *power of* **attorney** and the title **Attorney** *General*. A British person calling himself or herself a **lawyer** is probably a **solicitor**, who advises clients, draws up documents, and briefs **barristers**; a **solicitor** in the USA is the officer responsible for the legal affairs of a town. A **barrister** in England and Wales, or an **advocate** in Scotland, belongs to the smaller and rather more prestigious branch of the profession, being qualified to plead in the higher courts; **barrister** is also a less common American English word for **lawyer**. **Counsel** means a **barrister**, or in the USA a **lawyer/attorney**, while actually in court: *counsel for the prosecution*; *to be represented by counsel*.

lay, lie

Other forms of these two verbs are **laid, laid**, and **lay, lain** respectively. The two have been confused: *Bill went and laid down*; *She lay the book on the table*. The confusion is probably caused by the fact that **lay** is also the past of **lie**; but **lain** is not part of **lay**, and **laid** is not part of **lie**. **Lay** is almost entirely transitive (*Please lay the table*; *I don't know how to lay bricks*; *The scene is laid in wartime London*), with one or two intransitive uses, as in *The hens have stopped laying* (ie laying eggs). **Lie** is only intransitive: *lie on the floor*. In the following examples **lie** is used correctly: *I like to lie* (not *lay*) *down in the afternoons*; *I'm lying* (not *laying*) *down now*; *I lay* (not *laid*) *down yesterday afternoon*; *I've never lain* (not *laid*) *down in the morning*. A third verb, **lie** meaning 'tell a lie', has other forms **lied, lied** (*She lied to me*), but this does not seem to cause difficulties.

lb

This means 'pounds weight', not 'pounds sterling', for which the symbol is £.

lead, led

To go first and invite people to follow is to **lead**, rhyming with *weed*. Its related noun is pronounced and spelled in the same way: *to lead the expedition*; *to take the lead*. The heavy metal is spelled **lead** and pronounced to rhyme with *bed*, and so is its related verb: *lead pipes*; *leaded window frames*. But the past tense and participle of the verb about going first is spelled **led** and rhymes with *bed*: *He led the way*; *She had led the procession*.

leadership

Ths properly means either the office of a leader (*He resigned the leadership*) or the period of being a leader (*during her leadership*). The word is now widely used when *leaders* might be more appropriate, as in *The Soviet leadership has rejected the proposal*.

leading question

In law, this has the precise meaning of 'a question so phrased as to suggest the expected answer'. It does not mean a 'principal', 'embarrassingly direct', 'unfair', or 'difficult' question. A true **leading question** is helpful rather than hostile in intention.

leaf

Leaves is the plural of the noun, but is not part of the verb: *She leafs through the book*.

leak, leek

A **leak** is a crack through which a gas or liquid gets in or out. A **leek** is an onionlike vegetable. **Leak**, both as noun and verb, is also correctly used of the unauthorized disclosure of secret information: *a security leak*; *He leaked the story to the press*.

lean

Leaned and **leant** are equally common in British English for the past tense and participle, but **leaned** is the American form. The British often pronounce **leaned**, as well as **leant**, like *lent*.

leap

Leaped and **leapt** are equally common for the past tense and participle, in both British and American English, **Leaped,** as well as **leapt,** is often pronounced as 'lept'.

learn

1 Learned and **learnt** are equally common in British English for the past tense and participle, but **learned** is the preferred American form. **Learned** is often pronounced like **learnt**.

2 Do not use **learn** to mean 'teach': *I learned French from her*; *She taught me* (not *learned me*) *French*.

learned

When **learned** means 'memorized', as in *a learned response*, it has one syllable. When it means 'erudite', as in *a learned professor* or *learned studies*, it has two.

least

1 Least should not be used for contrasting only two items: *I don't know whether John or his wife was less* (not *least*) *to blame*.

2 Least of all means 'especially not', and belongs in negative sentences: *No one, least of all the children, paid attention*. It should be carefully distinguished from *most of all*, which means 'especially' and belongs in questions and positive statements: *What reason can you* *offer for your action, and most* (not *least*) *of all for your failure to inform us of it?*

leastways, leastwise

These expressions are now more or less confined to regional dialect. Use *at least*.

leave, let

1 Leave should not be used for **let** in the sense of 'allow to do something': *Let* (not *leave*) *me go!*; *Let* (not *leave*) *him be*. (In the sense of 'stop holding', *let go of* the handle is preferable to *leave go of* it, but both are common in speech. Probably people who say *Leave me go!* mean 'stop holding me' rather than 'Allow me to depart'.) The two verbs are partially interchangeable with *alone*. *Let me alone* means 'Stop bothering me', and *leave me alone* can correctly mean that too. But *leave alone* can also mean 'allow to remain in solitude', as in *We can't go out and leave the baby (all) alone*, where **let** could not be used, and *let alone* can mean 'still less', as in *He can't even walk, let alone run*, where **leave** would be inappropriate.

2 *Leave severely alone* is a CLICHÉ.

lectern

See PODIUM.

lectureship

This is the usual word for the position of an academic lecturer. The word *lecturership* might seem more logical, but it is very rarely used.

led

See LEAD.

leek

See LEAK.

leeward

Sailors pronounce the first syllable 'loo' rather than 'lee', but there is no reason to do this when on land. It means 'on the side sheltered from the wind', and always ends in *-ward*, not in *-wards*.

leftward(s)

Before a noun, use **leftward**: *a leftward turn*. After a verb, use the form with an *s* in British English (*glanced leftwards*) and the one without an *s* in American English.

legal

See LAWFUL.

legend, myth

These are both traditional stories handed down; but while a **legend** may have some historical basis, such as the **legend** of Alfred and the cakes, a **myth** exists to account for something, as with the **myth** of Pandora's box which explains the existence of evil. **Myth** is often used of a fictitious person or thing or a false belief or statement: *His story about the TV having fallen off a lorry was a complete myth.*

legible, readable

These words end in -*ible* and -*able* respectively. A piece of writing is **legible** if it can be deciphered (*His handwriting was scarcely legible*), **readable** if it is interesting to read and not too technical. Avoid using **readable** for **legible**.

legionary, legionnaire

They are both members of *legions*. An ancient Roman soldier was a **legionary**. A member of the French foreign legion is a **legionary** or **legionnaire**, and so is a British or American ex-serviceman, the Americans preferring **legionnaire**.

legislation, legislature

Legislation is the making of laws, or else a body of actual or prospective laws. The **legislature** is the body of people, such as Parliament in Britain, who make the laws.

legislator

The word ends in -*or*, not -*er*.

legitimate (*adjective*)

See LAWFUL.

legitimate (*verb*)

This means 'give legal authority to', and is perhaps preferable to the alternatives *legitimatize* and *legitimize*, for the reasons discussed at -IZE.

leisure, leisurely

1 Both are spelled -*ei*-, not -*ie*-.

2 The first syllable is pronounced in British English only with the short *e* of *fed*, but American English has the choice between the sound of *fed* and that of *feed*.

3 Leisurely is correctly used as either an adjective (*a leisurely stroll*) or an adverb (*drive there leisurely*).

length

1 This should not rhyme with *tenth*. Pronounce the *ng* fully.

2 It is VERBOSE to say that something is a *metre in length*; it is shorter to say *a metre long*.

lengthways, lengthwise

Both forms are standard.

lengthy

This is best used in the sense of 'tediously long; too long' and not merely as a synonym of *long*.

lens

Lens is the singular of which **lenses** is the plural: *This lens is broken*; *a new pair of lenses*.

lento

See LARGO.

lese majesty, lèse majesté

Both the French and the anglicized spellings are in use. The expression is used less of actual treason than of a presumptuous affront to someone's dignity.

less

1 Correctly, *fewer* applies to things that can be counted, and **less** to quantities and abstractions: *less opportunity*; *less beer and fewer cigarettes*. But the rule cannot be stated quite so simply. **Less** is correct with either 'numbers' that give the size of a quantity, or the word *number*: *less than six weeks* (ie a length of time); *less than £50* (ie a sum of money); *The number of people was less than usual*; but *Fewer than 50 people came*. There is an increasing tendency for **less** to replace *fewer* even with countable plurals: *'more pay, less hours'* engineering claim (*Daily Telegraph*); *emerging from the mêlée with less wounds than his brothers* (Alan Sillitoe). See FEW.

2 Less is much used in such educational EUPHEMISMS as *less able*, *less academic*, and *less talented*. These are not actual comparisons (*less able* than whom?) but are a kindly, and therefore presumably justifiable, way to avoid calling anyone *stupid*.

3 For *much less*, see MUCH.

-less

Words ending in **-less**, such as *harmless*, are spelled as one word unless there are three *l*'s, as in *bell-less* or *will-less*. A hyphen is not generally used where there are only two *l*'s, as in *tailless*.

lessee, lessor

A **lessee** holds property under a lease. A **lessor** is the owner of that property.

lest

This formal word is correctly used with *should* (*lest he should forget*) or with the subjunctive form of the verb (*lest he forget*). Do not write *lest he will forget*, *lest he would forget*, or *lest he forgets*.

let

1 Let introducing a request or proposal is correctly followed by object pronouns: *Let me* (not *I*) *see*; *Let us* (not *we*) *pray*. This is true even when two or more objects are involved: *Let John and me* (not *I*) *do it*; or when another verb follows of which the pronoun might be thought to be the subject: *Let them* (not *they*) *that made the mess clear it up*. The rule is often broken in speech, where **let** introduces a proposal rather than a request: *Let* (or *let's*) *you and I discuss the matter quietly*. Or *you and I* can be introduced later: *Let us go then, you and I* (T S Eliot).

2 Let *us* is shortened to **let's** only when it introduces a proposal including the person addressed: *Come on Mary, let's dance!* When it makes a request, it must be **let** *us*: *Please let us go now!* The negative of **let's** is *let's not*, in both British and American English: *Let's not have lunch yet*. British English has also *don't let's*, and American sometimes *let's don't*. The more formal equivalent of all these is *let us not*.

3 See LEAVE.

letter endings

In British English, the standard complimentary ending before the signature is *Yours sincerely*, which is normal in letters to acquaintances and to strangers addressed by name and is often used in business letters. The more formal ending is *Yours faithfully*, which is also used in letters to strangers and in business letters and is normal for letters printed in newspapers. *Yours faithfully* is usual when the greeting does not contain the name of the recipient of the letter, as with *Dear Madam* or *Dear Editor*. Other less common endings that are still more formal are *Yours truly*, the somewhat less distant *Yours very truly*, and the deferential *Yours respectfully*. For close friends, common endings include *Yours ever*, *Yours*, and *Best wishes*.

The standard ending in American English is *Sincerely yours*. More formal endings include *Very truly yours*, *Respectfully yours*, and *Respectfully*. More friendly and informal endings are *Cordially yours* and *Cordially*. For close friends, common endings include *As ever*, *Best wishes*, and *Best regards*. There are less formal but less usual variants in which *yours* comes at the beginning of the phrase, eg *Yours truly*. When *very* is added, it makes *sincerely* and *cordially* more informal, but makes *truly* and *respectfully* more formal.

leuk(a)emia

The name of this disease is spelled with the first *a* in British English, without it in American English.

levee, levy

A **levee** is either a formal reception or, in American English, an embankment. A **levy** is a tax or fine.

level

1 Other forms of the verb are **levelled, levelling** in British English, but the second *l* is usually omitted in American English.

2 The noun is somewhat OVERUSED is such expressions as *on the local level* (use *locally*); *a decision taken at Cabinet level* (use *by the Cabinet*); *to increase in noise level* (omit *level*, or rephrase as *to get noisier*).

lexicon

The plural is **lexicons** or, less usually, **lexica**.

liable

See APT.

liaison

1 The last syllable is now usually pronounced 'zon', rather than with a French nasal sound.

2 The noun has technical senses in cookery and phonetics, but chiefly means 'military or other cooperation' or 'secret sexual relationship'. The verb **liaise**, formed by BACK-FORMATION, is associated only with the 'cooperation' sense. People engaged in a sexual affair do not **liaise**.

liar, lyre

A **liar** tells lies; a **lyre** is a stringed musical instrument.

libation

This means a sacrifice of liquid to a god. It is FACETIOUS to use the word merely for 'beverage' or 'drink'.

libel, slander

1 Other forms of the verb **libel** are **libelled, libelling** in British English, but the second *l* is usually omitted in American English.

2 Both **libel** and **slander** are the harming of someone's reputation by false statement. **Libel** is written, broadcast, or in the form of pictorial representation. **Slander** is in the less public and permanent form of an oral statement or an offensive gesture.

liberal

Use a capital *L* for a member of the British political party, a small *l* for the other meanings, such as 'generous': *a liberal donation*.

liberality, liberalism

Liberality is generosity in giving. **Liberalism** is broad-mindedness or, with a capital *L*, the political principles of a Liberal party.

liberate

This means 'set free', but is also a jocular EUPHEMISM for 'steal' or 'loot'. It originated in the 1940s, when the soldiers engaged in **liberating** occupied Europe helped themselves to a few objects on the way, and has been preserved in the vocabulary of anarchistic youth with reference to shoplifting and the like.

libertarian, libertine

They both believe in liberty; but a **libertarian** is a noble advocate of tolerance, while a **libertine** is unrestrained by moral conventions, especially sexual ones.

library

Both the *r*'s are pronounced in careful speech.

libretto

The plural is either **librettos** or **libretti**.

licence, license

In British English the noun is **licence** (*my driving licence*) and the verb **license** (*to license the car*); in American English both noun and verb are spelled **license**. A British **licensed** establishment (ie place where one can drink alcoholic drinks) may spell the word **licenced**, suggesting that it has a **licence** (as *bearded* means 'having a beard') rather than that it has been **licensed**.

lichee, lichi

See LITCHI.

lichen

This word for a moss-like growth begins with the sound 'like' in American English, but with either 'like' or 'litch' in British English.

licit

See LAWFUL.

licorice

See LIQUORICE.

lie

See LAY.

lie, lye

A **lie** is a falsehood, or the position in which something lies (*the lie of the land*). **Lye** is an alkaline liquid used in soapmaking.

lieutenant

The first syllable is pronounced like *left* in British English and *loot* in American English. The British navy say 'l'tenant'.

life

1 The plural is **lives** except in the case of *still lifes*, pictures of inanimate objects.

2 Life- is somewhat OVERUSED in compounds such as *life-denying*, *life-enhancing*, which use **life** not in the biological sense but to mean something like 'spiritual freedom'. One's *life-style* is the way one lives, and the expression is popular with advertisers who seek to improve our way of living by adding to our possessions.

lifelong, livelong

Lifelong means 'lasting throughout one's life': *a lifelong fear of flying*. **Livelong** is an old-fashioned poetic word for 'whole, entire': *the livelong day*.

ligature

See DIPHTHONG.

light (*noun*)

In the light of means 'taking into consideration', and this, not *in light of*, is the conventional form of the idiom.

light (*verb*)

The past tense and participle is either **lighted** or **lit**. **Lit** is commoner except where the participle is used as an adjective before a noun: *I lit the candle*; *The fire's lit*; *a lighted cigarette*.

lightening, lightning

Lightening is the process of making lighter: *the lightening of my task*. **Lightning** is the electrical accompaniment to thunder.

like (*preposition*)

1 When **like** is used as a preposition (*His house is like a barn*), one should ensure that one is actually comparing the things that one intends to compare. Do not write *Like her father, her chief interest was gambling*, because we are comparing her chief interest with her father's chief interest, not with her father himself. Write *Her chief interest, like her father's, was gambling*. The same is true of **unlike**: *Unlike many children's books* (write *those in many children's books*), *the characters are realistic*.

2 *Feel* **like** meaning 'be in the mood for', as in *I feel like a drink*, is a well-established idiom. **Like** here does not mean 'similar to'.

3 Like is sometimes formally used as an adjective equivalent to *likely*: *the one discipline like to give accuracy of mind* (Harold Laski). This is not a mistake.

4 For **like, as**, see AS (9).

like (*verb*)

1 In British English the more traditional and more formal *should like* in *I should like to ask a question* is often replaced by *would like*, which is usual in American English. In speech and informal writing, however, the shortened form *I'd like* is adequate. See SHOULD.

2 *If you like* is irritatingly OVERUSED, particularly in broadcasting, to introduce metaphors, clichés, flights of fancy, and almost anything else that the speaker feels like introducing: *The negotiations have ground, if you like, to a halt.*

3 One **likes** things to happen, but it is an American regionalism to say that one **likes** *for* things to happen. Write *I'd like you* (not *for you*) *to read it.*

-like

Words ending in **-like**, such as *childlike*, are usually spelled as one word unless there are three *l*'s, as in *cell-like*. Where there are only two *l*'s, practice is divided between, for instance, *owllike* and *owl-like*.

lik(e)able

The word is spelled either with or without the first *e*.

likely

In formal British English, **likely** meaning 'probably' is not used alone, but only in the combinations *quite likely, very likely, more likely, most likely, more than likely*, and *as likely as not*. The use of **likely** alone is somewhat more widely accepted in American English: *They will likely betray themselves by heavy breathing.* There is nowhere any objection to **likely** standing alone as an adjective meaning 'probable' (*a likely story*), or to *They are likely to go.* See APT.

likewise

This means 'similarly': *Go and do likewise.* It should not be used to replace *and* or *together with*, as in *His appalling temper, likewise* (write *and*) *his unpleasant appearance, discouraged them from inviting him.*

417

limb, limn

A **limb** is an arm, a leg, or a branch. The archaic verb **limn** (same pronunciation) means 'draw or paint'.

limbo

The plural is **limbos**.

lime

This is really three words of quite different origins. There is the chemical mixture **lime**, obtained from shells or limestone, used in mixing plaster and in agriculture; there is the European tree called either **lime** or *linden*; and there is the tropical **lime**, a tree cultivated for the juice of its citrus fruit.

limit, delimit

One **limits**, that is 'restricts', people or activities: *to limit one's spending*. One **delimits**, that is 'fixes', boundaries or distances: *to delimit the terms of a problem*.

lin(e)age, lineage

Lin(e)age, pronounced 'line-idge', is the number of lines of printed matter. It is spelled with or without the first *e*. **Lineage**, pronounced 'linny-idge', is descent or pedigree.

lineament, liniment

A **lineament** is a distinctive feature or contour, particularly of the face. **Liniment** is a medicated liquid to be rubbed on the skin.

lingerie

In British English, this is pronounced with the stress on the first syllable, sounding more or less like 'lan', and the last syllable sounding like 'ree'. The pronunciation with the stress on the last syllable, pronounced 'ree' or 'ray', is American.

lingo

The plural is **lingoes**.

linguistics

See GRAMMAR.

linked genitives

Genitive nouns and possessive pronouns (used as determiners) may be connected with a following noun phrase: *That is the* **accountant's** *opinion*; **His** *analysis was the best*. They may also function independently: *That opinion is the* **accountant's**; **His** *was the best analysis*. Most possessive pronouns have a different form when they are independent: *mine, ours, yours, hers, theirs* (rather than *my, our, your, her, their*). The exceptions are *his* and *its*, which have the same form for both uses. (*Its*, however, is rare as an independent possessive.) (See PARTS OF SPEECH for determiners and possessive pronouns.)

Problems arise when two or more possessives are linked to the same noun:

(1) The linking may result in ambiguity. *The chairman's and the treasurer's proposals* may mean either the same as *the joint proposals of the chairman and the treasurer* or the same as *the proposal(s) of the chairman and that* (or *those*) *of the treasurer*. The meaning may well be clear in the context; but if not, prefer the longer constructions.

(2) The omission of the genitive inflection in *the chairman and the treasurer's proposal* (intended to indicate a joint proposal) is not fully acceptable in formal English. Prefer one of the constructions in (1).

(3) Linking of two possessive pronouns is possible, but seems clumsy: *your and her proposals*. It is better to introduce the independent possessive as the second unit: *your proposal(s) and hers*. Both constructions indicate separate proposals. If a combinatory meaning is required, rephrase; for example, *the proposals which you and she have jointly formulated*. Rephrasing is preferable for both meanings when three possessive pronouns would otherwise be linked. Instead of *your, her, and my proposals*, it is better to use *the proposals which you, she, and I have* (*separately* or *jointly*) *put forward*.

(4) It is not correct to put an independent possessive first: *yours and the treasurer's proposals*; *yours and her proposals*. Instead, use rephrasings such as are given in (3) above.

links

See GOLF COURSE.

liqueur, liquor

The second syllable of **liqueur** usually rhymes with *pure* in British English but with *her* in American English. A **liqueur** is a sweetened and flavoured spirit, such as Cointreau or Benedictine. **Liquor**, particularly in American use, is any alcoholic drink, distilled rather than fermented.

liquidate, liquidize

Besides its technical meanings in finance and commerce, **liquidate** is a sinister EUPHEMISM for 'kill', used especially of the killing of its own citizens as a ruthless political measure by a totalitarian government. **Liquidize** means literally 'make liquid', as when one reduces fruit or vegetables to a puree.

liquorice, licorice

Liquorice is the British spelling, **licorice** the American. The word ends with the sound of either *kiss* or *wish*.

lira

The usual plural of the Italian **lira** is **lire**, but that of the Turkish or Syrian **lira** is **liras**.

lists

Lists should name things of the same kind. One would not write *yellow, purple, autumn, and mountain flowers*, since *yellow* and *purple* are colours, *autumn* a season, and *mountain* a habitat. Similarly, one should be careful with the sort of 'open-ended' list introduced by *such as* or followed by *etc*. It is sensible to write *paper clips, typewriter ribbons, etc*, because the reader can easily see that the list might be extended to include further items of stationery; but *paper clips, ice cream, etc*, or *items such as dogs and violins* would leave the reader wondering.

lit

See LIGHT (*verb*).

litany, liturgy

A **litany** is a prayer consisting of a series of petitions and responses. A **liturgy** is a whole form of public worship.

litchi, lichee, lichi, lychee

The commonest spelling for this Chinese fruit is **litchi**, but the others are acceptable variants. Nobody seems sure how to pronounce it, but the consensus is 'LIE-chee' or 'lie-CHEE' (British) and 'LEE-chee' (American).

literal, literally

Do not use these words in formal English to mean 'in effect, virtually':

She was literally tearing his hair out. They are appropriate when used to emphasize something both true and striking: *He literally screamed with rage*.

literate, literal, literary

Literate means 'able to read and write; educated'. **Literal** means 'not metaphorical'. **Literary** means 'concerning literature'.

literature

Some people have objected to the use of **literature** to mean any kind of printed matter, such as sales brochures and campaign leaflets, but the usage is now well established and too convenient to be abandoned.

litre, liter

The word is spelled **litre** in British English, **liter** in American English.

littoral, literal

Littoral means 'of the seashore'. **Literal** means 'not metaphorical'.

liv(e)able

The first *e* is usually omitted in American English, but may be retained in British English.

livelong

See LIFELONG.

livid

As a colour, this means variously 'black-and-blue, like a bruise', or 'pallid', or 'reddish'. The chief use of **livid**, however, is in the informal sense of 'angry'.

living

Living in a fool's paradise is a CLICHÉ.

living room

See SITTING ROOM.

llama

See LAMA.

421

Lloyd's

The association of London underwriters is spelled like this; not *Lloyds* (which is the name of a British commercial bank) or *Lloyds'*.

load

See LODE.

loaf

Loaves is the plural of the noun, but is not part of the verb: *He loafs around all day*.

loan

As a verb, **loan** (*loan me a book*) is usually avoided in formal British English, though it was once as correct as *lend* and is coming back through American influence, especially in financial contexts. It is entirely correct in American English, particularly in the participle (*pictures loaned to the gallery*) where it is preferred to *lent*. Americans may be reluctant to use *lent* because they are in general uneasy about participles that end in *t*; American English prefers *spelled* to *spelt* and *dreamed* to *dreamt*.

loathe, loath, loth

Loathe is the verb meaning 'dislike greatly'. The adjective meaning 'reluctant' is spelled **loath** or **loth**: *I was loath/loth to argue*. **Loath** is the preferred spelling for the adjective, particularly in American English.

locale, locality, location

These all refer to 'place', and are partly interchangeable. A **locale** is a 'venue', the place where something happens: *the actual locale of a crime*. A **locality** is a 'situation', a position considered geographically: *heavy rainfall in this locality*. A **location** is a particular position, or an occupied 'site', such as a factory or an Australian sheep station. The word is also used when a film is shot *on location*.

locate

This means 'find', but only with reference to a particular thing of fixed position. One may **locate** the enemy's camp but not, correctly, a stolen car or even a good parking place (since any good parking place would do). **Located** means 'situated', so that a house may be **located** on the river bank. In American but not in British English, to **locate** may mean 'to settle oneself somewhere': *The company decided to locate in Ohio*.

loch

See LOUGH.

locus

The plural is **loci**.

lode, load

A **lode** is an ore deposit; a **load** is a burden or cargo. *Lodestar*, meaning 'something that serves as a guide', is sometimes spelled *loadstar*. *Lodestone*, meaning 'a magnet', is perhaps more often spelled *loadstone*.

-logue

Words ending in **-logue** often have an alternative spelling with **-log** in American English: *analog(ue); dialog(ue)*.

lone

When it needlessly replaces *only* or *single* (*a lone tree*), this word smacks of old-fashioned poetry.

lonelily

Although it ends with **-ly** like *quickly* and *easily*, *lonely* is not an adverb but an adjective: *a lonely road*. The related adverb **lonelily** (*He sighed lonelily*) looks and sounds so odd that it is probably better to rephrase the sentence as *He gave a lonely sigh*.

long

As long as and *so long as* mean 'up to the end of the time that; while': *The different key words that we must use are all interconnected, and so long as some remain vague, others must . . . share this defect* (Bertrand Russell). They can also mean 'providing': *Go there so long as you don't drink too much*. In American, rather than in British, use, they can mean 'in view of the fact that; since': *As long as you're going, I'll go too*.

long s

This character, rather like an *f*, was used until the 19th century in some but not all of the places where we use *s*; that is, at the beginning or in the middle of a word but not at the end: *ʃave; ʃuppoʃe; troops*. It was not, of course, pronounced 'f'.

423

look

When it is followed by an adverb, **look** describes a way of using one's eyes: *Please look carefully*. When followed by an adjective, it means 'appear when seen': *It looks dirty*; *You look cold*. To **look** *well* (besides meaning 'to use your eyes carefully') may mean either 'to appear healthy' or 'to appear attractive'. To **look** *good* may also mean 'to appear attractive', as well as bringing in all the other meanings of *good*: *That kipper looks good*. Try to avoid confusion here, perhaps by using **look** *good* for the 'attractive' sense. See GOOD.

looker-on

The plural is **lookers-on**.

loose, loosen, lose

To **loose** is to 'release' or 'detach'. The commoner verb **loosen** means 'make looser'; one **looses** the dogs or an arrow but **loosens** one's belt. Neither verb should be confused with **lose**, meaning 'fail to find', 'be deprived of', etc: *She always loses her glasses*.

loot

The standard meaning is either the spoils of war or something taken by violence. To use the word simply for any money or valuables (*lots of lovely loot*) is decidedly informal.

lord

See TITLES OF PEOPLE.

Lord's, Lords

Lord's is a cricket ground in London; *the* **Lords** is the House of Lords, the upper house of the British parliament.

lose

1 *Lose no time in* doing something may mean either that one should do it as soon as possible or that it would be a waste of time to do it at all. Avoid this expression if it is ambiguous in context.

2 The informal combination *lose out* means 'be at a disadvantage'. If you work in the evenings you *lose out on* your social life. *Lose out* should not be used simply for 'undergo defeat' in sport, where **lose** alone is adequate.

3 See LOOSE.

loss, lost

In British English, though not in American, it is old-fashioned to pronounce these with the vowel sound of *law*.

lot

The use of *a* **lot** and **lots** as in *a lot of money*; *lots of friends*; *drive a lot faster* is somewhat informal, but as good plain English is acceptable in all but the most elevated contexts, where *much* and *many* are better.

loth

See LOATHE.

lotus

The plural is **lotuses**.

louche

See FAROUCHE.

loud, loudly

These can both mean 'noisily': *Don't talk/shout/laugh so loud(ly)*; *He's playing it very loud(ly)*. **Loudly** is the usual word for a figurative sense, such as 'vociferously' (*He complained loudly about the food*) or 'obtrusively' (*loudly dressed in orange velvet*).

lough, loch

These are the Irish and the Scottish words, respectively, for 'lake'. They are pronounced identically, with the 'ch' sound which many speakers of standard English have to say as 'k'.

lounge

See SITTING ROOM.

lour

See LOWER.

louvre, louver

The word is spelled **louvre** in British English, **louver** in American English.

lov(e)able

This is usually spelled **lovable**, but **loveable** also exists.

lovelily

Although it ends with **-ly** like *quickly* and *easily*, *lovely* is not an adverb but an adjective: *lovely weather*. The related adverb **lovelily** (*She sings lovelily*) looks and sounds so odd that one may prefer to rephrase the sentence as *Her singing is lovely*.

lover

How should one speak of the sexual partner with whom one lives outside marriage? *My lover* sounds too emotional, *my man* or *my woman* too primitive and earthy, and *my mate* far too biological. *Boyfriend* and *girlfriend* are possible, but slightly coy. *My friend* is vague. *Cohabitant* and *cohabitee* sound like legal jargon. *Concubine* would be an interesting choice, but one can scarcely imagine its becoming popular. What is needed is a word expressing an equal relationship, which older expressions such as *my mistress* do not. An American English alternative that meets this requirement is *posslq* (pronounced 'possl cue'), short for 'person of the opposite sex sharing living quarters', but this has not achieved general circulation. Likewise, the Scottish word *bidie-in* has limited currency. Most people are obliged simply to refer to the person by name and expect others to infer the relationship.

low (*noun*)

Some people dislike the use of **low** to mean 'a lowest point', as in *Sales reached a new low*.

low, lowly

Low can be either an adjective (*a low shelf*) or an adverb (*aim low*). **Lowly** is chiefly an adjective meaning 'humble' (*his lowly status*). In the rare cases where **lowly** is used as an adverb (*bow lowly*) it means 'humbly' or 'in a low position'.

low-budget, low-cost

These are EUPHEMISMS for *cheap*: *a low-budget movie*; *low-cost housing*.

lower, lour

When **lower** means 'scowl; look threatening' it may be spelled **lour** (*a louring sky*) and rhymes with *hour*. When **lower** is an adjective meaning 'relatively low', or a verb meaning 'make low', it rhymes with *mower*.

low profile

A high building has a high 'profile'; it is noticeable on the horizon because it sticks up. The opposite of this is a **low profile**, an expression used figuratively to mean the policy of remaining unnoticed on purpose: *The Government has been keeping a low profile over the disturbances* (*The Guardian*). The expression is useful, but perhaps OVERUSED by those who are anxious to avoid noisy confrontation. A **low profile** may of course conceal either sinister underground activity or failure to do anything at all.

lucre

The word is spelled like this in both British and American English; not *-er*. It is a FACETIOUS word for 'money', as in *filthy lucre*.

lull

Lulled into a false sense of security is a CLICHÉ.

lumbar, lumber

Lumbar refers to the loins. **Lumber** is surplus articles, or (in American English) timber.

lunch(eon)

Lunch is now the ordinary word for this midday meal. **Luncheon** is formal and may seem PRETENTIOUS.

lustful, lusty

Lustful means 'full of sexual lust'. **Lusty** means 'vigorous'.

lustre, luster

It is spelled **lustre** in British English, usually **luster** in American English.

luxuriant, luxurious

Luxuriant means 'growing profusely': *luxuriant hair/grass*; or, figuratively, 'exuberantly ornamented': *luxuriant prose*. **Luxurious** comes from *luxury* and means 'rich and costly': *luxurious meals/ cushions*.

-ly

1 Adjectives ending in *-ical* (*practical*) form adverbs with **-ly** (*practically; politically*) and adjectives ending in *-ic* usually add **-ally** (*scenically; sarcastically*). The only well-known words ending in *-icly* are *publicly* and the variant spelling *franticly*.

2 A series of **-ly** words sometimes sounds clumsy. Rephrase *practically inevitably* as *almost inevitably*.

3 See FIRSTLY. For the choice between *clear* and *clearly*, *high* and *highly*, etc, see the words concerned.

lychee

See LITCHI.

lye

See LIE.

lyre

See LIAR.

lyric(al)

The adjective **lyric** is used of poetry expressing personal emotion. A **lyric** is a **lyric** poem, such as Wordsworth's familiar piece about daffodils; but the word is now chiefly used in the plural for the words of a popular song or musical. The adjective **lyrical** is sometimes used for **lyric**, but it chiefly means 'full of enthusiasm': *He was lyrical about the beauties of the countryside*.

Mm

-m-, -mm-

Many words ending in *-gram* double the *-m-* even when a word of more than one syllable is not accented on the last syllable: *epigram(matic)*.

Such words therefore disobey rule (2) given under DOUBLING. See also PROGRAM(ME).

Mac-, Mc-

Make sure of the spelling of these names. Harold *Macmillan* spelled his name with **Mac-**, Marshall *McLuhan* spelled his with **Mc-**.

macabre

The word is spelled with *-re*, not *-er*, in both British and American English. As most English speakers find it difficult to end with the sound 'br', this word is often pronounced to rhyme with *harbour*, which seems a reasonable compromise.

machismo, macho

These OVERUSED words mean 'an excessive sense of masculine pride'; **macho** can also be an adjective meaning 'aggressively virile'. Perhaps a word for this idea is more needed since masculine pride has been challenged by the women's movement. The *ch* is pronounced either as in *chip* or as in *character*.

mad

This means 'crazy', as in *It sounds mad, but it's true*; or 'frantic', as in *He made a mad dash for cover*. The word is no longer used technically to mean 'insane' in psychiatric circles. The use of **mad** to mean 'angry' (*She was mad at him*), though very common, is too informal for serious writing.

madam(e)

Madam is the English title, used in the opening of a formal letter (*Dear Madam . . .*) or before a woman's title of office (*Madam Mayor*). The keeper of a brothel is a **madam**, and so in British use is a conceited minx: *She's a proper little madam*. **Madame** is the equivalent of *Mrs* for married women of non-English-speaking countries and particularly of French nationality: *Madame Curie*. (It is also sometimes assumed by English-speaking women for professional purposes.) **Mesdames** is the plural of **madame** and also, somewhat jocularly today, of **madam** as a form of address; in serious use prefer *ladies* there.

madding

This word is known to most of us only from Thomas Gray's line *Far from the madding crowd's ignoble strife*, from which Thomas Hardy borrowed the title of a novel. It means 'frenzied', not 'infuriating'.

maestro

The plural is either **maestros** or **maestri**.

Mafia

The name of this secret criminal society is now used, and even OVERUSED, figuratively with reference to any too influential clique by those who feel victimized by it: *The literary mafia will plug it even if it is rubbish* (*The Bookseller*).

magdalen(e)

Magdalen or **magdalene**, pronounced with three syllables, is an old-fashioned word for a reformed prostitute. The Oxford college is **Magdalen** and the Cambridge one **Magdalene**, both pronounced like *maudlin*.

Magna C(h)arta

Charta is on the whole the preferred American spelling. **Carta** is the British one. They are both pronounced with 'k'.

magnate, magnet

A **magnate** is an influential or wealthy person. A **magnet** attracts iron.

magneto

The plural is **magnetos**.

magnifico

The plural is either **magnificoes** or **magnificos**.

magnitude

Though it is properly used in technical senses, as when classifying stars by their brightness, this can seem rather a PRETENTIOUS word when used merely for *size* (*We must not underestimate the magnitude of the problem*); and *of the first magnitude* is a CLICHÉ.

Mahomet

See MUHAMMAD.

maize, maze

Maize is Indian corn. A maze is a labyrinth.

major

Besides its technical senses in music and education, this means not only 'greater' (*major road*) but 'considerable; big and important' where no explicit comparison need be involved: *major surgery*; *a major chemical company*. It is sometimes OVERUSED, and may be better replaced by *important*, *serious*, or *principal*. *Major portion* can be neatly replaced by *most*.

majordomo

The plural is **majordomos**. It means the head steward of a large household.

majority, plurality

1 In American political use, a **majority** is more than half the total number of votes cast, for more than two candidates, which the British would call an *absolute majority*; while a **plurality** is a winning number of votes that is still less than half the total.

2 Strictly speaking, a **majority** is the greater number of a group rather than the greater part of a quantity. In this use it often takes a plural verb. One might say *The majority of my friends live* (not *lives*) *in London,* or *The majority of the population lives* . . . (or *live*, because *population* is a collective noun), but not *The majority of the book is too technical.*

3 Do not use *the majority of* when *most* will do. *In the majority of instances* is a VERBOSE way of saying *usually* or *mostly*.

malefactor

The word ends in *-or*, not *-er*.

mall

The chief American pronunciation rhymes with *hall*, and the word is used in the USA for what in Britain is called a *shopping precinct*. The pronunciation like the first syllable of *mallet* is equally common in Britain. It is the correct one for the street name *Pall Mall*.

-man

For the use of this ending, see FEMININE FORMS. In its most familiar combinations, such as *postman* and *milkman*, **-man** is pronounced with a reduced vowel sound rather than like the word *man* in isolation. But see BUSINESSMAN.

manageable, managing

The first is spelled with the final *e* of *manage*, the second without it.

mandarin

This word is used in the sense of 'reactionary high-ranking bureaucrat': *Just because they can't deliver on tax cuts and spending cuts, Whitehall's mandarins mustn't presume that all other organisations are equally ineffectual (Daily Mail)*. This carries the implication that the British Civil Service are aloof and élitist.

maneuver

See MANOEUVRE.

mango

The plural is either **mangoes** or **mangos**.

mania, phobia

Apart from the technical senses, a **mania** is an unreasonable craze for something, while a **phobia** is an equally unreasonable fear of something: *a mania for fast cars*; *a phobia about spiders*.

manifesto

The plural is either **manifestos** or **manifestoes**.

manifold

This means 'various, diverse', rather than meaning 'many times' in the way that *threefold* means 'three times'.

mankind, humankind

1 Some feminists prefer to use **humankind** for our species, and to use **mankind** only for men as distinguished from women (in the way that *womankind* would be used). This preference arouses criticism from those who find **humankind** a ridiculous word, though having existed since the 17th century it cannot be called a novelty. See SEXISM.

2 These words are used with either singular or plural verbs and pronouns, the singular being probably the safer choice for the careful writer: *Mankind learns its* (rather than *learn their*) *first language in early childhood*. Do not in any case use *his* here.

manner

This word is a fruitful source of VERBOSITY. You can usually replace *in a careful manner* by *carefully*, *in a gentle manner* by *gently*, and *in a manner similar to* by *like*.

manoeuvre, maneuver

The former is the British spelling, the latter the American. Other forms of the verb are **manoeuvred, manoeuvring** and **maneuvered, maneuvering** respectively.

man-of-war

The plural is **men-of-war**.

manpower

It means 'people available to do a job'. For the feminist objection to this and other *man* words, see SEXISM.

manqué

The word is spelled with the accent. It means 'that could have been but failed to be': *a poet manqué*.

mantel, mantle

A **mantel**, sometimes spelled **mantle**, is the frame round a fireplace or the shelf above it. A **mantle** is a cloak.

many

Although **many** is normally plural (*How many are coming?*) or attached to plural nouns (*Many years have passed*), it takes a singular verb when it means 'each of a large number': *Many's the time I've wondered; Many another student has had this idea; There's many a true word spoken in jest*.

margarine

This is almost always pronounced like *Margery* except by its British manufacturers and advertisers. Their pronunciation, which is like *Margaret*, will probably never become popular with a public that is now used to the British shortened form *marge*.

marginal

This is a useful word in many senses, particularly in economics, but OVERUSED to mean no more than 'slight' or 'small': *a marginal but*

433

important improvement; *The cost will be marginal*. The same is true of *marginally*: *He is marginally* (use *slightly*) *more likely to win*.

marionette

See PUPPET.

marital, martial

Marital refers to marriage, **martial** to war.

mark, marque

Mark used with a number specifies a particular model in serial order of a weapon, machine, etc: *a Mark 4 racing car*. **Marque**, also used of cars, is not a French way of spelling this word, but means 'make, brand'.

marquess, marquis

The preferred spelling is **marquess**, with *marchioness* rather than *marquise* for the feminine.

marriageable

It is spelled like this, retaining the final *e* of *marriage*.

marry

People either **marry** other people or are **married** *to* them. Both constructions are correct, but they should be used consistently. Do not write: *Henry VIII married six times: first to Catherine of Aragon* ...

marshal

Both noun and verb are spelled with one *l*. Other forms of the verb are **marshalled, marshalling** in British English, but the second *l* is usually omitted in American English.

marten, martin

The **marten** is an animal like a large weasel. The **martin** is a bird of the swallow family.

martial

See MARITAL.

martyr

Since **martyr** is a verb as well as a noun, it is better to use it rather than to form an unnecessary verb *martyrize*: *He was martyred for his faith.*

marvel

In British English other forms of the verb are **marvelled, marvelling**, and the adjective is **marvellous**. In American English the second *l* is usually omitted.

Mary

The plural is *Marys*; the rule that words ending in -*y* form their plural with -*ies* does not apply to names.

mask, masque

A **mask** covers one's face. A **masque**, sometimes also spelled **mask**, was an entertainment of the 16th and 17th centuries.

massacre

1 The word is spelled with -*re*, not -*er*, in both British and American English.

2 A **massacre** properly involves killing a lot of people. It is better not to write *He threatened to massacre me.*

massage

In British English this is usually pronounced with the stress on *mass*, in American English with the stress on *age*. The word may end with a final 'j' sound, or with 'ahzh'.

massive

There is nothing wrong with this useful word, but it has been OVERUSED in the figurative sense (*a massive victory; a massive research programme*) and may be better replaced by *extensive, overwhelming, vigorous*, etc.

masterful, masterly

These two words should not be encouraged to spread into each other's territory. **Masterful** chiefly means 'dominating and authoritative': *a masterful king who put down the lawless barons.* **Masterly** chiefly means 'very skilful': *masterly handling of a complex topic.*

materialize

Strictly, this means 'make material' (*words materialize ideas*) or 'appear in bodily form' (*Spirits materialized during the exorcism*). By extension, it is used of a physical object to mean 'become tangible': *The bicycle I was promised never materialized.* It should not be used in serious writing to mean simply 'happen', as in *The committee meeting never materialized*, or 'turn up', as in *We waited till seven but he failed to materialize.*

matériel, material

Matériel, often spelled without the accent, is equipment and supplies in contrast with personnel, particularly in a military context. It cannot replace **material** in any other sense.

mathematics

1 This is used with a singular verb when speaking of the science of numbers: *Mathematics is my best subject.* When it means the mathematical operations involved in a problem or field of study it is often treated as a plural: *The mathematics of this subject are complex.*

2 The common British abbreviation *maths* takes either a singular or a plural verb, in the same way as **mathematics**. The American form *math* is straightforwardly singular.

matinée

The accent is sometimes omitted, particularly in American English.

matins, mattins

The spelling **mattins** is used more in the Church of England than elsewhere, perhaps to distinguish its Morning Prayer from the Roman Catholic dawn service.

matrix

1 The plural is either **matrices** or **matrixes**.

2 Matrix has many specialized meanings in technology, anatomy, mathematics, linguistics, computing, and elsewhere. In its most general sense of 'environment within which something develops' (*to provide a better matrix for international understanding*) it has become jargon, and is used to mean no more than 'setting' or even something less definite than that.

matt, mat, matte

Matt is the preferred British spelling for this adjective meaning 'not shiny', and **mat** the preferred American one. **Matte** is a third possibility.

matter

1 *In the matter of* . . . is rather VERBOSE. It can be replaced by *concerning* or *about*.

2 *No matter* can mean 'regardless of': *She would be calm, no matter what the provocation; I won't go, no matter who asks me.* If you have to insert another preposition such as *to* or *by*, be careful to put it in the right place. Write *It would be late, no matter who(m) I sent it to* or *no matter to whom I sent it*, but not *to no matter whom I sent it*.

mature

This means 'grown-up, adult'. It is more polite than *adult*, suggesting mellow wisdom and experience. It is also often a EUPHEMISM for 'middle-aged' (*clothes for the mature figure*), though middle-aged people grew up a long time ago.

matzo

The plural can be **matzoth** or **matzot** or **matzos**. It means unleavened bread.

mausoleum

The plural is either **mausoleums** or **mausolea**. It means a large elaborate tomb.

maximal, minimal

These are OVERUSED words for 'most comprehensive' and 'least possible' respectively. Consider replacing *the maximal use of our resources* by *the best use*, and *takes a minimal interest in the project* by *takes very little interest*.

maximize, minimize

These words are also OVERUSED. They are useful when they really mean 'increase to the maximum' and 'reduce to the minimum', but elsewhere they can often be replaced by *increase*, *enlarge*, or *improve*, and by *reduce*, *lessen*, or *diminish*. Do not write *greatly minimize the effort*, since a minimum is not a matter of degree.

maximum, minimum

1 The plurals are either **maxima, minima** or **maximums, minimums**.

2 These two words are sometimes curiously confused. A *maximum decrease* in an amount reduces the amount to the smallest possible, or *to the minimum*. A *minimum decrease* leaves it as close as possible to the original amount.

may, might

1 May *have* and **might** *have* have some overlap of meaning: *I may/ might have seen him, but I can't remember. He may have been drowned* must mean 'perhaps he has been drowned', but *He might have been drowned* usually means that the possibility of drowning existed but that he survived. Do not use **may** *have* for **might** *have*, as in the following: *Mr Guy Hodgson . . . said that if a fire break had been constructed, the 'difficult problems which eventually came about may* (change to *might*) *well have been avoided'* (*Daily Telegraph*); *Why the BBC chose Italy . . . I cannot say. Albanians, Finns, or even Turks may have been a more eccentric choice, but Italians it is* (*Hampstead & Highgate Express*). In this second example, it should be **might**, because the Albanians, Finns, and Turks were in fact not chosen.

2 Since one sense of **may** is 'perhaps', as in *He may go home* or *We might miss the train*, it is somewhat TAUTOLOGOUS to write **may/might** *perhaps* (or *possibly*). These combinations are often used for emphasis in speech, but in writing it is better to use either **may/might** alone or *will/would perhaps*.

3 For **may** or **can**, see CAN.

maybe

1 This is a standard though less formal alternative to *perhaps*: *Maybe they forgot*. It is better to use *perhaps* before an adjective: *a perhaps* (not *maybe*) *unnecessary objection*.

2 When *may be* is used as a verb, it must be spelled as two words: *They may be thirsty*.

mayor, mayoress

A **mayoress** is the wife of a mayor, or someone who acts as hostess at mayoral functions. She is not a female mayor. See FEMININE FORMS.

maze

See MAIZE.

Mc-

See MAC.

me

For *as me*, *than I*, etc see CASE, GRAMMATICAL (4).

meagre, meager

It is spelled **meagre** in British English, **meager** in American English.

mean (*noun*)

See AVERAGE.

mean (*verb*)

One can correctly **mean** something to happen, or **mean** *that* something should happen, but not **mean** *for* something to happen. Write *I didn't mean you* (not *for you*) *to hear*.

meaning

Words mean what the users of the language at a given time understand them to mean. It is an odd misconception to think that a word has only one true meaning: everyday words in particular have many meanings, as one can see by glancing at any large dictionary. It is also a mistake to think that the true meaning of a word is to be found in its etymology, the study of its origins and development. Words frequently change their meanings, and their meaning at an earlier period or in the foreign languages from which they were borrowed is not necessarily relevant to their use today. *Meat* once referred in English to food in general (a meaning still found in the proverb 'One man's meat is another man's poison'); *girl* was once used for young persons of either sex; *silly* once meant 'fortunate' or 'happy'; *stove* comes from an old German word meaning 'heated room'; *cider* can be traced back to a Hebrew word for strong drink, *alcohol* to an Arabic word for a substance used by women to darken their eyelids, *hysteria* to a Greek word for the womb, *edify* to a Latin word meaning to build (a meaning retained in the noun *edifice*).

A new meaning is sometimes condemned by those who insist that the word should be used in only one way, its original meaning. Some writers object to the extended use of *alibi* because it comes from the Latin word for 'elsewhere' and was once restricted to the legal defence that the accused was in another place when the crime was committed; it has been extended in nonlegal contexts to an excuse of any kind, though usually an invented excuse. *Alternative* comes from the Latin *alter* 'other of two', and therefore some people object to the use of

439

alternatives for three or more choices. *Decimate* comes from a Latin word meaning 'to kill one of every ten', and some criticize the use of the extended meanings 'to kill a large number' or 'to destroy a large part'. If objections to a use are sufficiently widespread, it is safer to avoid it in formal writing. For guidance on disputed meanings, see the entries for specific words in this book or in a general dictionary.

meaningful

This perfectly respectable word is nevertheless OVERUSED in such phrases as *meaningful experience* and *meaningful relationship*. To give it a rest, one can use *useful*, *fruitful*, or *important*.

means

1 When this means 'method', it is correctly treated as either singular or plural: *by this/by these means*. When it means 'wealth', as in *beyond my means*, it is plural: *His means were much reduced*.

2 *By means of* is usually VERBOSE. Write *We made a hole with* (not *by means of*) *a needle*.

meantime, meanwhile

These words are interchangeable. It is commoner, though, to use **meantime** as a noun (*They rested in the meantime*) and **meanwhile** as an adverb (*Meanwhile, they rested*).

measles

This is usually treated as a singular noun (*Measles is very unpleasant*), although it can be a plural (*Measles are . . .*). It is rather old-fashioned to say *the measles*.

Mecca

The name of the Islamic holy city is often used (and indeed OVERUSED) with a small *m* to mean the centre of any activity: *Lord's, the cricketer's mecca*. Such secular uses are harmless enough, and should not displease Muslims, but to use the word in connection with other religions than Islam would be absurd and very possibly offensive.

mechanization, automation

Mechanization is making machines do what human muscles used to do. **Automation** is making machines do what human brains used to do, in controlling other machines.

medal, meddle

A **medal** is a commemorative disc. To **meddle** is to interfere.

media

This is the plural of **medium**, but in the sense of 'means of mass communication' it is sometimes treated as a singular noun. Avoid this practice, and write *The media are* (not *is*) *responsible*. Do not write *a* **media**, or use the plural *medias*.

medi(a)eval

See AE-.

median

See AVERAGE.

mediate

This is a jargon word from psychiatry, often used for *influence*, *bring about*, or even *provide*, as in *counselling services mediated by the local authority*.

mediocre

This means 'neither good nor bad'. In that sense things either are or are not **mediocre**, and one should not call them *more mediocre* or *very mediocre*. But the word can also mean 'not good enough, poor', which is what we mean when we speak of *a very mediocre performance*.

Mediterranean

The word is spelled with one *t* and two *r*'s.

medium

In most senses, the plural is either **mediums** or **media**. It is **mediums** when the word is used for someone who claims to communicate with the dead, but usually **media** when it refers to a means of communication, such as television. See MEDIA.

meet

To greet the arrival of someone is to **meet** him or her: *I'll meet you off the train*. To encounter someone by chance is also to **meet**, and for British English this is a safer choice in formal writing than the much-criticized phrases **meet** *up* and **meet** *up with*: *I met (up with) him at the zoo*; *We'll try to meet (up) after the concert*. To experience or be

441

subject to something is to **meet** it, and even here conservative British speakers prefer not to use **meet** *with*: *His efforts met (with) much criticism.* **Meet** *up*, **meet** *up with*, and **meet** *with* are more acceptable in American English.

meet, pass

Things that come together from opposite directions **meet** (*The cars met in a head-on collision*), and one moving object going in the same direction as another may **pass** it. **Pass** is a better word than **meet** for what happens when vehicles move past each other from opposite directions without colliding, as with two cars on the northbound and southbound carriageways of a motorway. As *We passed a white Volkswagen* has these two meanings, one should make it perfectly clear, for instance in describing an accident, whether or not both vehicles were going the same way.

melodic, melodious

The distinction between these words is sometimes blurred, but **melodic** is chiefly a descriptive term meaning 'of melody' in the technical sense, while **melodious** is appreciative and means 'pleasantly tuneful'.

melody

See HARMONY.

melted

See MOLTEN.

membership

This means the state of being a member (*resign my membership*) or the number of members (*a drive to increase our membership*). The word is now widely used where *members* might be better, as in *Our membership may refuse to discuss the matter.*

memento

The plural is either **mementos** or **mementoes**.

memo

The plural is **memos**.

memorandum

The plural is either **memorandums** or **memoranda**. **Memoranda** is sometimes treated as a singular noun, but it should not be. Write *this* **memorandum** or *these* **memoranda/memorandums**, not *this* **memoranda** or *these* **memorandas**.

ménage

The word is spelled with the accent. It means 'household'.

mendacity, mendicity

Mendacity is telling lies. **Mendicity** is being a beggar.

menial

This word can no longer be used of a domestic helper. As a modern adjective it means 'lowly and degrading' (*menial tasks*) and may sometimes be jocular or offensive.

mental

Do not use this word in serious writing to mean 'crazy' or 'mad'.

mentality

In practice this is generally used in a disparaging sense. We speak of someone's *low mentality* or *provincial mentality*. It is convenient to have a word like this, but we can no longer use it if we want to praise or to be neutral: *her brilliant intellect* (not *mentality*).

mental telepathy

Since **telepathy** is communication between minds, **mental telepathy** is a TAUTOLOGY.

mentor

The word ends in *-or*, not *-er*. It means 'adviser'.

merchandise

Both noun and verb are spelled like this, not *-ize*, in British English. The verb is sometimes spelled *merchandize* in American English.

mercifully

Besides meaning 'in a merciful way' (*They mercifully pardoned the prisoners*), this now commonly means 'it is a matter for relief that'. In this sense it is used just like *thankfully*, and is open to the same objections and dangers of ambiguity. See SENTENCE ADVERBS.

mercy

Leave to the tender mercies of . . . is a CLICHÉ.

meretricious, meritorious

Meretricious means 'falsely and vulgarly attractive; specious': *meretricious ornaments*. It has nothing much to do with merit. **Meritorious** means 'deserving honour': *meritorious industry*.

merino

The plural is **merinos**. It is a kind of sheep with fine wool.

mésalliance

The word is spelled with the accent. It means 'marriage with a social inferior', and cannot be exactly replaced by the English form **misalliance**, which is more widely applied to any unsuitable union.

mesdames

See MADAM(E).

Messrs

This plural of *Mr* (*Messrs Jones, Brown, and Robinson*) is appropriate in commerce but not in ordinary letters.

metal (*verb*)

Other forms are **metalled, metalling** in British English, but the second *l* is usually omitted in American English.

metal, mettle

Metal is a substance. **Mettle** is 'vigour' or 'stamina': *The trucks had proved their mettle in army transport*.

metallurgy, metallurgist

They are usually pronounced with the stress on *tal* in British English, but on *met* in American English. **Metallurgy** is the science and technology of metals.

metamorphosis

The plural is **metamorphoses**. The stress is usually on *mor*, but some British speakers stress the *phos*.

metaphor

Our language is full of words and expressions that are metaphorical in origin: *He flew into a temper*; *She agreed to foot the bill*; *I sat at the head of the table*; *They are making pigs of themselves*; *He hung on every word she uttered*; *She was greatly attached to her youngest brother*. Such metaphors are dead metaphors, so widely used that we no longer think of them as metaphors. Experienced writers sometimes revive them effectively to renew their metaphorical force. But in serious writing be careful not to associate dead metaphors accidentally with words or expressions that might revive the metaphor and produce absurd associations with the literal meanings: *As soon as he entered the plane, he flew into a temper*; *The waiter handed him the bill, but she agreed to foot it*; *The gallows were seldom empty when the camp was in full swing*; *Thompson, not the most open of athletes, has been keeping the condition of his leg injury close to his chest since he arrived here last week* (*Daily Telegraph*).

Introduce your own metaphors only when the implied comparison helps readers: if it expresses an idea concisely and vividly, if it clarifies what you are saying. Unnecessary or inappropriate metaphors distract readers from the content to the wording.

Avoid mixed metaphors, unless you intentionally wish to be funny:

It has been difficult to raise money for the last stage in the construction of the hospital. A year ago we were *back on our own goal line* and we had *a long row to hoe*; but we are now *on the threshold of success*.

' . . . You must forgive *the new broom*, I have to *learn the ropes*,' he added, getting confused among the metaphors (Graham Greene).

'So long as there is a crock of gold at the end of the garden the spur to sink or swim is blunted' (quoted in *The Times*).

metaphysics

It takes a singular verb: *Metaphysics is* (not *are*) *a branch of philosophy*.

meter, metre

American English uses only the spelling **meter** for all senses. In British English the situation is more complicated. Here the metric unit is **metre**, and so are all its combinations: *centimetre*; *kilometre*. Measured rhythm in verse is **metre** when the word stands alone (*ballad metre*) but **-meter** in combination: *pentameter*. Measuring instruments are spelled **meter**, whether the word is used alone or in combination: *gas meter*; *barometer*; *speedometer*.

method

There's method in my madness is both a CLICHÉ and a MISQUOTATION.

methodology

This is the systematic procedure proper to a particular field. It is a word for serious scholarship, so that one may suitably refer to *the methodology of dialectical materialism*, but it might seem PRETENTIOUS to talk about *the methodology of making salad*. Use *way* or *method* here.

meticulous

This word has come up in the world. From meaning 'timidly overfussy', it is now chiefly used in the appreciative sense 'admirably careful and thorough': *a meticulous scholar*.

métier

The word is spelled with the accent. It means 'trade, profession'.

mettle

See METAL.

mews

This British word is usually treated as a singular noun. A **mews** is a yard or lane lined with stables and coach houses that are now usually converted into dwellings and garages.

mid, midst

Both forms of this preposition are correct: *mid(st) the leafy gardens*. But they belong to old-fashioned poetic language; in ordinary writing *among* is the appropriate word.

midwifery

The second syllable is pronounced 'wiff' in British English, 'wife' in American English.

mien

This is a formal word whose only sense is 'bearing, demeanour': *that mien of a commercial traveller who has been everywhere* (Arnold Bennett). Do not confuse it with any of the many senses of *mean*.

might

See MAY.

mighty

As an adverb, **mighty** means 'very': *mighty scarce*; *a mighty filling meal*. This informal use of the word is particularly common in American English, and conveys a chatty, down-to-earth, rural quality as the colourless *very* could not. It is inappropriate to formal prose.

migraine

The first syllable is usually pronounced like *me* in British English, like *my* in American English.

migrant

See EMIGRANT.

mil

This means 0.001 of an inch, and the word is also used for *thousand* in certain technical contexts: *a salinity of 38.4 per mil*. It should not be confused with any of the many senses of *mill*.

mil(e)age

The word is spelled either with or without the first *e*.

milieu

The plural is either **milieus** or **milieux**; in either case, it is usually pronounced like an ordinary English -*s* plural. The word means 'environment': *three studies of women, each from a different milieu* (Edmund Wilson).

military (*noun*)

This word has been established for centuries as a chiefly plural noun meaning 'the army' or 'soldiers': *The military were popular with the local girls*. It has been objected that **military** is properly only an adjective, but if we were to be influenced by such arguments we should never be able to form any nouns such as *comic*, *bitter*, or *final* from their related adjectives. See CONVERSION.

militate

See MITIGATE.

milk (*verb*)

This now often means 'extract too much money': *He needs to milk the profits of this nationalised industry to balance the Treasury books* (*Daily Mail*). It is a useful extension of the literal meaning of the word.

millennium

The plural is either **millennia** or **millenniums**. It means a period of 1000 years, but chiefly the period when, according to Revelation, Christ is to reign on earth. This word and the associated adjective *millennial* are spelled with two *l*'s and two *n*'s; but *millenary* and *millenarian*, which have similar meanings, have only one *n*.

milli-

See KILO-.

milliard

See BILLION.

mimic (*verb*)

Other forms are **mimicked, mimicking**.

mincemeat

In modern use, this usually means the meatless mixture of fruit, suet, etc that goes into mince pies. It is clearer not to use **mincemeat** to mean *minced meat*, which is also called *mince* or, in American English, *ground meat* or *hamburger*.

mine

In modern English, this is a pronoun: *friends of mine*. If you want to use the archaic adjective form, perhaps when writing period dialogue, note that it occurred only before a vowel or *h* (*mine enemy, mine host*) or after a noun: *O mistress mine, where are you roaming?* (Shakespeare).

miner

See MINOR.

minimal

See MAXIMAL.

minimize

See MAXIMIZE.

minimum

See MAXIMUM.

minister

See PRIEST.

minor, miner

A **minor** (*noun*) has not yet reached the legal age of majority, and **minor** (*adjective*) means 'inferior in importance'. A **miner** works in a mine.

minority

1 When it means 'a smaller number within a group', **minority** usually takes a plural verb: *Only a minority of the shareholders object* (not *objects*).

2 Do not use the word to mean merely 'a small number', as in *We discussed only a minority of* (write *a few*) *cases*. A **minority** may be anything less than half a total, in fact, quite a large number. A *large minority* means 'a number approaching half'.

3 Do not use **minority** to refer to a single member of an ethnic **minority**, as in *She was the only minority who attended the meeting*. In the ethnic sense, as elsewhere, *three minorities* means three groups, not three people.

minus

It is slightly FACETIOUS to use **minus** for *without*, as in *He arrived breathless and minus his hat*.

minuscule

This is commonly but incorrectly spelled and pronounced *miniscule*.

minutia

The plural is **minutiae**. It means 'a small detail', and is usually used in the plural.

miracle play, mystery play, morality play

These are all types of medieval drama. A **miracle** play was based on a

Bible story, or on the life of a saint, and such a play when centring on the life of Christ was often called a **mystery** play. They are sometimes revived, especially in cities such as York where particular cycles of these plays originated. The **morality** plays belong to a rather later period and are allegorical, with characters personifying such abstractions as Pride or Youth.

mis-

Do not hyphenate words formed with **mis-**, even when the original word begins with *s*: *misspell; misspent.*

misanthrope, misogamist, misogynist

A **misanthrope** hates people. A **misogamist** (a rarer word) hates marriage. A **misogynist** hates women.

mischief, mischievous

Both words are spelled *-ie-*, not *-ei-*. **Mischievous** should not be spelled or pronounced with four syllables as *mischievious*.

misdemeano(u)r

This is spelled with the *u* in British English, without it in American English.

misquotations

Certain familiar quotations from famous sources are constantly bandied about in wrong forms that are better known than the originals. We may indeed feel that it would be pedantic to get them right. Nevertheless, it may be of interest to record the correct forms of the following selection. Others, not listed here, can be found in a dictionary of quotations:

All power corrupts. Lord Acton actually wrote, 'Power tends to corrupt, and absolute power corrupts absolutely'.

Blood, sweat, and tears. Churchill's famous wartime speech offered the British nation 'blood, toil, tears, and sweat'.

Cloud no bigger than a man's hand. This omen of disaster is referred to in I Kings 18:44 as 'There ariseth a little cloud out of the sea, like a man's hand'.

The devil can quote Scripture. Antonio in *The Merchant of Venice* said, 'The devil can cite Scripture for his purpose'.

Fresh fields and pastures new. Milton wrote in *Lycidas* 'Tomorrow to fresh woods, and pastures new'.

Gild the lily. Salisbury in *King John* said, 'To gild refined gold, to paint the lily'.

The last infirmity of noble minds. Milton in *Lycidas* called Fame 'that last infirmity of noble mind'.
A little knowledge is a dangerous thing. Pope wrote, 'A little learning is a dangerous thing'.
Money is the root of all evil. St Paul in I Timothy 6:10 said, 'The love of money . . . .'.
A poor thing, but mine own. Touchstone in *As You Like It* spoke of his girlfriend as 'An ill-favoured thing, sir, but mine own'.
Pride goeth before a fall. In Proverbs 16:18 'Pride goeth before destruction, and an haughty spirit before a fall'.
There's method in my madness. Polonius in *Hamlet* observed 'Though this be madness, yet there is method in't'.
Water, water, everywhere, and not a drop to drink. Coleridge in *The Ancient Mariner* wrote, ' . . . nor any drop to drink'.

Miss

The formal plural is **Misses**, so that Jane and Ann Brown are correctly *the Misses Brown*; but *the Miss Browns* is now more usual and perfectly permissible. See also MR.

missal, missile, missive

A **missal** is a Roman Catholic book of masses. A **missile** is a thrown or projected weapon. **Missive** is a formal or FACETIOUS word for a written communication.

missing

The expression *go missing*, meaning 'disappear', is disliked by some people and should not be used in formal writing.

misspell

Do not misspell it as *mispell*.

mistak(e)able

The first *e* is usually omitted.

mitre

This word for a bishop's ceremonial hat or a join in wood or cloth is spelled **mitre** in British English and **miter** in American English.

mitigate, militate

To **mitigate** something is to make it less bad: *to mitigate the harshness of the law*. To **militate** is to have significant effect, usually *against*

451

something: *His boyish appearance militated against his chances of early promotion*. Be careful not to use **mitigate** for **militate**; the reverse mistake is less common.

mix (*noun*)

This is rather OVERUSED in the sense of 'mixture': *the right mix of jobs, people, and amenities (The Times)*. You could vary it by using *combination* instead.

mixed metaphor

See METAPHOR.

moat

See MOTE.

mobile

The last syllable of both the adjective and the noun rhymes with *Nile* in British English. In American English, the adjective usually ends like the end of *marble*, but the noun for a moving decorative structure ends like *wheel*, perhaps under the influence of *automobile*. See also MOV(E)ABLE.

mobilize

This is OVERUSED in the sense of 'marshal for action'. One can **mobilize** facts, financial resources, or support for a proposal. It is also a popular political word with the Left: *to mobilize the Labour movement*.

modality

This word has technical senses in grammar and logic. It is pretentiously OVERUSED in contexts where it might be better replaced by *procedure, method, system*, or *characteristics*: *the political modalities of negotiating a cease-fire*.

model (*verb*)

Other forms are **modelled, modelling** in British English, but the second *l* is usually omitted in American English.

model (*noun*)

Besides its usual senses of 'replica', 'pattern', etc, **model** can mean 'description used to help visualize something', as when we try to imagine the structure of the atom which cannot be directly observed.

This is closely related to the sense 'description of a possible system of human relationships', in which **model** is somewhat OVERUSED: *his revolutionary new model of an election procedure.*

moderator

The word ends in -*or*, not -*er*.

modicum

This means 'a small amount': *a claim without even a modicum of truth in it.* Replace *a modicum of* by *some* or *any* or *a little* where possible.

module

This is a section or standardized unit of almost anything from a building or a spacecraft to a computer program or educational course. The word has been much OVERUSED by people who mean little more than *group*, *class*, *period*, or *topic*.

modus operandi, modus vivendi

The first means 'method of procedure' and the second means 'practical compromise between conflicting parties'. Although **modus vivendi** is 'manner of living' in Latin, the phrase is not used like that in English. Use these LATINISMS with restraint.

Mogul, Mongol

The **Moguls** were a Muslim dynasty that ruled India from the 16th to the 18th century. With a small *m*, a **mogul** is an important or wealthy person: *Hollywood moguls.* The **Mongols** are members of the People's Republic of Mongolia, or people of the Asian racial stock that includes Malays, Eskimos, and some American Indians. With a small *m*, **mongol** means a sufferer from Down's syndrome, but it is offensive to use **mongol** in this sense.

Mohammed

See MUHAMMAD.

moiety

This is a formal and perhaps rather PRETENTIOUS word for 'half'. It should be confined to legal and learned contexts.

moisturize

Advertisers of cosmetics use **moisturize** rather than *moisten*, but the ordinary word is more suitable elsewhere.

mold, molt

See MOULD.

mollusc, mollusk

The word is spelled with a *c* in British English, but usually with a *k* in American English.

molten, melted

Molten is used, rather than **melted**, of things that melt at very high temperatures: *molten lead/lava*; *melted chocolate/ice*.

moment

Moment of truth, originally the final swordthrust in a bullfight, is often and legitimately used for the moment of testing on whose outcome everything depends. *At this/that moment in time*, however, are VERBOSE expressions for *now/then*.

momentarily

In *I was momentarily stunned by the blow*, **momentarily** means 'for a moment'. American English uses the word also to mean 'in a moment': *We will be landing momentarily at Kennedy Airport*; but this use arouses some confusion or resentment among British listeners.

momentary, momentous

Momentary means 'lasting only a moment': *a momentary glimpse*. **Momentous** means 'of great significance': *a momentous decision*.

monarchic(al), monarchal

Monarchical is the usual adjective from *monarch* and *monarchy*, with **monarchic** as an alternative form. The rarer word **monarchal** means 'royal, kingly': *monarchal splendour*.

money

1 This word usually has no plural. Where one is used, the usual plural is **moneys**, but **monies** also exists.

2 Sums of money may be written in either words or figures. Simple amounts are perhaps better written in words, unless actual arithmetic is involved: *a thousand pounds*; *ten cents*; or with the £ or $ sign: *£8 million* rather than *£8,000,000*. It is TAUTOLOGOUS to use both the symbol and word for the currency. Write *£10* (not *£10 pounds*) or *$25* (not *$25 dollars*). Beware of using the abbreviations £10m (ten million pounds) and £10K (ten thousand pounds) where they might not be understood. For the use of the singular verb in *Five pounds is all I have on me*, see NUMBER AGREEMENT (10).

Mongol

See MOGUL.

mongoose

The plural is **mongooses**, not *mongeese*.

monitor

The word ends in *-or*, not *-er*.

monogram, monograph

A **monogram** is a design formed of interwoven initials. A **monograph** is a learned treatise on a specialized subject.

monologue, soliloquy

They both mean a long talk by one speaker. **Soliloquy**, rather than **monologue**, is talking to oneself when thinking out loud. A **monologue** may be a dramatic sketch performed by one actor, or a long speech that monopolizes a conversation.

monseigneur, monsignor

The first is the title of a French dignitary, the second of a high-ranking Roman Catholic priest. The plurals are **messeigneurs**; and **monsignors** or **monsignori**.

moonlight, moonlit

1 Use **moonlight** in the phrase *moonlight night*, and when it means 'done by moonlight': *moonlight revels*. Use **moonlit** when speaking of the visual effect: *the moonlit ocean*.

2 As a verb, **moonlight** is now well established in the sense 'hold a second job'.

moot

This adjective means 'open to doubt': *a moot question*. It does not mean 'theoretical', and should not be confused with *mute* (ie 'silent'). A *moot point* is a 'debatable' one, not a 'silent' one.

moral, morale

The **moral** of a story is its practical significance. **Morals**, in the plural, are standards of conduct: *a man of loose morals*. **Morale** is one's enthusiasm and confidence: *The morale of the troops was low after the withdrawal*.

morality play

See MIRACLE PLAY.

moratorium

The plural is either **moratoriums** or **moratoria**. It means 'a suspension of activity': *ordered a moratorium on arms sales*.

more

1 Be careful to avoid confusion when using **more** before an adjective. *Here are three more interesting people for you to meet* would be better rephrased as either *three people who are more interesting* or *three other interesting people*, according to which you mean. Similarly, confusion may arise where **more** can be construed as either a noun or an adjective, as here: *The more people know about AIDS, the less likely it is to spread* (DHSS leaflet). If this means 'the greater the amount of information that people know', it would be better expressed as *The more that people know*; if it means 'the greater the number of people who know', one should say *The more people who know*.

2 *More than one* is conventionally singular, whether or not a noun follows it: *More than one boy was rejected*; *More than one has passed*; but *More than fifty people were killed*.

3 It would of course be absurd to write **more** *better* or **more** *fatter*, since *better* and *fatter* themselves express the idea of more; it may be less obvious that one should not write **more** *preferable* either, as *preferable* itself means 'more desirable'.

4 *More or less* means 'fairly' or 'almost': *He more or less insisted*; *more or less certain*; *It's more or less over*. Do not use it where it means 'either more or less', as in *Will you earn more or less money?*, but write *more money, or less*.

5 For *The cost has been more than halved*, see HALVE. For *more stupid* or *stupider*, see COMPARISON, GRAMMATICAL (1). For *more well-known*, see WELL-. For *much more*, see MUCH.

moreover

This word is appropriate to formal writing. Elsewhere, replace it by *and* or *also* or *besides*, or merely leave it out.

mores

It is pronounced 'more-ease' or 'more-rays'. Use *customs* or *conventions* where this word might seem too PRETENTIOUS.

morgue

See MORTUARY.

Mormon

In official contexts, the **Mormons** are properly referred to as members of the *Church of Jesus Christ of Latter-Day Saints*.

morphia, morphine

They are the same narcotic drug, but **morphine** is the scientific term.

morphology

See GRAMMAR.

mortar

See CEMENT.

mortgagee, mortgagor

The **mortgagee** is the bank, building society, etc that lends money on the security of a property. The **mortgagor** is the house buyer who borrows money on that security.

mortician

This word, originally a GENTEELISM, is now well established in American though not in British English. If *undertaker* seems too plain, an alternative is *funeral director*.

mortise, mortice

Mortise is the more usual spelling. It is the groove or cavity that receives the projection called a *tenon*.

mortuary, morgue

Both are places where dead bodies are kept before burial or cremation. A hospital or an undertaker's establishment has a **mortuary**. **Morgue** is commoner in American than in British English, and may be another word for **mortuary** or may mean the place where bodies found dead await identification by the relatives.

Moslem

See MUHAMMAD.

mosquito

The plural is **mosquitoes** or, less usually, **mosquitos**.

most

1 Use *more*, not **most**, to contrast only two items: *I don't know whether Paul or Susan was more* (not *most*) *embarrassed.*

2 Before a noun, **most** can mean 'the greatest number of' (*most people*) or 'the greatest extent of' (*She has the most intelligence*). It cannot replace *biggest*: *They have the biggest* (not *the most*) *navy.*

3 Most can properly replace *very* before adjectives and adverbs that convey a judgment of feeling or opinion: *a most beautiful day*; *John argued most persuasively.* It is not used like that before other adjectives or adverbs: *a very* (not *most*) *tall girl*; *she works very* (not *most*) *quickly.* Do not use **most** for *very* where it could be taken to mean 'more than all the others'. *John argued most persuasively* could mean that, in some contexts.

4 Most is used for *almost* in informal American English: *Most anybody can play*; but it is not appropriate for serious writing.

5 For *most well-known*, see WELL-.

mostly

This means 'for the greatest part': *The land is mostly desert*; or 'usually': *We mostly watch TV at night.* Use *most*, not **mostly**, for the sense 'to the greatest degree': *The people most* (not *mostly*) *in need of help do not ask for it.*

mote, moat, motte

A **mote** is a speck, particularly of dust: *motes dancing in the sunlight.* A **moat** is a ditch round something, such as a castle or a modern zoo

enclosure. **Motte** is the technical word for the fortified mound of a
Norman castle.

Mother's Day

This is a Sunday appointed for the honouring of mothers; in Britain it is
the fourth Sunday in Lent, also called *Mothering Sunday*, and in the
USA it is the second Sunday in May.

motif, motive

A **motif** is a recurring theme in a work of music or literature, or a
repeated design in a work of art. The word is sometimes anglicized into
motive, but the chief meaning of **motive** is 'that which causes one to
act'.

motion pictures

See CINEMA.

motivate

To **motivate** someone is to make him or her want to do something. The
word is OVERUSED in managerial contexts, where the employer wants the
staff to work hard and hopes to achieve this end by making them want
to as well: *to motivate and stimulate our sales force*; *Candidates must
be money-motivated* (in plain English, *greedy*). Do not use **motivate**
where *make* or *cause* would do instead. The plain English for *What
motivated his action?* is *What made him do it?*

motto

The plural is **mottoes** or, less usually, **mottos**.

mould, moult

The words are spelled like this in British English but usually **mold,
molt** in American English.

m(o)ustache

The word is spelled **moustache** in British English, **mustache** in
American English.

mov(e)able, mobile

1 The spellings **movable** and **moveable** are both correct.

2 A **movable** thing is less so than a **mobile** one. A wooden hut which could be taken down and reerected elsewhere is **movable**, but a *mobile library* is actually in a van, on wheels.

movement

This can mean 'an organized effort to promote something', as in the *civil rights movement*. As an extension of this sense, the word is used of various organizations of the political Left, though less usually of the Right: *the Labour movement*; *the trades union movement*. It is a way of suggesting irresistible dynamic force.

movies

See CINEMA.

mow

The participle is either **mowed** or **mown**. It is usually **mowed** when used as part of a verb (*I've just mowed the lawn*), but **mown** when used as an adjective (*new-mown hay*).

M.P.

The letters are an ABBREVIATION for Member of Parliament (*Mary Jones, M.P.*); but in fact the term is used only of members of the House of Commons, though the House of Lords is also part of the British Parliament.

Mr, Mrs, Miss

1 **Mr** and **Mrs** are the commoner British forms, **Mr.** and **Mrs.** the American ones.

2 On whether to refer to yourself, or to your own husband or wife, as *Mr Smith* or *Mrs Jones*, see NAMES OF PEOPLE.

3 Conventionally, **Mrs** is used with the husband's first name (*Mrs John Jones*) rather than with the wife's own name (*Mrs Mary Jones*), unless she is a peer's daughter (*Lady Mary Jones*); this remains true if the woman is widowed, but not if she is divorced. This rule is becoming old-fashioned, although some women maintain a strong preference for it.

4 **Miss** is often used of a married woman, particularly an actress, in connection with her career. **Miss** and **Mrs** are not used with other titles, so that a woman doctor is *Dr Jones* and a woman mayor may be *Madam Mayor*. **Mr**, by contrast, is often used (particularly in American English) in such combinations as *Mr President* and *Mr Ambassador*.

Ms

1 This is usually pronounced 'miz', and has a full stop after it in American English.

2 This title shows that the person named is a woman, just as *Mr* indicates a man, but it conceals her marital status. It is used either with or without her first name, though not with her husband's first name: *Ms Brook; Ms Carol Brook.* Married professional women may use it in association with their maiden names; so that *Mr Jack Lemmon* and *Ms Carol Brook* may turn out to be husband and wife.

Theoretically, **Ms** would be a useful form of address when you simply do not know whether the woman you are writing to is married and do not wish to offend her by using *Mrs* if she is not or *Miss* if she is. But because **Ms** is associated with the feminist movement from which it sprang in the 1970s, it has attracted a good deal of abuse from people of both sexes outside the movement. It has become less common in newspapers than in the first flush of its novelty, and is outlawed by the style books of both *The Times* in Britain and *The New York Times*. Do not write to a woman as **Ms** unless you know that she likes it.

much

1 For *much interested* or *very interested*, see VERY.

2 *Much more* and *much less* are curiously easy to confuse, and when we get them the wrong way round we say the opposite of what we mean. *Much less* means 'and certainly not': *I can't even walk, much less run*. It is sometimes misused in sentences where the writer meant to say 'and even more so': *It's difficult for me to walk, much less* (it should be *more* difficult, not *less*) *to run*; *It took at least a week even to address the envelopes, much less* (it means *more* than a week, not *less*) *to type the letters*.

muchly

This is FACETIOUS. Use *much*.

mucous, mucus

Mucous is the adjective, **mucus** the noun: *The mucous membrane secretes mucus*.

Muhammad, Muslim

The name of the founder of Islam is correctly spelled **Muhammad**, though the old-fashioned spellings **Mahomet** and **Mohammed** may look more familiar. The adherents of Islam are now usually referred to as **Muslims**, rather than the older form **Moslems**.

mulatto

The plural is either **mulattoes** or **mulattos**. It is an outdated word for a person of mixed black and white ancestry.

mumps

This is usually treated as a singular noun (*Mumps is potentially serious*), although it can be plural (*Mumps are . . .*). It is a little old-fashioned to say *the mumps*.

municipal

This is best pronounced with the stress on the second syllable, not on the third.

munitions

See AMMUNITION.

music, musical

People of those occupations usually call themselves *music teachers* and *music critics*. **Musical** here would sound as if they were boasting about their talent for music. In any case it is usual to put a noun before *teacher*, as in *history teacher*.

music centre

See GRAMOPHONE.

Muslim

See MUHAMMAD.

must

Except in formal writing, this is correctly used as a noun to mean 'something necessary': *A crash helmet is a must for motorcyclists*. It is somewhat more informal to use the word as an adjective meaning 'necessary', as in *a piece of must legislation*.

mustache

See M(O)USTACHE.

mutual, reciprocal, common

1 Mutual and **reciprocal** both mean 'directed by each towards the other': *mutual affection between mother and daughter*. **Reciprocal** carries, in addition, the idea of one of the two parties repaying in kind: *I admire her and she has a reciprocal respect for me*. In older English, **mutual** also meant 'shared', as when Sir Walter Scott wrote *Communication between them was cut off at night by the mutual door being shut*. In modern use, however, it is better to express this idea by **common**, except in expressions such as *mutual friend* where **common** might be taken to mean 'inferior'. Dickens' use of the title *Our Mutual Friend* may have made the phrase more acceptable.

2 It is TAUTOLOGOUS to speak of *mutual cooperation* or of *mutually helping each other*. Omit *mutual* and *mutually* there.

myself

Myself should not be used in formal writing to replace *I* or *me*, as in *John and myself are grateful*. See REFLEXIVE.

mystery play

See MIRACLE PLAY.

myth

See LEGEND.

Nn

-n-, -nn-

See DOUBLING.

'n'

This means 'and' in some advertisements and menus: *chicken 'n' chips*. Do not use it in serious writing, except in *rock 'n' roll*.

nadir, zenith

In astronomy the **nadir** is the point in the heavens vertically below the observer, and the **zenith** is vertically above. The words are used figuratively for 'low point' and 'high point': *the nadir of moral degradation*; *the zenith of her career*.

naïf, naïve

Naïf is the French masculine form of the word, but **naïve** is now used in English for both masculine and feminine. It can be spelled either with or without the dots on *i*, and pronounced 'nah-eve' or 'nigh-eve'. This borrowed French word expresses a shade of meaning not otherwise covered in English. It means 'unworldly; artless'. Scientists and sociologists now use it of creatures not previously subjected to a particular experimental procedure: *made the test with naïve rats*.

The related noun can be spelled in a variety of ways: *naivety, naïveté, naiveté, naivete, naïvety*. The first two forms are probably the best.

names for groups

There are numerous names that popular and technical usage have established for people, animals, or things that are together in a group, such as *a* **flock** *of birds*. Here are some examples:

actors: a company or troupe

aeroplanes: a flight or squadron

angels: a host

bees: a swarm

bells: a peal

bishops: a bench

cards: a pack or (chiefly American) deck

cars: a fleet

cattle: a herd or drove

chickens: a brood

concerts: a series

cubs: a litter

dancers: a troupe

deer: a herd

dogs: a kennel

flowers: a bunch, bouquet, or nosegay

foxes: a skulk

geese: a gaggle or (in flight) a skein

gnats: a swarm or cloud

grapes: a bunch or cluster

hounds: a pack

keys: a bunch

larks: an exaltation

leopards: a leap

lions: a pride

loaves: a batch

magistrates: a bench

monkeys: a troop

oxen: a yoke, drove, team, or herd

partridges: a covey

porpoises: a school

pups: a litter

sheep: a flock

ships: a fleet, squadron, or flotilla

stars: a cluster or constellation

steps: a flight

thieves: a gang

whales: a school, gam, or pod

wolves: a pack, rout, or herd

worshippers: a congregation

It is always possible to invent facetious names, perhaps *a jubilation of fans, a pride of scholars, a cacophony of singers.*

names of people

1 First name or surname?

It is now much commoner than it was in past generations to speak to, or about, people by their first names, both at work and within the family. It is more general in American than in British English, but everywhere it may apply more naturally to contemporaries and juniors than to seniors, so that it is only in fairly 'progressive' companies and families that the secretary calls the boss by the first name and children so address their parents. In more traditional families, children may be encouraged to say *Uncle Bill* and *Auntie Mary* to their parents' friends who are not relations at all. Just because the one-way use of the first name implies a somewhat stereotyped one-way relationship, a modern

465

middle-class housewife may be shy of using it to a cleaning woman of her own age.

Some adults are undecided over what to call their father-in-law or mother-in-law. The choice is between the first name, a title such as *Dad/Mum/Ma*, and as a third choice (in formal families) *Mr/Mrs Brown*. Another problem is how to speak of (rather than to) one's husband or wife. One can say *Bill thinks* . . . only to people who know who *Bill* is. *Mr Brown thinks* . . . is no way to refer to one's husband today, as it sounds pompous and old-fashioned. *My husband thinks* . . . is the best choice when speaking to strangers. On the other hand, when referring to the spouse of the person you are talking to, unless you know both parties well enough to ask *What does Bill think?* it may be more civil to call him *Mr Brown* rather than *your husband*. See MR.

There is no fixed answer to the modern question of how to announce oneself on the telephone. Should it be *This is Mr Brown speaking*, or *John Brown*, or just *Brown*? If a title is involved, should it be *Professor Brown, Professor Mary Brown*, or, again, *Mary Brown*? The use of *John Brown/Mary Brown* is widespread, perhaps particularly at the upper end of the social scale and particularly in American use.

It was common a generation ago for men of equal status to speak to and about each other by the surname alone, but the practice is now old-fashioned, though it survives in some schools and among some male groups (eg in sports clubs). Women used to be referred to by their surnames only if they were servants or criminals, but there is a recent tendency to write about women in this form in scholarly or critical articles: *Frink's new exhibition at Burlington House* (for *Elizabeth Frink*). Sportswomen are sometimes treated likewise in the press: *Navratilova had an easy win in straight sets*.

It is common in broadcasting, though not elsewhere, to address people by their full name. The device is particularly important on radio panel shows, where the participants are invisible to the listening audience and the compere has constantly to make it clear who is going to speak next: *Perhaps you'd like to comment on that, John Selwyn Gummer*. The same style is quite often used in addressing letters to strangers who are to some degree public figures (*Dear Mary Whitehouse*), though it is fair to say that the recipients of the letter are not always pleased.

2 The form of the name.

People are sensitive about their own names, so be careful to spell and pronounce them right. Give the name, for serious purposes, in the form they prefer themselves: *Arthur C. Clarke*, not *Arthur Clarke* or *Arthur Charles Clarke*. (One would not, of course, prohibit the jocular nicknaming of public figures. Her own supporters, as well as her adversaries, call Margaret Thatcher *Maggie*.) If the preferred form is that of initials and surname alone, it leaves the sex unspecified. Do not assume it to be male. You would be wrong over, say, the historian *C.V. Wedgwood* (*Cicely Veronica*). See FEMININE FORMS.

The names of firms have also their idiosyncrasies. The publishers of this book call themselves *Longman*, not *Longmans* or *Longmans'*, whereas *Barclays* Bank is not *Barclay* or *Barclays'*. One should try to get these forms right. See also TITLES OF PEOPLE; FALSE TITLES.

narcissus

The plural is **narcissus** or **narcissuses** or **narcissi**.

narcotics

This is the plural of the singular noun **narcotic**. Heroin is a **narcotic**, heroin and marijuana are **narcotics**. **Narcotics** is therefore not used with a singular verb, unlike *mathematics*.

narrate, narrative

These are formal words for *tell* and *story*. In general use they may sound PRETENTIOUS.

nary

This dialect word meaning 'not one single' (*They spoke nary a word*) is FACETIOUS when used in general writing.

nasturtium

This has an ordinary English plural, **nasturtiums**.

nation

This takes a singular verb in American English and usually in British English: *The whole nation was* (rather than *were*) *alarmed*. See COLLECTIVES.

nationalize, naturalize

To **nationalize** is to bring under public ownership: *to nationalize the railways*. To **naturalize** is to admit to citizenship (*a naturalized British subject*), or to introduce foreign plants and animals into a region or words into a language.

native

It is offensive to call a non-European national a **native**, although *Native American* is an accepted way of referring to an American Indian. It is

467

reasonable, however, to speak of a **native** *of* a place (*a native of Yorkshire*), and the word can be used in suitable contexts for 'permanent resident': *Only the natives (of our village) understand the local bus timetable*.

naturalist, naturist

A **naturalist** is a student of natural history, especially one who works out of doors rather than in a laboratory; or an artist or writer who portrays life realistically. A **naturist** is a nudist.

nature

For the use of **nature** for *kind* or *sort*, see CHARACTER.

naught

See NOUGHT.

nauseated, nauseous

In British English, **nauseated** usually means 'disgusted' (*I was nauseated by their sentimentality*) and **nauseous** means 'disgusting' (*a nauseous smell*). In American English, **nauseated** is used to mean 'suffering from nausea' and **nauseous** to mean 'causing nausea'; however, **nauseous** is often used in the same sense as **nauseated**, though this use meets with disapproval. The British use *sick* to mean 'suffering from nausea' (*I feel sick*), whereas *sick* in American English applies to general bad health; see ILL. The American physical sense of **nauseated** is not common in British English.

nautilus

The plural is either **nautiluses** or **nautili**.

naval, navel

Naval refers to the *navy*. The **navel** is the depression in the abdomen; a *navel orange* has a similar depression at the top.

navigable

The word is spelled without an *e* in the middle.

navigator

The word ends in *-or*, not *-er*.

nay

In rather formal and archaic use, this means 'not merely this but also': *The letter made him happy, nay, ecstatic.* **Nay** means 'no' only in some regional dialects, and as the opposite of *aye* when votes are being counted.

near

Near is used for *nearly* in adjective and noun combinations such as *near-perfect, a near-disaster, near silk.* These are usually hyphenated, but there is no consistency in the matter.

nearby, near by

As an adjective before a noun, it is spelled **nearby**: *a nearby café.* As an adverb, it can be spelled as one word or two: *to live nearby; to stay at a farm near by.* Do not use it as a preposition: *living near* (not *nearby*) *the seaside.*

neath

This word for *beneath* (as in *neath the spreading foliage*) belongs to old-fashioned poetic language (see POESY).

nebula

The plural is either **nebulas** or **nebulae**.

née

This is spelled with or without the accent. It is conventionally used before the former surname, not the first name, of a married woman: *Mrs Thomson, née Wilson* (not *née Sarah Wilson*). By extension, **née** is sometimes used for 'formerly' in general (*Sri Lanka, née Ceylon*), but this is a FACETIOUS practice.

need

1 Need combines in two ways with another verb. (a) in negatives and questions, or in phrases with a negative implication, it can have the invariable form **need** and be followed by the simple infinitive without *to*: *Need I go?*; *He need not answer*; *The hole is deeper than it need be.* (b) in any circumstances, it can have the forms **needs** and **needed**, and be followed by *to* and the infinitive: *He needed to go*; *Do I need to go?*; *He does not need to go.* Where there is a choice of forms, as in negatives and questions, American English rather prefers *He doesn't need to* and *Do I need to?*, while British English favours *He needn't* and *Need I?* Both are perfectly correct, but they should not be mixed. Write *They need no longer be* (not *to be*) *ashamed.*

2 Do not use **need** with a past participle, as in *This needs changed.* Write either *This needs changing* or *This needs to be changed.*

3 *Need be* and *if need be* are convenient idioms for use in the present or future: *We'll go by bus if need be.* They sound clumsy in the past, so replace them by *(if) necessary: He left earlier than was necessary* (not *than need have been*).

4 *Needs must* and *must needs* mean 'must necessarily'. The form is always **needs**, not **need**, and the expression is usually used ironically: *He knew they were vegetarians, and he must needs take them to a steak house.*

ne'er

This contraction of *never* (as in *He ne'er forgave the wrong*) belongs to old-fashioned poetic language.

negation

1 too many negatives
2 subject with *all* or *every* followed by negative
3 with linked clauses

1 too many negatives
When there are several negative words in the same sentence, the sentence may become difficult to understand:

The company shall *not* insure the Policyholder in respect of damage occurring while the vehicle is being driven by the Policyholder *unless* he holds a licence to drive such vehicle and is *not disqualified* from holding such a licence.

You can make this sentence easier to understand by substituting positives as well as by making some other improvements:

The company will insure you for damage occurring while you are driving the vehicle, provided that you hold a licence to drive the vehicle and are permitted to hold the licence.

2 subject with *all* or *every* followed by negative
If the subject of a negative sentence contains *all* or *every*, the sentence may be ambiguous: **All** *the members of the committee have* **not** *signed the petition* may mean either that none have signed (all have failed to do so) or that some have signed (there are some that have not done so). If the meaning of such a sentence is not clear, rephrase it as *None of the*

members of the committee have signed . . . or *Some of the members of
the committee have not signed . . .*

3 with linked clauses

It is easy to make mistakes when you link two clauses, the first of
which is negative. Here are some examples:

(a) You may want to apply the negative to the second clause but fail
to do so: *The company has decided to introduce its own training
schemes and will therefore employ school leavers who have not learnt
to type and* **are experienced** (are not experienced, or are
inexperienced) *in using computers.* The first negative is between an
auxiliary (*have*) and a main verb (*learnt*) and does not carry over to the
second clause. It carries over if it takes the auxiliary with it: *They have
not learnt to type and* **use** (ie they have not learnt to use) *computers*
(but better *and to use computers* or *or to use computers*, to avoid the
meaning 'and they use computers'); *They have not learnt to type or*
used (ie they have not used) *computers.* Even if the same auxiliary
appears in the second clause, the negative does not carry over: *They
have not learnt to type and* **have used** *computers* (ie they have used).

(b) You may not want to apply the negative to the second clause but
you may unintentionally do so: *They did not want to help her persuade
the workers to join the trade union and in fact* **hinder** (hindered) *her
from doing so.* If you use *hinder*, the negative carries over (ie did not
want in fact to hinder her).

(c) You may mistakenly seem to carry over a negative subject to the
second clause: *No alcoholic drinks are allowed in the public rooms but
can be* (but alcoholic drinks can be) *taken into the bedrooms. But* here
suggests a contrast. You need to introduce a positive subject.

(d) If a negative that is not the subject (*not only* in the following
example) begins the first clause and the auxiliary (*would*) consequently
comes before the subject (*she*), you need to repeat the subject in the
second clause: *Not only would she be involved in the selection of the
short list of candidates but* **could** (she could) *also be present at the
interviews.* Contrast the preference for leaving out the subject when the
negative is inside the clause: *She would not only be involved in the
selection of the short list of candidates but* **could** *also be present at the
interviews.* You can see the same effect for two linked clauses in the
contrast between a statement (*She will be there and* **could** *help us*) and
an equivalent question (*Will she be there and could she help us?*).

(e) Certain main verbs, such as *think, suppose, expect, believe,
imagine, seem*, and *appear*, may take the negative even though the
negation applies to what follows: *I do* **not believe** *that they have yet
drawn up the contract* means roughly the same as 'I believe that they
have *not* yet drawn up the contract'; *Your figures do* **not seem** *to be
correct* ('Your figures seem *not* to be correct'); *I don't think* *so* ('I
think *not*'). If two linked clauses follow this type of negative, you have

471

to be careful not to allow the negative to carry over unintentionally to the second clause: *I do **not think** that your arguments have convinced the others and should therefore be rephrased.* The solution is to put the negative in the one clause to which it belongs: *I think that your arguments have **not convinced** the others and should therefore be rephrased.*

See also DOUBLE NEGATIVE.

negative, positive

1 *The answer was in the negative* is a PRETENTIOUS way of saying that it was 'no'.

2 Negative is OVERUSED in the sense of 'hostile', and **positive** in the sense of 'favourable'. Advertisers try to create a *positive attitude* to a product, meaning to get people to like it. A *negative audience reaction* to a play probably means that they booed.

negligee, negligé(e)

The preferred spelling is **negligee** with no accent, particularly in American English.

negligible, negligent

Negligible means 'not worth care; trifling': *a matter of negligible importance.* **Negligent** means either 'careless' or 'pleasantly casual': *She conversed with negligent ease.*

negotiate

The third syllable is generally pronounced 'she'. An alternative pronunciation 'see' exists, but may sound rather too genteel to ears that are not used to it. Compare APPRECIATE (1).

Negro, Negress

See BLACK; FEMININE FORMS.

neigh

The word is spelled *-ei-*, not *-ie-*.

neighbo(u)r, neighbo(u)rhood

1 These are spelled with the *u* in British English, without it in American English.

2 *In the neighbourhood of*, as in *It cost in the neighbourhood of £60*, is a VERBOSE way of saying 'about'.

neither

It should be followed by *nor*, not by *or*: *Neither the steak nor* (not *or*) *the salad was paid for*. For *neither is/are* and other points, see EITHER.

nem. con.

See UNANIMOUS.

neologism

Neologisms are new words or phrases (also called nonce words) or new usages. The term usually expresses disapproval of their novelty. If they become established in the language, they are no longer neologisms. Some writers, however, may continue to avoid certain expressions that they recognize as recent neologisms, eg *to impact, to update, ongoing, input* (meaning 'contribution' or 'advice').

nephew

The first syllable is pronounced 'nef' in American English, but often 'nev' in British English.

nerve-(w)racking

It is usually spelled without the *w*. See RACK.

-ness, -ty, -ion

The endings **-ness** and **-ty** are attached to adjectives to form nouns meaning a state or quality: *correctness*; *cruelty*. It is clumsy and unnecessary to form a **-ness** word such as *anxiousness* or *loyalness* where a suitable **-ty** word such as *anxiety* or *loyalty* already exists. Sometimes, however, a pair of such words have developed different meanings, so that both are needed. *Casualness* is the quality of being casual, but a *casualty* is an injured person or thing. *Enormousness* is the quality of being enormous, but an *enormity* may be a wicked act.

The ending **-ion** is attached to verbs to form nouns meaning either a process or the result of a process: *validation*; *regulation*. There are a few pairs of similar words ending in **-ion** and **-ness** which have different meanings and need to be distinguished, such as *completion* and *completeness*, *correction* and *correctness*.

net(t)

When it means 'remaining after deductions' (*net earnings*), the spelling **net** is correct everywhere, but **nett** is a British alternative.

neuralgia, neuritis, neurosis, neurasthenia

Neuralgia and **neuritis** are both physical ailments. **Neuralgia** is spasmodic pain along the course of a nerve. **Neuritis** entails not only pain but impaired reactions and sensory disturbances. **Neurosis** is an emotional disorder involving phobias, compulsions, and anxiety. **Neurasthenia** is an old-fashioned word for *nervous breakdown*, a state of great fatigue and anxiety that prevents one from coping with life.

never

This is often used simply for *not*, where no question of time is involved. It is a convenient form of emphasis: *I never knew* (stronger than *I didn't know*) *he cared*; *I never remember hearing it mentioned*. It is useful to be able to say *he never used to*, if one finds *he usedn't to* and *he didn't used to* equally awkward. There can be no reason for objecting to these harmless combinations.

new

It is TAUTOLOGOUS to refer to a *new innovation* or *a new swimming record*, except perhaps when **new** means 'recent' in contrast with an earlier innovation or record.

news

It takes a singular verb: *No news is* (not *are*) *good news*.

next

See FIRST.

nexus

The plural is either **nexuses** or **nexus**. It means 'a link': *It makes money seem the only social nexus* (*National Review* (Melbourne)).

nice

The commonest sense of **nice** is 'pleasant': *a nice day; be nice to him*. There is nothing wrong with this blanket term of approval and it would be a great mistake, even if it were possible, to confine the word to its earlier sense of 'precise': *a nice distinction*. Careful writers of serious prose, though, usually seek for a more specific word, such as *beautiful, pleasant, amusing, tasty*, or *interesting*, according to the kind of 'niceness' they have in mind.

nicety

Unlike *niceness*, this noun does not carry the popular sense of the adjective *nice*. We can speak of a *nice* day, but not of the **nicety** of the day. **Nicety** chiefly means a 'subtlety': *the niceties of English grammar*.

nicknames

Some additional names for people, places, or things have become sufficiently established to be generally recognizable: *the Union Jack* (British flag); *the Stars and Stripes* (American flag); *William the Conqueror* (William I of England). Most, however, may not be known to all readers: *the Big Apple* (New York); *the City of Gold* (Jerusalem); *the Swan of Avon* (Shakespeare); *the sport of kings* (horse-racing). These should be used only if in their context they are likely to be clear to your intended readers. Overuse of such nicknames is irritating.

niece

The word is spelled *-ie-*, not *-ei-*.

nigger

See BLACK.

nigh

This is reasonably current in the combinations *well-nigh* (*She well-nigh fainted at the news*) and *nigh on* (*nigh on fifty years*), although they sound rather quaint or affected and are better replaced by *almost* or *nearly*. When it stands alone, meaning 'near' (*The end draws nigh*), it belongs to old-fashioned poetic language (see POESY).

-nik

This ending came from Yiddish into American English. It means 'person who is something or does something', and it forms several new informal words. A *computernik*, for instance, is someone who works with computers.

nimbus

The plural is either **nimbi** or **nimbuses**. It is a halo, or a raincloud.

ninish, ninth

There is no *e* in these words.

nitre, niter

The word is spelled **nitre** in British English, **niter** in American English.

no

1 The usual plural is **noes**, but **nos** is not wrong.

2 Write *no worse a thing*, not *a no worse thing*, and *his considerable achievement*, not *his no small achievement*. **No** cannot be preceded by *a, the, this, that*, or by *his, her, my*, etc. It is used instead of them.

nobody, no one

See ANY (1).

nohow

This means 'in no way', as in *I could nohow read it*. It almost always, however, appears incorrectly in DOUBLE NEGATIVES: *They couldn't get that cow out of the ditch nohow*. This has given the word an aura of being bad English, so that it is much better not to use it at all.

noisome

This means 'disgusting': *a noisome smell*. It has nothing to do with 'noise'.

nom de plume

The plural is **noms de plume**. It is better to use the English words *pen name* or *pseudonym*.

nomenclature

1 This is usually pronounced with the stress on *men* in British English, but on *nom* in American English.

2 It is not a grand word for 'name', but means 'a system of names', as for plants, animals, or chemical compounds. Write *A club has been formed under the name* (not *the nomenclature*) *of the Brighton Snooker Club*.

non-, in-, un-

1 Words beginning with **non-** are nearly always spelled as one word in American English: *nonreturnable*; *nonalignment*; but hyphenated forms such as *non-returnable*, *non-alignment* are equally common in British English.

2 Non- is often used lazily to escape having to think of a true opposite. Where one exists, it is better to use it: *amateur* rather than *nonprofessional*, *negative* rather than *nonpositive*, and *failure* rather than *nonsuccess*.

3 Non-, **in-**, and **un-** all mean 'not', but while **non-** expresses simple negation, **in-** and **un-** often express active opposition. *Nonscientific* means 'not connected with science', but *unscientific* is 'slovenly as regards science'. See IN-.

nonce

For the nonce, meaning 'for the time being', is a FACETIOUS phrase which is best avoided.

nonce word

See NEOLOGISM.

none

None may be followed by a singular or a plural verb as the sense requires: *None of the telephones is* (or *are*) *working*, but it would be absurd to write *is* in place of *are* in *None of them are better singers than the Welsh*. Plural verbs and pronouns often accompany **none** where it is followed by *of* and a plural noun (*none of the telephones*), and particularly where one wishes to avoid the awkward *he or she*. *None of the members have paid their subscriptions* may sound more natural than *has paid his or her subscription*. See NUMBER AGREEMENT (7).

nonmoral

See AMORAL.

nonplus (*verb*)

Other forms are **nonplussed, nonplussing** in British English, but the second *s* is usually omitted in American English.

nonreligious

See IRRELIGIOUS.

nonsense

This can mean not only 'foolish language or thinking' but 'a piece of foolish behaviour', particularly a muddle or mix-up caused by bungling: *Lyne made a nonsense of the embarkation* (Evelyn Waugh);

the . . . nonsenses which are causing the crisis (*The Economist*). This use of the word is well established in British English, but apparently less usual in American English.

nonsocial

See ANTISOCIAL.

no one

This means 'no person, nobody': *No one replied to my advertisement.* (In this sense, the hyphenated form *no-one* is acceptable but less usual.) Confusingly, the same two-word combination means 'no single': *No one room is big enough.*

noplace

This American English word is more informal than *anyplace*, *everyplace*, or *someplace*. In writing, use *nowhere*.

nor, or

1 It is often perfectly legitimate, and very effective, to begin a sentence or even a paragraph with **nor** or **or**.

2 Use **nor**, not **or**, after *neither*: *He neither wrote nor telephoned.* After other negative words, there is often a choice between **nor** and **or**: *He did not write nor/or telephone*; *He never wrote nor/or telephoned.*

3 Nor is used for *than* only in regional dialect. Write *He's no better than* (not *nor*) *I am.*

normalcy

Although this word is used in standard English, careful writers nevertheless prefer *normality*.

north, northern

Clear divisions of the earth's surface and particularly political ones are often called **north**, **south**, **east**, or **west**, and vaguer ones **northern**, **southern**, **eastern**, **western**: *South Africa, southern England*; *the North Pole, northern Europe*; *East Germany, eastern counties.* But note the exceptions *Northern Ireland, Western Australia.*

northward(s)

Before a noun, use **northward**: *a northward direction.* After a verb, use the form with an *s* in British English (*pointing northwards*) and the one without the *s* in American English.

nostrum

The plural is **nostrums**, not *nostra*. It means a medicine or remedy.

nos(e)y

The spellings **nosy** and **nosey** are both correct.

not

1 It is normal in speech and informal writing to shorten *could not* to *couldn't, had not* to *hadn't*, etc. It is in fact rather prim not to.

2 Be careful how you combine **not** and *all*. *Not all teachers can manage the computer* decidedly means that only some of them can. *All teachers cannot manage the computer* means that too, and is perfectly idiomatic English, but for some people it may also mean 'no teachers can'. See NEGATION (2).

3 It is legitimate to write *not un-* and *not in-*, as in *not uncommon* and *not inconsiderable*. Such combinations cannot be censured as being DOUBLE NEGATIVES. They are 'double', certainly, but the one negative cancels out the other as is intended, producing an effect of cautious understatement: things that are *not uncommon* are less common than *common* things. However, this stylistic device should not be used so often that it becomes a mannerism.

4 For *not all that*, see ALL (2). For *not about to*, see ABOUT (1). For *not because*, see BECAUSE (2). For *not . . . but*, see BUT (5).

notable, noticeable, noted, notorious

Notable means 'worthy of notice'. **Noticeable** means 'perceptible'. A *notable improvement* must be quite large, but a *noticeable improvement* may be rather small. **Noted** means 'celebrated', applying to people or things that not merely deserve notice but have received it: *a noted authority on tropical diseases*. All the preceding words should be clearly distinguished from **notorious** and its associated noun *notoriety*, which usually imply disreputable fame: *a notorious liar*.

notary public

The plural is **notaries public**.

nothing

1 Use a singular verb after *nothing but*, even when a plural noun follows: *Nothing but trees was* (not *were*) *to be seen* (or *Nothing was to be seen but trees*).

2 *Nothing like*, as in *It's nothing like as cold*, is rather informal. In serious prose, write *not nearly*.

notify

This is a rather formal word for 'inform': *If you have any complaints, please notify the manager*. It can seem PRETENTIOUS to use it in less formal contexts where *tell* or *let know* will do.

notorious

See INFAMOUS; NOTABLE.

nought, naught

Nought is the usual British spelling of the word meaning *zero*, or *0*, and **naught** is its American spelling. In both British and American use, **naught** is an archaic or literary word for *nothing* or *nothingness*: *Our hopes came to naught*.

noun

Most nouns have a plural form: *manager, managers* (see PLURALS OF NOUNS; FOREIGN PLURALS). Many also take the genitive: *the manager's report, the managers' meetings* (see GENITIVE; APOSTROPHE; CASE, GRAMMATICAL).

    Concrete nouns refer to people, places, or things: *secretary, office, typewriter*; **abstract nouns** refer to qualities, states, or actions: *honesty, knowledge, destruction*. (See ABSTRACT NOUNS.) **Proper nouns** are specific names of people, places, and the like: *Jennifer Robin, Captain Maynard, Americans, Edinburgh, the Suez Canal, Monday, January, Christmas, the House of Commons, the Pentagon, the Tate Gallery, The Economist, The New York Times*. (See CAPITALS; TITLES OF BOOKS AND NEWSPAPERS; TITLES OF PEOPLE.) Nouns that are not proper nouns are **common nouns**.

    See also PARTS OF SPEECH for uses of nouns.

nouveau riche

The plural is **nouveaux riches**, pronounced in the same way as the singular. It means a crudely ostentatious newly rich person.

now

When used as an adjective before a noun, **now** is informal when it means 'existing now' (*the now president*) and even more so when it means 'excitingly up-to-date' (*now clothes*). Both should be avoided in serious writing.

no way

See WAY (3).

nowhere near

As with *nothing like*, this is rather informal. Write *not nearly ready* rather than *nowhere near ready*.

nowheres

This American word does not belong in writing. Use *nowhere*.

noxious

See OBNOXIOUS.

nth

From being a mathematical term, **nth** has passed into the phrase *to the nth degree*, which just means 'to the utmost, extremely': *boring to the nth degree*. It seems a legitimate extension of meaning.

nuclear

Pronounce it like *new clear*, not as three syllables with the last two like *circular*.

nucleus

The plural is **nuclei** or, less usually, **nucleuses**.

number

1 When it means 'several, some', **number** takes a plural verb: *There are* (not *is*) *a number of reasons against it*; *A number of them prefer tea*. When **number** is used in a sentence commenting on the size of the total, it takes a singular verb: *The number of visitors increases every year*. See AMOUNT.

2 *In number*, as in *few in number*, *twelve in number*, is VERBOSE. Use *few* or *twelve* alone.

number agreement

1	general	**9**	*one of those who*, etc
2	attraction	**10**	phrases of measure and
3	linking with *and*		quantity
4	*each, every*	**11**	introductory *there*
5	linking with *as well as* and	**12**	titles of works and cited
	other prepositions		expressions
6	linking with *or* and *nor*	**13**	*what, whatever*
7	*everybody*, etc	**14**	singular nouns in *-s*
8	*who, which, that*	**15**	*many a, more than one*

1 general

The general rule for number agreement between the subject and the verb is simple: a singular subject requires a singular verb, and a plural subject requires a plural verb: *Your letter* **has** *been forwarded to your new address*; *Your letters* **have** *been forwarded to your new address*. The number difference applies chiefly to present forms of verbs; the past form *had* is therefore used whether the subject is singular or plural: *Your letter/letters* **had** *been forwarded to your new address*. The verb *be* is exceptional in that it provides a number choice even in the past, between singular *was* and plural *were*. Most auxiliaries (eg *may, can, will*) are exceptional in another way, since they do not provide a number choice at all: *Your letter/letters* **will** *be forwarded to your new address*.

2 attraction

The number of the subject depends crucially on its noun or (if the subject is a phrase) the main noun. If another noun immediately precedes the verb, there is a danger that the verb will be falsely 'attracted' to that nearer noun, perhaps resulting in wrong number agreement. The choice is wrong in these sentences because of false attraction: *The first* **payment** *to both your clients* **were** *made on the last day of the month* (correct to *was*, since *payment* is the main noun); *The* **terms** *of the contract that you sent to my client* **has** *not met with his approval* (correct to *have*, since *terms* is the main noun).

3 linking with *and*

The subject is plural if two or more singular units are linked with *and*: *The heat and the humidity* **deter** *tourists from visiting the country during the summer*. It is plural even if *and* is absent, provided that it could be present: *The house, the garden, the view* **were** *just what they wanted*.

The subject is treated as plural when one of an implied pair of nouns is left out: *Regular and decaffeinated coffee* **taste** *the same to me* (regular coffee and decaffeinated coffee); *Both the immature and the* *precocious student* **need** *individual attention* (both the immature student and the precocious student).

On the other hand, the linked units may refer to one thing, in which case the subject is singular: *My closest colleague and best friend* **has** *recently divorced her husband* (My closest colleague is my best friend); *Her first and best essay* **has** *won a prize* (Her first essay is her best essay).

Two linked units may sometimes be viewed either as separate or as combined into one whole. According to the interpretation, the plural or the singular may be used: *Law and order* **have/has** *been re-established in the country* (both law and order/the rule of law and order); *Bread and butter* **is** *all that is provided with the tea* (bread spread with butter); *Bread and butter* **are** *sold in the shop on the corner* (both bread and butter); *Their respect and admiration for her* **are/is** *unlimited*. See AND (3).

The singular is required when *and* introduces something in parenthesis: *The head of my department – and perhaps her spouse –* **is** *expected to attend the reception*; *Your style, and even your handwriting,* **needs** *to be improved*. Whether or not *and* is present, the singular is required if the second unit is negative, the meaning being then clearly singular: *A boy, not a woman,* **is** *playing the part*.

4 *each, every*
It seems at first sight curious that linked units introduced by *each* or *every* require a singular verb: *Each room and corridor in the building* **has** *been painted in the same colour*; *Every man and woman* **is** *required to complete two years of national service*. The reason for the singular is that *each* and *every* focus on the individual units separately. Similarly, without any linking: *Each of the men/Every one of the men* **is** *required to complete two years of national service*. In contrast, a plural subject followed by *each* elsewhere in the sentence requires a plural verb in accordance with the general rule: *The employees* **were** *each given a bonus at the end of the year for increased productivity*.

5 linking with *as well as* and other prepositions
Some prepositions have a similar meaning to *and*, but the linking does not make the subject plural. They include *as well as*, *with*, *together with*, *in addition to*. The verb must be singular: *My son, as well as my daughter,* **is** *at college*. So also with other prepositions that do not resemble *and* in meaning: *One child after another* **has** *complained of the cold*; *Perseverance rather than intelligence* **ensures** *success in this type of position*.

6 linking with *or* and *nor*
There is no problem in deciding the number of the verb if both units are singular or if both are plural: *Their house or their business* **is** *in Manchester*; *Neither cats nor dogs* **are** *allowed in the building*. If the

units differ in number, the verb follows the number of the unit nearest to it: *Either my carpets or my furniture* **is** *going to be replaced this year* (singular *my furniture* is nearest); *Neither cheese nor eggs* **were** *on the menu.*

As with *and* (see (3) above), *or* may link units that refer to the same thing. The number of the verb follows the first unit: *London's green belt, or the parks and farmlands that encircle London, is gradually being eroded by major construction companies.*

7 everybody, etc

Use a singular verb with the following pronouns: *anybody, anyone, everybody, everyone, somebody, someone, nobody, no one, either, neither, each.* There is a danger of attraction to the plural when a plural noun comes between one of these pronouns and the verb; see (2) above. The singular is correct in *Neither (of the amendments)* **was** *passed*; *Each (of my friends)* **has** *sent me congratulations.* In informal style, *neither* may also take a plural verb.

Use the singular or plural with these pronouns, depending on whether a singular or plural noun is present or implied in the context: *all, none, some, half*, and other fractions. The singular is correct in *The company has ordered more coal, but none of the coal* **has** *yet arrived* (compare *The coal* **has** not yet arrived); *The town has often suffered from flooding, and this year nearly half* **is** *under water* (The town **is** under water); *Some of the merchandise sent by mail order* **was** *judged to be defective* (The merchandise **was** defective); *All the beer* **is** *warm.* On the other hand, the plural is correct in *The survivors were given a thorough medical examination, and all* **were** *without serious injury* (The survivors **were** without serious injury); *Some of the documents* **are** *missing*; *About half of the children* **were** *severely undernourished*; *None of the workers in this factory* **have** *gone on strike.* In this last sentence with *none*, singular *has* would also be correct, since *none of the workers* can be viewed as equivalent to the singular *not one of the workers* (Not one **has** gone on strike).

8 who, which, that

The relative pronouns *who, which,* and *that* have the same number as the noun or pronoun they refer back to. The singular is correct in *The civil servant who* **was** *convicted of leaking confidential documents to the press is now writing a book about the case* (The civil servant **was** convicted); *I objected to the wording of the memorandum that* **was** *circulated in our department* (The memorandum **was** circulated). The plural is correct in *The stories she wrote in her childhood, which* **were** *discovered only after her death, have now been published* (The stories **were** discovered); *Those who* **are** *convicted of driving while under the influence of alcohol or drugs should have their licences suspended for a minimum of one year.*

Which sometimes refers back to more than one word or phrase; it is then always singular: *We have not been able to persuade him to resign, which* **means** (and that means) *that we may have to face a court case.*

9 *one of those who*, etc

After expressions such as *one of those who* and *one of the few that*, choose the plural verb if the focus is on the group: *My daughter is one of those students who* **like** *to study late at night* (Some students **like** to study late at night and my daughter is one of them). Choose the singular if the focus is on the individual: *My daughter is the only one of the students in her class who* **is** *likely to obtain a distinction in English Language* (Only my daughter **is** likely to obtain a distinction in English Language).

10 phrases of measure and quantity

Plural phrases of measure or quantity may be viewed as a single unit, in which case a singular verb is used: *Five miles* **was** (That distance **was**) *as far as they went that day*; *Ten dollars* **is** (That amount **is**) *the price of the cheapest ticket*; *Ten years* **is** (That period **is**) *the maximum sentence for that offence.* Similarly: *Two hundred people* **was** (That number **was**) *all that the room could hold.*

11 introductory *there*

There is often an introductory word rather than a word meaning 'in that place'. In formal English the number of the verb depends on the subject that follows: *There* **is** *a flaw in his argument*; *There* **are** *several flaws in his argument.* Similarly in questions: **Has** *there been any serious complaint from the members?*; **Have** *there been any serious complaints from the members?*

12 titles of works and cited expressions

The title of a book, film, etc is counted as singular even though it is a plural phrase: '*Porgy and Bess*' **has** (The opera **has**) *recently been revived on Broadway*; '*Great Expectations*' **is** (The novel **is**) *to be made into a film again.* Plural titles of collections of stories, poems, etc may be viewed as either singular (a collection) or plural (individual works): '*Lamb's Tales*' **was/were** *my first introduction to Shakespeare's plays.* If an expression is mentioned as such rather than used in the normal way, it is always singular: '*Children*' **is** (The word **is**) *an irregular plural*; '*My apologies*' **was** (The expression **was**) *all he could say.*

13 *what, whatever*

Use a singular or a plural verb with *what* depending on the meaning: *What* **disturbs** *the council* **is** *the hostile attitude of many citizens towards the police* (The thing that **disturbs** the council **is**); *They live in what* **were** *once army barracks* (in places that **were** once army barracks); *What they do* **is** *no concern of mine* (Anything they do **is**).

485

Whatever as a pronoun is always singular: *You may eat whatever* **pleases** *you* (anything that **pleases** you). But *what* and *whatever* may be used before a plural noun: *You may eat what/whatever foods* **please** *you.*

14 singular nouns in -s

Some nouns ending in -*s* are often singular. *News* is always singular: *The news* **is** *good today*. Nouns denoting a field of study or activity such as *athletics, economics, gymnastics, mathematics, physics* are singular: *Physics* **is** *a prerequisite for that course*; *Athletics* **was** *their favourite subject*. But some of these nouns are plural when used in a different sense: *Your statistics* **are** *inaccurate* (Your collection of quantified data). Names of diseases, such as *measles, mumps, shingles*, are usually singular: *Measles* **is** *a highly infectious disease*. Names of games such as *billiards* and *dominoes* are singular: *Dominoes* **is** *the only game I play at home*; contrast *The dominoes* **are** *on the floor* (The individual pieces **are**).

15 *many a, more than one*

Phrases beginning with *many a* and *more than one* are plural in meaning, but are singular in grammar because the main noun of the phrase is singular. The singular is therefore correct in *Many a day* **has** *been passed in leisurely reading*; *More than one error* **was** *discovered in the wording of the document.*

See also COLLECTIVES; PERSON AGREEMENT.

numbers

1 figures or words	**3** in thousands
2 at beginning of sentence	**4** separating figures

1 figures or words

It is usual to write numbers as figures in scientific, technical, and statistical material. In other types of writing the general rule is to write small numbers as words and large numbers as figures. Small numbers are often taken to be numbers under 100 (ie numbers that can be expressed in one or two words: *fifteen* or *thirty-six*, but *110, 240*); but for many writers and printers small numbers are under 20 and for others under 10. However, do not mix figures and words (*from 15 to 100*, not *from fifteen to 100*).

2 at beginning of sentence

Write large numbers as words at the beginning of a sentence: *Three hundred people have died as a result of the floods*. If the number is long, it is better to reword the sentence so that the number does not come at the beginning: *The floods have killed 324 people.*

3 in thousands

It is usual to mark off thousands in figures by commas: *1,500*; *10,200*; *2,300,500*. In scientific and technical writing a space is generally used instead: *2 300 500*. In American English, a *billion* is a thousand million, the meaning now widely used in British English. Outside scientific and technical writing it is clearer to use *a thousand million* in British English. The traditional British term *billion* means a million million, the American equivalent being *trillion*.

4 separating figures

Since commas are used to separate thousands in figures, do not put figures next to each other that might be misunderstood as part of the same number: *The hall can hold 700, 150 of whom would have to sit on folding chairs*. Rephrase as: *The hall can hold 700, of whom 150 . . . .*

See also ADDRESSES; DATES; HYPHEN (for number compounds); MONEY; TIMES OF DAY.

numerator, denominator

They are the figures in a fraction. In 5/7, 5 is the **numerator** (the part above the line) and 7 the **denominator** (the part below the line).

numerous

This is an adjective. You can say *numerous reasons* but not *numerous of the reasons*. If you want to use the *of* construction, say *many of the reasons*.

nuptials

This is a FACETIOUS word. Prefer *wedding*.

Oo

O, oh

Oh is the usual form, except in poetic and religious contexts: *O wild west wind*; *oh dear!*. *Oh Lord* is probably an exclamation whereas *O Lord* begins a prayer. Note that **O** is usually capitalized. **Oh** is followed by a comma if it is a separate unit: *Oh, is that what you mean?.*

-o plurals

There is no fixed rule as to whether words ending in *-o* make their plural with *-s* or *-es*, but see PLURALS OF NOUNS (2).

oasis

The plural is **oases**.

oath

The plural **oaths** rhymes with *clothes*.

obeisance

The word is spelled *-ei-*, not *-ie-*. It means a respectful bow, or attitude of deference.

obiter dictum

The plural is **obiter dicta**. This LATINISM means 'an incidental remark made by a judge', or broadly 'a remark made in passing'.

object (*verb*)

One can either **object** *to* things or **object** *to doing* things, but not **object** *to do* things: *They objected to paying* (not *pay*) *the full amount.*

object, grammatical

See CASE, GRAMMATICAL.

object, objective

1 When the desired meaning is 'a strategic position to be attained', use **objective**: *military objectives.* When it is no more than 'goal' or 'purpose', prefer **object**: *The object is to avoid damaging the roots.*

2 *The object of the exercise* is a CLICHÉ.

objector

The word ends in *-or*, not *-er*.

objet d'art

The plural is **objets d'art**. It is a small article of artistic value.

obligate, oblige

They can both mean 'bind legally or morally': *She felt obligated to abide by the contract*; *He was obliged to find money for his taxes.* Avoid using **obligate** merely to express gratitude: *I am much obliged* (not *obligated*) *to you for all your help.*

obliqueness, obliquity

They are both nouns formed from *oblique*, which itself can mean either 'slanting; diagonal' or 'inexplicit': *an oblique line across the page*; *an oblique angle*; *He made an oblique reference to his colleague's rudeness.* Use **obliquity** for 'inexplicitness', and also in its own formal sense of 'moral deviousness'. It also has a specialized meaning in astronomy. Use **obliqueness** about angles.

oblivious

1 It is followed by *of* rather than *to*: *oblivious of* (not *to*) *the risk he ran.*

2 Some people maintain that **oblivious** should mean only 'forgetful', and not 'unaware'. Usually, however, the observer does not know whether the **oblivious** person has forgotten, or never knew, whatever he or she is **oblivious** of, so that the distinction is necessarily blurred. Use the word in either sense.

obnoxious, noxious

Obnoxious means 'highly unpleasant': *obnoxious smells*; *obnoxious views on race.* **Noxious** means 'injurious', either physically (*noxious industrial waste*) or morally (*noxious political doctrines*).

oboe

The player of this woodwind instrument is an **oboist**.

obscene

This word for 'repulsive and indecent' is OVERUSED as a blanket term of disapproval: *I think it's basically obscene that there is only one radio station in London putting out pop music* (a disc jockey).

observance, observation

Both nouns are formed from *observe*. **Observance** is the 'observing' of a ceremony, rule, or law: *the observance of the speed limit*; *pious observances.* **Observation** is 'observing' in the sense of 'watching and noticing', or of 'comment': *under observation at the hospital*; *a very childish observation.*

obsolescent, obsolete

Obsolescent means 'in process of going out of use'. **Obsolete** means 'no longer in use; outdated'; it is a stage beyond **obsolescent**.

obtain

This means 'gain possession of' in suitably formal contexts. Elsewhere, it can sound PRETENTIOUS, and may be better replaced by *get*: *get/obtain tickets for the ballet*.

obtrude

See INTRUDE.

obverse

See REVERSE.

obviate

To *obviate an objection* is to anticipate and dispose of it in advance. To *obviate the need for arriving early* is to make it unnecessary. The word should not be used simply for 'remove', as in *obviate difficulties*.

occasion

The word is spelled with two *c*'s and one *s*.

occupied, preoccupied

When they are used of people, **occupied** means 'busy' (*He was occupied in writing letters*), and **preoccupied** means 'absorbed in thinking about something to the exclusion of everything else' (*He was preoccupied all evening with what happened at work during the day*).

occur

1 Other forms are **occurred, occurring**.

2 It means 'happen', but do not use it in that sense where there might be a confusion with other meanings. *That would never occur to me* could mean either that it would never happen to me or that I should never think of it, but of course the meaning might be clear in the context. Like *happen*, **occur** refers particularly to unplanned events. For what is planned, prefer *take place*: *When did the accident happen/ occur?*; *When will the wedding take place?*

occurrence

In British English, the second syllable is pronounced with the short *u* of *current*, not as in *occur*. In American English, **occurrence** begins like *occur*.

ochre, ocher

This yellowish pigment is spelled **ochre** in British English, **ocher** in American English.

octavo

The plural is **octavos**. It is a size of paper.

octopus

The preferred plural is **octopuses**. The alternatives **octopodes** and **octopi** are pedantic, **octopi** being simultaneously pedantic and wrong.

oculist

See OPHTHALMOLOGIST.

odd

When it is used after a number to mean 'rather more than', as in *thirty-odd people*, there should always be a hyphen to avoid confusion; *thirty odd people* might mean 'thirty peculiar people'.

odious, odorous

Odious means 'hateful', **odorous** means 'having a smell'.

odo(u)r

1 This is spelled **odour** in British English, **odor** in American English; but words formed from it, such as *odorous* and *odorize*, never have a *u*.

2 This is the right word in the phrase *in bad odour*, meaning 'out of favour'. In its literal sense, **odour** is a GENTEELISM; prefer *smell*.

oe-

See AE-.

oedema

The word is usually spelled like this in British English, but **edema** in American English.

Oedipus

This mythological Greek monarch's name is spelled like this in both British and American English, and so is the *Oedipus complex* which is named after him. The first syllable rhymes with *weed* in British English, with *weed* or *wed* in American English.

o'er

This contraction of *over* (as in *travel o'er hill and dale*) belongs to old-fashioned poetic language (see POESY).

oesophagus

The word is usually spelled like this in British English, but **esophagus** in American English.

oestrogen

The word is spelled like this in British English, but **estrogen** in American English.

of

1 Do not write **of** for *have*: *I might have* (not *of*) *known. Have* is an auxiliary verb, as in *I have known.* The jocular *What is she a doing of?* is allowable only as a FACETIOUS imitation of Cockney grammar.

2 It has been argued that an expression such as *that long nose of his* is allowable only if he has several noses. But it clearly means 'the nose which is his', and is a well-established construction that only pedants would criticize.

3 When **of** expresses the idea of possession by people, and a noun is involved, there is a choice between, for instance, *a friend of the king* and *a friend of the king's*. The second form would not be used about inanimate things: *the crew of a liner* (not *liner's*). Sometimes there is a difference of meaning. *A picture of John* represents him, but *a picture of John's* belongs to him or was painted by him. (*John's picture* may mean any of the three.) See GENITIVE.

4 For *the most beautiful of any English cathedral*, see ANY (2). For *a boy of twelve years old*, see OLD (1).

of course

See COURSE (2).

off

1 In British English, though not in American English, it is old-fashioned to pronounce this as 'awf'.

2 Use *from*, not **off**, when something is transferred from one person to another: *I bought it from* (not *off*) *a friend*; *Take the ball from* (not *off*) *her*; *Get the answer from* (not *off*) *one of the other boys*. It is not wrong to say *claim it off tax*, where what is meant is a deduction or subtraction.

3 The combination *off of* does not belong in good writing, even where **off** itself would be correct, as in *step off* (not *off of*) *the platform*. It is used in educated American speech, but is much less acceptable in Britain.

offence, offense

The word is spelled with a *c* in British English, with an *s* in American English.

official, officious

Official means 'of one's duty and position' (*an official title*; *on official business*) or 'authorized' (*the official account*). **Officious** means 'offering unwanted help; fussy' (*officious waiters*).

offspring

The usual plural is **offspring**: *'Is she your only offspring?' 'No, we have two other offspring'* (not *offsprings*). When applied to one's children, it is a rather jocular word, but it can be used seriously to mean 'result, issue', as in *The bomb is the offspring of modern physics*.

oft

This word for *often* (as in *many a time and oft*) belongs to old-fashioned poetic language (see POESY).

often

1 In British English, though not in American English, it is old-fashioned to pronounce the first syllable as 'awf'. The *t* may be either pronounced or silent.

2 It can mean either 'frequently' (*We often go there*) or 'in many cases' (*They often die young*). Where either meaning might be understood, as in *The houses are often painted white*, rephrase as *Many of them are painted white* or *The houses are painted white at frequent intervals*.

oh

See O.

old

1 Write *a boy of twelve*, or *a twelve-year-old boy*, but not *a boy of twelve years old*. You can, however, write *The boy is twelve years old*.

2 You can say *He died of old age*, but not *at an old age*. The expression is then *at a great age*, or *at an advanced age*.

3 Although **old** chiefly means 'advanced in years', nobody misunderstands *old friend* (ie one of long standing), or *his old* (ie former) *students*. If the friend or the students are in fact elderly, you must make it quite clear in some other way.

olden, olde-worlde

They both reflect nostalgia for the past. **Olden**, as in *olden days* and *olden times*, is poetic (see POESY). The pseudo-antique spelling of **olde-worlde** is supposed to suggest picturesque quaintness, and the expression is sometimes used seriously in travel brochures (*narrow olde-worlde streets*), but its chief use is now jocular, especially when it is pronounced as if it were spelled 'oldy-worldy' (*modern hotels decorated with olde-worlde junk*).

older

See ELDER.

omelet(te)

Omelette is the commoner British spelling, **omelet** the commoner American one.

omit

Other forms are **omitted, omitting**.

on

1 on, onto. The central meaning of **on** as a preposition is to convey the idea of position (*on the table*) or state (*on holiday*). It is very often, and quite correctly, used also to convey the idea of motion, but may be less vivid than **onto**: *jump on/onto the table*. *He drove on the pavement* is, of course, different from *He drove onto the pavement*. See ONTO.

2 on, upon. **On** is either a preposition (*on the table*) or an adverb (*Now read on*). **Upon** is only a preposition, and can replace **on** only in formal contexts. It is used in the fixed phrase *once upon a time*, and in certain placenames though not others: *Stratford-upon-Avon*; *Stoke-on-Trent*.

3 On sometimes expresses relationships for which no more precise word may exist. When there is such a word, it is better to use it: *She reassured me about* (rather than *on*) *my health*; *his apathy towards* (rather than *on*) *the subject*. But how else could you express *Please phone me on 435 8862?*

4 For **on** or **in** a train or street, see IN (4).

one

1	**ones** and **one's**	**4**	singular or plural?
2	**one** or **he**	**5**	fractions
3	**one** for **I**	**6**	unnecessary **one**

1 The plural is **ones**: *We've eaten all the soft ones* (not *one's*). The genitive is **one's**: *to do one's best*. **One's** also means 'one is' or 'one has': *One's blue and one's red*; *One's got a hole in it*.

2 In British English, the indefinite pronoun **one**, meaning 'anybody', should be followed by **one, one's, oneself** (*One must do one's best*) rather than by **he, him, his, himself**. American English is more tolerant of **he** and **his** here: *One must do his best*. (This raises the further problem of whether it should be *his* or *her best*, to escape the charge of SEXISM.) It is better to avoid repeating **one's, oneself**, etc several times in the same sentence. A sentence like *One is free to do as one likes so long as one's habits do not irritate one's companions* should be rephrased to avoid clumsiness. A common alternative is to use *you* and *your*: *You are free to do as you like*. This is appropriate in all but really formal writing, but be careful that your reader or listener does not think *you* means himself or herself. Never change in midstream by writing *One is free to do as you like* or *as they like*.

When **one** is used as an actual number, it is followed by **he, she**, or **it**, not by **one** and **one's**: *One of them is scratching his nose*; *Only one in three washes her hair*.

3 It is an affectation to use **one** when you mean **I**: *One's whole ministry has been along ecumenical lines* (an archbishop).

4 Use a singular verb when the number **one** is the subject: *One in every five learns* (not *learn*) *French*; *One of the stolen cars was* (not *were*) *recovered*. But generally use a plural verb in this kind of sentence after *who, which, or that*: *He's one of those who are* (not *is*) *always grumbling*; *It's one of the hardest tasks that have* (not *has*) *been* *attempted*. Here, the verbs refer to the plurals *those* and *tasks*. See NUMBER AGREEMENT (9).

5 In writing fractions, the style *a pint and a half, a million and a quarter* is an alternative to *one and a half pints*, *one and a quarter million*. See HALF (2).

6 Where there is a choice, write *Do you want these trousers or those?* rather than *or those ones*; write *The story is not suitable* (rather than *is one not suitable*) *for children*. But this kind of **one** is sometimes needed to show the difference between singular and plural: *What nice shirts! Which one/ones shall we buy?* Here, *Which shall we buy?* might be too vague. Are we buying a single shirt, or more?

one another

See EACH OTHER (2).

oneself, one's self

It is better spelled as one word, but both forms exist.

ongoing

This is OVERUSED, particularly in the phrase *ongoing situation*. It can often be replaced by *in process* or *continuing*.

only

1 In careful speech, pronounce the *l*. It should not rhyme with *pony*.

2 The natural place for **only** in a sentence is often next to the verb. In normal speech, including the speech attributed to characters in a story, that is the place to put it: *I only met you at a party* (Iris Murdoch). When people are talking, the intonation of the sentence helps to make the meaning clear. But in formal writing, **only** should come next to the word it concerns: *Only John* (ie no one else) *saw the lion*; *John only saw* (ie he didn't shoot) *the lion*; *John saw only the lion* (ie not the tiger).

A badly placed **only** can give rise to confusion, particularly in the condensed style of public notices: *Cooked Shellfish Only In This Fridge* (ie not raw shellfish, or nothing but cooked shellfish, or no cooked shellfish anywhere else?); *This Basin Only For Cleaning Brushes* (does this mean that brush-cleaning is the only use of this basin, or that this is the only basin to be so used?). Even in a full written sentence, there may be problems: *The condition can only be alleviated by drugs* (does it mean that it can be alleviated in no other way, or that drugs can only alleviate but not cure it?).

3 In formal writing, **only** should not be used for 'but', or 'were it not for the fact that': *They look very attractive, but* (not *only*) *we cannot afford them.*

onto, on to

The relation between **onto** and *on* is the same as that between *into* and *in*, but **onto** as a single word is rather less well established. Some people still prefer to write **on to**. The rule is that when it means 'so as to be on', it may be written either as one word or two: *The cat jumped onto* (or *on to*, or just *on*) *the table*. Where **on** is an adverb meaning 'forward' or 'ahead', followed by *to*, the words must be separate: *They walked on to Berwick*; *He went on to discuss another problem.*

onward(s)

Before a noun, use **onward**: *the onward course of events*. Otherwise, use the form with *s* in British English (*from her childhood onwards*) and the one without an *s* in American English.

op. cit.

This means 'in the same book, article, etc as was mentioned before'. It is always preceded by the author's name, and usually followed by a page number: *Smith, op. cit., p. 76*. Compare IBIDEM.

operate

Surgeons **operate** *on* people; they do not, properly, **operate** them. Write *I'm afraid he'll have to be operated on* (not merely *he'll have to be operated*).

operation

The word has many legitimate uses, but its sense of 'a military manoeuvre' has been extended and OVERUSED in commerce and industry to cover any fairly large-scale business transaction: a plant or factory is called a *production operation*, a sales manager is said to be in charge of *sales operations*.

operative *(adjective)*

This is OVERUSED in the sense of 'most important, key': *She may come, and 'may' is the operative word.*

operator, operative *(noun)*

1 The word **operator** ends in *-or*, not *-er*.

2 Both **operators** and **operatives** may operate machines, but **operator** is wider in scope, since it may also be someone who runs a business: *a tour operator*. Telephone **operators** run telephone switchboards. An **operative** is usually a factory worker, but in American use the word also means 'private detective' or 'secret agent'.

ophthalmologist, oculist, optician, optometrist

A physician specializing in diseases and defects of the eye is an **ophthalmologist**, for which **oculist** is a more old-fashioned word. An **optician** makes and deals in optical goods (including, for instance, microscopes) as well as spectacles; but in Britain the word is usually taken to refer to an **ophthalmic optician** (who, though not a doctor, is qualified to test eyesight and prescribe lenses) or a **dispensing optician** (who merely supplies spectacles). **Optometrist** is an alternative word, especially in American English, for an **ophthalmic optician**.

opine

This word for 'state' or 'say' is so formal as usually to sound FACETIOUS.

opinion

The word gives rise to VERBOSITY. *In my opinion* means no more than 'I think', and *She was of the opinion that . . .* means 'She thought . . .'.

opportunity

Correctly, you *take the* **opportunity** *for doing* something (a verb), *of doing* something, or *to do* something, but you *take advantage of* something (a noun). Write *I took the opportunity of asking him*, but *I took advantage of* (not *the opportunity of*) *his visit to ask him*.

opposite

There is some confusion over prepositions after **opposite**. When the word is a noun, write *His character is the opposite of* (not *to*) *hers*. When it is an adjective, write *They live in the opposite house to* (or *from*, but not *of* or *than*) *ours*. You can also say *They live opposite us* (where it is a preposition) or *They live opposite to us* (where *opposite to* is a preposition).

optician

See OPHTHALMOLOGIST.

optimal, optimum

These words are OVERUSED to mean simply 'best': *under optimal conditions*. It is perfectly proper to use either of them for the rather complex idea of 'most favourable as the product of conflicting requirements'. The **optimum** or **optimal** size for a town reconciles the need for proper urban facilities with the desire to be near the countryside.

option

The rather VERBOSE phrase *I have no option but to* can be more concisely replaced by *I have to*.

optometrist

See OPHTHALMOLOGIST.

opus

The plural is **opera** or, less usually, **opuses**. The first syllable is usually pronounced as in *soap* rather than as in *sop*.

or

See NOR. For verbs after **or**, see NUMBER AGREEMENT (6).

-or, -our

As a rough rule, spellings such as *armor, honor, favor, color* are American and *armour, honour, favour, colour* are British; but the matter is not quite so simple.

1 Certain words, including *pallor, tremor, horror, terror*, have no *u* in either kind of English.

2 Words that retain the *u* in British English usually drop it before *-ate, -ation, -ize*, and *-ous*: *coloration; vaporize; humorous* (but *honourable, colourful*).

3 American English prefers the spelling *glamour* rather than *glamor*, and uses *honour* in certain formal contexts, such as invitations.

oral

See AURAL; VERBAL.

orate

This BACK-FORMATION from *oration* means 'hold forth pompously'. Do not use the word to mean 'make a speech' unless you intend to be a little impolite.

orator

The word ends in *-or*, not *-er*.

oratorio

The plural is **oratorios**.

orbit (*verb*)

Other forms are **orbited, orbiting** in both British and American English.

orchestrate

This is a technical term in music, meaning 'to compose or arrange for an orchestra'. By extension, it now often means 'organize for maximum effect': *to orchestrate a pressure group*; *a carefully orchestrated campaign*.

ordeal

It is usually, but not always, pronounced with the stress on *deal*.

order

1 After *in order that* use *may* or *might*, or sometimes *shall* or *should*, but not *can*, *could*, *will*, or *would*: *He spoke slowly in order that they might* (not *could*) *follow him*. But the phrase can easily be replaced by *so that*, or less formally by *so* alone, and these are not subject to the restriction.

2 *In order to* is rather formal. It is often better replaced by *so as to* or merely by *to*: *Jack and Jill went up the hill to* (rather than *in order to*) *fetch a pail of water*.

3 *In/on/of the order of* are phrases with a technical use in connection with *order of magnitude*, which means a range extending from some value to ten times that value. In ordinary use, as in *something of the order of five thousand people*, they are a VERBOSE way of saying 'about'.

orderly

Apart from its noun sense (*a hospital orderly*), this is usually used only as an adjective, not as an adverb, even though it ends with **-ly** like *quickly* and *easily*. An *orderly person* behaves in an *orderly way*, but should not be said to behave **orderly**. There is no word *orderlily*.

order of words

The order in which you place words or longer units is likely to have an
effect on meaning, clarity, or emphasis. See ADVERBS, POSITION OF;
AMBIGUITY; CLARITY(4, 10); CORRELATIVE (2); INVERSION.

ordinance, ordnance, ordonnance

An **ordinance** is an authoritative decree or enactment: *a positive
ordinance . . . that there should be no sketching till lessons were done*
(Arnold Bennett). **Ordnance** is artillery and military supplies.
Ordonnance is both an old word for **ordinance**, and also the
systematic arrangement of a literary or artistic work: *There are design
and ordonnance in it* (C Day Lewis).

orient, orientate

The two words mean exactly the same thing. **Orient** is the main form,
with **orientate** a variant more prevalent in British than in American
use. Both are greatly used, even OVERUSED, not so much in the literal
sense of 'cause to face the east' (*orient a church*) as loosely for 'direct
towards' (*humanistically oriented scholars*) or 'adjust to the
surroundings' (*help school leavers to orient themselves in the working
environment*).

orifice

Except in really formal writing, replace this PRETENTIOUS word by the
more direct *hole* or *opening*.

origin of words

1 original vocabulary	5 compounding
2 borrowings from foreign languages	6 from proper names
	7 onomatopoeia
3 borrowings from other varieties of English	8 mistakes
4 derivation	9 inventions

1 original vocabulary

The Germanic tribes that settled in Britain in the 5th and 6th centuries
(traditionally identified as Angles, Saxons, and Jutes) brought with
them the dialects of German that they had spoken in their home
territories (thought to be in parts of what are now Germany and
Denmark). As far back as the earliest written records in the language
(dated about 700) their language was called English, a name derived
from that of the tribe of the Angles. Many of the basic words in our

language are Germanic, retained from the early English period; for example, *man*, *woman*, *child*, *father*, *mother*; *home*, *house*, *room*, *bed*, *door*; *body*, *head*, *arm*, *leg*, *foot*; *eat*, *drink*, *be*, *have*, *go*, *come*; *and*, *but*, *if*, *so*, *yet*; *day*, *night*, *week*, *month*, *year*; *bread*, *milk*, *meat*, *fish*.

2 borrowings from foreign languages

English has always been hospitable to words borrowed from other languages. The largest number of borrowings have come from Scandinavian, French, and Latin. Scandinavian words came into English after Scandinavian invaders settled in the north and east of England in the late 9th century; common borrowings from Scandinavian include *are*, *birth*, *call*, *egg*, *ill*, *skin*, *sky*, *they*. The Norman Conquest in 1066 led to the replacement of English by French as the language of the royal court and the upper classes for about three centuries. Towards the later part of this period thousands of French words entered English, among them *government*, *parliament*, *court*, *tax*, *crime*, *prison*, *army*, *peace*, *dress*, *city*, *honest*, *nice*, *poor*, *real*, *safe*. Latin was the normal language for learned and official writing in England until well into the 17th century. When English came to replace Latin for this purpose, numerous words were borrowed from Latin (some through French) and to a lesser extent from Greek (usually through Latin or French); these generally belong to the learned vocabulary. The establishment of British colonies in various parts of the world introduced words from the languages of peoples with whom the colonists were in contact, such as *bungalow* and *canoe*. Finally, cultural influences have contributed numerous words to English from dozens of other languages; nowadays these borrowed words are spread rapidly through the mass media. See FOREIGN PLURALS for nouns that still show their foreignness by their plural forms.

3 borrowings from other varieties of English

There are differences in the vocabularies of the various English-speaking countries, though these are relatively minor in proportion to the total vocabulary that is common to all English speakers. Words and phrases from one English-speaking country are sometimes adopted by the others. American English has been particularly influential on other national varieties during this century. Words may also be borrowed into the standard language from local dialects or from slang (eg *fun*, *mob*, *snob*, *jazz*).

4 derivation

Derivation, in the technical sense, is the creation of a new word from an existing word. New words are frequently derived from existing words by the addition of a prefix (eg *hypersensitive* from *sensitive*; *unwind* from *wind*; *coexist* from *exist*) or a suffix (eg *terrorist* from *terror*; *employee* from *employ*; *noisy* from *noise*). A very common type of derivation is **conversion**, where there is no change in the form of the word (eg the verb *service* from the noun *service*; the noun *hit* from the verb *hit*; the verb *back* (as in *back the car*) from the adverb *back*). An infrequent type of derivation is **back-formation**, where what was thought to be a suffix was removed to form a new word (eg *edit* from *editor*; *televise* from *television*; *enthuse* from *enthusiasm*).

5 compounding

New words are frequently formed by combining existing words to form *compounds* (eg *paperback*, *ghostwriter*, *outpatient*). These often contain Latin or Greek roots, sometimes combined with established English roots or with English prefixes or suffixes (eg *hologram*, *hydroplane*, *stereophonic*). When parts of the words are combined, the resulting words are **blends** (eg *smog* from *smoke* and *fog*; *brunch* from *breakfast* and *lunch*; *telex* from *teleprinter* and *exchange*). When initial letters of words or parts of words are combined, the resulting words are **acronyms** (eg *LSD* from **l**y**s**ergic **a**cid **d**iethylamide; *TV* from **t**ele**v**ision; *radar* from **ra**dio **d**etection **a**nd **r**anging). Some compounds are **clipped** (eg *photo* from *photograph*), though not all clipped words are compounds (*flu* from *influenza*).

6 from proper names

A name of a person or place may give rise to a new word, called an **eponym**. Examples are *bikini*, *boycott*, *lynch*, *pasteurize*, *sandwich*. This is an infrequent source of new words, as are the sources that follow.

7 onomatopoeia

The sounds of some words are felt to suggest their meaning, eg *burp*, *chatter*, *hiss*, *squelch*. Some are **reduplicatives**, compounds that consist of identical or nearly identical elements, eg *tick-tock*. Reduplicatives commonly suggest movement or more abstract notions such as instability or nonsense, eg *flip-flop*, *hocus-pocus*, *gobbledygook*, *wishy-washy*. Many children's words are reduplicatives, some used only within a particular family.

8 mistakes

The forms of a few words are due to popular etymology, mistaken beliefs in the origins of the words, eg *help-mate* (from *help meet*), *shamefaced* (from *shamefast* 'shame-fixed'), *bridegroom* (from *bridegome*; the obsolete *gome* meant 'man'). In some instances a faulty division of words has added *n* from the indefinite article *an* to the beginning of the word (eg *newt*, *nickname*) or removed the *n* from the word because it was wrongly thought to belong to a preceding *an* (eg *adder*, *umpire*).

9 inventions

Comparatively few words are complete inventions (though some onomatopoeic words may be; see (7) above). Among recent inventions are *googol* (term in mathematics) and *quark* (term in physics).

See also CHANGE OF MEANING for new meanings.

orphan

Although there is no other word for a child who has lost only one parent, an **orphan** will usually be taken to have lost both. It is not at all clear, either, at what age people are too old to be called orphans. It is thus rather a vague word. You can use *fatherless* or *motherless* if you have to be more specific.

orthop(a)edic

This is usually spelled with the *a* in British English, without it in American English. See AE-.

oscillate, osculate

To **oscillate** is to move to and fro like a pendulum. **Osculate** is a FACETIOUS word for *kiss*.

ostensible, ostentatious

1 Ostensible ends in *-ible*, not *-able*.

2 Ostensible means 'professed, declared': *The ostensible purpose of the procession was to celebrate their independence, but it was really a public demonstration against the regime*. It means more than 'apparent', since it implies a deliberate intention to conceal something, so write *the apparent* (not *ostensible*) *similarity of the two hotels*. It should not be confused with **ostentatious**, which means 'deliberately conspicuous; showing off': *She took an ostentatious interest in local affairs*.

other

1 Other is correctly followed by *than*, not by *but* or *except*: *in any other country than* (not *but*) *ours*; *I could do no other than* (not *except*) *climb the wall*. (Alternatively, you can say *in any country but ours* or *I could do nothing except climb the wall*.) Except in formal writing, though, it is reasonable to use **other** . . . *from* like *opposite* . . . *from*: *They live on the other side of London from us*.

2 Careful writers use *otherwise than* rather than **other** *than* for the meaning 'in any other way than': *We can't get there otherwise* (not *other*) *than by swimming*. See OTHERWISE (1). Similarly, *apart from*, *aside from*, or *in other respects than* is better here: *He has a slight headache, but apart from* (not *other than*) *that he's feeling fine*.

3 When **other** means 'additional', it introduces more things of the same kind. We say *John and three other boys*, or *John and three* (not *three other*) *girls*. Although this may seem obvious enough, writers of longer sentences often go wrong in this respect: *Plato, Jesus, Marx, Lenin, Mao, Hitler and the numerous other nationalist demagogues of the last hundred years . . .* (Ferdinand Mount). Not all the historical figures mentioned have lived in the last hundred years, nor are they all nationalist demagogues.

4 See EACH OTHER. For *any other*, see ANY (2). For *on the other hand*, see CONTRARY (2).

otherwise

1 Just as **otherwise** *than* should be preferred in certain circumstances to *other than* (see OTHER (2)), so *other than* should be preferred to **otherwise** *than* where the sentence requires an adjective: *How can I be other* (not *otherwise*) *than grateful?*

2 The combinations *and* **otherwise**, *or* **otherwise** are often used like *and not*, *or not*: *mothers, both married and otherwise*; *The question turns on her capacity or otherwise to understand the instructions*; *Please confirm or otherwise your intention to come.* Conservative writers of English have argued that because **otherwise** is an adverb it should be linked in this way only to another adverb, such as *rightly* in *He decided, rightly or otherwise, to refuse.* But the linking of **otherwise** to words other than adverbs (here, *married, capacity*, and *confirm*) is too common in good writing to deserve continued censure. Those who dislike the *or* **otherwise** construction can generally escape it by using a negative or opposite form (here, *and unmarried, or incapacity, or deny*).

ottoman

See SOFA.

ought

1 The negative of **ought** is correctly expressed by *ought not*: *You ought not to/oughtn't to do it.* The question form is as in *Ought we to tell him?* The combinations *didn't ought* and *hadn't ought* are incorrect. Write *I ought to ask, oughtn't I?* (not *didn't I?*).

Some people nevertheless find these negative and question forms too formal. Knowing that they must avoid *didn't ought* and *hadn't ought*, they escape the dilemma by using *should* instead: *You shouldn't have done it*; *Should I go?* The solution is not entirely satisfactory, because *should* expresses a somewhat weaker sense of moral 'obligation' than **ought**.

2 Ought should be followed by *to*: *He ought to* (not merely *He ought*) *and could have told me*. See ELLIPSIS. *You ought not go* is an American regionalism.

ours

This means 'the one belonging to us': *The house became ours* (not *our's*).

ourselves

See REFLEXIVE.

out

The use of **out** as a preposition like *out of* (*The cat jumped out the window*) is standard in American English, but in British English is felt to be either American or rather informal. Compare OUTSIDE OF.

outcome

It is TAUTOLOGOUS to write *The outcome of the strike will lead to a decline in our exports*. Either the **outcome** will *be* a decline, or the *strike* will *lead to* one.

outdoor, outdoors

Before a noun, use **outdoor** or **out-of-door**: *outdoor games*. After a verb, use **outdoors**, or **out of doors**: *to go outdoors/out of doors when it's raining*.

outfit (*verb*)

Other forms are **outfitted, outfitting** in both British and American English.

outgoing

It is somewhat OVERUSED in the sense of 'warm and responsive'. **Outgoing** people are good at getting on with other people; in other words, they are *friendly* or *sociable*.

outré

The word is spelled with the accent. It means 'violating convention, eccentric'.

outside of

The situation is the opposite of that for *out the window*; see OUT.

Outside of is common and almost standard in American English, but British English much prefers **outside** to be used alone as a preposition: *standing outside* (not *outside of*) *the door*; *observers outside the industry*.

outstanding

1 This can mean 'unsettled': *left several bills outstanding*; or 'distinguished': *a really outstanding student*. To avoid ambiguity in a sentence such as *Some of the results are outstanding*, use *still outstanding* for one meaning and some word like *remarkable* for the other.

2 Things either are **outstanding** (in either sense) or they are not. It seems tautologous to refer to *one of the world's most outstanding ski resorts*. Even if *most* were omitted here, the praise would be fervent enough.

outward(s)

Before a noun, use **outward**: *the outward voyage*. After a verb, use the form with *s* in British English (*to peer outwards*), and the form without *s* in American English. Note also the combination *outward-bound*.

outwit

Other forms are **outwitted, outwitting**.

over

It is perfectly reasonable to use **over** for 'more than', as in *over £10*. Do not use the word for comparisons involving a decrease: *a considerable reduction from* (or *on*, but not *over*) *last year's price*.

overall

This is OVERUSED as an adjective meaning 'including everything, comprehensive': *the overall result*; *an overall reduction*. It can usually be replaced by *total, general, as a whole*, etc, or simply omitted.

overflow, overfly

Overflow has the past tense and participle **overflowed**, and refers mostly to water: *The river overflowed its banks*; *The meeting overflowed into the corridor*. **Overfly** has the past tense and participle **overflew, overflown**, and refers to aircraft: *The bomber overflew enemy territory*.

overlay, overlie

The past tense and participle of **overlay** are **overlaid**, **overlaid**; those of **overlie** are **overlay**, **overlain**. They mean, as one might suppose, 'lay over' and 'lie over' respectively, and are as easily confused as *lay* and *lie* themselves; see LAY. Compare: *She overlaid* (ie covered) *the primer with a thin undercoat*; *The sandstone overlies* (ie lies over) *the coal*. Both verbs are used indiscriminately in the sense of suffocating a baby by lying on it: *The sow overlay/overlaid her piglets*.

overlook

This can mean not only 'fail to notice' but also, and quite correctly, 'supervise'. If there is any danger of confusion between these two almost opposite senses, do not use the word at all, but prefer *neglect* or *disregard* for the first and *oversee* for the second.

overly

This means 'excessively' in both American and Scottish English. There is nothing wrong with it, but alternatives to *overly cautious* and *overly zealous* are *overcautious*, *overzealous*, and even *too cautious*, *too zealous*.

oversight

This can mean not only 'inadvertent error' but also, and quite correctly, 'supervision'. The second sense is of course related to *oversee* and is used here: *The Home Office (in England and Wales), the Scottish Home and Health Department, and the Northern Ireland Office are responsible for the general oversight of electoral law* (HM Stationery Office).

overtone, undertone

They both mean that something has more in it than is apparent. While an **overtone** is an additional secondary effect (*the unpleasant overtones of his speech*), an **undertone** is usually an unexpressed communal state of mind (*undertones of pessimism in the City*).

overused words

There are fashions in words, as in anything else. Though there is nothing necessarily wrong with these fashionable words, it is a mark of the insensitive writer to use them too frequently and indiscriminately. The words may start their life as slang, or as technical terms, or as academic or bureaucratic jargon, and then find their way into journalism and advertising copy. When they have been with us long enough, they become burnt-out CLICHÉS.

A selection from the many words referred to in this book as OVERUSED, perhaps only in particular senses, will show what we mean.

angle	obscene
astronomical	ongoing
ballgame	operation
case	overall
crash	parameter
escalate	permissive
feedback	situation
image	spectrum
input	syndrome
integrate	target
low profile	traumatic
marginal	viable
motivate	-wise

ovum

The plural is **ova**.

owing to

Modern convention allows **owing to** to be used as a preposition meaning 'because of': *Owing to the fog we missed the train*. (All the same, it is better not to write the longwinded *owing to the fact that* instead of *because*.) See DANGLING PARTICIPLE, and for **owing to** and *due to* see DUE TO.

Pp

-p-, -pp-

Words ending in *-p* double the *-p-* even when a word of more than one syllable is not fully accented on the last syllable, if that last syllable has some degree of accent. Such words therefore disobey rule (2) given under DOUBLING. Thus, *handicap(ped)*, *horsewh   d)*, *sideslip(ped)*; but *gossip(ed)*, *gallop(ed)*. *Worship* makes *worshipped*, *worshipper* in British English, but can also make *worshiped*, *worshiper* in American English.

package

Both the noun and the verb are useful with reference to things that must be accepted or rejected as a whole: *a package holiday*; *to package a TV series*. The sense is well established.

pact

This chiefly means an international treaty (*nonaggression pact*), but in journalese the word is used for any kind of agreement.

paean, peon

A **paean** is a hymn of praise or triumph. A **peon** is a farm labourer in Spanish America, or an Indian or Sri Lankan soldier or messenger.

p(a)ed-

Words formed from **p(a)ed-**, meaning 'child', are chiefly spelled with the *a* in British English (*paediatric*; *paedophilia*) but without it in American English.

pair

1 The commoner plural is **pairs** rather than **pair**: *two pairs* (rather than **pair**) *of shoes*; *several pairs* (rather than **pair**) *of skis*. Always use **pairs** in those rare cases where no number or other word precedes it to show that it is plural: *Pairs of socks should be pinned together.*

2 When it means 'two people', **pair** takes a plural verb: *The happy pair are just leaving for their honeymoon.*

pajamas

See PYJAMAS.

pal(a)eo-

Words formed from **pal(a)eo-**, meaning 'old', can be spelled with or without the second *a*.

palate, palette, pallet

The **palate** is the roof of the mouth, or the sense of taste: *Dry wines suit my palate.* An artist mixes paints on a **palette**, and the word is also used of an artist's range of colour, and even of the range of available elements in some nonvisual art such as music. Among other things, a **pallet** is a platform for storing or moving things on in a warehouse, or a temporary bed.

palpable

This means 'capable of being touched', but also 'perceptible by the intelligence; manifest': *a palpable lie*. In this sense it is a vivid though perhaps bookish word, suggesting that the lie is so obvious that one could physically touch it. It could be confusing to use it of things that could in another sense be really touched, such as *palpable rubbish*.

pampas, prairie, savanna(h), steppe, veld(t)

They are all words for grassy plains: the **pampas** in South America, the **prairie** in North America, the **steppe** in eastern Europe and Asia, and the **veld** or **veldt** in southern Africa. **Savanna** or **savannah** is tropical grassland anywhere, but particularly in Africa.

panacea

This means a cure for all diseases, both literally and figuratively. One can refer to *a panacea for our economic problems*, but not to *a panacea for flu* or *a panacea for boredom*. These ills are too specific.

pandemic

See ENDEMIC.

pander

To **pander** *to* people or their desires is to provide gratification for them: *The audience is vulgar and stupid, you've got to pander to them* (Herman Wouk). A person who does this is a **panderer** or a **pander**, but as the noun **pander** preserves its earlier literal sense of a 'pimp' or 'go-between', **panderer** is probably the safer choice.

pandit, pundit

They are alternative spellings of the same Hindi word. Use **pandit** as a Hindu title (*Pandit Nehru*), but **pundit** as a slightly irreverent word for 'critic, authority': *We did what all the pundits said was impossible*.

panel (*verb*)

Other forms are **panelled**, **panelling** in British English, but the second *l* is usually omitted in American English.

panic (*verb*)

Other forms are **panicked**, **panicking**.

pants, knickers, panties, trousers, underpants, shorts

In British English, **pants** or **underpants** are a man's undergarment, and the equivalent for women is called **knickers**, **panties**, or **pants**; **trousers** are a man's outer garment, and the equivalent for women is **trousers** or **pants**. In American English, the man's undergarment is called **underpants** or **shorts**, and the equivalent for women is **panties**; **pants** are a man's or woman's outer garment. **Knickers** in American English are short trousers gathered at the knee, not an undergarment at all.

pantsuit

See SUIT.

papier-mâché

The word is spelled with the accents.

paradigm

Besides having a technical meaning in grammar, this is an OVERUSED word for 'pattern' or 'model' or 'archetype' or 'framework of argument'; to *overthrow the conventional paradigm* is to set up a whole new range of possibilities that changes all the rules. Unless that is really what you mean, steer clear of the word.

paradise

The usual form of the related adjective is **paradisiacal**, but **paradisiac**, **paradisaic**, **paradisaical**, and **paradisal** also exist.

paraffin

See KEROSENE. **Paraffin** has one *r* and two *f*'s.

paragraphs

The end of a paragraph provides a resting-place for readers, a place at which they can pause. Modern taste favours short paragraphs, to provide more resting-places. Good paragraphing can make the structure of the writing easier to follow by grouping sentences that are more closely connected. There can be no precise rules for deciding on paragraph breaks, except that the break should not separate sentences that are more closely connected than the other sentences that are next to them.

Paragraphs are usually indented (set in from the edge of the page) in handwritten and printed material, except that in print the first paragraph of a chapter or section is usually not indented. Especially in typewritten material and computer printouts, there is the alternative convention of leaving a line between paragraphs, but it should be noted that this convention does not make it clear when a paragraph begins on a new page.

parallel

1 The word is spelled with two *l*'s, then one. Other forms of the verb are **paralleled**, **paralleling**, in both British and American English.

2 Lines and surfaces are said to be **parallel** *with*, or **parallel** *to*, each other.

parallelism

Parallelism brings together words or larger units that are alike grammatically, to focus on their similarity or contrast in meaning. It promotes economy and clarity, and introduces a pleasurable rhythm. The closer the units are in their form, the greater the balance in the parallelism. Here are some examples:

> We here highly resolve that . . . government *of the people*, *by the people*, and *for the people*, shall not perish from the earth. (Abraham Lincoln's Gettysburg address)

> One trusts *one's lawyer*, *one's doctor*, *one's priest*, I suppose. (Graham Greene)

> I was impressed and oddly touched by this hulking, powerful man, *so domineering and yet so insecure, so overwhelming and yet so vulnerable*. (Henry Kissinger)

> She was *a bit thin*, *a bit bony*, but she walked well. (Paul Scott)

> *We shall fight* on the beaches, *we shall fight* on the landing grounds, *we shall fight* in the fields and in the streets, *we shall fight* in the hills; we shall never surrender. (Winston Churchill)

> And so, my fellow Americans: *ask not what your country can do for you – ask what you can do for your country*. (John Kennedy's inaugural address)

See also CORRELATIVE; ELLIPSIS.

paralyse, paralyze

The word is spelled **paralyse** in British English, **paralyze** in American English.

paralysis

The plural is **paralyses**.

parameter, perimeter

Parameter has technical senses in mathematics and statistics. In more general but still correct use, it means a measurable factor among others, as when one says that temperature, pressure, and density are **parameters** of the atmosphere. This has developed into a vague OVERUSE of the word where *limit*, *scope*, *boundary*, or sometimes *characteristic* would do perfectly well, as in *We must work within the parameters* (use *limits*) *of time and budget*. In this loose sense it can be confused with **perimeter**, which is literally the outer edge or circumference of something: *the perimeter fence round the airfield*; *beyond the perimeter of my field of vision*.

paramount

It means 'supreme, primary'. If something is *the paramount issue* it is not merely an important one but the most important.

paraphernalia

This can take not only a plural verb but also a singular one, particularly in the informal sense of 'complicated rigmarole': *All the paraphernalia of getting planning permission is taking longer than we expected*.

paratroops

A member of the **paratroops** should be called a **paratrooper**, not a **paratroop**.

parcel (*verb*)

Other forms are **parcelled**, **parcelling** in British English, but the second *l* is usually omitted in American English.

pardon

This is sometimes thought to be a GENTEELISM when used as an apology or a request for repetition. Instead of **Pardon!** or *Pardon me?* you can say *I'm sorry!* or *What did you say?*

parenthesis

The plural is **parentheses**. The related adjective is **parenthetic** or **parenthetical**. See also BRACKETS.

pariah

This is usually pronounced to rhyme with *Isaiah*; the pronunciation rhyming with *carrier* is old-fashioned and chiefly British. It means an outcast.

parlay, parley

The noun **parlay** is American English for the type of bet that the British call an *accumulator*, and the related verb to **parlay** can mean 'to exploit successfully': *tried to parlay this Russophobia into a parliamentary career* (*Newsweek*). A **parley** is a discussion of disputed points, particularly of proposed terms with an enemy, and to **parley** is to hold such a discussion.

parlo(u)r

The word is spelled **parlour** in British English, **parlor** in American English. It is a rather old-fashioned word except in such combinations as *beauty parlour*, *funeral parlour*, and the US *parlor car* (a luxurious railway carriage).

parlous

Outside suitably formal contexts (*the parlous state of international relations*) this is rather a FACETIOUS word. Use *dangerous* or *hazardous*.

parricide, patricide

Parricide is the murder of either of one's parents, or of a near relative. **Patricide** is specifically the murder of one's father.

parson

See PRIEST.

part

1 *On the part of* is VERBOSE; use *by* or *among*.

2 *Part and parcel* is a CLICHÉ.

3 See PORTION.

partake

To **partake** *of* something is to take a share of it. You can *partake of* someone else's supper, or a meal in company with others, but it is silly to say *I partook of a solitary cup of coffee*. The word may in any case seem rather PRETENTIOUS in this sense, though less so in the sense 'have some attributes of': *The story itself ceases to be melodramatic, and partakes of true drama* (T S Eliot).

partial

This can mean either 'biased' or 'not total'. A sentence such as *He offers a partial solution to the problem* is ambiguous, so replace **partial** here by *biased* or *prejudiced*, or else by *incomplete*, according to which you mean.

participle

See DANGLING PARTICIPLE.

particular

This is a word that can often be left out, to the benefit of the sentence. You usually lose little or nothing by writing *this house* instead of *this particular house*, *in my case* instead of *in my particular case*, and *the person I mean* instead of *the particular person I mean*.

particularly

In careful speech all five syllables should be pronounced. There are two *l*'s in the word.

parting

The parting of the ways is a CLICHÉ.

partly, partially

Where either word will do, prefer the more ordinary **partly**: *It's only partly* (rather than *partially*) *painted*. There is a slight difference of meaning here. **Partly** is particularly appropriate to material things or places, meaning 'in part': *It's partly wood and partly plastic*; *He lives partly in London and partly in Paris*. **Partially** is suitable for conditions, and means 'to some degree': *partially blind*. To say that a meal is **partly** cooked suggests that some of its components are cooked and others are not; to say that it is **partially** cooked suggests that all of it is undercooked. Avoid **partially** where it might erroneously be taken to mean 'in a biased way', as in *I can advise you only partially* (use *in part* here).

parts of speech

Words are classified into **parts of speech**. There is more than one way of classifying words, and the classes can also be divided into subclasses.

Four of the classes are readily open to additions of new words: nouns, full verbs, adjectives, and adverbs.

(1) noun
It is chiefly used as the main (or only) word in a phrase functioning as subject (*The* **attempt** *was unsuccessful*), object (*Take your* **dog** *away*), subject complement (*Their most profitable crop is* **coffee**), or complement of a preposition (*This is for* **Gloria**). Nouns can also modify other nouns (*a* **staff** *meeting*).

(2) full verb
It is the main (or only) verb in the verb phrase: *He* **laughed** *at the idea*; *I am* **going** *now*; *We have been* **thinking** *about you*; *Norman will* **help** *you*; *The office has been* **redecorated**.

(3) adjective
It is chiefly used to modify a noun (*a* **new** *member*; *the* **former** *president*) or as subject complement (*Her solution was* **elegant**; *My decision is* **final**). Most adjectives are easily distinguishable from nouns because they can be modified by *very*: *very simple*, *very pleasant*, *very interesting*. (But see GRADABILITY.)

(4) adverb
The adverb class is the most miscellaneous. Adverbs are chiefly used to modify adjectives (**very** *comfortable*, **quite** *clever*, **economically** *feasible*), other adverbs (**very** *quickly*, *often* **enough**, **more** *leisurely*), verbs (*dressed* **carelessly**, *played* **well**, *smoked* **incessantly**), clauses or sentences (**Luckily**, *no one was hurt*; *there will*, **however**, *be an official inquiry*).

(5) auxiliary verb
It is used before the full verb as part of the verb phrase to convey notions such as time, possibility, permission, obligation: **has** *taken*, **will** *go*, **may** *tell*, **must** *write*. Auxiliaries may be combined: **may be** *calling*; **has been** *informed*; **should have been** *playing*. When an auxiliary is used by itself, the full verb is understood from the context: *Everybody has signed, and you* **should** *too* (should sign).

(6) pronoun
It is a subclass of the noun, generally used as a substitute for a noun (or its equivalent) to avoid repetition: *she*, *they*, *itself*, *yours*, *this*, *any*, *each*, *which*. Some pronouns can also refer directly to people or things (**That's** *my dog*, said while pointing at a dog), and some (in particular the pronoun *I*) are always used that way.

(7) preposition
It links its complement – a noun (or its equivalent) – to another part of the sentence: *in*, *at*, *for*, *without*, *across*. The complement generally

follows the preposition: *in Edinburgh, for you, without any doubt, across the road, by saying that.* Some prepositions are combinations of words: *owing to, because of, in spite of.*

(8) conjunction

It generally links one **clause** to another clause: *You take one* **and** *I'll take the other; They will take you* **if** *you are ready; We know* **that** *she approves.* Some conjunctions (particularly *and* and *or*) also link parallel words or phrases: *him* **and** *her; your brother* **or** *your sister.*

(9) determiner

It introduces a noun or noun phrase, coming before adjectives or adjective phrases (if any): **that** *house,* **my** *best subject,* **any** *early reports,* **some** *extremely attractive proposals.* Many dictionaries classify most determiners as adjectives.

(10) article

It is a subclass of the determiner. There are two articles: the definite article (*the*) and the indefinite article (*a, an*).

(11) demonstrative

Demonstratives may be used either as pronouns (**This** *is the best*) or determiners (**This** *method is the best*). There are four demonstratives: *this, that, these, those.*

(12) possessive pronoun

There are two sets of possessive pronouns. One set is used as determiners: *my, your, his, her, its, our, their* (*Here is* **your** *coat*). The other set is used as pronouns: *mine, yours, his, hers, ours, theirs* (*Is this* **yours**?); they are used independently, not introducing a noun phrase.

(13) interjection

It is a class of emotive words that are not part of the structure of the sentence: *oh! ah! ouch! boo!* Some grammarians include in this class exclamatory greetings, oaths, and the like: *Hello! Cheers! Blast! Hear, hear!*

(14) numeral

The class of numerals divides into the cardinal numerals (*one, ten, fifty-two, three thousand*), ordinal numerals (*first, tenth, twenty-first*), and fractions (*a half, two-thirds, nine-tenths*). There are also the three multipliers: *once, twice,* and the somewhat archaic *thrice.*

Many words belong to more than one class. *Attempt* is a noun in *The attempt was unsuccessful,* but a verb in *I would not attempt it; well* is an adjective in *She looks well,* but an adverb in *She plays well; past* is an adverb in *He strolled past,* but a preposition in *He strolled past our house; after* is a preposition in *I left after lunch,* but a conjunction in *I left after the meeting ended.* See CONVERSION.

See also GRAMMATICAL ANALYSIS.

party

This can mean a single person in legal and quasi-legal contexts: *a party to the transaction*; *the guilty party*; *the injured parties*. Elsewhere, the use of **party** in this sense is jocular: *He is a shameless and determined old party* (Winston Churchill). In serious use, write *Several people* (not *parties*) *were detained in hospital*.

pass

See MEET.

passable, passible

These are different words, not variant spellings. **Passable** means either 'tolerable' (*a passable meal*) or 'capable of being travelled on' (*roads were barely passable*). The rarer word **passible** means 'able to feel or suffer'. They sound the same in American English; but those British speakers who pronounce *pass* with a long 'a' use that sound in **passable,** while rhyming the *pass* of **passible with** *ass*.

passé

The word is spelled with the accent. It means 'out-of-date; faded'.

passed, past

Passed is the past tense and participle of the verb to *pass*: *We passed the house*; *She has passed her exam*. **Past** is an adjective, as in *the past fortnight*; or a preposition, as in *They drove past the house*; or an adverb, as in *The bus went past without stopping*; or a noun, as in *memories of the past*. People sometimes confuse the adjective **past** with the participle **passed.** Compare: *The day was past* (ie adjective); *The day has passed* (ie verb); *Because of the long time already passed* (ie that has passed), *it is too late to do anything*; *Time present and time past* (ie that is past) *Are both perhaps present in time future* (T S Eliot).

passerby

The plural is **passersby**.

passive

We recommend the active unless there is good reason for using the passive. Excessive use of the passive makes writing more difficult to understand because it reverses the more natural order of subject–verb–object (active *My secretary will answer your questions*) for an order in which the subject and object switch places (passive *Your questions will be answered by my secretary*), so that the active object becomes the passive subject. The active order of subject-verb-object commonly follows the natural order of meaning: agent (doer of the action) – action – person or thing affected by the action.

A useful occasion for the passive is when we do not know the agent (the doer of the action) or when we want to repress mention of the agent. Thus when:

(1) The identity of the agent or agents is unknown: *Many substances* **have been shown** *to cause cancer in animals.*

(2) The identity of the agent is not important: *I* **have been told** *that Chinese is a difficult language for Americans to learn.*

(3) The identity of the agent is obvious from the context: *Our golden retriever would not allow other dogs into his territory. Once a Doberman pinscher trespassed onto our land and* **would have been killed** *if I had not intervened.*

(4) The writer wants an impersonal tone: *In one experiment, pregnant rats* **were allowed** *to deliver their pups and to nurse them for four weeks.* In scientific and technical writing, writers often use the passive to place the emphasis on processes or experimental procedures. The passive allows the writer to avoid the constant repetition of *I* or *we* as subject, and it contributes to the objective tone that many scientists wish to convey. Nevertheless, it is preferable to reduce the heavy frequency of the passive in such writing. The subject *we* is particularly appropriate when the writing represents the work of a team.

(5) The writer wishes to avoid mentioning the agent: *The refrigerator door* **has** *not* **been** *properly* **closed**. The reason may be to avoid assigning responsibility in order to be polite or tactful. But the motivation may be more reprehensible – to avoid accepting responsibility for an assertion or falsely to suggest that an opinion is held generally: *It* **has been suggested** *that the government is not negotiating in good faith.*

But there are occasions when it is convenient to use the passive while expressing the agent (with a *by*-phrase). For example:

(1) to place emphasis on the agent of the action: *He refused to vote for Ron Tulworth as leader, and he was privately and publicly scourged for that decision* **by his former comrades**.

(2) to avoid a long active subject: *The city is governed* **by a Democratic mayor and a city council that is divided equally between Democrats and Republicans**.

(3) to retain the same subject in a coordinated clause: *The chairman proposed changing the rules for admitting new members, but he was overruled* **by the rest of the committee** (also . . . *but was overruled* **by the rest of the committee**).

past

1 See PASSED.

2 It is TAUTOLOGOUS to speak of *past history* and *past athletic records* unless there is reason to contrast them with those of the present or future.

pastor

See PRIEST.

pasty

See TART.

pâté

The word is spelled with the accents. It is used both for a rich savoury paste and for a small pie.

patent

In British English the first syllable often rhymes with *hat* in technical contexts: *the Patent Office*; *to file a patent*; *to patent an invention*; but it usually rhymes with *hate* in non-technical contexts (*patent leather*; *patent medicine*) and in the general sense of 'readily visible': *her patent dislike of the scheme*. American speakers tend to prefer the *hat* pronunciation.

pathos

See BATHOS.

patio

The plural is **patios**.

patricide

See PARRICIDE.

patrol (*verb*)

Other forms are **patrolled, patrolling**.

patronize

Since this can mean 'treat with condescension', it should be used only with caution in its other meaning of 'be a customer of', as when you **patronize** a hairdresser or greengrocer.

paucity

This formal noun means 'fewness' or 'smallness': *the paucity of help accorded to me* (Rudyard Kipling). It can seem PRETENTIOUS, and is better replaced by *small amount*, *scarceness*, or some phrase with *few*, *small*, or *little*.

pavement

In British English this means the surfaced walk for pedestrians beside a road; the American English word for this is *sidewalk*. In American English **pavement** means the surface of a road. Some international confusion may be caused by instructions not to walk, or alternatively not to park, on the **pavement**.

pay

1 The past tense and participle are both **paid**, except in the nautical sense. You can (but need not) write *We payed out the rope*.

2 The idioms are *pay attention (to)*, *take notice (of)*. Do not write *He paid no notice*. One may either *pay heed to* something, or *take heed of* it.

peaceable, peaceful

1 Peaceable is spelled like this, retaining the final *e* of *peace*.

2 Peaceable usually applies to people or their intentions, meaning 'not inclined to quarrel; quietly behaved': *peaceable citizens going about their business*. **Peaceful** can mean 'without physical violence' (*peaceful demonstration*) or can suggest a state of rest and tranquillity: *a peaceful rural scene*.

peal, peel

The ringing of bells is a **peal**; the skin or rind of a fruit is the **peel**. The medieval fortified towers along the Scottish–English border are **peel** *towers*.

peasant

Do not call country people in modern English-speaking countries **peasants.** The word is not a reliable translation for some similar words in other European languages, which imply a better social status.

peccadillo

It means 'a trifling offence'. The plural is either **peccadillos** or **peccadilloes.**

pecuniary

This formal and perhaps PRETENTIOUS adjective can usually be replaced by some phrase with *money*.

ped-

See P(A)ED-.

pedal, peddle

1 Other forms of **pedal** as a verb are **pedalled, pedalling** in British English, but the second *l* is usually omitted in American English.

2 To **pedal** is to use a foot pedal, or to ride a bicycle. To **peddle** is to sell from place to place: *peddling dope*. **Peddle** is a BACK-FORMATION from **peddler,** which is the usual spelling for someone who pushes drugs and is also the American spelling for **pedlar.**

pee

Although nobody seems to mind pronouncing the *P* of PTO or of MP as 'pee', some British hearers dislike it as the spoken form of *p* meaning *penny* or *pence*. To escape criticism, say *pence* for the plural and *one penny* for 1p.

peel

See PEAL.

peer, pier

1 To look closely at something is to **peer** at it. A **peer** is a nobleman, or an equal. A **pier** is a landing place, or a support for a bridge.

2 Your **peers** are your equals and not your superiors, so that something **peerless** has no equal, not merely no superior. *Peer group* is sociological jargon for a set of people equal in age or status, but it is perhaps the only short way to express that idea.

peeve

As both a verb meaning 'irritate' and a noun meaning 'a grudge', this BACK-FORMATION from *peevish* is too informal for serious writing.

pejorative

This is usually pronounced with the stress on the second syllable, rather than on the first. It means 'disparaging, derogatory'.

pellucid

This formal and perhaps rather PRETENTIOUS word can usually be replaced by *clear* or *transparent*.

pen *(verb)*

This is FACETIOUS. Instead of *pen an epistle*, prefer *write a letter*.

pencil *(verb)*

Other forms are **pencilled, pencilling** in British English, but the second *l* is usually omitted in American English.

pendant, pendent

The noun meaning a hanging ornament is usually **pendant**. The adjective meaning 'hanging' (*pendent icicles*) is usually **pendent**.

pending

Convention permits the use of this formal word not only as an adjective meaning 'not yet dealt with', as in *decisions still pending*, but as a preposition meaning 'while awaiting': *The decision was delayed pending further information*. See DANGLING PARTICIPLE. If the word seems PRETENTIOUS in the context, recast the sentence so as to be able to use *until*.

pendulum

The plural is **pendulums**.

peninsula(r)

Peninsula is the noun and **peninsular** is the adjective: *the Peninsular War*.

penman, penmanship

These refer to handwriting, not to authorship. It is FACETIOUS to call an author a **penman**.

penny

The plural of the British monetary unit is **pence** when you speak of a sum of money (*The ticket cost 40 pence*), but **pennies** with reference to the coins themselves (*a heap of pennies*). When it means a US or Canadian cent, the plural is always **pennies**.

peon

See PAEAN.

people

1 This replaces **persons** as the usual plural of **person**, at least in British English: *There were 400 people at the wedding*. Some American writers, more conservative in this respect, prefer to use **persons** where a number is mentioned, particularly a small number (*Seven persons were killed*), and **people** only for an indefinite group, as in *Some people don't like it*. In British use **persons** is very formal, and appropriate only to legal contexts (*murder by a person or persons unknown*) or with reference to the Christian Trinity (*God in three Persons*).

2 When **people** means 'a group united by a common culture', it is an ordinary singular noun with a regular plural: *the peoples of Africa*. In this sense, the singular as a COLLECTIVE may take a plural verb (chiefly) in British English: *a nomadic people who follow their herds*. In all its other senses, **people** is treated as plural: *These people are busy*; *The people have rebelled against the nobles*.

per

This is appropriately used in formal contexts where it means 'for each': *£60 per head per week*; although the same idea can quite well be expressed by *a*, as in *an apple a day*. The use of **per** for 'by means of' (*send it per rail*) or 'according to' (*per list price*; *as per my letter*) should be confined to business English.

peradventure

As an adverb it means 'perhaps', and as a noun it means 'a doubt, chance': *without the vestige of a peradventure*. Either way, this is an archaic word.

per annum, per capita, per diem

They mean, respectively, 'for each year', 'for each person' (*the highest income per capita*), and 'for each day'. Where possible, use the English equivalents *a year*, *a head*, *a day*.

perceive

The word is spelled *-ei-*, not *-ie-*.

per cent, percentage

1 Per cent (two words) is the usual British spelling, **percent** the American one. The symbol is %.

2 If 0.5% is expressed in words as *point five per cent* it may sound too technical, but some people dislike the formulation *half a per cent*. A good alternative is *half of one per cent*.

3 An expression such as *increase the rate from 3 to 5 per cent* may mean that it is now 3% and will become 5%, or that it is to be increased by a proportion somewhere between 3% and 5%. Spell it out carefully, according to which you mean: either *from 3% to 5%* or *by 3–5%*.

4 Per cent and **percentage** are followed by a singular or plural verb according to the noun concerned: *30% of her income goes in rent*; *30% of the children live in Cambridge.*

5 Do not use *a* **percentage** to mean 'some', as in *The method has been successful in a percentage of cases*. A **percentage** is more than 'none'. It may be more than 'all', since 300% is also a **percentage**. To achieve more precision, write *a small* or *a low percentage*, or *a large* or *high percentage*. Or use plain English and write *some*, *a few*, *many*, or *most*. Compare PROPORTION.

perceptible, perceptive, percipient, perceptual

What one can *perceive* is **perceptible**: *a perceptible change in her tone*. **Perceptive** means 'able to *perceive* keenly': *a perceptive scholar*. **Percipient** is a rarer formal word for **perceptive**. **Perceptual** is a learned term meaning 'of sensory experience'.

perchance

This word meaning 'perhaps' belongs to old-fashioned poetic language, as in Hamlet's *To sleep, perchance to dream.*

percolator

The word ends in *-or*, not *-er*.

per contra

It means 'on the other hand; by way of contrast'. Where possible, use the English equivalents.

père

This is spelled with the accent. But use *senior* except with reference to a Frenchman: *Dumas père*. It distinguishes a father from a son (eg *Dumas fils*) of the same name.

peregrinations

This is a FACETIOUS word for *travels*.

peremptory, perfunctory

1 Peremptory is usually pronounced with the stress on the second syllable, not the first.

2 Peremptory means 'dictatorial': *a peremptory command*. **Perfunctory** means 'cursory, superficial': *gave it a perfunctory glance*.

perennial

See ANNUAL.

perfect

Since there can presumably be no degrees in perfection, some people think it absurd to say *more perfect*, *most perfect*, *very perfect*, *less perfect*, or *least perfect*. The combination *more perfect* seems better established than the others, as when the US Constitution refers to *a more perfect union*, but it may still arouse comment. There can be no objection to *nearly perfect*.

perfectible

The word ends in *-ible*, not *-able*.

perfect infinitive

The perfect infinitive is correctly used to refer to a situation occurring before that indicated by the main verb: *I should like* (now) *to have met them* (yesterday); *We seem to have made a mistake*. When the situation of the main verb is in the past there is often no need for the perfect infinitive: *They appeared to like us*; *She wanted to live in London*. The perfect infinitive is justified, however, when the situation it indicates happened earlier: *They appeared to have found the mistake*. If the main verb has the perfect *have*, there is a tendency to repeat the *have* by using the perfect infinitive: *She would have liked to have lived in London, but she couldn't afford the rent*. The tendency should be suppressed; correct to *She would have liked to live in London, but she couldn't afford the rent*. Similarly, write *I should have liked to meet them if I had known that they were in town* (not *I should have liked to have met them*).

527

perfunctory

See PEREMPTORY.

perhaps

It is perfectly normal to pronounce it 'praps' in rapid Southern British speech. American speakers are less likely to do this; probably because, like the Scots, they usually pronounce *r* before *h*.

peril, perilous

These can sound FACETIOUS. If in doubt, use the more ordinary *danger, dangerous*.

perimeter

See PARAMETER.

period

1 This is VERBOSE in such expressions as *for a period of ten years*, or *a short period of time*. Write *for ten years*; *a short time*.

2 The adjective **period** means, vaguely, 'of more than half a century ago': *period costume; a period décor*. It is almost meaningless unless you specify which period.

period (*punctuation mark*)

See FULL STOP.

periodic(al)

Both **periodic** and **periodical** can mean 'recurring at regular intervals': *periodic(al) outbreaks of flu*. **Periodic** is used with reference to a measured literary style (*periodic sentence*) and in such scientific terms as *periodic acid, periodic function, periodic table*. **Periodical** (adjective and noun) is the word for magazines published at fixed intervals.

periphrasis

See CIRCUMLOCUTION.

permanence, permanency

Both words, particularly **permanence**, mean 'the quality of being permanent'. In addition, a **permanency** is 'something permanent': *Her new job isn't a permanency*.

permeate, permute

To **permeate** something is to penetrate or diffuse through it: *a room permeated with tobacco smoke*. To **permute** something is to arrange it in all possible different ways, as with teams in the football pools.

permissible, permissive

1 Permissible ends in *-ible*, not *-able*.

2 Permissible means 'allowed, not prohibited'. **Permissive** means 'allowing, tolerant'. **Permissive** is OVERUSED in the sense of 'accepting a relaxed social and sexual morality': *the permissive society*; *parents who are too permissive*.

permit

1 Other forms are **permitted**, **permitting**.

2 In sentences like this, *of* is optional: *the facts permit (of) no other explanation*.

3 It can seem PRETENTIOUS to use **permit** where *let* will do, as in *permit them to go home*.

perpendicular, vertical

They both mean 'at right angles to the horizon': *the perpendicular/vertical descent of a waterfall*. **Perpendicular**, rather than **vertical**, also mens 'at right angles to a given line or surface'. A line or plane can be **perpendicular** without being **vertical**, if it is at right angles to something not horizontal.

perpetrate, perpetuate

To **perpetrate** is to commit (something bad): *Terrorists perpetrated another outrage*. To **perpetuate** is to cause to continue: *to perpetuate a noble tradition*. The related nouns are **perpetrator**, **perpetuator**.

perquisite, prerequisite

Perquisite is the formal word for *perk*, an incidental extra gain or profit: *perquisites such as the use of a company car*. A **prerequisite** is a requirement that must be satisfied in advance: *Physical stamina is a prerequisite for success in politics*.

per se

It means 'in itself or oneself; as such': *I don't enjoy driving per se*. Use the English equivalents, or nothing at all.

persecute, prosecute

To **persecute** is to harass and cause to suffer, usually because of race, religion, or political beliefs: *The Nazis persecuted the Jews*. To **prosecute** is to institute legal proceedings against: *Trespassers will be prosecuted*. The related nouns are **persecutor**, **persecution**; **prosecutor**, **prosecution**.

persistently

See CONSISTENTLY.

person

1 This has become a popular word in the vocabulary of feminism, to replace *man* in such expressions and slogans as *the man in the street* or *one man, one vote*. Combinations such as *salesperson*, *congressperson*, and *draughtsperson* have come into use, partly because of the official policy both in Britain and in the USA of devising nonsexual job descriptions, and partly, as with *sportsperson*, to avoid the implication that women are excluded. It is noticeable, however, that a woman is more likely to call herself a *chairperson* or *spokesperson* while a man appointed to the same position will often use *chairman* and *spokesman*.

Such jokes as *personhole* for *manhole*, *snowperson* for *snowman*, and *Personchester* for the city of Manchester are invented not by the feminist movement but by its detractors. See FEMININE FORMS.

2 For the plural **persons**, see PEOPLE.

persona

Personae (plural) are the characters in a play, novel, or other fictional work, as used in the expression *Dramatis Personae*. In Jungian psychology the **persona** means the social façade reflecting someone's public role, in contrast to the person's private character. The word is OVERUSED in this sense, whose plural is either **personae** or **personas**.

persona (non) grata

Persona grata means 'personally acceptable', and **persona non grata** is the opposite. These phrases are used in English like adjectives, and should properly have no plural form: *They'll be persona grata on the committee with their fund-raising experience*; *Her new book made her persona non grata with the Russians*. But use these LATINISMS sparingly.

personage, personality, VIP

They are all important people. A **personage** is more likely to be a member of the royal family, a **personality** (the commoner word) a celebrity in the entertainment world, and a **VIP** a high official.

person agreement

The verb must agree with the subject where the verb makes person distinctions. There are three grammatical persons and they interact with the distinction in number between singular and plural:

1st person (person or persons addressing): singular *I*; plural *we*

2nd person (person or persons addressed): *you*

3rd person (person or persons referred to): singular *he*, *she*, *it*, and all singular nouns; plural *they* and all plural nouns

For all verbs other than the verb *be*, the 3rd person singular pronouns *he*, *she*, and *it*, like singular nouns, take the form in *-s* (*She* **manages** *the business*), while the other personal pronouns, like plural nouns, take the form without *-s* (*I/We* **manage** *the business*). The verb *be* has a three-fold person distinction in the present tense (1st person singular: *I* **am** *ready*; 3rd person singular: *She/He/It* **is** *ready*: others: *We/You/They* **are** *ready*).

When two or more items are linked by *or*, *either* . . . *or*, or *neither* . . . *nor*, there may be a conflict over which form of the verb to choose. In such cases, you may choose the form that agrees with the last item: *Either you or I* **am** *likely to be nominated*; *My wife or I* **am** *responsible for what happened*; *Neither I nor anyone else* **blames** *you*. However, it is better to avoid the conflict by rephrasing the sentence: *Either you or I will probably be nominated*; *Either my wife is responsible for what happened or I am*; *I do not blame you, nor does anyone else*.

personal, personally

Personal is VERBOSELY used in such combinations as *personal charm*, *personal friend*, *my personal opinion*. So is **personally** in the sense of 'as far as I am concerned': *Personally, I don't think much of it*. It is reasonable to use **personally** for 'not through a deputy' (*attend to the matter personally*) or for 'directed against a person' (*Don't take my remarks personally*).

personalty

This legal term means 'personal property', ie moveable or temporary possessions (goods or money). For all the other senses of *personal*, the related noun is *personality*.

personate, personify

See IMPERSONATE.

personnel

This is either a body of people employed somewhere, or the division of an organization concerned with the welfare of the employees. The word should not be used with a definite number, as in *six personnel*, but only with reference to an indeterminate group: *All the personnel have studied the regulations*. It originated in the armed forces (*RAF personnel*), and in civilian life is rather a stiff word. Apart from its second sense (*personnel department*; *personnel manager*), it is often better replaced by *staff*, *employees*, or just *people*.

perspective, prospective

Perspective is the way solid objects in space are represented on a flat surface. By extension it means 'aspect; relationship': *see events in their historical perspective*. **Prospective** means 'likely to happen or be': *the prospective benefits of this law*; *a prospective mother*.

perspicacious, perspicuous

These are both formal words. **Perspicacious** means 'able to discern clearly, astute'. The noun is *perspicacity*. **Perspicuous** means 'plain to the understanding, clear'. The noun is *perspicuity*. A **perspicacious** person (or argument) is intelligent; a **perspicuous** argument (or person) is comprehensible.

perspire

This is a GENTEELISM for *sweat*.

persuasion

It is correct though rather old-fashioned to use this word about a particular religious belief: *of the Protestant persuasion*. The extension to mean 'kind, description', as in *gentleman of the racing persuasion*, is FACETIOUS.

[persue]

This is an incorrect spelling of **pursue**.

pertain

This verb is common in the formal style of dictionaries, where *perceptive* may be defined as *of or pertaining to perception*. In more general use it may sound PRETENTIOUS, and be better replaced by *belong* or *refer to*. Books *pertaining to* birds are books *about* birds.

peruse, perusal

In formal use, **peruse** means 'study in detail': *peruse a contract*. It can seem PRETENTIOUS or FACETIOUS to use **peruse** and **perusal** merely for *read* and *reading*.

perverse, pervert

Perverse means 'obstinate, wrongheaded'. **Perverted** means 'corrupt', often in a sexual sense.

peseta, peso

In English, the stressed second syllable of **peseta** usually rhymes with *gate*, although the Spanish pronounce it like *set*. The **peseta** is the monetary unit of Spain and Andorra. The **peso** (plural **pesos**) is the unit of Bolivia, Chile, Colombia, Cuba, the Dominican Republic, Guinea-Bissau, Mexico, the Philippines, and Uruguay.

petite

This French adjective is used in English only in its feminine form, never as the masculine *petit*, and always of women or of certain feminine accessories. It is, for instance, the term for a clothing size for small women.

petit four

The plural is usually **petits fours**, but **petit fours** is sometimes used. They are small fancy cakes or biscuits.

petrel, petrol

A **petrel** is a kind of seabird. **Petrol** is the British word for the petroleum product which is called gasoline in American English.

phalanx

The plural is either **phalanxes** or **phalanges** when it means a body of troops or close-ranked mass of creatures, but always **phalanges** when it is a bone of the finger or toe.

phantasy

See FANTASY.

pharisaic(al)

Either form is correct; note the *-ai-* spelling. It refers to the *Pharisees* in the Bible, and also means 'hypocritically self-righteous'.

pharmacop(o)eia

The spelling with *o* before *e* is the only British and the chief American one.

pharynx

The plural is either **pharynges** or **pharynxes**. See LARYNX.

phase, phrase

A **phase** is a stage in something; part of a sequence. A **phrase** is a short expression, a group of related words, and the term is also used of a group of musical notes. Since groups of words or notes often form part of a sequence, there is some danger of using **phrase** for **phase**: the next *phase* (not *phrase*) *in our development programme*. See also FAZE.

phenomenon

The singular is **phenomenon**; **phenomena** is its plural (except in the sense 'exceptional person or thing', where **phenomenons** is more usual). Write *this phenomenon*, but *these* (not *this*) *phenomena*.

Philippines

The word is spelled with one *l* and three *p*'s.

philology

See GRAMMAR.

philtre, philter

The word is spelled **philtre** in British English, **philter** in American English. It means a love potion, and is not a grander spelling for the *filter* through which gas, liquid, etc are passed.

phobia

See MANIA.

Phoebe, Phoenician, phoenix

All three words are spelled *-oe-* in American as well as in British English.

phone

This is standard as a CLIPPED form of *telephone*, and should not be spelled *'phone*. It is still rather informal when it stands for *earphone* or *headphone*.

phonetics

See GRAMMAR.

phon(e)y

It is usually spelled **phoney** in British English, **phony** in American English; and is too informal for serious writing.

phonograph

See GRAMOPHONE.

photo

The plural is **photos**. This CLIPPED form of *photograph* is rather informal.

phrasal verb

See PREPOSITION (3).

phrase

See PHASE.

phrases

There are five kinds of grammatical phrases:

(1) noun phrase: *a rather chilly day for this time of the year*. (The main word *day* is a noun.)

(2) verb phrase: *should have been working*. (The main word *working* is a full verb.)

(3) adjective phrase: *far more comfortable*. (The main word *comfortable* is an adjective.)

(4) adverb phrase: *very pleasantly*. (The main word *pleasantly* is an adverb.)

(5) prepositional phrase: *in the sun*. (The introductory word *in* is a preposition; *the sun* is a noun phrase.)

See GRAMMATICAL ANALYSIS; PARTS OF SPEECH.

phylum

The plural is **phyla**. It is the technical word for a major division in the classification of plants, animals, or languages.

physic, physique

Physic is an old-fashioned word for a medicine, especially a laxative, and also survives in a few phrases (*Regius Professor of Physic*) as an archaic word for the science of medicine. One's **physique** is one's bodily makeup.

physician, physicist

1 Technically, the word **physician** should be used of a medical doctor who is not a surgeon. It can sound rather PRETENTIOUS to use it in everyday situations where *doctor* would do.

2 A **physician** is concerned with medicine, a **physicist** with physics.

physiognomy

This is FACETIOUS when it means 'features' or 'face', but the word is more often used figuratively: *the physiognomy of a political party*.

pianissimo

The plural is either **pianissimi** or **pianissimos**.

piano

As the name of the musical instrument (with the plural **pianos**), this is pronounced with the short *a* of *man*; but as a musical instruction to play softly, with the long *a* of *father*.

piazza

It rhymes with *hats a* or *dads a* in British English, with *has a* or *pa's a* in American English. The plural is sometimes **piazze** when it means a square in an Italian town, but always **piazzas** when it is an American word for a verandah or porch, or a British word for a covered passageway.

pibroch

This is a kind of music for the Highland bagpipe. It is not a musical instrument.

picaresque, picturesque

A **picaresque** novel, such as Henry Fielding's *Jonathan Wild*, deals with the career of a rogue. The commoner word **picturesque** means 'quaintly charming' (*picturesque village*) or 'vivid' (*picturesque language*).

piccolo

The plural is **piccolos**. It is a small flute.

pick

As a noun this can mean 'choice' (*take your pick*) or 'best' (*the pick of the students*), but these senses of the word should be avoided in serious prose. Write *take your choice* and *the best of the students*. The verb **pick** is similarly less formal than *choose* when their meanings coincide, but it suggests a more random selection: *pick the most expensive restaurant; choose the most appropriate course of action*.

picket (*verb*)

Other forms are **picketed**, **picketing** in British as well as in American English. The related noun is **picketer**.

picnic (*verb*)

Other forms are **picnicked**, **picnicking**. The related noun is **picnicker**.

pictures

See CINEMA.

pidgin, pigeon

A **pidgin** is a mixed language used for trade between people with different native languages. The bird is a **pigeon**, and that spelling is also used in the informal expression *not my pigeon*, where the word means 'business, duty'.

pie

See TART.

piebald, skewbald

There is some vagueness here; but a black and white horse is usually called **piebald**, a brown and white one **skewbald**.

pièce de résistance

This is spelled with the accents and the plural is **pièces de résistance**. It means 'a showpiece' or 'the chief dish of a meal'.

pied-à-terre

This is spelled with the accent, and the plural is **pieds à terre**. It means 'a secondary or temporary lodging'.

pier

See PEER.

pigeon, dove

They are the same bird, but **dove** is the word preferred in poetical and symbolic contexts, and as part of the names of certain pigeons such as the *stock dove* and *turtledove*. See also PIDGIN.

pigmy

See PYGMY.

pilaf

Probably this is the commonest spelling, but this Oriental rice dish also figures on menus as **pilaff**, **pilau**, **pilaw**, and **pilao**.

pilaster, pillar

They are both upright columns. A **pilaster** is usually rectangular in section and is embedded in the face of a wall. A **pillar** has no lateral support, can be any shape in section, and either supports something or stands alone as a monument.

pilot (*verb*)

Other forms are **piloted**, **piloting**.

pincers, pliers

Both are tools for grasping things. **Pincers** have rounded jaws with a circular space between them. The jaws of **pliers** are long and somewhat tapering, and can bend and cut wire.

Pinyin

This is a way of writing Chinese in Roman characters, phonetically spelled. It is now the officially recommended spelling for international use, and is becoming common in Western writing. In the **Pinyin** system, for instance, the city formerly referred to as *Peking* becomes *Beijing*, *Canton* is *Guangzhou*, the river *Yangtze* is the *Chang Jiang*, and the political leader *Mao Tse-tung* is *Mao Zedong*.

piqué, piquet

Piqué, usually spelled with the accent, is a fabric. It is pronounced 'PEE-kay' in British English and 'pi-KAY' in American English. **Piquet** is a card game, pronounced 'pi-KET' or 'pee-KAY'.

pistachio

The plural is **pistachios**.

pistil, pistol, pistole

A **pistil** is the female part of a flower. A **pistol** is a firearm. A **pistole** was a former Spanish gold coin.

pitiful, pitiable, piteous

They can all mean 'deserving pity', but are not otherwise quite interchangeable. If you mean 'shameful', choose **pitiful** or perhaps **pitiable**: *pitiful wages*; *a pitiable hulk of the man he once was*. If you mean 'lamentable', choose **pitiable**: *The poor old man was in a pitiable condition*. The rarer **piteous** often means 'seeking pity': *piteous cries for help*. **Pitiful** has also the archaic sense of 'feeling pity'.

place

1 As a verb, **place** is more formal than *put*. It has several senses where *put* would be wrong, including the American English one of 'come in one of the top places in a competition': *This horse placed in several races last year*; but do not use it where *put* will do.

2 Careful writers use *where* rather than **place** in the American English combinations *anyplace*, *everyplace*, *no place*, *someplace*. *Go places* is informal, both in its literal sense and when it means 'succeed'. Use *succeed* in writing.

plague

Other forms of the verb are **plagued, plaguing**; the related adjective is spelled either **plaguey** or **plaguy**.

plaid, tartan

A **plaid** (pronounced 'plad') is, correctly, a length of tartan fabric worn over the shoulder as part of Highland dress. Outside Scotland **plaid** is often used loosely for **tartan**, which is a Scottish textile design patterned to designate a particular clan. **Tartan** fabric can be made into **plaids**, kilts, and various other garments.

plain, plane

As nouns, both words can mean 'a flat surface', but a **plain** is only an area of flat country. **Plane** is used of a level surface in mathematics, and also of a more abstract 'level': *on a high intellectual plane* (not *plain*). Use the spelling **plain** in the expression *plain sailing*, meaning easy unobstructed progress: *Once that is solved the rest will be plain sailing*. **Plane sailing** was the original form of the phrase, but it now seems very pedantic.

plaintiff, plaintive

A **plaintiff** starts a civil legal action. **Plaintive** means 'melancholy, mournful'.

plan

1 In formal writing, prefer the construction *plan to do* something, rather than *plan on doing* it.

2 Plan and **planning** give rise to a number of TAUTOLOGOUS expressions. Since plans refer to the future, it is usually unnecessary to say *future plans* or *advance planning*. However, it is reasonable to speak of plans that one expects to make in the future as *future plans*, in contrast with *present plans* ('plans currently held') and *past plans* ('plans held in the past').

plantain

This is the name of two unrelated plants. The **plantain** of temperate latitudes is a wild plant and common garden weed, with spikes of tiny brownish flowers. The tropical **plantain** is a kind of banana, a staple food.

plastic

The first syllable is usually pronounced to rhyme with *gas*. The British pronunciation like *plaster* is now old-fashioned.

plateau

The plural is either **plateaus** or **plateaux**.

platonic

Platonic love was originally conceived by Plato as a love ascending from feeling for the individual to the contemplation of the universal. It came later to mean nonsexual affection between people of opposite sexes. This has since given rise to a use of the adjective **platonic** for 'nominal, theoretical', so that one can speak of a nation as taking purely **platonic** action over some issue rather than proposing to fight about it. The sense is now established. Sir Herbert Beerbohm Tree said of an actress: *I don't like her. But don't misunderstand me: my dislike is purely platonic*.

platypus

The plural is **platypuses** or, less usually, **platypi**.

plausible

The word ends in *-ible*, not *-able*.

plc

This is an ACRONYM for *public limited company*. Since the 1981 Companies Act, which implemented a directive of the European Community, it distinguishes British companies which are eligible to be listed on the Stock Exchange from those which are not. Formerly, both public and private British companies were merely *limited*, or *Ltd*.

plead

1 The past tense and participle are **pleaded**. The alternative past tense **pled** or **plead** (pronounced 'pled') is an American or Scottish variant.

2 In law one *pleads not guilty*; one does not *plead innocent*.

pleasantry, pleasantness

A **pleasantry** is an agreeable remark or little joke. The quality of being pleasant is **pleasantness**.

please

The expressions *please find* (*Enclosed please find our latest report*) and *please be advised that* (*Please be advised that your order is now ready*) are old-fashioned business English. The first can be replaced by *Here is* or *I enclose*, and the second omitted altogether.

pleasure

The idea of 'I am glad to do this' can be formally expressed by *I have the pleasure of* . . . or by *I have pleasure in* . . . , and you can politely reply, when thanked: *It's a pleasure*; or *my pleasure*. (These replies are alternatives to the American *You're welcome*.) But since one's **pleasure** may be understood to mean one's 'wish' or 'desire' (*detained during Her Majesty's pleasure*), you must say *I had pleasure in attending* (not *It was my pleasure to attend*) *the centenary celebration*. It is reasonable to speak of someone else's **pleasure** in the sense of 'wish': *Is it your pleasure that I sign the minutes as correct?*

plebiscite, referendum

1 The last syllable of **plebiscite** is pronounced like either *sit* or *site*.

2 Both words mean a vote by all the people of a district or country. In practice, **plebiscite** has been used particularly of a vote to choose a ruler or a form of government, while a **referendum** may be held on any measure put to the electorate.

plectrum

The plural is either **plectra** or **plectrums.** It is the small object for plucking the strings of a guitar, lute, zither, etc.

plenitude

This can seem a rather PRETENTIOUS word for *plenty* or *abundance*. The form *plentitude* is incorrect.

plenteous

This us a formal word, somewhat evocative of old-fashioned poetry. Prefer *plentiful*.

plenty

This is a noun, also used informally as an adjective or adverb. In writing, use **plenty** *of* for the adjective: *plenty of midges on the moor*; *plenty of work to be done* (not *plenty midges* or *plenty work*). Replace the adverb by *quite* or *very*: *quite* (not *plenty*) *warm enough*; *very* (not *plenty*) *hungry*.

plethora

This is a superfluity, not merely a large number or quantity, and is used disparagingly: *a plethora of trivial regulations*. For a more neutral effect, use *plenty*.

pliers

See PINCERS.

plough, plow

Plough is the British spelling, **plow** the American.

plurality

See MAJORITY.

plurals of nouns

1 words ending in *-y*	**6** words ending in *-f* or *-fe*
2 words ending in *-o*	**7** singular words ending in *-s*
3 compounds	**8** plural only
4 letters and figures	**9** animal names
5 proper nouns	

1 words ending in *-y*

If the word ends in a consonant plus *y*, form the plural by changing the
y to *i* and adding *-es*: *cry*, *cries*; if a vowel comes before the *y*, simply
add *-s*: *tray*, *trays*. Words ending in *-quy* are an apparent exception in
that they end in *-ies* (*soliloquy*, *soliloquies*), but the vowel *-u* is merely
an automatic spelling partner of *q*. Names ending in *-y* form their
plurals in *-ys*: *the Kennedys*; *the two Germanys*. Two compounds
ending in *-by* likewise have plurals in *-ys*: *lay-bys*; *stand-bys*.

2 words ending in *-o*

Most words ending in *-o* form their plurals in *-os*: *radio*, *radios*. A few
end in *-oes*: *domino*, *dominoes*; *echo*; *embargo*; *go*; *hero*; *Negro*; *no*;
potato; *tomato*; *torpedo*; *veto*. Some others may end in either *-os* or *-oes*, eg *cargo*; *innuendo*; *motto*. If you are in doubt, the safest method
is to use *-os* except for the few listed above that form their plurals only
in *-oes*. See also Italian plurals under FOREIGN PLURALS.

3 compounds

Most compounds pluralize only the last word of the compound: *book
reviews*; *cigar smokers*; *killer sharks*; *window-cleaners*; *word-
formations*; *boat-rides*; *songwriters*; *food-deliveries*. The first words in
most of these particular examples refer to more than one thing (cleaners
of windows; smokers of cigars), but nevertheless do not have a plural
form. The same generally applies to compounds expressing a quantity
that modify a following noun: *a three-mile race*; *a two-day conference*;
a ten-pound note. Notice also the plural in the last part of *gin-and-
tonics* and *whisky-and-sodas*. Compounds ending in an adverb
generally add *-s* to the end: *close-ups*; *stand-ins*; *push-ups*; also *lay-bys*

and *stand-bys* under (1) above. Words ending in *-ful* usually take their plural at the end: *spoonfuls*; *cupfuls*; *mouthfuls*; but the first part may take the plural instead (*spoonsful*).

Some compounds pluralize only the first part. They include compounds ending in a prepositional phrase (*grants-in-aid*), those with a personal noun followed by an adverb (*passers-by*), and those borrowed from French that end in an adjective (*notaries public*). Other examples: *commanders-in-chief*; *rights of way*; *heirs presumptive*; *listeners-in*. Some French borrowings allow the plural on either part: *courts martial*, *court martials*; *attorneys general*, *attorney generals* (and other compounds ending in *general*): *poets laureate*, *poet laureates*. Compounds ending in *-in-law* pluralize the first part in formal writing: *mothers-in-law*; *brothers-in-law*; but may take a regular plural informally: *mother-in-laws*; *brother-in-laws*.

A few compounds pluralize both parts. They refer to people, and their first part consists of *man* or *woman* (*men doctors*; *women doctors*) or contains those words (*gentlemen farmers*).

4 letters and figures
The plurals of letters and figures are formed by adding *s*: *B.A.s*; *I.O.U.s*; *1980s*. There is no need for an apostrophe before the *s*, unless there is danger of confusion: *Dot your i's*; *She has three A's*.

5 proper nouns
The plurals of proper nouns (names) end in *-s*: *the Robinsons*; *the Joneses*. Do not add an apostrophe after the *s*.

6 words ending in *-f* or *-fe*
Some words ending in *-f* or *-fe* make their plural in *-ves*: *calves* (less commonly *calfs*); *elves*; *halves*; *knives*; *leaves*; *lives*; *loaves*; *-selves* (for words ending in *-self*; eg *themselves*); *sheaves*; *shelves*; *thieves*; *wives*; *wolves*. A few have either *-ves* or the regular plural: *dwarfs*, *dwarves*; *hoofs*, *hooves*; *scarfs*, *scarves*; *wharfs*, *wharves*. Others have only the regular plural, eg *beliefs*; *roofs*; also *still lifes*, pictures of inanimate objects.

7 singular words ending in *-s*
Some words normally end in *-s*, but are singular. The most common is *news*. Others name (a) diseases, which may also be plural, eg *mumps*, *measles*; (b) fields of study or activity, eg *statistics*, *economics*, *athletics*; (c) games, eg *billiards*, *darts*; (d) proper nouns naming places, countries, or organizations, eg *Athens*, *Wales*, *the United States*, *the United Nations*. Some of the words under (b) and (c) have different senses in which they have a singular without *-s* as well as a plural with *-s*: *That is a useful statistic* (a single item in a set of statistics); *You have left a dart* (an individual missile) *on the table*.

8 plural only

A few nouns are used as plurals but have no plural ending: *people*
(normal plural of *person*), *police*, *cattle*, *poultry*, *livestock*, *vermin*.
Folk is often used as a plural (as in *the country folk*).

9 animal names

Some animal names commonly use the same form for singular and
plural, especially when the animals are referred to collectively: *They
are out shooting duck*; *We did not catch any fish that day*. In the
following common animal names, always use the same for singular and
plural: *cod*, *deer*, *grouse*, *salmon*, *sheep*, *swine*.

See also COLLECTIVES; FOREIGN PLURALS; NUMBER AGREEMENT.

plus

1 As a preposition, **plus** means 'with the addition of'. Its presence
should not affect the question of whether a following verb should be
singular or plural, which depends on the plurality of the first item
mentioned: *His earnings plus his pension come* (plural) *to £100*; *His
pension plus his earnings comes* (singular) *to £100*.

2 In serious writing, do not use **plus** to mean 'and moreover': *plus he
has to watch what he says* (*Punch*). Do not use it to mean 'additional
and welcome': *Another plus factor is its nearness to the shops*.

p.m.

See TIMES OF DAY.

podium, lectern

A **podium** is a platform for a speaker or orchestral conductor; the
plural is either **podiums** or **podia**. A **lectern** is a reading desk, such as
that from which the Bible is read in church.

poesy

People who call poetry **poesy** are employing a sort of antiquated high-
flown language which has long fallen out of favour with most poets,
but which is still available to journalists (and to the rest of us) for
certain heightened effects. This kind of writing is not always to be
censured. It is part of the craft of an accomplished writer to be able to
slide smoothly between the levels of language, introducing deliberately
an unexpectedly pompous or colloquial expression with results that
may be either moving or genuinely funny. What matters is that one
should know what one is doing. Expressions such as the following, if
used indiscriminately, appear either FACETIOUS or simply out of place:

beauteous for beautiful

ere for before

haply for perhaps

isle for island (except in place-names)

nigh for near

perchance for perhaps

thither for there.

poetess

Most women poets would rather be called *poets*. See FEMININE FORMS.

poet laureate

The plural is either **poets laureate** or **poet laureates**.

point

At this point in time and *at that point of time* are CLICHÉS. Use *now* and *then* respectively.

point of view, standpoint, viewpoint

All of these can give rise to VERBOSITY. Expressions such as *inconvenient from the cleaning point of view* can be more concisely rephrased as *inconvenient for cleaning*.

politic(al)

Politic means 'shrewd; expedient': *a politic decision*. The adjective from *politics* is **political**.

politics

Use it with a plural verb when it means 'political sympathies': *Her politics are nothing to do with me*. Use a singular verb elsewhere: *Politics is a controversial topic; politics was my chosen career*.

polity, policy

Polity is a formal word for 'a politically organized unit', or 'a form of political organization'. In the first sense Britain is a **polity**, in the second sense monarchy is a **polity**. Do not use the word instead of the commoner **policy**, which is a plan for a course of action.

poltergeist

The word is spelled -*ei*-, not -*ie*-.

pomegranate

It has usually three syllables (like 'pom-gran-it') in American English, but should properly have four (like 'pom-i-gran-it') in British English.

pommel, pummel

The noun, meaning a knob on a sword or saddle, is usually **pommel**, the verb more often **pummel**. Both spellings of the verb have other forms **-elled**, **-elling** in British English, but the second *l* is usually omitted in American English.

poncho

The plural is **ponchos**.

pontiff

He may be a bishop, or an ancient Roman priest. The word is unnecessarily used as an ELEGANT VARIATION for *pope*.

poof, poove, pouf, pouff, pouffe

Poof, **poove**, and **pouf** are derogatory and chiefly British words for 'male homosexual'. A **pouf**, **pouffe**, or (less usually) **pouff** is a large solid cushion for sitting on, a type of hairstyle, or a padded part of a dress.

pore, pour

You **pore** over a book or manuscript. You **pour** liquids.

portable, transportable

With reference to microcomputers, the difference is that a **portable** computer can run on batteries, while a **transportable** one can be packed up for transport, but runs only on the mains.

portentous, pretentious

Portentous means 'foreshadowing a coming and often dreadful event, ominous', or else 'pompous, weighty': *regarded all these things with a portentous solemnity* (H. G. Wells). This second sense should not be confused with **pretentious**, which may also imply pomposity, but in the sense of pretending to be grand or making excessive claims: *pretentious frauds who assume a love of the classics*.

portfolio

The plural is **portfolios**.

portico

The plural is either **porticoes** or **porticos**.

portion, part

A **portion** is a share, such as a helping of food, allotted to someone. A **part** is a limited quantity taken from a whole, and this is the more general word. Do not use **portion** where **part** will do: *Part* (not *a portion*) *of the office is being painted*.

portmanteau

The plural is either **portmanteaus** or **portmanteaux**. This word for an old-fashioned kind of suitcase now usually means something that combines two uses or qualities. BLENDS such as *motel* are often called *portmanteau words*.

position

1 *I am/am not in a position to* can seem a PRETENTIOUS way of saying *I can*, or *I cannot*.

2 To **position** things or people implies more than merely to *put* them somewhere. It suggests care in the exact placing: *to position a vase on the mantelpiece*; *to position oneself where one can see out of the window*. Do not use the verb **position** where *put* or *place* will do.

3 See JOB. For **position** in the general sense of 'situation', see SITUATION.

positive

This word is popular and rather OVERUSED in many contexts where it might be replaced by *constructive* (*positive advice*) or *cheerful* (*take a positive attitude towards his illness*) or *effective* (*a positive influence for good*). See also NEGATIVE.

possessed

To be **possessed** *of* something is to have it: *possessed of dogged determination*. To be **possessed** *by* or *with* something is to be mastered by it: *possessed by a sudden fury*.

possessive

See GENITIVE.

possessive pronouns

Some possessive pronouns (see PARTS OF SPEECH) end in -s (*ours*, *yours*, *his*, *hers*, *its*, *theirs*). They do not take APOSTROPHES: *Its eyes were red*; *This car is ours*. The possessive pronouns are sometimes confused with other words that are pronounced similarly.

(1) Distinguish *his* from *he's*, a contraction of *he is* (*He's not in*) or *he has* (*He's paid for it*).

(2) Distinguish *its* from *it's*, a contraction of *it is* (*It's raining*) or *it has* (*It's stopped raining*).

(3) Distinguish *their* from *they're*, a contraction of *they are* (*They're on their way*), and from *there*, the opposite of *here* (*My slippers are not there*).

(4) Distinguish *your* from *you're*, a contraction of *you are* (*I don't think you're ready*).

Whose, the genitive of *who* (*a woman, whose courage I admire*), is sometimes confused with *who's*, a contraction of *who is* (*Who's there?*) or *who has* (*Who's taken my tie?*).

Other pronouns make their genitive by adding *-'s*, eg *one's*, *somebody's*. They therefore have the same form for the genitive as for the contraction of *is* or *has*: *One should stand up for one's rights* (genitive); *If one's in trouble* . . . (*one is*); *When one's made a promise* . . . (*one has*).

possessor

The word has four *s*'s and ends in *-or*, not *-er*.

possible

1 The word ends in *-ible*, not *-able*.

2 Since things either are or are not **possible**, some people object to expressions such as *even less possible*. Avoid these combinations in careful writing.

3 Possible means 'that may happen' or 'that can be done'. You are repeating yourself if you write that anything is *possible to happen* or *possible to be done*; say that it is **possible**, or that it *may happen*, or that it *can be done*.

4 Although *as little money as possible* and *as much time as possible* are good idiomatic English, *more money than possible* and *less time than possible* are not. Write *than necessary*, *than is unavoidable*, etc.

postmaster general

The plural is usually **postmasters general**, but **postmaster generals** is sometimes used.

postprandial

This is FACETIOUS. In serious contexts, use *after-dinner*.

postulate (*verb*)

Outside logic and mathematics, this is a PRETENTIOUS word. Use *assume*, or *take for granted*, in such contexts as *We can postulate that it won't freeze*.

potato

The plural is **potatoes**.

potent, potential, potentiality

Potent means 'powerful': *potent drugs*; *a potent argument*. **Potential** as an adjective means 'existing as a possibility but not yet developed': *potential benefits*; *potential musical ability*. As a noun, **potential** like **potentiality** is the inherent capacity for development, or something that has this capacity. We usually speak of either **potential** or *a* **potential**, and of either **potentiality** or **potentialities**: *She has great musical potential/potentiality*; *They have a potential/have potentialities for violence*.

pouf, pouf, pouffe

See POOF.

pour

See PORE.

p.p.

This stands for the Latin *per procurationem*, and is used when someone signs a letter by proxy. The form is *Linda Smith, pp Mary Black* if Miss Smith signs because Miss Black is absent.

practical, practicable

One sense of **practical** is 'sensible, prudent'. **Practicable** can mean 'usable' (*a practicable weapon*) but chiefly means 'possible', of an action. A plan, method, or suggestion may be both **practical** and **practicable**, so that the two words are virtually interchangeable in some contexts. One can reasonably say, though, that it is **practicable** but scarcely **practical** to go hiking in bedroom slippers.

practically

The use of **practically** for 'almost, virtually' is well established: *We've practically finished*; *Practically everyone went to the party*. But since it can also mean 'in a practical way', **practically** should be avoided in such phrases as *practically trained mechanics*, where either meaning might be understood.

practice, practise

In British English, the noun is spelled **practice** (*We need lots of practice*) and the verb **practise** (*practise the piano*). In American English, **practice** is the commoner spelling of both noun and verb, with **practise** as a rarer alternative for both.

prairie

See PAMPAS.

pre-

This means 'before, in advance'. Words such as *prearrange, precondition, preplanning, prerequisite* are now established in the language, even though some people object that arranging, conditions, planning, and requisites must all of their nature take place or be complied with in advance.

precede, proceed

To **precede** is to go before or ahead of: *He preceded me up the stairs*. To **proceed** is to advance or continue.

precedence, precedent

1 In British English, **precedence** is pronounced with the stress on the first syllable, which sounds like *press*. In American English, the stress may alternatively be on the second syllable, sounding like *seed*.

2 Precedence is 'priority': *A baron takes precedence over a baronet*. A **precedent** is an earlier occurrence of something that may serve as a rule for a later one: *the precedent of resigning after three years*.

preceding

This is a formal word, and phrases such as *the preceding day*, *the preceding paragraph* may in suitable contexts be replaced by *the day before*, *the last paragraph*. Since **preceding** refers to what comes immediately before, it cannot be replaced by vaguer words such as *earlier* or *former*.

precipitate, precipitous

Precipitate means 'hasty, sudden': *a precipitate departure*.
Precipitous means 'very steep': *a precipitous slope*.

précis

The word is spelled with the accent, and the plural is also **précis**. It means 'a concise summary'.

preconceive

The word is spelled *-ei-*, not *-ie-*.

precursor

The word ends in *-or*, not *-er*. It means 'a forerunner'.

predecease

Outside legal contexts, use *die before*.

predecessor

The word ends in *-or*, not *-er*.

predicate, predict

Predicate as a formal verb means 'assert as an attribute' (*to predicate intelligence of our species*), and **predicated** usually means 'based, founded': *China's . . . modernisation programme is predicated on cheap Japanese loans* (*The Observer*). The word shares no sense with the commoner verb **predict**, meaning 'foretell'.

predominant, predominate (*adjective*)

They mean the same thing. **Predominant** is the commoner adjective form.

pre-empt

This is spelled either as one word or with the hyphen, but in any case is pronounced with two syllables. It means 'invalidate by taking action in advance': *The government's decision to build an airport pre-empted the council's plans.*

prefer, preferable

1 Other forms of **prefer** are **preferred**, **preferring**.

2 Prefer and **preferable** are best followed by *to*: *I prefer swimming to riding*; *Our method is preferable to theirs.* To avoid having two consecutive *to*'s in a sentence however, as in *I'd prefer to swim to to ride*, introduce *rather than* if necessary (*I'd prefer to swim rather than to ride*) or rephrase the sentence as *I'd rather swim than ride.* Do not use *than* alone after **prefer** or **preferable**, as in *Swimming is preferable than riding.*

3 Preferable is usually pronounced with the stress on the first syllable.

4 Preferable itself means 'more desirable'. Do not write *more preferable* or *most preferable*.

prefix, preface (*verb*)

To **prefix** is to provide (something) as a beginning: *to prefix an introduction to an article.* To **preface** is to add a beginning to (something): *to preface an article with an introduction.*

pregnant

There are many interesting EUPHEMISMS and synonyms here. **Expectant** belongs only to the phrase *expectant mother*, who is also a **mother-to-be**; **with child** is almost biblical; **enceinte** is an old-fashioned roundabout expression; **expecting** and **in the family way** are roundabout but rather more contemporary; **in the club** and **preggers** are jocular British slang. Fortunately, people no longer feel so shy as they did about just saying **pregnant.** But unfortunately, the useful figurative sense of **pregnant** 'full of something unexpressed' (*a pregnant pause*; *pregnant with meaning*) may now be taken to have something to do with literal pregnancy.

prejudice

One has a **prejudice** *against*, or more rarely *in favour of* something, not *to* it. Do not write *a prejudice to eating snails*.

preliminary, preparatory, previous

Things are **preliminary** or **preparatory** if they are in some way introductory to something else. It can sound PRETENTIOUS to use *preliminary to*, *preparatory to*, or *previous to* where *before* will do (it can always replace *previous to*), and dubiously correct if they are made to function as prepositions, as in *I cleaned my teeth preparatory to going to bed.*

553

premature

See IMMATURE.

premier

As a noun, it means a prime minister. As an adjective, it means 'foremost': *England's premier duke*. Avoid using it as a loose word of general praise: *a premier split-level residence*.

première

The word can be spelled either with or without the accent. As a noun, it means a first public performance. It often functions as a verb (*to premiere a film*), but some people dislike this usage.

premise

1 It is sometimes spelled **premiss** as a legal term for the preliminary part of a deed, and also in the sense of something assumed in logic. The common use of the word is in the plural form **premises**, a formal word for 'buildings, property'.

2 As a verb, it is always spelled **premise**, and often pronounced 'prim-EYES' rather than (like the noun) 'PREM-iss'. It means 'base on certain assumptions' or 'presuppose': *The efficiency of the system is premised on regular funding by the local authority*. Do not use the rather PRETENTIOUS *is premised on* when *assumes* will do.

preoccupied

See OCCUPIED.

preparatory

See PRELIMINARY.

prepared to

In official jargon, *I am not prepared to* may be a necessary device for refusing to do something without curtly saying *I will not* or *I do not*: *The Department is not prepared to admit your claim*. Even so, the phrase should be used with restraint. There seems to be no good reason for using *I am prepared to* rather than saying *I am willing to* or *I will*, or just leaving it out. Try to confine *I am prepared to* to cases in which you have actually made preparations to do something: *I am now prepared to answer your questions*.

preposition

1 general	5 repeated prepositions
2 prepositions in idioms	6 omitted prepositions
3 prepositional verbs and phrasal verbs	7 objective case with prepositions
4 ending with a preposition	

1 general

A preposition links a noun or its equivalent to another part of the sentence or to the sentence as a whole:

Send a copy to *David*.

The majority of *the people* tolerate the hardships.

The government abolished exchange controls in *1979*.

You can start the machine by *pushing the red button*.

We were not satisfied with *what he said*.

A prepositional phrase consists of a preposition and its complement, ie the noun or equivalent that the preposition links to something else. In the first example, *to David* is a prepositional phrase, *to* a preposition, and *David* its complement. One prepositional phrase may be embedded inside another: *the majority* **of** *the people* **in** *this country*. Here, **of** *the people in this country* is a prepositional phrase containing **in** *this country*. But two adjacent phrases may be independent of each other: *The last conference was held* **in** *London* **in** *1984* (Compare: *The last conference was held* **in** *1984* **in** *London*.)

A preposition may consist of more than one word: *because of*, *owing to*, *in need of*, *in addition to*. For example: *Food is more expensive* **because of** *the damage done to crops by heavy thunderstorms*.

2 prepositions in idioms

Numerous idioms consist of a verb, adjective, or noun with a preposition: *resort* **to**, *conceive* **of**, *ply* **with**, *take advantage* **of**, *pride* **in**, *aptitude* **for**, *incompatible* **with**, *averse* **to**, *conscious* **of**. Sometimes there is a choice, usually involving a difference in meaning: *agree* **to/with**, *discriminate* **against/between**, *angry* **at/with/about**. This book gives information on many idiomatic combinations under the entries for individual verbs, adjectives, and nouns. If you are in doubt about other idioms, consult a large dictionary.

3 prepositional verbs and phrasal verbs

Idioms consisting of verb plus preposition (*arrive at* in *arrive at a solution*) are prepositional verbs, while those consisting of verb plus adverb (*make up* in *make up a story*) are phrasal verbs. Prepositional verbs require a complement: *We have looked into* **the matter**; *They dispensed with* **his services**; *My assistant cannot cope with* **the work**; *I have invested in* **some shares**. The complement may become subject of a passive sentence, hence leaving the preposition at the end (see 4 below): **The matter** *has been looked into*: **His services** *were dispensed with*.

Phrasal verbs may be intransitive (without an object): *They will not* **give in**; *Sales have* **fallen off**; *The deal has* **fallen through**. Sentences with phrasal verbs may have an object, but if so the adverb is separable from the verb: it can come after the object: *I have handed* **in** *my name*. – *I have handed my name* **in**. Phrasal verbs tend to be informal, and in formal writing it is advisable to replace some of them with single verbs where possible: *give in – surrender*; *fall off – decline*.

Here are some more complex examples of idioms with prepositions or adverbs: *I will* **confine** *my remarks* **to** *the amendment* (*to* is a preposition); *You have not* **made allowance for** *interest payments* (*for* is a preposition); *They are no longer prepared to* **put up with** *his frequent absences* (*up* is an adverb, *with* a preposition); *We must* **cut down on** *waste* (*down* is an adverb, *on* a preposition); *I can* **supply** *you* **with** *details shortly* (*with* is a preposition).

4 ending with a preposition

It is normal for a preposition to precede its complement (see 1 above): **on** *modern art*, **behind** *the door*, **under** *suspicion*. But it is sometimes natural for prepositions to follow their complements, and then the sentence may end with a preposition: *What was the lecture* **on**? Good writers have ended a sentence with a preposition since English was first written. Sometimes there is no alternative for the sentence as it stands: *The details have been attended* **to**; *Her suggestions were easy to comment* **on**; *The money was not worth arguing* **about**; *She hinted at what they objected* **to**; *What are they* **like**?; *I have not been told which visitors he is to look* **after**. There is no good reason to avoid ending a sentence with a preposition, but some writers avoid the usage in formal writing when there is a choice. The second example in these pairs is the formal alternative:

I cannot remember the name of the drug he was addicted **to.**

I cannot remember the name of the drug **to** which he was addicted.

They expect to hear soon about the grants they applied **for.**

They expect to hear soon about the grants **for** which they applied.

For the less formal usage, the preposition is not necessarily at the end of the sentence; it is merely alone, without its complement, after the verb: *He did not say what he wanted to talk* **about** *this time*: *The letter I am hoping* **for** *has not yet arrived.*

Less common and longer prepositions tend not to come at the end: *She was in Venice for the whole summer*, **during** *which she completed* *her first novel*; *It rained heavily that morning,* **because of** *which they cancelled the afternoon visit.*

5 repeated prepositions

Be careful not to repeat an earlier preposition as in these sentences: *The environment* **in** *which children live* **in** *affects their attitudes when they are adults*; *The saturated fat contained in the milk* **from** *which the yoghurt was made* **from** *has been shown to raise cholesterol levels.* The error occurs because writers want to put the preposition in the more formal position, but then repeat it in the more natural position (see 4 above).

6 omitted prepositions

The reverse error is to omit necessary prepositions, as in these sentences: *They need constant practice in writing, more than they are accustomed* (*to* required at the end); *He experienced a great deal of teasing at first, which after several months he learned to cope* (*with* required, either before *which* or at the end).

7 objective case with prepositions

Where the distinction applies, the complement of the preposition (see 1 above) must be in the objective case: *in* **him**, *under* **them**, *between* **us**. Mistakes of HYPERCORRECTION occur mostly when two words are linked with *and* or *or*: *for* **you and she** (correct to **and her**), *to* **my sister or I** (correct to **or me**), *between you* **and I** (correct to **and me**). The correct case is clear when only the one pronoun is present: *for* **her**, *to* **me**, *between* **us**. When the complement is a clause, the *wh*-word (such as *who* or *whom*) is of course not the complement and its case depends on its use in its own clause: *to* **whoever** *wants it* (*whoever* is the subject of *wants it* – compare **She** *wants it* – and therefore must be subjective); *to* **whom(ever)** *you want* (*whom* or the formal *whomever* is the direct object of *you want* – compare *You want* **her** – and therefore must be objective). See also CASE, GRAMMATICAL; CLARITY (7).

preposition, proposition

A **preposition** is a word or word group such as those just discussed. A **proposition** is a statement to be proved, or something to be considered, accepted, or otherwise dealt with: *We debated the proposition that there should be no restrictions on the right to free speech.* See PROPOSAL.

prepositional phrase, prepositional verb

See PREPOSITION.

prerequisite

See PERQUISITE.

prescience, presentiment

Pronounce **prescience** with the stress on the first syllable, 'press' or 'presh', not as if you were saying *science*. It means 'foreknowledge' or 'foresight' in general. A **presentiment** is a feeling that something specific is going to happen, a 'foreboding': *I had a presentiment* (not a *prescience*) *that we would lose.*

prescribe, proscribe

To **prescribe** is to lay down a rule, to advise or specify: *prescribe a course of injections.* Its related noun is *prescription.* The rarer word **proscribe** means 'condemn as harmful, prohibit': *proscribe a dangerous drug.* The noun is **proscription**. The two pairs of words are thus more or less opposites.

prescriptive right

In law, this is a right founded on long and unchallenged custom, which does not give it any more sanctity than any other sort of right. The expression is popularly used in the sense of 'unchallengeable right': *The old man had a prescriptive right to the seat by the fire.* There is nothing wrong with this use, which is perfectly well understood.

presence

This is OVERUSED in a sense that means not much more than 'having someone there': *to establish a British presence in a largely foreign-controlled industry.*

present (*adjective*)

At the present time is longwinded and OVERUSED. Prefer *at present*, or simply *now.*

present (*verb*)

1 One **presents** someone *with* something. Write *He was presented with a watch*, not *He was presented a watch.* But the slightly less formal *He was given a watch* is correct.

2 In medical contexts, a patient is said to *present* (ie come forward) *with abdominal pains*, and a tumour may *present* (ie appear) *as an axillary mass.* This usage has been taken up in sociological jargon, where *look* or *appear* or *seem* would be simpler and better: *He presents as a dull child*.

presentiment

See PRESCIENCE.

present incumbent

See INCUMBENT.

presently

In standard southern British English this means 'soon': *He'll be back presently*. The equally ancient use of **presently** for 'now, at present', as in *He's presently writing his memoirs*, has always been current in Scotland, is common in American English, and is being revived in standard British use, particularly in industry and commerce. There seems little chance of confusion between the two meanings, as the 'soon' sense is normally accompanied by a future tense, but there is opposition to the 'now' usage, both in the USA and in Britain. Avoid using **presently** for 'now' where it may cause offence and avoid using it in either sense in contexts where it may be ambiguous. *He's presently coming back from China* might mean that he is coming either 'now' or 'soon'. The use of **presently** for 'at once, immediately' is archaic: *Dispatch it presently, the hour draws on* (Shakespeare).

present tense

The present tense (*School* **finishes** *tomorrow*) is frequently used to describe situations that are certain to happen in the future: *Tomorrow* **is** *my birthday*; *The meeting* **starts** *at nine o'clock*; *We* **leave** *for Chicago next Monday*; *When* **is** *your wedding?* This use is perfectly normal, especially in spoken English. The future use of the present tense is regularly used in subordinate clauses referring to time (eg those introduced by *when*) and condition (eg those introduced by *if*): *They will let you know when they* **are** *ready*; *I will send you the books after I* **receive** *your payment*; *She will be here later today if the weather* **is** *fine*.

Various combinations with the present tense are also used to refer to future happenings. For example: *We* **are going to** *get married next month*; *It* **is going to** *rain later today*; *There* **is to** *be an investigation*; *The show* **is about to** *begin*; *He* **is bound to** *complain*; *They* **are sure to** *send you an invitation*.

present writer

The present writer is used as a rather formal self-important way of saying *I* in writing, and *I* is usually better. See WE.

preserve, reserve, reservation

1 It can seem PRETENTIOUS to use **preserve** when you mean *jam*.

2 **Preserve, reserve,** and **reservation** are all used for tracts of public land set aside for a special use. **Preserve** is particularly used of land set aside for regulated hunting and fishing, **reserve** is associated with the protection of plants and animals (*nature reserve*), and a **reservation** is land designated by treaty for the use of American Indians or, in Britain, a strip of land separating carriageways.

pressurize, pressure

Pressurize rather than **pressure** is used in the literal sense of 'maintain pressure in': *a pressurized aircraft cabin*. Both words are used for 'coerce': *The hunger strike pressurized/pressured the authorities into action.*

prestige

Although this word is derived from a Latin one meaning 'conjuror's tricks', its modern meaning is 'high social standing', and the related adjective **prestigious** applies to what enhances that standing: *a prestige company car*; *a prestigious London address*; *A career in pure science is still more socially prestigious, in Britain, than one in engineering* (*The Times*). **Prestigious** would probably be misunderstood today if it were used in connection with conjuring.

presume, assume

Both verbs can mean 'suppose'. **Presume** is used particularly when one supposes something naturally from the evidence: *Dr Livingstone, I presume?* **Assume** takes something temporarily for granted without proof, as a basis for argument: *Assuming/Let's assume you don't marry, what will the tax position be?* The same is true of the related nouns **presumption** and **assumption**.

presumptive, presumptuous

Presumptive is a legal term meaning 'based on probability', as in *heir presumptive*; see HEIR. The commoner word **presumptuous** means 'too bold, insolent': *It would be presumptuous to criticize so great a musician.*

pretence, pretense, pretension

1 The word is spelled **pretence** in British English, **pretense** in American English.

2 Pretence is 'make believe': *They saw through his pretence of indifference*. But since people often 'make believe' to be grander or cleverer than they are, the word is often used almost interchangeably with **pretension**, which is 'laying claim to something': *He makes no pretence to learning*; *His pretensions to learning are without foundation*. See also PORTENTOUS.

pretentious

See PORTENTOUS.

pretentious words

The rich vocabulary of English often provides us with several ways of expressing the same idea. One way may be more specific than another, as *scarlet* is more specific than *red*. Or one may be more technical, as when the doctor refers to a *broken collarbone* as a *fractured clavicle*. Many words differ from their synonyms purely in being more formal, as *purchase* is more formal than *buy* or *gratuity* than *tip*. When such a word sounds too grand for the everyday occasions on which some people employ it, it is 'pretentious' in the same way that it is pretentious to wear a dinner jacket for the sort of party where everyone else is in jeans.

Probably no word is pretentious all the time. We use these words properly in their technical senses, as when the lawyer refers to someone under eighteen as an *infant*, which does not necessarily mean a *baby*. We may also have reason to sound dignified and authoritative, perhaps in a formal business letter, where we may rightly use *endeavour* rather than *try* or *beverage* rather than *drink*. We may even feel that the plainer word is too frank, as when the dictionary defines the anus as an *aperture* or *orifice* rather than as a *hole*.

The danger is that this kind of writing may become such a habit that we are unable to discard it when there is every reason to be simple and human. What is appropriate in the special language of the law may be frightening and mystifying when the law must be interpreted to the public, and the medical language in which doctors talk to each other is no use when the doctor discusses symptoms with the patient.

The less pretentious way of saying something is not always the shortest. It takes longer to say *acquaint* me *with* a fact than *tell* me it, but *put up with* is actually longer than *tolerate*. For the different and equally important distinction to be made between concise and longwinded ways of expressing oneself, see VERBOSITY. Meanwhile, a small selection of the many words referred to in this book as PRETENTIOUS will demonstrate the kind of writing against which this article is directed:

pretentious	simple
abode	home
ascertain	find out
commence	begin, start
deceased	dead
deem	think
desist	stop
dwell	live
edifice	building
employ	use
furnish	give
garments	clothes
impecunious	poor
notify	tell
peruse	read
reside	live
sufficient	enough
terminate	end
utilize	use

preternatural

See SUPERNATURAL.

pretty

As an adverb, **pretty** means 'fairly, rather', and is used with adjectives and other adverbs: *pretty comfortable*; *drove pretty fast*. It can be replaced by *fairly* or *rather* in formal writing, but is not inappropriate there: *The arguments for buying expensive books have to be pretty cogent* (*Times Literary Supplement*). The adverb meaning 'in a pretty way' is not **pretty** but *prettily*: *prettily dressed*; *thanked them prettily*.

prevaricate, procrastinate

These are formal words for things you might do to avoid committing yourself. To **prevaricate** is to speak evasively, so as to hide the truth. To **procrastinate** is to delay a necessary action or purpose.

prevent

You can **prevent** *me from* doing something, or **prevent** *my* doing it: *We tried to prevent his drinking/him from drinking*. The construction *prevent him drinking* is common in speech, but some people object to it in formal writing; see FUSED PARTICIPLE. See also AVOID.

prevent(at)ive

Preventive and **preventative** are equally acceptable. The shorter form is commoner.

previous

See PRELIMINARY.

price

See COST.

priest, minister, pastor, parson

The clergy in the Roman Catholic, Orthodox, and Anglican churches are **priests**. Women who are admitted to the Christian priesthood are **priests** too, the feminine form **priestess** being confined to female priests of some non-Christian religions. A **minister** in the religious sense is usually a Protestant or nonconformist clergyman, and so is a **pastor**, these words implying a less sacramental view of the office. **Parson** is a jocular word for an Anglican or nonconformist clergyman. See also RECTOR.

prima donna

The plural is **prima donnas**. The first syllable is pronounced 'preem' in British English, 'preem' or 'prim' in American English.

prim(a)eval, primitive

1 Primeval is an accepted spelling everywhere; **primaeval** is an older British variant.

2 Primeval means 'existing from the beginning; very old': *primeval forest*. **Primitive** means 'of an early stage of development; little evolved': *primitive technology*. In music criticism, for instance, the two words may be used almost interchangeably to suggest a quality of savage violence.

prima facie

It means 'apparent, self-evident': *a prima facie duty*. Do not use too many of these LATINISMS.

primarily

In British English, this is usually pronounced with the stress on the first syllable. In American English the stress more often falls on the second syllable.

principle, principal

Principle can be only a noun. It means 'universal law' (*the principles of physics*) or 'rule of conduct' (*a man of principle*). **Principal** is either a noun or an adjective. As a noun it means 'person in authority' (*the principal of the school*), or 'leading performer', or 'original sum of money' when this must be distinguished from the income derived from it. **Principal** as an adjective means 'main, chief'.

prior to

This is a formal and perhaps rather PRETENTIOUS phrase. It is more nearly justified when it means 'in preparation for': *resting prior to the evening performance*. Do not use **prior to** when *before* will do.

prise

See PRIZE.

pristine

From meaning 'original' (*the hypothetical pristine lunar atmosphere*), this came to mean 'uncorrupted by civilization' (*pristine innocence*) and then by a natural transition 'unsullied, fresh and clean': *the pristine, air-conditioned new building* (*The Times*). This latter sense is very common, and appears in reputable contexts, but its users should know that some people object to it. There are several synonyms, such as *spotless*, *unsoiled*, and *brand-new*, which one can use without fear of criticism.

privacy

In British English the first syllable is usually pronounced as in *privilege*. In American English it is pronounced as in *private*.

privatize

Privatize, like *denationalize*, means 'remove from public ownership'. It may be used for local as well as national bodies. Certain services may also be **privatized** by local authorities (eg refuse collection) or by public institutions such as hospitals (eg cleaning). See -IZE (2).

prize, prise, pry

There is one verb meaning 'force with difficulty': *prize the box open*; *prize information out of her*. This is spelled **prize**, with **prise** as a British variant and **pry** as an American one. The other **prize** verb, meaning 'value', is always **prize**.

pro

The plural is **pros**. This CLIPPED word for *professional* is informal. It can, but need not, mean 'professional prostitute'.

probability

In all probability is rather VERBOSE. Prefer *probably* or *very likely*.

probable

An event may be **probable**, meaning that it is *likely to happen*, but you cannot correctly say that it is *probable to happen*.

probe

Apart from its other senses, this is journalese for 'investigation, inquiry' and as a verb for 'explore, investigate'. Avoid it unless you are writing a headline.

problem

This is OVERUSED before a noun for 'presenting a problem' (*problem child*; *problem area*) and as a main noun for anything at all that goes wrong. You have a *weight problem* if you are too fat, a *drink problem* if you cannot keep off the stuff, and a *communication problem* if you are shy or tongue-tied. Try to express the idea in some other way.

proboscis

The plural is either **proboscises** or **proboscides.** It is a technical word, properly used in zoology to refer to the trunk of an elephant or the projecting mouth-parts of certain insects, but FACETIOUS when used for the human nose.

procedure, proceedings

A **procedure** is a way of doing something, usually in a series of ordered steps: *the procedure for renewing a passport*. A **proceeding** is something that is done, and in the plural it can mean 'events, goings-on' or 'a legal action': *divorce proceedings*.

proceed

This can seem PRETENTIOUS as a synonym for *go*, *walk*, or *travel*, though suitable when it means 'go ahead'. (It can also mean 'continue in the same direction', so that to **proceed** backwards in a car is to go on reversing.) Used with *to*, as in *She proceeded to read the minutes*, it is often superfluous; here one might say merely *She read the minutes*. But **proceed** *to* may usefully convey an ironical flavour: *He proceeded to lecture me on how it should be done*. See also PRECEDE.

process

The noun, and most senses of the verb, are pronounced with the stress on *pro*: *the process of growth*; *to process an insurance claim*. But in the British English sense of 'move in a procession' it is a BACK-FORMATION, and the stress is on *cess*.

procrastinate

See PREVARICATE.

proctor

The word ends in *-or*, not *-er*.

procure

This has the special sense 'get women for prostitution', and otherwise implies some effort in getting something: *At last I managed to procure this rare book*. It can seem PRETENTIOUS to use **procure** where *get* will do.

prodigy, progeny

They can both be applied to children. A very talented child such as the infant Mozart is often called a **prodigy**. **Progeny** means merely 'offspring, descendants'.

produce, product, production

Things produced on a farm are **produce**. Things produced by industry are **products**. The noun **production** applies to both: *the production of eggs/of cars*.

productive

To say that something is *productive of* something else is a VERBOSE way of saying that it *produces* it.

profession

Traditionally a **profession** is a calling such as medicine or the law that demands long training, specialized academic knowledge, and paper qualifications. The term has been widened to mean almost any sort of paid occupation: *He's a salesman by profession.* There seems no reason to quarrel with this usage, if it is felt to lend dignity to people's employment.

professor

In Britain, this is the title of a university staff member of the highest rank. In the USA the term is used more widely of teachers at universities and colleges; but even there it should be applied only to those (assistant, associate, or full professors) who have the title *professor*.

proffer

Other forms are **proffered, proffering**. Do not use this formal word where *offer* will do.

profile

This is OVERUSED in contexts where *data*, *specification*, or even *impression* would be good alternatives. A *job profile* is merely a description of the job. Sometimes, but by no means always, **profile** refers to the kind of information that can be represented on a graph (*our sales profile*) and thus has literally a visible **profile** or 'outline'. See also LOW PROFILE.

progeny

See PRODIGY.

prognosis

The plural is **prognoses.** It means 'prospect of recovery from a disease', or more generally 'forecast'.

program(me)

Both the noun and the verb are spelled **programme** in British English, except in the context of computers, but always **program** in American English. Other forms of both spellings of the verb are **programmed, programming** in British English; the second *m* is sometimes omitted in American English, but less usually when referring to computers.

progression

See ARITHMETICAL, GEOMETRICAL PROGRESSION.

prohibit

See INHIBIT.

prolific

This means 'fruitful, productive', and properly applies to what produces rather than to what is produced. Cats or writers are **prolific** if they produce many kittens or books. The kittens and books are often said (but not usually by careful writers) to be **prolific** too if they are produced abundantly.

promise

Some people dislike the use of the verb **promise** about present or past facts to mean 'assure', as in *I promise you it was at least eight feet long*. It is probably better to use the word only with reference to the future.

prone, prostrate, supine

Prone and **prostrate** correctly mean 'lying face downwards', and **prostrate** carries the added implication of doing it to express adoration or submission. Both words are used loosely to mean 'lying flat', particularly where **prostrate** means 'physically overcome': *prostrate with jaundice*. Careful writers make the distinction where necessary by using the rare precise word **supine** for 'lying face upwards'; but this would seem odd in connection with illness or exhaustion.

pronoun

The pronoun is a subclass of the noun (see PARTS OF SPEECH). Pronouns fall into a number of classes.

(1) personal pronouns. Most have two forms, subjective and objective: *I, me*; *we, us*; *you*; *he, him*; *she, her*; *it*; *they, them*. See CASE, GRAMMATICAL for the choice between the two forms; PRONOUN AGREEMENT; AMBIGUITY.

(2) possessive pronouns: *mine, ours*; *yours*; *his, hers*, (rare) *its*; *theirs*. The term also applies to related words that function as determiners, eg *my* in *my closest friend*: *my, our*; *your*; *his, her, its*; *their*. See POSSESSIVE PRONOUNS; PRONOUN AGREEMENT; AMBIGUITY.

(3) reflexive pronouns: *myself, ourselves, yourself, yourselves, himself, herself, itself, themselves, oneself.* Do not use the nonstandard forms *hisself* or *theirselves.* See REFLEXIVE.

(4) demonstrative pronouns: *this, that, these, those.* These can be either pronouns (**These** *are my books*) or determiners (**These** *books belong to me*).

(5) reciprocal pronouns: *each other, one another.*

(6) interrogative pronouns: *who, whom, whose, what, which.* See CASE, GRAMMATICAL for the distinction between *who* and *whom.*

(7) relative pronouns. These introduce relative clauses (*the person* **who** *told me*): *who, whom, whose, which, that.* Closely related to these are the pronouns (*whoever, whatever, whichever,* etc) that introduce clauses that can be a subject or object such as *You can take whatever you want.* See CASE, GRAMMATICAL (6).

(8) indefinite pronouns. There are a large number of these. Examples: *some, any, both, all, each, either, none, somebody, everybody.* See NUMBER AGREEMENT; PRONOUN AGREEMENT.

pronoun agreement

1 singular nouns referring to a class
2 indefinites
3 *one*
4 collectives
5 *or, nor*

1 singular nouns referring to a class
A singular noun that ordinarily refers to an individual may be used to refer to a class (**The British worker** *is more conservative than* **the American worker**; **A young child** *needs encouragement*). The choice of pronouns to agree with such nouns becomes a problem if the nouns refer both to males and to females. Traditionally, the masculine pronouns have been used: *A student who wishes to apply for a grant must send in* **his** *application form before the session begins.* Although the plural pronouns are sometimes used informally, they are regarded as incorrect for formal writing. Recent changes in attitude have led many to regard the use of the masculine as an indication of sexist bias, and often it is now replaced by *he or she* (*his or her application form* in the above sentence). This alternative is, however, felt to be clumsy if the pronouns have to be repeated. You can evade the problem by using plurals instead: *Students who wish to apply . . . must send in their application forms . . .*

2 indefinites

Indefinite pronouns (eg *anybody*) and other indefinite words (eg *every*) raise the same problem. Again, the singular can generally be replaced by a plural: *Any candidate who fails to obtain the specified percentage of votes will forfeit* **his** *deposit* (*Candidates who fail . . . will forfeit their deposits*); *I wonder if anyone would lend* **his** *car for a day or two* (*. . . if any of you would lend me your car . . .*). Since *none* can be treated as either singular or plural, use the plural in such circumstances: *None can remember where they were that day.*

3 one

In British English, the indefinite pronoun *one* is followed by *one*: **One** *does not have the time to do all that* **one** *wants to do.* In American English, *one* is more usually followed by *he*: **One** *does not have the time to do all that* **he** *wants to do.* See ONE (2).

4 collectives

Singular *it* is common with collectives: *The committee is conducting* **its** *business behind closed doors.* The plural pronoun should be used if the plural verb is chosen: *Her family still have to make up* **their** *minds whether* **they** *will attend the wedding.* In American English the plural pronoun is also correct even though the singular verb is used (as is normal with collectives): *Her family still has to make up* **their** *minds whether* **they** *will attend the wedding.* But consistency in pronouns is necessary, and therefore it is wrong to write *Her family still have to make up* **their** *minds whether* **it** *will attend the wedding.*

5 or, nor

If you wish to avoid using the masculine pronoun to refer to both sexes, you will need to rephrase the sentence: *I do not know whether either Nancy or Michael types* **his** *own letters* (*. . . whether Nancy and Michael type their own letters*); *Neither Ruth nor her brother is willing to change* **his** *attitude* (*Ruth is not willing to change her attitude, nor is her brother willing to change his*; *Both Ruth and her brother are not willing to change their attitudes*).

See also SEXISM.

pronounceable

The word is spelled like this, retaining the final *e* of *pronounce*.

pronunciation

(Do not either spell or pronounce this word as *pronounciation*.) There is considerable regional variation in the pronunciation of English in the British Isles, and also within the regions there is variation that is associated with social class and educational level. One type of pronunciation in particular that is not restricted regionally has acquired social prestige. It is **Received Pronunciation**, abbreviated to **RP**, the accent (type of pronunciation) used by those educated in the public schools. At one time it was the only pronunciation used by radio and television announcers and newsreaders, but a variety of accents may now be heard from announcers and newsreaders as well as from prominent public figures. Even within RP there are differences in pronunciation. For example, some pronounce the vowel in *off*, *cross*, and similar words as if written 'orf'; and for some there is no difference between *pore* and *poor*. As with other features of language, people tend to adapt their accent to the accent of the group they regularly associate with, and may use different accents in their employment and in their social circle. There is no reason for people to change an educated regional accent that they feel comfortable with, since educated regional accents enjoy general acceptance. See also SPELLING PRONUNCIATION.

propaganda, publicity

1 Propaganda is a noun with no plural: *A lot of propaganda is published*.

2 Both these words mean 'the organized spreading of information'. **Propaganda** is usually used disparagingly, with the implication that someone is trying to sway public opinion by disseminating false or biased news. The word is used more of information spread by a government or a political party than, say, by private industry or advertisers. What they do is to **publicize** something or give it **publicity**, which are more neutral words.

propel

Other forms are **propelled**, **propelling**.

propellant, propellent

The noun is usually spelled **propellant** and the adjective **propellent**, but it is not wrong to reverse them.

propeller, propellor

Both spellings are correct, but the first is more usual.

prophecy, prophesy

The noun is a **prophecy**; the verb is to **prophesy**.

proportion

1 Do not use *a proportion* to mean 'some'. as in *The audience*

571

contained a proportion of teachers. To achieve more precision, write *a
small* or *a large proportion* or *the greater proportion*. Or use plain
English and write *some*, *part of*, *a few*, *many*, or *most*. Compare
PERCENTAGE.

2 Proportions in the plural can mean 'size, extent'. It is perfectly
standard to refer to *an event of epic proportions*.

proposal, proposition

They can both mean 'a suggestion; plan put forward for consideration'.
An application for insurance is a **proposal**. A business project worked
out in some detail is a **proposition**: *Their proposition involves a 10%
reduction in overheads*. An offer of marriage is a **proposal**, while an
invitation to sex outside marriage is a **proposition**, with the related
verb to **proposition** someone. See also PREPOSITION.

proprietor

The word ends in *-or*, not *-er*.

pro rata

It means 'in proportion', and it may be better to say so in English. Do
not use too many of these LATINISMS.

prosaic, prosy

Prosaic means 'unimaginative and commonplace'. **Prosy** means
'longwinded and wearisome'. Neither of them means merely 'written
in prose'.

proscribe

See PRESCRIBE.

prosecute

See PERSECUTE.

proselyte, proselytize

To make converts is to **proselytize**. The use of *to* **proselyte**, as a verb,
is standard in American but not in British English.

prospective

See PERSPECTIVE.

prospector

The word ends in *-or*, not *-er*.

prospectus

The plural is **prospectuses**.

prosthesis

The plural is **prostheses**. It means an artificial limb, tooth, etc.

prostrate, prostate

Prostrate means 'lying down'; see PRONE. The **prostate** is a gland at the neck of the bladder in male mammals.

prosy

See PROSAIC.

protagonist

The Greek word from which this comes means 'first actor'. Some writers have consequently objected both to the idea that there may be more than one **protagonist** in anything, and to the use of the word to mean 'supporter'. If we write *She is one of the most enthusiastic protagonists of devolution*, we offend against both these rulings.

The 'supporter' sense seems to have arisen from a misunderstanding of the word's construction, by people who thought that since an *antagonist* is 'against' or 'anti-' something, a **protagonist** must be 'for' or 'pro-' it, whereas in fact the word is formed from *prot-* (ie 'first') as in *prototype*, not from *pro-* (ie 'favouring') as in *pro-American*. Nevertheless, this sense is now so well established, and so few people know Greek, that if you use the word in the 'first actor' sense you will probably be misunderstood. Either have the courage to use it for 'supporter' or avoid it altogether.

protector

The word ends in *-or*, not *-er*.

protégé(e)

Both the masculine **protégé** and the feminine **protégée** are spelled with accents. It means 'person under someone's protection or patronage'.

protein

The word is spelled *-ei-*, not *-ie-*.

protest

1 People act *in* **protest** *against* or *at* something: *He resigned in protest against* (not *of*) *their views.*

2 In American but not in British English, the verb **protest** is used for **protest** *against*: *They protested the arrest of their leaders.*

protester, protestant

People who make a protest are **protesters** or **protestors**. It is better not to call them **protestants**, which even without a capital *P* might be confused with the religious sense.

protractor

The word ends in *-or*, not *-er*.

protrude

See INTRUDE.

provable

The word is usually spelled without the final *e* of *prove*, but the form **proveable** also exists.

prove

Other forms are **proved**, and either **proved** or **proven**.
The participle **proven**, once rare except in the Scots
legal phrase *not proven*, is becoming commoner, particularly in
American English and particularly when it is used as an adjective rather
than as part of the verb. Even British writers who prefer *He's proved*
(rather than *proven*) *his point* will nevertheless refer to *a proven* (rather
than *proved*) *record of successful management.*

provided, providing

1 They both imply a clear stipulation for some desirable condition to be
fulfilled ('if and only if'): *You may come, provided/providing that you
pay for yourself.* Neither word can be used everywhere for *if*; you must
write *It wouldn't have happened if* (not *provided*) *we'd known the
truth.* Where *if* is all that you mean, it should probably be preferred as
being the simpler word. As for choosing between **provided** and
providing, some conservative writers prefer **provided** in formal
writing, but there is now little difference between the two.

2 Both these words are conventionally allowed to occur in sentences

such as *Providing it's fine, we can go*, without any suggestion that 'we'
are doing the providing. See DANGLING PARTICIPLE.

province

See FIELD.

proviso

The plural is either **provisos** or **provisoes**.

prox.

This is old-fashioned business English for 'next month'. It is better to
write the name of the month.

proximity

In close proximity is a VERBOSE way of saying *close* or *near*.

prudential, prudent

Prudential means 'based on prudence': *He refused the offer on
prudential grounds*. It is not merely a grander word for **prudent**,
which means 'wise, cautious, discreet'. **Prudential** is descriptive,
prudent appreciative.

pry

See PRIZE.

PS

This stands, among other things, for *postscript*. A second or
subsequent postscript is PPS.

psychoanalyse, psychoanalyze

The word is spelled **-lyse** in British English, **-lyze** in American
English.

psychological moment

In its popular sense of 'the appropriate time to do or say anything', this
is a CLICHÉ.

psychology, psychiatry

Psychology is the study of the mind. **Psychiatry** is the treatment of
mental disorders.

psychosis

The plural is **psychoses**.

public (*noun*)

In British, though not in American, English, this can take a plural verb: *Her public expect/expects her to sing.* See COLLECTIVES.

publicity

See PROPAGANDA.

publicly

The word ends in -*ly*, not -*ally*.

puerile

See JUVENILE.

puisne

Despite the spelling, this is pronounced like *puny*. It means 'lower in rank', and is used of the lower judges of the British High Court.

pulchritude, pulchritudinous

These are FACETIOUS words for *beauty* and *beautiful*.

pummel

See POMMEL.

punctuation

1 general	**3** comma or semicolon
2 full stop or semicolon	**4** commas, dashes, or brackets

1 general

It is a common misconception that some punctuation marks, particularly the comma, represent pauses in speech. For example, the sentence that follows would be spoken or read with a pause after the subject (here italicized), but the rules do not allow a comma to separate the subject from the verb (except for a pair of commas enclosing a parenthesis):

> *Interpreting the range of choices expressed by a group of people* is a common problem for psychologists. (*New Scientist*)

We would similarly expect two or three pauses in this unpunctuated
sentence:

> Managers at all levels ought to be told to stop grumbling about the
> need to pay large salaries to attract specialised skills into the civil
> service. (*The Economist*)

Putting punctuation between the subject and the verb breaks a
punctuation rule. But very often you can choose between different
punctuation marks or decide not to have any. Good punctuation is the
art of making the best choices in particular instances, choices that will
best help the reader to understand the intentions of the writer. The uses
of punctuation marks are discussed under the entries for each mark.
Here something will be said about choices.

2   full stop or semicolon
Consider the division of sentences in the following paragraph.

> America gave the world denim. Asia undercut it with cheap labour.
> Europe now plans to fight back with robots and hope. Several
> European companies are developing new techniques that might allow
> them to make new and cheaper denim garments. The market is big
> but shrinking. The average American buys about two pairs of jeans a
> year; the European buys two every 18 months. (*The Economist*)

The first three sentences could have been combined into one sentence,
punctuated by semicolons, in which a contrast would be made between
America, Asia, and Europe; but combining the third sentence with the
two before it would have separated it from the fourth sentence about
Europe. The third sentence is linked both to the first two sentences and
to the fourth sentence, but the fourth is linked to the third and (more
loosely) to the fifth. The best solution is for all five to be separate
sentences. The final sentence could have been split into two; but to do
so would have separated the parallel statements, and would have put
each of them on an equal level with the fifth sentence. It is such
considerations that careful writers take into account when deciding
whether to use a full stop or a semicolon.

3   comma or semicolon
The comma is the normal punctuation mark when two or more clauses
or three or more phrases are linked by coordinators such as *and* and
but. (Two linked clauses are often left unpunctuated.) The semicolon
replaces the comma to mark the more important break when the
presence of other commas threatens to obscure the structure of the
sentence. The semicolon before *but* in the first of the following
sentences illustrates this use; in the second sentence a comma can be
used because no other commas are present:

> It is not difficult to dissociate out-of-date euphemisms from their

related objects or activities and to dismiss them as quaint, ridiculous or coy; but when we hear a word consistently applied, we tend to identify the name with what it describes, and to use it and think of it as inseparable from that thing. Words with more than one meaning may cause some confusion in the adult's mind, but the context will generally clarify which meaning is appropriate. (C. Storr in *Fair of Speech*, ed. by D. J. Enright)

There is not the same justification for the semicolon in the next example; it does no more than suggest a sharper break between the two clauses than a comma would:

Much about the process of evolution is still unknown; but I have no doubt that natural selection provides the justification for teleological answers. (O. R. Frisch in *The Encyclopaedia of Ignorance* by R. Duncan and M. Weston-Smith)

4 commas, dashes, or brackets

A pair of commas is the normal mark for phrases or clauses that are loosely attached or parenthetical:

Large classes of school children, for example, often break into groups of about seven.

If one of the pair coincides with a major punctuation mark, such as a full stop or semicolon, there is only one comma:

Educationalists see the new scheme as an attempt by government to impose its own curricula in schools, traditionally the right of local education authorities.

After many months of talking, the project was given political and scientific backing.

Commas are always used for loosely attached units at the beginning of a sentence. Elsewhere, dashes or brackets mark sharper breaks or are used where other commas in the sentence would obscure which commas enclose the parenthesis:

Examples of delegated legislation can be found in the nineteenth century, but it is essentially a twentieth century device, justified by reference to the necessity for speed (particularly in emergencies), flexibility (in revising legislation to take account of changed circumstances), and complexity (because Parliament does not possess the necessary technical skills or specialist knowledge). (G. Alderman. *Modern Britain, 1700–1983*)

Dashes are more informal than the other marks. They suggest a dramatic pause. As with commas, one of the pair may be superseded by a major punctuation mark:

The moisturizing formulations are designed to put back into the skin – particularly the face – what the sun has taken out.

The commander said later that he was disappointed with the abortion of the mission – but pleased that the shut-down equipment had worked.

Both dashes and brackets, but not commas, can enclose a parenthetical sentence; only brackets can enclose more than one sentence. Brackets are the strongest signal of parentheses and are therefore used for digressions:

Legler has recently found a way to dye the weft with indigo, though the company will not say how. (It is no good just dunking the final undyed fabric into the indigo bath, because the dye is then unable to penetrate properly.) The dyed weft is being sold to knitters who are using the yarn to make jerseys, as well as being woven into fabric. (*The Economist*)

Brackets are usual for note-like references, such as page numbers, publications, dates, percentages, or brief explanations.

The following example illustrates the use of all three markers of loose attachment:

Roman legionary centuries often numbered fewer than 100 men, usually 80 – a multiple of the basic fighting and catering unit, the contabernium (con = together, tabernium = hut), of eight men. (*New Scientist*)

The outermost marker is the initial comma before *usually*, the concluding comma being superseded by the full stop. Then the dash introduces an explanation of why the century was usually 80, the concluding dash also being superseded by the full stop. The Latin name and its etymology are enclosed in a pair of commas. Within that enclosure, the Latin etymology and the English equivalents are surrounded by brackets.

See also ACCENT MARKS; APOSTROPHE; BRACKETS; CAPITALS; COLON; COMMA; DASH; EXCLAMATION MARK; FULL STOPS; HYPHEN; ITALICS; PARAGRAPHS; QUESTION MARK; QUOTATION MARKS; RUN-ON SENTENCE; SEMICOLON; SENTENCE FRAGMENT; SQUARE BRACKETS.

pundit

See PANDIT.

pupa

The plural is either **pupae** or **pupas**. It is the stage in the life of some insects between larva and adult.

pupil, student, scholar

In older but recent British use, a schoolchild was a **pupil**, and the word **student** was reserved for young adults at college or university. American English extends the age-range of **student** down to those considerably too young for college (*high school students*), and this use is now quite common in British English. A person of any age being directly instructed by a barrister, musician, or painter is his or her **pupil**. **Scholar** as a word for a schoolchild may have dropped out of favour because of the danger of confusion with the word's other senses of 'learned person' and 'holder of a scholarship'.

puppet, marionette

Strictly speaking, the ones moved from above on wires are **marionettes**, and **puppets** are the ones with a cloth body that fits over your hand, or the kind moved on rods from below or appearing as shadows on a screen; but **puppet** is often used loosely for all kinds.

purchase *(verb)*

It can seem PRETENTIOUS to use this word where *buy* will do, as it usually will.

purée

This is usually, but not always, spelled with the accent.

purloin

This is a PRETENTIOUS or FACETIOUS word for *steal*.

purport *(verb)*

This means 'be intended to seem; profess to be': *a book that purports to be an objective analysis*. It can be used of a person, but only when a person *purports* (ie 'seems') *to be* something: *men purporting to be citizens*. It should not be used of a person who makes a 'claim' in words. Write *She claims to have found* (not *She purports to have found*) *the document in an old trunk*. Do not use the verb in the passive form *is purported to*, in the way that you use *is supposed to*; use **purports** or **purporting**: *a document purporting* (or *that purports*, but not *purported* or *that is purported*) *to contain all the information*. It is perhaps less unreasonable to use **purported** as an adjective meaning 'thought to be, reputed': *a purported biography*.

purpose

It is VERBOSE to use *for the purpose of* when *for* or *to* will do.

purposely, purposefully, purposively

Purposely means 'on purpose, not accidentally'. **Purposefully** means 'with determination, resolutely' or 'with a definite aim'. **Purposively** comes from the formal adjective *purposive*, which means 'serving a purpose, useful'.

pursuant to

This is jargon. It means 'in conformance with', and is used in legal contexts. Elsewhere, use *by* or *under*.

purveyor

The word ends in *-or*, not *-er*. It is a formal word for a victualler or caterer.

pusillanimous

The word is spelled with two *l*'s. It is a formal or FACETIOUS word for *timid* or *cowardly*.

putrefy

This is spelled with an *e*; not like *purify, horrify,* etc.

pygmy, pigmy

Pygmy is the more usual spelling.

pyjamas, pajamas

The word is usually spelled **pyjamas** in British English, **pajamas** in American English.

qua

This rather formal Latin word means 'in the role of': *I dislike him not qua chairman but qua person*; *Money, qua money, cannot buy happiness*. It is used when someone or something can be regarded from more than one point of view, and a statement is to be limited to only one of these. It should be used only when the two nouns or pronouns concerned are both clearly present in the sentence and it is important to emphasize their whole-and-part relation. Otherwise, use *as*: *Speaking as a* (not *qua*) *beginner, I am mystified*. In any case, *money qua money* is probably better replaced by *money as such*.

Quaker

In formal and official contexts, the **Quakers** should be referred to collectively as the *Society of Friends*, and individually as *Friends*.

quantity

Like *amount*, **quantity** is correctly used of nouns with no plural and of abstractions that cannot be counted, but *number* should be used of plurals: *a quantity of sand/of information*; *a number of people/of mistakes*.

quantum

The plural is **quanta**. In physics, this means 'the minimum unit of energy, momentum, etc'. The expressions *quantum leap* and *quantum jump*, which strictly mean 'the abrupt transition of a particle or atom from one energy state to another', have become popular in journalese in the sense 'a sudden spectacular advance or increase': *a quantum leap in oil prices*. Similarly, in such phrases as *quantum improvement* the meaning of **quantum** is 'large', not 'small'.

quarrel (*verb*)

Other forms are **quarrelled**, **quarrelling** in British English, but the second *l* is usually omitted in American English.

quarto

The plural is **quartos**. It is a size of paper.

quash

This rather formal word means 'nullify' (*quash a verdict*) or 'suppress' (*quash a rebellion*). It is not merely another way of spelling *squash*, though they have some overlap of meaning.

quay

See KEY.

queer

It is risky to use this adjective of a person, to mean 'odd, eccentric', because of the derogatory slang sense of 'homosexual'.

query

Prefer the simpler words *question* for both noun and verb, and *ask* for the verb, where they are appropriate. The use of the verb to mean 'ask questions of', as in *They queried the President about his intentions*, is standard in American but not in British usage.

question

1 When **question** is followed by an actual 'question', it is better not to use *question of* or *question as to*. Write *the question whether* (not *of whether* or *as to whether*) *she's reliable*. But when **question** is followed by a noun, it must be linked to that noun by something. Here, *question of* is correct when question means 'problem' or 'matter' (*It's a question of money*) but *question as to* when it means 'doubt' (*There's some question as to her reliability*). The combination *no question*, meaning 'no doubt', can give rise to ambiguity, as in *There's no question that these films are being rented by children*. This may be taken to mean that they certainly are, or that they certainly are not, being rented. To make the matter clear, use *no question but that* if you mean that they certainly are, and *no question of these films being rented* if you mean that they certainly are not; or else avoid using **question** here altogether.

2 See also BEG THE QUESTION.

question mark

1 to signal questions
2 to express doubt
3 to express a request

1 to signal questions
A question mark at the end of a sentence signals that the sentence is a question: *Did you see the match?*; *What did they say to you?*. The question may be tagged on to the end of a statement: *The bank has given you a loan, hasn't it?*. Occasionally the question is in the form of a statement: *You have not yet replied?*.

It is wrong to use a question mark for a reported question: *She asked whether you saw the match?*; *I asked them what they said to you?*. It is also wrong to use a question mark for similar constructions that raise a question about information or lack of information: *She did not know whether you saw the match?*; *He told me what they said to you?*. Similarly, it is a mistake to put a question mark at the end of *Guess what I saw?*, since *guess* is imperative, and at the end of *Tell you what? I'll lend you the money*, since the sentence is an elliptical statement (I'll tell . . .). All these sentences should end with full stops. On the other hand, the question mark is correct in *Know what? They married yesterday*, since the first part is an elliptical question (Do you know what?). Similarly, the question mark is correct in these elliptical questions: *Seen my sister?*; *Want anything?*.

2 to express doubt

A question mark enclosed in brackets is used to express doubt or surprise about a part of the sentence that comes immediately before it: *The capital of Zaire, formerly the Belgian Congo (?), is Kinshasa*. The question mark should be used sparingly in this way. Avoid using it to underline sarcasm: *That was a clever (?) answer*.

3 to express a request

You may replace the question mark with a full stop if the question is being used as a request: *Would you please send me another ten copies of your report so that I can give one to each member of my staff*. A question mark is also correct and should be used with short sentences of this kind: *Would you please reply at once?*.

questionnaire

It always begins with the pronunciation 'kw' in American English, and usually in British English. The pronunciation beginning with 'k' alone is old-fashioned.

quiche

See TART.

quick

Quick, **quicker**, and **quickest** are often used as adverbs, particularly after verbs of motion; *Come quick*; *We'll get there quicker*. But prefer *quickly*, *more quickly*, *most quickly* in formal writing.

quiet(en)

The verb **quiet** is chiefly American. The verb **quieten** is British.

quilt, eiderdown, comforter, duvet, continental quilt

They are padded bed coverings. A **quilt**, **eiderdown**, or (American English) **comforter**, is designed to be used over other bedclothes. A

duvet, or (British English) **continental quilt**, usually has a removable cover, and it replaces the top sheet and blankets.

quire

This means 24 sheets of paper. A group of singers is a *choir* (same pronunciation); the alternative spelling *quire* is archaic for this sense, except perhaps in reference to angels.

quit

The past tense and participle are either **quit** or **quitted**. On the whole, **quit** is the American preference and **quitted** the British. The word is popular in journalese as an alternative to *leave*.

quite

1 It can legitimately mean 'entirely, absolutely': *quite alone*; *quite dead*; *quite different*. Or it can, equally legitimately (except in negative sentences), mean 'rather, fairly': *quite good*; *quite happy*; *I quite enjoyed it*. When it is used with 'all-or-nothing' adjectives there is no chance of confusion, since you cannot be *rather alone* or *fairly dead*. But elsewhere, confusion is possible. *Quite happy* can mean 'perfectly happy' or 'moderately happy' (although *not quite happy* can only mean 'not entirely satisfied'); *quite cold* can mean (of weather) 'a bit chilly' or (of coffee) 'having completely cooled'. Avoid using **quite** where you may be misunderstood.

2 *Quite a* is correctly used before adjectives (*quite a small house*; *quite an old man*) and the phrases *quite a few*, *quite some time* are well established. The use of *quite a*, *quite some* before other nouns, with no intervening adjective, is informal: *quite a girl*; *quite some party*.

quiz

This conveniently short word is used in headlines as the journalese for *interrogate*. Its cheerful association with general knowledge competitions makes it, perhaps, rather unsuitable for the police interrogation of suspects.

quondam

This is a FACETIOUS word. Use *former*.

quorum, quota

A **quorum** is the minimum number of people sufficient to transact a piece of business; the plural is **quorums**. A **quota** is either a minimum

amount required (*the factory's production quota*) or a maximum
amount allowed (*an immigration quota*).

quotable

The word is spelled like this, without the final *e* of *quote*.

quotation marks

1 general	**3** for titles of works
2 for direct speech and quotations	**4** for referring to words or parts of words

1 general

Quotation marks open and close the quotations. It is all too easy to
forget the closing marks.

British English (where quotation marks are also called **inverted
commas**) generally uses single quotation marks in the first instance,
and double quotation marks for a quotation within a quotation:

> Jonathan told me, 'One young man shouted out "Fire!" and
> everyone rushed to the exits'.

American English generally follows the reverse practice:

> Jonathan told me, "One young man shouted out 'Fire!' and
> everyone rushed to the exits".

In both British and American English, full stops and commas are
inside the closing quotation marks for direct speech:

> 'If you wish,' she said, 'I can show you the way.'

But British English puts full stops and commas outside the closing
quotation marks in other circumstances.

> He has been called 'the finest thriller writer alive'.

> My dictionary does not yet include 'glitz', but I expect it will be in
> the next edition.

American English, on the other hand, puts them inside the quotation
marks:

> He has been called "the finest thriller writer alive."

> My dictionary does not yet include "glitz," but I expect it will be in
> the next edition.

In both British and American English, semicolons and colons are
outside the quotation marks:

She said, 'Excuse me'; then she picked up the telephone.

The position of other marks depends on whether they belong to the direct speech:

Dorothy asked, 'Is that what it means?'

Did she say 'It's against my religious principles'?

They all shouted, 'We want Dennis!'

He actually said, 'I'm too busy to see you'!

'I have done my share,' she said, 'but you –'

His conversation is lively and fluent – you never heard from his lips 'you know' or 'you see' – though his intonation is monotonous.

If both the direct speech and the sentence as a whole are questions, it is clearer to use only one question mark, either inside or outside the quotation marks:

Did she say, 'Is that what it means?'

Did she say, 'Is that what it means'?

2 for direct speech and quotations

Quotation marks are used not only for direct speech, which tends to be accompanied by a reporting clause such as *she said*. They are also used for brief quotations that draw attention to a significant few words:

The researchers described the new mathematics curriculum as emphasizing 'mental technique, not rote'.

They also indicate that you as writer are not responsible for this form of words and that you think they are not appropriate for a reason that should be obvious from the context:

He was 'without signs of life' when he was pulled ashore after 30 minutes in the rough sea. Two full ambulance crews worked for six minutes to achieve a first spontaneous gasp from him. He is now back in his office without any indication of brain damage.

You can similarly use quotation marks for expressions that you do not attribute to anyone in particular:

The lake's rich marine life seems doomed by the 'progress' of polluting industries.

The quotation marks suggest that you do not agree with the evaluation offered by some people.

One extension of this use is to mark expressions as being inappropriate in the context, for example because they are slang. The effect is to suggest that some would put it that way, though you are aware that it is not right to do so. It is better to take responsibility for what you write, and substitute what you think is appropriate:

> When you travel on business, you need a 'go-anywhere' telephone.

> He feels guilty because he lacks 'zip'.

The quotation marks are legitimate for newly coined terms that fit stylistically into the context:

> We travelled by 'cushion class' to Shanghai.

3 for titles of works

Quotation marks are regularly used for some titles: articles in newspapers, magazines, or journals, chapters or sections of books, short stories, short poems, songs, and radio or television programmes. They are sometimes used instead of underlining – or of italics, the equivalent in printed material – for the titles of books and other works; but underlining is clearer, especially if apostrophes or other quotation marks are needed in the context. See ITALICS; TITLES OF BOOKS AND NEWSPAPERS.

4 for referring to words or parts of words

When you mention words or parts of words rather than using them in the normal way, you should enclose them in quotation marks or underline them. (As in 3 above, italics is the printed equivalent of underlining.)

> The plural of 'oasis' is 'oases'.

Prefer underlining, which is clearer.

> Underline foreign words, but put translations in quotation marks:

> *Perennial* 'perpetual' or 'recurring' has its roots in the Latin *per* ('through') and *annus* ('year').

quote (*noun*)

In serious writing, prefer a *quotation* (not *a quote*) *from Shakespeare*. **Quote**, besides meaning *quotation*, can mean *quotation mark*, and is sometimes indispensable in speech: *The Prime Minister said quote we have beaten inflation unquote.* You never need to use this sense of **quote** in writing, because quotation marks ('') are available.

quoth

It means 'said', and precedes its subject: *quoth the raven.* It belongs to old-fashioned poetry, not to ordinary writing.

Rr

r

In the sort of neutral British accent most often heard on the BBC, and represented in British English dictionaries, the sound 'r' is pronounced only before vowels, so that we hear it in *rabbit* and *barrow* but not in *morning* or *order*. It is usually pronounced before a vowel that begins a following word, as in *far away*. In the standard American speech usually represented in American dictionaries, and also in Scottish English and southwest dialects of England, 'r' is pronounced wherever it occurs in the spelling. Some speakers dislike the pronunciation of a nonexistent *r* ('intrusive *r*') between words, as in *law (r) and order* and *I saw (r) a man*, or in words like *drawing*.

-r-, -rr-

See DOUBLING.

race

The use of **race** and **racial** in the strict anthropological sense (*the Mongoloid race*) has led to much abuse and misunderstanding, so that it is probably safer to avoid these words even with reference to physical characteristics. **Race** is loosely and perhaps harmlessly used where a sovereign state is involved (*the British race*). Available alternatives are *nation*, which need not imply political statehood (*the Gipsy nation; the Navaho nation*), *people* (*nomadic peoples*), and *community*, which often applies to an identifiable group within a larger society (*the Polish community in London*).

racism

There are a number of derogatory terms that are sometimes applied to ethnic or religious groups in Britain or America, eg *honkie, kike, nigger, spic, wog, wop*. Some abbreviated terms, eg *Chink, Jap*, are also felt to be disparaging. All these and the use of derived pejorative verbs such as *to welsh* are offensive to members of the groups concerned and are rightly resented by them. Avoid using such words. Ethnic and religious groups are also sensitive to unnecessary identification of discreditable members, for example those accused or convicted of crimes.

racism, racialism

These both mean the belief, or practices based on the belief, that some races are naturally superior to others; particularly, of course, that one's own race is best. Some writers seek to draw a distinction between **racism** as a scientific theory and **racialism** as racial prejudice, but the two seem generally to be used indiscriminately. **Racialism** is the older of the two words, and **racism** is commoner today.

rack, wrack

These two spellings are often confused. You **rack** your brains, and things can be *nerve*-**racking**. It is usually **wrack** *and ruin* but sometimes **rack** *and ruin*. Suitcases go on a **rack**; the instrument of torture is a **rack**; scudding clouds are **rack**; it is **rack** of lamb; seaweed is **wrack**.

racket, racquet

The implement used in tennis is a **racket** or **racquet**. In the other senses, such as 'noise' or 'illegal enterprise', it is always spelled **racket**. The use of the word for 'occupation' (*She's in the publicity racket*) is informal, and may offend people who hear it applied to their legitimate profession.

radiator

The word ends in *-or*, not *-er*.

radical, radicle

The adjective is always **radical**: *radical principles*. So is the noun, except for the technical senses in chemistry, where it may be spelled **radicle**, and in botany and anatomy, where it must be.

radio

The plural of the noun is **radios**. Other forms of the verb are **radios**, **radioed**, **radioing**. **Radio** has practically superseded the older British word *wireless*.

radius

The plural is **radii** or, less usually, **radiuses**.

railroad, railway

Railroad is not used in British English except as a verb: *railroad a bill through Parliament*. American English uses chiefly **railroad**, but prefers **railway** for a short line or for one designed for light rolling stock.

raiment

This word (which is not spelled *rainment*) is either FACETIOUS, or old-fashioned and literary. The modern word is *clothes*.

raise, rise

1 Do not confuse these two verbs. They are **raise**, with the past tense and participle **raised**, and **rise**, with the past tense and participle **rose** and **risen**. **Raise** takes an object: *raise the rent; raise a cheer*. **Rise** takes no object; you cannot **rise** something: *Prices rose; The Rhine rises in Switzerland*. See also RAZE.

2 The use of **raise** for 'rear' is standard in American English, but in British English is still felt to be more informal than *breed* (for animals) and *bring up* (for children).

3 An increase in salary is usually a **raise** in American use and a **rise** in British use.

raison d'être

The word is spelled with the accent. It means 'reason for existence', not just 'reason'. But do not overuse such FOREIGN PHRASES.

rallentando

The plural is either **rallentandos** or **rallentandi**.

Ralph

The older pronunciation of the name rhymes with *safe*. It is often pronounced as it is spelled, as a SPELLING PRONUNCIATION.

ranco(u)r

The word is spelled **rancour** in British English, **rancor** in American English. The related adjective is **rancorous** in either case.

rapacious, voracious

Rapacious means 'grasping, covetous', and applies particularly to money: *a rapacious landlord*. It is more derogatory than **voracious**, which means 'very hungry; insatiable': *a voracious appetite*; *a voracious reader*.

rapport

It is a rather OVERUSED word for 'a sympathetic relationship'. You have *rapport* **with** someone: *to establish a closer rapport with my students*.

rapt, wrapped

Rapt means 'enraptured; engrossed': *They listened in rapt silence*. **Wrapped** is 'bundled up'; but to be *wrapped up in* something is to be 'engrossed' too: *He's completely wrapped up* (not *rapt up*) *in his daughter*.

rare, scarce

Uncommon and perhaps valuable things are **rare**: *rare books*; *a rare coin*. Common useful things that we are short of, perhaps only temporarily, are **scarce**: *Potatoes were scarce that winter*. **Rare**, but not **scarce**, can mean 'infrequent': *one of my rare visits to Paris*.

rarefy

Note the spelling, unlike *purify, solidify*, etc.

rarely

Do not write *rarely ever*; and do not write *rarely or ever*, which is nonsense. Instead, use **rarely** alone, or the combinations *rarely if ever*, *rarely or never*: *They rarely if ever/or never go out*.

rase

See RAZE.

rat(e)able

The first *e* is usually included in British English and omitted in American English.

rates

See TAX.

rather

1 To express preference, *I would rather* is common but *I had rather* is also correct. *I'd rather* is the shortened form of either of them.

2 Rather is sometimes used, particularly in British English, to downgrade a strong adjective: *rather extraordinary; rather exquisite.* This device belongs more to speech than to formal writing; but it is useful when you wish, perhaps through modesty, to 'downgrade' a striking situation: *We were really rather pleased when we won the Nobel prize.*

3 *Rather a* and *a rather* are equally correct. *Rather a* is the only possible order where no adjective intervenes before the noun: *rather a pity*; *felt rather a fool*; *a rather cold day*; *rather a cold day*.

ratio

The plural is **ratios**.

ravage, ravish

To **ravage** is to devastate and destroy: *The enemy ravaged the countryside*; *houses ravaged by fire*; *a face ravaged by age*. To **ravish** is to abduct, or to rape. **Ravish** also means 'to enchant', and this is the only current sense of the adjective **ravishing**: *a ravishing smile.*

ravel

Other forms are **ravelled**, **ravelling** in British English, but the second *l* is usually omitted in American English. Confusingly, it means either 'entangle' (usually *ravel up*) or 'disentangle' (usually *ravel out*). It is clearer to use *unravel* for the second.

raze, rase

It is now usually spelled **raze,** and means 'destroy completely': *buildings razed to the ground.* Do not confuse it with *raise*.

re

This preposition belongs to legal writing and to business English. Elsewhere, use *concerning*, *with regard to*, or simply *about*.

re-

1 Words beginning with **re-** are usually spelled as one word: *rewrite*, *reassemble*. In American English, though less often in British English, this is true even when *e* follows: *re(-)elect*. A hyphen is put in to distinguish, for instance, *re-cover* (cover again) from *recover* (get better), or *re-form* (*Ice re-formed on the lake*) from *reform* (change for the better). Sometimes, however, two such words are distinguished only by their context and by pronunciation. The first syllable of *recount* (tell a story) is usually pronounced with the short sound of *rick*, but *recount* (count again) has the longer sound of *reek*.

2 Do not use *back* or *again* with **re-** words that already contain that meaning. Write *The ice re-formed*, not *re-formed again*.

-re, -er

For *center/centre*, etc, see -ER.

reaction

In scientific use, a stimulus has a **reaction** *on* or *upon* something, which in its turn has a **reaction** *to* or *reacts against* the stimulus. When **reaction** means merely 'response to circumstances' it is used with *to* (*What was their reaction to his proposals?*), or with *against* or *from* when it means 'backlash' (*He took to crime as a reaction from his strict upbringing*). Careful writers may prefer to confine **reaction**, which is rather OVERUSED in its figurative sense, to automatic rather than considered responses (*my instant reaction*) and to use *opinion* or *impression* where these are appropriate.

readable

See LEGIBLE.

readership

This can mean a particular body of readers, and is often used where *readers* might be better, as in *It will appeal to an intelligent readership*.

real, really

1 The use of **real** for *very*, as in *real sorry*, is decidedly informal. It is commoner in American and Scottish English than in southern British use.

2 Real is often an unnecessary word. It can be omitted from such combinations as *real danger, real life*, and *real dairy butter* with little loss of meaning. This is even more true of **really**, which is OVERUSED as a meaningless filler.

realistic

This is somewhat OVERUSED in such phrases as *realistic prices, realistic terms, a realistic figure*. You could use *sensible, practical*, or *reasonable* for a change.

realm

See FIELD.

realty

This legal term means 'real property; real estate'. Do not confuse it with *reality*.

rear

At the **rear** *of* is sometimes a VERBOSE way of saying 'behind'; but one may wish to distinguish between a troop of pipers *at the rear of* a procession and the children trotting along *behind* it.

rearward(s)

For the noun and adjective, use **rearward**: *a rearward glance; to the rearward of the marching column.* For the adverb, use the form with an *s* for British English (*glanced rearwards*) and the one without an *s* for American English.

reason

We speak of *the reason for* something, and of *the reason that* something happens. It is also perfectly correct to refer to *the reason something happens* or *the reason why it happens*. (Only very conservative writers object to *the reason why*.) When giving a 'reason', write *The reason he failed was that he was ill*. It is TAUTOLOGOUS to write *The reason was because he was ill*, or *The reason was due to/ attributed to/on account of his illness*. It is VERBOSE to write *for the reason that* when *because* will do, or *by reason of* for *because of*.

rebel (*verb*)

Other forms are **rebelled**, **rebelling**.

rebound, redound

To **rebound** is to spring back, like a ball or an echo: *Their hatred rebounds on themselves*. **Redound** means 'contribute to' (*Your behaviour will redound to your credit*), but it also means 'become reflected on', a sense which is close to **rebound** but should be distinguished from it: *The President's action redounds on his party*.

rebut

Other forms are **rebutted**, **rebutting**.

receipt

1 The word is spelled *-ei-*, not *-ie-*.

2 A set of instructions for making something is a *recipe*. It is old-fashioned to call this a **receipt**. A **receipt** is a written acknowledgment of having received something.

3 *In receipt of* is business English for 'having received'. Write *We have received* (not *We are in receipt of*) *your order*.

receive

1 The word is spelled *-ei-*, not *-ie-*.

2 You can often replace this formal word by *get* or *be*, as when you change *receive injuries* to *get hurt*.

recess

The preferred British pronunciation stresses *cess*, but the one with the stress on *re* is at least equally common in American English.

réchauffé, recherché

Both words are spelled with accents.

recipient

This is a formal word. It may seem PRETENTIOUS to write *She was the recipient of an award* if you mean simply that she *received* (less formally, *got*) one.

reciprocal

See MUTUAL.

recital

See CONCERT.

reckless

See FECKLESS.

reckon

It is informal or a regionalism to use **reckon** for *think*, *guess* or *suppose*, as in *I reckon they're not coming*.

recognizance

See RECONNAISSANCE.

recognize

In careful speech, the *g* should be pronounced.

reconcilable

The word is spelled like this, without the final *e* of *reconcile*.

recondite

The stress may correctly fall on either the first or the second syllable.

reconnaissance, recognizance

A **reconnaissance** is a preliminary exploratory survey, as of enemy territory. **Recognizance** is a legal term for a bond requiring someone to do something.

reconnoitre, reconnoiter

The word is spelled **reconnoitre** in British English, **reconnoiter** in American English.

record

It is usually TAUTOLOGOUS to speak of an *all-time record*; or a *new record* (except in contrast with an *earlier record*). A **record**, in this sense, must go beyond anything previously recorded.

recorder

In a musical context, this may mean an end-blown wind instrument, or it may be short for *tape recorder*. Make it clear if necessary.

record player

See GRAMOPHONE.

recourse, resource, resort

These three words overlap in one meaning, but are used in different idiomatic constructions. In the sense that concerns us, **recourse** and **resource** are only nouns, and **resort** is either a noun or a verb. To have **recourse** *to*, to have **resort** *to*, and to **resort** *to* all mean 'turn to when needed': *We were obliged to have recourse/resort to the law; He resorted to prayer*. The person or thing that one turns to in such need is

597

a **resource** or **resort**: *Flight was my only resource*; *In the last resort we shall fight*. It is a common confusion to use **resource** where **recourse** or **resort** is needed: *to succeed without recourse/resort* (but not *resource*) *to the law*.

recto

See VERSO.

rector, vicar

Both a **rector** and a **vicar** are Church of England or Episcopal clergymen. The historical distinction was that **rectors** received their tithes directly, while **vicars** did not, but this is no longer relevant. **Rector** is also the title of the heads of certain universities, while a **vicar** may be an administrative deputy of various kinds.

recur

Other forms are **recurred**, **recurring**, and the related noun and adjective are **recurrence** and **recurrent**. As it means 'occur again', there seems no need for the variant form *reoccur*.

redound

See REBOUND.

redskin, Red Indian

Do not use these impolite words for American Indians. Call them American Indians or (chiefly American use) Native Americans.

reduce

People are **reduced** *to doing* something, not *to do* it. Write *She was reduced to apologizing* (not *to apologize*).

redundant, redundancy

Redundant means 'superfluous'; and when used of language, 'verbose'. In British use, these words have taken on a special sense in connection with employment, where to be *made redundant* is to be dismissed from a job because you are no longer needed, and a **redundancy** is a dismissal for this reason. The concept implies that the dismissed person will not be replaced, so the words are indispensable.

refer

1 Other forms are **referred**, **referring**.

2 The phrase *refer back* is TAUTOLOGOUS unless it is important to show that one is not **referring** forwards. Use **refer** alone.

3 Do not use *referring to* to introduce a topic, as in *Referring to your letter, the goods have already been dispatched*; see DANGLING PARTICIPLE. You could use *with reference to*, but even better would be some simple phrase of acknowledgment such as *Thank you for your letter*.

referee, umpire

There is usually no difference in the function of these officials. **Referee** is the term used in football and boxing, **umpire** in cricket, baseball, and tennis. In American football the **referee** is in overall charge of the game, the **umpire** controls equipment and players' conduct.

reference

Several formal phrases centre on this word. Like *with regard to*, *with reference to* and *in reference to* are useful in introducing a topic for discussion; but it is shorter and often neater to replace them by *regarding*, *respecting*, *on*, or *about*, and to replace *have reference to* by *be about* or *mean*. See also REGARD; ALLUSION.

references

1 general
2 in the text
3 in the bibliography

1 general
There are various ways in which writers refer to other publications. Whichever you choose, apply it consistently. The simplest and clearest method is the one that is generally used in the natural and social sciences. It is illustrated below.

2 in the text
Enclose in brackets the last name of the author and the year of publication: (Smith 1985) (Jones 1972, 1983, 1986)
You may wish to add a reference to page numbers or chapters: (Smith 1985, 25–34) (Jones 1972, ch.4) (Jones 1972, ch.4; 1983, ch.6)
If there is more than one author refer to two or three authors by name, but for more than three authors add 'et al.' after the name of the first author: (Smith, Jones, and Clarke 1982) (Smith et al. 1984)
For two authors in the same family, repeat the name: (Clarke and Clarke 1981)

If they do not belong to the same family, add initials: (J. P. Clarke and
T. Clarke 1983)
Add initials also when you need to refer to different works by authors
with the same last name.

If you refer to people rather than to their publications, only the
publication date and page numbers or chapters are in brackets: Smith
(1985) compared . . . Smith and Jones (1982) maintain . . . Smith
(1985, 25–34) explains . . .

3 in the bibliography

In the bibliography, list alphabetically all the publications you refer to
in the text. If an author has more than one publication, list them in
order of publication date, and use letters for more than one publication
in the same year: Smith, Charles R. (1983a); Smith, Charles R. (1983b);
Smith, Charles R. (1984).
Put single-author entries before multiple-author entries with the same
first author: Smith, Charles R. (1984); Smith, Charles R. and Johnson,
Paul (1981); Smith, Charles R., Johnson, Paul and Clarke, Ian (1980).
Do not use 'et al.' in the bibliography.

Use single quotation marks (double in American English) for articles
or other works not published separately, and italics (underlining stands
for italics in manuscript) for books and periodicals. For articles, give
the volume number and (separated by a comma) the page numbers. For
books, give the place of publication and (separated by a colon) the
name of the publisher. Here are a few examples:

> Lodge, David (1984). *Language of Fiction* (2nd ed.). London:
> Routledge & Kegan Paul.

> Fiske, John and Hartley, John (1978). *Reading Television*. London
> & New York: Methuen.

> Bok, Sissela (1980). *Lying: Moral Choice in Public and Private
> Life*. London: Quartet Books.

> Borges, Jorge Luis (1974). 'The Garden of Forking Paths', in
> *Labyrinths*, 44–54. Harmondsworth: Penguin. Orig. publ. in
> Spanish 1956.

> Miller, J. Hillis (1980). 'The figure in the carpet', *Poetics Today* 1,
> 107–18.

> Lambert, Wallace E. (1967). 'A social psychology of bilingualism',
> *The Journal of Social Issues* 23, 91–109.

referendum

The plural is **referendums** or, less usually, **referenda**. See also
PLEBISCITE.

reflection, reflexion

Both spellings are permissible in British English, but **reflection** is commoner, and is the only American form.

reflective, reflexive

Reflective means either 'thoughtful' or 'reflecting light'. **Reflexive** is used in grammar and mathematics.

reflector, refractor

Besides being merely a surface that *reflects*, a **reflector** is a telescope using a mirror to focus the light rays, while a **refractor** is one that uses a lens.

reflexive

Reflexive pronouns end in *-self* for the singular (eg *myself*, *yourself*) and *-selves* for the plural (eg *ourselves*, *yourselves*). The reflexive has four uses:

(1) You must use it to refer back to a noun (or its equivalent) if the reflexive and the noun refer to the same person or thing and if the noun is the subject of the sentence or clause:

Justin is behaving *himself*.

Doris looked at *herself* in the mirror.

I asked *Robert and Benjamin* to wash *themselves* (*Robert and Benjamin* is the subject of *to wash*).

David and I are preparing *ourselves* for the meeting.

If you are not careful, you may hurt *yourself* (or *yourselves* if there is more than one person).

The reflexive is occasionally used after prepositions expressing space even though a personal pronoun is equally correct:

They slammed the door behind *themselves* (also: behind *them*).

Sarah tied the rope around *herself* (also: around *her*).

(2) You may use it for emphasis with another noun (or its equivalent), which need not be the subject:

I myself once stayed there ('I and nobody else').

I spoke to the Prime Minister *herself*.

They wanted *us* to finish the job *ourselves*.

If the noun is the subject, you may put the reflexive next to it or in a later position:

I once stayed there *myself*.

It is wrong to enclose the emphatic reflexive in commas: *I, myself, once stayed there* (remove the commas).

(3) You may use it for emphasis as the equivalent of *you yourself, she herself*, etc.

Henry is keen on sport, and like *himself* all his friends watch football on T.V. (also: like *him*).

The first and second person reflexives need not refer back to another noun when they are used after certain prepositions:

No one knows the rules better than *yourselves* (also: than *you*).

Except for *ourselves*, nobody was there (also: except for *us*).

Like *yourself*, we have signed the petition (also: like *you*).

(4) The reflexive is sometimes used as the second part of a coordinated phrase:

The chocolate is for your sister and *yourself* (also: for your sister and *you*).

It is also used in place of *I* and *me*; but some object to this use, which they feel to be a genteel evasion of the choice between *I* and *me*. It is better then to avoid *myself* both for this use and that described in (3) when you are writing formally:

Leslie and *myself* are playing next (prefer *I*).

She refuses to speak to Doreen and *myself* (prefer *me*).

With certain verbs you can leave out the reflexive with little or no change in meaning:

Justin is behaving (himself) today.

David and I are preparing (ourselves) for the meeting.

This possibility can lead to a confusion between the uses of the reflexive in (1) and (2) if the emphatic reflexive is placed after the verb:

Jeremy doesn't worry *himself*.

In such instances it is better to put the emphatic reflexive next to the subject: *Jeremy* **himself** *doesn't worry*.

refrigerator

The word ends in *-or*, not *-er*.

refute

To **refute** a statement is to disprove it, not merely to deny it. To **refute** a person is to produce evidence supporting your argument, not merely to contradict.

regalia

The word is correctly used with a plural verb. It means the emblems and insignia of royalty, or of some office or order: *a mayor's regalia*.

regard, regarding

1 Regard gives rise to the formal phrases *in regard to*, *with/without regard to*, and *as regards*. There is nothing wrong with these, and they are useful in introducing a topic for discussion: *With regard to your suggestion, we are examining the various alternatives*; but it is shorter and often neater to use *regarding*, *respecting*, or *concerning*, or even *on* or *about*. Do not use the 'mixed' expressions *in regards to*, *as regards to*, and *with regards to*. When the noun means 'aspect, respect' it is usually more appropriate to write *in this respect*, *in some respects*, rather than using **regard, regards**. See also IRREGARDLESS.

2 When the verb **regard** means 'consider in a particular way', it is correctly used as in *He regarded them as his superiors*; *He regarded them highly*; *He regarded them with admiration*. Do not write *He regarded them his superiors*, or *He regarded them to be his superiors*. You can use *consider*, but not **regard**, in those patterns: *He considered them (to be) his superiors*. Prefer *consider* where **regard** would lead to two consecutive *as*'s in the sentence: *They regarded him as* (use *They considered him*) *as conscientious as the others*.

regardless

This is conventionally used with *of*: *He swam across, regardless of the cold*. As an adverb meaning 'despite everything' (*carry on regardless*), the word is somewhat informal.

régime

The accent is usually omitted.

regret

Other forms are **regretted**, **regretting**.

regretful, regrettable

Regretful and **regretfully** mean 'showing regret': *He sighed* *regretfully*. **Regrettable** and **regrettably** mean 'causing regret': *a regrettably high rate of unemployment*. If you mean 'it is a pity that', use **regrettably**: *Regrettably* (not *regretfully*), *I had forgotten her name*.

regularly

In careful speech pronounce all four syllables; not 'reguly'.

regulate

See RELEGATE.

rehabilitate

Although the word applied originally to people, and meant 'restore to a former good state', its use of things is also well established. You can **rehabilitate** a slum area, as well as criminals or the disabled.

rein, reign

1 Both words are spelled *-ei-*, not *-ie-*.

2 To **reign** is to rule, a **rein** is for controlling horses. Confusion arises over the figurative extensions of **rein**: *to hand over the reins* (not *reigns*) *of government*; *to give free rein* (not *reign*) *to your imagination*.

reiterate

It means 'repeat'. *Reiterate again* is a TAUTOLOGY.

relate

This is rather formal. Prefer *tell* for the sense 'recount a story'. There is a flavour of psychiatric jargon about the use of **relate** for 'have a relationship; respond' (*patients who cannot relate*), but it has passed into general usage: *try to relate to this kind of music*.

relative, relation, relationship

People with whom we are connected by ancestry, marriage, or adoption are our **relations** or **relatives**. For some reason, we speak of *rich* or *poor relations*, but of *elderly relatives*. The fact or degree of being connected with these people is a **relationship**: *He's my first cousin, which is quite a close relationship*. **Relationship** is also used of other kinds of human connection: *a purely platonic relationship*; but more abstract connections are usually called a **relation**: *the close relation between Blake's painting and his poetry*. Actual dealings or

transactions are **relations**: *the relations between landlord and tenant*.
Since a phrase like *We have professional relations* is ambiguous, it is
safer to use **relatives** for one's aunts and cousins where **relations** might
be taken to mean **relationship**, and to use **relationship** where
relations might be taken to mean **relatives**.

relative clauses

1 restrictive and nonrestrictive clauses
2 relative pronouns

1 restrictive and nonrestrictive clauses

Most relative clauses modify nouns, the clauses always following the
nouns. For example *price* is a noun, and the *that*-clause following it in
this example is a relative clause: *a price* **that everyone can afford**.
The two major types of relative clauses are *restrictive* relative clauses
and *nonrestrictive* relative clauses. Restrictive clauses identify more
closely what the noun refers to: *that they play* in the phrase *the games*
that they play is a restrictive clause identifying which games they are;
they may contrast with (say) *the games* **that they watch**.
Nonrestrictive clauses do not identify; they provide additional
information: *which I bought only last year* in the phrase *my car,* **which
I bought only last year** is a nonrestrictive clause; if I own only one
car, the word *my* identifies the car.

The two types of clauses differ in their meaning, and careful writers
signal the difference through the presence or absence of separating
punctuation. Nonrestrictive clauses should be punctuated, generally by
a pair of commas – unless the final comma is superseded by a full stop
or some other major punctuation mark. The punctuation in the sentence
The research, **which involved over a dozen scientists**, *was funded by
charitable foundations* indicates that the relative clause should be
understood as nonrestrictive, the research having been identified in the
previous context.

Names are normally uniquely identifying, requiring no further
identification. Relative clauses after names are therefore normally
nonrestrictive: *The city fathers are discussing a plan to save Venice,*
which suffers from several floods each year. Occasionally, names
are further specified by a restrictive clause: *I remember with nostalgia
the Paris that I visited as a teenager*.

2 relative pronouns

It is usual for a relative clause to contain a relative pronoun (such as
who or *which*) that refers back to the noun or the noun equivalent that
the clause modifies; for example *which* in *my car,* **which** *I bought only
last year* refers back to *my car*. The pronoun usually begins the relative
clause, as in this example, but a preposition may precede the pronoun:

the documents **for which she is responsible** (contrast: *the documents* **which she is responsible for**).

In nonrestrictive relative clauses the relative pronoun is always a word beginning with *wh*: *who, whom, whose, which*. Restrictive clauses have those relative *wh*-words, but in addition they may be introduced by *that* or by nothing. Hence, these two clauses are restrictive: *We checked the measurements* **that had been supplied**; *It was a book* **I should have read long ago**.

In many instances the context makes the meaning clear even if the punctuation is wrong, but occasionally the interpretation depends crucially on the punctuation. In the sentence *We should ban television advertisements*, **which appeal to the baser instincts**, the comma indicates that the clause is nonrestrictive, in which case the plea is for a ban on all television advertisements and the claim is that they all appeal to the baser instincts. If the comma is omitted, the restrictive interpretation makes the proposed ban apply only to those television advertisements appealing to the baser instincts. In consequence, where there may be a danger of misunderstanding a restrictive as a nonrestrictive clause it may be wise to use *that*: *We should ban television advertisements* **that appeal to the baser instincts**.

In some nonrestrictive clauses the relative pronoun *which* refers back not to a noun but to a larger unit: *He failed his driving test three times,* **which must be discouraging** (his having failed his driving test three times must be discouraging). Where it may be unclear which unit the relative pronoun refers to, it would be better to rephrase the sentence: *He failed his driving test,* **which annoyed him** (Did the failure or the test annoy him?). Rephrase: *He failed his driving test, and the failure annoyed him.*

See APPOSITION; CASE, GRAMMATICAL (6).

relative to, relating to

These are formal and even PRETENTIOUS phrases. In most contexts, prefer *about*.

relatively

See COMPARATIVELY.

relay (*verb*)

There are two verbs. **Relay** meaning 'lay again' has the past tense and participle **relaid**: *They relaid the track.* **Relay** meaning 'retransmit' has the past tense and participle **relayed**: *The programme is being relayed by satellite.*

relegate, regulate

1 To **relegate** is to move to a lower status, so do not use the word
(except facetiously) when somebody or something makes a step up
rather than down. Normally, things or people are **relegated** *to* a place:
relegate the old furniture to the children's room. There is a special
sense in British football, 'demote to a lower division of the football
league', where the verb is used alone: *Our team's been relegated.*

2 Do not confuse **relegate** with **regulate**, which means 'adjust, put
right': *regulate the tyre pressures.*

relevant

Normally things are **relevant** *to* (ie applicable to) other things: *Your
remarks are scarcely relevant to the subject.* See IRRELEVANT.

relic, relict

A **relic** is something surviving from the past, particularly something
preserved for veneration. **Relict** is an archaic word for *widow,* and has
also technical senses in ecology and geology.

relief, relieve

Both words are spelled *-ie-,* not *-ei-.*

relocate

This is business jargon for *move* or *transfer*: *The successful candidate
must be prepared to relocate to Brussels.* Prefer *move* where possible.

remain

1 It is old-fashioned to end a letter with *I remain* or *We remain.* See
LETTER ENDINGS for alternatives.

2 *Continue to remain* is a TAUTOLOGY, because **remain** itself means
'continue to be'.

remains

As a EUPHEMISM for *corpse*, this has become outmoded and quaint.
Prefer *body.*

remediable, remedial

Remediable means 'able to be remedied': *remediable defects in vision.*
Remedial means 'used as a remedy': *remedial eye exercises.*

607

remembrance, reminder

1 Remembrance is pronounced with three syllables; not 'remember-ance'.

2 A **remembrance** is a memory: *I had only a dim remembrance of the event*. A **reminder** is something that reminds you: *He tied a knot in his handkerchief as a reminder*; but a memento or keepsake is a **remembrance**: *He sent her his photograph as a remembrance*.

remit (*verb*)

Other forms are **remitted**, **remitting**.

remittance, remission, remittal, remit

These words are related to the verb **remit**. **Remittance** is rather a PRETENTIOUS word for a sum of money sent; prefer *payment* or *money*. **Remission** is release from guilt (*remission of sins*), or the reduction of a prison sentence, or a period of diminished severity in a disease. The rarer word **remittal** chiefly means 'referral of a case to another court'. **Remit** as a noun has the fashionable sense 'area of responsibility', so that one may write *It is within the remit of this committee to investigate the salary structure for the whole staff*.

remunerate, remuneration

These are formal words, which often PRETENTIOUSLY replace the simpler *pay* and *payment*. In the business world, however, **remuneration** may include quite substantial fringe benefits as well as actual money, so that the word is needed.

renaissance, renascence

Renaissance is the commoner spelling, and (with a capital *r*) the only one for the rebirth of European learning in the late Middle Ages. The variant form **renascence** is sometimes preferred for 'rebirth' in general.

render

There are many legitimate senses of **render**, as well as other senses which are formal and even PRETENTIOUS. Prefer *make* where that will do: *enough rain to make/render irrigation unnecessary*. Similarly, prefer *sing* or *perform* or *give* where they will do, as in *render a duet*.

rendezvous

As a noun, this has the plural **rendezvous**. It also functions as a well-established verb, whose other forms are **rendezvouses** (rhyming with *whose*), **rendezvoused** (rhyming with *rude*), and **rendezvousing** (rhyming with *doing*): *They rendezvoused at the beach.*

rendition

It means 'translation' or 'performance': *her rendition of the aria*. There is nothing wrong with **rendition**, but conservative writers prefer the more ordinary word *rendering*.

rep

When it means 'sales representative' or 'repertory theatre' it is informal. When it means 'reputation' it is American slang. It can also mean a fabric with a corded surface, and is then often spelled **repp**.

repairable, reparable

Material things are **repairable**: *These shoes aren't repairable/are unrepairable*. Loss, damage, and injury are **reparable**: *a misfortune that is scarcely reparable/that is irreparable*.

repeat

Do not write *repeat again*. It is a TAUTOLOGY. Use *repeat* alone.

repel, repulse

1 Other forms of **repel** are **repelled**, **repelling**.

2 Disgusting things **repel** you, and are **repellent** or (the stronger word) **repulsive**; they make you feel **repulsion**. Fabrics that **repel** moisture are **repellent** or (less usually) **repellant**, not **repulsive**. You **repel** or (the stronger word) **repulse** an invading enemy, who undergoes a **repulse**.

repertoire, repertory

A **repertoire**, rather than a **repertory**, is the list of items that someone can perform, or that are available for performance: *our modern orchestral repertoire*. A theatre company that presents several different plays alternately is a **repertory** company.

repetition of sounds and words

Do not put words near each other if they sound the same or almost the same but have different meanings:

Churches illustrate how symbolic *effects affect* behaviour.

The survey has not *proved* that primary school children have *improved* their writing.

The public was *informed* that a *formal* inquiry would soon be held.

The television *show showed* how diamonds are mined in South Africa.

Avoid also repetition of several words containing the same sounds:

The new design facilitates the detec*tion* of varia*tion* in ioniza*tion*.

*M*ainly *m*inor revisions re*m*ain to be *m*ade in the final draft.

You may repeat related words containing identical sounds if you are intentionally contrasting the words:

Coal prices can now compete with oil prices. What was once *uneconomic* is now *economical*.

You may also repeat identical words if the repetition is necessary for your purpose:

Either the flats were reasonably priced but children were not accepted, or children were accepted but the flats were not reasonably priced.

The amount of work imposed on them was *intolerable. Intolerable*, too, was the way that their employers treated them.

Indeed, you should repeat a word rather than substitute another expression that might be misinterpreted as referring to something else:

The sequence of human errors and mechanical failures began two weeks before *the accident. The mishap* itself was caused by the failure of a pump. (The accident itself . . .)

See ELEGANT VARIATION.

repetitious, repetitive

Both these adjectives are related to *repetition*. **Repetitious** is derogatory, suggesting needless boring repetition: *His jokes tend to become repetitious*. **Repetitive** is a more neutral word: *a repetitive job on an assembly line*.

replace

This has two important meanings, and you may have to make it clear which you are using. Write *We put back the textbooks* or *We substituted some new textbooks*, because *We replaced the textbooks* might mean either. See DISPLACE; SUBSTITUTE.

replaceable

The word is spelled like this, retaining the final *e* of *replace*.

replete, complete

Replete with means 'abundantly supplied': *a bedroom replete with every modern convenience. Complete with* means 'with nothing lacking': *bought a house complete with furniture.*

replicate

This formal word means 'duplicate; repeat exactly': *to replicate a statistical experiment.* It can seem PRETENTIOUS to use it when *copy* or *repeat* will do.

reportedly

This means 'as is reported'. The word has been sneered at for no good reason. It is a common way of distinguishing what has been asserted from what has been verified, is no worse than *allegedly* or *reputedly*, and usefully carries the particular implication that something has been *reported* by the media.

reported speech

1 direct speech
2 indirect speech
3 sequence of tenses

1 direct speech

You use direct speech when you quote the actual words that others have used:

> The institute commends a report, produced in 1980 by researchers at Leeds Polytechnic for the now disbanded Noise Advisory Council, as the 'best executed and most relevant work'.   (*New Scientist*)

Or that they might use:

> Ask a restauranteur about the dish which has made the most rapid advance in popularity since the beginning of the decade, and he might well answer 'Scallops!'   (*New Scientist*)

Or that you yourself have used on a previous occasion:

> 'The reason why I came,' I began – and a wave of horror crossed the table.   (*William Safire*)

Or that you might use:

> Well, they would indeed, and the rest of us could turn to our companions and say 'Well, fancy that'.   (*New Scientist*)

In quoting written material, you must reproduce the original spelling and punctuation, unless you explicitly say that you have corrected spelling and punctuation errors or have made changes to bring the text in line with some different system.

If you wish to draw to your readers' attention that an error or peculiarity appears in the original and is not a mistake that you (or printers) have introduced, put [sic] (Latin for *thus*) after the expression. Similarly, use SQUARE BRACKETS to enclose comments or explanations of your own, and to mention that you (and not the author) have italicized or underlined some part, eg [my emphasis] or [emphasis added].

> Interestingly a local newspaper . . . says of a woman who died two days after being turned away from a hospital, that she '*may* [emphasis mine] have lived if doctors had heeded advice at an inquest four years ago . . . ' I would have used *might* here. (Robert Ilson)

If you want to omit part of a quotation, insert three ellipsis dots to mark the omission. The above example illustrates this use; we have provided the first set, and Dr Ilson the second. It is important to ensure that omissions do not distort the meaning of the original. See FULL STOPS.

QUOTATION MARKS are used to enclose direct speech. They are not necessary if you centre the direct speech. They are omitted in plays, reports of meetings, and reports of formal interviews. The name is usually followed by a colon or full stop:

> RICH (*voice cracking*): You look at me as though I were an enemy!
>
> MORE (*puts out a hand to steady him*): Why, Richard, you're shaking.
>
> RICH: I'm adrift. Help me.
>
> MORE: How?
>
> RICH: Employ me.
>
> MORE: No.
>
> (Robert Bolt, *A Man for All Seasons*)

The direct speech of each new speaker in a dialogue begins on a separate line. In narrative writing it is set out as a paragraph with indentation:

> She did not turn completely to face me. She turned her head so that her profile was outlined against the worn tapestry.
>
> 'It is enough.'
>
> 'What is?'

612

'The two of us.'

'Why?'

'It is enough. That's all.'

(William Golding, *The Paper Men*)

In plays and reports, you may either indent or begin at the margin. See QUOTATION MARKS.

2 indirect speech

Instead of quoting (*He wrote to me, 'I was too nervous to take the test today'*), you may report the words of a person indirectly: *He wrote to me that he was too nervous to take the test that day*. Quotation marks are not used for indirect speech. Reported questions in indirect speech do not take question marks: *She asked how I liked the climate.* Exclamation marks also cannot occur as part of an indirect statement or command: *She told me to go home* (compare the command 'Go home!'). See QUESTION MARK; EXCLAMATION MARK.

3 sequence of tenses

In indirect speech, the tense of the verb bears some relation to the tense of the reporting verb (eg *said* in *she said*). The verb in indirect speech commonly follows a rule of sequence of tenses. What would be present tense in direct speech (*likes*) becomes past (*liked*):

She said, 'I *like* the climate'.

She said (that) she *liked* the climate.

What would be past (*lived*; *was*) either remains past or (less commonly) becomes past perfect (*had lived*; *had been*):

He said, 'We *lived* in Edinburgh when I *was* a child.'

He said that they *lived* in Edinburgh when he *was* a child.

He said that they *had lived* in Edinburgh when he *had been* a child.

What would be present perfect (*have seen*) **becomes past perfect** (*had seen*):

He replied, 'We *have* not *seen* them for years.'

He replied that they *had* not *seen* them for years.

If the situation still applies when the sentence is spoken or written, you may keep the present or the present perfect:

She said that their son *lives* in New York (if he still lives there).

She said that they *have written* to her many times (if it is possible that they will continue to write).

It is useful to retain the present tense in such instances, since you can then convey additional information: *She said that their son lived in New York* does not indicate whether he still lives there or not.

For recent reports or reports from well-known sources, the reporting verb may be in the present: *She **says** that most women drive carefully*; *He **tells** me that he will soon be promoted*; *Aristotle **says** that perfect happiness lies in contemplation*. Where relevant, the verb in the indirect speech may be in the past or the present perfect: *The Bible says that the world **was** created in six days*; *She tells me that they **have** just married*.

report to, work to

These are fashionable management jargon. They both mean 'be directly responsible to', in a structured hierarchy of authority: *You would report to the Sales Manager*; *I work to Jane Briggs*.

repository

See DEPOSITARY.

reprehensible

The word ends in *-ible*, not *-able*.

reprieve

The word is spelled *-ie-*, not *-ei-*.

republican

Use a capital *R* for the US political party or its members, a small *r* with reference to republics in general.

repulse

See REPEL.

reputable

This is usually pronounced with the stress on *rep*, not on *put*.

request

As a verb, **request** is more formal than *ask*, which should often replace it. You can **request** someone *to do* something (*He requested them to excuse him*; passive, *He requested to be excused*); you can **request** something *from* or *of* someone (*He requested some information from us*), or **request** *that* something happens or *that* someone should do

something (*He requested that she should leave*). You cannot, correctly,
request someone *for* something; or **request** *for* someone *to do*
something; or **request** someone *do* something or *should do* something
(since *that* is required after **request** in these cases); or **request** *to do* or
to be something. When **request** is a noun, however, a **request** *for*
information is correct.

require

Require should not be followed, as *need* and *want* can be, by *to* and
another verb. Write *You do not need to*(not *You do not require to*) *reply
immediately*. **Require** may be followed by an object and a *to-*
infinitive: *I require you to reply immediately*. Hence it is also used
correctly in the passive: *You are required to reply immediately*.

requisite, requirement

Physical objects that are needed are usually **requisites**: *toilet
requisites*. Demands that must be met are **requirements**: *the
requirements for admission to the college*. In many contexts, though,
the two words are interchangeable: *The essential requirements/
requisites* (or *prerequisites*) *for the job are energy and adaptability*.

research

Some British listeners dislike the pronunciation that stresses *re*, though
it is common in British as well as in American use.

resentment

One feels **resentment** *at* or *against* things, not *to* them: *the resentment
I feel at their proposal*.

reserve, reservation

See PRESERVE.

reside

Where possible, replace this PRETENTIOUS word by *live*.

resident

See CITIZEN.

resin, rosin

Resin is a sticky plant secretion, or a synthetic substance with similar physical properties. **Rosin** is one kind of natural resin, used particularly for rubbing on violin bows.

resistance

Resistance *to* is followed by an *-ing* participle, not by an infinitive. You can say *resistance to being amalgamated*, but not *resistance to be amalgamated*.

resister, resistor

A person who resists is a **resister**. A **resistor** is an electrical component.

resource, resort

1 See RECOURSE.

2 In British English, **resource** is usually pronounced with the stress on *source*. The pronunciation stressing *re* is at least equally common in American English.

respect

The correct formal phrases here are *in respect of* and *with respect to*. Like *with regard to*, they are useful in introducing a topic for discussion: *With respect to your last letter, the goods have already been dispatched*; but it is shorter and often neater to use *regarding, respecting, on,* or *about*. Avoid the 'mixed' combination *in respect to*. See REGARD.

respectable, respectful, respective

Respectable means 'deserving respect; proper; acceptable': *respectable clothes*; *a respectable amount of work*. **Respectful** means 'showing respect': *They listened in respectful silence*. **Respective** means 'of each; separate': *They returned to their respective homes*.

respectfully

Yours respectfully is an old-fashioned way of ending a letter, and can sound somewhat servile. See LETTER ENDINGS.

respecting

Modern convention permits the use of the somewhat formal **respecting** for 'with respect to': *Respecting the recent flood, please report the extent of the damage.*

respective(ly)

The proper use of **respective** and **respectively** is to clarify the relationships between two or more groups. In *He and I sat by our respective telephones*, **respective** is necessary to show that he sat by his and I by mine. It might otherwise seem that we sat together surrounded by a group of telephones. (Even here, however, the sentence could be rephrased as *We each sat by our own telephone*.) In *He was educated at Harrow and Trinity respectively*, only one man is involved, so that **respectively** is unnecessary. It should be omitted, or the sentence be rephrased to read *(both) Harrow and Trinity*. In *The boys and girls play football, tennis, and badminton respectively*, **respectively** is positively bewildering, since the three games are distributed between the two sexes. Write *The boys play football and the girls play tennis and badminton*, if that is what you mean.

responsible

The word ends in *-ible*, not *-able*.

restaurateur

This is commonly but incorrectly spelled *restauranteur*.

restive, restless

Restive means 'resistant to control, refractory'. It is particularly used, however, of animals (or children, or adults) that move when they ought to keep still, rather than keeping still when they ought to move, so that it has come to mean also 'fidgety', which is one sense of **restless**. You can be **restive** or **restless** from boredom, but only **restless** from pain. We speak of a *restless night*, and the *restless ocean*.

restrain

See CONSTRAIN.

restrictions

One imposes **restrictions** (ie limitations) *on* people or facilities: *restrictions on the use of company cars*. There are also **restrictions** (ie regulations) *against* activities: *restrictions against bringing dogs into Britain*.

restrictive clauses

See APPOSITION; RELATIVE CLAUSES.

result

1 Events **result** *from* a cause, and **result** *in* a consequence: *injuries resulting from skiing*; *errors that resulted in tragedy*.

2 The phrases *as a result of* and *with the result that* are slightly VERBOSE. They can often be replaced by *because of*, and by *so that* or *so*.

résumé

This noun meaning a summary is spelled with both accents in British English. They are sometimes omitted in American English.

retain

Apart from the special senses (*retain a barrister*; *Lead retains heat*) this may seem rather a PRETENTIOUS word. Where possible, use *keep*.

retire, retreat

1 In military use, to **retire** is to withdraw as a matter of strategy, but to **retreat** is to draw back when things are going badly. The distinction is preserved in ordinary life.

2 It is a GENTEELISM to use **retire** for 'go to bed'.

retrieve, retrieval, retriever

These words are spelled *-ie-*, not *-ei-*.

retrograde, retrogressive

Both these adjectives can mean simply 'moving backwards' (*a retrograde/retrogressive step*). The associated verbs are to **retrogress**, which particularly means 'to decline', and the rarer **retrograde**, meaning chiefly 'to recede'. Glaciers can **retrograde**. The usual noun is **retrogression.**

return back

This is a TAUTOLOGY. Use **return** alone.

rev (*verb*)

Other forms are **revved, revving**.

revel (*verb*)

Other forms are **revelled, revelling** in British English, but the second *l* is usually omitted in American English.

revenge

See AVENGE.

reverent, reverential, reverend

Reverent and **reverential** both mean 'showing reverence', but **reverent** implies that the reverence is really felt: *reverent disciples*; *a reverential bow*. By contrast, **reverend** means 'deserving reverence', and is used as a title for clergymen, abbreviated to *Rev.* or sometimes *Revd*. The title should be used with an initial or first name, or with *Mr* or *Dr*: *(The) Rev. J. Smith*; *(The) Rev. John Smith*; *(The) Rev. Mr/Dr Jones*. It is now common, but still incorrect, to write simply *Rev. Smith* and to speak of *Reverend Smith*. It is wrong to call a clergyman simply *the Reverend*.

reversal, reversion

The process of *reversing* something (ie turning it round) is **reversal**, not **reversion**: *the reversal of our economic policy*. **Reversion** is connected with the verb *revert* (ie to return), and is used technically in law, insurance, and biology.

reverse, inverse, converse, obverse

All these words express some sort of 'oppositeness'. **Reverse** is the most general, and the safest word to use if one is unsure of the delicate distinctions between the others: *a day that is the reverse of fine is a wet day*. **Inverse, converse,** and **obverse** all have technical meanings in formal logic. In more ordinary use, however, **inverse** is used particularly in the sense 'upside down': *inverse snobbery*. **Converse** usually applies to the reversal of an action or event: *The man bit the dog* is the **converse** of *The dog bit the man*. The **obverse** is the necessary counterpart that accompanies a fact: *Their rise was merely the obverse of the Empire's fall* (A J Toynbee). As applied to coins, the **obverse** is the side with the head and main inscription, the **reverse** is the other side.

reversible

The word ends in *-ible*, not *-able*.

revert back

This is a TAUTOLOGY. Use **revert** alone.

review, revue

A **review** is an examination or inspection. It may be a military inspection, a legal examination of a verdict, or a critique of literary or artistic work. A **revue** is an entertainment involving dances and satirical songs and sketches. **Revue** is sometimes spelled **review**, but this can cause unnecessary confusion.

reviewer

Your **reviewer** is a rather formal self-important way of saying *I* when writing a review.

revise

This is the only correct spelling in both British and American English; not *-ize*.

revolting

The verb *revolt* means 'rebel', but the adjective **revolting** can mean 'disgusting'. Although you can write *The students revolted* without being misunderstood, it is unwise to write *The students are revolting* or *the revolting students*. Use the verb *rebel* or the adjective *disgusting*, according to which you mean.

rewarding

This word is OVERUSED in such contexts as *a rewarding experience* or *a rewarding job*. It can often be replaced by *valuable*, *satisfying*, or *gratifying*.

rhetorical questions

When speakers or writers use rhetorical questions, they do not expect an answer. They assume that hearers will agree that only one answer is possible, an answer that they will give mentally. The rhetorical question has the effect of a forceful statement, an effect all the more emphatic because hearers are induced to arrive at the mental answer by themselves: *Is there anybody here who will not fight to the finish?* (Everybody here will fight to the finish); *Who could defend such a view?* (Nobody could defend such a view). Rhetorical questions misfire if hearers (or some of them) do not agree with the assumed answer. If you use a rhetorical question, you must be sure that you know that your readers or hearers share your views.

rhino

The plural is **rhinos**. This CLIPPED form of *rhinoceros* is rather informal.

rhinoceros

The plural is **rhinoceroses** or, less usually, **rhinoceri**; but one may speak of *a herd of rhinoceros* collectively.

rhomboid, rhombus

These are oblique-angled four-sided geometrical figures. A **rhombus** (sometimes called a **rhomb**) has four equal sides, like the diamond on playing cards; the plural is either **rhombuses** or **rhombi**. A **rhomboid** has only its opposite pairs of sides equal, like a squashed oblong.

rid

The commoner past tense is **rid**: *He rid the town of rats*. **Ridded** is old-fashioned.

right, rightly

1 Right is correctly used as an adverb meaning 'in the right way'. It should not be replaced by **rightly** is such combinations as *treat them right*; *do it right*; *guessed right*. It can also mean 'exactly', 'straight', or 'immediately': *right in the middle*; *go right home*; *right after lunch*; *blew right out of the window*. This use, however, particularly in the phrases *right here*; *right there*; *right away*; *right now*; *I'll be right over*; *He'll be right down*, belongs rather to speech than to formal writing. The use of **right** for *very* survives in certain titles such as *The Right Worshipful*, and in *welcomed them right royally*, but is otherwise archaic or regional. Do not write *right pretty*.

2 Rightly can mean 'and this is (or was) right'. It makes a comment on the whole sentence: *Rightly, he refused* (ie he did right to refuse); *He rightly guessed that they had gone home*; *They believed, rightly or wrongly, that the shop was shut*.

right-of-way

The plural is **rights-of-way**.

rightward(s)

Before a noun, use **rightward**: *a rightward turn*. After a verb, use the form with an *s* in British English (*gazed rightwards*) and the one without an *s* in American English.

rigorous, vigorous

Rigorous means 'strict, precise': *rigorous standards of hygiene*. **Vigorous** means 'strong, forceful': *a vigorous plant*; *vigorous* *exercise*. There is no overlap of meaning, though one may certainly speak of either **rigorous** or **vigorous** *measures*, or *policies*, or *enforcement of the law*.

rigo(u)r

The word is spelled **rigour** in British English when it means 'inflexibility', or 'precision', or 'harshness' (*the rigours of a Highland winter*), but **rigor** when it means 'muscular rigidity'. It is spelled **rigor** for both meanings in American English. The related adjective is always **rigorous**.

ring

There are two **ring** verbs. The past tense and participle of one are **rang** and **rung**: *He rang* (not *rung*) *the bell*; *I have rung you up several times*. The other, meaning 'encircle', has **ringed** as its past tense and participle: *Police ringed the building*.

riot (*verb*)

Other forms are **rioted**, **rioting**.

rip off

It means 'rob, steal, or cheat'. It is slang, and so is its associated noun, a **rip-off**.

rise

See ARISE; RAISE.

risqué

The word is spelled with the accent. It means 'rather indecent': *risqué jokes*.

rival (*verb*)

Other forms are **rivalled, rivalling** in British English, but the second *l* is usually omitted in American English.

rivet (*verb*)

Other forms are **riveted, riveting**.

road, street

A highway between towns is a **road**, and often takes its name from the place it goes to: *the Bath road*. An exception is that the great Roman roads of Britain have names with **street**: *Watling Street*. A thoroughfare in a town between rows of buildings is a **street**: *a street party*; *Regent Street*; but the name **Road** is often retained in the suburbs, or when a road leading out of a town has become built up: *the Old Kent Road*. Both roads and streets can have names with *Avenue*, *Lane*, *Grove*, etc.

rób

Correctly, thieves **rob** (ie steal from) a person or a place: *rob a bank*. **Rob** is sometimes used like *steal* (*rob the jewels*), but not in good modern writing. ·

rock, stone

Any piece of stone small enough to throw must usually be a **stone** in British English, but in American use the word **rock** is correctly applied to a mere pebble, and this is beginning to influence British speakers: *throwing stones/rocks at the birds*.

rode, rowed

They sound exactly the same, although **rode** comes from *ride* and **rowed** from *row*. In some spoken contexts they can be confused: *We rowed* (rode?) *along the shore*.

rodeo

The plural is **rodeos**.

roentgen, röntgen

The unit of radiation is usually, but not always, spelled **roentgen** in English.

roguish

The word is spelled without the final *e* of *rogue*.

rôle, roll

Role is more often spelled without the accent. It means an actor's part, or broadly a usual function (*Their role is to provide information*). A **roll** is something rolled up, or a list of names, or a small shaped piece of bread.

Romania

The country of southeastern Europe is best spelled like this, rather than
Rumania or **Roumania**.

Roman numerals

As fewer and fewer people understand these, it is wise to use ordinary
Arabic numerals whenever you have a choice. The Roman system is
conventionally used for the names of monarchs (*Henry VIII*), in
reference to acts and scenes of plays (*Hamlet* V i), and often for the
introductory pages of books and for the numbering of volumes of
learned periodicals. It appears on war memorials and old clocks.

Roman numerals may be either capitals (I, X, C) or small letters (i,
x, c). If you have to use (or interpret) them, they go as follows:

I, II, III, IV, V (five), VI, VII, VIII,
IX, X (ten), XI, XII, XIII, XIV, XV, XVI,
XVII, XVIII, XIX, XX (twenty).
L is 50, C is 100, D is 500, M is 1000.

Many of these numbers are represented by subtraction. You add
identical letters, so that III is 3, and you add a smaller letter following a
larger one, so that VI is 6; but you subtract a smaller letter preceding a
larger one, so that IV is 4. A line above a letter multiplies its value by
one thousand: V̄ is 5,000.

The date 1988 appears as MCMLXXXVIII.

rondeau, rondo

A **rondeau** (plural **rondeaux**) is a three-stanza poem in a complicated
verse form with only two rhymes. **Rondeau** is also a less usual spelling
of **rondo** (plural **rondos**), a piece of music with a recurring refrain.

roof

The plural is **roofs**, not *rooves*.

room

This is pronounced either with the short vowel sound of *foot* or with the
long sound of *food*.

root, rout

Both **root** (rhyming with *boot*) and **rout** (rhyming with *out*) can mean
'poke around' or 'dig out': *rooting around in the desk for paper clips*;
routed out some old photographs. Only **root** is used in the American
sense of 'support vociferously' (*rooting for the team*) or in the vulgar
Australian sense of 'have sexual intercourse'. See also ROUT.

rosin

See RESIN.

rostrum

The plural is either **rostrums** or **rostra**.

rota(to)ry

Both **rotary** and **rotatory** mean 'turning round on an axis', but the shorter form is commoner: *a rotary cutter*.

rote

For *by* **rote**, see HEART.

rouble, ruble

It is not clear why **rouble** should be the preferred British spelling, and **ruble** the American one, for the unit of Soviet currency, but that is the fact. **Ruble** is the older form; **rouble** was adopted from the French.

roué

The word is spelled with the accent. It means a debauched man.

round

See AROUND.

rouse

See AROUSE.

rout, route

Rout (rhyming with *out*) can mean 'disorganize; defeat; drive away'. **Route** as a verb (rhyming with *boot* in British use but with either *boot* or *out* in American English) means 'send by a chosen route'. The past tense of both verbs is spelled **routed**: *Their party was routed at the polls*; *All business was routed through his colleague*. See also ROOT.

rowboat, rowing boat

The first is the American form, the second is British.

rowed

See RODE.

royal (*noun*)

The sense of **royal** meaning 'a royal person' is well established, and there is no sound basis to the objection that **royal** is properly only an adjective.

Rs

This may be short for *rupees*, the Indian currency unit. It is written, as £ and $ are, before the sum of money (Rs 1000) and is often uttered in that order in Indian use: *It cost rupees one thousand*.

ruble

See ROUBLE.

rucksack, backpack, knapsack, haversack

The modern hiker carries a **rucksack**. **Backpack** is a chiefly American synonym. The **knapsack** or **haversack** was an earlier and less developed version, used particularly by soldiers and often having only one strap.

rudimentary

See VESTIGIAL.

rule

For *the exception proves the rule*, see EXCEPTION.

rule the roost/roast

Rule the roast was the original form, but *rule the roost* is overwhelmingly commoner. It would be pedantic to insist on *roast*.

rumo(u)r

The word is spelled **rumour** in British English, **rumor** in American English.

runner-up

The plural is **runners-up**.

run-on sentence, comma splice

If you join two sentences into one sentence without a coordinating conjunction (*and*, *or*, *but*) or certain other linking words (*neither*, *nor*, *so*, *yet*), you must put a punctuation mark between them. If you omit the punctuation mark, the result is a run-on sentence:

> These accidents do not happen because of the malfunction of instruments they happen because of human error (insert a semicolon: *malfunction of instruments*; *they happen*).

It is a mistake, sometimes termed a comma splice, to insert merely a comma between the two sentences; a weightier punctuation mark is required, generally a full stop or a semicolon:

> A popular method of waste disposal is by incineration, this method is used where land is scarce (*by incineration. This method is*).

> It is not clear if these special schools are intended for disruptive students, if they are, I am not in favour of them (*for disruptive students*; *if they are*).

The mistake is most likely to occur when a conjunctive adverb (eg *therefore*, *nevertheless*) or a conjunctive prepositional phrase (*as a result*, *in spite of that*) comes between the two sentences:

> He is not the world's leading authority on coins, however he is often consulted by foreign buyers (*on coins*; *however, he is*).

See COMMA (2).

Russian, Soviet

Russia is the largest of the constituent republics of the USSR, the Union of Soviet Socialist Republics. The post-revolutionary country is properly *the Soviet Union*, and the people are properly **Soviets**, but **Russia** and **Russians** are commonly used instead. The official language of the Soviet Union is **Russian**. There is no language called **Soviet**.

Ss

-s

1 The use of **-s** to form adverbs from nouns, as in *He's always at home Sundays*; *They go to the beach weekends* (for *on Sundays, at the* *weekends*) is commoner in American than in British English. The British, however, also say *We go there most Sundays*, and *to work nights*.

2 The commonest use of **-s** is to form plurals. These should not be spelled with an apostrophe (*a pound of apple's*). The only exceptions are the plurals of abbreviations, letters, figures, and dates. These can, but need not, take the apostrophe: *MC's* or *MCs*; *B's* or *Bs*; *4s* or *4's*; *the 1980's* or *the 1980s*. Numbers written as words do not take an apostrophe: *hundreds*; *thousands*; *dozens*; *sixes and sevens*.

-s-, -ss-

For the rules about whether to double a final *-s* before adding an ending, see DOUBLING; but comparatively few monosyllables end in a single *-s* after one vowel, and their behaviour is erratic. *Gas* makes *gases* or *gasses*, *gaseous*, *gassed*, *gassing*. *Focus* makes *focused* or *focussed*, *bias* makes *biased* or *biassed*, and *bus* makes *buses* or *busses*.

-'s

1 For the most part, nouns which take *'s* for the possessive refer to people and living creatures: *the boy's socks*; *the dog's dinner*; *children's books*; *the girls' room*. The **-'s** possessive is also used of periods of time: *a morning's work*; *an hour's delay*; *today's paper*; *last week's article*; *my life's ambition*; and in certain fixed phrases: *out of harm's way*; *to his heart's content*; *get your money's worth*. See APOSTROPHE. Since *girl's* and *girls'* sound the same in speech, it may be necessary to rephrase expressions such as *the doctor's opinion* and *the teachers' room* if you need to make it clear whether there is more than one doctor or teacher.

2 The **-'s** should not normally be used of inanimate or abstract nouns, though it often is so used as a journalistic spacesaver: *the car's wheels*; *London's traffic*. In normal use, prefer *the wheels of the car* or *the car wheels*, and *the traffic of London* or *London traffic*. See GENITIVE.

3 Where a group of words form one unit, the **-'s** possessive normally comes at the end of the unit: *my daughter-in-law's job*; *the man next door's dog*. Where such a group is longer and of looser construction, though, it is clumsy to put an apostrophe at the end and it is therefore better to write *the house of the people you met yesterday* rather than *the people you met yesterday's house*. For constructions such as *John and Mary's daughter*, see LINKED GENITIVES. For *someone else's* and *who else's*, see ELSE.

4 For the choice between *a friend of the king* and *a friend of the king's* see OF (3). Both are possible forms, but not in sentences such as *Their ears are longer than those of the rabbit's*. This should be rephrased as either *than those of the rabbit* or *than the rabbit's*.

5 Many firms and organizations choose to spell their names with -*s* alone, rather than with -**'s.** It is *Barclays Bank*, not *Barclay's* or *Barclays'*. The same is true of some placenames: *St Andrews*. It is important to check the correct form if you have to write it. See NAMES OF PEOPLE (2).

Sabbatarian, sabbatical

A **Sabbatarian** is a strict observer of the Sabbath. **Sabbatical** as an adjective usually refers to the Sabbath (*sabbatical laws*), but a **sabbatical** or a **sabbatical** *term* or *year* is a period of paid leave, such as may be granted to a university teacher for research.

Sabbath

This is Saturday for Jews and Seventh Day Adventists, Friday for Muslims. Christians who call Sunday the **Sabbath** are usually those who observe the fourth commandment strictly.

sabotage

This is malicious damage to property; or, figuratively, deliberate subversion of a plan or project: *to sabotage the peace talks*. The word should be used only of intentional action. Impersonal or accidental destruction is not **sabotage**.

sabre, saber

The word is spelled **sabre** in British English, **saber** in American English.

sac, sack

A fluid-filled pouch inside an animal or plant is a **sac.** Any other kind of bag is a **sack.** The chiefly British use of **sack** as a verb meaning 'dismiss' and as a noun for 'dismissal' (*He was given the sack*) is informal.

saccharin(e)

The chemical compound is **saccharin.** The adjective, meaning 'mawkishly sweet', is **saccharine.**

said

Said and the compounds *aforementioned* and *aforesaid* are used as adjectives in legal contexts to mean 'previously mentioned': *the said Simpson*. Do not use them elsewhere, except humorously: *the said pub*. It is almost always adequate to use *the* alone.

sailor

The word ends in *-or*, not *-er*.

Saint

The abbreviation is *St.* (plural *Sts.*) or, less usually, *S.* (plural *SS.*). The French feminine form **Sainte** is abbreviated to *Ste*. The full stop is often omitted from all these in modern British use.

sake

1 It is permissible, but not necessary, to use the plural **sakes** after another plural. There may be a slight difference of meaning. We write *go to the seaside for the children's sake* because a common purpose is implied, but *do it for both our sakes* if 'our' aims might be supposed to differ. An alternative is *for the sake of the children* or *for the sake of both of us*.

2 For expressions such as *for goodness sake*, see APOSTROPHE (1f).

sal(e)able

Both **salable** and **saleable** are correct spellings, but the *e* is more often omitted in American than in British use.

sales representative, traveller, commercial traveller

A person who travels to get orders for goods is today usually called a **sales representative** or merely a **representative**, or in informal British use a **rep**. **Traveller**, **commercial traveller**, and **bagman** are old-fashioned, and rather lowly in their implications, suggesting a humble pedestrian with a bag of samples rather than a smart executive in a big car. **Salesperson**, **salesman**, and **saleswoman** may be avoided in British use because they suggest that the person stands behind a counter in a shop.

salon, saloon

A **salon** is a drawing room, a hall for art exhibitions, or a stylish business establishment: *a beauty salon*. A **saloon** is a public room on a ship, or a bar (see BAR), or the (now rather rare) British word for an enclosed (sedan) car.

salubrious, sanitary, salutary

They all mean 'promoting health'. **Salubrious** refers (rather formally or facetiously) to air and climate: *a salubrious seaside resort*. **Sanitary** implies cleanliness and freedom from infection. **Salutary** is chiefly used in a figurative sense, meaning 'beneficial': *an unpleasant but salutary experience*.

salvo

The plural is either **salvos** or **salvoes**.

same

1 The use of **same** or *the* **same** for *it* or *them* is old-fashioned business English: *He ordered a drink and refused to pay for same*. Avoid it in normal prose.

2 When **same** is an adjective, either *as* or *that* may follow it, or nothing at all: *the same shoes (as/that) I wore yesterday*. See SIMILAR.

sanatorium, sanitarium

Sanatorium is the only British word. **Sanatarium**, **sanitorium**, and **sanitarium** are American variants. The plural is either **-iums** or **-ia**.

sanction

As a noun, **sanction** has two almost opposite meanings: either 'official approval' (*gave her sanction to the marriage*) or 'penalty used to enforce behaviour' (*economic sanctions*). The verb **sanction** means only 'give approval'.

sanitary

See SALUBRIOUS.

sans

This is a FACETIOUS word. Use *without*.

sarcophagus

The plural is **sarcophagi** or, less usually, **sarcophaguses**. It is a stone coffin.

sari, sarong

The **sari**, or **saree**, is the six- or nine-yard length of cloth worn by Hindu women as a combination of long skirt and head or shoulder covering. The **sarong** is also a length of cloth, draped to form a skirt only and worn by both sexes in Malaysia and Polynesia.

sartorial

This is a rather FACETIOUS word about men's clothing: *sartorial elegance*. Unfortunately, it has no simpler synonym, but the word can easily be avoided by rephrasing the sentence. It can scarcely be a necessary word, since there is no equivalent for women.

satire, satyr

Satire is writing that uses mockery to attack vice and folly. A **satyr** is either a minor Greek god with the legs of a goat, or else a lecherous man.

satisfied, happy

Both these words can mean 'convinced': *We're now quite satisfied/ happy that the murder occurred at 5.30 pm.* But since they can also mean 'pleased', one should perhaps avoid using them to mean 'convinced of something bad'. It sounds heartless to ask *Are you satisfied that they're all dead?* Use *sure, certain, convinced*, etc.

sauté

The word is spelled with the accent. The verb has the other forms **sautéing, sautés,** and **sautéed** or **sautéd,** and means 'fry in shallow fat'.

savanna(h)

See PAMPAS.

save

This is a formal word when it is used as a preposition (*no survivor save one*) or a conjunction (*He would have protested save that he was afraid*). Prefer *but* or *except*.

savio(u)r, savo(u)r, savo(u)ry

These words are spelled with the *u* in British English, but without it in American English.

saw (*verb*)

The participle is either **sawed** or **sawn**. It is usually **sawed** when used as part of a verb (*I've sawed down the tree*), but **sawn** in British English and **sawed** in American English when used as an adjective (*sawn/sawed wood*).

scampi

The singular and plural have the same form; one prawn is a **scampi**, and a dozen prawns are also **scampi**.

scan

This means either 'glance through hastily' (*scan the small ads looking for a job*) or 'examine minutely' (*scan the hills carefully with binoculars*). Both senses are correct, but make sure that the word is not ambiguous in the context.

scant

This literary and rather PRETENTIOUS word means 'barely sufficient', and is used particularly with abstract nouns: *scant attention*; *scant regard*. In general, prefer *small* or *little*.

scapula, spatula

A **scapula** is a shoulder blade; the plural is either **scapulae** or **scapulas**. A **spatula** is a flat tool for spreading, mixing, or scooping; the plural is **spatulas**.

scarce(ly)

As an adverb (*scarce a moment*) **scarce** is archaic; use *scarcely*. See HARDLY. For **scarce** as an adjective, see RARE.

scarf

Both **scarves** and **scarfs** are correct plurals for the strip or square of cloth. The technical word **scarf**, for a joint or notch in timber, has the plural **scarfs**.

scarify

This means 'scratch the surface': *scarify an area for vaccination*. The word has nothing to do with *scare*.

scenario

1 The plural is **scenarios**.

2 In British English, the second syllable is usually pronounced to rhyme with *far*; but the pronunciation rhyming with *fare* is perhaps commoner in American English.

3 Scenario is rather OVERUSED in contexts where *plan*, *prediction*, *scheme*, or *development* might make a welcome change: *On this scenario, unemployment could reach 5 million by 1990.*

sceptic, skeptic, septic

Sceptic is the British and **skeptic** the American spelling for a person who mistrusts or disbelieves. They are both pronounced 'sk', which distinguishes them from **septic** meaning 'poisoned, infected'.

sceptre, scepter

The word is spelled **sceptre** in British English, **scepter** in American English.

schedule

The usual British pronunciation begins with the sound 'sh', the usual American one with 'sk'.

schism, schismatic

The first part is pronounced like either 'siz' or 'skiz', but not 'shiz'. **Schism** is separation into opposing factions.

schiz-, schizo-

This means 'split, divided'. It forms words such as *schizophrenia*, which all begin with the same sound 'skits'.

scholar

See PUPIL.

school, college

School is often used in American English for places of higher education which the British would call **colleges**. In this sense, universities such as Harvard or Princeton are **schools**. In both British and American English a **school** can also be a specialized part of a university: *the London School of Economics*; *the Yale Law School*; or it can be an establishment for nonacademic instruction: *a driving school*. The British use **college**, perhaps more than the Americans, for certain secondary schools: *a sixth-form college*; *Eton College*; and for nonspecialized units within a university: *Balliol College, Oxford*;

King's College, London. In American English, **college** is used for institutions of higher learning that (unlike American universities) are wholly or largely restricted to educating undergraduates: *four-year colleges*; *Swarthmore College*; *Dartmouth College*; and for specialized units within a university: *college of letters and science*; *college of engineering*.

scissors

It is correctly a plural, and takes plural verbs: *Where are* (not *is*) *the scissors?* For the singular, say *a pair of scissors*, not *a scissors*.

scone

It is pronounced either with the short 'o' of *pot* or with the long 'o' of *note*. The *pot* pronunciation is preferred in Scotland, where scones were invented.

Scottish, Scots, Scotch

The people of Scotland prefer to use the adjective **Scottish** (*the Scottish universities*; *Scottish scenery*; *their Scottish blood*), or **Scots** in particular contexts (*Scots law*; *a Scots engineer*; *she married a Scotsman*). Many Scots dislike the use of **Scotch**, the older term which was once used both by themselves and by outsiders: *I'm pure Scotch . . . the correct term is Scottish, but that sounds so pompous* (Margaret, Duchess of Argyll). **Scotch** is correctly used of whisky, and in some combinations such as *Scotch broth*. See also BRITISH.

scrip, script

Certificates entitling the holder to something, such as a piece of land or a number of bonds, are **scrip**. **Script** is lettering, characters (*Russian script*), or a printed or written text (*a film script*).

scull, skull

A **scull** is a kind of oar, or a light racing boat. A **skull** is the bones of the head.

sculptor, sculptress

Sculptress is not an offensive term, but a woman might nevertheless prefer to be called a **sculptor.**

sculpture

The usual verb is **sculpture**: *to sculpture a monument*. An alternative is the BACK-FORMATION **sculpt**.

séance

The word is spelled with the accent.

seasonable, seasonal

Seasonable means 'normal for the time of year': *Frost in January is seasonable*. It also means 'opportune, timely': *seasonable advice*. **Seasonal** means 'depending on the season; happening at particular seasons': *seasonal bird migration*; *seasonal employment at seaside hotels*.

second

1 This is usually abbreviated to *2nd* in British English, but to *2d* in American use.

2 Both when it means *2nd*, and when it is a verb meaning 'support, endorse', the stress is on the first syllable: *to second a motion*. The British verb **second**, meaning 'transfer for temporary duty', is pronounced 'si-KOND'.

3 For **second, secondly** see FIRSTLY.

secretary

It is usually pronounced 'SEK-re-try' in British English. The pronunciation 'SEK-re-terry' is standard in American English.

sector

The word ends in -*or*, not -*er*.

secular, sectarian

Secular means 'worldly; not religious': *secular music*. **Sectarian** means 'involving religious sects': *sectarian violence in Northern Ireland*.

secure

As a verb, this means 'gain the safe possession of' in suitably formal contexts. Elsewhere, it can sound PRETENTIOUS, and may be better replaced by *get*: *get/secure our seats well in advance*.

-sede

See -CEDE.

see

1 The past tense and participle are **saw** and **seen**: *I saw* (not *I seen*) *the accident*, but *I've seen the film*.

2 It is the sign of an inept speaker to have to keep filling in time by saying *you see*.

3 *I see where*, as in *I see where they've cancelled the match*, is nonstandard. Prefer *I see that . . .* or just *I see . . .*

4 See SEEING.

seed

Seed is generally a noun like *sugar*, with no plural: *a sack of grass seed*. The plural **seeds** is used for small or specified quantities: *to grow a few seeds in a saucer*; *There are 10,000 seeds in this sack*.

seeing

Modern convention permits the use of **seeing** for 'in view of the fact; since': see DANGLING PARTICIPLE. It should be followed by *that* or by nothing at all, but not by *as* or *as how*: *Seeing (that) the handle was broken, the pump was unusable*.

seek

This is more formal than *try*, and may sound PRETENTIOUS. It is often used as a journalistic spacesaver, where *look for* would be the normal choice.

seem

In formal writing, avoid the combination *cannot seem to*. Rather than *He cannot seem to understand*, write *He seems unable to understand*, or *It seems (that) he cannot understand*, or simply *He cannot understand*.

[seige]

This is an incorrect spelling of *siege*.

seismic, seismology, seize, seizure

These words are spelled *-ei-*, not *-ie-*.

seldom

1 In modern use, **seldom** is an adverb (like *rarely*), not an adjective (like *rare*). Where Thackeray wrote *My Lord D ... entertainments were both seldom and shabby*, a writer today would use *rare*.

2 Do not write *seldom ever*; and do not write *seldom or ever*, which is nonsense. Instead, use **seldom** alone, or the combinations *seldom if ever*, *seldom or never*: *He seldom if ever/or never gets a letter*.

select, selection

These are more formal than *choose* and *choice*, and may sound PRETENTIOUS.

self

1 One may properly make out a cheque to **self**, but elsewhere **self** should not be used to replace *I* or *me* or *you*, as in *They invited self and wife* or *an invitation for self and friend*.

2 Many words beginning with **self-** could drop it without any loss of meaning. This is true, for instance, of *self-conceit* and *self-confessed*; but **self-** is meaningful in *self-defence*, *self-employed*, *self-service*, and *self-addressed* (ie by or of or to oneself) and in *self-sealing*, *self-raising* (ie automatically). In each case, think whether **self-** is necessary.

3 For the **-self** pronouns, see MYSELF and REFLEXIVES.

semi-, demi-, hemi-

These all mean 'half': *semicircle*; *demigod*; *hemisphere*. Of the three, **semi-** is the only one freely available for making new words: *semigovernmental*.

semicolon

1 for joining	**2** for listing

1 for joining
The semicolon (;) joins two or more sentences into one sentence:

> Before 1948 the earliest known manuscripts of the Hebrew Bible dated from about A.D. 900; now we have texts of most of the Hebrew Bible that are about 1,000 years older.

In this example, a comma would be wrong, unless we insert *and* or *but* between the sentences (see RUN-ON SENTENCE). Similarly, a semicolon is required when the linking expression is merely a conjunctive adverb (eg *however, therefore, besides*) or a conjunctive prepositional phrase (eg *as a result, in consequence, for example*):

A number of technical reforms have been suggested; *however*, there is no consensus on any of them.

A party of that type requires too much preparation; *in any case*, no one would come.

Even where a comma is possible, you may use a semicolon if you want to indicate a sharper break:

The game department is supposed to regulate hunting by controlling the number of licences issued and setting limits as to how many animals may be shot; but law enforcement is negligible. *(The Sunday Times Magazine)*

Prefer a semicolon if you have used commas for other purposes. In the next example, the semicolon before *but* marks the major division in the sentence:

Several times, when fortune seemed harsh, he contemplated suicide; but when the weather changed, or when a dollar or two arrived, his mood would change, and he would wait.

See explanations under COLON.

2 for listing

You should use a semicolon instead of a comma for listing items or sets of items in a series when there are other commas within one or more items or sets:

Stockists include Joseph of Sloane Street, London SW1; The Beauchamp Place Shop of Beauchamp Place, London SW3; Stephen King, Kings Road; Jones, Kings Road; Simpsons; Harrods; and branches of Whistles. *(The Sunday Times Magazine)*

The guests at the party were Susan Blake, a novelist; Robert Lundley, one of the biggest property owners in Manchester; Ruth Maynard, a business executive; and David Ronwall, M.P.

See COMMA (4).

semimonthly

See BIMONTHLY.

semiweekly

See BIWEEKLY.

senator

The word ends in *-or*, not *-er*.

señor, señora, señorita

The 'tilde' mark over the *n* is often omitted. They are the equivalents of *Mr*, *Mrs*, and *Miss* when you are addressing Spanish-speaking people, as *Signor* etc are for Italians.

sensational

This is OVERUSED in the sense of 'very impressive, marvellous', as in *a sensational victory*, or *You look sensational*.

sensible, sensitive, sensibility

Sensible chiefly means 'reasonable, judicious'. The related noun here is *sense*, or the rarer *sensibleness*. It has also the more formal meanings of 'perceptible' (*a sensible difference*) or 'aware' (*I am sensible of my limitations*). **Sensitive** means 'responding readily to a stimulus', and can be used of inanimate things: *a photographic emulsion sensitive to red light*. When used of people, it can mean 'easily distressed' or 'acutely aware of subtleties'. A **sensitive** issue is one needing tactful handling. The related nouns are *sensitiveness* and *sensitivity*. These are close in one meaning to **sensibility**, which means 'susceptibility to emotional or artistic feeling'. It is not the quality of being **sensible** in the sense of 'reasonable'.

sensual, sensuous

They both apply to what we experience through our senses. **Sensual** is chiefly physical, referring to the pleasures of food, drink, and particularly sex. It is often rather derogatory. **Sensuous** is aesthetic, and used of the beauties of colour and sound, as when we speak of **sensuous** poetry, music, or painting.

sentence adverbs

Despite their name, many adverbs are not specifically connected with a verb. Sentence adverbs are related to the sentence as a whole or perhaps to a clause within the sentence. They include:
    (1) conjunctive adverbs, ie those having a linking function:

The petition attracted over half a million signatures; *however*, the embassy refused to accept it.

The pound was weakening, and we *therefore* did not change our pounds into dollars.

(2) adverbs that comment on the language used:

Frankly, he was never able to control his children.

Quite simply, the answer is completely wrong.

(3) adverbs that comment on the content:

Inevitably, the trustees ordered an investigation.

Happily, nobody was hurt.

Some adverbs are used in more than one function. For example, *simply* is an adverb expressing manner in *He spoke quite simply*, and *happily* is a manner adverb in *She was singing happily when I saw her*. Some writers object to certain sentence adverbs (in particular *hopefully*, but also *thankfully* and *mercifully*) because they are also manner adverbs and readers may therefore be unsure whether they are intended as sentence adverbs or manner adverbs (see the entries for these words). Avoid using them in contexts where they are ambiguous.

sentence fragment

In formal writing, one should generally not punctuate a part of a sentence as a separate sentence:

We should recognize that science and technology have solved some problems. *And created others*. (better: *problems, and*)

They had to turn away many people. *To comply with safety regulations*. (*people, to comply*)

Their party was a success. *For a change*. (*a success – for a change*)

Sentence fragments are correct in written dialogue:

Caroline asked, 'When will you come to my office?'

'*Tomorrow*,' replied Doris.

They may be appropriate occasionally in fiction to suggest the process of thinking, to indicate a dramatic pause, or to represent an afterthought:

Two cloaked figures, cowled and faintly monastic, hove into sight. *Shepherds*. (John Fowles)

A small room, austere, remarkably unboylike. That was Perron's impression until he remembered that Edward hadn't slept or played here for several months. (Paul Scott)

Advertisers use sentence fragments profusely, often setting them out as separate paragraphs:

The 740's unique rear suspension and orthopaedically designed seats ensure an eminently comfortable ride.

While power steering and a quieter, more responsive engine make the car a joy to drive.

Especially out of the showroom. (Volvo advertisement)

sentient, sententious

Sentient means 'capable of sensation, conscious'. **Sententious** chiefly means 'pompously moralizing', though it has the almost opposite additional sense of 'tersely pithy'.

sentiment, sentimentality

Sentiment, in one sense, is sincere emotional feeling, though perhaps of an indulgently romantic or nostalgic kind: *We kept the photo on the mantelpiece for reasons of sentiment.* The adjective **sentimental,** and still more the noun **sentimentality**, imply a false and maudlin degree of **sentiment**.

septic

See SCEPTIC.

septic(a)emia

The word is spelled **septicaemia** in British English, **septicemia** in American English. It means 'blood poisoning'.

sepulchre, sepulcher

The word is spelled **sepulchre** in British English, **sepulcher** in American English. It means a tomb.

sequence of tenses

See sequence of tenses under REPORTED SPEECH (3).

seraglio

The plural is **seraglios**. The *g* is silent; see ITALIAN SOUNDS. It means a harem.

serendipity

It means the accidental finding of agreeable things. The related adjective **serendipitous** is sometimes used, incorrectly, of a discovery that is merely fortunate without being also accidental.

serf, surf

A **serf** is a kind of slave. **Surf** is breaking waves.

serge, surge

Serge is a fabric. **Surge** means 'toss and swell'.

sergeant, serjeant

The first syllable rhymes with *large*. For the army and police rank, the word is spelled **sergeant**. In legal, and British parliamentary, contexts the official spelling is **serjeant**. There is an officer of Parliament called the *serjeant-at-arms*.

serial

See CEREAL.

series

Since the plural is spelled the same as the singular, you can correctly write *This series is complete* or *These series are complete*; but not *This series are complete*.

servant

See STAFF.

service (*verb*)

One **services** things that require periodical attention: *to service a vacuum cleaner/a debt*. A bull **services** (ie copulates with) a cow. This verb should not replace any of the many senses of the more general word *serve*. Write *Three schools serve* (not *service*) *the area*.

serviceable

The word is spelled like this, retaining the final *e* of *service*.

session

See CESSATION.

sestet, sextet

A **sestet** is the last six lines of a sonnet. A **sextet** is six musicians, or a musical composition for them.

set, sit

The past tense and participle of **set** are **set, set**, and those of **sit** are **sat, sat**. Do not use **set** for **sit**: *The collar sits* (not *sets*) *awkwardly*; *The food sat* (not *set*) *heavily on his stomach*. The two verbs have a few senses in common. You can **set** or **sit** a baby in its pram, and a hen **sits** or **sets** while her eggs are hatching. **Set** usually takes an object (*set your hair/your watch/an example*), though cement **sets** and so does the sun. **Sit** usually takes no object, though you can **sit** a horse or an examination. See also SIT.

settee, settle

See SOFA.

sew, sow

The past tense of **sew** is **sewed**, and the participle either **sewn** or **sewed**. It means 'make stitches'. The past tense of **sow** (same pronunciation) is **sowed**, and the participle either **sown** or **sowed**. It means 'scatter or plant seed'.

sewage, sewerage

The waste matter itself is usually called **sewage**, but sometimes **sewerage**. The system for disposing of it, and also of surface rainwater, is **sewerage**.

sexism

The feminist movement has drawn attention to problems of masculine bias in the use of the language. Careful writers avoid expressions that might be understood as confirming stereotypes of sex roles in society, in particular expressions that reflect or reinforce tendencies to judge women and men unequally in matters that have nothing to do with differences in sex.

The major problem in grammar arises from the absence of a singular pronoun that can refer equally to both sexes. Traditionally, formal English has used *he* to refer to both: *If a researcher wishes to use human subjects in* **his** *experiments,* **he** *should first apply for written permission from this committee*. You can avoid implying that the researcher must be a male by adopting various strategies:

(1) Substitute the plural for the singular, since plural *they* is sex-neutral: *If* **researchers** *wish to use human subjects in* **their** *experiments,* **they** *should first apply for written permission from this committee*.

(2) Rephrase to avoid pronouns: *A researcher wishing to use human subjects in experiments should first apply for written permission from*

this committee. You can often substitute *the* for *his*: *The candidate must send* **his** *references with* **his** *application* (*the* references with *the* application).

(3) Substitute *he or she* or *she or he* (or corresponding combinations such as *him or her*, *his or her*): *If a researcher wishes to use human subjects in* **his or her** *experiments,* **he or she** *should first apply for written permission from this committee.* This combination, however, is awkward when it has to be repeated.

(4) Use abbreviated forms with a slant – *he/she, she/he* or *s/he* – or with brackets *(s)he*. The last two are possible only in writing and only for the subject pronouns, and some writers object to their use in formal writing. The first two have corresponding objective and possessive forms (*him/her; his/her*): *If a researcher wishes to use human subjects in* **his/her** *experiments,* **he/she** *should first apply for written permission from this committee.*

(5) Alternate masculine and feminine pronouns, perhaps in alternate paragraphs. Avoid this practice, since it is likely to confuse or disconcert readers.

(6) After one of a set of indefinite words the plural *they* is commonly used in speech: *If* **anyone** *wishes to use human subjects in* **their** *experiments,* **they** *should first apply for written permission from this committee.* But this use of *they* is not yet established in formal writing. The indefinite words are *everyone, everybody; someone, somebody; anyone, anybody; no one, nobody; either, neither; each, every.*

Careful writers also try to use words that are neutral in sex-reference to avoid the suggestion that the expected occupant of a position or role must be male or that the roles of men and women are different. Examples of neutral expressions are *supervisor* for *foreman; flight attendant* for *steward* or *stewardess; worker*, not *workman*. In the sentence *When* **businessmen** *want advice about computers, they consult our magazine*, there is an assumption that business is a male occupation; replace *businessmen* with *business people*. Similarly, replace the generic use of *man* with equivalents that clearly include women: *human achievements* (instead of *man's achievements*); *the man in the street* (*the average person, ordinary people*); *man hours* (*working hours* or *work-hours*). Unless it is relevant to the point you are making, you should not refer to the sex of a person (*lady doctor, woman driver, female lawyer, male teacher, male nurse*). See FEMININE FORMS.

sextet

See SESTET.

sez

Some writers use this spelling of *says* to suggest illiterate speech, though it does in fact correspond exactly with the standard pronunciation of the word.

shade, shadow

Shade is any place sheltered from the sun. A **shadow** is the clear shape made by the **shade** of something, whereas **shade** has no particular shape. People and objects *cast* **shadows.**

shall, will

In formal British English south of the Border, **shall** has traditionally been used to express the 'pure' future in the first person: *I shall be late home tonight, I'm afraid*; and to express commands and promises in the second and third persons: *You shall not steal* (*New English Bible*); *You shall go to the ball, Cinderella.* Conversely, **will** has expressed intentions and promises in the first person: *Give me my robe, for I will go* (Shakespeare), and the pure future in the second and third persons: *England expects that every man will do his duty* (Nelson).

This distinction is dying out. **Will** and **won't** commonly replace **shall** and **shan't**, particularly in American English. It is acceptable, except in very formal prose, to write *We will arrive on Wednesday*. Indeed, the distinction between 'pure' future and 'intention' is often hard to make.

Shall I? and *shall we?* are still commonly used in questions. A useful distinction can be made between *Shall I open the window?* (ie do you want me to?) and *Will I need a passport?* (ie will it be necessary?), and between *Shall we get a drink?* (ie would you like one?) and *Will we get a drink?* (ie do you know whether they will give us one?). Another distinction can be made between *Shall you join us?* (ie are you going to?) and *Will you join us?* (ie please do!). However, those who seldom or never use **shall** have other perfectly adequate ways of making such distinctions. When they immediately follow the subject, both **shall** and **will** are replaced in less formal contexts by the neutral **'ll** (*I'll go*), which serves either meaning.

shampoo

The plural of the noun is **shampoos**. Other forms of the verb are **shampoos, shampooed, shampooing**.

shan't

This short form of *shall not* is rarer than *shall*, and nonexistent in American English. It may strike some people as affected. See SHALL.

shant(e)y

See CHANT(E)Y.

sharp, sharply

Apart from its musical sense (the opposite of *flat*) the adverb **sharp**, rather than **sharply**, is correctly used in the sense of 'abruptly' (*turn sharp left*; *pull up sharp*) and 'punctually' (*four o'clock sharp*). It cannot replace **sharply** in other senses: *speak sharply to him*; *sharply contrasted colours*.

shave

The past tense is **shaved** (*He shaved off his beard*) and the participle either **shaved** or **shaven**. But **shaved** is the usual past participle of the verb (*I haven't shaved this morning*) and **shaven** is chiefly used as an adjective: *clean-shaven*.

she

1 When we call a ship **she** we are using 'personification', referring to a thing as if it were a person. This is a common way to express affection for something inanimate, such as one's car. It is old-fashioned and slightly flowery to use **she** of nations and cities. Prefer *Britain revised its* (rather than *her*) *agricultural policy*. If you do personify something, do so consistently, writing either *Britain, who revised her policy* or *Britain, which revised its policy*, but not *who . . . its* or *which . . . her*. See GENDER, GRAMMATICAL.

2 For the choice between **she** and *her*, see CASE, GRAMMATICAL.

sheaf

The plural is **sheaves**.

shear, sheer

1 The past tense of **shear** is **sheared** (*He sheared the sheep*) and the participle either **shorn** or **sheared**. The normal past participle is **shorn** for hair and for the abstract senses, particularly in adjectival use (*his shorn head*; *The king was shorn of his authority*), but **sheared** is used of metal (*The bolt has sheared off*).

2 Sheer is chiefly an adjective meaning 'diaphanous' (*sheer tights*) or 'utter' (*sheer ignorance*). As a verb, it means 'swerve, deviate': *The runaway vehicle sheered* (ie veered) *away from the precipice*.

sheik(h)

When it means an Arab chief it should be spelled **sheikh**, but the spelling **sheik** is more usual for the wider sense of a romantically dashing man. The pronunciation 'shake' is to be recommended in British English, at least for the first sense, but 'sheek' is a very common alternative.

shekel

It is FACETIOUS to use this word to mean simply 'money': *raking in the shekels*. The usage should be avoided, since the **shekel** is the official monetary unit of modern Israel.

shelf

The plural is **shelves**.

shepherd

This is the usual British word. People who look after sheep on the open ranges of the American West are *sheepherders*.

shew, shewn

See SHOW.

shibboleth

From its biblical origin, as a word whose correct pronunciation was used as a test to distinguish the Gileadites from their enemies, this has come to be a rather derogatory word for any entrenched and mindlessly observed custom or dogma: *the ancient shibboleths of the Labour Movement*. It should not be used as a synonym for *platitude*, as in *the shibboleth that crime does not pay*.

shield

The word is spelled *-ie-*, not *-ei-*.

shier, shyer, shily, shyly

Both **shier** and **shyer** are correct spellings for 'more shy'. **Shyly** is far more usual than **shily**.

shine

The past tense and participle are **shone**, except in the sense of 'polish': *The sun shone; She shone her torch into the corner; He shined his shoes*.

shingles

As the name of a disease, this is usually treated as a singular noun (*Shingles is very unpleasant*), although it can be a plural (*Shingles are . . .*).

ship

See BOAT.

shoe (*verb*)

Other forms are **shoeing**, and **shod** or occasionally **shoed**. Use **shod** when the participle is used with a noun: *a racehorse shod with plates*.

shoot, chute

Both spellings are correct for a sloping channel down which something is moved (*a rubbish shoot/chute*) or for a slide into a swimming pool. **Chute** is the British preference.

shop (*verb*)

Other forms are **shopped, shopping.** In American English, you can **shop** a store or its merchandise rather than shopping *at* the store or *for* the goods: *shop the stores for Christmas gift ideas.* This use is, however, avoided by careful American writers. The British sense of **shop,** 'inform against', is informal too: *the robber who changed sides and shopped his mates* (*Daily Mirror*).

short, shortly

1 The adverb **short** is used in such phrases as *cut short, stop short, run short, sell short.* **Shortly** means 'soon' (*shortly after lunch*) or 'abruptly', or 'briefly', so there is little overlap of meaning.

2 *In short supply* can seem a PRETENTIOUS way of saying 'scarce'.

shorts

See PANTS.

should, would

When **should** and **would** are used in 'reported speech' to represent the 'pure' future, the distinction between them has traditionally been the same as that between *shall* and *will*; see SHALL. **Should** was used for the first person, so that *We shall come* became *We said we should come*, and **would** for the second and third persons, so that *They will come* became *I thought they would come*.

This distinction is dying out. **Would** and **'d** commonly replace **should,** particularly in American English, just as *will* replaces *shall,* and *I said I would come* is now acceptable. The process may have been hastened for the good reason that **should** can also mean 'ought to', in all three persons: *You should see a doctor; It shouldn't be allowed.* If you use **should** with *I* or *we* you may introduce an unintended element of 'ought'. A British politician wrote in *The Times* that if something or other happened *we should be building in the wrong place and at the wrong time.* He did not mean that we ought to build in the wrong place. The ambiguity would have been avoided if he had written *we would.* (For the use of **should** to replace *ought,* see OUGHT.)

Should is correctly, though rather formally, used after *if: if it should snow* (for *if it snows*); *if you should be late* (for *if you're* late). Here there can be no implication of 'ought'. Nor is there any ambiguity over the polite phrase *I should think,* which is less dogmatic than *I think.* It is very common, though, in British as well as American English, to write *I would like, I would prefer, I would be inclined,* etc rather than using **should** in such phrases, and the practice does not seem to attract criticism.

Should is commonly used in *that*-clauses after expressions that express a future necessity, plan, or intention or that convey an emotional reaction to a future event: *I have arranged that you should drive; They prefer that I should chair the meeting; It is regrettable that she should be absent during the negotiations.* This use of **should** may give rise to ambiguity: *They insisted that the reforms should be implemented immediately.* In such instances, rephrase to avoid the ambiguity: *They insisted that the reforms be implemented immediately* or *They insisted that the reforms ought to be implemented immediately.*

shovel

Other forms are **shovelled, shovelling** in British English, but the second *l* is usually omitted in American English.

show

1 The past tense is **showed**, and the participle either **shown** or **showed**. (The archaic spellings *shew, shewn* survive almost solely in legal use.) Use **shown**, not **showed**, in the passive: *We were shown some photographs.* Otherwise, **showed** is equally correct but less common: *They've shown/showed us the photographs.*

2 The American English use of **show** to mean 'put in an appearance' (*He failed to show for the award*) is informal.

shriek

The word is spelled -ie-, not -ei-.

shrink

The past tense is **shrank** or sometimes **shrunk**, and the participle **shrunk** or **shrunken**. **Shrunken** is the adjectival form: *My socks shrank; They have shrunk; shrunken heads.*

shrivel

Other forms are **shrivelled, shrivelling** in British English, but the second *l* is usually omitted in American English.

shrouded

Shrouded in mist/fog/secrecy is a CLICHÉ.

shyer, shyly

See SHIER.

sibling

This word is useful to those professionals who have to refer to a brother or sister irrespective of sex. For general purposes, prefer *brother, brothers, brother and sister*, etc.

sic

This means 'intentionally so written'. It is used, in square brackets, to show that a quoted item exactly reproduces the original and is not a mistake by the copier. Do not use it to jeer at uneducated language, as in *He said he seed [sic] the whole thing.*

sick

See ILL.

sickly

This is an adjective. The related adverb should be *sicklily*, but this sounds so clumsy that it is better to rephrase *smile sicklily* as *smile in a sickly way* or *with a sickly smile.*

siege, sieve

Both words are spelled -ie-, not -ei-.

[sieze]

This is an incorrect spelling of **seize**.

sight, site, cite

Sight is vision or something seen, a **site** is a location, to **cite** is to refer to.

signal, single

1 Other forms of the verb **signal** are **signalled, signalling** in British English, but the second *l* is usually omitted in American English.

2 The correct phrase is *single out* (ie 'select from a group'), not *signal out*.

significant, significantly

These are OVERUSED in such phrases as *a significant improvement* or *significantly faster*. For a change, use *important, marked, considerably, appreciably*, etc.

signor, signora, signorine

The *gn* is pronounced like the *ni* of *onion*; see ITALIAN SOUNDS. These are the equivalents of *Mr, Mrs,* and *Miss* when you are addressing Italian-speaking people, as *Señor* etc are for the Spanish.

silk, silken, silky

Use **silk** as an adjective for things actually made of silk: *a silk scarf.* **Silken** is somewhat literary, and is used figuratively of delicate or luxurious things: *The cat moved with silken grace.* **Silky** can be used of things that feel like silk: *silky cotton.*

silly, sillily

Silly can be used not only as an adjective (*silly boy*) but informally as an adverb (*Don't talk so silly*). The more formal **sillily** (*to giggle sillily*) sounds awkward, so it may be better to write *foolishly* or *in a silly way*.

silo

The plural is **silos**. The word is used, not only in an agricultural sense, but to mean a store for guided missiles.

similar, same

1 Use **similar** with *to* and not with any other word: *dressed in similar* *clothes to mine* (not *as mine*), or *to those I was wearing*. But prefer the simpler word *like* where the sentence allows it. Clothes *similar to mine* are clothes *like mine*.

2 Same means either that the items under consideration are really one (*They take their children to the same doctor*) or that they correspond so closely as to be indistinguishable (*two brothers with the same nose*). **Similar** means that the items are alike in certain respects. You can say that things are *exactly* or *almost the same*, or that they are *very, rather,* or *somewhat similar*, or you can speak of a *slight* or *great similarity*.

simplistic

1 This means 'oversimplified, affectedly naive'. It should not be confused with the often appreciative word *simple*. We speak of *a nice simple explanation* but of *a stupid simplistic generalization*.

2 Since **simplistic** itself contains the idea of 'too much', it is a TAUTOLOGY to call things *oversimplistic*.

simply

The position of **simply** in a sentence affects its meaning. When preceding the part of the sentence it concerns, it means 'only, merely' (*I simply asked*) or 'unquestionably' (*simply marvellous*). When following the relevant part, it may mean 'only', but it may also mean 'in a simple way'. A sentence such as *He eats simply to keep alive* might mean either that that is the only reason he eats, or that his health obliges him to live on a simple diet. Rephrasing is needed to make the meaning clear.

simulate

See DISSIMULATE.

simultaneous

This is an adjective: *simultaneous translation*. The adverb is **simultaneously**: *The speech was relayed simultaneously* (not *simultaneous*) *in the five official languages*.

since

1 When it means 'during the time after', or 'from then till now', expressions with **since** are correctly accompanied by a verb in the perfect tense (ie with *have, has, had*): *He has since become* (not *He since became*) *rich*; *We haven't met* (not *We didn't meet*) *since 1978*. But you can say *It's a long time since breakfast*, or *How long is it since you met?* A verb following **since** is usually, but not always, in the past tense. You can say *It's been very quiet since Bill left*, but also *We've been very busy since Bill's been here*, meaning that he is still here. **Since** can also correctly mean 'because', and is then used with any tense: *Since Peter didn't know, I asked Mary.* See BECAUSE.

2 The adverb **since** is used like *ago* in the expression *long since*: *I've long since forgotten*. Prefer *ago* elsewhere, as in *He went out half an hour ago* (rather than *since*). Do not write *ago since*; see AGO.

sincerely

Yours sincerely (chiefly British), or *Sincerely yours* (chiefly American), is the standard complimentary ending to a letter. See LETTER ENDINGS.

sinecure, cynosure

A **sinecure** is a job involving little or no actual work. A **cynosure** (formal) is a centre of attraction, as in the CLICHÉ *She was the cynosure of all eyes*.

sine die, sine qua non

Prefer the ordinary English word *indefinitely* for **sine die** (*The meeting adjourned sine die*) and *necessity* or *essential* for **sine qua non** (*Strong boots are a sine qua non*).

sing

The past tense and participle are **sang** and **sung**: *They sang* (not *sung*) *his praises*; *They have sung some carols*.

singe

Other forms are **singed, singeing**. *Singing* would be part of the verb *sing*.

single

See SIGNAL.

Sinhalese, Singhalese, Cingalese

Sinhalese is the preferred spelling of this word for the people and language of Sri Lanka (formerly Ceylon).

sink

The past tense and participle are **sank** (or, rarely, **sunk**) and **sunk**: *They sank* (rather than *sunk*) *a frigate*; *The frigate has sunk*. The related adjective *sunken* is the usual choice before a noun: *sunken cheeks*; *a sunken garden*.

sinus

The plural is **sinuses**.

Sir, Dame

Sir is the title of a British knight or baronet; **Dame** is the female equivalent. One can use these titles before the person's first name (*Sir Laurence*; *Dame Edith*), or before the whole name (*Sir Laurence Olivier*; *Dame Edith Evans*), but not before the surname alone (ie not *Sir Olivier*, *Dame Evans*). See TITLES OF PEOPLE.

sit

The past tense and participles are both **sat**: *She sat on the floor*; *The court has sat for a week*. For the literal sense of 'resting on one's buttocks', the adjective is *seated* rather than *sat*: *a seated model*; *Please be seated*. Write *I sat* (not *I was sat*) *there all afternoon*. See also SET.

site

See SIGHT.

sitting room, living room, drawing room, lounge

The room where you relax in your home is the **sitting room** or **living room**. **Living room** may be the better word if the only other rooms are kitchen, bathroom, and bedrooms. **Drawing room** is a rather formal word, and suggests a large grand room. **Lounge** in this sense is something of a GENTEELISM, though it is the established word for a room for sitting in a public place: *a hotel lounge*; *an airport departure lounge*.

situate(d)

The adjective **situate** is very formal, used in such contexts as *a parcel of land situate in the village of Seathwaite*. Outside legal contexts use **situated** (which commonly occurs in the language of estate agents), or just leave it out.

situation, position

Both words are OVERUSED in the sense 'state of affairs'. Instead of *a crisis situation* one can say just *a crisis*; instead of *in a face-to-face situation*, just *face to face*; instead of *if the position arises*, simply *if it happens*. The combination *ongoing situation* has been particularly criticized.

sixth

In careful speech, the *th* should be pronounced. Otherwise it sounds like *six*.

size

1 It is VERBOSE to call things *large in size* or *large-sized*; use *large* alone.

2 Either **-size** or **-sized** is correct as part of a compound adjective, but one or the other may be more normal in particular combinations: *bit-size(d) biscuits*; *a life-size(d) statue*; *outsize clothing*; *a medium-sized house*.

siz(e)able

This can be spelled either with or without the first *e*.

skein

The word is spelled *-ei-*, not *-ie-*.

skeptic

See SCEPTIC.

skewbald

See PIEBALD.

ski

1 This is usually pronounced 'skee'. The British variant 'shee' is old-fashioned and rare.

2 The usual plural is **skis** rather than **ski**. Other forms of the verb are **skied, skis, skiing**. The related noun is **skier**.

skil(l)ful, skilled

1 The word is spelled **skilful** in British English, **skillful** in American English.

2 **Skilful** implies dexterity and ingenuity, and is used of people and behaviour: *skilful debater*; *skilful handling of the problem*. **Skilled** suggests mastery of a craft, and can apply to the craft as well as to the worker: *a skilled carpenter*; *skilled trades*.

skull

See SCULL.

slack, slacken, slake

To be lazy is to **slack**: *The boss caught them slacking*. To make something, or to become, less or slower or looser is to **slacken**: *slacken the rope*; *slacken speed*; *Our enthusiasm slackened*. You can **slake** or **slack** lime, but you **slake** your thirst.

slander

See LIBEL.

slang

See VARIETIES OF ENGLISH.

slash

When used of prices and reductions, this is journalese. *Cut* or *reduce* should be used in ordinary writing.

slate (*verb*)

In informal British English, this can mean 'censure, criticize'. In American English it can mean 'schedule; destine': *slated for President*. A headline such as *Peace Talks Slated* may therefore be interpreted very differently in the two countries.

slattern

See SLUT.

slay

The past tense and participle are normally **slew** and **slain**. Curiously enough, this verb can be either literary in flavour (*St George slew the dragon*) or journalese (*Mad Axeman Slays Nine*), besides being informal in the sense 'overwhelm', where the past is *slayed*: *His jokes really slayed me*. Usually *kill* is a more appropriate word.

sledge, sled, sleigh

These are all vehicles that slide on runners over snow. **Sledge** is the commonest word in British English, both for the small downhill toboggan and for the larger vehicle that is pulled by dogs, horses, or reindeer. In American and Canadian English **sled** is preferred for the smaller vehicle and **sleigh** for the larger, particularly when it has seats and is drawn by a horse.

sleep

The sleep of the just is a CLICHÉ.

sleight

This is pronounced to rhyme with *light*, and spelled *-ei-*, not *-ie-*.

slew

This is the past tense of **slay**; but see SLOUGH.

slier, slily

See SLYER.

sling, slink

The past tense and participle are **slung** and **slunk**, not *slang* or *slank*.

slough, slew

A swamp or marshy pool is a **slough**, rhyming with *now* in British English, but it is a **slough** or **slew** or **slue**, rhyming with *too*, in American English. The verb meaning 'shed', and the noun meaning 'cast-off skin' are **slough** or sometimes **sluff**, both pronounced 'sluff'. The verb meaning 'skid sideways' is **slew**.

slovenly

See SLUT.

slow, slowly

Slow as an adverb is less formal than **slowly**. It is particularly used with *go*, as in the industrial sense of *go slow*, and is probably commoner in American than in British use. Both **slow** and **slowly** are usually possible, particularly in the imperative, but **slowly** is the more formally correct: *Please drive slow/slowly*; *to speak slower/more slowly*. Only **slowly**, not **slow**, can precede a verb: *He slowly opened the box.*

slut, slattern, slovenly

They all refer to a dirty negligent person. Only a woman can be a **slut** or **sluttish**, a **slattern** or **slatternly**. **Sluts** are even dirtier than

slatterns, and may be sexually immoral too. Men as well as women can be **slovenly**, but the noun **sloven** is rare.

slyer, slier, slyly, slily

Both **slyer** and **slier** are correct spellings for 'more sly'. **Slyly** is commoner than **slily**.

small-scale, small-sized

Small-scale applies properly to maps. When used of other things than maps, it implies 'narrow in scope': *a small-scale statistical survey*. It is VERBOSE to use it, or **small-sized**, merely for 'small'.

smell (*verb*)

1 The past tense and participle are either **smelt** or **smelled** in British English, but **smelled** is much the commoner American form.

2 When it means 'have a specified smell', **smell** is followed by an adjective, not an adverb (*It smells funny*), or else by a phrase (*It smells of onions*). When it means 'stink', the verb may be used either alone (*His breath smells*) or with an expression that describes the degree of 'stink': *The meat smelled slightly so I threw it away*. You can correctly say either *The room smells horrible* (ie that is the smell it has) or *The room smells horribly* (ie that is how much it stinks).

smok(e)y

The *e* is usually omitted.

smo(u)lder

The word is spelled **smoulder** in British English, **smolder** in American English.

sneak (*verb*)

The past tense and participle are **sneaked**. The past tense **snuck** is American English only, and is nonstandard or jocular.

so

1 **so** for **very**	**5** **so** *far as*; see FAR (1)
2 purpose and result	**6** **so** *long as*; see LONG
3 **so** meaning 'therefore'	**7** **so** *nice a*; see SUCH (3)
4 *do* **so**	**8** **so** or **as**; see AS (2)

1 The use of **so** for **very**, as in *I'm so glad to see you*, is more appropriate to speech than to writing. In the wrong context it can sound rather gushing.

2 So can express, among other things, the ideas of both 'purpose' and 'result'. A sentence such as *They turned off the radio so he could sleep* may explain either 'their' purpose in turning it off, or the fortunate consequence of 'their' action. If it is necessary to make the distinction, rephrase the sentence as *so that he would be able to sleep* or *so as to let him sleep* or *to let him sleep* (purpose), or *so that he was able to sleep* (result).

3 So can also mean 'consequently, therefore': *We were tired and so went to bed*. There is nothing wrong with this use, but you should avoid it if it might create confusion with one of the other meanings of **so**. Before an adjective, it might be taken to mean 'very'. In *The witness was biased and so unreliable*, **so** should be changed to *very* or *therefore*, according to the intended meaning. When this kind of **so** begins a sentence, as it sometimes does, do not put a comma after it. *So(,) what shall we do now?*

4 The expression *do so* is conveniently used to avoid repetition of a verb. It means 'act in this way': *I didn't wash my hair today but I will do so tomorrow*. Make sure that there is, in fact, a verb to which *do so* obviously refers. Do not write *He is kind to children unless it is too much trouble to do so*, but use *be* **so**, or leave out the phrase. Do not write *I know nothing about chess but I hope to do so*, because it sounds rather as though you 'hope to know nothing'. Rephrase it, perhaps as *but I hope to learn*.

soar

See SORE.

so-called

1 The expression means that something has no right to its name. Do not use it of people or institutions that unquestionably are what they are called, just because you dislike them. *So-called pop music* is pop music, even if you hate it.

2 Do not combine it with quotation marks. Write either *a so-called militant* or *a 'militant'*.

sociable, social

Sociable is an appreciative word for 'fond of companionship' or 'friendly': *We're very sociable in our office*. **Social** is neutral, meaning merely 'of society': *social history; a busy social life*. Confusion is commonest when we speak of a *social evening* or a *social club*. These may or may not be also **sociable** (ie friendly).

social disease

This is a rather old-fashioned EUPHEMISM for *venereal disease*. Use the plainer expression.

socialism, socialist

Use a capital *S* for a political party or its members, a small *s* for the political principles in general or their adherents.

sofa, settee, couch, davenport, chesterfield, settle, ottoman

A **sofa** has a back and two arms. A **settee** need not have arms, and is generally less upholstered than a **sofa**. **Couch** is another word for **sofa**, but a **couch** may also have one raised head-end and be meant for reclining on. A large sofa is a **davenport** in American English. A **chesterfield** is a tightly padded usually leather sofa, with upright armrests often the same height as the back. A **settle** is a more primitive benchlike affair, with wooden arms and a high wooden back. An **ottoman** is an upholstered box, with no arms and usually no back.

soft, softly

Soft can be an adverb, but it is so used chiefly in literary contexts: *How soft the poplars sigh* (A E Housman). It cannot replace **softly**, the usual adverb, as in *whistle softly*.

soi-disant

This French expression means 'self-styled, professed', rather than merely 'so-called': *a soi-disant sculptor*. Do not use it when a person is called something by other people. In any case, prefer an English word where possible.

soigné(e)

This is spelled with the accent, and has the feminine form **soignée** when used of a woman. It means 'well-groomed' or 'elegant'.

soiled

This is a GENTEELISM: *soiled laundry*. Prefer *dirty*.

soirée

The accent is usually omitted.

sojourn

In British English, the first *o* is pronounced like the sound of *lodge* or of *budge*. In American English, it sounds like 'soh'. This is an old-fashioned or PRETENTIOUS word for *stay*.

solicitor

The word ends in *-or*, not *-er*.

soliloquy

See MONOLOGUE.

solo

The plural is usually **solos**; the rare plural **soli** is only for the musical sense.

soluble, solvable

Soluble means 'can be dissolved': *soluble pills*. Both **soluble** and **solvable** mean 'can be solved': *soluble/solvable problems*.

sombre

The word is spelled **sombre** in British English, **somber** in American English.

sombrero

The plural is **sombreros**. It is a wide-brimmed Mexican hat.

some

1 When **some** is used with a number, to mean 'about', the number is not intended to be precise. Write *some 300 people*, but not *some 293 people*.

2 Some is used, more in American than in British English, to mean *somewhat* or *rather* or *sometimes*: *He felt some better*; *It rained some*; *We play tennis some*. Except in the phrase *some more* (*It rained some more in the evening*), this is decidedly more appropriate to speech than to serious writing. The use of **some** to mean 'an enormous, an amazing' as in *That was some party!* is informal too, but it can be extremely effective, as in Churchill's *Some chicken! Some neck!*.

somebody, someone

See ANY (1).

someday

This one-word spelling of *some day* is correct in American but not in British English. It means 'at some indefinite future time', as in *We'll go there someday*. But write *We'll choose some day* (not *someday*) *that suits us both*.

someone

This means 'some person, somebody': *Someone has borrowed my pen*. **Some one** means 'some single': *Choose some one subject to study*.

someplace

This is correct in American English for all except formal writing, and *some place* (two words) is correct at all levels of American use. British English prefers *somewhere*.

sometime, sometimes

As an adjective, **sometime** is a correct but rather old-fashioned word for 'former': *the sometime chairman*. It is correctly used, in both British and American English, as an adverb meaning 'at some unspecified time', but *some time* (two words) can also be used here. *We'll meet sometime* (or *some time*) *next week*. *Some time* (not **sometime**) also means 'an appreciable length of time': *The fire burned for some time*. **Sometimes** means 'occasionally'.

someway, someways

These are informal American words. Prefer *somehow* in British English, and in all writing.

somewhere(s)

Somewhere is the correct form; **somewheres** is nonstandard.

sooner

After *no sooner*, use *than*, not *when*: *I had no sooner sat down than the phone rang*. See CORRELATIVE (3).

soprano

The plural is **sopranos**.

sore, soar

Sore means 'painful'. The archaic adverb (*sore afraid*) belongs to old-fashioned poetic language; use *sorely*, *much*, etc. **Soar** means 'fly high'.

sorrow

More in sorrow than in anger is a CLICHÉ.

sort

See KIND.

soufflé

The word is spelled with the accent.

sound (*verb*)

1 When it means 'seem when heard', **sound** is followed by an adjective: *The story sounds incredible.* In formal writing it should not be followed by *to* and a verb: *He sounded furious* (not *to be furious*).

2 *Sound out* in the sense of 'test by questioning' is a well-established idiom, an alternative to using **sound** alone: *We sounded him (out) about the new proposals.*

sound, soundly

Both these adverbs can mean 'thoroughly', but **sound** is used almost entirely in connection with sleep: *sound asleep*; *You'll sleep the sounder for it.* Elsewhere, use **soundly**: *scolded them soundly.*

south, southern

See NORTH.

southward(s)

Before a noun, use **southward**: *a southward flight.* After a verb, use the form with an *s* in British English (*sailing southwards*) and the one without an *s* in American English.

Soviet

See RUSSIAN.

sow

See SEW.

spark (*verb*)

In the sense 'precipitate; incite' (*spark off a riot*) **spark** is popular with journalists but is too general to be called journalese. It is a vivid addition to the language.

spatula

See SCAPULA.

spearhead

Prefer *head*, *lead*, or *direct* as a change from this OVERUSED verb: *to spearhead our new sales programme.*

speciality, specialty

Something in which one *specializes*, or at which one is particularly skilled, is usually a **speciality** in British English and a **specialty** in American English: *Yorkshire pudding was mother's speciality.* In both British and American English, a distinguishing characteristic of something is its **speciality**, and a legal agreement embodied in a sealed document is a **specialty.**

special(ly), especial(ly)

Specially is commoner than **especially**, but some careful writers recognize a distinction. They prefer to confine **special** and **specially** to the sense 'for a particular purpose' (*a special train*; *This is specially for you*) and use **especially** and the rarer **especial** for the sense 'to an unusual degree' (*an especial friend*; *not especially clever*).

specie, species

1 The *c* in both words is pronounced either 'sh' or 's', but some British speakers dislike the second.

2 Specie is a rare word for money in coin. A **species** (plural **species**) is a biological category (*the human species*). **Species** is used loosely as another word for *kind*: *a dangerous species of criminal.*

spectator

The word ends in *-or*, not *-er*.

spectre, specter

The word is spelled **spectre** in British English, **specter** in American English

spectrum

The plural is either **spectra** or **spectrums**. This word is OVERUSED in such contexts as *a wide spectrum of interests*, where *range*, for instance, would be a welcome change.

speculator

The word ends in *-or*, not *-er*.

speed (*verb*)

The past tense and participle are either **sped** or **speeded**. **Sped** is not used in connection with traffic offences, nor in the combination *speed up*: *We've speeded up the process*.

spell

1 The past tense and participle of the verb meaning 'form words' are **spelled** or **spelt**, but **spelt** is an almost entirely British form. The other verb, meaning 'relieve for a time', allows only **spelled**: *The two guards spelled each other*.

2 Spell *out* may mean 'make explicit': *spell out the implications of the new law*. It is perfectly standard in that sense.

spelling

1	origins	**3**	British and American spellings
2	spelling reform	**4**	spelling rules

1 origins

Most of the common words in our vocabulary come from two sources: the Germanic words of Old English, and the Romance words introduced from Norman-French in the period after the Norman Conquest when it was the language of the upper class. Numerous words have been borrowed from foreign languages in later periods – particularly from French, Latin, and Greek –and new words have been and are still being created by combining classical roots. Our spelling reflects a mixture of the Old English and Norman-French spelling systems, together with spellings introduced by loanwords from other languages. So we have the same sound represented by different spellings (**s**ell from Old English, **c**ertain from French, **ps**ychology from Greek), and the same spelling representing different sounds (**g**et from Old English, **g**em from French). Loanwords of relatively recent vintage are often recognizable by the unusual relationship between their spelling and pronunciation: *khaki, potpourri, cuisine, reservoir, pterodactyl, mnemonic, bureau*. A further complication is that some spellings were changed, usually by analogy with Latin and Greek words, to bring them nearer to what were thought to be their original spellings: *b* was added in *debt* and *doubt*, *l* in *fault* and *vault*, *c* in *indict*.

Our present spelling was in general fixed by the early printers in the late fifteenth century, although further stabilized by printers and compilers of dictionaries in the three centuries that followed. But important sound changes have affected the English vowel system since the end of the fifteenth century and these are not reflected in the present spelling system.

These two historical factors – the mixed spelling systems and the failure of spelling to follow sound change – have resulted in a modern English spelling that is generally thought to be chaotic. It is easy to point to eccentricities such as the different pronunciations of final -*ough* in *cough, though, through, rough, thorough, bough, hiccough*. The sound 's' in *sell* is also spelled *ss* (*pass*), *c* (*cell*), *sc* (*science*), *se* (*lapse*), *ps* (*psalm*), *st* (*whistle*), *sw* (*sword*), *z* (*waltz*), and it is the second of two sounds spelled by the letter *x* (*box*). Many further examples can illustrate that English spelling is not phonetic. At the same time we should not ignore the numerous regularities in the system, some of which will be illustrated below. We should also recognize that there still exist very many variant correct spellings. Here are just a few examples: *acknowledgment, acknowledgement; bulrush, bullrush; characterize, characterise* (and numerous similar pairs); *disyllable, dissyllable; forebode, forbode; gradable, gradeable; partisan, partizan; primeval, primaeval; sergeant, serjeant*. Dictionaries list variants, generally indicating if one of them is the preferred or more frequent spelling. Widespread use of spelling checkers as an aid to word processing may lead in the future to greater uniformity in spelling.

2 spelling reform

Over the centuries many reformers have unsuccessfully advocated spelling systems that would make English spelling conform more closely with English pronunciation. The most serious problem in devising a phonetic system is that pronunciation differs considerably between and within English-speaking countries; spellings that would suit one region would not necessarily suit the others. It has also been pointed out that existing spellings are sometimes able to convey meaning relations that are obscured by different pronunciations of the words: *medicine, medical; nation, national; photograph, photography; sign, signature*. Nevertheless, some simplifications are possible and some anomalies can be removed while preserving international intelligibility and relations in meaning between words.

3 British and American spellings

There are differences in spelling between British and American English, though in some instances the two spellings occur in both national varieties. Here is a list of common American spelling usages or preferences, with the preferred British spellings in brackets. The words listed are merely examples. Further examples appear under the general entries, such as DOUBLING, elsewhere in this book, and also in the entries for individual words.

(a) doubling before a suffix follows the regular rule for *l*: *signaled* (*signalled*), *traveler* (*traveller*)

(b) -or, (-our): *labor* (*labour*), *color* (*colour*)

(c) -ize (-ise): *civilize* (*civilise*), *naturalize* (*naturalise*); *-ize* is increasingly the preferred form in British English, and *-ization* is now usual

(d) -e- (-ae-, -oe-): *medieval* (*mediaeval*), *diarrhea* (*diarrhoea*); the simpler American spelling is increasingly common in British English

(e) -ection (-exion): *inflection* (*inflexion*), *reflection* (*reflexion*); the American spelling is becoming the norm for British English

(f) -er (-re): *center* (*centre*), *meter* (*metre*)

Here are American spellings for some common words, most of which have the British spelling (in brackets) as an alternative:

ax (*axe*)	*intrust* (*entrust*)
catalog (*catalogue*)	*naught* (*nought*)
check (*cheque*)	*offense* (*offence*)
cigaret (*cigarette*)	*pajamas* (*pyjamas*)
curb (*kerb*)	*practice* as verb (*practise*)
defense (*defence*)	*pretense* (*pretence*)
draft (*draught*)	*program* (*programme*;
enroll (*enrol*)	except in computing)
fulfill (*fulfil*)	*story* (*storey*) 'floor in
gray (*grey*)	a building'
inclose (*enclose*)	*tire* (*tyre*)
inquiry (*enquiry*)	

4 spelling rules

Despite the notorious vagaries of English spelling, there are some general rules that are useful to remember for avoiding common mistakes.

(a) doubling of consonant before suffix

This rule accounts for the double *r* in *preferred* and the single *r* in *preference*. See DOUBLING.

(b) dropping -e before suffix

If a word ends with a silent *-e* (*fame*), we drop the *e* when we add a suffix beginning with a vowel (*-ous*). Examples: *famous, having, curable, refusal*. In four words ending in *ie*, we also change the *i* to *y*: *dying* (*die*), *lying* (*lie*), *tying* (tie), *vying* (*vie*).

We exceptionally retain the *e* in *dyeing* (from *dye*), *singeing* (from *singe*), and *swingeing* (from *swinge*), to distinguish these words from *dying* (from *die*), *singing* (from *sing*), and *swinging* (from *swing*). Similar exceptions are *hoeing* (from *hoe*), *canoeing, shoeing, toeing*. We also retain the *e* in *ce* (*peace*) and *ge* (*courage*) when the suffix begins with *a* (*-able*) or *o* (*-ous*) to preserve the 's' sound in *c* and the 'j' sound in *g*: *peaceable, traceable, noticeable, courageous, advantageous, knowledgeable*.

There are also some exceptions where we drop the *e* before a consonant. The *e* is dropped in *argument, awful, duly, truly, wholly*. In several words where the suffix is added to *-dge*, spellings with or without *e* are correct: *abridg(e)ment, acknowledg(e)ment, judg(e)ment*. See -E-.

(c) changing *y* to *i* before suffix

If a word ends in a consonant plus *y* (*happy*), we change the *y* to *i* (*happily*) before any suffix except *-ing* (*studying*) or *'s* (*spy's*, in contrast to *spies*). Examples: *beautiful, mysterious, amplification, emptiness*. The same rule applies to plurals of nouns (*worries*), and to verb forms (*dries, dried*).

We exceptionally retain the *y* in a few words before the suffix *-ness*: *dryness, shyness, slyness*. We also keep the *y* in *busyness* 'the state of being busy' to distinguish it from *business*.

There are also a few exceptions where the word ends in a vowel before *y*, and we nevertheless change the *y* to *i*: *daily, laid, paid, said, slain*.

(d) *i* before *e* except after *c*

If the sound is 'ee', spell *ie* except after *c*. We therefore have *niece, priest*, and *siege*; but *deceive, receive, ceiling*. Exceptions with the spelling *ei*: *seize, weird*, and (where one pronunciation has 'ee') *either* and *neither*. In words where the sound is 'ay' as in *say*, the order is *e* before *i* (*weigh, reign*). See I BEFORE E. For plurals ending in *-ies*, see PLURALS OF NOUNS (1).

(e) adding *-ally* to adjectives in *-ic*

To form adverbs from adjectives, add *-ally*, even though the first syllable (*-al*) is generally not sounded in conversation: *basically, realistically*. The exception is *publicly*.

(f) adding *-ful* to nouns

The suffix is *-ful*, not *full*: *beautiful, successful.* Notice also the spellings *fulfil* and *fulfilment*, spelled in American English *fulfill* (also *fulfil*) and *fulfillment*.

(g) problem words

Here are some words that often cause difficulty: *accommodate, acknowledge, allege, argument, calendar, cemetery, committee, concede, conscience, embarrass, exceed, existence, February, foreign, government, harass, inoculate, language, library, necessary, neighbour, occasion, parliament, persuade, precede, privilege, proceed, professor, pronunciation, pursue, recede, recommend, reference, science, secede, secretary, succeed, supersede, surprise, suspicious, therefore, Wednesday.*

See also POSSESSIVE PRONOUNS; PLURALS OF NOUNS; EYE DIALECT.

spelling pronunciation

The spread of literacy has encouraged new pronunciations that are based on the spelling of the words. Some of these spelling pronunciations ousted older pronunciations long ago: the 'h' sound in *host*, where *h* was once silent and still is in words like *hour*; the 'th' sound in *author*, which replaced an earlier *t* sound; the 'l' sound in *fault*, not pronounced in earlier periods. Numerous spelling pronunciations exist side by side with traditional pronunciations, in some instances gradually displacing them: *forehead* (traditionally pronounced 'forrid'), *often* ('offen'), *Monday* and many other words ending in *-day* (the final vowel traditionally pronounced as in *trendy*), *arctic* ('artic'), *pulpit* ('pulp it'), *constable* ('cunstable'), *appreciate* (*c* traditionally pronounced 'sh', but now often 's'). As long as they are currently in wide use, both pronunciation variants are correct. It you are in doubt about the pronunciation, consult a dictionary.

sphere

See FIELD.

spill

The past tense and participle are either **spilt** or **spilled**. **Spilt** is the preferred British form, **spilled** the American one: *spilt/spilled milk; The train spilled/spilt its passengers onto the platform.*

spin

The past tense and participle are **spun**. The past tense **span** is archaic.

spiral (*verb*)

1 Other forms are **spiralled, spiralling** in British English, but the second *l* is usually omitted in American English.

2 Spiral can correctly mean 'increase uncontrollably': *spiralling costs*. It is not necessary to say *up* or *upwards* here.

spire, steeple

A **spire** is a roof that tapers to a point, often on top of a tower. **Steeple** is often used as another word for **spire**, particularly when it is part of a church, but it can also mean the tower itself, with or without a spire.

spiritual, spirituous

They are both adjectives from *spirit*. **Spiritual** refers to the soul (*our spiritual needs*) and **spirituous** to alcohol.

spirt

See SPURT.

spit

The past tense and participle of the verb meaning 'expectorate' are **spat** or **spit**. **Spat** is the usual past tense in British English, but **spit** is a common American form: *He spat/spit at me*. The other verb, meaning 'impale', makes **spitted.**

spitting image

This is derived from *spit and image*, but it would be rather pedantic to spell it like that.

splendiferous

This informal word may sound FACETIOUS. In serious contexts, use *splendid*.

splendo(u)r

The word is spelled **splendour** in British English, **splendor** in American English. The related adjective is **splendorous** or, less usually, **splendrous.**

split infinitives

When words come between *to* and a following infinitive, the infinitive is said to be split: *They were urged to **seriously** reconsider their stand;*

You ought to **of course** *apply for the position.* Although splitting the infinitive occurs fairly frequently, there are widespread objections to the practice and split infinitives should therefore be avoided in formal writing whenever possible. A lengthy interruption is conspicuous and especially open to criticism: *The political will is lacking to* **resolutely and wholeheartedly** *reform the tax system.*

Occasionally the split infinitive cannot be avoided without rephrasing the sentence: *He persuaded us to* **more than** *double the asking price* (that we should more than double the asking price); *He was ashamed to* **so much as** *mention it to his wife* (He was so ashamed that he would not even mention it to his wife). Sometimes, avoiding a split infinitive results in ambiguity: *Her major objective is to* **not** *make any further concessions whatever* (*is not to* could mean the same as *isn't to*, the negation of the main verb); *They would like to* **really** *learn the language* (*would like really to learn* could mean the same as *would really like to learn*); *I asked them to* **merely** *explain their reasons* (*I asked them merely to explain* could mean the same as *I merely asked them to explain*).

There is no reason for objecting to inserting words elsewhere in an infinitive phrase other than immediately after *to*: *to be* **badly** *treated*; *to have* **perhaps** *confessed.* Nor should there be any objections to insertions in verb phrases other than infinitive phrases: *may* **then** *say*; *have* **suddenly** *remembered.*

spoil

The past tense and participle are either **spoilt** or **spoiled**. **Spoiled** is the preferred American form but **spoilt** is equally common in British use: *The heavy rain spoilt/spoiled the crops*; *spoiled/spoilt children.*

spokesman

It means 'a person who speaks on behalf of others'. For the alternative *spokesperson*, see PERSON.

sponge

The idiom for 'acknowledge defeat' is *throw up the sponge* or *throw in the sponge*, or *throw in the towel*.

spontaneity

The third syllable is pronounced either 'nee' or 'nay'.

sport, sports, sporting

1 As a verb, **sport** means 'flaunt; show off': *He sported a green cravat.* Do not use it merely for 'wear' (*to sport a dirty raincoat*).

2 The adjective form before nouns is **sports** in British English, but often **sport** in American English: *a sports/sport car*; *sports/sport equipment*. The adjective **sporting** chiefly means 'fond of sports' (*sporting nations*) or 'risky', in the phrase *a sporting chance*. It is not much used in the sense 'concerned with sport', and in American English it often suggests dissipation and particularly gambling. A *sporting house* is a brothel.

spouse

The word is often needed as a blanket term for 'husband or wife', particularly when something must be done for or about the husbands of women employees as well as the wives of men employees: *invite all the pensioners and their spouses*. It is FACETIOUS to use it where *husband* or *wife* will do, as in *take some roses to his spouse*.

sprain, strain

In common parlance, **sprain** applies particularly to ankles and wrists. It is more serious than a **strain**, which usually entails the stretching but not tearing of a muscle or tendon rather than a ligament.

spring

As the name of a season this is not usually capitalized.

spring (*verb*)

The past tense is **sprang** or (less often) **sprung**, with **sprung** as the only past participle: *Factories sprang/sprung up all over the area*; *The lid had sprung open*.

spry

Other forms are either **spryer, spryest** or **sprier, spriest**.

spurt, spirt

Spurt is the chief American spelling. **Spirt** is a British variant form, but for the meaning 'gush, jet' (*a spirt/spurt of milk*; *The blood spurted/spirted out*), not for the meaning 'burst of effort'.

squalor

The word ends in *-or*, not *-our*, in both British and American English.

square

1 An area *three miles square* is a square with sides three miles long.

Three square miles is an area measuring three miles by one, and need be no particular shape.

2 Square in the sense 'conventional' or 'conventional person' is informal as well as being rather old-fashioned.

square brackets

This is the term for [ ] in British English. In American English they are called simply 'brackets'.

Use square brackets to add comments to or explanations on someone else's words, especially in quotations:

> It [the continental shelf] is scored by deep troughs between which banks and islands rise.

> 'When I first met Tom [Repton], he was just about to sit for his exams', she said.

Sic, Latin for *thus*, is enclosed in square brackets. It indicates that a peculiarity in the wording goes back to the original:

> Frank wrote in his examination paper, 'John [sic] Washington was the first president of the United States of America'.

You must point out to the reader any change in the wording or form of the original. If you add underlining for emphasis to part of a quotation, you should make it clear that you have done so by a comment in square brackets.

You may use square brackets instead of brackets to enclose digits or letters that mark listed items or sections. See BRACKETS.

-st

There is a choice in British English between *amid* and *amidst*, *among* and *amongst*, *while* and *whilst*. *Amid* and *amidst* are somewhat literary words, often better replaced by *among*. They are still used to combine the meanings of *among* and *during*, and here British English may prefer *amidst*: *He escaped amidst the confusion*.

stadium

The usual plural is **stadiums**. **Stadia** is pedantic.

staff

Those who have resident domestic employees face a problem of linguistic etiquette in deciding what to call them. **Servant** is no longer an appropriate word, and **maid** is also disliked in Britain, though not in the USA. In British English a foreign girl paid to help in the house may be called an **au pair**, which implies a more egalitarian relationship with the householder, but this will not do, for instance, for a middle-aged couple of the employer's own nationality. Such people could be called collectively the **staff**, an inoffensive word that could apply to everyone in paid employment, or the employer might get round it by saying of a single employee 'she helps me', or by using the more specific words *cook*, *gardener*, *nanny*, *housekeeper*. See also CLEANER.

staffs, staves

1 The plural of **staff** meaning any kind of stick is **staffs**, or sometimes **staves**. When it means 'group of employed people' it must be **staffs**. A set of spaced lines on which music is written is often called a **stave** rather than a **staff**, particularly in British English.

2 In formal writing, refer to *a staff member* or *one of the staff*, rather than using *a staff* for a single person, as in *The juniors must be accompanied by a staff* or *by two staff*.

stag

(ie on the Stock Exchange). See BEAR.

stalactite, stalagmite

Stalactites hang down. **Stalagmites** stick up.

stamen

The usual plural is **stamens**. The plural **stamina** is pedantic; and besides, it has the important meaning, as a singular, of 'endurance'.

stanch

See STA(U)NCH.

stand

1 In American use you *run* for public office, while in British English you **stand** for it.

2 Besides meaning 'represent', as in *'MP' stands for 'Member of Parliament'*, *stand for* means 'permit', as in *I won't stand for it*. This is different from the use of **stand** for 'endure', as in *stand the pain* or, rather informally, *She can't stand her boss*. Both forms are therefore needed. Avoid the use of **stand** in the negative for 'remain firm in the face of' (*stand a siege*) where it might be taken to mean 'tolerate', as in *He couldn't stand the test*.

standard English

Standard English is the type of English that is used by educated people throughout the English-speaking world. It is a variety with distinctive features of vocabulary and grammar, and not an accent (type of pronunciation); standard English is therefore spoken by people with different accents. There is no authority that decides what is standard English; it has acquired its value as the non-regional variety used by people of social prestige. It is the English that is taught in the education system of English-speaking countries and is also taught to foreigners; it is the variety that appears in print and (for most serious purposes) in the spoken language of the mass media.

Standard English is not completely uniform. There are differences between the national standards (eg in Britain, America, and Australia) and also variation within each English-speaking country. For example, within the British standard, there are features typical of Northern England, Scotland, and Northern Ireland. The most firmly established national standards are British and American English, the others tending to follow the usages of these two. Differences in spelling and punctuation between the two standards are relatively minor; more occur in grammar, and more still in vocabulary. We point out many differences under general entries, such as SPELLING, and under individual words.

In many areas of the world English is not a native language, but a second language with official status used in education and administration and for communication between speakers of other languages. Second-language speakers have also contributed a considerable quantity of creative writing in English. Most of the countries where English is a second language were formerly British territories (eg India, Nigeria, and Ghana). Many people in these countries think of themselves as speaking British English, but their use of the language diverges considerably from the British standard English, and not only in pronunciation. It is possible that some national varieties such as Indian and Nigerian English will eventually acquire independent norms and then have their own national standards. It is to be hoped that the varieties of English will not diverge to the extent of impeding international communication in English.

standpoint

See POINT OF VIEW.

stanza

See VERSE.

star (*)

See ASTERISK.

starlight, starlit

Use **starlight** in the phrase *starlight night*, but **starlit** with reference to the visual effect: *a starlit scene*.

state

1 The rather formal verb means 'declare, announce': *to state one's intentions*; *He stated that he was a French citizen*. Do not use it where *say* will do.

2 As a noun, **State** takes a capital *S* in the titles of politically organized countries, or constituent units of a federal nation: *the State of Texas*. Otherwise use a small *s*: *the welfare state*; *a police state*.

3 The use of **state** for 'condition of tension', as in *Don't get in a state about it*, is informal.

stately

Although it ends with *-ly*, this is an adjective: *a stately procession*. Do not use **stately** or *statelily* as an adverb, but prefer *impressively* or *with dignity*.

stationery, stationary

Stationery is paper, envelopes, etc. **Stationary** means 'not moving'. They are most often confused when **stationery** is used as an adjective, as in *the stationery department*.

statistic

It is quite correct to speak of a single item in a collection of *statistics* as a **statistic**. It is a BACK-FORMATION.

statue, stature, statute

A **statue** is a piece of sculpture. Your **stature** is your height or (figuratively) your status: *a painter of international stature*. A **statute** is a law.

status

1 The pronunciation of the first syllable like *stay* is to be recommended for British English, but the one with the vowel of *rat* is well established, particularly in American speech.

2 This word is commonly used in the sense of 'condition in the eyes of the law': *tax status*; *marital status*. It is used, not to say OVERUSED, in the phrase *status symbol*, for a prestigious possession, and by sociologists in the sense of 'rank in a hierarchy of prestige'. For instance, a child who is despised by other children is said to suffer from *status deprivation*.

sta(u)nch

You **stanch** or **staunch** blood or tears, but the adjective meaning 'steadfast' is usually **staunch** rather than **stanch**.

staves

See STAFFS.

stay, stop

Careful writers prefer to use **stay** for the meaning 'lodge temporarily': *to stay at a hotel*; *We're staying with friends*. **Stop** is correctly used of a short break in a journey: *stop somewhere for lunch*.

steady, steadily

Steady is used as an adverb after certain particular verbs, as in *hold steady*; *go steady*. It cannot usually replace **steadily**, as in *steadily increasing prices*.

steeple

See SPIRE.

stencil (*verb*)

Other forms are **stencilled, stencilling** in British English, but the second *l* is usually omitted in American English.

step

1 The verb **step** can certainly mean 'go on foot', but you should avoid saying *Please step this way* if *Come in* will do.

2 *Take steps* should be used with restraint. It is reasonable to write *Steps are now being taken to increase our office space*, meaning that the process has begun, but it can seem PRETENTIOUS to write *We will take steps to* when all you mean is that *we will*.

step-

See -IN-LAW.

steppe

See PAMPAS.

stereotype, stereotypical

Since the noun *type* has so many other meanings, it is perhaps clearer to use **stereotype** or *archetype* rather than *type* for the sense 'person or thing conforming to a standardized pattern': *He is the stereotype* (or *the archetype*) *of the small businessman.* It seems PRETENTIOUS, however, to call such a person a *stereotypical small businessman.* The simpler adjective *typical* is perfectly suitable here.

stewardess

A woman organizer on a racecourse would be a *steward.* **Stewardesses** on aircraft are beginning to be called *flight attendants.* See FEMININE FORMS.

stigma

In the religious, botanical, and medical senses the plural is **stigmata**. For the sense 'disgrace', it is **stigmas**: *the stigmas of poverty and ignorance.*

stile, style

A **stile** is a step for getting over a wall. **Style** is the way of doing or expressing something.

stiletto

The plural is either **stilettos** or **stilettoes**.

still

1 *Still and all* (as in *She's young, but still and all she should know better*) is informal, and somewhat VERBOSE. For serious writing, use **still** alone, or *nevertheless*, or *even so*.

2 It is strictly TAUTOLOGOUS to say that something *still continues*, or *remains*, or *persists*, since these words include the idea of 'even as before'. You could omit **still** here.

still life

The plural is **still lifes**. It means a picture of an inanimate object.

stimulant, stimulus

Both a **stimulant** and a **stimulus** (plural **stimuli**) *stimulate*, but drinks and drugs are usually called **stimulants**, whereas a **stimulus** is an abstract incentive: *The approach of Christmas acted as a stimulus to finish the job.* **Stimulus** is also the word for whatever excites a muscular contraction, a glandular secretion, etc in an organism.

sting

The past tense and participle are **stung**, not *stang*.

stink

The past tense is **stank** or **stunk**, with **stunk** as the only participle: *The gas stank/stunk the house out; It has never stunk so badly.*

stipend

Clergymen and some magistrates receive **stipends**. Other people are generally paid *salaries*, *wages*, *fees*, etc.

stoic(al)

Stoic and **stoical** overlap in meaning. Some writers, however, distinguish between **stoic** for the sense connected with the *Stoic* philosophers of the ancient world, and **stoical** as meaning 'not affected by pain or sorrow': *Stoic logic; the Stoic virtues; a stoical explorer; her stoical indifference to cold.*

stone

Leave no stone unturned is a CLICHÉ. See also ROCK.

stop

See STAY.

storey, story

A floor level of a building is a **storey** (plural **storeys**) in British English, but a **story** (plural **stories**) in American English. A narrative is always a **story**, plural **stories.**

straight, straightly

Use **straight** not only for the adjective (*straight hair*) but for the adverb: *go straight home; straight after breakfast.* The adverb **straightly** is rare.

strain

See SPRAIN.

strait (*adjective*)

This means 'narrow, constricted': *straitlaced*. To **straiten** is to 'restrict': *in straitened circumstances*. These rather archaic words do not share any meanings with the commoner words *straight* and *straighten*, but nevertheless *strai(gh)tjacket* and *strai(gh)tlaced* are legitimately spelled either with or without the *gh*.

strata

This is the plural of *stratum*, but in the sense of 'level of society' it is often treated as a singular: *this strata of society*. This usage should be avoided; write *this stratum* or *these strata*.

strategy, tactics

In warfare, **strategy** is the overall plan, and **tactics** the detailed procedures involved in carrying it out in the face of the enemy. In civilian life the difference becomes blurred, but it is still possible to think of your whole marketing policy as **strategy** and of the way you set about implementing it as **tactics.**

stratum

See STRATA.

street

See ROAD.

strength

This should not rhyme with *tenth*. Pronounce the *ng* fully.

strew

The past tense is **strewed** (*Children strewed flowers in their path*) and the participle **strewn** or **strewed** (*parks strewn/strewed with litter*).

stride

The past tense and participle are **strode** and **stridden**; but **stridden** is rare, merely because one seldom has occasion to express the idea.

strike

The past tense is **struck** (*The clock struck*) and the participle **struck** or **stricken**. **Struck** is the ordinary participle (*The clock has struck four*, *I was struck by its economy*), and **stricken** is used almost entirely in the sense of 'afflicted' (*stricken by a heart attack*).

string

The past tense and participle of the verb are **strung**: *They strung lanterns between the trees*; *highly strung nerves*. The adjective **stringed** means 'having strings'. It comes from the noun **string**, and is used of *stringed instruments*.

strive

The usual past tense and participle are **strove** and **striven**: *We strove to increase our profits*; *I have striven in vain*. The form **strived** is archaic in British English, but it remains an alternative in American English, especially for the participle. **Strive** is a rather old-fashioned and literary word which could be replaced by *try*.

strong, strongly

The use of **strong** as an adverb is confined to certain fixed phrases, such as *still going strong*.

student

See PUPIL.

studio

The plural is **studios.**

stupefy

This is spelled with an *e*; not like *purify*, *horrify*, etc.

stupor, torpor

1 These words end in -*or*, not -*our*, in both British and American English.

2 They both mean a sluggish state, but **stupor** is largely mental, being typically caused by drugs or shock, while **torpor** is a physical condition, as of an animal in hibernation.

sty(e)

Pigs live in a **sty**, plural **sties**. An inflamed swelling on the eyelid is a **sty** or **stye**, plural **sties** or **styes**.

style

See STILE.

suave

It is usually pronounced with the 'a' of *father* rather than with that of *cave*. It means 'smoothly polite'.

subconscious, unconscious

In ordinary use, as distinct from their technical senses in psychology, **subconscious** means 'imperfectly conscious' (*a subconscious realization of the truth*), whereas **unconscious** means either literally 'not conscious' (*He was unconscious for three days*) or 'unintentional' (*an unconscious bias*). You can be **unconscious** (ie not aware) *of* something, but not **subconscious** *of* it.

subject

See CITIZEN.

subject, grammatical

See CASE, GRAMMATICAL; COLLECTIVES; NUMBER AGREEMENT; PERSON AGREEMENT.

subject and verb

See CLARITY (10).

subject to

Do not write *He is very subject to ill health.* See GRADABILITY.

subjoin

This formal word means 'append': *He subjoined a statement of expenses to his report.* In ordinary use it can seem PRETENTIOUS; use *attach* or *add*.

sub judice

It means 'not yet judicially decided'. Outside legal contexts, prefer *under consideration.* In general, avoid these LATINISMS.

subjunctive

Subjunctives are forms of verbs that are primarily used to convey conditional relationships or to refer to situations that are desired or feared. They occur more frequently in American English, but the British use is increasing. There are two subjunctives: the present and the past. For most verbs the present subjunctive occurs only in the third person singular (*she* **leave** as in *It is urgent that she* **leave** *at once*), where it contrasts with the indicative, the usual form (*she* **leaves**); the present subjunctive of the verb *be* is *be*, which is used for all persons: (*I/you/he/we/they* **be**). The past subjunctive is **were** and is limited to the first and third person singular of **be** in the past tense (*I/it* **were**).

There are two main uses of the present subjunctive:

(1) The present subjunctive is sometimes used in subordinate *that*-clauses after expressions of demanding, persuading, and the like:

They proposed that she *leave* before the vote was taken.

It is vital that I *be* co-opted to the committee.

The management stipulates that any person under 18 *be* accompanied by a parent or guardian.

It is this use of the subjunctive that is increasing in British English, though it is felt to be more formal than in American English. The more popular British equivalent has *should*: *They proposed that she* **should leave** *before the vote was taken*. Prefer the subjunctive or *should* to the indicative in formal writing: *They proposed that she* **leave/should leave** (not *left*); *It is vital that I* **be/should be** (not *am*) *co-opted*; *The management stipulates that any person under 18* **be/should be** (not *is*) *accompanied*.

(2) The present subjunctive is used in certain set expressions: *God* **save** *the Queen!*; *Heaven* **forbid!**; *God* **bless** *you!*; *Long* **live** *the Republic!*; **come** *what may*; **be** *that as it may*. The subjunctive here generally expresses a similar meaning to the use of *may* or *let* (*May God save the Queen*; *Let come what may*).

The present subjunctive is occasionally used in subordinate clauses that express notions such as condition or concession: *If it* **be** *your wish*; *Though it* **be** *late*; *Even though it* **seem** *presumptuous*. These are old-fashioned and are better replaced by the indicative (*is; seems*).

The past subjunctive *were* is used as a more formal variant of *was* for expressing hypothetical situations; that is, situations that are contrary to fact or that are unlikely to come about:

If I *were* a rich man (but I am not), I would take a world trip.

I wish she *were* here (but she is not).

If I *were* to tell you what I saw, you would be shocked (but I am not going to tell you).

Use *were* rather than *was* for this purpose in formal writing. You should always use *were* in the fixed expressions *as it were* ('so to speak') and *if I were you*. In very formal style, it is possible to leave out *if* and put *were* in front: *Were I a rich man; Were I to tell you*.

Use indicative and not subjunctive *were* if the condition is viewed as open, that is realizable:

If she *was* elected (and she may have been), she will tell us.

If he *was* supposed to arrive in London last night (and we can assume that he did so), why have we not yet heard from him?

Do not use subjunctive *were* when *if* is equivalent to *whether*: *Let me know if my son **were** responsible for the damage* (correct to *was*).
The main verb with hypothetical conditions is generally *would:*

If he *were* in London (but I think he is not), he *would* phone us.

If I *were* your mother, I *would* not allow it.

The open condition has *will* (*If he **is** in London, he **will** phone us*). Do not mix the two constructions (*If he **were** in London, he **will** phone us*). *Would* is also generally used with hypothetical conditions that have past forms and not the subjunctive:

If she *liked* me (but she probably doesn't), she *would* tell me.

If I *had* been there (but I wasn't there), I *would* have prevented it.

submersible

The word ends in *-ible*, not *-able*.

submit

1 Other forms are **submitted, submitting**.

2 It can mean 'offer for decision': *submit a question to the panel*; *submit a bid on a contract*. It can seem rather PRETENTIOUS to use it where *put* or *send* will do, or to use it for *suggest* (*We submit that the charge is not proved*) unless you are a lawyer in court.

subp(o)ena

It is always spelled **subpoena** in British and usually in American English, but **subpena** exists as an American variant. It means a writ commanding someone to appear in court, and the verb means 'summon with such a writ'.

subsequent, consequent, consequential

Subsequent means 'following in time': *the weeks subsequent to the wedding*. **Consequent** means 'following as a result': *the expenses consequent on getting married*. **Consequential** should not be used as a mere grander alternative to **consequent**. It has a technical sense of 'entailed as an indirect result' (as in *consequential loss*, often provided against by insurance policies), and can also mean 'important' (*a grave and consequential event*) or 'self-important'.

subsequent(ly)

Events are **subsequent** *to*, or happen **subsequently** *to*, other events: *a discussion subsequent to the lecture*; but avoid these formal and rather PRETENTIOUS words where *then*, *after*, or *later* will do.

subsidence, subsidy

1 Subsidence is pronounced with the stress on either *sub* or *sid* (pronounced like *side*).

2 Subsidence is the process of *subsiding*, ie sinking or caving in: *roads liable to subsidence*. A **subsidy** is a grant of money. The writer of the notice *Buses Delayed due to Road Subsidy* had got them the wrong way round.

substantial, substantive

Both these adjectives are related to *substance*. Both can mean 'not imaginary; firm and solid': *There's no substantial/substantive reason to disbelieve her story*. The chief meaning of **substantial**, however, is 'considerable, ample': *We won by a substantial margin*. Unlike **substantive**, it can refer to concrete things: *a substantial meal*. **Substantial**, but not **substantive**, can mean 'true in the main, virtual': *We are in substantial agreement*; or 'influential and prosperous': *substantial farmers*. **Substantive**, but not **substantial**, has a technical sense in grammar, when it denotes a noun or an item used like a noun; and in law, where it designates what is to be enforced as contrasted with the procedure for enforcing it. *Substantive rank* in the Services is permanent rather than temporary or acting.

substitute, replace

When saccharin is used instead of sugar, it is **substituted** *for* or **replaces** sugar, and the sugar is **replaced** *by* or *with* saccharin. **Substitute** is increasingly used instead of **replace**, particularly in the passive and particularly in scientific and technical contexts: *Sugar was* *substituted by/with saccharin*; but it is clearer to preserve the distinction.

subtract

This is not spelled *substract*.

succeed

You **succeed** *in doing* something: *We succeeded in ousting* (not *to oust*) *our rivals*. See also ACCEDE.

successful(ly), successive(ly)

Successful(ly) means 'with *success*'. **Successive(ly)** means 'in *succession*'.

succo(u)r

The word is spelled **succour** in British English, **succor** in American English. It is a formal word. It can seem PRETENTIOUS, and is often better replaced by *aid*, *help*, etc.

succubus

The plural is **succubi** or, less usually, **succubuses**. This was a female demon who was believed to have sexual intercourse with sleeping men. The male equivalent is INCUBUS.

such

1 It is formal, but not wrong, to use **such** for 'those people; such people', as in the biblical *of such is the kingdom of God*. You can correctly write *Such as wish to leave may do so*, or *Such of the girls as went enjoyed it*, or *Such was the result of our efforts* (where **such** means 'that thing or event'). Avoid, however, using **such** where *it* or *them* or *what* can conveniently replace it: *It is not the fault of those who show violence on television but of parents who allow their children to watch such* (use *it*); *He watched such as he could see of the carnival* (use *what he could see*).

2 When **such** introduces an example or comparison it should be followed by *as*, not by any other word: *such cases of hardship as* (not *that* or *which*) *I encounter in my profession*. In formal writing, **such** *as* is appropriate for introducing examples, but elsewhere *like* can often replace it: *a subject such as/like physics*. See AS (8). **Such** *as* means 'of a kind like', not 'in the way that': *to change our out-of-date, unfair* *rating system such as* (omit *such*) *Liberals have been suggesting for many years.* (It is the change, and not the system, that the Liberals have been suggesting).

3 Such *a* is normal before adjectives, where *so* would be rather formal: *I've never met such a charming boy* (formal *so charming a boy*). But the use of **such** *a* for *a very*, where no comparison is involved, as in *He's such a nice boy!* is more appropriate to speech than to writing. It can sound rather gushing.

4 *as* **such**; see AS (5).

suchlike

This is rather informal: *tea, sugar, and suchlike* (or *and suchlike groceries*). In formal prose you can use *and the like*, or *and similar things*, or *and so on*, or even *etc.*

suède

The accent is usually omitted.

suffer

To **suffer** *from* a disease or disability is simply to have it, with or without any attendant discomfort: *She suffers from varicose veins.* To **suffer** *with* it is to undergo actual pain: *She's been suffering a lot with her bad leg.* Do not use **suffer** *with* for 'having a disease'.

suffice

This appears in the CLICHÉ *Suffice it to say* . . . Elsewhere, too, it is PRETENTIOUS. Use *be enough*, or *do*.

sufficient

See ENOUGH.

suffragan

The *g* is usually pronounced as 'g', not 'j'. It means a kind of subordinate bishop.

suggestible

The word ends in *-ible*, not *-able*.

suicide

This is better used as a noun than as a verb: *He committed suicide*, rather than *He suicided* or *He suicided himself*.

suit, suite

Suit is used for a set of clothes, sails, or playing cards, for a lawsuit, and for an entreaty or petition. A **suite** is a retinue, a set of rooms or of furniture, or a kind of musical composition.

suit, trouser suit, pantsuit, costume

A man's matching jacket and trousers is a **suit**, a woman's is a **trouser suit** (British English) or **pantsuit** (American English). A woman's matching jacket and skirt is a **suit** too, but some older women still call this a **costume**.

suitor

The word ends in *-or*, not *-er*.

sulphur, sulfur

A whole group of words begin with **sulph-** in British English and with **sulf-** in American English: *sulpha drugs*; *sulphate*; *sulphide*; *sulphuric acid*.

summer

This is not usually capitalized.

summon(s)

To **summon** is to call upon to come: *summon a doctor*. It is more formal than *send for*, which can often replace it. To **summons** is to command to appear in court, by means of a written notification, a **summons** (plural **summonses**). The verb **summon** can be used for **summons** but not the other way round.

sums of money

See MONEY.

sunk, sunken

See SINK.

supercilious, superficial

Supercilious means 'disdainful, haughty'. **Superficial** means 'not thorough or serious; shallow': *superficial wounds/charm*.

superior

Things are **superior** *to*, not *than*, other things: *She has superior ideas to mine*. *Most superior* is not wrong, but it means 'very superior', not 'superior to all others': *a most superior candidate*. **Superior** is often used commercially as a general word of praise: *a superior detached bungalow*. See GRADABILITY.

superlative

See COMPARISON, GRAMMATICAL.

supermarket, hypermarket

The distinction between these two words for a self-service shop or store is somewhat blurred. On the whole, though, a **supermarket** need not be very large, and it can sell only one type of goods: *a furniture supermarket*. A **hypermarket** is a very large supermarket, selling a wide range of consumer goods, typically food, clothes, toys, and electrical equipment, provided with a car park and usually situated on the outskirts of a large town. In Britain, **hypermarket** is also used of an indoor market with stalls under separate ownership but selling the same kind of goods: *an antique hypermarket*.

supernatural, preternatural

They both mean 'beyond what is natural'. **Supernatural** is used particularly of gods, spirits, and devils, or their manifestations: *something supernatural, a stirring as it were of the roots of the hair* (W B Yeats). **Preternatural** has come to be used chiefly for 'extraordinary, exceptional': *the child's preternatural grasp of mathematics*.

supersede

See -CEDE.

supervise

This is the only correct spelling, in both British and American English; not -*ize*.

supervisor

The word ends in *-or*, not *-er*.

supine

See PRONE.

supplement

See COMPLIMENT.

support (*noun*)

It forms the phrase *in support of*: *Russia mobilized in support of* (not *for*) *Serbia*.

supportive

This means 'giving support': *supportive evidence for the charge*. In the more specific sense 'giving emotional and moral support' it has become OVERUSED: *He was very supportive during her convalescence*. The phrase *is supportive of* is used unnecessarily where *supports* will do.

suppose, supposing

1 Both these words can indicate a proposal (*Suppose/Supposing we wait a bit*) or introduce an imaginary situation (*Suppose/Supposing they saw you*). **Supposing**, but not **suppose**, is also used like *if*: *Even supposing they're late, we can always sit in the bar*.

2 Supposed *to* (not *suppose to*) means 'intended to; allowed to': *They're not supposed to have visitors*.

supposititious, suppositious

These two formal and perhaps PRETENTIOUS words can both be replaced by *hypothetical* or by *spurious*, their two shared meanings: *the earth as seen by a supposit(it)ious observer on Mars*; *supposit(it)ious evidence which is now discredited*.

supra

It means 'earlier in this writing'; but prefer the plainer words *earlier* or *above*.

[suprise]

This is an incorrect spelling of **surprise**.

surcease

The noun is very formal and usually seems PRETENTIOUS. Prefer *pause* or *respite*. The verb means 'discontinue', and is archaic.

sure, surely

British English uses the adverb **sure** in *sure enough*; and in the informal *as sure as* (*as sure as eggs are eggs*); and for *certainly*, but only in an informal reply: *Sure, I'll be there*. Informal American English uses both **sure** and **surely** for *certainly*: *I sure/surely am tired*. In British English, *certainly* would be the more usual word there, **surely** being chiefly confined to situations where you hope to set a doubt at rest: *Surely you must be tired?*; *We'll surely hear from them soon*. Only **surely**, not **sure**, can mean 'safely, confidently' in the expression *slowly but surely*.

surf

See SERF.

surfeit

The word is spelled *-ei-*, not *-ie-*.

surge

See SERGE.

surly

Though it ends with **-ly**, this is an adjective. The related adverb would be **surlily**; but this sounds clumsy, so rephrase *He growled surlily* as *He gave a surly growl*. Or use *sullenly*, *gruffly*, etc.

surmise

This is the only correct spelling, in both British and American English; not *-ize*. It is rather a formal word.

surprise

1 This is the only British spelling. **Surprize** is a rare alternative in American English, and is best avoided.

2 Surprised can mean not only 'taken unawares' but 'astonished'. In the one sense it is followed by *by*, in the other by *at* or by a clause: *The burglars were surprised by a policeman*; *I'm surprised at you!*; *I'm surprised (that) he didn't answer*.

3 For *I wouldn't be surprised if it didn't rain*, see DOUBLE NEGATIVE.

surveillance

The word is spelled *-ei-*, not *-ie-*, and the second syllable is usually pronounced like *veil*.

surveyor, survivor

Both words end in *-or*, not *-er*.

susceptible

1 The word ends in *-ible*, not *-able*.

2 When it means 'capable of', **susceptible** is followed by *of* or *to*: *a theory susceptible of/to proof*. When it means 'unresistant', it requires *to*: *a city susceptible to air attack*; *a man highly susceptible to beauty*.

suspect, suspicious

These adjectives both mean 'giving rise to suspicion': *He died in suspect/suspicious circumstances*. **Suspicious**, but not **suspect**, can also mean 'feeling suspicious, distrustful': *He's suspicious of strangers*. The adverb must be *suspiciously* in either sense, so that *He glanced at me suspiciously* is ambiguous.

suspected

See ACCUSE.

suspense, suspension

Suspense is mental uncertainty: *a novel of suspense*. **Suspension** has several senses, of which that is not one. It means 'temporary withholding or abolition' (*the suspension of a bus service*), or the springs supporting a car body on its axles, or (in chemistry) a liquid or gas mixture with solid particles dispersed in it.

suspicion

Do not use this word as a verb. Use *suspect*.

sustain

It is correct, though formal, to use **sustain** for 'suffer, undergo': *to sustain injuries/heavy losses/a broken rib*. It can sound PRETENTIOUS, so say instead *He broke a rib*. Perhaps **sustain** is better confined to its other senses of 'support' (*a sustaining meal*), 'endure bravely' (*sustain a siege*), and 'keep up' (*sustain a conversation*).

swap, swop

Use *exchange* in most serious contexts. The variant spelling **swop** is British rather than American.

swat, swot

The two spellings are sometimes interchanged, but to kill an insect is usually to **swat** it, and to study hard is to **swot** in informal British use. The Americans would say *grind*.

swell

The past tense is **swelled** (*The population swelled*), and the participle either **swollen** or **swelled**. **Swollen** is the usual word when the implication is of harmful excess (*rivers swollen by flood water from the mountains*), and **swelled** for more neutral or pleasant increase (*Our numbers were swelled by the arrival of the Yorkshire contingent*). **Swollen** is the usual adjective form before a noun (*swollen ankles*), but *swelled* is an alternative in the phrase *swelled head*. See VERBS, PRINCIPAL PARTS.

swim

The past tense and participle are **swam** and **swum**: *He swam* (not *swum*) *the Hellespont*; *She has swum* (not *swam*) *the Channel*.

swine

It is used either technically (*swine vesicular disease*) or in literature (*a swineherd who married the Princess*) for *pig*. The chief use of **swine** for most of us is as a term of abuse.

swing

The past tense and participle are **swung**. **Swang** is a rare past tense form, to be avoided. **Swinging** in the sense of 'lively and up-to-date' is informal.

swing(e)ing

This is usually spelled **swingeing**, to avoid confusion with the *swinging* that comes from *swing*. This British word means 'severe, thumping': *swingeing cuts in public spending*.

swivel

Other forms are **swivelled, swivelling** in British English, but the second *l* is usually omitted in American English.

swop

See SWAP.

swot

See SWAT.

syllabus

The plural is usually **syllabuses**. The plural **syllabi** is rather pedantic.

symbol

See CYMBAL.

sympathy

You have or feel **sympathy** *for* someone in the sense of 'pity, compassion'. You are in **sympathy** *with* someone in the sense of 'agreement, loyalty': *They came out in sympathy with the miners.* See also EMPATHY.

symposium

The plural is either **symposia** or **symposiums.** This is a formal word for a discussion or short conference.

syndrome

This has the important meaning in medicine and psychiatry of a group of signs and symptoms, or of emotions and actions, that together form an identifiable pattern. It is OVERUSED to mean 'condition' or 'attitude': *a hitherto unrecognized emotional ailment: the motorcycle syndrome* (*Time*).

synergy

In technical use, this means cooperative action between two or more agencies, such as drugs, producing a combined effect greater than the sum of their separate effects. It is OVERUSED elsewhere, particularly in business jargon, to mean no more than 'cooperation' or 'collaboration': *Our success depends on synergy between the production and marketing departments.*

synonym

See HOMOGRAPH.

synopsis

The plural is **synopses**.

syntax

See GRAMMAR.

synthesis

See ANALYSIS.

synthetic

See ARTIFICIAL.

systematic, systemic

Systematic means 'presented as a system' (*systematic classification*) or 'thorough and methodical' (*a systematic search*). **Systemic**, a rarer word, means 'affecting a whole system', and particularly 'affecting the whole body or organism' (*systemic pesticides*).

Tt

-t-, -tt-

See DOUBLING.

table (*verb*)

In British English to **table** a motion is to place it on the agenda for consideration, but in American English it means to remove it from the agenda indefinitely. The different uses may be a source of misunderstanding.

tableau

The plural is either **tableaux** or **tableaus**.

table d'hôte

This is spelled with the accent. It means a meal consisting of a set number of courses, served at a fixed price; by contrast, an *à la carte* meal is ordered from a menu that prices each item separately.

tactics

See STRATEGY.

tailor

The word ends in *-or*, not *-er*.

take

1 *Take into consideration* can often be advantageously shortened to *consider*.

2 *Take it easy* is the established form of the idiom; not *easily*.

3 *Take place* is more formal than *happen*, which can sometimes replace it, but it is also more suitable for planned events: *When will the wedding take place?*

4 See BRING.

talisman

The plural is **talismans**, not *talismen*. It is a magical object that brings luck.

tangible

The word ends in *-ible*, not *-able*. It means 'able to be grasped physically', but like PALPABLE is often extended to whatever can be 'grasped' by the intellect, so far as to be almost meaningless: *tangible advantage*; *tangible motives*. It can often be omitted from such phrases.

target

Although it is often used, and perhaps OVERUSED, for 'goal', the word does still exist in the literal sense of 'object to be fired at'. Since some people may be aware of this literal sense, it may sound slightly odd to speak of *achieving*, *raising*, or *exceeding* one's **target.** If you want to express these ideas, use *goal*, *aim*, *objective*, or *quota*, as appropriate.

tarry

As a synonym for *delay*, *stay*, or *linger*, the verb **tarry** (rhyming with *marry*) is archaic or jocular; see POESY. It is not to be confused with the adjective **tarry**, meaning 'covered with tar' and rhyming with *starry*.

tart, pie, flan, quiche, pasty

In British use, **pies** are covered with pastry or something similar, and are fairly deep. Shallow ones with the top left open are **tarts**, whether the contents are sweet or savoury: *an apple tart; a cheese tart.* The word **tart** is rarer in American English, and used only of small sweet ones, so that an American speaks of *blueberry pie* or *pumpkin pie* whether it is open or covered. A **flan** is open, and its base material may be either pastry or cake. A pastry **flan**, filled with a savoury custard and other ingredients such as ham or spinach, is a **quiche**. Pasty is an old word for **pie**, but in modern use a **pasty** is made by folding a circle of pastry round its contents.

tartan

See PLAID.

taste

When it means 'have a specified flavour', **taste** is followed by an adjective (*It tasted nasty*) or else by a phrase (*It tastes of fish*). An adverb used with **taste** describes the way someone tests a flavour: *She tasted it cautiously.*

tasteful, tasty, tasteless

Despite appearances, **tasteful** and **tasty** are not a pair of synonyms of which **tasteless** is the opposite. People or their creations are **tasteful** if they show discrimination (*a tasteful colour scheme*) and are often called **tasteless** if they lack it (*a tasteless joke*), although some careful writers prefer to confine **tasteless** to the meaning 'insipid'. Food and drink are **tasteless** if they lack flavour (*a tasteless meal*) and **tasty** if they have a pleasant (usually savoury) taste. By informal extension of this sense, a 'juicy' bit of gossip is **tasty** too.

tattoo

The plural of the noun is **tattoos**. Other forms of the verb are **tattooed, tattooing**.

taught, taut, taunt

Taught is the past tense and participle of *teach*. **Taut** means 'tight' or, in a nautical context, 'kept in proper order': *a taut ship*. **Taunt** (noun and verb) means 'jeer'.

tautology

Tautology is the unnecessary repetition of an idea, generally in different words. The repetition may occur in the same phrase, one expression repeating an idea implied in the other:

sad misfortune	widow *woman*
past history	eliminate *altogether*
final end	*puzzling* mystery

A special kind of tautology is the combination of synonymous expressions, where one alone is sufficient:

(8) a.m. in the morning	sufficient enough

This kind of tautology appears in some clichés:

each and every	in this day and age

Avoid tautology in your writing. It is padding that wastes the time and effort of your readers.

Some repetitions of the same idea are deliberate and acceptable. Definitions are a familiar type, whether expressed as in the first sentence in this entry (*Tautology is* . . .) or through APPOSITION (*tautology, the unnecessary repetition* . . .). Repetition may also be deliberately used for stylistic effect in PARALLELISM; in this next quotation, the repetition conveys forcefully the determination not to surrender:

> We shall go on to the end, we shall fight in France, we shall fight on the seas and oceans, we shall fight with growing confidence and growing strength in the air, we shall defend our island, whatever the cost may be, we shall fight on the beaches, we shall fight on the landing grounds, we shall fight in the fields and in the streets, we shall fight in the hills; we shall never surrender. (Winston Churchill)

Here are some further examples of tautology:

It *adds additional* weight to their complaints. (It adds weight)

Since the 1960s a *growing* awareness of consumer rights and interests has *increased* in the United States. (Since the 1960s awareness . . . has increased)

The Chancellor *chose* to *pick* inflation as the first topic of his lectures. (The Chancellor chose inflation)

Other cases are described in individual entries in this book. See, for example, BECAUSE (1); BUT (2); REASON.

tax, duty, rates, excise, customs, toll

Tax was formerly levied directly on people, and **duty** on goods and transactions, but there is no longer any distinction between the two, at least in Britain; **tax** is the commoner word, and we speak of *value-added tax* as well as *income tax*. **Rates** are the taxes charged by a British local authority and assessed on the value of property; the American equivalent is *property tax*. **Excise** is, strictly speaking, the internal tax on goods (such as Scotch whisky in Britain) produced within the country, and **customs** (usually called **duty**) the tax on goods (such as French brandy) imported from abroad, though the two are sometimes loosely confused. The most familiar use of **toll** is for the charge on using a bridge or a road.

taxi

The plural of the noun is **taxis** or, less usually, **taxies**. Other forms of the verb are **taxied**, and **taxiing** or **taxying**: *aircraft taxiing/taxying down the runway*.

team

See TEEM.

technique, technics

Technique is the usual word for 'method of doing something'.
Technics, with the stress on *tec*, is another word for *technology*, 'applied science'.

teem, team

Teem is two verbs. One means 'abound': *rivers teeming with fish*. The other means 'pour' or 'rain hard': *It's simply teeming down*. Neither word should be confused with the noun and verb **team**, meaning 'a group of people or animals' or 'to join in a team': *We're teaming up with our neighbours for a night out*.

televise

This is the only correct spelling in both British and American English; not *-ize*. The word is a BACK-FORMATION from *television*.

temerity, timidity

They are similar in appearance and almost opposite in meaning.
Temerity is rashness, recklessness. **Timidity** is lack of courage or adventurousness. A rash person is *temerarious* (rather a formal word);

the adjectives related to **timidity** are *timid* or *timorous*, the latter perhaps emphasizing shrinking hesitation.

temperature, fever

It is common usage to say that someone *has a temperature*, meaning one that is above normal. The expression is slightly odd because, after all, everyone must have some temperature even if it is a normal one.

tempo

The plural is either **tempi** or **tempos**. Outside musical contexts, the word is used figuratively for 'pace' or even 'activity': *the increased tempo of urban life*.

temporal, temporary

Temporal is opposed to *eternal*, and thus to *spiritual* or *ecclesiastical*. In the House of Lords, the *Lords Temporal* are those who are not bishops. **Temporary**, the commoner of these two words, means 'transient', or 'not meant to last': *a temporary wooden structure*.

temporary, temporarily

In British English, both words are usually pronounced with the stress on *temp*. In careful speech, both *r*'s are sounded, and **temporary** usually has three syllables. The pronunciation stressing *rar* is usual in American English, particularly for **temporarily**.

temporize

See EXTEMPORIZE.

tend

In formal writing, use *attend to*, or **tend** alone, but not **tend** *to*, for 'see to': *to tend the sheep*; *to attend to his bruises*. See ATTEND. **Tend** is correctly used with *to*, and often with another verb, in the sense of 'have a tendency': *His books tend to/towards dullness*; *She tends to get angry about it*.

tender (*verb*)

This formal word means 'present for acceptance' (*tender my resignation*) or 'make a bid' (*Six firms tendered for the contract*). It can seem rather PRETENTIOUS to use it where *offer* or *give* will do, as in *tender my services*.

tenor

The word ends in -or, not -our, in both British and American English.

terminable, terminal

Terminable means 'capable of being ended': *The agreement is terminable at a week's notice*. **Terminal** as an adjective means 'coming at the end' (*terminal buds*) or 'causing an end, fatal' (*terminal cancer*).

terminal, terminus

In American English, **terminus** (plural either **termini** or **terminuses**) and **terminal** are completely interchangeable. In British English, there is a technical distinction: a **terminus** is the end of a route, whereas a **terminal** is a point of access to vehicles or of interchange between different vehicles or different forms of transport. Hence the British usually speak of an *air terminal* but of a *railway terminus*, although both words are used with reference to buses, and the distinction is by no means always clear.

terminate

Outside legal or quasi-legal contexts, as in *terminate an agreement*, this word can seem PRETENTIOUS. Use *end*, *stop*, *finish*, or *bring to an end* where possible. However, **terminate** is the only possible word in such contexts as *This train terminates at Glasgow*, because *stop* would there mean something quite different. **Terminate** can also be a sinister EUPHEMISM for 'kill, assassinate'.

terms

In terms of means 'with regard to' or 'in relation to'. It is legitimately used where one factor is to be isolated for special consideration: *They are not rich in terms of actual money, but they have a large farm*. It is VERBOSE to use it in place of a specific word to express a particular relationship: *They are well equipped in terms of* (use *with*) *rolling stock*; *The design of the hall is unsuitable in terms of* (use *for*) *indoor games*.

testatrix

This still has some currency in legal contexts for a female *testator*, a woman who leaves a will, but is often replaced by *testator*.

tête-à-tête

This is spelled with the accents. It means 'in private' or 'a private conversation between two people'.

textual, textural

Textual refers to texts, **textural** to textures: *textual problems in Shakespeare*; *the textural quality of the rocks*.

than

1	**than** *I*	**3**	*as* . . . **than**
2	**than, then**	**4**	misplaced **than**

1 In formal writing, the forms *She is fatter than I/he/we/they* are preferable to *She is fatter than me/him/us/them*. See CASE, GRAMMATICAL (4).

2 Do not misspell **than** as **then**, or vice versa. They sound similar in rapid speech, but write *now and then*, *more than ever*.

3 Do not write *He is as old or older than Jane*. Instead, write *He is as old as or older than Jane* or *He is as old as Jane, or older*. See ELLIPSIS.

4 Than is used after comparatives: *kinder than*; *more convenient than*; *worse than*; *rather than*. Besides **than** with comparatives, correct combinations are *other than*, *otherwise than*, *else than*, and *elsewhere than*. Do not write **than** where *as* is required: *nearly twice as many students enrolled than* (write *as*) *last year*. For further situations where **than** should be avoided, see DIFFERENT (1); HARDLY; PREFER (2); SUPERIOR.

thankfully

Besides meaning 'in a thankful way' (*She collapsed thankfully on the sofa*), this now very commonly means 'it is a matter for relief that': *Thankfully things have changed*. The situation is the same as with the better-known case of *hopefully*. There is a prejudice against the new usage both in Britain and in the USA. Its users may justify their decision by analogy with adverbs such as *happily*, which can mean either 'in a happy way' (*He smiled happily*) or 'it is fortunate that' (*Happily he was not badly hurt*). If you use **thankfully** in this way, be careful to leave no room for ambiguity. *Thankfully she closed the door* may mean either that she felt thankful or that it is a good thing she closed it. See SENTENCE ADVERBS.

thanks, thank you

1 Thanks is somewhat informal as an expression of gratitude, and a little perfunctory on its own, without *many* or *very many*; *I thank you* is decidedly formal; the neutral one is **thank you**.

2 *Thanks to* is correctly used for 'because of, owing to': *Thanks to the fine weather we got the hay in early*. It is ironically used of misfortunes: *Thanks to all that rain, the hay was ruined*.

3 Thank you should be spelled as two words when it is used to show gratitude: *Thank you* (not *thankyou*) *for your letter*. It is correct to hyphenate it when it is used as an adjective, as in *a thank-you letter*.

4 There is no accepted answer in British English to expressions of thanks, but *That's all right, Not at all*, and *Don't mention it* are all available. The standardized phrase *You're welcome* is chiefly American but is coming into British use.

that

1 omission of **that**	**5** *doubt* **that**; see DOUBT
2 unnecessary **that**	**6** uncertain reference; see
3 **that** or **who, which, whom**	THIS
4 **that** for **very**	**7** *and* **that**; see WHICH (3)

1 omission of that

When an introductory **that** can be left out, it is shorter and usually neater to omit it, particularly before short clauses: *I'm glad (that) I came; Take anything (that) you want*. The choice of whether to leave it out chiefly depends on the relative formality of an introducing verb. Compare: *He said he'd come; He asserted that he would come; I suppose you're right; I assume that you are right; She believes it's true; She postulates that it is true*. Try not to use two consecutive **that**'s: *He says (that) that method is unreliable*.

Do not leave out **that** where confusion may result. If it is omitted in *She said (that) before we left (that) we must pay the bill*, it is not clear whether her words were 'Pay the bill' or 'Pay the bill before you leave'. On the other hand, it is also possible to cause confusion by including **that**. If it is included in *I don't believe (that) Mr Spedding knows anything about it*, it may not be clear in some contexts (at least in writing) whether I am referring to him scathingly as *that Mr Spedding*, or whether the included **that** could have been omitted to produce *I don't believe Mr Spedding knows anything about it*. In speech, the difference is made by the full pronunciation of the *a* in the **that** of *that Mr Spedding*.

2 unnecessary that

It is a common mistake to introduce an extra **that** when another clause has intervened: *It seems that, if we are to finish in time, that* (omit *that*) *we shall have to work over the weekend*. Perhaps this most often occurs where there is a danger that the final clause will seem too 'absolute': *We've always found that if we both work and aren't too extravagant, (that) we have no difficulty in keeping up the mortgage payments*. Omission of the bracketed **that** here might suggest to an inattentive listener or reader that we have, in fact, no difficulty in keeping up the payments; but the sentence must be corrected, and the clearest way to do it is to change the order of the clauses: *We've always found that we have no difficulty in keeping up the payments if* . . .

3 that or who, which

That is rather less formal than **who, which,** and **whom,** but it is perfectly correct to use it of people as well as of things, and it is often useful when you wish to refer to both: *the children and parcels that filled the car*. **That**, not **who**, must be used in the phrase *that was*, referring to a woman's maiden name: *Mrs Molesworth, Miss Green that was*. **That** cannot be used after a preposition. You can write either *the women with whom I work* or *the women whom I work with*, but only *the women (that) I work with*. **That** cannot introduce a restrictive relative clause, but **who, whom, whose,** and **which** can introduce either a restrictive or a nonrestrictive one. Compare: *I saw the car that/ which ran over your cat*; *I saw the car, which* (not *that*) *was very fortunate*. See RELATIVE CLAUSES.

4 that for very

The use of **that** for **very** is normal in conversation after negatives, but is inappropriate for formal writing: *It's not that cold*; *We don't go there that often*. It seems to raise the question, As cold as what? Rephrase as *It's not very cold*. Without a negative, the use of **that** for **very** (*I'm that hungry!*) is nonstandard and should be avoided.

the

1 In conversation **the** is often pronounced in its stressed form, like *thee*, while the speaker pauses to select the following word: *You should apply to the – appropriate authority*. This trick of speech should, however, be avoided in the formal reading of prepared material. Broadcasters sometimes adopt it, to the irritation of some listeners, as if in imitation of spontaneous conversation. **The** is always pronounced in its stressed form, however, when it means 'the famous one': *You can't be the Dustin Hoffman!*

2 The should be capitalized if it is part of a title: *The Times*. See CAPITALS (4).

3 Most people who speak English as their mother tongue have no hesitation as to where **the** is necessary and where it can be left out. We say, correctly, *the Mississippi, the Hague*, and *the 1980s*, but *Paris*,

Easter, and *Westminster Abbey*. There is some variety of practice over
a few words: *I'm always cold in (the) winter*; *a matter solely for (the)
government*; *students of (the) film*. In such cases either choice is
reasonable, although conservative speakers would probably retain **the**.
Omission of **the** may sometimes cause confusion. A phrase such as *the
old men and women* may be ambiguous, and should then be changed to
the old men and the old women or to *the old men and the women*,
according to whether the younger women are supposed to be included.
For omitted **the** in phrases such as *footballer Matthew Green*, see FALSE
TITLES.

theatre, theater

This is spelled **theatre** in British English, but usually **theater** in
American English.

thee, thou

Writers who have occasion to use these archaic forms, perhaps when
composing period dialogue, should note that **thou** is the subjective
form (like *I*), **thee** is objective (like *me*), and **thy, thine** are genitive
(like *my, mine*). They are singular forms, the plural of **thou** being *ye*.
   The exception is the special grammar of old-fashioned Quakers, who
use **thee** (in the singular) throughout: *Is thee* (not *Art thou*) *ready?*

[theif]

This is an incorrect spelling of *thief*.

their

See THEIRS; THEY; THERE.

theirs

This means 'the one belonging to them': *The house became theirs* (not
their's).

[theirselves]

This is not standard English. Use *themselves*, as in *They might hurt
themselves*.

them

1 See THEY. For *as they, than them,* etc, see CASE, GRAMMATICAL (4).

2 Do not use **them** for *those*: *those* (not *them* or *them there*) *things*.

themselves

See REFLEXIVE.

then

1 The use of **then** as an adjective for 'existing at that time', as in *the then Secretary of State*, is a well-established and economical way of expressing that idea. There seems no reason to object to it.

2 See IF (4).

3 See THAN (2).

thence

For *from* **thence**, see FROM (1).

there, their, they're

1 These all sound the same. **There** means (among other things) 'not here'; **their** means 'of them'; **they're** is short for *they are*. Write *He insisted on their being admitted*, which resembles *our being admitted*; but *He insisted on there being* (ie that there should be) *separate toilet facilities*.

2 **There** can express the idea of existence: *What is there to eat? There seem to be only eggs*. Before a plural it should correctly be *there are/were*, although *there is* is common in spoken English: *There's two experts in the studio*. When **there** introduces a list of items of which the first is singular, usage is divided: *There are/is Bill and the children to consider*. Here **are** is correct, though it may be felt to sound odd before the singular *Bill*.

3 Some confusion may arise in writing between the two meanings of *there's Peter* (ie 'he exists', and 'I can see him'), but the difference would be clear in speech, and the occasions for confusion in writing would be rare.

4 *That* **there** and *those* **there** (*that there book*) are always wrong; but there is nothing wrong with *that book there* and *those children there*.

thereabout(s)

It is usually spelled with the *s*: *a week or thereabouts*.

thereby, therein, thereof, thereto, therewith

These and others like them are formal words. Except for **thereby**, they are also archaic, at one time normal in legal contexts: *the conditions* *attaching thereto*. They sound PRETENTIOUS if they are used where *in that*, *with that*, etc would do.

therefor, therefore

The one is not a misspelling of the other. **Therefor** is a very formal word for 'for that': *She commissioned a full audit and gave her reasons therefor*. **Therefore** means 'consequently': *I was tired and therefore irritable*.

these

See THIS (2). For *these kind*, see KIND (1).

thesis

The plural is **theses**. See also DISSERTATION.

thespian

This is a FACETIOUS word for *dramatic* or *actor*: *the thespian art*; *enthusiastic thespians*. Prefer the plainer words.

they, them, their

1 For the use of these after *each, either, neither, none, any, every, anybody, everybody, nobody*, and *somebody*, see NUMBER AGREEMENT (7).

2 It is perfectly legitimate to use **they** for 'people in general' (*They say we'll have a hard winter*) or for 'the authorities' (*They took my licence away*). It is often better to do this than to rely constantly on the passive, as in *My licence was taken away*.

thief

The word is spelled *-ie-*, not *-ei-*, and the plural is **thieves**.

think

1 The use of *think to* for 'remember to' is rather informal: *I didn't think to ask him*. **Think** as a noun meaning 'an act of thinking' (*have a think*) is informal too.

2 It is perfectly acceptable to write *I don't think he'll come*, meaning that I think he will not come. See NEGATION (3e).

708

third

1 It is usually abbreviated to *3rd* in British English, but to *3d* in American use.

2 For **third, thirdly** see FIRSTLY.

this, that

1 This conventionally refers to what is about to be said (*Listen to this!*) or to what is near (*Hold this*). Both **this** and **that** can refer to something previously mentioned: *Who told you this/that?* Here, **this** perhaps gives more feeling of immediacy. Whichever word you use, it is important that the thing, concept, or state of affairs referred to should be clearly identifiable: *The children will perform their own musical version of Cinderella. This* (Cinderella? the version? the idea of performing it?) *was decided on last term.* A Social Services Secretary said the opposite of what he presumably meant in the following: *Ministers want to be kept fully aware of what our most active members think. This letter, factsheet and questionnaire is the first in a series designed to change that.*

2 Both **this** and **that**, and their plural forms **these** and **those**, are often used rather than *a*, *the*, or *your* to give a feeling of intimacy. A story may begin *There were these two Scotsmen . . . .* Or an advertiser may advise you to buy *that last-minute Christmas gift* at a particular shop. The habit is harmless in its proper place, but that place is not formal prose.

3 The use of **this** and **that** for 'to this degree' and 'to that degree' is normal in conversation: *I didn't expect to wait this/that long.* In formal writing prefer *as long as this* and *as long as that*.

thither

See HITHER.

tho

This spelling of *though* is either very informal or poetic.

those

See THIS (2). For *those kind*, see KIND (1).

thou

See THEE.

though, although

1 Though is somewhat less formal than **although**, but there is no difference in meaning: *Though/Although it rained every day we enjoyed ourselves*; *We enjoyed ourselves, though/although it rained every day*. **Though** can be used at the middle or end of a clause or sentence: *We found, though, that it rained every day*; *We enjoyed ourselves, though* (not *although*). *However* and *nevertheless* are more formal substitutes for this use of **though**.

2 There is a delicate choice to be made between **(al)though** and *but* as connecting words. If we say *She looks happy, though rather thin* we emphasize the fact of her happiness; the emphasis on her happiness is even greater if we change the position of the clauses: *Though rather thin, she looks happy*. If we prefer to say *She looks happy, but rather thin* we express greater concern over her thinness.

threshold

The word is spelled with only one *h*, but is pronounced either 'thresh-old' or 'thresh-hold'.

thrice

This word is archaic. In ordinary contexts use *three times*.

thrive

The past tense is either **thrived** or **throve** (*The business thrived/throve*), and the participle either **thrived** or **thriven** (*The farm has never thrived/thriven*).

throes, throws

Throes are spasms or struggles: *in the throes of revolutionary change*. **Throws** is part of the verb *throw*.

through

1 The use of **through** for 'finished' (*I'm not through with the book*; *I'm through with tennis*) or 'done for' (*As a politician she's through*) is appropriate in all except very formal prose, but is perhaps more popular in American than in British English.

2 Through in the sense of 'up to and including' (*Monday through Friday*) is a useful Americanism which the British are beginning to adopt. If you say *from Monday to/till Friday* it is not clear whether Friday is included.

thru

Avoid this spelling of *through*, except in *thruway*, which is now an official American word for an urban motorway.

thus

As **thus** is itself an adverb, there is no need for the FACETIOUS variant *thusly*.

-tiate

See -CIATE.

tidbit

See TITBIT.

tight, tightly

Like **tightly**, **tight** can be an adverb meaning 'fast, firmly': *shut tight/ tightly*; *hold tight/tightly*. **Tightly** is preferred before past participles (*tightly clasped*) except in certain established compounds formed from nouns: *tight-lipped* (ie with tight lips); *tightfisted* (with tight fists). Only **tight** is used in the phrase *sleep tight*.

till

See UNTIL.

timber, timbre

They are not two spellings of the same word. **Timber** (rhyming with *limber*) is wood, often called *lumber* in American English. **Timbre** (rhyming with *clamber* or *limber*) is the distinctive resonance of a sound.

time

For *until such time as*, see UNTIL (4).

timely

This can be not only an adjective (*timely intervention*) but occasionally an adverb (*arrived timely*), and the awkward adverbial form *timelily* is not used. If you find **timely** uncomfortable as an adverb, and do not wish to reword your sentence to say *their timely arrival*, use *opportunely* or *seasonably*, or *in (good) time* or *at the right time*.

times

It is misleading to say that production is *six times greater* (or *more*) *than in 1985*. Does this mean that six times, or seven times, as many tons of the product have been produced? The clear way to express the idea is to say that it is *six times* (or *seven times*) *as great as in 1985*. *Six times less* is positively mysterious, because **times** implies multiplication. Instead of referring to a lake as *six times smaller* than Lake Constance, say *a sixth of the size*. There is a definite oddity in the advertisements for a brand of peat said to be *compressed to 2½ times normal volume*.

times of day

For hours and fractions of an hour, give the time in words: *five o'clock*; *half past one*; *a quarter to eight*. *O'clock* goes with the exact hour only: not *half past seven o'clock*.

If you include minutes, use figures: *7.25 a.m.* (or *am*; in American English *7:25 a.m.*); *2.40 p.m.* (or *pm*; in American English *2:40 p.m.*). If you add *a.m.* or *p.m.* to the hours or fractions, use figures: *5 p.m.*; *1.30 p.m.*; *7.45 p.m.* The abbreviation *a.m.* stands for *ante meridiem* (Latin for 'before noon') and refers to the period from midnight to before noon; *p.m.* is an abbreviation of *post meridiem* (Latin for 'after noon') and refers to the period from noon to before midnight. Hence *12 a.m.* is midnight, and *12 p.m.* is noon; but since these are often confused, prefer the explicit *12 midnight* and *12 noon*.

In formal writing, use *o'clock* with the words only (*six o'clock*), not with figures (*6 o'clock*). Do not use *o'clock* with *a.m.* or *p.m.* (*eight o'clock a.m.*; *ten o'clock p.m.*); instead use expressions such as *in the morning/afternoon/evening* and *at night*: *eight o'clock in the morning*; *ten o'clock at night*. Since *a.m.* and *p.m.* indicate the two halves of the day, it is TAUTOLOGOUS to write *10.40 a.m. in the morning*; correct to *10.40 a.m.* or *10.40 in the morning*.

Note that 11.45 is *a quarter to 12* in both British and American use, but Americans also say *a quarter of 12*. 12.15 is *a quarter past 12* in both British and American use, but Americans also say *a quarter after 12*. 12.30 is *half past 12* in both British and American use, but the British also say *half 12*.

The 24-hour clock is common in transport timetables and military usage: *7.25* (7.25 a.m.); *19.25* (7.25 p.m.); *12.00* (12 noon); *24.00* (12 midnight); *12.45* (12.45 p.m.), *00.45* (12.45 a.m.).

timidity

See TEMERITY.

timpani

See TYMPANUM.

tin

See CAN.

tinge (*verb*)

Other forms are **tinged** and either **tingeing** or **tinging**.

tiptoe

Other forms are **tiptoed, tiptoeing**.

tire

See TYRE.

titbit, tidbit

Titbit is the usual form in British English, **tidbit** in American English.

titillate, tit(t)ivate

To **titillate** is to excite pleasantly, and often sexually: *titillating pictures of nudes*. *To* **titivate** or **tittivate** is to smarten up: *titivate oneself for the party*.

titles of books and newspapers

1 These titles, and those of plays, films, musical compositions, and works of art may be referred to in italics (which means underlining them in manuscript): Tolkien's *The Lord of the Rings*; the film *Gone With the Wind*; or alternatively they may be enclosed in double or single inverted commas: a chapter of ''Treasure Island''; Gainsborough's 'Blue Boy'.

A popular modern practice is to use italics for the titles of full-length and separately published works (including newspapers and journals), and inverted commas for short works, sections of works, and radio and TV programmes: BBC's ''Tomorrow's World''; the third chapter of *Treasure Island* is entitled 'The Black Spot'. Musical works identified by the form in which they are written are often shown without either italics or inverted commas: Beethoven's Quartet in D Minor.

2 For the use of capital letters in these titles, see CAPITALS (4).

3 Titles are always singular: *'Romeo and Juliet' is* (not *are*) *set in Verona.*

titles of people

Anyone may have occasion to write to an MP, or to greet suitably a distinguished visitor to an institution or the guest of honour at some public occasion. An exhaustive list of titles and forms of address would be beyond the scope of this book, but the following indications may be helpful.

Lord and Lady are used with the first name for the sons and daughters of dukes and marquesses: *Lord Charles*; *Lady Sarah*. They are used with the surname elsewhere.

The Hon. (short for *Honourable*) is used with the first name for the children of viscounts, barons, and life peers and peeresses, and for the younger sons of earls: *The Hon. Michael Black*.

By American convention, **Mr** is used in addressing various people who in Britain might be addressed by their titles alone; *Mr Minister* and *Mr President* rather than merely *Minister* and *President*.

In British use, 'My dear' is less appropriate to formal letters than 'Dear', while in American English the reverse is true.

person	envelope	opening of letter	verbal address
The Queen	Correspondence addressed to 'The Private Secretary to Her Majesty the Queen'		Your Majesty; Ma'am (Pronounced 'mam')
The Duke of Edinburgh	As for the Queen: to his secretary		Your Royal Highness
The Queen Mother	As for the Queen: to her secretary		As for the Queen
Royal Princes & Princesses	His Royal Highness, The Prince Charles, Prince of Wales; Her Royal Highness, The Princess Anne, Mrs Mark Phillips (etc)	Your Royal Highness	Your Royal Highness; Sir/Ma'am
duke, duchess	The Duke/Duchess of Dorset	Dear Duke/Duchess (of Dorset)	Duke/Duchess
marquess, marchioness	The Marquess/Marchioness of Broughton	Dear Lord/Lady Broughton	Lord/Lady Broughton
earl, countess	The Earl/Countess of Chell	Dear Lord/Lady Chell	Lord/Lady Chell
viscount, viscountess	The Viscount, Viscountess Brown	Dear Lord/Lady Brown	Lord/Lady Brown
baron, baron's wife	The Lord/Lady Simon	Dear Lord/Lady Simon	Lord/Lady Simon

person	envelope	opening of letter	verbal address
hereditary peeress	The Countess of Bannockburn (her husband is 'Mr')	Dear Lady Bannockburn	Lady Bannockburn
life peer, life peer's wife	The Lord/The Lady Camden	Dear Lord/Lady Camden	Lord/Lady Camden
life peeress	Baroness Camden (her husband is 'Mr')	Dear Lady Camden	Lady Camden
baronet, baronet's wife	Sir Thomas Black, Bt./Lady Black	Dear Sir Thomas/Dear Lady Black	Sir Thomas/Lady Black
knight, knight's wife	Sir Thomas Black/Lady Black	Dear Sir Thomas/Dear Lady Black	Sir Thomas/Lady Black
dame	Dame Edith Evans	Dear Dame Edith	Dame Edith
untitled people (British)	John Webster (but see ESQ) Mrs John/Mary Webster Miss Mary Webster (but see MS, and MR, MRS, MISS)	Dear Mr/Mrs Webster; Dear Sir/Madam	Mr/Mrs/Miss Webster
Prime Minister	The Prime Minister	Dear Prime Minister	Prime Minister (or eg Mrs Thatcher)
Secretaries	The Home/Foreign (etc) Secretary	Dear Home/Foreign Secretary	Home/Foreign Secretary (or name)
Ministers	John Jones, MP	Dear Minister	Minister (or name)

M.P.'s	John Jones, MP	Dear Mr Jones	Mr Jones
High Court Judge	The Hon. Mr/Mrs Justice Jones	Dear Judge/(Dear) Madam	Sir John/Dame Mary
Circuit Court Judge	His/Her Honour Judge Jones, QC	(Dear) Sir/Madam	Judge Jones
admiral	Admiral William Jones	Dear Admiral Jones	Admiral Jones
other naval officers	Captain (etc) William Jones, R.N.	Dear Captain Jones	Captain (Jones)
general	Major-General (etc) William Jones	Dear General (Jones)	General (Jones)
other Army officers	(as for Navy)		
Royal Air Force	(as for Navy, R.A.F. may follow the name.)		
archbishop	The Most Reverend and Rt Hon The Lord Archbishop of Canterbury/York	Dear Archbishop	Archbishop
bishop	The Right Reverend the Lord Bishop of Durham (the Bishop of London is 'The Right Rev and Rt Hon')	Dear Bishop	Bishop
dean (of Cathedral)	The Very Reverend, the Dean of Barchester	Dear (Mr) Dean	Dean
archdeacon	The Venerable the Archdeacon of Barchester	Dear (Mr) Archdeacon	Archdeacon
vicars & rectors; & Church of Scotland ministers	The Reverend John Smith	Dear Mr Smith	Mr Smith

person	envelope	opening of letter	verbal address
Chief rabbi	The Chief Rabbi Dr Israel Brodie	Dear Chief Rabbi	Chief Rabbi
other rabbis	Rabbi P. Wiseman	Dear Rabbi Wiseman	Rabbi Wiseman
the Pope	His Holiness the Pope	Your Holiness	Your Holiness
cardinal	His Eminence the Cardinal Archbishop/Bishop of Oxbridge	Your Eminence	Your Eminence
Catholic archbishop	His Grace the Archbishop of Armagh	Your Grace	Your Grace
Catholic bishop	His Lordship the Bishop of Castletown	My Lord Bishop	My Lord
Catholic priests	The Reverend John O'Brien	Dear Father O'Brien	Father
abbot	The Right Reverend the Abbot of Oxbridge	My Lord Abbot	Father Abbot
Sister Superior	The Reverend Sister Superior	Dear Reverend Sister	Sister Superior
lord mayor (including women mayors)	The Rt Hon the Lord Mayor of London/York	My Lord Mayor	Lord Mayor

lady mayoress (ie a lord mayor's wife. A mayor's or lord mayor's husband is the (Lord) Mayor's Consort or Escort, but is addressed by name.)	The Lady Mayoress of Castletown	My Lady Mayoress	Lady Mayoress
mayor	The Right Worshipful the Mayor of Liverpool	Dear Mr/Madam Mayor	Mr/Madam Mayor
councillor	Councillor John/Mary Jones	Dear Councillor	Councillor (or name)
ambassador	His Excellency the American Ambassador	Your Excellency	Your Excellency
consul	Mr John Jones, American Consul	Dear Sir	(name)
university vice-chancellor	The Vice-Chancellor	Dear Vice-Chancellor	Vice-Chancellor
head of college	The Master/Provost/Principal	Dear Master (etc.)	Master (etc.) (or name)
professor	Professor Fry	Dear Professor Fry	Professor (or Professor Fry)

person	envelope	opening of letter	verbal address
The American President	The President	Mr President	Mr President
US cabinet officers	The Secretary of State (etc)	My Dear Mr Secretary	Mr Attorney General (etc)
US senator	The Honorable John Jones	My Dear Senator	Mr Senator
congressman/-woman	Honorable John/Mary Jones	Dear Sir/Dear Madam	Mr/Mrs Jones
US judge	The Honorable John Jones	My Dear Judge Jones	Judge Jones
US state governor	The Honorable Edward Brook	Dear Sir	Governor
US mayor	The Honorable Edward Brook	Dear Mr/Madam Mayor	Mr/Madam Mayor

to

1 To as a preposition must be followed by *me, us, him, her, them*, not by *I, we, he, she, they*. Write *to us* (not *we*) *geologists*; *to John and me* (not *I*). See CASE, GRAMMATICAL; HYPERCORRECTION.

2 It is perfectly legitimate to leave out the verb after **to** in contexts like *He asked me to come but I don't want to.* You need not write *want to come* or *want to do so*.

3 It is an elementary spelling mistake to confuse **to** with **two** the number, or with **too** meaning 'also' or 'excessively'.

4 To can correctly be either included or omitted in sentences such as *All he had to do now was (to) pack his bag.*
For omitted **to** elsewhere, see DARE; HELP; NEED; WRITE.

5 For *to really understand* etc, see SPLIT INFINITIVE.

toboggan (*verb*)

Other forms are **tobogganed, tobogganing**.

together

For *together with*, see WITH.

togetherness

This is OVERUSED to mean a warm feeling of closeness to other people. For a change, *intimacy* is a possible alternative.

toilet, lavatory

Toilet, originally a GENTEELISM, has perhaps become the most general British word, both for the fixture and for the place, rather than **lavatory**. **Water closet** and its abbreviation **WC** are understood everywhere but rarely used. A popular informal British word is **loo**. **Bathroom** and **washroom** are American rather than British EUPHEMISMS, but there are more synonyms than could possibly be listed here: the **bog** or **karzy** (British slang); the **can** or **john** (American slang); the **head** or **heads** (nautical, or American); the **jakes** (slang); the **privy** (American, or suggestive of an outdoor one without plumbing). The American **rest room** and **comfort station** (for a public toilet) may be misunderstood in Britain, where **ladies** and **gents** are the usual terms. A public **convenience** is a municipal one in the street. A **latrine** is usually a mere hole dug in the ground, as used in a camp. **Powder room** is another EUPHEMISM (for a ladies' toilet), and even more so are all those jocular expressions like *little boy's room*.

toilette, toilet

The process, or the result, of dressing and attending to one's hair and face is a **toilette** or **toilet**. **Toilette** cannot replace the other sense of **toilet**, as in *toilet paper*.

token

By the same token means 'furthermore and for the same reason', and can seem rather PRETENTIOUS.

toll

See TAX.

tomato

The plural is **tomatoes**.

tome

This is most frequently used to refer to a large scholarly book. Its use as a mere synonym of *book* is an ELEGANT VARIATION which is better avoided.

tomorrow

It is not wrong to use the present tense when referring to **tomorrow** as a date in an inevitable sequence: *Tomorrow is Tuesday/is the first of May/is my birthday*. One may prefer to speak of **tomorrow** as a future event when considering predictions or future arrangements: *Tomorrow will be a busy day/will be wet*.

ton, tonne, tun

Ton and **tonne** (pronounced the same) are large units of weight. A **ton** is 2000 lbs (a short ton, used in the USA) or 2240 lbs (a long ton, used in Britain). A **tonne**, or *metric* **ton**, is 1000 kg. A **tun** is a large cask, or a liquid capacity unit of 210 imperial gallons.

tongue

In the sense of 'language', this refers to speech rather than writing and to local dialect as well as to national standard. Do not use the word where (as in *foreign tongues*) *language* will do.

too

1 Too is correctly used before ordinary adjectives and adverbs: *too old*; *too quickly*. Before the *-ed* form of verbs it needs to be supplemented by an intervening adverb: *too greatly admired*; *too far removed* (not *too admired/removed*). Some *-ed* forms, however, have come to be treated as ordinary adjectives, and these can take **too** alone: *too tired/ bewildered/limited*. In marginal cases it is safer to insert an adverb, at least for formal writing: *too (much) occupied*. Compare VERY.

2 *Not* **too** is informally used for *not very*, as in *He wasn't too pleased*. There is nothing wrong with this, but there is some danger of ambiguity in such statements as *I cannot speak too highly of his contribution*. Was his contribution great, or only mediocre? The use of **too** for *very* as in *It's too marvellous* is informal, and may sound rather gushing.

3 As **too** can mean either 'excessively' or 'also', you may have to separate it from the rest of the sentence by commas to avoid confusion. Compare: *Ann, too, often interrupted* (ie she also); *Ann too often interrupted* (ie excessively often).

4 too, to, two; see TO (3).

top (*adjective*)

This is perhaps OVERUSED for *foremost* or *leading* (*top journalists*) and for *highest* (*top prices*). It is firmly established, however, in all but the most formal contexts, and has at least the virtue of brevity.

tormentor, tormenter

Tormentor is the commoner spelling.

tornado

The plural is either **tornadoes** or **tornados**.

torpedo

The plural of the noun is **torpedoes**. Other forms of the verb are **torpedoed, torpedoing**.

torpor

See STUPOR.

torso

The plural is either **torsos** or **torsi**.

tort, torte

Tort is a legal word for a wrongful act. A **torte** (plural **torten**) is a rich elaborate cake.

torturous, tortuous

The two words are easily confused, because *torture* can mean 'twist, distort' and **torturous** means 'involving *torture*', but in the sense of being agonizing: *I spent torturous hours looking at his holiday slides.* The one that means 'winding' or 'devious' is **tortuous**: *tortuous lanes*; *tortuous mental processes.*

total (*verb*)

Other forms are **totalled, totalling** in British English, but the second *l* is usually omitted in American English.

totality

This word leads to VERBOSITY. Do not write *the totality of* when *all* will do, as in *The totality of his plan was rejected.*

totally

It is OVERUSED in, for instance, *totally unnecessary*, and could often be omitted from such combinations as *totally destroyed* and *totally demolished.* Use *completely*, *entirely*, *quite*, or nothing at all.

touché

The word is spelled with the accent. It is used to acknowledge a hit in fencing or the success of an argument or accusation.

tour de force

This means 'a remarkable feat', and it may be better to say so in English.

toward(s)

The preposition is usually spelled **towards** in British use, though often **toward** in American English: *with his back toward(s) me*; *toward(s) the end of the afternoon.* There is also a rare and archaic adjective meaning 'afoot' or 'imminent', which is usually **toward**.

track record

It is hard to see how a **track record** (as in *Applicants must have a* *proven track record in sales management*) differs from a *record*, and apart from being tautologous the phrase has become OVERUSED.

tractor

The word ends in *-or*, not *-er*.

trade(s) union

Trade union is the commoner form. The variant **trades union** occurs chiefly in the title of the British *Trades Union Congress*. The commoner American expression is *labor union*.

traffic (*verb*)

Other forms are **trafficked, trafficking**.

tragedy

This word has been devalued. It should perhaps not be used for an event, such as a defeat on the football field, that involves neither death nor lasting misery.

tragic(al)

Tragic is the chief form of this adjective. If **tragical** is used at all it is in the sense of 'gloomy': *his tragic death; in a tragical/tragic mood.*

trait

It rhymes with *wait* in American English. Some British speakers dislike this pronunciation, but the alternative pronunciation like *tray* seems pretentious to others.

traitor

The word ends in *-or*, not *-er*. See also TREASON.

tramp

To the British this usually means a vagrant, but to the Americans it means a promiscuous woman. In American English a vagrant is a *bum* or *hobo*.

tranquil(l)ity, tranquil(l)ize

Tranquillity and **tranquility** are both acceptable spellings, but the former is more usual. **Tranquillize** is spelled with two *l*'s in British English, but the second *l* is usually omitted in American English.

725

transcendent, transcendental

In general use, **transcendent** chiefly means 'pre-eminent, surpassing': *a pianist of transcendent genius*; while **transcendental** chiefly means 'abstruse, exalted': *that transcendental phraseology which defies exact translation* (Herbert Read).

Theologians use **transcendent** with reference to God, meaning that He exists independently of the universe. **Transcendental** has a technical meaning in mathematics. Both words are used, with different meanings, in Kantian philosophy.

transfer (*verb*)

Other forms are **transferred, transferring**. The related adjective can be spelled either **transferable** or **transferrable**.

transgressor

The word ends in *-or*, not *-er*.

transient, transitory

These adjectives both mean 'lasting only a short time'. They are more or less synonyms. **Transient** may suggest that the shortness of duration is caused by rapid movement: *transient guests at a hotel*. **Transitory** emphasizes the too swift passing of something pleasant: *the transitory rewards of fame*. Most writers would prefer **transience** (or perhaps its variant **transiency**) for the noun, since **transitoriness** is an unwieldy word: *the transience of earthly pleasures*.

transistor

The word ends in *-or*, not *-er*.

translate, transliterate

To **translate** a word is to turn it into another language. To **transliterate** it is to write it in the characters of another alphabet. Hence the Greek word πολεμος is translated as 'war' and transliterated as 'polemos'.

translator

The word ends in *-or*, not *-er*.

transmit

Other forms are **transmitted, transmitting**. It is rather PRETENTIOUS to use this word where *send*, *post*, or *pass on* will do, as in *Please transmit my good wishes to your mother*.

transparent, translucent

They both describe the property of letting light through. Frosted glass is **translucent**, because it diffuses the light so that objects cannot be seen clearly. Clear glass is **transparent**. Only **transparent** is used figuratively to mean 'obvious': *a transparent lie*.

transpire

This means 'become known': *It later transpired that he had been absent at the time*. For centuries the word has also been used, and often by good writers, to mean merely 'occur' or 'turn out to happen': *Nobody will ever know what transpired at the banquet*. There is, however, an ancient prejudice against the use of **transpire** in this second and quite well established sense, so that it is perhaps wiser to use it only as in our first example.

transport, transportation

British English has traditionally used **transport** for the system of conveying (*Ministry of Transport*) and for a means of conveying (*Hospitals cannot provide transport for outpatients*), for both of which American English uses **transportation.** The American form is coming into Britain but is still felt to be an Americanism. British and Americans alike speak of *transports of joy* (meaning 'strong emotions'), and of the **transportation** of convicts to penal colonies.

transportable

See PORTABLE.

transverse, traverse

Transverse is an adjective, and means 'across': *transverse beams in the roof*. **Traverse** is a rather formal verb meaning 'cross': *The bridge traverses a brook*. Both words can be used as a noun for something that crosses, in which case a **transverse** is a crosswise section or part of something, while a **traverse** is usually a way across, or a sideways movement.

trauma

1 The first syllable can rhyme with either *for* or *how*, but purists prefer the former choice.

2 In medical and psychological contexts this word means an injury to living tissue, or a disordered state resulting from shock, and its more technical plural is **traumata**. In everyday use the plural is **traumas**, and the word with its associated adjective **traumatic** has been loosely OVERUSED to describe any upsetting experience: *a traumatic love affair*.

travel

In British English, other forms are **travelled, travelling**, and the related noun is **traveller**, but the second *l* is usually omitted in American English.

traveller

See SALES REPRESENTATIVE.

traverse

See TRANSVERSE.

tread

The past tense and participle are **trod** and **trodden**. See VERBS, PRINCIPAL PARTS. An alternative participle **trod** was once equally correct: *being trod to death like a frog* (Jonathan Swift). Today this use of **trod** (*You've trod on my foot*) is common but informal.

treason, traitor, treachery

The legal term for the offence against one's country is **treason**, and the offence is **treasonable** or, less usually, **treasonous**. A **traitor** is a person who commits this offence, or anyone who in a wider sense betrays a trust. Betrayal in this wider sense is **treachery**, or is **traitorous** or **treacherous**. **Treacherous** and **treacherousness** can also describe what is unreliable: *the treacherousness of the ice*.

treble, triple

Both words express the idea of 'threeness' as noun, adjective, and verb, and are largely interchangeable. **Triple** is perhaps commoner as an adjective (*a triple fence*), and American English tends to prefer **triple** for the verb where British English would use **treble**: *to treble/ triple our profits*. In music the meanings are sharply distinguished, **treble** referring to pitch and **triple** to rhythm.

trefoil

The first syllable is pronounced either 'tree' or 'treff'.

trek

1 Other forms of the verb are **trekked, trekking**.

2 Both noun and verb imply a long and arduous journey. Do not use the word merely for *journey* or for *go*.

tremor

The word ends in *-or*, not *-our*, in both British and American English.

tri-

When **tri-** is used in measurements of time (*triweekly*; *trimonthly*), there is often doubt as to whether it means 'every three' or 'three times in one'. It is often safer to avoid such combinations, and say *every three weeks*, *three times a month*, etc.

triad

See TRILOGY.

tribute

The word is legitimately used in the sense of 'evidence of the worth of something': *The vote was a tribute to their good sense*. It should refer only to something praiseworthy. Do not write *The vote was a tribute to their lack of vision*, except ironically.

trigger (*verb*)

This is rather OVERUSED in the sense of 'initiate': *an indiscreet remark that triggered off a fight*. It is appropriately so used except in really formal contexts, but *precipitate* or *set off* could be used for a change.

trillion

In British English the older use of **trillion** to mean a million million million (10^{18}) is increasingly giving way to its use to mean a million million (10^{12}), which is standard in American and international scientific English. Compare BILLION.

trilogy, trio, trinity, triad

These words all mean 'set of three'. A **trilogy** is usually three literary works, and cannot be used of people. A **trio** (plural **trios**) is a musical composition for three performers, but it is also the most general word for a group of three people or things. **Trinity**, apart from its Christian religious sense, can also be used of three people or things, so that

Macbeth's three witches were a **trio** or **trinity**. **Triad** is a rarer word, with technical senses in music and in medieval Welsh literature.

triple

See TREBLE.

triumphant, triumphal

Triumphant means 'victorious', and can be used of a notable achievement or of the people who rejoice in it: *her triumphant success*; *the triumphant team*; *grinned triumphantly at me*. **Triumphal**, a rarer word, means only 'in honour of a victory': *a triumphal arch*.

troop, troupe

A **troop** is a group of soldiers or scouts, and also more generally of people or creatures: *a troop of children*; *a troop of kangaroos*. A **troupe** is a group of actors. A **trooper** is a cavalry soldier or a mounted policeman, but a **trouper** is an actor, especially a veteran one, or (particularly in the phrase *old trouper*) a loyal or dependable person.

troublous

This is an archaic synonym for *troubled* (ie agitated) rather than for *troublesome* (ie causing trouble). It may seem PRETENTIOUS or excessively formal.

trousers

See PANTS.

trouser suit

See SUIT.

trousseau

The plural is either **trousseaux** or **trousseaus**.

truculent

The chief modern sense is 'defiant, pugnacious' rather than the older meaning of 'savage, scathing'. It is a small but definite CHANGE OF MEANING.

truly

For *Yours* **truly** and similar phrases, see LETTER ENDINGS; FAITHFULLY.

trustee, trusty

A **trustee** (plural **trustees**) is a person legally appointed to administer property in trust. A **trusty** (plural **trusties**) is a trustworthy convict allowed special privileges.

try

There are two ways of using **try** which have occasioned some dispute. One is the fixed combination *try and* followed by a second verb, as in *try and stop me*. This has been long established in the language, and is appropriate everywhere except in very formal writing, where it should be replaced by *try to*. In any case, it cannot be used in some constructions, where *to* has to replace *and*: *I shall try not to* (not *and*) *shout*; *She tries/tried to jump* (not *tries and jumps* or *tried and jumped*). The other disputed use is that of **try** as a noun. Leaving aside its technical sense in rugby, it can mean 'an attempt': *give it a try*; but formal prose would demand *make an attempt*.

tryst

This is either literary or FACETIOUS. Use *date*, *assignation*, or *appointment*. The word is pronounced to rhyme with either *list* or *priced*.

T-shirt

See VEST.

tubercular, tuberculous

The difference between these two words is too technical to be consistently observed in laymen's writing. Strictly, **tubercular** refers to *tubercles*, which are knobby protuberances, and **tuberculous** is associated with the disease *tuberculosis*; but often **tubercular** is also used in this second sense.

tumo(u)r

The word is spelled **tumour** in British English, **tumor** in American English.

tumulus

The plural is **tumuli**. It is a burial mound.

tun

See TON.

tunnel (*verb*)

Other forms are **tunnelled, tunnelling** in British English, but the second *l* is usually omitted in American English.

turbid, turgid

Turbid means 'cloudy' or 'muddy', and **turgid** means 'swollen'. A river in flood can therefore be both **turbid** and **turgid**; and so, figuratively, can confused and inflated speech or writing. Nevertheless the words are not synonyms.

turf

The plural is either **turfs** or **turves**; the latter is used mainly in British English.

tutor

The word ends in *-or*, not *-er*.

twilight (*adjective*), twilit

Twilight can mean 'at the time of twilight' (*a twilight scene*), or figuratively 'in a period of decline' (*the twilight years of the Roman Empire*). It is also the recognized form in the combinations *twilight sleep* and *twilight zone*. **Twilit** means 'lighted by twilight': *a twilit room*.

two

See TO (3).

-ty

See -NESS.

tympanum, tympani

A **tympanum** is part of the ear, or else an architectural feature; the plural is **tympana** or, less usually, **tympanums**. **Tympani** is a variant spelling of **timpani**, which means a set of kettledrums.

type

1 Do not use **type** for *type of*, as in *that type person* or *a new type dishwasher*. The similar construction in which a hyphen joins **type** to a noun is common in fairly technical contexts: *Roquefort-type cheese.* Elsewhere, it is somewhat informal: *Goon-type funny voices.*

2 Like **kind** and **sort**, in formal writing **type** should be treated as an ordinary singular noun. One should write *This type of tree needs pruning* and *That type of person is dull*, although the plural construction *Those type of people are dull* may be common in speech.

typo

The plural is **typos**. It is an informal word for a printing error.

tyrannize

One can either **tyrannize** *over* people or just **tyrannize** them. Both constructions are correct.

tyre, tire

The rubber ring round a wheel is a **tyre** in British English but usually a **tire** in American English.

Uu

uglily

Although it ends with **-ly**, *ugly* is an adjective and not an adverb: *the ugly duckling*. The adverb **uglily** does exist, but it looks and sounds so clumsy that you may prefer to rephrase *uglily dressed*, perhaps as *unattractively dressed* or *dressed in ugly clothes*.

ult.

This is old-fashioned business English for 'last month'. It is better to write the name of the month.

ultimate

It combines the ideas of 'latest' and 'maximum', and is perhaps OVERUSED as an advertisers' word: *the ultimate in modern living*. **Ultimately** is more formal than *finally* or *in the end*.

ultimatum

Ultimatums is the usual plural. **Ultimata** is pedantic.

umpire

See REFEREE.

un-

There is sometimes confusion between two possible meanings of **un-** words ending in *-ed* that derive from verbs. An *unwrapped* parcel has either been taken out of wrappings or not been *wrapped*. An *unwashed* shirt, on the other hand, has not been *washed* (it is impossible to *unwash* something), so that there is no confusion here. See also UNBENDING. Before you form a negative by attaching **un-** to a word, make sure that the resultant meaning is clear.

  For *not* **un-**, see NOT (3).

unaccountable, unaccounted

Things that cannot be explained are **unaccountable**. Things that are merely not, or not yet, explained are **unaccounted** *for*. Do not write *unaccountable for*.

unanimous, nem. con.

A motion is said to be carried **unanimously** if everyone votes for it. If there are some abstainers but nobody votes against it, it is carried **nem. con.**, which means 'with no one contradicting'.

unapt

See INAPT.

unaware(s)

Unaware is the adjective, usually followed by *of* or *that*: He was unaware of my presence; *She is unaware that the plane has left*. The adjective does not (in this sense) precede a noun, but it can be used for 'insensitive to one's surroundings': *politically unaware people*; see AWARE. The adverb form is **unawares** (or often **unaware** in American English), meaning 'inadvertently' or 'without warning': *The storm took us unawares; We came upon it unawares*.

unbeknown(st)

Both **unbeknown** and **unbeknownst** are in standard though slightly

PRETENTIOUS use, meaning 'without someone's knowledge'. They require *to*: *Quite unbeknown(st) to his father, he had left his job.*

unbending

This can mean 'inflexible': *unbending discipline*. It can also come from the verb *unbend*, which gives it the almost opposite meaning of 'behaving informally': *the boss unbending at the office party*. See UN-.

unbias(s)ed

This is spelled with either one or two *s*'s.

uncharted, unchartered

See CHART.

unconscious

See SUBCONSCIOUS.

underachiever

This is a child who fails to achieve his or her scholastic potential. The word is a popular EUPHEMISM in educational circles, often applied to those who could not be expected to achieve more.

underestimate

A kind of DOUBLE NEGATIVE is produced by using **underestimate** where *overestimate* is meant, as in *The role played by her husband in her success cannot be underestimated* (write *should not be underestimated* or *cannot be overestimated*).

underhand(ed)

Underhand is the chief form, for both adjective and adverb and both for the sense 'underarm' and for 'deceitful', but **underhanded** is not wrong. **Underhanded** also means 'shorthanded, understaffed'.

underlay, underlie

The past tense and participle of **underlay** are both **underlaid**; those of **underlie** are **underlay** and **underlain**. They mean 'lay under' and 'lie under' respectively, and are as easily confused as *lay* and *lie* themselves; see LAY. Compare: *We underlaid the carpet with felt* (ie put felt under it); *The coal underlies* (ie lies under) *the sandstone*. *Underlying* can be used before a noun: *the underlying problem*.

underpants

See PANTS.

undershirt

See VEST.

undersigned

It is PRETENTIOUS to refer to yourself outside legal contexts as *the undersigned*. Use *I* or *we*.

undertone

See OVERTONE.

under way

See WAY (4).

undiscriminating, indiscriminate

Undiscriminating is the only British form, but **indiscriminating** is an American variant. Both forms mean 'lacking in judgment; not making careful distinction', and **indiscriminate** can mean that too: *her undiscriminating/indiscriminate reading habits*. **Indiscriminate** also means 'random, haphazard', with little or no reference to the person who might be expected to exercise the *discrimination*: *indiscriminate killing of soldiers and civilians alike*.

undue, unduly

In such contexts as *There is no need for undue alarm*, or *Do not be unduly concerned*, these words seem only to mean that there is no reason to be or do something unreasonable, and they could be omitted. Use them only where it is really necessary to say that something is excessive. To *exert influence* is harmless enough, but to *exert undue influence* is a different matter. Do not use **undue** or **unduly** to mean simply 'great', as in *It did not require undue intelligence to foresee the result*.

uneatable

See EATABLE.

uneconomic(al)

Both **uneconomic** and **uneconomical** mean 'costly, wasteful'. There is no difference, as there is between *economic* and *economical*.

unequal

One may be **unequal** *to* a task, or **unequal** *to* performing it, but not **unequal** *for* it or *to* perform it: *She was quite unequal to making* (not *make*) *the decision*.

unequal(l)ed

The word is spelled with two *l*'s in British English, with one in American English. See DOUBLING.

unequivocally

The word is not spelled *unequivocably*.

unexceptionable, unexceptional

Unexceptionable means 'beyond criticism, irreproachable'. **Unexceptional** means 'commonplace, ordinary'.

unintelligible, unintelligent

Unintelligible ends in *-ible*, not *-able*. It means 'impossible to understand'. **Unintelligent** means 'stupid, ignorant'.

uninterested

See DISINTERESTED.

unionized, un-ionized

Unionized means 'formed into a trade *union*'. The hyphen is obligatory in **un-ionized,** because it means 'not converted into chemical *ions*'. The reviewer in *New Scientist* who wrote *The central atoms of a planet must remain unionised* must have confused his readers.

union jack, union flag

A **union jack** is, strictly speaking, a ship's *jack* (a small national flag) emblematic of any two or more sovereignties. For more than a century, however, the national flag of the UK has been called the **Union Jack**, even when it is not on a ship, and that is now the only term for it that would be generally understood.

unique

1 Unique has traditionally been applied to people or things that are the only one of their kind. In this sense, things either are **unique** or they are not. The Sphinx is **unique**. You can correctly speak of the **unique**

copy of an unpublished manuscript. **Unique** is very often used, however, for 'unusual' or 'exceptional': *London is one of the most unique ecology areas in the world* (*Punch*). The combinations *very*, *more*, *most*, *rather*, *somewhat*, and *comparatively* **unique** have aroused a great deal of adverse criticism, and should be avoided in formal writing. Instead, use *rare*, *remarkable*, etc. There is nothing to be said against *quite*, *almost*, *nearly*, *more nearly*, *absolutely*, *perhaps*, or *surely* **unique**. **Uniquely** is often loosely used to mean something like 'specially', as in *a hotel uniquely situated on the lake shore*. This should be avoided too.

2 Write *a* (not *an*) *unique statue*.

United Kingdom

See GREAT BRITAIN.

universal

It means 'including everyone or everything or everywhere': *universal cultural habits*. Things either are **universal** or they are not. Do not write *a more universal genius*, or *most universally appreciated*.

unlawful

See LAWFUL.

unless and until

As with the commoner pair *if and when*, it is usually unnecessary to use **unless** and **until** together. Write *There will be no reform unless* (or *until*, not *unless and until*) *the nation demands it*.

unlike

See LIKE (*preposition*) (1).

unmoral

See AMORAL.

unprecedented

1 The second syllable is usually pronounced 'press' rather than 'preess'.

2 It means 'having never happened before'. Do not use **unprecedented** for events that are merely unusual.

unqualified, disqualified

Unqualified means 'without the necessary qualifications'. A driver with no driving licence is **unqualified**. **Disqualified** means 'made ineligible, banned'. A driver whose licence has been taken away is **disqualified**.

unravel

Other forms are **unravelled, unravelling** in British English, but the second *l* is usually omitted in American English. It means 'disentangle'. See RAVEL.

unreadable

See ILLEGIBLE.

unreligious

See IRRELIGIOUS.

unrepairable

See IRREPARABLE.

unrival(l)ed

The word is spelled with two *l*'s in British English, but with one in American English.

unsanitary, insanitary

They mean the same thing. **Insanitary** is almost the only British form, but **unsanitary** has some currency in American use.

unsatisfied

See DISSATISFIED.

unsociable, unsocial

See ANTISOCIAL.

unstructured

This OVERUSED word means 'informal, not highly organized', often in an appreciative sense: *unstructured college courses*. It must be the opposite of *structured*, so that it is curious that that is often an appreciative word too.

unthinkable

From meaning 'inconceivable' or 'out of the question', **unthinkable** has come to be used, like *preposterous* or *monstrous*, of things that actually exist or are happening: *It's unthinkable that you're still paying all that tax.* There is a certain lack of logic here, but the extension of meaning is standard.

until, till

1 Until is rather more formal than **till**, but the words are used interchangeably. Do not spell **till** as *'til.*

2 Until and **till** can be ambiguous in negative sentences. *We didn't sleep till morning* might mean either that we were awake till then, or that we woke up before then. Consider the following report on the findings of an industrial tribunal: *Staff should not be put at risk until someone is hurt or killed in a raid* (*Daily Telegraph*). The writer of the report, of course, is afraid that only injury or death will be a sufficient incentive to start protecting the staff properly. But it sounds as though we must protect the staff until someone is hurt but can then stop worrying about it. The report needs to be rephrased; perhaps as *Staff should be protected now, or someone may be hurt . . . .*

3 The combination *up until* is unnecessary. It is neater to use **until** alone: *(Up) until now I've scarcely worn my wellies.*

4 *Until such time as* is another usually VERBOSE way of saying **until**. It is sometimes useful, though, to convey the idea that the event in question is a long time in the future and may never happen at all: *You can use the garage until such time as* (not *that*) *the Council takes over the whole property.* See also UNLESS AND UNTIL.

untimely end

This is a CLICHÉ.

unto

This is an archaic word; use *to*.

untoward

This is pronounced with three syllables in British English. It has usually only two in American speech.

unveil

This word is popular in journalese: *unveil their plans for the new docks.* For a change use *tell, reveal, announce*, etc.

unwieldy

The word is spelled -ie-, not -ei-.

unwonted

This is a formal and perhaps PRETENTIOUS word for 'unusual, unaccustomed'. Do not confuse it with *unwanted*.

up

1 As a verb, **up** is informal: *to up the prices; He upped and married a showgirl.*

2 *Up to* is appropriate everywhere except in formal prose: *My German isn't up to reading Schiller; I wonder what they're up to?* Both *up to* and (in British use) *down to* can mean 'the responsibility of': *It's up to/ down to you to collect the money.*

upon, on

See ON (2).

upstage

This means the back of the stage, so that to **upstage** an actor is to force him or her to face away from the audience, by holding a dialogue from behind. By extension, informally it has come to mean 'treat someone snobbishly' and as an adjective to mean 'haughty and aloof'.

uptight

It means 'tense and nervous', or 'indignant', or 'rigidly conventional', and is informal.

upward(s)

1 Before a noun, use **upward**: *an upward movement.* After a verb, use the form with *s* in British English (*to glance upwards*) and the one without *s* in American English.

2 *Upward adjustment* and *upward revision* are EUPHEMISMS for a rise in prices.

3 *Upwards of* means 'more than': *They cost upwards of £50.* It is a standard though not very formal expression.

urban, urbane

Urban means 'of a city': *urban development; urban driving.* **Urbane** means 'smooth in manner; confidently courteous': *an urbane car* *salesman*. It is sometimes used derogatorily by those who distrust very polished manners.

Urdu

See HINDI.

us

For *as we, than us*, etc, see CASE, GRAMMATICAL (4).

usage, use *(noun)*

1 Usage is the usual word for 'treatment': *received some rough usage*. In connection with language, **usage** is the way in which words and phrases are actually used in accepted practice, as distinct from what abstract theory might predict: *modern English usage*. **Use** is using or being used, and should be preferred to **usage** in this wider sense (*excessive use of coal*) and for 'usefulness' or 'purpose' (*What's the use of worrying?*).

2 *No use* is a standard expression, as in *It's no use worrying*.

use *(verb)*

1 *Winters used to be colder* means that they were formerly colder. The usual negative form of this was once *They used not to be* or informally *They usedn't to be*, but the commoner negative in both British and American English has become *They didn't use to* or (perhaps better) *They didn't used to*. Writers who dislike all these forms can escape an awkward choice by preferring *They never used to*. The common question form is *Did they use(d) to?* although *Used they to?* is the traditionally correct form. Similarly, the usual negative question is *Didn't they use(d) to?*, rather than *Used they not to?* or *Usedn't they to?*: *Didn't they use(d) to live in Sheffield?*; *They used to live in Sheffield, didn't they?*.

2 To **use** a person or organization can mean 'exploit for one's own ends': *He feels he is being used and manipulated for political purposes*. The sense is standard. You may want to say 'do something by means of' in a harmless sense, as in *use girls to sell cosmetics*, but be careful that you are not misunderstood.

3 *He had used to be* and *He used to could* are not standard English. Avoid them, and write *He used to be* and *He used to be able to*.

us(e)able

This can be spelled either with or without the first *e*.

user

This is OVERUSED in compounds such as *user-oriented* and *user adequacy*, which express concern for the needs of the user. The commonest is the convenient expression *user-friendly*, applied initially to computer systems that provide jargon-free step-by-step guidance, and by extension to any machine or textbook that is easy to use.

usherette

She shows people to their theatre or cinema seats. Any other kind of woman usher would be called an *usher*. See FEMININE FORMS.

utilize

It can seem PRETENTIOUS to use **utilize** where *use* will do, and it nearly always will do. There is some excuse for **utilize** in the sense of 'put to unexpected practical use' (*utilize an old bathtub as a drinking trough*).

uvula

The plural is **uvulas** or, less usually, **uvulae**.

vacant, vacuous

Applied to human expressions and behaviour, **vacant** means 'empty of thought, expressionless': *a vacant stare*. **Vacuous** means 'stupidly vacant, fatuous': *a vacuous giggle*. Intelligent people can be **vacant** but not **vacuous**.

vaccinate, inoculate

In technical parlance these words are synonyms. **Vaccinate**, however, is often used for smallpox, and **inoculate** for other diseases.

vacuum

The usual plural is **vacuums**. **Vacua** is pedantic, and would be absurd if by **vacuums** you mean vacuum cleaners.

743

vade mecum

The plural is **vade mecums**. It means a manual for ready reference.

vagary

The pronunciation stressing the first syllable (like *vague*) is on the whole to be recommended for British English; but that which stresses the second syllable (like *air*) is also common, particularly in American use.

vagina

Vaginas is the usual plural, **vaginae** being pedantic. It is a deficiency of the language that there is no neutral word for this passage. **Vagina** is rather technical, and all the other words are rude. The same deficiency applies, in fact, to the sexual and excretory parts and processes in general.

vain, vane, vein

Vain means 'worthless' or 'conceited'. A **vane** revolves in air or water: *weather vane*. A **vein** is a blood vessel, or a deposit of ore, or a mode of expression: *wrote in romantic vein*.

vale, veil

A **vale** is a valley. Apart from its use in placenames (*the Vale of Evesham*), the word belongs to old-fashioned poetry. A **veil** is a cloth over the head.

valet

This is pronounced either 'vallit' or 'vallay'. Other forms of the verb are **valeted, valeting** in both British and American English.

valid, validate, validity

These are OVERUSED: **valid** in the sense of 'relevant' or 'sound' (*a valid study programme*), **validate** for 'confirm' (*to validate his academic competence*), and **validity** for 'standing' or 'merit' (*question her validity as a performer*). There can be no objection to **valid** when used in the senses in which we speak of a *valid inference* or a *valid passport*.

valo(u)r, valorous

These are spelled **valour, valorous** in British English, and **valor, valorous** in American English.

value

Although we may ask *What use is it?* or *What good is it?*, the word **value** is not correctly used in that way. Write *Of what value is it?* or *It is of no value*.

van

See D'.

vane

See VAIN.

vantage

See ADVANTAGE.

vapo(u)r, vaporize, vaporous

The noun is spelled **vapour** in British English, **vapor** in American English. The related words are always spelled as shown.

variance

Things are *at variance with*, not *from*, each other: *ideas totally at variance with hers*. Do not spell this expression *at variants*.

varieties of English

English is not a monolithic language. Some variation in vocabulary and grammar largely depends on who the users are: where they live, what socio-economic group they belong to, what education they have acquired. Varieties of English defined by such variation are regional or social **dialects**. (Pronunciation varieties of this kind are regional or social **accents**.) The national regional dialects (British, American, Australian English, and so on) can be further differentiated regionally (Scots, Yorkshire, Midwest). The dialects have enough in common for it to make sense to call them all English. Many English speakers are comfortable in using or understanding several dialects. Some people move permanently from one area to another; some belong to more than one social group.

There is also variation that depends on choices that people make, when they adapt their language to particular situations. This stylistic variation depends on the medium (spoken or written), on attitude to others (level of formality), and on the type of activity (giving instructions, writing letters, drawing up legal documents). The three types of choices are interrelated; legal documents, for example, are written, are very formal, and contain features that are peculiar to legal language. When it is most formal, spoken English is closest to written English; conversely, at its least formal, written English is closest to spoken English.

In formal letters, for example, it would be inappropriate to use words and expressions such as *OK*; *kind of* (*I kind of like them*); intensifying *pretty* (*We wanted it pretty quickly*); *you know* (*He looks like me, you know*). Contractions (*I'm sorry about the mistake*) or omission of words (*Hope to see you soon*) would not be expected.

At the most informal end of the scale are **slang** words, which are intended to be irreverent. They are usually confined to particular regions or groups and often have a short life. Here are a few examples in contemporary use: *booze*, *grotty* (British), *jerk* (American). The slang of an occupation group (thieves, jazz musicians) is sometimes known as an **argot** or a **cant**. Some words that were once slang (*mob*, *blurb*) have acquired respectability.

When a specialized vocabulary is condemned as incomprehensible, it is often known as a **jargon** (medical jargon, political jargon). Some jargons have their own names: *legalese*, *computerese*, *bureaucratese*. Specialized vocabulary has its place when it is addressed to specialists, and indeed it is more economical and precise than nontechnical vocabulary. But a manual for home computers, for example, should be written in a language that potential users can easily understand; it should not be overburdened with technical terms. In some cases, the difficulties in intelligibility are due to the complexity of the grammar, a fault ascribed to **gobbledygook**, an incomprehensible jargon associated with government employees. **Journalese** is criticized for its overuse of certain expressions (*breakthrough*, *card-carrying*, *critical* meaning 'ill or injured', *laid off* for workers, *saga* for a story appearing more than once) and for some oddities of grammar (eg the creation of ad hoc titles such as *approved-schoolmaster Ivor Cook* or *horror film actress Patricia Ann Walsh*).

See also DIALECT; STANDARD ENGLISH.

various

Do not use **various** as a pronoun. *I asked various of the children* can be rephrased as *some* or *several of the children*, or *various children*.

varsity

In British English this is an old-fashioned word for *university*, current only in referring to a sporting fixture between Oxford and Cambridge (*varsity match*). In current American English it means a principal college or school team.

vase

In British English, this is pronounced with the vowel sound of *father*.
In American English it usually rhymes with either *face* or *daze*.

vehicle

This formal word is indispensable in the language because it is so
general. If you know what kind of vehicle you are talking about, prefer
car, *bus*, etc.

veil

See VALE.

vein

See VAIN.

veld(t)

See PAMPAS.

venal, venial

Venal means 'corrupt': *a venal judge*. **Venial** means 'pardonable': *a
venial fault*.

vendor, vender

Vendor is the chief British spelling, and **vender** a chiefly American
variant.

vengeance

See AVENGE.

ventilator

The word ends in *-or*, not *-er*.

venue

It is commonly used, and perhaps OVERUSED, to mean the scene of any
event: *this most unlikely venue for vodka production* (*The Observer*).
You could use *scene* or *place* for a change.

veranda(h)

This is spelled either with or without the *h*.

verb

See COLLECTIVES; NUMBER AGREEMENT; PERSON AGREEMENT; VERBS, PRINCIPAL PARTS.

verbal, oral

Verbal means 'of words': *a verbal distinction*. **Oral** means 'spoken' or 'of the mouth': *oral hygiene*. **Verbal** is often used to mean 'in spoken words, in contrast to written ones'. This can be confusing. Where the distinction is important, as in *a verbal contract*, it is clearer to use **oral** for spoken words and *written* for writing, and to avoid **verbal** altogether.

verbiage, verbosity

They both mean 'wordiness', in either speech or writing. Some writers try to distinguish written **verbiage** from spoken **verbosity**, but they are more or less synonyms.

verbosity

This means 'longwindedness'. It is the use of more words than are necessary.

There are sometimes good reasons against saying something in the shortest possible way. We may deliberately avoid the concise technical term, and choose instead to go the long way round to make the matter clear to a lay audience. Instead of advising visitors to a cathedral to look at the carvings on the *misericords*, we might speak of the *ledges under the hinged choir stalls*, which are the same thing but may be easier for the visitors to find. We may deliberately avoid too direct a word, and prefer the polite EUPHEMISM that is less embarrassing, as when we say *pass away* or *fall asleep* for *die*, or comment that someone has been *economical with the truth* rather than accusing him of lying. Or in preparing material to be spoken, we may intentionally pad it out with repetitions, jokes, illustrative anecdotes, anything that will help the listeners to keep up with the speaker, since they may not be able to absorb densely packed material fast enough, and cannot go back as readers do to recover what they have missed.

In general, though, it is a good rule to express oneself as briefly as possible. The economical utterance is nearly always the most effective one. Such economy is achieved partly by avoiding TAUTOLOGY, the repetition of the same idea, as in *bisect in two* (where *in two* should be omitted because *bisect* means the same thing); partly by the kind of device recommended in the article CIRCUMLOCUTION, which suggests some ways to concise expression.

verbs, principal parts

Regular verbs have four forms:

1 the simple form: *play*

2 the *-s* form: *plays*

3 the *-ing* form: *playing*

4 the *-ed* form: *played*

The uses of these forms are listed below.

1 The simple form, which has no inflection, is used for:

(a) the present tense for all except the third person singular (which has the *-s* form): *I/You/We/They play football.*

(b) the imperative: *Play with us.*

(c) the infinitive with *to*: *He wants to play chess.*

(d) the infinitive without *to*: *She may play with us.*

(e) the present subjunctive: *His parents requested that he play with me.*

2 The *-s* form is used for the third person singular in the present tense: *She/He/It plays well.* To make the *-s* form from the simple form, add *-s* (*plays* from *play*) or *-es* (*washes* from *wash*). Exceptions: *has* (from *have*) and *is* (from *be*). See SPELLING and DOUBLING for further details.

3 The *-ing* form is used:

(a) to combine with the verb *be* to make the progressive: *She was playing well; We are playing later.*

(b) to make a phrase that functions as subject or in some other way than as the main verb of the sentence: *Playing the piano is my only hobby; Playing cautiously, we managed to win the game.*

To make the *-ing* form from the simple form, add *-ing* (*playing* from *play*). See SPELLING and DOUBLING for further details.

4 The *-ed* form has two sets of uses:

(A) the past tense: *We played the match yesterday.*

(B) the *-ed* participle (also called the past or passive participle), which is used:

(a) to combine with the verb *have* to make the perfect: *I have often played with them; She has played hockey.*

(b) to combine with the verb *be* to make the passive: *The final match was played last week.*

(c) to make a phrase that is attached to the sentence or to part of it: *Played well, the game provides plenty of exercise; The game played last week ended in a draw.*

Verbs are regular if from the simple form we can work out by rules the other three forms. All new verbs are regular, so if we are given a verb *glate*, we know that it makes *glates, glating, glated.*

Verbs are irregular if the *-ed* form cannot be predicted from the simple form. For example, the *-ed* form of *make* is *made*; from the rules for regular verbs we would expect *maked*. A further complication is that many irregular verbs have two *-ed* forms; they distinguish the past tense from the *-ed* participle; so *see* makes *saw* (*I saw them yesterday*) and *seen* (*I have seen the film*). In addition, some verbs have regular as well as irregular forms: *mow* can be regularly *mowed* or it can have past *mowed* and participle *mown* (*I mowed the lawn yesterday*; *I have already mowed/mown the lawn*).

To use irregular verbs we therefore have to know their past and *-ed* participle as well as the simple form. These three forms of an irregular verb are called the *principal parts* of the verb and they are always given in this order: simple form – past – *-ed* participle. There are some differences in irregular verbs between British and American English. For example, *dived* and *dove* both occur as pasts of *dive* in American English, while *dived* is the only past in British English; both *smelled* and *smelt* occur in British English, but only *smelled* in American English.

Here is a list of the principal parts of verbs that may cause difficulty. Correct alternatives are also given. For those verbs that have '(E)' after them, consult the individual entries.

simple form	past	-ed participle
awake	awoke	awoken
bear	bore	borne
begin	began	begun
beseech	besought, beseeched	besought, beseeched
bet	bet, betted	bet, betted
bid (E)	bid	bid
bite	bit	bitten, bit
bleed	bled	bled
blow	blew	blown
break	broke	broken
burn	burnt, burned	burnt, burned
bring	brought	brought
catch	caught	caught
choose	chose	chosen
cleave (E)	cleaved	cleaved, cloven
come	came	come
cost	cost	cost
creep	crept	crept
dig	dug	dug
dive (E)	dived	dived
do	did	done
draw	drew	drawn

simple form	past	-ed participle
dream	dreamt, dreamed	dreamt, dreamed
drink	drank	drunk
drive	drove	driven
eat	ate	eaten
fall	fell	fallen
flee	fled	fled
fling	flung	flung
fly	flew	flown
forget	forgot	forgotten
forgive	forgave	forgiven
freeze	froze	frozen
give	gave	given
go	went	gone
grow	grew	grown
hear	heard	heard
hide	hid	hidden
hurt	hurt	hurt
keep	kept	kept
kneel	knelt, kneeled	knelt, kneeled
know	knew	known
lay	laid	laid
lean	leant, leaned	leant, leaned
leap	leapt, leaped	leapt, leaped
learn	learnt, learned	learnt, learned
lie	lay	lain
light	lit, lighted	lit, lighted
make	made	made
mistake	mistook	mistaken
mow	mowed	mown, mowed
pay	paid	paid
plead (E)	pleaded	pleaded
prove	proved	proved, proven
put	put	put
quit	quit, quitted	quit, quitted
rid (E)	rid, ridded	rid, ridded
ride	rode	ridden
ring (eg bell)	rang	rung
ring (eg building)	ringed	ringed
rise	rose	risen
run	ran	run
saw	sawed	sawed, sawn
say	said	said
see	saw	seen

simple form	past	-ed participle
sell	sold	sold
sew	sewed	sewn
shake	shook	shaken
shave	shaved	shaved, shaven
shear	sheared	shorn, sheared
shine	shone, shined	shone, shined
shoe	shod, shoed	shod, shoed
shoot	shot	shot
show	showed	shown, showed
shrink	shrank, shrunk	shrunk
shut	shut	shut
sing	sang	sung
sink	sank	sunk
sit	sat	sat
slay	slew	slain, slayed
sleep	slept	slept
sling	slung	slung
slink	slunk	slunk
smell	smelt, smelled	smelt, smelled
sow	sowed	sown, sowed
speak	spoke	spoken
speed	sped, speeded	sped, speeded
spell	spelt, spelled	spelt, spelled
spill	spilt, spilled	spilt, spilled
spin	spun, span	spun
spit	spit, spat	spit, spat
spoil	spoilt, spoiled	spoilt, spoiled
spring	sprang	sprung
stand	stood	stood
steal	stole	stolen
stick	stuck	stuck
sting	stung	stung
stink	stank	stunk
strew	strewed	strewn, strewed
stride	strode	stridden
strike (E)	struck	struck, stricken
string	strung	strung
strive (E)	strove, strived	striven, strived
swear	swore	sworn
sweep	swept	swept
swell	swelled	swelled, swollen
swim	swam	swum
take	took	taken
teach	taught	taught

simple form	past	-ed participle
tear	tore	torn
tell	told	told
think	thought	thought
thrive	thrived, throve	thrived, thriven
throw	threw	thrown
tread	trod	trodden
wake	woke, waked	woken, waked
wear	wore	worn
weave (E)	wove, weaved	woven, weaved
weep	wept	wept
wet	wetted, wet	wetted, wet
win	won	won
wind (E)	wound, winded	wound, winded
write	wrote	written

vermin

It is usually treated as a plural, and there is no plural form *vermins*: *These vermin are a problem.* It may occasionally refer to one as well as to more than one creature: *Foxes are vermin*; *That fox is vermin*; *You vermin!* (addressed to one person).

vermouth

In British English the stress is usually on *ver*. In American English it is on *outh*, rhyming with *tooth*.

vernacular

This meant originally the local mother tongue as contrasted with a learned or literary language. In the Middle Ages it might be English as opposed to Latin, a use which survives when we speak of the **vernacular** name of a plant (*snapdragon*) in contrast with its botanical Latin name (*antirrhinum*). **Vernacular** has come to be applied to commonplace or colloquial speech: *his gumption, to use the vernacular word* (William James). A **vernacular** style of building is the common style of a place.

verruca

The usual plural is **verrucas**. **Verrucae** is pedantic.

verse, stanza

Verse is poetry, or a poem, or (technically in prosody) a line of a poem, or a short division of the Bible. Most people also use **verse** for what is technically called a **stanza**, a series of lines forming one division of a poem. This is surely a case where everyday usage should be respected outside technical contexts.

verso, recto

The **verso** is the back of a printed or manuscript page, or the left-hand page of a book. The **recto** is the front, or right-hand page.

vertex, vortex

A **vertex** is the highest point, or summit. A **vortex** is a whirlpool or whirlwind. The plurals are **vertices, vortices** or, less usually, **vertexes, vortexes**.

vertical

See PERPENDICULAR.

very

It is correctly used before ordinary adjectives and adverbs: *very young*; *very quickly*. Before the *-ed* form of verbs it should be replaced by *much* or used with another adverb: *was much* (or *very much*, but not *very* alone) *admired*; *The story has been very greatly exaggerated* (not *very exaggerated*) *by the Press*. Some *-ed* forms have come to be treated as ordinary adjectives, and these can take **very** alone: *very tired/pleased/limited*. Indeed the same form can be used as a verb or an adjective, so that *It was a very exaggerated story* is correct. In marginal cases it is safer to use *much* or *very much* or some other adverb, at least for formal writing: *much distressed*, *very much inconvenienced*, *greatly absorbed* (in her book). Compare TOO. For *too* = **very**, see TOO (2).

vessel

This is a very formal word. Outside technical contexts prefer *ship*, *cup*, etc according to the sense.

vest, waistcoat, undershirt, T-shirt

In British English a **vest** is a sleeveless (or occasionally short-sleeved) undergarment. In American English a **vest** is what the British call a **waistcoat**, and the undergarment is an **undershirt** or **T-shirt**. **T-shirt** may also mean an outer shirt of similar design, and that is its only meaning in British English.

vestigial, rudimentary

Vestigial refers to the remaining traces left by something that has vanished: *vestigial beauty in her aging face*. **Rudimentary** means 'not yet fully developed; crude': *a rudimentary knowledge of physics*.

However, a creature may be said to have a **vestigial** or a **rudimentary** tail, with much the same meaning, in comparison with the more fully developed tails of similar creatures.

vet

This is standard everywhere as a CLIPPED form of *veterinary surgeon*. In American English it is also short for *veteran*, meaning an ex-serviceman. The verb **vet**, meaning 'appraise expertly', is chiefly British: *vetting the manuscript for possible breach of the Official Secrets Act* (*The Sun*).

veto

The plural of the noun is **vetoes**. Other forms of the verb are **vetoes, vetoed, vetoing.**

via

This means 'by way of', and is properly applied to routes: *fly to Bombay via Frankfurt*. It is better to replace it by *by* or *through* where a means of transport or a method of communication is concerned: *send the goods by* (rather than *via*) *rail*; *send a message through* (rather than *via*) *the milkman*.

viable

In biology this means 'able to survive and develop': *a viable foetus*; *viable seeds*. By extension, we can say *The colony is now a viable state*. **Viable** is OVERUSED where *workable*, *sound*, *effective*, or *practicable* would make a welcome change: *a viable alternative*; *not economically viable*.

vial, viol

A **vial** is a small bottle, also called a *phial*. A **viol** is a stringed musical instrument.

vibrator

The word ends in *-or*, not *-er*.

vicar

See RECTOR.

vice, vise

Vice is immorality. A **vice** is also a carpenter's clamp in British English, but this is spelled **vise** in American English.

vicinity

In the vicinity, or *in the immediate vicinity of*, is a VERBOSE way of saying *about* or *near*.

vicious, viscous

Vicious means 'depraved, evil'. **Viscous** means 'sticky'.

victor

The word ends in *-or*, not *-er*.

victuals

This is pronounced 'vittles'; but it is a quaintly FACETIOUS word, better replaced by *food* or *provisions*.

videlicet

See VIZ.

view

There are three common expressions involving **view**. *With a view to* and *with the view of* refer to future intentions: *study the subject with a view to finding* (not *to find*) *a solution*. The rather similar phrase *in view of* refers to existing circumstances: *In view of the weather, the show will take place in the tent*. But *in view of the fact that* can be more concisely replaced by *because* or *since*.

viewpoint

See POINT OF VIEW.

vigo(u)r, vigorous

These are spelled **vigour, vigorous** in British English, and **vigor, vigorous** in American English. See also RIGOROUS.

villain, villein

A **villain** is a scoundrel. A **villein** was a medieval serf.

viol

See VIAL.

violoncello

This is not spelled *violincello*. The usual word is *cello*, in any case.

VIP

See PERSONAGE.

virago

The plural is either **viragoes** or **viragos**. It means an overbearing noisy woman. Feminists are trying to revive the archaic nonderogatory sense of a woman who is big and strong and brave, and if they succeed it will be an interesting CHANGE OF MEANING.

virtuoso

The plural is either **virtuosos** or **virtuosi**. It means a highly skilled performer.

virus

The plural is **viruses**.

vis-à-vis

This is spelled with the accent. Although it means 'face to face' in French, in English the phrase can correctly mean 'in relation to; towards': *the company's position vis-à-vis the union*.

viscous

See VICIOUS.

vise

See VICE.

visibility

This means not only the quality of being visible, or 'visibleness', but clarity or range of vision: *Visibility is down to 20 yards*. It is coming to be OVERUSED in managerial contexts for 'noticeableness, conspicuousness': *a high-visibility job*.

visible, visual

Things that can be seen are **visible**: *visible symptoms*. **Visual** means 'used in seeing' (*visual organs*) or 'done or achieved by sight' (*visual impressions*; *visual navigation*) or 'involving sight' (*visual aids in education*; *the visual focus of a lens*; *a visual display unit*).

visionary

This is a rather derogatory word, meaning 'impractical, utopian': *a visionary scheme*. It cannot replace *imaginative* or *farsighted*.

visitation

A **visitation** is a much more formal and official affair than a mere *visit*. It might be a visit of an inspector. The word can also mean an affliction, such as a plague, believed to be sent by God.

visitor

The word ends in *-or*, not *-er*.

visit with

This informal American expression has been adversely criticized in Britain. It cannot be replaced by *visit* alone in American English because it means 'have a chat with'.

visor, vizor

Both spellings are correct.

visual

See VISIBLE.

vitamin

The first syllable rhymes with *fight* in American English, but usually with *sit* in British English.

viz, i.e.

The abbreviation **viz** is short for *videlicet*, and means 'namely', which usually replaces it in speech. It is less commonly used than **i.e.**, which stands for the Latin *id est*, 'that is'. Careful writers sometimes make a delicate distinction, using **viz** to introduce a list of items composing a previously mentioned whole, and **i.e.** to supply a paraphrase or interpretation: *three full members, viz Tom, Dick, and Harry*; *three full members, i.e. people who have paid their dues*.

vizor

See VISOR.

vocabulary size

How many words are there in the English language? This seems a
simple question, but is in fact difficult to answer. First, what words do
we count as belonging to English? Do we disregard words that are now
obsolete? Do we include words from all the national varieties of
English, not only British and American English but also words used in
the many other varieties, such as Australian, Caribbean, or Indian
English? When do we regard a foreign word as established in the
language? Do we count dialect words and slang? Do we count all
scientific and technical words? If not, which of them belong to the
general vocabulary? It has been estimated that there are over six million
chemical compounds, each of which has a name, and more compounds
are continually being added to the list. And of course there are
specialized words in many other fields, such as medicine and law.

Secondly, do we count combinations as separate items? The
Longman Dictionary of the English Language (published in 1984) lists
as separate entries 34 combinations with the verb *get*, such as *get
ahead*, *get away with*, *get out*; in addition, several other combinations
(eg *getting one's own back*) are listed as idioms under the main entry
for *get*.

Thirdly, many words have more than one meaning. The Longman
Dictionary lists 21 main definitions for the verb *give*. If we count all
the subsidiary definitions, the total increases to 39. At least some of
those definitions we may want to regard as representing separate
words; for example, *give* in *give a doll to a child* and *give* in *give a
concert*. But it is not clear where we draw the line between different
meanings and different words.

Fourthly, do we count the same form in different parts of speech as
different words? *Answer* and *end* can be either a verb or a noun. *Well*
and *slow* can be either an adjective or an adverb.

Finally, do we count separately the grammatical forms? Are *speak*,
speaks, *speaking*, *spoke*, *spoken* separate words for this purpose? And
what about *he, him, his*; or *man, man's, men, men's*; or *go* and *went*?

One approach to answering the original question is to look at the
largest dictionary of currently used English, Webster's Third New
International Dictionary (published 1961). This American dictionary
claims to have over 450,000 words. It lists some, but not all,
combinations as separate entries. All the definitions of (say) *give*
appear under that entry. It provides separate entries for irregular forms
of the same part of speech, such as *gave* and *spoken*, cross-referring
them to the main entry; it is not clear whether these are included in the
general total. Different parts of speech (the verb *answer* and the noun
answer) have their own entries.

Although an American dictionary, Webster's Third includes British
words, and to a lesser extent words from other English-speaking

759

countries. It is by no means complete for slang or dialect, and it excludes much specialized vocabulary. Since its publication, many thousands of new words have been added to the language, and many more additions can be expected every year.

We use only a limited number of the words in the dictionary, and perhaps in addition dialect, slang, or specialized words that do not appear in a general dictionary. We also understand words that we do not use ourselves. It has been estimated that undergraduate students have a vocabulary of 40,000 to 50,000 words that they understand, though not necessarily use.

vocation

See AVOCATION.

voice

It is not wrong to use **voice** for 'express', even when the expression is written rather than spoken: *He voiced his opinion in a letter to The Times*.

volcano

The plural is either **volcanoes** or **volcanos**.

voluntarily

This is pronounced with the stress on either *vol* or *ar*. The second is easier to say.

von

See D'.

voracious

See RAPACIOUS.

vortex

See VERTEX.

vulnerable

In careful speech, the first *l* should be pronounced.

wage(s)

The singular and plural forms have much the same meaning: *This is a low wage*; *My wages are low*. The plural **wages** is the commoner word for 'payment for work', except before other nouns as in *wage earner*, *wage packet*, *wage scale*. **Wages** is no longer used as a singular noun, in spite of the biblical text *The wages of sin is death*.

wag(g)on

Wagon is the commoner spelling everywhere. **Waggon** is a British variant.

waist, waste

The **waist** is the narrow part of the body. **Waste** is refuse, or careless squandering.

waistcoat

See VEST. In Britain, where the word is chiefly used, **waistcoat** is usually pronounced more or less as spelled, rather than with the older pronunciation 'weskit'.

wait, await

1 In modern English, the rather formal verb **await** must take an object: *I am awaiting your decision* (or *waiting for it*, but not *awaiting to hear it*). **Wait** generally takes no object.

2 *Wait on/upon* usually means 'act as an attendant to': *We waited on them hand and foot*. It should not normally replace *wait for* in the sense of **await**: *waiting for* (not *on*) *a bus*. There is, however, a slight difference of emphasis between *waiting for the Government to act* and *waiting upon the Government to act*, the latter suggesting an unwelcome lingering and delay, so that *wait on/upon* may sometimes be justified.

waive, wave

To **waive** is to relinquish or dismiss: *waive one's rights*; *waive the formalities*. It is sometimes confused with a figurative sense of **wave**: to *wave* (not *waive*) *something aside* is to dismiss it as unimportant.

waiver, waver

A **waiver** is the legal renouncing of a right. To **waver** is to sway, or falter.

wallop (*verb*)

Other forms are **walloped, walloping** in both British and American English.

want

1 The standard constructions with **want** are *I want you to go*; *I want this changed*; *I want this to be changed*; *This wants changing*. Do not write *I want for you to go*, *I want this changing*, or *This wants changed*. In some regional varieties of English it is possible to distinguish between *Do you want your chicken cooked?* (ie do you want a cooked one?) and *Do you want your chicken cooking?* (ie shall I cook it for you?). In standard writing, however, this distinction must be made in some other way.

2 Want in the sense of 'lack' (*He wants courtesy*) is old-fashioned, and may lead to actual confusion with the commoner sense of 'desire'. *They want food and shelter* would certainly be taken to mean that they wish for those things.

3 The use of **want** for *ought* (*You want to see a doctor about that*) is rather informal. So are *want in* and *want out* (*The cat wants out*), which are chiefly found in American and Scottish English.

4 For **want** or *wish*, see WISH.

-ward(s)

This ending usually takes the form **-ward** in adjectives: *the homeward journey*; *The child was backward*. Adverbs usually end with **-wards** in British English: *sailing northwards*. American English, and older British writing, often use **-ward** for adverbs, with the curious result that American forms such as *afterward* may appear old-fashioned (rather than American) to a British reader. There are, however, some irregularities; see FORWARD(S).

warn

Traditionally you **warn** someone *of*, *about*, or *against* something; or you **warn** someone *to do* or *not to do* something, or *that* something may happen. The verb can be used with no object, meaning 'give a warning'. Wordsworth wrote *A perfect woman, nobly planned, To warn, to comfort, and command*, so that this intransitive construction cannot be said to be peculiar to journalese, but it is common there: *Minister Warns Of Future Cuts*.

warp, woof, weft, web

In weaving, the **warp** is the lengthways threads, the **woof** or **weft** is the crosswise threads, and the **weft** or **web** is the resultant fabric.

was

See WERE.

wash up

In British English it means 'wash the dishes'. In American English it means 'wash your face and hands'.'

wastage, waste

Wastage is is loss by rotting, leaking, evaporation, and so on, but not by human 'wastefulness'. It is not a grander synonym for the noun **waste**, as in *a waste of time*. While **waste** implies some moral censure, **wastage** does not. We speak of a reduction in the staff of an organization by *natural* **wastage**, which means by retirement or resignation rather than by dismissal.

waste

See WAIST.

wave

See WAIVE.

waver

See WAIVER.

wax

This verb is often used for *grow* or *become*. If you use it (usually humorously) like that, it must be followed by an adjective, not an

adverb: *He waxed lyrical* (not *lyrically*) *about the beauties of Bognor.*
Those who use **wax** with an adverb presumably think it means 'speak'.

way

1 The use of *ways* for **way** (*a long ways from town*) is American, and is
avoided in good American writing.

2 For *way above*, *way back*, see AWAY.

3 *No way* is an informal way of expressing forceful refusal or
contradiction: *no pictures in the nude, no way* (*Punch*). It is vivid, but
would be unsuitable in a serious context.

4 *Under way*, not *under weigh*, is the right way to spell the expression
that means 'in progress': *Preparations were under way.* In nautical
contexts it also means 'not anchored'. The confusion between the two
spellings probably arose from the existence of the phrase *weigh anchor*;
which incidentally means to raise it, not to drop it.

we

1 editorial use	4 royal **we**
2 inclusive authorial use	5 **we** for **you**
3 indefinite use	

1 editorial use
This use of **we** is only justified when it refers to the view of an editorial
board or some other collective body (*We recommend that . . .* ; *In our
view*). It is regrettable that in formal scientific writing many single
authors still feel the need to avoid *I* and prefer instead to use **we** or to
cast their sentences into the passive (*As we have indicated above . . .* ;
As has been indicated above). Another coy strategy for avoiding *I* is for
authors to refer to themselves – and sometimes also to readers – in the
third person (*The author wishes her readers to know . . .* ; *As your
correspondent must realize . . .*). If you are writing as a single
individual, use the first person pronoun: *As I have indicated above . . .*

2 inclusive authorial use
An author may wish to draw the reader into the discussion by using **we**:
We now turn to the next argument . . . ; *Let us consider the evidence in
greater detail.* This appeal to the reader's involvement is normal and
commendable, and frequently used in academic writing.

3 indefinite use
In another justifiable extension, **we** refers indefinitely to people in
general, perhaps the nation or all human beings: *We have a*

responsibility to care for the elderly among us; We now know that space wars are possible.

To avoid confusion, do not put two uses of **we** in the same sentence: *We believe that we must no longer inflict our problems on other countries.* The first **we** is the editorial **we**; the subsequent indefinite **we** and *our* refer to the nation.

4 royal **we**
This appears to be dying out. Even in formal contexts Queen Elizabeth II speaks of *my husband and I* and *my government.*

5 **we** for **you**
We is occasionally used by people addressing children or the sick: *Now we must finish our food, mustn't we?; How are we feeling today, Mr Jones?* This may seem condescending.

weak, week

Weak means 'not strong'. A **week** is seven days.

wean

This literally means 'accustom to food other than mother's milk', so that you can **wean** a baby *on* a specified food. In figurative use, you can correctly either **wean** someone *from* a cause of emotional dependence, or **wean** someone *on* a dominating influence: *a generation weaned* (ie reared) *on television.*

weather

See WHETHER (1).

weave

There are two **weave** verbs. The one connected with cloth has the past tense and participle **wove, woven**, and is also used figuratively: *He wove the stories into a continuous narrative.* The other verb has the past tense **weaved**, and means 'lurch waveringly': *Drunken sailors weaved down the street.*

week

See WEAK.

weft, web

See WARP.

weigh, weight *(verb)*

1 Both words are spelled *-ei-*, not *-ie-*.

2 To **weigh** is to find out how heavy something is, or to register a specified weight: *The baby weighs* (not *weights*) *ten pounds*. To **weigh** an anchor is to raise it, not to lower it. To **weight** is to load, literally or figuratively: *a wage structure weighted in favour of junior employees*. Both verbs can mean 'oppress': *weighed/weighted down with cares*.

weir, weird

1 Both words are spelled *-ei-*, not *-ie-*.

2 Weird strictly means 'mysteriously frightening, uncanny'. It has been OVERUSED in a looser sense which could often be expressed as *odd*, *strange*, *unusual*, etc.

well

1 For **well** or *good*, see GOOD.

2 *As well as* can mean 'as proficiently as': *She sings as well as you do*. It can also mean 'in addition to': *You'll have to pay as well as Peter*; *You'll have to pay as well as help* (or *helping*) *with the tea*. (For the choice between *as well as I* and *as me*, see AS (1)). Be careful not to create confusion between these two meanings of the phrase. *The women swim as well as the men* may mean that they also swim, or that they swim equally well.

Sometimes the subject of a sentence is directly followed by *as well as*. Here, the added phrase should make no difference to whether the verb is singular or plural. It is not like a plural subject joined by *and*. Compare: *The cat as well as the kittens climbs trees*; *The cats as well as the kittens climb trees*; *The cat and the kittens climb trees*. The phrase *as well as the kittens* can be, but need not be, separated off by commas.

3 It is perfectly correct to write *not as well as*. See AS (2).

well-

Do not write *more well-behaved*, *most well-known*, etc, but *better-behaved*, *best-known*. See COMPARISON, GRAMMATICAL.

well-nigh

See NIGH.

Welsh

See BRITISH.

Welsh rabbit, Welsh rarebit

The older name of this cheese dish was **Welsh rabbit**, but **Welsh rarebit** may now be just as common. People seem to think that *rabbit* is a corruption of *rarebit*, rather than the other way round.

weltanschauung, weltschmerz

These words of German origin mean 'philosophy of life' and 'sentimental pessimism' respectively. The *w*'s are pronounced as 'v'. Do not overuse such FOREIGN PHRASES.

were

In formal writing, use **were** rather than *was* to express a state of affairs that is contrary to fact: *I wish it were finished* (but it isn't); *Suppose it were true* (but it is false); *He behaves as though he were a millionaire* (but he isn't). Similarly for hypothetical conditions after *if*: *If John were here he would know*; *If it were to rain we should get wet*; *If it were not for her illness she would go*; *He spoke as if I were deaf*.

In all of the above, *was* is common in less formal styles. But even when you are not attempting formality, **were** is the only choice in inverted sentences (*Were this true it would be very alarming*) and in the set phrase *as it were*. Do not use **were** after *if* in the sense in which *if* can be replaced by *whether*: *I wondered if/whether he was coming*; *to find out if/whether it was true*; *There is some doubt if/whether he was really her son*. See SUBJUNCTIVES. For *if* and *whether*, see IF (1).

west, western

See NORTH.

westward(s)

Before a noun, use **westward**: *a westward view*. After a verb, use the form with an *s* in British English (*flying westwards*) and the one without an *s* for American English.

wet (*verb*)

The past tense and participle are either **wetted** or **wet**: *Billy's wet/wetted the bed*. It is clearer to use **wetted** as the participle after *be* or *get*, where **wet** might be taken to be an adjective. Compare: *The bed was wet* (ie not dry); *The bed was wetted* (ie by Billy).

wh-

Many forms of standard English make no difference between the pronunciation of *wh* and of *w* alone. Educated speakers of Southern British English pronounce *whales* like *Wales* and *which* like *witch*. The distinction is more often preserved in American English, and by Scottish and Irish speakers.

wharf

The plural is either **wharfs** or **wharves**.

what

1 When **what** means 'things that' or 'ones that' it is followed by a plural verb: *eating what appear to be peaches*. If it can be interpreted either as 'the thing that' or as 'the things that', the following verb can accordingly be either singular or plural: *What he enjoys is/are geography and French*; *What really matters is/are the children*. Traditionally, however, the singular verb has been favoured in such cases.

2 Do not use **what** for *that*, *which*, or *who*, as in *the man what lives next door*.

3 What . . . *for* is an informal substitute for *why*: *What did you do that for?* Avoid it where it might cause confusion. *What did he sell it for?* might mean either 'why?' or 'for how much?'.

4 what or **which**. Use **what** as an interrogative where the choice is open: *What's this?*; *What salary do they pay?*. Use **which** where there is a finite choice: *Which is your house?*; *Which colour do you want, red or blue?*.

whatever

When it means 'what in the world' it should be written as two words: *What ever do you mean?* See EVER (1).

when

1 Confusion can arise between different senses of **when**. It is likely to be understood in its commonest sense of 'at the time that'; but it can mean 'and then', and may there be better replaced by *and then* or *whereupon*: *He retired from the navy, when he decided to take up astronomy*. It can mean 'in spite of the fact that', and may there be better replaced by *although*: *She gave up politics, when she might have done well in it*.

2 In everyday language, **when** is probably the commonest way of introducing a definition of anything at all abstract: _Telepathy is when people communicate directly with each other's minds_. In formal writing, however, the rule is the same as that which governs the making of dictionaries; a noun such as _telepathy_ must be paraphrased by another noun: _Telepathy is communication directly from one mind to another_.

3 For **if and when,** see IF (3).

whence

For _from_ **whence,** see FROM (1).

whenever

When it means 'when in the world' it should be written as two words: _When ever did you find the time?_ See EVER (1).

where

1 Where means '_at_ what place' and also '_to_ what place'. It is unnecessary to write _Where are you going to?_ (omit _to_) and clumsy to write _Where is it at?_ (omit _at_). **Where** does not mean '_from_ what place', so that _Where do you come from?_ is the only way of expressing that idea.

2 For _see where_, see SEE (3).

whereabouts

This is used with either a singular or plural verb: _His present whereabouts is/are a secret_.

whereas

This rather formal word may be preferred to _while_ to emphasize contrast: _Welding is easy for an expert, whereas_ (rather than _while_) _it is dangerous for a novice. While_ may be misunderstood to refer to time rather than to contrast. See WHILE (2).

whereat, wherein, whereof, whereon, whereto

These and those like them are formal archaic words, at one time normal in legal contexts: _citizens of the United States and of the State wherein they reside_ (US Constitution). They sound PRETENTIOUS if used where _of which, to which_, etc would do.

wherever

When it means 'where in the world' it should be written as two words: *Where ever did you go?* See EVER (1).

whether

1 Whether is like *if*; see IF (1). **Weather** is the state of the atmosphere.

2 If *or not* can be omitted after **whether**, it is neater to leave it out: *It depends on whether he's ready (or not).*

3 A second or even a third **whether** may be needed after *or* in a list of 'alternative' clauses if the clauses have their own subject: *We cannot decide whether to sell the flat now or whether* (do not omit *whether*) *it will fetch more money later*; . . . *whether we should sell the car now or whether* (do not omit *whether*) *we should wait till the spring*; . . . *whether we should sell the car now or* (no *whether* here) *wait till the spring.*

which

1	referring to a sentence	**3**	*and* **which**
2	**which** and **who**	**4**	*of* **which**

1 referring to a sentence

Which may introduce a RELATIVE CLAUSE attached to one word, as in *They keep a large dog, which bit me.* Here, **which** refers to the dog. But it is also perfectly correct for **which** to refer to a whole sentence, as in *He can sing, which is an advantage.* Here, **which** refers to the fact that he can sing. Avoid this device if it might lead to ambiguity. In *She crashed the car, which was expensive*, it is not clear whether *expensive* refers to the car or to the crashing. Some writers use **which** to refer even to a preceding sentence: . . . *can be overcome by basing these programs on need not race. Which is fine (Nation Review* (Melbourne)). This device seems legitimate, but it should not be allowed to become a mannerism.

2 which and who

Which normally performs the same function in respect to things as **who** or **whom** do for people. We say *the dog which* but *the boy who*. **Which**, however, is used in questions about people as well as about things: *Which girl/Which of the girls do you mean?* (For the choice between **which** and *what* in questions, see WHAT (4)). **Which** is often used in reference to human groups: *a tribe which has aroused much interest among anthropologists*; *The Education Secretary yesterday met the Council for Local Education Authorities which he had promised to* *consult before drafting the White Paper* (*Times Educational Supplement*). See WHO (2).

Which is used of single people in constructions like this: *the policeman, which he obviously was* ... Here, **which** refers to his profession, and could be replaced by *and this*. (For the choice between **which** and *that*, see THAT (3)).

3 *and* which

See AND (2). If one of two linked parts of the same sentence entails a *who*, **which**, or *that*, then the other part must have a *who*, **which**, or *that* too, referring to the same thing. It is a common error to use *and which* (perhaps more often than *and that* or *and who*) where no previous *which* has been introduced: *'Sherry Flip' the revue I had written some sketches for and which was about to begin rehearsal* (S J Perelman); *Mr Reagan bends over to inspect two birds presented to him by the Californian Turkey Industry Board and which will grace the table at the President-elect's Pacific Palisades home.* Both these examples need another **which**: *the revue for which I had written* ... ; *birds which were presented to him* .... The following would be more difficult to correct: *I write as the widow of X whose grave is on the west side of Highgate Old Cemetery and in which I too hope to rest.* Here, she would have to write *in whose grave on the west side of Highgate Old Cemetery I too hope to rest.* It is possible to link two verbs, quite correctly, with one **which**: *He offered her a chocolate which she accepted and ate* (not *and ate it*).

4 *of* which

Where possible, replace *of which* by *whose*. It is correctly used of things as well as of people: *the factory in whose construction* (rather than *in the construction of which*) *they were involved*. See WHOSE.

while, whilst

1 Whilst is not used at all in American English, but in British English it remains a common alternative to **while**. Its rather archaic appearance perhaps leads people to believe that it is more formal or elegant.

2 Besides meaning 'during the time that' (*take a nap while I'm out*), **while** can quite correctly mean 'whereas' or 'although'. It may be better to replace it by one of those words if confusion might arise. *While he is young, he will do the job admirably* could mean either 'although he is young' or 'until he gets older'. **While** can also be replaced in one sense by *and*, and this should indeed replace it if there is any absurd suggestion that two incompatible activities are being carried on simultaneously: *Sir James Harker conducted the first part of the concert, while* (use *and*) *Dame Anthea Briggs conducted the second part.*

3 While sometimes introduces a DANGLING PARTICIPLE: *While not disagreeing with your summary, would it be possible to introduce a few modifications?* (correct to *while I do not disagree*, or else to *might I introduce*).

whir(r)

The spelling with two *r*'s is a chiefly British variant, but in either case other forms are **whirred, whirring**.

whisk(e)y

Whisky from Scotland and Canada is correctly spelled with no *e*. The kind produced in Ireland and in the USA is spelled **whiskey**.

white

Do not capitalize **white** with reference to race: *white minorities*. See CAUCASIAN.

white paper, blue book, green paper

They are all British Government reports on a topic. A **white paper** is usually a fairly brief statement of policy. A **blue book** is a longer document, typically a report from a government department, Royal Commission, or Committee of Inquiry. A **green paper** is more tentative, a set of proposals put out for public comment before they are used as a basis for legislation.

whither

This somewhat archaic word can usually be replaced by *where*. Instead of *the place whither it was posted*, write *the place to which it was posted* or (less formally) *the place it was posted to*. Compare HITHER, THITHER.

whitish

The word is spelled without the final *e* of *white*.

who, whom

1 **who** and **whose**	5 **who** *he was*
2 **who** or **which**	6 **who** *else's*; see ELSE (1)
3 **who** for **whom**	7 *and* **who**; see WHICH (3)
4 **whom** for **who**	8 *than* **whom**; see CASE, GRAMMATICAL (4)

1 who and whose

The possessive form of **who** is spelled **whose**: *the girl whose* (not *who's*) *flat I'm sharing*.

2 who or which

Who, **whom**, and **whose** normally perform the same function in respect to people as **which** does for things. We say *the car which* but *the girl who*. (But see WHICH (2).) There is some doubt as to whether **who** should properly refer to animals (*a cat who's had lots of kittens*), or to countries (*Syria, who was partly to blame*), or to ships (*Hotspur, who had lost her rudder*). It is a matter of attitude and style. For further discussion of this topic, see SHE (1). **Who** is often used, rather than **which**, in reference to human groups when they are thought of as a collection of individuals. It then requires a plural verb. Compare: *a family who constantly quarrel among themselves*; *a family which is mentioned in the earliest records*.

It is as important as it is with **which** (see WHICH (1)) to make it clear who is meant by **who**. A sentence like the following is not clear: *He was a busy doctor with a large family who had no time for external commitments*. This must be rephrased to show whether it was the doctor or the family who had no time.

3 who for whom

Who often replaces the more formal **whom** in questions: *Who did you see?* It is particularly justified if the question ends with a preposition: *Who were you with?*; *Who are you writing to?*; *Who was it aimed at?* In such cases *with whom*, *to whom*, *at whom* would be distinctly pedantic. Elsewhere than in direct questions, at any rate in formal writing, **who** should be replaced by **whom** or (where possible) by *that*: *a man whom/ that it is natural to admire*.

Writers who prefer to avoid the formal **whom** have often the further option of using no linking word at all: *a man (whom) I have always admired*. See CASE, GRAMMATICAL (6).

4 whom for who

Whom should not be used for **who** with the verb *to be*. Write *Who* (not *whom*) *do you think you are?* and *You know who* (not *whom*) *I am*. It is common, but nevertheless incorrect, to use **whom** for **who** in constructions such as the following: *a creature whom* (it should be *who*) *we pretend is here already* (E M Forster); *someone whom* (it should be *who*) *they imagined would be a more vigorous President* (Winston Churchill). The choice of **whom** for **who** in such circumstances is usually made because the pronoun is felt to be the object of the inserted verb *pretend* or *imagine*, whereas it is in fact the subject of *is here* and *would be*. If the extra element is thought of as segregated inside imaginary brackets (even though it contributes to the meaning), the mistake can be avoided: *a creature who (we pretend) is here already.*

Whom is the right choice where such sentences involve a verb in the infinitive, the *to-* form: *a man whom they understood to be extremely rich*; compare *They understood him to be extremely rich.*

5 who *he was*
Unless **who** and *was* can be brought fairly close together, the verb should directly follow **who**: *We wondered who the conductor was*; *We wondered who was the first person to swim the Channel.* A distinction of meaning is possible in a theatrical context, where someone who asked *who was Hamlet* might be answered by 'Laurence Olivier', whereas someone who asked *who Hamlet was* would be told 'The Prince of Denmark'.

whoever, whomever

1 Whoever means 'anyone who' (*Whoever invests in that company is an optimist*) or 'no matter who' (*I'll speak to whoever is in charge*). In questions, when the sense is 'who in the world', the two-word form *who ever* is preferred: *Who ever can it be?* See EVER (1).

2 Although **whomever** exists as the objective form of **whoever**, it is rarer and even more formal than *whom*. Except in the most formal prose, do not be afraid to write *Choose whoever you like*, or *Give it to whoever you want.* **Whomever** is sometimes wrongly used where **whoever** would be correct, as in *Invite whomever likes jazz.* Here **whoever** is correct because it is the subject of the verb *likes.* See CASE, GRAMMATICAL (6).

wholly

See HOLEY.

who's, whose

Who's is short for *who is* (*Who's coming?*) or *who has* (*Who's eaten it?*). **Whose** is the possessive form of *who*: *the girl whose flat I'm sharing.*

whose

1 This can be used of things as well as people. It is much neater to write *mountains whose peaks are covered with snow* and *the factory in whose construction they were involved*, rather than *mountains the peaks of which* and *the factory in the construction of which.*

2 It is as important as it is with *which* (see WHICH (1)) to make it clear who or what is meant by **whose**. The following is not clear: *Sir Thomas* *is much annoyed at this evidence of Mrs Norris's interference, whose existence he had never suspected* (Elizabeth Jenkins). This needs to be rephrased to show whether it was the evidence, the interference, or even Mrs Norris that surprised him by its or her existence.

3 For **whose** *else's*, see ELSE (1).

why

It is quite correct to refer to the *reason why* something happens, but **why** can also be omitted there. See REASON.

wide

See BROAD.

wide, widely

Wide as an adverb is chiefly used in the fixed combinations *far and wide*; *wide open*; *wide awake*; *wide apart*. It cannot replace **widely**, whose chief meaning is 'over a broad range or area': *travel widely*; *fluctuate widely*. **Widely** is used with past participles: *widely separated*; *widely known*.

widow

It is TAUTOLOGOUS to say *widow of the late X*. If she is his **widow** he must be dead. Write *widow of X*.

wield, wiener

Both words are spelled *-ie-*, not *-ei-*.

wife

The plural is **wives**.

will

See SHALL.

wil(l)ful

The word is spelled **willful** in American English, **wilful** in British English.

win (*noun*)

This is properly used in sporting contexts: *an away win for Tottenham*

Hotspur. It is better not to use **win** as a noun for political victories, and particularly for military ones.

wind (*verb*)

There are three verbs. The one that means 'bend' or 'twist' rhymes with *kind*, and its past tense and participle are **wound**. The rarer one that means 'blow a horn' also rhymes with *kind*, and its past tense and participle are either **winded** or **wound**. The one meaning 'follow by scent', or 'make short of breath' rhymes with *tinned*, and its past tense and participle are **winded**.

windward

It means 'on the side exposed to the wind', and the form is **-ward**, not **-wards**, for adjective, adverb, and noun.

wink at

See BLINK.

winter

This is not usually capitalized. *Winter of our discontent* is a CLICHÉ, as commonly used in a way that somewhat distorts its original use by Shakespeare; but it is useless to quarrel with *winter of discontent* as a familiar label for the political situation in Britain in the winter of 1978–79.

-wise

The process of tacking **-wise** meaning 'with regard to' onto nouns to form adverbs has attracted a good deal of criticism. People who do it at all tend to OVERUSE the resultant words. Although *careerwise*, *taxwise*, *saleswise*, and *jobwise* are certainly more concise than *from a tax point of view* and *when it comes to sales*, you should probably avoid such words in serious writing.

wish

1 Wish is more formal than *want*, and less direct. The choice between the two arises, however, only where they will both fit the same grammatical pattern. You can say *The manager wants* (or *wishes*) *to thank you*, and *I wish* (or *want*) *you to read it*. It is a GENTEELISM to use **wish** where only *want* will fit, as in *Does Madam wish some more gravy?* or *Do you wish it sent by rail?*. If *want* is too plain here, use *wish for more gravy*, or *wish it to be sent*.

2 For *I wish it were*, see WERE.

wit (*verb*)

This archaic and literary verb survives chiefly in the phrase *to wit*. Use *namely*.

with

1 A singular subject to which something else is linked by **with**, or by *together* **with**, should correctly take a singular verb: *The Queen, with her entourage, has* (rather than *have*) *just arrived*.

2 The use of **with** for 'employed by' suggests a job in at least middle management. The person who says *I'm with ICI* is not in its typing pool.

withal

This belongs to old-fashioned poetic language (see POESY). Use *with* or *besides* instead.

withhold

It has two *h*'s.

within

This is rather more formal than *inside*, but it may seem appropriate in association with large places: *within the castle* but *inside the matchbox*. See also INSIDE OF; IN (2).

without

In serious prose, do not use **without** for *unless*, as in *He won't know without you tell him*. It is a regionalism. The journalist who wrote *Rarely a day goes by without he dictates between 20 and 30 letters* could have expressed it better as *without his dictating* or *when he does not dictate*.

witness (*verb*)

Although it need not be confined to its legal sense, as in *witness a will*, this word does emphasize the idea of seeing something for oneself at first hand: *to witness this historic event*. It should not be used indiscriminately for *see* or *watch*.

wolf

Wolves is the plural of the noun, but is not part of the verb: *He wolfs the pie*.

woman

See LADY.

wonder (*verb*)

1 Expressions of wonder are not direct questions and therefore should not end in a question mark: *I wonder who she is* (not *who she is?*).

2 *I shouldn't wonder* often gives rise to a DOUBLE NEGATIVE: *I shouldn't wonder if it didn't snow* (write *if it snowed*).

wondrous

This archaic word can now only sound FACETIOUS, as in *wondrous to relate*. In serious contexts use *wonderful*.

wont, wonted, won't

Wont and **wonted** mean 'custom' and 'accustomed': *as was his wont; They are wont to be tedious; wrote with his wonted clarity*. **Won't** is short for *will not*.

woof

See WARP.

wool(l)en, wool(l)y

These are spelled with two *l*'s in British English, but often with one in American English.

word citation

If you want to refer to words or parts of words as such, underline them (in print italicize them) or enclose them in quotation marks: *They could not find 'astronaut' in their dictionary*. See ITALICS and QUOTATION MARKS.

word order

See ORDER OF WORDS.

work to

See REPORT TO.

world

Of this world, as in *the Ronald Reagans of this world*, is a CLICHÉ.

778

worse

It can correctly be not only an adjective (*getting worse*) but an adverb (*raining worse than ever*). **Worsen** meaning 'get or make worse' is standard; but do not use the archaic word **worser**.

worship (*verb*)

Other forms are **worshipped, worshipping** in British English, but the second *p* is usually omitted in American English.

worst

1 *The two/three/hundred worst houses* is probably better than *the worst two/three/hundred houses*, since the superlative forms of other adjectives are used like that. We say *the three oldest women* or *the five most ridiculous answers*, not *the oldest three women* or *the most ridiculous five answers*.

2 The idiom is *if the worst comes to the worst. The* is sometimes omitted in American use.

worth, worthwhile

Worth can be a noun (*proved his worth*) or a preposition, and when it is a preposition it needs an object: *worth the effort*; *worth £50*; *not worth reading*. You cannot say merely that something is **worth**.

   Worthwhile is an adjective, like *useful* or *easy*, so that you can say *It's worthwhile to read this book* just as you would say *It's useful to read this book*. But do not say that the book is *worthwhile examining* any more than you would say it was *worthwhile a lot of money*. **Worthwhile** is sometimes spelled as two words. If it is spelled *worth while*, **worth** is a preposition and **while** is a noun, as they clearly are in *It is not worth your while reading this book*.

would

1 For **would** or **should**, see SHOULD.

2 Write *would have*, not *would of*. Do not use **would** or *would have* in the '*if*' part of a sentence: *If I had* (not *would have*) *known I would have told you*; *If it rained* (not *would rain*) *they would cancel the match*. The exception is where **would** is used of a person and means 'be willing to': *If you would only listen, I could explain*.

3 Would is often used to avoid too dogmatic a statement: *it would seem*; *I would have thought*; *I suppose that would be Mrs Beardmore*. But beware of sounding too timid.

4 For the incorrect combination *would better*, see BETTER (1); for *would rather*, see RATHER.

wrack

See RACK.

wraith

See WREATH (1).

wrapped

See RAPT.

wrath, wroth

Wrath is a noun: *the wrath of God*. It is also a rare variant of the adjectives *wrathful* and **wroth.** All these words, however, are either literary or FACETIOUS; prefer *anger* and *angry* for everyday use.

wreak, wrought

Wreak means 'inflict': *wreaked his vengeance*. It has no connection with the adjective **wrought**, which means 'worked': *wrought iron; carefully wrought essays*. Pleasant things can be **wrought**, but you can **wreak** only unpleasant ones, so do not write *wreak an agreeable transformation*.

wreath, wraith

1 A **wreath** is a garland. A **wraith** is a ghost.

2 Wreaths usually rhymes with *breathes* rather than with *heaths*, particularly in American English.

3 *Wreathed in smiles* is a CLICHÉ.

writ large

This is the proper form of the expression, not *written largely*. It means 'manifested on a larger scale': *The problems of modern totalitarianism are only our own problems writ large* (*Times Literary Supplement*).

write

In standard American English you can say *I wrote my mother* where British usage would require *I wrote to my mother*. There is no objection in British English to *I wrote my mother a postcard*, because here *postcard* is the direct object (what I wrote), and *my mother* is the indirect object. It is the same construction as *I gave my mother some roses*.

writer

The writer, *this writer*, and *the present writer* are rather formal self-important ways of saying *I* in writing: *This writer* (ie *I*) *was unable to gain admittance to the crypt*. See WE (1).

wrong, wrongly

Wrong may be an adverb meaning 'so as to be wrong', and then **wrongly** is an alternative: *guessed wrong*; *spelled it wrong*. It may also be an adjective after the linking verb *go*: *The washing machine went wrong*. **Wrongly** means 'in a wrong way' (*acted wrongly*), and is the only one that can precede a verb or participle (*a wrongly addressed letter*) or that can be used as a SENTENCE ADVERB: *Wrongly, he refused* (ie he did wrong to refuse).

wroth

See WRATH.

wrought

See WREAK.

Xmas

This spelling of *Christmas* should be confined to either commercial or casual writing. Most people prefer to say 'Christmas' when reading it aloud.

Yy

-y

Adjectives can be formed from nouns by adding **-y**: *dirty*; *sleepy*. If the noun ends with an *e*, the *e* is normally dropped: *icy*; *slimy*. Exceptions are:
(a) *Hole* makes *holey*. (This distinguishes it from *holy*, ie sacred.)
(b) Nouns ending in *-ue* keep the *e*: *gluey*.
(c) The following can either drop or keep their *e*: *game(e)y*, *hom(e)y*, *lin(e)y*, *mous(e)y*, *nos(e)y*, *stag(e)y*, *whit(e)y*. Note also *clay*, *clayey*; *day*, *daily*.

yang

See YIN.

Yank(ee)

In American use **Yankee** meant originally a New Englander, or a Northerner in the Civil War. **Yankee** and **Yank** have come to be used freely for any inhabitant of the USA. The words are only slightly impolite.

ye

This archaic spelling of *the* arose from the use by early printers of the letter *y* instead of Þ, the letter called *thorn* which was later replaced by *th*. **Ye** has been used from time to time to suggest picturesque quaintness, as in *Ye Olde Gifte Shoppe*, but such devices are now chiefly jocular.

yeah

This is used in writing to represent a casual pronunciation of *yes*. Most people probably drop the final *s* now and then in rapid speech.

yes

Yes can agree with a positive statement or contradict a negative one, so that the reply to both *She's French* and *She's not French* might be *Yes, she is!* (although this would probably be spoken with a different stress, according to which meaning is intended). It would be very odd to use **yes** to agree with a negative statement, and say *Yes, she isn't*. That is what *no* is for.

yet

1 *As yet* means the same as **yet** in the sense of 'so far', so that *as* can often be omitted, but it is better to retain it at the beginning of a sentence because **yet** alone would be understood as meaning 'nevertheless': *As yet, he had encountered few problems*; *He had encountered few problems (as) yet*.

2 In the sense of 'so far', **yet** and *as yet* are not used with the simple past tense except in informal American English: *Did you eat yet?* In formal writing, this would become *Have you eaten yet?*

yew

See EWE.

Yiddish

See JEW.

yield

The word is spelled *-ie-*, not *-ei-*.

yin, yang

In Chinese philosophy, **yin** is the feminine passive principle, associated with dark, cold, and wetness. **Yang** is the masculine active principle, associated with light, heat, and dryness. The two combine to produce the whole universe.

yodel (*verb*)

Other forms are **yodelled, yodelling** in British English, but the second *l* is usually omitted in American English.

yogurt

The *yog* rhymes with *bog* in British English, with *rogue* in American English. Other spellings are *yoghurt, yoghourt*.

yolk, yoke

The **yolk** is the yellow part of an egg. A **yoke** is either a sort of crossbar, such as that linking a pair of oxen, or else a tight part across the shoulders or hips of a garment.

yore

The phrase *of yore* is archaic, poetic, or FACETIOUS. Use *long ago*.

you

1 You is correctly used for *one* everywhere except in the most formal writing: *funny, when you come* (or *when one comes*) *to think of it*. In giving instructions, **you** is more direct and less clumsy than the repeated use of the passive. You should use either **you** or *one* consistently throughout the same passage. Do not write *If you want to learn French, one ought to go to France*.

2 You may be either the subject or the object of a verb, whereas *I* is only the subject and *me* is only the object: *You love me and I love you*. It is important when combining them to ensure that *you and I* is used for *we* (*You and I are ready*) and *you and me* for *us* (*They've invited you and me*; *a present for you and me*). See CASE, GRAMMATICAL (3).

young

Do not write *at a young age*. The phrase is *at an early age*.

your, you're, yours

Your means 'belonging to you': *your job*. **You're** means 'you are': *You're wrong*. **Yours** means 'the one belonging to you': *The house became yours* (not *your's*).

yourself, yourselves

See REFLEXIVE.

youth

When used of an individual, **youth** means a young male, and is often used disapprovingly: *youths loitering at street corners*. The word can also be a collective noun for young people of both sexes, used with a singular verb (or often in British English a plural verb) and often before other nouns: *The youth of the nation demands a hearing*; *youth culture*; *youth clubs*.

-yse, -yze

For verbs with this ending, see -IZE.

Zz

-z-, -zz-

See DOUBLING.

zeitgeist

It is spelled *-ei-*, not *-ie-*. This word of German origin means 'the spirit of the age'.

zenith

See NADIR.

zero

1 The plural of the noun is either **zeros** or **zeroes**. Other forms of the verb are **zeroes, zeroed, zeroing**.

2 Zero is used in American English for saying telephone numbers, where British English uses *oh*. The number 5104 would be five one zero four.

3 Except in technical writing there is no reason to add zeros when you refer to the full hour of the day (*5 p.m.*, not *5.00 p.m.*) or to rounded sums of money (*£12*, not *£12.00*; *$31*, not *$31.00*).

zoology

Some speakers prefer to pronounce the first of the four syllables as 'zoh'; but the pronunciation 'zoo' is now much commoner, and cannot be considered incorrect.

zoom

Some people would confine this word to the specialized aeronautical sense of 'climb steeply', but that is an unreasonable restriction. **Zoom** is used freely and appropriately in such contexts as *The car zoomed past the house* and *The pigeon zoomed down from the roof*, as well as in the sense of operating a camera with a **zoom** lens.